Chaos, Confusion, —•✦•— and —✦•— Political Ignorance

June 28-August 5, 1914: The Untold Truth About the Start of World War II

John Hance

Order this book online at www.trafford.com
or email orders@trafford.com

Most Trafford titles are also available at major online book retailers.

Printed in the United States of America.

ISBN: 978-1-4907-2878-0 (sc)
ISBN: 978-1-4907-2879-7 (e)

Trafford rev. 03/05/2014

 www.trafford.com
North America & international
toll-free: 1 888 232 4444 (USA & Canada)
fax: 812 355 4082

I respectfully dedicate this book to all those who paid in blood, So those who fabricated the lies will live with the shame and guilt of knowing the truth but not exposing the truth for what it is.

To my wife who endure my countless hours at the library and research on the internet to find the material and resources to make this book possible.

To Mr. Marchese, my former high school history teacher, who took countless phone calls from me to not only help out but to clarify my interpretations. Without his help, I would only second guess these historical documents.

I feel Mr Hance has captured the essence of the political intrigue of the time. His comprehension of the ignorance displayed by high government shows the chaos of the world scene at that moment in history, when a little "common sense" would have saved the people much pain.

Mr Vinnie Marchese
History Professor

"You know the truth and the truth will set you free"
John 8;32

What is Historical truth?

History is recorded by the Victors!
History is based of personnel viewpoints!
History is driven by biased opinions!
History recorders are blind to closed minds and misconceptions of political leaders!
History is recorded with the presence of a lie and a confrontation toward the absolute truth!

Contents

Foreword

How did I start this book?

I have been a student of World War 2 since I was about eight or nine years old. Starting out with the attitude of "Kill the dirty Jap", and the "Barbaric Hun," I then progressed to learn more about the battles and equipment each nation used during this conflict. Then my curiosity got me to research about the people involved with the war. Finally, I wanted to know how this war was started, so I started with Dec 7, 1941. There were no answers with this date; it was just when the U.S. officially entered the war. Therefore, I backed up to September 1, 1939; this date just shows when the war in Europe officially started. From this date, I went back in history slowly and carefully. When I got to 1933, Hitler's rise to power in Germany, no answers were found with this date, and backing up a few more years, I still found no answers. At this point, I went to the end of World War 1 with the Treaty of Versailles. This document proves World War II is a continuation of World War I. I still came across no answers on how World War II was started, but I found evidence to the origins of both conflicts when researching the historical documents from this period.

The biggest evidence is that World War I was a war of jealousy, revenge and greed. This stems from the end of the Franco-Prussia War of 1870: when France started this was because of a statement made by the King France's wife to the King, and lost the capital city of Paris by the Prussia (current day Germany) army. From this point I was able to trace through history political action and inaction with treaties that were signed and violated. The most intriguing evidence was all of the secret co-operation and treaties being made against one another in Europe and Russia. In the time frame of 1871 to 1910, several wars had been averted because several nations had not been organized enough to continue with an arm conflict because several nations had not been organized enough to continue with an arm conflict. These averting of wars could have been contributed to such factors as no economic means, no raw materials needed to feed the war machine, lack of a strong industry, or no allies to protect one's interest. In fact, at this point, only Great Britain, Germany and United States had all three of these ingredients. Even so, these three countries were very opposed to global war in June of 1914. As I moved back through history, I begun to find more and more evidence that showed a constant attitude from the same countries and their attitude toward one or two countries in Europe and Russia.

My attempt is to bring these historical documents to life and prove that the start of World War 1 is a misconception of the truth while hiding a lie. By tracing these documents through time, the truth can be revealed and show that the guilty are innocent and the innocent is guilty of wars against peace and welfare of the word population by starting this war. By no means am I saying what these countries did to other cultures or beliefs is right. My attempt is to show how World War II really started

Chapter One
June 28, 1914

On June 28, 1914, Archduke Ferdinand journeyed to Bosnia without the usual protection against assassins. He remarked that all was in the hands of God. In Sarajevo, he was assassinated. The assassins were members of the Black Hand group.

The Assassination of Archduke Franz Ferdinand

Borijove Jevtic, one of the leaders of the Narodna Odbrana, who was arrested with Gavrilo Princip immediately after the assassination, gave this firsthand account of the killing.

A tiny clipping from a newspaper mailed without comment from a secret band of terrorists in Zagreb, capital of Croatia, to their comrades in Belgrade was the torch that set the world afire with war in 1914. That bit of paper wrecked old, proud empires. It gave birth to new, free nations. I was one of the members of the terrorist band in Belgrade who received it. The little clipping declared the Austrian Archduke Francis Ferdinand would visit Sarajevo, the capital of Bosnia, on June 28 to direct army maneuvers in the neighboring mountains. It reached our meeting place, the café called *Zlatna Moruna*, one night the latter part of April 1914. To understand how great a sensation that little piece of paper caused among us when it was passed from hand to hand almost in silence and how greatly it inflamed our hearts, it is necessary to explain just why the *Narodna Odbrana* existed, the kind of men who were in it, and the significance of that date, June 28, on which the archduke dared to enter Sarajevo. As everyone knows, the old Austria-Hungarian Empire was built by conquest and intrigues, by sales and treacheries, which held [...] men of the upper classes, who were ardent patriots. They were dissimilar in everything except hatred of the oppressor. Such were the men into whose hands the tiny bit of newsprint was sent by friends in Bosnia that April night in Belgrade. At a small table in a very humble café, beneath a flickering gas jet, we sat and read it. There was no advice or admonition sent with it. Only four letters and two numerals were sufficient to make us unanimous, without discussion, as to what we should do about it. They were connived [sic] in Sarajevo, all the twenty-two conspirators were in their allotted positions, armed and ready. They were distributed five hundred yards apart over the whole route along which the archduke must travel from the railroad station to the town hall. When Francis Ferdinand and his retinue drove from the station, they were allowed to pass the first two conspirators. The motor cars were driving too fast to make an attempt feasible and in the crowd were many Serbians; throwing a grenade would have killed many innocent people. When the car passed Gabrinovic, the compositor, he threw his grenade. It hit the side of the car, but Francis Ferdinand, with presence of mind, threw himself back and was uninjured. Several officers riding in his attendance were injured. The cars sped to the town hall, and the rest of the conspirators did not interfere with them. After the reception in the town hall, General Potiorek, the Austrian commander, pleaded with Francis Ferdinand to leave the city, as it was seething with rebellion. The archduke was persuaded to drive the shortest way out of the city and to go quickly. The road to the maneuvers was shaped like the letter V, making a sharp turn at the bridge over the River Milgacka. Francis Ferdinand's car could go fast enough until it reached this spot, but here it was forced to slow down for the turn. Here Princip had taken his stand. As the car came abreast, he stepped forward from the curb, drew his automatic pistol from his coat, and fired two shots. The first struck the wife of the archduke, the Archduchess Sofia, in the abdomen. She was an expectant mother. She died instantly. The second bullet struck the archduke close to the heart. He uttered only one word, "Sofia"—a call to his stricken wife. Then his head fell back and he collapsed. He died almost instantly. The officers seized Princip. They beat him over the head with the flat of their swords. They knocked him down, they kicked him, scraped the skin from his neck with the edges of their swords, tortured him, all but killed him. The next day they put chains on Princip's feet, which he wore till his death....I was placed in the cell next to Princip's, and when Princip was taken out to walk in the prison yard, I was taken along as his companion.... Awakened in the middle of the night and told that he was to be carried off to another prison, Princip made an appeal to the prison governor:

"There is no need to carry me to another prison. My life is already ebbing away. I suggest that you nail me to a cross and burn me alive. My flaming body will be a torch to light my people on their path to freedom."

At the same in Pokrovskoe, Russia minister to Nicholas II, Gregori Rasputin, was almost assassinated by a disgruntled female. Rasputin's involvement in the war involved being Nicholas's personnel confidant and advisor to the Tsar. Without his ability to talk sense into the Russia leader, war proponents in Russia would have their way with the Tsar.

Primary Documents: Archduke Franz Ferdinand's Assassination, 28 June 1914

The assassination of Archduke Franz Ferdinand, heir to the Austro-Hungarian throne, on 28 June 1914, set in train a series of diplomatic events that led inexorably to the outbreak of war in Europe at the end of July 1914.

Ferdinand and his wife, Sophie, were killed by Serb nationalist Gavrilo Princip while on a formal visit to Sarajevo. Princip shot Ferdinand at point-blank range while the latter was travelling in his car from a town hall reception having earlier that day already survived one assassination attempt. Standing on the car's sideboard was Count Franz von Harrach. A witness to Ferdinand's assassination, he subsequently recounted the events of the day. A portion of his translated memoir is reproduced below.

Memoir of Count Franz von Harrach

As the car quickly reversed, a thin stream of blood spurted from His Highness's mouth onto my right check. As I was pulling out my handkerchief to wipe the blood away from his mouth, the Duchess cried out to him, "For God's sake! What has happened to you?" At that, she slid off the seat and lay on the floor of the car, with her face between his knees. I had no idea that she too was hit and thought she had simply fainted with fright. Then I heard His Imperial Highness say, "Sophie, Sophie, don't die. Stay alive for the children!" At that, I seized the archduke by the collar of his uniform to stop his head dropping forward and asked him if he was in great pain. He answered me quite distinctly, "It is nothing!" His face began to twist somewhat but he went on repeating, six or seven times, ever more faintly as he gradually lost consciousness, "It's nothing!" Then came a brief pause followed by a convulsive rattle in his throat, caused by a loss of blood. This ceased on arrival at the governor's residence. The two unconscious bodies were carried into the building, where their death was soon established.

Chapter Two
June 29, 1914

No. 1
Ritter von Storck, Secretary of Legation, to Count Berchtold.
Belgrade, June 29, 1914.

Under the terrible shock of yesterday's catastrophe, it is difficult for me to give any satisfactory judgment on the bloody drama of Sarajevo with the necessary composure and judicial calm. I must ask you, therefore, to allow me for the moment to limit myself to putting on record certain facts.

Yesterday, the 15/28, the anniversary of the battle of the Amselfeld, was celebrated with greater ceremony than usual, and there were celebrations in honour of the Serbian patriot, Milos Obilic who, in 1389 with two companions, treacherously stabbed the victorious Murad.

Among all Serbians, Obilic is regarded as the national hero. In place of the Turks, however, we are now looked on as the hereditary enemy, thanks to the propaganda that has been nourished under the aegis of the Royal Government and the agitation that has for many years been carried on in the press.

A repetition of the drama on the field of Kosovo seems, therefore, to have hovered before the minds of the three young criminals of Sarajevo—Princip, Cabrinovic, and the third person still unknown—who also threw a bomb. They also shot down an innocent woman and may therefore think they have surpassed their model.

For many years, hatred against the Monarchy has been sown in Serbia. The crop has sprung up and the harvest is murder.

The news arrived at about 5 o'clock; the Serbian Government at about 10 o'clock caused the Obilic festivities to be officially stopped. They continued, however, unofficially for a considerable time after it was dark. The accounts of eye witnesses say that people fell into one another's arms in delight, and remarks were heard such as: "It serves them right. We have been expecting this for a long time," or "This is revenge for the annexation."

No. 1.
From: M. Yov. M. Yovanovitch, Minister at Vienna.
To: M. N. Pashitch, Prime Minister and Minister for Foreign Affairs.
Vienna, June 29, 1914.
(Telegraphic)

The *Vienna Press* asserts that the magisterial enquiry has already shown that the Sarajevo outrage was prepared at Belgrade; further, that the whole conspiracy in its wider issues was organized at Belgrade among youth inspired with the Great Serbian idea, and that the Belgrade Press is exciting public opinion by publishing articles about the intolerable conditions prevailing in Bosnia. Press articles of this kind, according to the *Vienna Press*, are exercising a strong influence, as Serbian newspapers are being smuggled in large quantities into Bosnia.

Chapter Three
June 30, 1914

No. 2.
Ritter Von Storck, Secretary of Legation, to Count Berchtold.
(Telegraphic) Belgrade, June 30, 1914.

To-day I sent an enquiry to Herr Gruic, General Secretary of the Foreign Office, to ask the obvious question what measures the Royal police had taken, or proposed to take, in order to follow up the clues to the crime that notoriously are partly to be found in Serbia.

The answer was that the matter has not yet engaged the attention of the Serbian police.

No. 2.
From: Yov. M. Yovanovitch, Minister at Vienna.
To: M. N. Pashitch, Prime Minister and Minister for Foreign Affairs.
Vienna, June 30, 1914.
(Telegraphic)

The tendency at Vienna to represent, in the eyes of Europe, the outrage committed upon the Austro-Hungarian Crown Prince as the act of a conspiracy engineered in Serbia is becoming more and more apparent. The idea is to use this as a political weapon against us. The greatest attention ought, therefore, to be paid to the tone adopted by our press in its articles on the Sarajevo outrage.

No. 3.
From: Dr. M. Yovanovitch, Chargé d'Affaires at Berlin.
To: M. N. Pashitch, Prime Minister and Minister for Foreign Affairs.
Berlin, June 30, 1914.
(Telegraphic)

The Berlin Press, in publishing articles based on information from Vienna and Budapest, in which the Sarajevo outrage is connected with Serbia, is misleading German public opinion.

No. 4.
From: **Dr. M. Yovanovitch, Chargé d'Affaires at Berlin.**
To: **M. N. Pashitch, Prime Minister and Minister for Foreign Affairs.**
Berlin, June 30, 1914.
(Telegraphic)

The hostility of public opinion in Germany toward us is growing and is being fostered by false reports coming from Vienna and Budapest. Such reports are being diligently spread in spite of the contradictions issued by some newspapers and news agencies.

No. 5.
From: **M. Yov. M. Yovanovitch, Minister at Vienna.**
To: **M. N. Pashitch, the Prime Minister and Minister for Foreign Affairs.**
Vienna, June 30, 1914.

Sir,

As Count Berchtold was not able to receive me when I called, I spoke to the Under-Secretary of State at the Ministry for Foreign Affairs concerning the Sarajevo outrage. In the course of our conversation, I adopted the following line of argument: "The Royal Serbian Government condemns most energetically the Sarajevo outrage and on their part will certainly most loyally do everything to prove that they will not tolerate within their territory the fostering of any agitation or illegal proceedings calculated to disturb our already delicate relations with Austria-Hungary. I am of opinion that the Government is prepared also to submit to trial any persons implicated in the plot, in the event of its being proved that there are any in Serbia. The Royal Serbian Government, not withstanding all the obstacles hitherto placed in their way by Austro-Hungarian diplomacy (creation of an independent Albania, opposition to Serbian access to the Adriatic, demand for revision of the Treaty of Bucharest, the September ultimatum, etc.), remained loyal in their desire to establish a sound basis for our good neighborly relations. You know that in this direction something has been done and achieved. Serbia intends to continue to work for this object, convinced that it is practicable and ought to be continued. The Sarajevo outrage ought not to and cannot stultify this work."

Baron Macchio has taken note of the above and promised to communicate to Count Berchtold all that I said to him.

On the same day, I communicated to the French and Russian Ambassadors the substance of this conversation.

No. 6.
From: **M. M. Georgevitch, Chargé d'Affaires at Constantinople.**
To: **M. N. Pashitch, Prime Minister and Minister for Foreign Affairs.**
Constantinople, June 30, 1914.

Sir,

I had to-day a long conversation with the Austro-Hungarian Ambassador here concerning the Sarajevo outrage. I expressed the hope that this regrettable event—whatever is said about it in certain diplomatic circles—would not unfavorably influence the relation between Serbia and Austria-Hungary, which lately had shown considerable improvement.

He replied that such an eventuality was impossible, and ought not to be contemplated. He was also of opinion that Serbo-Austro-Hungarian relations had much improved lately. He added that the work in that direction ought to be persevered in. He informed me that from his latest conversations with Count Berchtold he understood that the latter was satisfied with the attitude adopted by the Serbian Government, and that he, on his part, sincerely desired friendly relations with Serbia.

Primary Documents: Kaiser Wilhelm on Austria's Ultimatum, July 1914
Updated: Saturday, 24 May 2003

Reproduced below are a series of telegrams sent by Baron Tschirschky, German ambassador in Vienna, to the German kaiser, Wilhelm II. Tschirschky reported upon events in Vienna surrounding preparation currently underway for presentation of a strict ultimatum to Serbia in retaliation for the murder of Archduke Franz Ferdinand a few days earlier in Sarajevo. Of most interest, however, are the kaiser's annotated notes upon the telegrams. These are indicated in the text in italics.

Telegrams from Baron Tschirschky to Kaiser Wilhelm II, 30 June–14 July 1914
30 June 1914

Count Berchtold has told me to-day there was every indication that the threads of the conspiracy of which the archduke was the victim centre at Belgrade. The affair was so cleverly designed that very young persons had been expressly selected to execute the crime, since they could not be sentenced to more than secondary penalties. *(I certainly hope this is not the case.)* The minister spoke with intense bitterness of the Serbian plots. I have heard even, people of moderation and responsible judgment expresses a desire to settle once for all Austria's account with the Serbs. *(Now or never!)* They think one should submit to the Serbs a series of conditions, and in case they do not accept them, should take vigorous measures. I am seizing every opportunity to dissuade people quietly but seriously from precipitate measures. *(Who has authorized that? Utterly stupid! It's none of his business! It is for Austria alone to decide what she considers it necessary to do. If things go wrong later, they will say: Germany opposed! Let Tschirschky do me the favor to drop such foolishness. The Serbs must be settled with as soon as possible. That is self-evident. It is something that requires no argument.)* First of all, it is important for people to know precisely what they wish. Up to the present, I have heard nothing but very vague and confused impressions. It would be well to weigh carefully the possible results of any act, and to bear in mind that Austria-Hungary is not the only country in the world; that she must show due consideration for her allies and keep in view the European situation as a whole; especially that she should not lose sight of Italy's and Rumania's attitude in matters concerning Serbia.

Chapter Four
July 1, 1914

No. 3.
M. Jehlitschka, Consul-General, to Count Berchtold.
Uskub, July 1, 1914.

On 28 June, the Feast of St. Titus (Corpus Christi Day), which on this occasion coincided with the 525th anniversary of the battle of the Amselfeld (1389), was for the first time officially celebrated as the "Festival of the Liberation" of the Serbian nation.

For four months, a special committee had worked at making this celebration an especially solemn and magnificent demonstration of Serbian nationality.

The propaganda connected with this at the same time extended to Croatia, Dalmatia, and Bosnia, but especially to Hungary; those who took part in it received free passes on the Serbian State railways; food and lodging at low prices, maintenance by public bodies, etc., were promised.

The agitation was carried on with energy and was with a definite end in view.

The visitors to the celebration at Prestina were brought in special trains.

The various speeches ran riot in historical reminiscences, which were connected with the scene of the celebration, and dealt under different aspects with the well-known theme of the union of all Serbia and the "liberation of our brethren in bondage" beyond the Danube and the Save, even as far as Bosnia and Dalmatia.

When, during the course of the evening, the news of the horrible crime of which Sarajevo had been the scene was circulated, the feeling that animated the fanatical crowd was, to judge by the numerous expressions of applause reported to me by authorities in whom I have absolute confidence, one that I can only characterize as inhuman.

In view of this attitude of the population, which was also displayed at Uskub, all attempts of the Serbian press to divest Serbia of the moral responsibility for a deed that was received by a representative gathering with such unvarnished satisfaction, collapse miserably.

No. 7.
From: M. M. S. Boschkovitch, Minister in London.
To: M. N. Pashitch, Prime Minister and Minister for Foreign Affairs.
London, July 1, 1914.
(Telegraphic)

Basing their information upon reports coming from Austrian sources, nearly all the English newspapers attribute the Sarajevo outrage to the work of Serbian revolutionaries.

No. 8.
From: M. N. Pashitch, Prime Minster and Minister for Foreign Affairs.
To: All of the Royal Serbian Legations abroad.
Belgrade, July 1, 1914.

The Austrian and Hungarian press are blaming Serbia more and more for the Sarajevo outrage. Their aim is transparent, viz., to destroy that high moral reputation Serbia now enjoys in Europe, and to take the fullest advantage politically against Serbia of the act of a young and ill-balanced fanatic. But, in Serbia itself, the Sarajevo outrage has been most severely condemned in all circles of society, inasmuch as all, official as well as unofficial, immediately recognized that this outrage would be most prejudicial not only to our good neighborly relations with Austria-Hungary but also to our co-nationalists in that country, as recent occurrences have proved. At a moment when Serbia is doing everything in her power to improve her relations with the neighboring Monarchy, it is absurd to think that Serbia could have directly or indirectly inspired acts of this kind. On the contrary, it was of the greatest interest to Serbia to prevent the perpetration of this outrage. Unfortunately this did not lie within Serbia's power, as both assassins are Austrian subjects. Hitherto Serbia has been careful to suppress anarchic elements, and after recent events she will redouble her vigilance, and in the event of such elements existing within her borders will take the severest measures against them. Moreover, Serbia will do everything in her power and use all the means at her disposal in order to restrain the feelings of ill-balanced people within her frontiers. But Serbia can on no account permit the Vienna and Hungarian press to mislead European public opinion, and lay the heavy responsibility for a crime committed by an Austrian subject at the door of the whole Serbian nation and on Serbia, who can only suffer harm from such acts and can derive no benefit whatever.

Please act in the sense of the above views, and use all available channels in order to put an end as soon as possible to the anti-Serbian campaign in the European press.

No. 9.
From: M. Yov. M. Yovanovitch, Minister at Vienna.
To: M. N. Pashitch, Prime Minister and Minister for Foreign Affairs.
Vienna, July 1, 1914.
(Telegraphic)

There were demonstrations last night in front of the Legation. I may say that the police showed considerable energy. Order and peace were maintained. As soon as I obtain positive information that the Serbian flag has been burned, I will lodge a complaint in the proper quarters. I will report to you the result. Hatred against Serbians and Serbia is being spread among the people, especially by the lower Catholic circles, the Vienna press, and military circles. Please do what is possible to prevent demonstrations taking place in Serbia, and to induce the Belgrade press to be as moderate as possible in tone. The tendency toward us here is still the same. It is expected that the decision as to the attitude to be adopted toward Serbia and the Serbians will be taken after the funeral.

Chapter Five
July 2, 1914

No. 10.
From: Dr. M. R. Vesnitch, Minister at Paris.
To: M. N. Pashitch, Prime Minister and Minister for Foreign Affairs.
Paris, July 2, 1914
(Telegraphic)

The French Government advise us to maintain an attitude of the greatest possible calm and composure in official circles as well as in public opinion.

M. Dumaine, French Ambassador at Vienna, to M. René Viviani, President of the Council, Minister for Foreign Affairs.
Vienna, July 2, 1914.

The crime of Sarajevo arouses the most acute resentment in Austrian military circles, and among all those who are not content to allow Serbia to maintain in the Balkans the position, which she has acquired. The investigation into the origin of the crime it is desired to exact from the Government at Belgrade under conditions intolerable to their dignity would, in case of a refusal, furnish grounds of complaint, which would admit of resort to military measures.

DUMAINE.

Autograph Letter of Franz Joseph to the Kaiser, Vienna, 2 July 1914

From Emperor Franz Joseph, Vienna, delivered to the Kaiser in Berlin on 5 July 1914, by the Austro-Hungarian ambassador, Count de Szogyeny-Marich. The annexed-memoire was drafted fully a month before Sarajevo. I sincerely regret that you should have been obliged to give up your intention of going to Vienna for the funeral ceremonies. I should have liked personally to express to you my sincerest thanks for your sympathy in my keen sorrow—a sympathy that has greatly touched me.

By Your warm and sympathetic condolence, you have given me renewed proof that I have in you a sincere friend worthy of confidence and that I may count upon you in every hour of grave trial. I should have liked very much to discuss with You the general situation, but as that has not been possible, I take the liberty of sending to You the subjoined mémoire prepared by my Minister of Foreign Affairs, which was drawn up before the terrible catastrophe of Sarajevo, and which now, following that tragic event, appears particularly worthy of attention. The attack directed against my poor nephew is the direct consequence of the agitation carried on by the Russian and Serbian Pan-Slavists, whose sole aim is the weakening of the Triple Alliance and the destruction of my Empire. By the foregoing declaration, it is no longer an affair at Sarajevo of the single bloody deed of an individual but of a well-organized conspiracy, of which the threads reach to Belgrade and if, as is probable, it be impossible to prove the complicity of the Serbian Government; nevertheless, it cannot be doubted that the policies leading to the reunion of all the Southern Slavs under the Serbian flag is favorable to crimes of this character and that the continuance of this state of things constitutes a constant danger to my house and to my realm. This danger is rendered more grave from the fact that Romania, despite the alliance with us, has entered into friendly relations with Serbia and, on her own territory, permits against us an agitation just as venomous as that allowed by Serbia. It is painful to me to suspect the fidelity and the good intentions of so old a friend as Charles of Romania, but he himself has twice declared during these last months to my Minister that by reason of the aroused and hostile sentiments of his people toward us he would not be in a position in case of need to carry out his obligations of alliance. Furthermore, the Rumanian Government encourages openly the activities of the *Kulturliga*, favors a rapprochement with Serbia and carries on, with Russian aid, the creation of a new Balkan alliance, which can only be directed against my Empire. Once before, at the beginning of the reign of Charles, such political fancies as these propagated by the *Kulturliga* disturbed the good political sense of Romanian men of state and the danger arose of seeing your realm launched on a policy of adventure. However, at that time, your venerated grandfather in an energetic and farsighted fashion intervened and pointed out to Romania the road, which assured to her a privileged place in Europe, and she became the strong support of the existing order. Now the same danger threatens this kingdom; I fear that counsel alone is insufficient and that Romania cannot be retained in the Triple Alliance unless, on the one hand, we make impossible the creation of the Balkan League under the patronage of Russia, by the entrance of Bulgaria into the Triple Alliance, and unless on the other hand, we make it clearly understood at Bucharest that the friends of Serbia cannot be our friends, and that Romania cannot consider us as allies unless she detaches herself from Serbia and represses with all her force the agitation directed in Romania against the existence of my Empire. The efforts of my government should in consequence be directed toward isolation and the diminishment of Serbia. The first step in that direction will be to strengthen the present situation of the Bulgarian Government in order that the Bulgars, whose real interests coincide with ours, shall be preserved from a return to friendship with Russia. If they realize at Bucharest that the Triple Alliance has decided not to abandon the alliance with Bulgaria, but that it is disposed to invite Bulgaria to an understanding with Romania and to guarantee its territorial integrity, we may perhaps succeed in bringing her back from the dangerous step to which she has been led by her friendship with Serbia and her understanding with Russia. If this should succeed, a reconciliation of Greece with Bulgaria and Turkey could be attempted. There would then arise, under the patronage of the Triple Alliance, a new Balkan alliance, the aim of which would be to put an end to the invasion of the Pan Slavist tide and to assure peace to our states. But this will not be possible unless Serbia, which is at present the pivot of Pan-Slavist policy, is eliminated as a political factor in the Balkans. In addition, you after this last terrible happening in Bosnia will see and know that one cannot think of smoothing out the differences that separate us from Serbia, and that the maintenance of peaceful policy by all the European Monarchies will be threatened as long as this focus of criminal agitation in Belgrade remains unpunished.

THE ANNEXE MEMOIRE.

Following the great disturbances of the last two years, the situation in the Balkans has cleared up to such a point that it is now possible to review the results of the crisis, and to establish in what measure the interests of the Triple Alliance, and more particularly those of the two Central Imperial Powers, have been affected by these events and what consequences result from them for European politics and for the Balkan policy of these Powers. If without prejudice we compare the present state of affairs with that existing before the crisis, we must decide that the result looked at from the point of view of Austria-Hungary, as well as from that of the Triple Alliance, cannot be considered in any way as favorable. The principal point is that following the development, which led to the second Balkan war, Bulgaria aroused herself from the Russian spell, and today can no longer be considered as an auxiliary of the Russian policy. The Bulgarian Government strives, on the contrary, to enter into more intimate relations with the Triple Alliance. To these favorable elements, however, are opposed the unfavorable factors that weigh more heavily in the balance. Serbia, whose policy has for years been animated by hostility toward Austria-Hungary and which is completely under Russian influence, has achieved an increase of territory and of population that exceeded by much her own expectations. Turkey, whose community of interests with the Triple Alliance was progressing well, and who constituted an important counterpoise against Russia and the Balkan States, has been almost entirely pushed out of Europe, and has seen her situation as a great power gravely compromised. Territorial proximity with Montenegro and the general strengthening of the Pan-Serbian idea have brought closer the possibility of a new expansion of Serbia by means of a union with Montenegro. Lastly, in the course of the crisis, the relations of Romania with the Triple Alliance have essentially changed....We see, on the other hand, that Russian and French diplomacy have carried on a unified action, in conformity with a preconcert plan to exploit the advantages obtained and to change certain factors that were from their point of view unfavorable....

The thought of freeing the Christian Balkan people from Turkish rule, in order to use them as a weapon against central Europe, has been for a long time the secret thought of Russian policy, by the traditional interest of Russia for these people. In these latter days has been developed the idea, put forward by Russia and taken up by France, of uniting the Balkan States into a Balkan alliance, in order by this means to put an end to the military superiority of the Triple Alliance. The first condition before the realization of this plan was that Turkey should be pushed back from the territory inhabited by the Christian nations of the Balkans, in order to increase the strength of these States and to render them free to expand to the west. This preliminary condition has been, on the whole, realized by the last war. On the other hand, after the end of the crisis, a division separated the Balkan States into two opposing groups of nearly equal strength: Turkey and Bulgaria on the one hand, and the two Serbian States, Greece and Romania, on the other. To put an end to this division in order to be able to use all the Balkan States or at least a decisive majority, to upset the balance of European power, was the latest task to which, after the end of the crisis, Russia and France applied themselves....There is no doubt of the basis upon which, according to the intentions of French and Russian diplomacy, these differences and rivalries might be reconciled and a new Balkan alliance created. What could be the actual aim of such an alliance in the present circumstances for the Balkan States? There is no longer reason to consider a common action against Turkey. It can, therefore, only be directed against Austria-Hungary and can only be accomplished on the basis of a program that should promise to all it members extensions of territory by a graduated displacement of their frontiers from the east to the west, at the expense of the territorial integrity of the Monarchy. A union of Balkan States upon any other basis would be impossible to imagine, but on this basis not only is it not impossible, but is in a fair way to be realized. One cannot question that Serbia under Russian pressure would consent to pay a considerable price in Macedonia for the entry of Bulgaria into an alliance directed against the Monarchy and looking forward to the acquisition of Bosnia and the adjacent territory....The relations of Austria-Hungary with Romania may be at this moment characterized by the fact that the Monarchy relies entirely upon its alliance and, before as since, is ready to uphold Romania with all its force if the *casus foedoris* shall arise, but that Romania detaches itself one-sidedly from its obligations of alliance and shows to the Monarchy only the prospect of neutrality. Even the neutrality of Romania is only guaranteed to the Monarchy by the personal affirmation of King Charles [a guarantee], which naturally is of value only for the duration of his reign and the accomplishment of which depends upon the King's keeping always the guiding hand on the direction of the foreign policy....Under these conditions, it is impossible to consider the alliance with Romania as of sufficient certainty and extent to serve Austria-Hungary as a pivot in her Balkan policy....To destroy, with the assistance of the Balkans, the military superiority of the two Imperial powers is the objective of Russia. But while France seeks the weakening of the Monarchy, because that is favorable to her ideas of *révanche,* the designs of the empire of the Tsar have a much greater extent....For Russia has recognized that the relation of her plans in Europe and in Asia, plans that correspond with internal necessities gravely affect the important interests of Germany, and must inevitably arouse her to resistance. The policy of Russia is determined by an unchanging situation, and is consequently constant and foresighted. Russia's policy of encirclement directed against the Monarchy, which does not pursue a world policy, has for its final aim to make it impossible for the German Empire to resist the aims of Russia or her political and economic supremacy. For these reasons those in charge of the foreign policy of Austria-Hungary are convinced that it is in the common interest of the Monarchy, as in that of Germany, to oppose energetically and in time in this phase of the Balkan crisis, the development foreseen and encouraged by Russia by a pre-concerted plan. The above mémoire had just been finished when there occurred the terrible events of Sarajevo. The complete extent of this abominable assassination can hardly be realized; at all events it appears undeniable proof, if indeed any were yet lacking, of the impossibility of extinguishing the hatred between the Monarchy and Serbia, as well as the danger and the violence of the Pan-Serbian propaganda, which hesitates at nothing. Austria-Hungary has not been lacking in good will and in the spirit of conciliation, to bring about reasonably good relations with Serbia, but it has just been shown that these efforts have been completely impotent and that the Monarchy must expect in the future to deal with the bitter, irreconcilable, and aggressive enmity of Serbia. In these conditions, the Monarchy must tear away with a strong hand the net in which its enemy seeks to entangle it.

Chapter Six
July 3, 1914

No. 11.
From: M. Yov. M. Yovanovitch, Minister at Vienna.
To: M. N. Pashitch, Prime Minister and Minister for Foreign Affairs.
Vienna, July 3, 1914.

Sir,

Yesterday being the day on which the remains of the Archduke Francis Ferdinand and his wife were brought from Sarajevo to Vienna, I gave instructions that the national flag at my residence should be hoisted at half-mast as a sign of mourning yesterday evening, on this account, protests were made by the concierge, the other tenants, the landlord's agent, and the landlord himself, who demanded the removal of the flag. Explanations prove of no avail, and the assistance of the police authorities was requested. The latter privately asked that the flag should be removed in order to avoid further disorders. The flag was not removed, and accordingly noisy demonstrations took place last night in front of the Legation. The conduct of the police was energetic, and nothing happened to the flag or to the building that might constitute an insult.

At 2 A.M. the crowd dispersed. To-day's papers, more particularly the popular clerical papers, publish articles under the heading "Provocation by the Serbian Minister," in which the whole incident is falsely described The flag on the Legation building remained flying the whole time up to the conclusion of the service at the Court Chapel. As soon as this ceremony was concluded, the flag was removed. People from all over the quarter in which I live went to the Prefecture, the Municipality, and the State Council to demand the removal of our flag.

The crowd was harangued by Dr. Funder, director in chief of the Catholic Reichspost, Hermengild Wagner, and Leopold Mandl, all of whom arc known as the chief instigators of the attacks in the Austrian and German press against Serbia and the Serbians.

No. 12.
From: M. Yov. M. Yovanovitch, Minister at Vienna.
To: M. N. Pashitch, Prime Minister and Minister for Foreign Affairs.
Vienna, July 3, 1914.

Sir,

In the course of a conversation I had with the Under Secretary at the Foreign Office on the subject of the Sarajevo outrage, Baron Macchio severely criticized the Belgrade press and the tone of its articles. He argued that the Belgrade press was under no control and created *die Hetzereien gegen die Monarchie.* I told him that the press in Serbia was absolutely free, and that as a result private people as well as the Government very often suffered; there were, however, no means of proceeding against the press except by going to law. I told him that in the present instance the fault lay with the Austrian and Hungarian press, which was controlled by the Austro-Hungarian Government. Was it not true that during the past two years, the Austrian and Hungarian press had been attacking Serbia, in such a manner as to offend her most sensitive feelings? The anniversary of the unfortunate war with Bulgaria had taken place a few days ago. I had myself witnessed the great lack of respect with which the Vienna press had written about Serbia and the Serbian army during and after the war, as well as in many other matters. The press in Belgrade was much more moderate. For instance, in the present case, a terrible crime had been committed and telegrams were being sent from Vienna to the whole world, accusing the entire Serbian nation and Serbia of being accomplices of the detestable Sarajevo outrage. All the Austrian newspapers were writing in that strain. Was it possible to remain indifferent? Even if the criminal was a Serbian, the whole Serbian nation and the Kingdom of Serbia could not be held guilty, nor could they be accused in such a manner.

Baron Macchio replied, "Nobody accuses the Kingdom of Serbia nor its Government, nor the whole Serbian nation. We accuse those who encourage the Great Serbian scheme and work for the realisation of its object."

I told him that it appeared to me that from the first the nationality of the criminal had been deliberately put forward in order to involve Belgrade and to create the impression that the outrage had been organised by Serbia. This had struck me immediately, as I knew that up till now the Serbians of Bosnia had been spoken of as *die Bosniaken, bosnische Sprache, die Orthodoxen aus Bosnien,* while now it was being said that the assassin was *ein Serbe,* but not that he was a Bosnian nor that he was an Austrian subject.

"I repeat," said Baron Macchio, "that we do not accuse the Serbian Government and the Serbian nation but the various agitators...."

I begged him to use his influence in order to induce the Vienna press not to make matters more difficult by its accusations in this critical moment, when Serbo-Austrian relations were being put to a severe test.

Chapter Seven
July 4, 1914

No. 4.
Count Szécsen to Count Berchtold.
(Telegraphic) Parts, July 4, 1914.

To-day I communicated to M. Poincaré the thanks of the Imperial and Royal Government for their sympathy.

In referring to the hostile demonstrations against Serbia among us, he mentioned that after the murder of President Carnot, all Italians throughout France were exposed to the worst persecutions on the part of the people.

I drew his attention to the fact that that crime had no connection with any anti-French agitation in Italy, while in the present case it must be admitted that for years past there has been an agitation in Serbia against the Monarchy fomented by every means, legitimate and illegitimate.

In conclusion, M. Poincaré expressed his conviction that the Serbian Government would meet us with the greatest willingness in the judicial investigation and the prosecution of the accomplices. No State could divest itself of this duty.

No. 13.
From: **Dr. M. R. Vesnitch, Minister at Paris.**
To: **M. N. Pashitch, Prime Minister and Minister for Foreign Affairs.**
Paris, July 4, 1914.

Sir,

I had a long conversation on Wednesday last on the subject of the Sarajevo outrage with M. Viviani, the new Minister for Foreign Affairs, who was somewhat concerned at what had occurred. I made use of this opportunity to describe to him briefly the causes that had led to the outrage, and that were to be found, in the first place, in the irksome system of Government in force in the annexed provinces, and especially in the attitude of the officials, as well as in the whole policy of the Monarchy toward anything orthodox. He understood the situation, but at the same time expressed the hope that we should preserve an attitude of calm and dignity in order to avoid giving cause for fresh accusations in Vienna.

After the first moment of excitement, public opinion here has quieted down to such an extent that the Minister-President himself considered it advisable in the Palais de Bourbon to soften the expressions used in the statement he had made earlier on the subject in the Senate.

No. 14.
From: **Dr. M. Spalaikovitch, Minister at Petrograd.**
To: **M. N. Pashitch, Prime Minister and Minister for Foreign Affairs.**
Petrograd, July 4, 1914.
(Telegraphic)

The Minister for Foreign Affairs tells me that the outrages committed upon Serbs in Bosnia will increase the sympathy of Europe for us. He is of opinion that the accusations made against us in Vienna will not obtain credence. The chief thing is for public opinion in Serbia to remain calm.

M. de Manneville, French Chargé d'Affaires at Berlin, to M. René Viviani, President of the Council, Minister for Foreign Affairs.
Berlin, July 4, 1914.

The Under-Secretary of State for Foreign Affairs told me yesterday, and has to-day repeated to the Russian Ambassador, that he hoped Serbia would satisfy the demands, which Austrian might have to make to her with regard to the investigation and the prosecution of the accomplices in the crime of Sarajevo. He added that he was confident that this would be the case because Serbia, if she acted in any other way, would have the opinion of the completely civilized world against her. The German Government does not then appear to share the anxiety that is shown by a part of the German press as to possible tension in the relations between the Governments of Vienna and Belgrade, or at least they do not wish to seem to do so.

DE MANNEVILLE.

Chapter Eight
July 5, 1914

Germany offers Austria war aid to fight against Serbia, otherwise known as the blank check.

Chapter Nine
July 6, 1914

No. 15.
From: M. Yov. M. Yovanovitch, Minister at Vienna.
To: M. N. Pashitch, Prime Minister and Minister for Foreign Affairs.
Vienna, July 6, 1914.
(Telegraphic)

The excitement in military and Government circles against Serbia is steadily growing owing to the tone of our press, which is diligently exploited by the Austro-Hungarian Legation at Belgrade.

No. 16.
From: M. Yov. M. Yovanovitch, Minister at Vienna.
To: M. N. Pashitch, Prime Minister and Minister for Foreign Affairs.
Vienna, July 6, 1914.

Sir,
The principal lines and tendencies to be found in the articles of the Vienna press on the subject of the Sarajevo outrage are as follows:

As long ago as Sunday afternoon, June 28 last, when the Vienna newspapers issued extra editions regarding the outrage upon the Crown Prince, the headlines announced that both the perpetrators were Serbians; moreover, this was done in such a manner as to leave the impression that they were Serbs from Serbia proper. In the later reports, which described the outrage, there was a marked tendency to connect it with Serbia. Two circumstances were especially emphasized and were intended to indicate Belgrade as the place of origin of the outrage, viz.: (1) the visit to Belgrade of both of the perpetrators; and (2) the origin of the bombs. As the third and last link in this chain of evidence, the Vienna papers began to publish the evidence given by the assassins at the trial. It was characteristic to find that the Hungarian Korrespondenzbureau, and the Hungarian newspapers, especially the *Az Eszt*, were alone in a position to know all about this "evidence." This evidence mainly tends to show: (1) that it has been established that the perpetrators, while in Belgrade, associated with the comitadji Mihaylo Ciganovitch; and (2) that the organizer and instigator of the outrage was Major Pribitchevitch.

Another tendency became apparent at the same time, viz.: to hold the Narodna Odbrana responsible for this outrage. Further, on Friday last, the latest announcement which the Hungarian Korrespondenzbureau made to the newspapers stated:

"The enquiries made up to the present prove conclusively that this outrage is the work of a conspiracy. Besides the two perpetrators, a large number of persons have been arrested, mostly young men, who are also, like the perpetrators, proved to have been employed by the Belgrade Narodna Odbrana in order to commit the outrage, and who were supplied in Belgrade with bombs and revolvers."

On the same day, late at night, the Hungarian Korrespondenzbureau sent the following request to the newspapers:

"We beg the Editor not to publish the report relating to the Sarajevo outrage, which appeared in our evening's bulletin."

At the same time the Vienna Korrespondenzbureau published the following official statement:

"We learn from authoritative quarters that the enquiries relating to the outrage are being kept absolutely secret. All the details, therefore, which have appeared in the public press should be accepted with reserve." Nevertheless, the Budapest newspapers continued to publish alleged reports on the enquiry. In the last "report" of the Budapest newspaper *A Nap,* which was reprinted in yesterday's Vienna papers, the tendency to lay the responsibility for the outrage on the Narodna Odbrana is still further emphasized. According to this report, the accused Gabrinovitch had stated that General Yankovitch is the chief instigator of the outrage.

6 July

The Kaiser departed for his annual North Sea cruise after completing his meetings with Hoyos and Szogyeny. The twenty-day cruise had been planned for months, and the Kaiser saw nothing in the events that would cause him to cancel it. Besides, it might appear that something was wrong should the cruise be cancelled.

M. Paléologue, French Ambassador at St. Petersburgh, to M. René Viviani, President of the Council, Minister for Foreign Affairs.
St. Petersburgh, July 6, 1914.

In the course of an interview, which he had asked for with the Austro-Hungarian Chargé d'Affaires, M. Sazonof pointed out in a friendly way the disquieting irritation, which the attacks of the Austrian press against Serbia, are in danger of producing in his country. Count Czernin, having given him to understand that the Austro-Hungarian Government would perhaps be compelled to search for the instigators of the crime of Sarajevo on Serbian territory, M. Sazonof interrupted him: "No country," he said, "has had to suffer more than Russia from crimes prepared on foreign territory. Have we ever claimed to employ in any country whatsoever the procedure with which your papers threaten Serbia? Do not embark on such a course."

May this warning not be in vain?

PALÉOLOGUE.

Primary Documents: Germany's "Blank Cheque" to Austria-Hungary, 6 July 1914

Below is the text of the telegram sent by the German chancellor, Theobald von Bethmann-Hollweg, to the German ambassador at Vienna.

The telegram effectively offered Austria-Hungary a "blank cheque" in terms of German support for whatever action Austria-Hungary chose to take in punishing Serbia for the assassination of Archduke Franz Ferdinand on 28 June 1914.

Confidential—For Your Excellency's personal information and guidance:

Berlin
6 July 1914

The Austro-Hungarian Ambassador yesterday delivered to the Emperor a confidential personal letter from the Emperor Francis Joseph, which depicts the present situation from the Austro-Hungarian point of view, and describes the measures which Vienna has in view. A copy is now being forwarded to Your Excellency. I replied to Count Szagyeny today on behalf of His Majesty that His Majesty sends his thanks to the Emperor Francis Joseph for his letter and would soon answer it personally. In the meantime His Majesty desires to say that he is not blind to the danger which threatens Austria-Hungary and thus the Triple Alliance as a result of the Russian and Serbian Pan-Slavic agitation. Even though His Majesty is known to feel no unqualified confidence in Bulgaria and her ruler, and naturally inclines more to ward our old ally Rumania and her Hohenzollern prince, yet he quite understands that the Emperor Francis Joseph, in view of the attitude of Rumania and of the danger of a new Balkan alliance aimed directly at the Danube Monarchy, is anxious to bring about an understanding between Bulgaria and the Triple alliance. […] His Majesty will, furthermore, make an effort at Bucharest, according to the wishes of the Emperor Francis Joseph, to influence King Carol to the fulfillment of the duties of his alliance, to the renunciation of Serbia, and to the suppression of the Rumanian agitations directed against Austria-Hungary. Finally, as far as concerns Serbia, His Majesty, of course, cannot interfere in the dispute now going on between Austria-Hungary and that country, as it is a matter not within his competence. The Emperor Francis Joseph may, however, rest assured that His Majesty will faithfully stand by Austria-Hungary, as is required by the obligations of his alliance and of his ancient friendship.

—Bethmann-Hollweg

No. 5.
Herr Hoflehner, Consular Agent to Count Berchtold.
Nish, July 6, 1914.

The news of the terrible crime at Sarajevo, which had been only too successful, created here a sensation in the fullest sense of the word. There was practically no sign of consternation or indignation; the predominant mood was one of satisfaction and even joy, and this was often quite open without any-reserve, and even found expression in a brutal way. This is especially the case with the so-called leading circles—the intellectuals, such as professional politicians, those occupied in education, officials, officers, and the students. Commercial circles adopted a rather more reserved attitude.

All explanations made by official Serbian circles or individual higher personalities purporting to give expression to indignation at the crime and condemnation of it must have the effect of the bitterest irony on anyone who has had an opportunity, during the last few days, of gaining an insight at first hand into the feelings of the educated Serbian people.

On the day of the crime the undersigned had gone to a coffee garden at about 9 o'clock in the evening without any suspicion of what had happened, and here received from an acquaintance his first information as to the very definite rumor which was being circulated. It was painful in the highest degree to see and hear what a feeling of real delight seized the numerous visitors who were present, with what obvious satisfaction the deed was discussed, and what cries of joy, scorn, and contempt burst out even one who has long been accustomed to the expression of political fanaticism which obtains here, must feel the greatest depression at what he observed.

Chapter Ten
July 7, 1914

Colonel House to the Kaiser
American Embassy
London, July 7, 1914
His Imperial Majesty,
Emperor of Germany, King of Prussia
Berlin Germany,

Your Imperial Majesty will doubtless recall our conversation at Potsdam and that with the President's consent and approval I came to Europe for the purpose of ascertaining whether or not it was possible to bring about a better understanding between the Great Powers, to the end that there might be a continuation of peace, and later a beneficent economic readjustment, which a lessening of armaments would ensure.

Because of the commanding position Your Majesty occupies, and because of your well-known desire to maintain peace, I came, as Your Majesty knows, directly to Berlin.

I can never forget the gracious acceptance of the general purpose of my mission, the mastery exposition of the worldwide political conditions as they exist today, and the prophetic forecast as to the future which Your Majesty then made.

I received every reasonable assurance of Your Majesty's cordial approval of the President's purpose, and left Germany happy in the belief that Your Majesty's great influence would be thrown in behalf of peace and the broadening of the world's commerce.

In France I tried to reach the thoughts of her people in regard to Germany and to find what hopes she nursed. My conclusion upon leaving was that her statesmen have given over all thoughts of revenge or of recovery of the two lost provinces. Her people in general still have hopes in both directions, but her better-informed rulers would be quite content if France could be sure of her autonomy as it now exist.

It was then, Sir, that I came to England and with high hopes, in which I have not been disappointed.

I first approached Sir Edward Grey, and I found him sympathetic to the last degree. After a two-hour conference, we parted with the understanding that we should meet again within a few days. This I inferred to mean that he wished to consult with the Prime Minister and his colleagues.

At our next conference, which again lasted for two hours, he had, to meet me, the Lord Chancellor, Earl Crewe, and Sir William Tyrrell. Since then I have met the Prime Minister and practically every important member of the British Government, and I'm convinced that they desire such an understanding as will lay the foundation of permanent peace and security.

England must necessarily move cautiously, lest she offered the sensibilities of France and Russia; but with the changing sentiment in France, There should be a gradual improvement of relations between Germany and that country which England will now be glad to foster.

While much has been accomplished, yet there is something still to be desired in order that there may be a better medium created for an easy and frank exchange of thought and purpose. No one knows better than Your Majesty of the usual ferment that is now going on throughout the world, and no one is in so a fortunate a position on to bring about a sane and reasonable understanding among the statesmen of the western peoples, so that our civilization may continue uninterrupted.

While this communication is, as Your Majesty knows, quite unofficial, yet it is written in sympathy with the well-known views of the president, and I'm given to understand, with hope from his Britannic Majesty's Government that it may bring a response from Your Majesty which may permit another step forward.

Permit me, sir, to conclude by quoting sentence from a letter which has come to me from the President:

"Your letter from Paris, written just after coming from Berlin, gives me a thrill of deep pleasure. You have, I hope and believe, begun a great thing and I rejoice with all my heart."

I have the honor to be, Sir, with the greatest respect, Your Majesty's very obedient servant.

—Edward M. House

"Thus was a last opportunity given to the Kaiser, who had the assurance of a disinterested outsider that if Germany sincerely desired peace she would have the active assistance of the United States and the co-operation of Great Britain. It was a definite answer to the allegations that Grey's policy aimed at the encirclement and isolation of the Germans. Alas! By the time Colonel House's letter reached Germany, Wilhelm II was already on his cruise in Norwegian waters whence he was recalled by the Austrian ultimatum to Serbia and to Serbia and the war-clouds that immediately gathered."

—Charles Seymour

Austria Declares War on Serbia

In 1914 Austria-Hungary launched its war against Serbia, believing it had the support of Germany. Russia chose to go to war to defend the Serbs from the Austro-Hungarians. Reproduced below are the official minutes of the Austrian Ministerial Council Meeting, which took place on 7 July 1914, some nine days following the assassination of Archduke Franz Ferdinand and his wife, Sophie, in Sarajevo on 28 June 1914. During the meeting, the prospect of war with Serbia was debated; aside from the Hungarian prime minister Count Tisza, all present favored presenting Serbia with a sufficiently severe ultimatum that could not be accepted. Its rejection would therefore prove grounds for a subsequent declaration of war.

Minutes of Ministerial Council on affairs of State held at Vienna on July 7, 1914, under the presidency of the Minister of the Royal and Imperial Household and Minister for Foreign Affairs, Count Berchtold.

Also were the Austrian Premier Count Sturkh, The Hungarian Premier Count Tisza, The Joint Minister for Finance Ritter von Bilinski, the War Minister, and Ritter von Krobatin.
Keeper of the Minutes: Councilor of Legation, Count Hoyos

Agenda: Bosnian Affairs—The Diplomatic Action against Serbia

The President opens the sitting by remarking that the Ministerial Council has been called in order to advise on the measures to be used in reforming the evil internal political conditions in Bosnia and Herzegovina, as shown up by the disastrous event at Sarajevo. In his opinion there were various internal measures applicable within Bosnia, the use of which seemed to him very appropriate, in order to deal with the critical situation; but first of all they must make up their minds as to whether the moment had not come for reducing Serbia to permanent inoffensiveness by a demonstration of their power. So decisive a blow could not be dealt without previous diplomatic preparation; consequently he had approached the German Government. The conversations at Berlin had led to a very satisfactory result, inasmuch as both the Emperor William and Herr von Bethmann Hollweg had most emphatically assured it is of Germany's unconditional support in the case of hostilities with Serbia. Meanwhile, we still had to reckon with Italy and with Rumania, and here he agreed with the Berlin Cabinet that it would be better to negotiate and be prepared for any claims to compensation which might arise. He was clear in his own mind that hostilities with Serbia would entail war with Russia. Russia, however, was now playing a far-seeing game, and was calculating on a policy of being able to unite the Balkan States, including Rumania, with the eventual objective of launching them at an appropriate moment against the Monarchy. He suggested that we must reckon on the fact that in face of such a policy our situation was bound steadily to deteriorate, and all the more if an inactive policy of laisser alley were to be interpreted as a sign of weakness by our own South Slavs and Rumanians, and were to be a direct encouragement to the power of attraction of the two neighbor States. The logical inference to be drawn from his remarks was that we must be beforehand with our enemies and, by bringing matters to a head with Serbia, must call a halt to the gathering momentum of events; later it would no longer be possible to do so. The Hungarian Premier agreed that during the last few days the results of our investigations and the tone of the Serbian press had put a materially new complexion on events, and emphasized the fact that he himself held the possibility of warlike action against Serbia to be more obvious than he had thought in the period immediately after the act at Sarajevo. But he would never give his consent to a surprise attack on Serbia without previous diplomatic action, as seemed to be contemplated and as had unfortunately already been made the subject of discussion by Count Hoyos at Berlin; were that done, in his opinion, our position in the eyes of Europe would be an extremely bad one, and in all probability we should have to reckon with the enmity of the whole Balkans, except Bulgaria, while Bulgaria herself being at present very much weakened would not be able to give us the necessary support. It was absolutely necessary that we should formulate demands against Serbia and only send an ultimatum in case Serbia failed to satisfy them. These demands must undoubtedly be hard, but should not be impossible of fulfillment. Should Serbia accept them we should be able to quote a dazzling diplomatic victory, and our prestige in the Balkans would be raised. Should our demands not be accepted he himself would then be for warlike action, but even at this point he thought it essential to lay stress on the fact that the object of such action ought to be the reduction of Serbia, but not her complete annihilation; first, because this would never be allowed by Russia without a life-and-death struggle, and also because he, as Hungarian Premier, could never consent to the annexation of part of Serbia by the Monarchy. It was not Germany's place to judge whether we should now deal a blow at Serbia or not. Personally, he was of opinion that it was not absolutely necessary to go to war at this moment.

At the present time we must take into account that the agitation against us in Rumania was very strong, that in view of the excited state of public opinion, we should have to reckon with a Rumanian attack. We must also remember that in the sphere of European politics the relation of French to German power would continually deteriorate because of the low birthrate, and that Germany would therefore continually have more troops at her disposal, as time went on, against Russia. These considerations ought all to be weighed on the occasion of a decision as important as the one to be taken to-day; he must, therefore, come back to this, that, in spite of the crisis of affairs in Bosnia, he would not make up his mind unconditionally for war.

The President remarked that the history of the last years had shown that while diplomatic successes against Serbia raised the reputation of the Monarchy for the time being, the actual tension in our relations with Serbia had only increased. Neither our success during the annexation crisis, nor at the creation of Albania, nor Serbia's submission later in consequence of our ultimatum of the autumn of last year, had altered the real situation in any way. He imagined that energetic action alone would suffice to solve once for all, the problem created by the systematic propaganda for a Greater Serbia encouraged from Belgrade, the disintegrating effects of which had made themselves felt as far as Agram and Zara. As regards the danger of a hostile attitude on the part of Rumania, mentioned by the Hungarian Premier, the President remarked that this was less to be feared now than later on, when the unity of interests between Rumania and Serbia would have become more pronounced. To be sure, King Carol had let fall doubts as to whether he would be able to fulfill his duty as an ally, should occasion arise, by sending active help. On the other hand, it was scarcely likely that he would allow himself to be so far carried away as to become involved in hostilities against the Monarchy, even supposing that public opinion did not itself oppose that. Further, there was Rumanian fear of Bulgaria; even as things stood at present this was bound to a certain extent to hamper Rumania's freedom of movement. As for the observation made by the Hungarian Premier on the relative strength of France and Germany, surely they had to remember that the decreasing birthrate of France was counter-balanced by the infinitely more rapid increase in the population of Russia, so that the argument that in future Germany would always have more troops at her disposal against France would not hold. The Austrian Premier remarked that to-day's Ministerial Council had actually been called for the purpose of advising about the internal measures to be taken in Bosnia and Herzegovina, in order to make effective the present inquiry into the assassination, on the one hand, and, on the other, to counteract the Greater Serbia propaganda. But now these questions must give way to the principal question: Should we solve the internal crisis in Bosnia by a demonstration of power against Serbia? Two considerations now made this principal question an immediate one; first, the Governor of Bosnia and Herzegovina was proceeding on the presumption, acquired in the course of inquiries and in consequence of his knowledge of Bosnian affairs, that no internal measures would be effective, unless we made up our minds to deal a forceful blow to Serbia abroad. In view of this report from General Potiorek we must ask ourselves whether the schismatic activities originating in Serbia could be stopped at all, unless we took action against the Kingdom.

During the last few days the whole situation had received a materially fresh complexion and a psychological situation had been created, which, in his opinion, led unconditionally to an issue of arms with Serbia. He certainly agreed with the Hungarian Premier that it was for us, and not for the German Government, to decide whether a war were necessary or not; he must nevertheless observe that our decision must be materially influenced by the fact that in the quarter which we were bound to regard as the greatest support of our policy in the Triple Alliance, unconditional loyalty was, as we were informed, promised to us and that, in addition, on our making inquiry, we were urged to act at once, Count Tisza ought to weigh this fact, and to consider that a hesitating, weak policy would run us into the danger of losing the certainty of this unconditional support of the German Empire on a future occasion. This was the second consideration, which was taken into account in forming our decision, and was additional to our interest in restoring order in Bosnia. How to begin the conflict was a question of detail and should the Hungarian Government be of opinion that a surprise attack "sans crier Bare," to use Count Tisza's expression, was not feasible, then they must needs think of some other way; but he did most earnestly hope that, whatever they might do, they would act quickly and our trade and commerce be spared a long period of unrest. All this was detail compared with the chief question as to whether it should in any case come to armed action or not, and here the authoritative interest was the reputation and stability of the Monarchy, whose South Slav provinces he held to be lost if nothing were to happen. They ought, therefore, to make up their minds to-day, in a general way, whether they meant to act or not. He, too, shared the President's view that the situation would not be in the least improved by a diplomatic success. If, therefore, international considerations caused them to adopt the method of an initial diplomatic action against Serbia, this would have to be done with the firm intention of allowing such action to end only in a war.

The Joint Finance Minister observed that Count Sturkh had referred to the fact that the Governor wanted war. For two years General Potiorek had held the view that we must match ourselves against Serbia, in order to be able to retain Bosnia and Herzegovina. We ought not to forget that the Governor, who was on the spot, could better judge the situation. Herr von Bilinski, too, was convinced that a decisive struggle was unavoidable sooner or later. The Hungarian Premier observed that he had the highest opinion of the present Governor as soldier, but, as regards the civil administration, it could not be denied that it had broken down completely and that reform was absolutely essential. He would not enter more fully into this question, especially as it was no time for big alterations; he would only observe that the most incredible conditions must be reigning among the police, to make it possible that six or seven persons known to the police should have been able to place themselves along the route of the procession on the day of the assassination, armed with bombs and revolvers without a single one of them being noticed or removed by the police. He could not see why the condition of Bosnia could not be materially improved by means of a thorough reform of the administration.

The Joint War Minister is of opinion that a diplomatic success would he of no value. Such a success would only be interpreted as a weakness. From the military point of view he must emphasize the fact that it would be better to wage the war now, rather than later, as the balance of power would move disproportionately against us later on. As for the procedure for beginning war, he might be permitted to remark that the two great wars of recent years, both the Russo-Japanese and the Balkan Wars, had been begun without previous declarations of war. His opinion was at first only to carry through their contemplated mobilization against Serbia, and let general mobilization wait until they knew whether Russia was going to take action or not. We had already neglected two opportunities of solving the Serbian question and had deferred decision on both occasions. If we did this again and took no notice of this latest provocation, this would be taken as a sign of weakness in every South Slav province and we should be inducing an increase of the agitation directed against us. It would be desirable from a military point of view if the mobilization could be carried out at once, and secretly, and a summons addressed to Serbia only after mobilization had been completed. This would also be a good thing as against the Russian forces, as just about this time the Russian frontier forces were not at their full strength on account of harvest-leave. Thereupon a discussion developed about the aims of warlike action against Serbia, and the Hungarian Premier's point of view was accepted, to the effect that Serbia should be reduced in size, but not, in view of Russia, entirely annihilated. The Austrian Premier emphasized the fact that it might also be advisable to remove the Karageorgevich dynasty and to give the Crown to a European prince, as well as to induce a certain condition of dependency of this reduced kingdom on the Monarchy in relation to military affairs. The Hungarian Premier still remained convinced that the Monarchy could adopt a successful Balkan policy by means of Bulgaria's adherence to the Triple Alliance, and pointed out what a frightful calamity a European war would be under present circumstances. The question of war was then further argued thoroughly in the course of a long discussion. At the end of this discussion agreement was reached:

(1) That all present wish for the speediest decision which is practicable in the conflict with Serbia, whether by means of war or peace.

(2) That the Ministerial Council is prepared to adopt the point of view of the Hungarian Premier to the effect that mobilization shall only follow after concrete

demands have been addressed to Serbia, and have been refused, and an ultimatum has further been sent.

(3) On the other hand, all present, excepting the Hungarian Premier, hold that a purely diplomatic success, even if ending in a startling humiliation for Serbia, would be without value, and that, therefore, the demands to be put to Serbia must be so far-reaching as to pre-suppose a refusal, so that the way would be prepared for a radical solution by means of military intervention. Count Tisza observes that he is desirous of meeting the views of all present, and therefore would be prepared to concede this much, that he would agree that the demands to be put to Serbia must be very hard, yet must not be of such a nature as to cause our intention of putting unacceptable demands to become obvious.

Otherwise, our legal position would be an impossible one for a declaration of war. The text of the Note would have to be most carefully formulated, and he must lay importance on the necessity of seeing the Note before its dispatch. He must further stress the necessity, as regards his own person, of taking the obvious action contingent on having had his point of view rejected. The meeting was now adjourned till the afternoon.

On the reassembly of the Ministerial Council, the Chief of the General Staff, and the Representative of the Navy Command [Admiral Kailer] were also present. By request of the President, the Minister for War addressed the meeting and put the following three questions to the Chief of the General Staff [Von Hoetzendorff]:

(1) Whether it would be possible to mobilize against Serbia first and only subsequently against Russia as well, if this should become necessary.

(2) Whether large bodies of troops should be retained in Transylvania to overawe Rumania.

(3) At which point the war against Russia would be begun. The Chief of the General Staff, in response to these inquiries, supplies information which is confidential, and therefore requests that it be omitted from the Minutes. A discussion of some length develops out of these explanations as to the relation of forces and the probable course of a European war, which, on account of its confidential character, could not be entered on the Minutes. At the end of this discussion the Hungarian Premier repeats his views on the question of war, and once more appeals to all present to weigh their decisions with care. A discussion followed on the points to be included in the demands to be put in the Note to Serbia.

The Ministerial Council took no definite decision as to these points; suggestions were simply made with a view to obtaining an idea of what demands might be put. The President sums up to the effect that though there still existed a divergence of view between all members and Count Tisza, yet they had come nearer agreement, inasmuch as the Hungarian Premier's own proposals would in all probability lead up to that armed conflict with Serbia, which he and the others at the meeting held to be necessary. Count Berchtold informs the meeting that he proposes to travel to Ischl on the 8th, and report to His Imperial Apostolic Majesty. The Hungarian Premier requests the President to submit also a humble memorial, which he would draw up, on his view of the situation. After a communiqué had been drawn up for the Press, the President closes the meeting.

Secretary: A. HOYOS (Signature)
BERCHTOLD (Signature)
I have noted the contents of these Minutes. Vienna, August 16, 1914.

FRANZ JOSEF (Signature)
Source: *Source Records of the Great War, Vol. I,* ed. Charles F. Horne, *National Alumni 1923.*

Russia believes it is necessary to mobilize against Germany as well as Austria-Hungary, in case Germany goes to war alongside Austria-Hungary. For the Germans this mobilization is a declaration of war. Military considerations have trumped diplomatic considerations, and the German nation approves of what it sees as a war of self-defense. Germany declares war on Russia, Aug 3, 1914.

No. 17.
From: **M. Yov. M. Yovanovitch, Minister at Vienna.**
To: **M. N. Pashitch, Prime Minister and Minister for Foreign Affairs.**
Vienna, July 7, 1914.

Sir,

In influential circles the excitement continues undiminished. Though the Emperor has addressed a letter to the Prime Ministers of Austria and Hungary respectively, and to the Minister of Finance, Herr Bilinski, in which an appeal is made for calmness, it is impossible to determine what attitude the Government will adopt towards us. For them one thing is obvious; whether it is proved or not that the outrage has been inspired and prepared at Belgrade, they must sooner or later solve the question of the so-called Great Serbian agitation within the Habsburg Monarchy. In what manner they will do this and what means they will employ to that end has not as yet been decided; this is being discussed especially in high Catholic and military circles. The ultimate decision will be taken only after it has been definitely ascertained what the enquiry at Sarajevo has brought to light. The decision will be in accordance with the findings of the enquiry.

In this respect, Austria-Hungary has to choose one of the following courses: either to regard the Sarajevo outrage as a national misfortune and a crime which ought to be dealt with in accordance with the evidence obtained, in which case Serbia's co-operation in the work will be requested in order to prevent the perpetrators escaping the extreme penalty; or, to treat the Sarajevo outrage as a Pan-Serbian, South-Slav and Pan-Slav conspiracy with every manifestation of the hatred, hitherto repressed, against Slavdom. There are many indications that influential circles are being urged to adopt the latter course: it is therefore advisable to be ready for defense. Should the former and wiser course be adopted, we should do all we can to meet Austrian wishes in this respect.

Chapter Eleven
July 9, 1914

No. 18.
From: M. N. Pashitch, Prime Minister and Minister for Foreign Affairs.
To: All the Serbian Legations abroad.
Belgrade, July 9, 1914.
(Telegraphic)

The Crown Prince Alexander is receiving threatening letters from Austria-Hungary nearly every day. Make use of this in course of conversation with your colleagues and journalists.

Chapter Twelve
July 10, 1914

Berchtold is complaining of Count Tisza's attitude, which makes it difficult to proceed vigorously against Serbia. Tisza pretends that they should act "like gentlemen." *(With assassins! After all that has happened! Stupidity!)*

Chapter Thirteen
July 11, 1914

M. d'Apchier le Maugin, French Consul-General at Budapest, to M. René Viviani, President of the Council, Minister for Foreign Affairs.
Budapest, July 11, 1914.

Questioned in the Chamber on the state of the Austro-Serbian question M. Tisza explained that before everything else it was necessary to wait for the result of the judicial inquiry, as to which he refused now to make any disclosure whatsoever. And the Chamber has given its full approval to this. He also showed himself equally discreet as to the decisions taken at the meeting of Ministers at Vienna, and did not give any indication whether the project of a *démarche* at Belgrade, with which all the papers of both hemispheres are full, would be followed up. The Chamber assented without hesitation. With regard to this *démarche,* it seems that the word has been given to minimize its significance; the anger of the Hungarians has, as it were, evaporated through the virulent articles of the press, which is now unanimous in advising against this step, which might be dangerous. The semi-official press especially would desire that for the word *"démarche,"* with its appearance of a threat, there should be substituted the expression *"pourparlers,"* which appears to them more friendly and more courteous. Thus, officially, for the moment all is for peace. All is for peace. In the press.

However, the public here believe in war and fears it. Moreover, persons in whom I have every reason to have confidence have assured me that they knew that every day cannon and ammunition were being sent in large quantities towards the frontier. Whether true or not this rumor has been brought to me from various quarters with details, which agree with one another, at least it indicates what the thoughts with which people are generally occupied are. The Government, whether it is sincerely desirous of peace, or whether it is preparing a coup, is now doing all that it can to allay these anxieties. This is why the tone of the Government newspapers has been lowered, first by one note, then by two, so that it is at the present moment almost optimistic. But they had themselves spread the alarm as it suited them *(à plaisir)*. Their optimism to order is in fact without an echo; the nervousness of the Bourse, a barometer which cannot be neglected, is a sure proof of this; without exception stocks have fallen to an unaccountably low level; the Hungarian 4 per cents. Were quoted yesterday at 79.95, a rate that has never been quoted since they were first issued.

D'APCHIER LE MAUGIN.

Chapter Fourteen
July 12, 1914

Announcement by the Russian Government.
St. Petersburg, July 12, 1914.

Recent events and the dispatch of an ultimatum to Serbia by Austria-Hungary are causing the Russian Government the greatest anxiety. The Government is closely following the course of the dispute between the two countries, to which Russia cannot remain indifferent.

Chapter Fifteen
July 14, 1914

From: Dr. M. Yovanovitch, Chargé d'Affaires at Berlin.
To: M. N. Pashitch, Prime Minister and Minister for Foreign Affairs.
Berlin, July 14, 1914.
(Telegraphic)

The Secretary of State has told me that he could not understand the provocative attitude of the Serbian press and the attacks made by it against Austria-Hungary, who, as a Great Power, could not tolerate such proceedings

No. 20.
From: M. N. Pashitch, Prime Minister and Minister for Foreign Affairs.
To: All the Serbian Legations abroad.
Belgrade, July 14, 1914.
(Telegraphic)

(1) The Austrian Korrespondenzbureau is showing a marked tendency to excite public opinion in Europe. This Bureau interprets neither correctly nor sincerely the tone adopted by the Belgrade press. It selects the strongest expressions from such articles as contain replies to insults, threats, and false news designed to mislead public opinion, and submits them to the Austro-Hungarian public.

(2) The Korrespondenzbureau quotes especially extracts from articles from those Serbian newspapers which are not the organs of any party or corporation.

(3) As far back as the annexation crisis, Austria-Hungary prohibited the entry into the country of all Serbian political and other newspapers, and thus our Press would not be in a position to excite public opinion in Austria-Hungary and Europe if the Korrespondenzbureau did not lay stress on and spread broadcast the items of news which it gathers from various Serbian papers, in every instance exaggerating them. Six days ago the entry into Austria-Hungary of the *Odyek,* the organ of the

Independent Radical Party, was prohibited, thus all our papers are now prevented from entering Austria-Hungary.

(4) With us the press is absolutely free. Newspapers can be confiscated only for lèse-majesté or for revolutionary propaganda; in all other cases confiscation is illegal. There is no censorship of newspapers in these circumstances; you should point out for their information, where necessary, that we have no other constitutional or legal means at our disposal for the control of our press. Nevertheless, when the articles in our papers are compared with those of Austria-Hungary, it is evident that the Austro-Hungarian papers originate the controversy, while ours merely reply. Please also emphasize the fact that public opinion in Serbia is relatively calm, and that there is no desire on our part to provoke and insult Austria-Hungary. No one in Europe would know what our newspapers were writing if the Korrespondenzbureau did not publish these items of news with the intention of doing as much harm as possible to Serbia.

No. 21.

From: M. N. Pashitch, Prime Minister and Minister for Foreign Affairs.
To: All the Serbian legations abroad.
Belgrade, July 14, 1914.
(Telegraphic)

During the past few days the Austro-Hungarian newspapers have been spreading reports to the effect that there have been demonstrations at Belgrade against the Austro-Hungarian Legation, that some Hungarian journalists were killed; that Austro-Hungarian subjects in Belgrade were maltreated and are now panic-stricken; that at the funeral of the late M. Hartwig Serbian students made a demonstration against the Austro-Hungarian Minister, etc. All these reports are absolutely untrue and imaginary. Complete calm prevails in Belgrade and there were no demonstrations of any kind this year, nor has there been any question of disorder. Not only do the Austro-Hungarian Minister and his staff walk about the town without being molested in any way, but no Austro-Hungarian subject has been in any way insulted, either by word or deed, as is reported by the Viennese papers; still less was any attack made upon the house of any Austro-Hungarian subject or were any of their windows broken. Not a single Austro-Hungarian subject has had the slightest cause for any complaint. All these false reports are being purposely spread in order to arouse and excite Austro-Hungarian public opinion against Serbia.

The whole of Belgrade and the entire diplomatic body were present to-day at the funeral of the late M. Hartwig; there was not the slightest sign of resentment shown by anybody. During the whole ceremony, exemplary order was maintained; so much, so that foreigners were impressed with the good behavior of the crowd, which was such as does not always prevail on similar occasions even in their own countries. Be good enough to communicate the above to the Government to which you are accredited and to the press.

No. 22.

From: M. Yov. M. Yovanovitch, Minister at Vienna.
To: M. N. Pashitch, Prime Minister and Minister for Foreign Affairs.
Vienna, July 14, 1914.

Sir,
Once more public opinion has been excited against us by the Literary Bureau of the Austro-Hungarian Ministry for Foreign Affairs. With the exception of the Zeit and the Arbeiter Zeitung, all the Austro-

Hungarian newspapers have obtained from that Bureau the material and tone of their articles on the subject of the Sarajevo outrage. You have yourself seen what kind of material and tone this is.

I am reliably informed that official German circles here are especially ill-disposed towards us. These circles have had some influence upon the writings of the Vienna press, especially upon those of the *Neue Freie Presse*. This latter paper is still anti-Serbian *à l'outrance*. The *Neue Freie Presse*, which is widely read and has many friends in high financial circles, and which—if so desired—writes in accordance with instructions from the Vienna Press Bureau, briefly summarizes the matter as follows: "We have to settle matters with Serbia by war; it is evident that peaceable means are of no avail. And if it must come to war sooner or later, then it is better to see the matter through now." The Bourse is very depressed. There has not been such a fall in prices in Vienna for a long time. Some securities have fallen 45 kronen. I have, &tc.

No. 19.
From: **Dr. M. Yovanovitch, Chargé d'Affaires at Berlin.**
To: **M. N. Pashitch, Prime Minister and Minister for Foreign Affairs.**
Berlin, July 14, 1914.
(Telegraphic)

The Secretary of State has told me that he could not understand the provocative attitude of the Serbian press and the attacks made by it against Austria-Hungary, who, as a Great Power, could not tolerate such proceedings.

No. 20.
From: **M. N. Pashitch, Prime Minister and Minister for Foreign Affairs.**
To: **All the Serbian Legations abroad.**
Belgrade, July 14, 1914.
(Telegraphic)

(1) The Austrian Korrespondenzbureau is showing a marked tendency to excite public opinion in Europe. This Bureau interprets neither correctly nor sincerely the tone adopted by the Belgrade press. It selects the strongest expressions from such articles as contain replies to insults, threats and false news designed to mislead public opinion, and submits them to the Austro-Hungarian public.

(2) The Korrespondenzbureau quotes especially extracts from articles from those Serbian newspapers which are not the organs of any party or corporation.

(3) As far back as the annexation crisis, Austria-Hungary prohibited the entry into the country of all Serbian political and other newspapers, and thus our Press would not be in a position to excite public opinion in Austria-Hungary and Europe if the Korrespondenzbureau did not lay stress on and spread broadcast the items of news which it gathers from various Serbian papers, in every instance exaggerating them. Six days ago the entry into Austria-Hungary of the *Odyek,* the organ of the Independent Radical Party, was prohibited, thus all our papers are now prevented from entering Austria-Hungary.

(4) With us the press is absolutely free. Newspapers can be confiscated only for lèse-majesté or for revolutionary propaganda; in all other cases confiscation is illegal. There is no censorship of newspapers

In these circumstances, you should point out for their information, where necessary, that we have no other constitutional or legal means at our disposal for the control of our press. Nevertheless, when the articles in our papers are compared with those of Austria-Hungary, it is evident that the Austro-Hungarian papers originate the controversy, while ours merely reply.

Please also emphasize the fact that public opinion in Serbia is relatively calm, and that there is no desire on our part to provoke and insult Austria-Hungary. No one in Europe would know what our newspapers were writing if the Korrespondenzbureau did not publish these items of news with the intention of doing as much harm as possible to Serbia.

No. 21.
From: **M. N. Pashitch, Prime Minister and Minister for Foreign Affairs.**
To: **All the Serbian legations abroad.**
Belgrade, July 14, 1914.
(Telegraphic)

During the past few days the Austro-Hungarian newspapers have been spreading reports to the effect that there have been demonstrations at Belgrade against the Austro-Hungarian Legation, that some Hungarian journalists were killed; that Austro-Hungarian subjects in Belgrade were maltreated and are now panic-stricken; that at the funeral of the late M. Hartwig Serbian students made a demonstration against the Austro-Hungarian Minister, &tc. All these reports are absolutely untrue and imaginary. Complete calm prevails in Belgrade and there were no demonstrations of any kind this year, nor has there been any question of disorder. Not only do the Austro-Hungarian Minister and his staff walk about the town without being molested in any way, but no Austro-Hungarian subject has been in any way insulted, either by word or deed, as is reported by the Viennese papers; still less was any attack made upon the house of any Austro-Hungarian subject or were any of their windows broken. Not a single Austro-Hungarian subject has had the slightest cause for any complaint. All these false reports are being purposely spread in order to arouse and excite Austro-Hungarian public opinion against Serbia.

The whole of Belgrade and the entire diplomatic body were present to-day at the funeral of the late M. Hartwig; there was not the slightest sign of resentment shown by anybody. During the whole ceremony exemplary order was maintained; so much so that foreigners were impressed with the good behavior of the crowd, which was such as does not always prevail on similar occasions even in their own countries.

Be good enough to communicate the above to the Government to which you are accredited and to the press.

No. 22.
From: **M. Yov. M. Yovanovitch, Minister at Vienna.**
To: **M. N. Pashitch, Prime Minister and Minister for Foreign Affairs.**
Vienna, July 14, 1914

Sir,
Once more public opinion has been excited against us by the Literary Bureau of the Austro-Hungarian Ministry for Foreign Affairs. With the exception of the Zeit and the Arbeiter Zeitung, all the Austro-Hungarian newspapers have obtained from that Bureau the material and tone of their articles on the subject of the Sarajevo outrage. You have yourself seen what kind of material and tone this is.

I am reliably informed that official German circles here are especially ill-disposed towards us. These circles have had some influence upon the writings of the Vienna press, especially upon those of the *Neue Freie Presse*.

This latter paper is still anti-Serbian *à l'outrance*. The *Neue Freie Presse,* which is widely read and has many friends in high financial circles, and which—if so desired—writes in accordance with instructions from the Vienna Press Bureau, briefly summarizes the matter as follows: "We have to settle matters with Serbia by war; it is evident that peaceable means are of no avail. And if it must come to war sooner or later, then it is better to see the matter through now."

The Bourse is very depressed. There has not been such a fall in prices in Vienna for a long time. Some securities have fallen 45 kronen.

14 July 1914

During the discussion to-day it was unanimously decided that it was advisable to wait until Poincare had left Russia before taking up matters with Belgrade. *(Too bad!)* For it is important, so far as is possible, to prevent the relations of those two Powers from being influenced, and perhaps determined, at St. Petersburg during the exhilaration of champagne dinners and demonstrations of fraternity by Poincare, Iswolsky, and the Grand Dukes. It would be better to have the toast over before the Ultimatum is sent. We shall be able to go ahead on July 25.

14 July 1914 (later)

Count Tisza called on me to-day after seeing Count Berchtold. He told me that he was a man who always counseled prudence, but that every day strengthened his opinion that the Monarchy must make up its mind to act energetically *(Certainly!)* in orders to prove its vigor and to end once for the entire deplorable situation on its southeastern border. The language of the Serbian press and of Serbian diplomats is insupportably arrogant. Tisza told me: "It has been disagreeable for me to advise war; but I am now fully convinced that it is necessary, and I shall exert myself to the utmost in behalf of the Monarchy." The final text of the note to be delivered to Serbia is not yet drafted. It will be ready Sunday (July 19). It has been decided that it will be better to wait until Poincare leaves St. Petersburg, that is, until July 25, before delivering it to Serbia. *(What a pity!)* But as soon as the period allowed Serbia to reply has elapsed, or in case she does not accept all the conditions without reservations, mobilization will be ordered. The note has been drafted in such a way that it will be practically impossible for Serbia to accept it. *(William II underlined this sentence twice.)*

[Tschirschky then explained that Berchtold was considering what demands had best be put forward to make Serbia's acceptance wholly impossible. To this the Kaiser noted] *Evacuate the Sandjak* (note: certain Turkish territory previously ceded by Austria to Serbia) *then the row will begin. Austria must without fail get it back so as to stop the unification of Serbia and Montenegro and the Serbs reaching the sea.*

Source: *Source Records of the Great War, Vol. I, ed. Charles F. Horne, National Alumni, 1923.*

July 14, 1914

The French socialists assembled in Paris for their annual Congress where, before government and public alike, they would reaffirm their unyielding opposition to war.

The weight of their responsibility fell heavily upon the conscience of the delegates. Could they really unleash a revolutionary strike against war? Would they strike ostracism and even repression? And if so, would the workers follow them? Frail but impassioned, the sixty-nine-year-old Guesde warned the Congress against the "nostrum" of the general strike, but his argument was now less anti-anarchist than anti-German, for if the general strike succeeded in France and not in Germany, he warned, as did the anti-socialist press, the nation would lie helpless before its enemy. At his side, paradoxically enough, stood Herve, the enfant terrible of the revolutionary left, who now insisted the patriotic workers would never respond to the call of the general strike. Thus, at the moment of crisis, the Marxist and the syndicalism, both of them foreshadowing their wartime nationalism, repudiate a lifetime of internationalism.

But not Jaures; his was the opposite route. "We have often agreed," he reminded the Congress, "that the general strike is one way of influencing and warning our rulers." Not a strike of French workers alone, he explained, which could paralyze France before an invader, but a coordinated proletarian effort in every belligerent country. "Thus, if France were exposed to the aggressions of German imperialism, Germany would be similarly threatened by Russia." Jaures' intervention prove to be decisive. Emboldened by his courage, the socialist agreed to use every means at their disposal, including general strike, to prevent a European war.

—Jean Jaures
France Socialist Congress

Chapter Sixteen
July 15, 1914

No. 23.
From: M. Yov. M. Yovanovitch, Minister at Vienna.
To: M. N. Pashitch, Prime Minister and Minister for Foreign Affairs.
Vienna, July 15, 1914.

Sir,

The most important question for us is, what, if any, are the intentions of the Austro-Hungarian Government as regards the Sarajevo outrage? Until now I have been unable to find this out, and my other colleagues are in a similar position. The word has now been passed 'round here not to tell anybody anything. The evening before last the Ministers of the Dual Monarchy held a meeting. It has not been possible to learn anything about the object and the result of this meeting. The communiqué issued on the subject was brief and obscure. It appears that the consequences of the Sarajevo outrage were discussed at length, but that nothing was decided. It is not clear whether the Chief of Staff and the Naval Commander-in-Chief were present, as was rumored. After this meeting, Count Berchtold has travelled to Ischl to report to the Emperor, who, after the funeral of Franz Ferdinand, had returned there to recover his health. In the Hungarian Parliament, Count Tisza has replied to the interpellations of the opposition concerning the Sarajevo incident; you are acquainted with his statements. His speech was not clear, and I believe it was intentionally obscure. Some people saw in it signs of an intention quietly to await the development of events and of calmness in the attitude of the Austro-Hungarian Government, while others saw in it hidden intentions for (I should say) an action as yet undecided. It was noted that there was no occasion for haste until the results of the magisterial enquiry were announced. Some time has now elapsed; the matter has been spoken of, discussed, written about, and distorted; then came the death of Hartwig and the alarm of Baron Giesl. In connection with this again came the interpellations addressed to Count Tisza in the Hungarian Parliament; you have read his reply. Many hold the opinion here that this second speech is much more restrained than the first, and that this is to be attributed to an order from the Emperor. (The Bourse has now recovered; both the War Minister and the Chief of Staff have gone on leave.) I am loath to express an opinion. In the above-mentioned speech, it is to be noted that the possibility of war is not excluded, in the event of the demands of Austria-Hungary in regard to the Sarajevo outrage not being complied with. One thing is certain: Austria-Hungary will take diplomatic steps at Belgrade as soon as the magisterial enquiry at Sarajevo is completed and the matter submitted to the Court. I have, &tc.

No. 24.
From: M. Yov. M. Yovanovitch, Minister at Vienna.
To: M. N. Pashitch, Prime Minister and Minister for Foreign Affairs.
Vienna, July 15, 1914.

Sir,

It is thought here that the magisterial enquiries and investigations have not produced sufficient evidence to justify bringing an official accusation against Serbia, but it is believed that the latter will be accused of tolerating within her borders certain revolutionary elements. Diplomatic circles here criticize and condemn the mode of procedure of the Austro-Hungarian Government, especially the attitude throughout of the Korrespondenzbureau and the Vienna press. There are many who consider our attitude to be correct and in accordance with the dignity of a nation. They find fault only with the views expressed in some of our newspapers, though they ad admit that it is provoked by the Vienna press. In spite of the fact that it appears that the German Foreign Office does not approve of the anti-Serbian policy of Vienna, the German Embassy here is at this very moment encouraging such a policy. I have, &tc.

No. 25.
From: M. Yov. M. Yovanovitch, Minister at Vienna.
To: M. N. Pashitch, Prime Minister and Minister for Foreign Affairs.
Vienna, July 15, 1914.

Sir,

What steps will be taken? In what form? What demands will Austria-Hungary make of Serbia? I do not believe that to-day even the Ballplatz itself could answer these questions clearly and precisely. I am of opinion that its plans are now being laid, and that again Count Forgach is the moving spirit. In an earlier report, I mentioned that Austria-Hungary has to choose between two courses: either to make the Sarajevo outrage a domestic question, inviting us to assist her to discover and punish the culprits; or to make it a case against the Serbians and Serbia, and even against the Jugo-Slavs. After taking into considerations all that is being prepared and done, it appears to me that Austria-Hungary will choose the latter course. Austria-Hungary will do this in the belief that she will have the approval of Europe. Why should she not profit by humiliating us, and, to a certain extent, justify the Friedjung and Agram trials? Besides, Austria-Hungary desires in this manner to justify in the eyes of her own people and of Europe the sharp and reactionary measures which she contemplates undertaking internally in order to suppress the Great Serbian propaganda and the Jugo-Slav idea. Finally, for the sake of her prestige, Austria-Hungary must take some action in the belief that she will thus raise her prestige internally as well as externally. Austria-Hungary wills, I think, draw up in the form of a memorandum an accusation against Serbia. In that accusation will be set forth all the evidence that has been collected against us since April 1909, until to-day; and I believe that this accusation will be fairly lengthy. Austria-Hungary will communicate this accusation to the Cabinets of the European Powers with the remark that the facts contained therein give her the right to take diplomatic steps at Belgrade, and to demand that Serbia should in the future fulfill all the obligations of a loyal neighbor. At the same time Austria-Hungary will also hand us a note containing her demands, which we shall be requested to accept unconditionally. I have, &tc.

M. Dumaine, French Ambassador at Vienna, to M. René Viviani, President of the Council, Minister for Foreign Affairs.
Vienna, July 15, 1914.

Certain organs of the Vienna Press, discussing they military organization of France and of Russia, represent these it two countries as incapable of holding their own in European affairs; this would ensure to the Dual monarchy supported by Germany appreciable facilities for subjecting Serbia to any treatment which it might be pleased to impose. The *Militärische Rundschau* frankly admits it. "The moment is still favorable to us. If we do not decide for war, that war in which we shall have to engage at the latest in two or three years will be begun in far less propitious circumstances. At this moment, the initiative rests with us: Russia is not ready, moral factors and right are on our side, as well as might. Since we shall have to accept the contest some day, let us provoke it at once. Our prestige, our position as a Great Power, our honor, is in question; and yet more, for it would seem that our very existence is concerned—to be or not to be—which is in truth the great matter to-day." Surpassing itself, the *Neue Freie Presse* of to-day reproaches Count Tisza for the moderation of his second speech, in which he said, "Our relations with Serbia require, however, to be made clear." These words rouse its indignation. For it, tranquility and security can result only from a *war to the knife* against Pan-Servism, and it is in the name of humanity that it demands the extermination of the cursed Serbian race.

DUMAINE.

Chapter Seventeen
July 16, 1914

1914 July 16: French president travels to Russia to meet with tsar.

No. 26.
From: Dr. M. Yovanovitch, Chargé d'Affaires at Berlin.
To: M. N. Pashitch, Prime Minister and Minister for Foreign Affairs.
Berlin, July 16, 1914.
(Telegraphic)

The Secretary of State has informed me that the reports of the German Minister at Belgrade point to the existence of a Great Serbian propaganda, which should be energetically suppressed by the Government in the interest of good relations with Austria-Hungary.

Gregori Rasputin's first telegram to Nicholas II.
July 16, 1914

When the time comes it will be necessary to declare war but the time has not yet come; your sufferings will be crowned, don't despair, my kind, dear one.

Chapter Eighteen
July 17, 1914

No. 27.
From: M. M. S. Boschkovitch, Minister at London.
To: M. N. Pashitch, Prime Minister and Minister for Foreign Affairs.
London, July 17, 1914.
(Telegraphic)

The Austrian Embassy is making very great efforts to win over the English press against us, and to induce it to favor the idea that Austria must give a good lesson to Serbia. The Embassy is submitting to the news editors cuttings from our newspapers as a proof of the views expressed in our press. The situation may become more acute during the next few weeks. No reliance should be placed in the ostensibly peaceable statements of Austro-Hungarian official circles, as the way is being prepared for diplomatic pressure upon Serbia, which may develop into an armed attack. It is probable that as soon as Austria-Hungary has taken action at Belgrade she will change her attitude and will seek to humiliate Serbia.

No. 28.
From: M. Ljub Michailovitch, Minister at Rome.
To: M. N. Pashitch, Prime Minister and Minister for Foreign Affairs.
Rome, July 17, 1914.
(Telegraphic)

I have obtained reliable information to the effect that the Marquis di San Giuliano has stated to the Austro-Hungarian Ambassador that any step undertaken by Austria against Serbia which failed to take into account international considerations would meet with the disapproval of public opinion in Italy, and that the Italian Government desire to see the complete independence of Serbia maintained.

Primary Documents: Austrian Report on Archduke's Assassination in June 1914

Reproduced below is the official Austrian report established to investigate the assassination of Archduke Franz Ferdinand and his wife, Sophie, in Sarajevo on 28 June 1914. Seizing the opportunity presented by Ferdinand's assassination (who in any event had not been viewed with any great favor, either by the Emperor Franz Josef or by his government), the Austro-Hungarian government decided to settle a long-standing score with near-neighbor Serbia. The official report was therefore accordingly slanted to throw most suspicion upon the involvement of the Serbian government.

Austria-Hungary's ultimate response—its ultimatum of 23 July—comprised a lengthy list of demands made upon the Serbian government.

The Official Austrian Report

Record of the District Court at Sarajevo, touching the proceedings there instituted against Gavrilo Princip and confederates on account of the crime of assassination perpetrated on June 28, 1914, on His Imperial and Royal Highness the Archduke Franz Ferdinand of Austria-Este and Her Highness the Duchess Sophie of Hohenberg.

Gavrilo Princip, Nedeljko Cabrinovic, Trifko Grabez, Vaso Cubrilovic, and Cetres Popovic confess that in common with the fugitive Mehemed Mehmedbasic they contrived a plot for the murder of the Archduke Franz Ferdinand and, armed with bombs and in the case of some of them with Browning pistols, laid wait for him on June 28, 1914, on his progress through Sarajevo for the purpose of carrying out the planned attack. Nedeljko Cabrinovic confesses that he was the first of the conspirators to hurl a bomb against the Archduke's carriage, which missed its mark and which on exploding injured only the occupants of the carriage following the Archducal motor car. Gavrilo Princip confesses that he fired two shots from a Browning pistol against the archducal motor car, by which the Archduke Franz Ferdinand and the Duchess Sophie of Hohenberg received fatal wounds. Both perpetrators confess that the act was done with intent to murder. These confessions have been fully verified by means of the investigations which have taken place, and it is established that the deceased Archduke Franz Ferdinand and the deceased Duchess Sophie of Hohenberg died as a result of the revolver shots fired at them by Gavrilo Princip. The accused have made the following declarations, which are essentially consistent, before the examining magistrate:

In April 1914, Princip, during his stay at Belgrade, where he associated with a number of Serbian students in the cafés of the town, conceived the plan for the execution of an attempt on the life of the late Archduke Franz Ferdinand. He communicated this intention to his acquaintance, Cabrinovic, who also was in Belgrade at the time. The latter had already conceived a similar idea and was ready at once to participate in the attempt. The execution of an attempt on the Archduke's life was a frequent topic of conversation in the circle in which Princip and Cabrinovic moved, because the Archduke was considered to be a dangerous enemy of the Serbian people. Princip and Cabrinovic desired at first to procure the bombs and weapons necessary for the execution of the deed from the Serbian Major Milan Pribicevic or from the Narodna Odbrana (see Note 1) as they themselves did not possess the means for their purchase. As, however, Major Pribicevic and the authoritative member of the said association, Zivojin Dacic, were absent from Belgrade at that time, they decided to try to obtain the weapons from their acquaintance Milan Ciganovic, who had formerly been a Komitadji and was at that time in the employment of the State railways. Princip, through the instrumentality of an intimate friend of Ciganovic, now got into communication with the latter. Thereupon Ciganovic called on Princip and discussed the planned attempt with him. He entirely approved it, and thereupon declared that he would like to consider further whether he should provide the weapons for the attempt. Cabrinovic also talked with Ciganovic on the subject of the weapons. At Easter Princip took Trifko Grabez, who also was in Belgrade, into his confidence. The latter is also shown by his own confession to have declared he ready to take part in the attempt.

In the following weeks, Princip had repeated conversations with Ciganovic about the execution of the attempt. Meanwhile Ciganovic had reached an understanding on the subject of the planned attack with the Serbian Major Voja Tankosic, who was a close friend of his and who then placed at his disposal for this object the Browning pistols. Grabez confesses in conformity with the depositions of Princip and Cabrinovic that on the 24th of May he, accompanied by Ciganovic, visited Major

Tankosic at the latter's request at his rooms. He says that after he had been introduced Tankosic said to him: "Are you the man? Are you determined?" Whereupon Grabez answered: "I am." Tankosic next asked: "Do you know how to shoot with a revolver?" and when Grabez answered in the negative Tankosic said to Ciganovic: "I will give you a revolver, go and teach them how to shoot." Hereupon Ciganovic conducted Princip and Grabez to the military rifle range at Topcider and instructed them in a wood adjoining the range in shooting with a Browning pistol at a target. Princip proved himself the better shot of the two. Ciganovic also familiarized Princip, Grabez, and Cabrinovic with the use of bombs which were given them.

On the 27th of May, 1914, Ciganovic handed over to Princip, Cabrinovic, and Grabez, as their confessions agree in stating, six bombs, four Browning revolvers, and a sufficient quantity of ammunition as well as a glass tube of cyanide of potassium with which to poison themselves after the accomplishment of the deed in order that the secret might be kept. Moreover, Ciganovic gave them some money. Princip had previously informed Danilo Ilic, at Easter, of his plan of assassination. He now begged the latter on his return to Sarajevo to enlist certain additional persons, in order to ensure the success of the attempt. Hereupon Ilic according to his confession enlisted Jaso Cubrilovic, Cetro Popovic, and Mehemed Mehmedbasic in the plot. Only one of the bombs was made use of in the execution of the attempt. The remaining five bombs came later into the possession of the police at Sarajevo. In the opinion of the judicial experts these bombs are Serbian hand-grenades which were factory-made and intended for military purposes. They are identical with the 21 bombs which were found in the Save at Brcko in the year 1913 and which were partly in their original packing, which proved without a doubt that they came from the Serbian arsenal of Kragujevatz. It is thus proved that the grenades which were used in the attempt against the Archduke Franz Ferdinand also came from the stores of the Army Depot at Kragujevatz. Grabez quite spontaneously calls the grenades which were handed over to him and his accomplices "Kragujevatz bombs." It is clear how far the criminal agitation of the Narodna Odbrana and those who shared in its views, has of late been primarily directed against the person of the hereditary Archduke. From these facts, the conclusion may be drawn that the Narodna Odbrana, as well as the associations hostile to the Monarchy in Serbia, which were grouped 'round it, recently decided that the hour had struck to translate theory into practice. It is noteworthy, however, that the Narodna limits itself in this way to inciting, and where the incitement has fallen on fertile soil to providing means of material assistance for the realization of its plans, but that it has confided the only dangerous part of this propaganda of action to the youth of the Monarchy, which it has excited and corrupted, and which alone has to bear the burden of this miserable "heroism." All the characteristics of this procedure are found in the history and origin of the profoundly regrettable outrage of the 28th of June.

Princip and Grabez are characteristic examples of young men who have been poisoned from their school days by the doctrines of the Narodna Odbrana. At Belgrade, where he frequented the society of students imbued with these ideas, Princip busied himself with criminal plans against the Archduke Franz Ferdinand, against whom the hatred of the Serbian element hostile to the Monarchy was particularly acute on the occasion of his tour in the annexed territories. He was joined by Cabrinovic, who moved in the same circles, and whose shifting and radically revolutionary views, as he himself admits, as well as the influence of his surroundings in Belgrade and the reading of the Serbian papers, inspired him with the same sense of hostility to the Monarchy, and brought him into the propaganda of action. Thanks to the state of mind in which he already was, Grabez succumbed very quickly to this milieu, which he now entered. But however far this plot may have prospered, and however determined the conspirators may have been to carry out the attempt, it would never have been affected, if people had not been found, as in the case of Jukic, to provide the accomplices with means of committing their crime. For, as Princip and Cabrinovic have expressly admitted, they lacked the necessary arms, as well as the money to purchase them. It is interesting to see where the accomplices tried to procure their arms.

Milan Pribicevic and Zivojin Dacic, the two principal men in the Narodna Odbrana, were the first accomplices thought of as a sure source of help in their need, doubtless because it had already become a tradition amongst those ready to commit crimes that they could obtain instruments for murder from these representatives of the Narodna Odbrana. The accidental circumstance that these two men were not at Belgrade at the critical moment doubtless balked this plan. However, Princip and Cabrinovic were not at a loss in finding other help, that of Milan Ciganovic, an exkomitadji, and now a railway official at Belgrade, and at the same time an active member of the Narodna Odbrana, who, in 1909, first appeared as a pupil at the school at Cuprija. Princip and Cabrinovic were not deceived in their expectations, as they at once received the necessary help from Ciganovic.

(Note 1) The chief Serbian society devoted to the cause of freedom for the Slavs in every land.

Source: *Source Records of the Great War, Vol. I, ed. Charles F. Horne, National Alumni, 1923.*

No. 27.

From: **M. M. S. Boschkovitch, Minister at London.**
To: **M. N. Pashitch, Prime Minister and Minister for Foreign Affairs.**
London, July 17, 1914.
(Telegraphic)

The Austrian Embassy is making very great efforts to win over the English press against us, and to induce it to favour the idea that Austria must give a good lesson to Serbia. The Embassy is submitting to the news editors cuttings from our newspapers as a proof of the views expressed in our press. The situation may become more acute during the next few weeks. No reliance should be placed in the ostensibly peaceable statements of Austro-Hungarian official circles, as the way is being prepared for diplomatic pressure upon Serbia, which may develop into an armed attack. It is probable that as soon as Austria-Hungary has taken action at Belgrade she will change her attitude and will seek to humiliate Serbia.

No. 28.

From: **M. Ljub Michailovitch, Minister at Rome.**
To: **M. N. Pashitch, Prime Minister and Minister for Foreign Affairs.**
Rome, July 17, 1914.
(Telegraphic)

I have obtained reliable information to the effect that the Marquis di San Giuliano has stated to the Austro-Hungarian Ambassador that any step undertaken by Austria against Serbia which failed to take into account international considerations would meet with the disapproval of public opinion in Italy, and that the Italian Government desire to see the complete independence of Serbia maintained.

Chapter Nineteen
July 18, 1914

No. 29.
From: Dr. M. Spalaikovitch, Minister at Petrograd.
To: M. N. Pashitch, Prime Minister and Minister for Foreign Affairs.
Petrograd, July 18, 1914.
(Telegraphic)

I have spoken to the Assistant Minister for Foreign Affairs on the subject of the provocative attitude of the Korrespondenzbureau and the Vienna press. M. Sazonof told me a few days ago that he wondered why the Austrian Government was doing nothing to put a stop to the futile agitation on the part of the press in Vienna which, after all, frightened nobody, and was only doing harm to Austria herself.

Chapter Twenty
July 19, 1914

M. Dumaine, French Ambassador at Vienna, to M. René Viviani, President of the Council, Minister for Foreign Affairs.
Vienna, July 19, 1914.

The Chancellor of the Consulate, who has sent me his half-yearly report, in which he sums up the various economic facts which have been the subject of his study since the beginning of the year, has added a section containing political information emanating from a trustworthy source. I asked him briefly to sum up the information, which he has obtained regarding the impending presentation of the Austrian note to Serbia, which the papers have for some days been persistently announcing. You will find the text of this memorandum interesting on account of the accurate information which it contains.

DUMAINE.

1914 July 19: Tsar told that Germany declared war on Russia.

No. 30.
From: M. Pashitch, Prime Minister and Minister for Foreign Affairs.
To: All Serbian Missions abroad.
Belgrade, July 19, 1914.
(Telegraphic)

Immediately after the Sarajevo outrage the Austro-Hungarian press began to accuse Serbia of that detestable crime, which, in the opinion of that press, was the direct result of the Great Serbian idea. The Austrian press further contended that that idea was spread and propagated by various associations, such as the "Narodna Odbrana," "Kolo Srpskich Sestara," etc. which were tolerated by the Serbian Government.

On learning of the murder, the Serbian Royal Family, as well as the Serbian Government, sent messages of condolence, and at the same time expressed severe condemnation of and horror at the crime that had been committed. All festivities which had been fixed to take place on that day in Belgrade were immediately cancelled.

Nevertheless, the press of the neighboring Monarchy continued to hold Serbia responsible for the Sarajevo outrage. Moreover, the Austro-Hungarian press began to spread in connection with it various false reports, designed to mislead public opinion, which provoked the Belgrade press to reply in self-defense, and sometimes to active hostility in a spirit of embitterment aroused by the misrepresentation of what had occurred. Seeing that the Austro-Hungarian press was intentionally luring the Belgrade press into a awkward and delicate controversy, the Serbian Government hastened to warn the press in Belgrade, and to recommend it to remain calm and to confine itself to simple denials and to the suppression of false and misleading reports. The action of the Serbian Government was ineffectual in the case of some of the less important papers, more especially in view of the fact that newly invented stories were daily spread abroad with the object of serving political ends not only against Serbia but also against the Serbs in Austria-Hungary.

The Serbian Government was unable to avert these polemics between the Serbian and the Austrian press, seeing that Serbian law, and the provisions of the constitution itself, guarantee the complete independence of the press and prohibit all measures of control and the seizure of newspapers. These polemics were further aggravated by the fact that the Vienna and Budapest journals selected passages from such of the Serbian newspapers as have practically no influence upon public opinion, strengthened still further their tone, and, having thus manipulated them, passed them on to the foreign press with the obvious intention of exciting public opinion in other European countries and of representing Serbia as being guilty.

Those who have followed the course of these polemics will know that the Belgrade newspapers merely acted in self-defense, confining their activities to denials and to the refutation of falsehoods designed to mislead public opinion, at the same time attempting to convince foreign Governments (which, being occupied with other and more serious affairs, had no time to go into the matter themselves) of the intention of the Austro-Hungarian press to excite public opinion in its own country and abroad. The Serbian Government at once expressed their readiness to hand over to justice any of their subjects who might be proved to have played a part in the Sarajevo outrage. The Serbian Government further stated that they had prepared a more drastic law against the misuse of explosives. The draft of a new law in that sense had already been laid before the State Council, but could not be submitted to the Skupshtina, as the latter was not sitting at the time. Finally, the Serbian Government stated that they were ready, as heretofore, to observe all those good neighborly obligations to which Serbia was bound by her position as a European State. During the whole of this period, from the date of the perpetration of the outrage until to-day, not once did the Austro-Hungarian Government apply to the Serbian Government for their assistance in the matter. They did not demand that any of the accomplices should be subjected to an enquiry, or that they should be handed over to trial. In one instance only did the Austrian Government ask for information as to the whereabouts of certain students who had been expelled from the Pakratz Teachers' Seminary, and had crossed over to Serbia to continue their studies. All available information on this point was supplied. The campaign against Serbia, however, was unremittingly pursued in the Austrian press, and public opinion was excited against her in Austria as well as in the rest of Europe. Matters went so far that the more prominent leaders of political parties in Austria-Hungary began to ask questions in Parliament on the subject of the outrage, to which the Hungarian Prime Minister replied. It is evident from the discussions in this connection that Austria is contemplating some action, but it is not clear in what sense. It is not stated whether the measures which are to be taken—more especially military measures—will depend upon the reply and the conciliatory attitude of the Serbian Government. But an armed conflict is being hinted at in the event of the Serbian Government being unable to give a categorically satisfactory reply.

On the sudden death of the Russian Minister, M. de Hartwig, at the residence of the Austrian Minister, the polemics in the newspapers became still more acute; nevertheless this sad event did not lead to any disorders even during the funeral of M. Hartwig. On the other hand, the Austro-

Hungarian Legation was so perturbed by certain false reports that Austrian subjects began to conceal themselves, some of them taking refuge in the Semlin and Belgrade hotels, and others in the Legation itself.

At 5 P.M. on the day of the King's birthday, which passed in the most orderly manner, I was informed by the Austrian Minister, through the Vice-Consul, M. Pomgraz, that preparations were being made for an attack that night on the Austrian Legation and on Austro-Hungarian subjects in Belgrade. He begged me to take the necessary steps for the protection of Austro-Hungarian subjects and of the Legation, stating at the same time that he held Serbia responsible for all that might occur. I replied that the responsible Serbian Government was not aware of any preparations of this kind being made, but that I would in any case at once inform the Minister of the Interior, and beg him at the same time to take such measures as might be necessary. The next day showed that the Austrian Legation had been misled by false rumors, for neither any attack nor any preparations for attack were made. Notwithstanding this, the Austro-Hungarian press took advantage of this incident to prove how excited public opinion was in Serbia and to what lengths she was ready to go. It went even further and tried to allege that something really had been intended to happen, since M. Pashitch himself had stated that he had heard of such rumors. All this indicates clearly the intention to excite public opinion against Serbia whenever occasion arises.

When all that has been said in the Hungarian Parliament is taken into consideration, there is reason for apprehension that some step is being prepared against us which may produce a disagreeable effect upon the relations between Serbia and Austria-Hungary. There is still further ground for such apprehension, as it is abundantly evident that the enquiry which is being made is not to be limited to the perpetrators and their possible accomplices in the crime, but is most probably to be extended to Serbia and the Great Serbian idea. By their attitude and the measures they have taken, the Serbian Government has irrefutably proved that they are working to restrain excitable elements, and in the interests of peace and the maintenance of good relations with all their neighbors. The Government has given its particular attention to the improvement and strengthening of its relations with the Austro-Hungarian Monarchy, which had lately become strained as a result of the Balkan wars and of the questions which arose there from. With that object in view, the Serbian Government proceeded to settle the question of the Oriental Railway, the new railway connections, and the transit through Serbia of Austro-Hungarian goods for Constantinople, Sofia, Salonica, and Athens. The Serbian Government consider that its vital interests require that peace and tranquility in the Balkans should be firmly and lastingly established. And for this very reason they fear lest the excited state of public opinion in Austria-Hungary may induce the Austro-Hungarian Government to make a démarche which may humiliate the dignity of Serbia as a State, and to put forward demands which could not be accepted. I have the honour therefore to request you to impress upon the Government to which you are accredited our desire to maintain friendly relations with Austria-Hungary, and to suppress every attempt directed against the peace and public safety of the neighboring Monarchy. We will likewise meet the wishes of the Austro-Hungarian Empire in the event of our being requested to subject to trial in our independent Courts any accomplices in the outrage who are in Serbia—should such, of course, exist.

But we can never comply with demands which may be directed against the dignity of Serbia, and which would be inacceptable to any country which respects and maintains its independence. Actuated by the desire that good neighborly relations may be firmly established and maintained, we beg the friendly Governments to take note of these declarations and to act in a conciliatory sense should occasion or necessity arise.

July 19, 1914
Rasputin wrote a short letter to Nicholas II:

"I believe [and] I hope for a peace," he continued, "they foreigners? Are preparing a great evil, but we are to blame, I know all your torments. It is very hard not to see each other. Friends are helpful secretly in the heart, can they help you?"

Rasputin was so upset by the prospect of war, as days past and the situation darkened, that he tore his bandages. He was especially appalled by talk of mobilization, an act the Germans and Austrians would view as a direct threat. Gregori's telegrams became bolder. "Do not declare war, evil will come to you and the tasrevich." Realizing this was having no effect, Gregori wrote a letter to the tsar. Gregori's primitive scrawl poured out an agonized vision:

> *Dear Friend:*
>
> *I will say again; a menacing cloud is over Russia; much sorrow and grief [are approaching,] it is dark and no lighting is to be seen. A sea of tears immeasurable are ahead and as to blood? What can I say? There are no words, the horror of it is in describable. I know they keep demanding war from you, evidently not knowing that it is destruction. Heavy is God's punishment; when he takes away reason, that is the beginning of the end. Thou are the Tsar, father of the people; don't permit the madness to triumph and destroy themselves and the people. Well, they will conquer Germany and what about Russia? If one thinks, then truly [it is clear that] there as not been a greater sufferer since the beginning of time[that Russia, and] she is all drowned in blood. Terrible is the destruction and without end to the grief.*
>
> *Gregori*

If Rasputin had been in St. Petersburg during the summer of 1914, there would have been a level head in Nicholas' to prevent the escalation of the events that led to World War I. The kaiser was all for peace and with Rasputin in St. Petersburg, Wilhelm II's case would have been made stronger with his presence. This is no guarantee that war would have been prevented, but its case would have been made weaker.

Chapter Twenty-One
July 20, 1914

No. 31.
From: M. Yov. M. Yovanovitch, Minister at Vienna.
To: M. N. Pashitch, Prime Minister and Minister for Foreign Affairs.
Vienna, July 20, 1914.

Sir,

It is very difficult, indeed almost impossible, to ascertain here anything positive as to the real intentions of Austria-Hungary. The word has been passed 'round to maintain absolute secrecy about everything that is being done. Judging by the articles in our newspapers, Belgrade is taking an optimistic view of the questions pending with Austria-Hungary. There is, however, no room for optimism. There is no doubt that Austria-Hungary is making preparations of a serious character. What is chiefly to be feared, and is highly probable, is, that Austria is preparing for war against Serbia. The general conviction that prevails here is that it would be nothing short of suicide for Austria-Hungary once more to fail to take advantage of the opportunity to act against Serbia. It is believed that the two opportunities previously missed—the annexation of Bosnia and the Balkan War—have been extremely injurious to Austria-Hungary. In addition, the conviction is steadily growing that Serbia, after her two wars, is completely exhausted, and that a war against Serbia would in fact merely mean a military expedition to be concluded by a speedy occupation. It is also believed that such a war could be brought to an end before Europe could intervene. The seriousness of Austrian intentions is further emphasized by the military preparations which are being made, especially in the vicinity of the Serbian frontier.

Sir Tyrrell, London
July 20, 1914

"From Sir Edward Grey, which was to the effect that he wished me to know before I sailed that the Austro–Serbian situation was giving him grave concern."

No. 1.
From: **Sir Edward Grey to Sir H. Rumbold, British Charge D' Affaires at Berlin.**
To: **Foreign Office.**
July 20, 1914.

Sir,

I asked the German Ambassador to-day if he had any news of what was going on in Vienna with regard to Serbia.

He said that he had not, but Austria was certainly going to take some steps, and he regarded the situations very uncomfortable.

I said that I had not heard anything recently, except that Count Berchtold, in speaking to the Italians Ambassador in Vienna, had deprecated the suggestion that the situation was grave, but had said that it should be cleared up.

The German ambassador, said that it would be a very desirable thing if Russia could act as a mediator with regard to Serbia.

I said I assumed that the Austrian government would not do anything until they had first disclosed to the public their case against Serbia, founded presumably upon what they had discovered at the trial.

The Ambassador said that he certainly assumed that they would act upon some case that would be known.

I said that this would make it easier for others, such as Russia, to counsel moderation in Belgrade. In fact, the more Austria could keep her demand within reasonable limits, and the stronger the justification she could produce for making any demand, the more chance there would be of soothing things over. I hated the idea of a war between the Great Powers, and that any of them should be dragged into a war by Serbia would be detestable.

The Ambassador agreed whole heartedly in this sentiment.

E. Grey

1914 July 20: Tsar signed declaration of war on Germany and Austria.

From: **Baron Giesl von Gieslingen, Austro-Hungarian.**
Memorandum.
(Extract from a Consular Report on the Economic and Political Situation in Austria.)
Vienna, July 20, 1914.

From information furnished by a person specially well informed as to official news, it appears that the French Government would be wrong to leave confidence in disseminators of optimism; much will be demanded of Serbia; she will be required to dissolve several propagandist societies, she will be summoned to repress nationalism, to guard the frontier in co-operation with Austrian officials, to keep strict control over anti-Austrian tendencies in the schools; and it is a very difficult matter for a Government to consent to become in this way a policeman for a foreign Government. They foresee the subterfuges by which Serbia will doubtless wish to avoid giving a clear and direct reply; that is why a short interval will perhaps be fixed for her to declare whether she accepts or not. The tenure of the note and its imperious tone almost certainly ensure that Belgrade will refuse. Then military operations will begin. There is here, and equally at Berlin, a party which accepts the idea of a conflict of widespread dimensions, in other words a conflagration. The leading idea is probably that it would be necessary to start before Russia has completed the great improvements of her army and railways, and before France has brought her military organization to perfection. However, on this point, there is no unanimity in high circles; Count Berchtold and the diplomatists' desire at the most localized operations against Serbia. But everything must be regarded as possible.

A singular fact is pointed out: generally the official telegraph agency, in its summaries and reviews of the foreign press, pays attention only to semi-official newspapers and to the most important organs; it omits all quotation from and all mention of the others. This is a rule and a tradition. Now, for the last ten days, the official agency has furnished daily to the Austro-Hungarian press a complete review of the whole Serbian press, giving a prominent place to the least known, the smallest and most insignificant papers, which, just on account of their obscurity, employ language freer, bolder, more aggressive, and often insulting. This work of the official agency has obviously for its aim the excitement of public feeling and the creation of opinion favorable to war. The fact is significant.

"An Ambassador's Memoirs"
By Maurice Paléologue
Day 1 in Russia with French President
Monday, July 20, 1914.

I left St. Petersburg at ten o'clock this morning on the Admiralty yacht and went to Peterhof. Sazonov, the Minister for Foreign Affairs, Isvolsky, the Russian Ambassador to France, and General de Laguiche, my military attaché, accompanied me. All four of us had been invited by the Tsar to lunch on the imperial yacht before going to meet the President of the Republic at Cronstadt. The staff of my Embassy, the Russian ministers and Court functionaries will go by rail direct to Peterhof.

The weather was cloudy. Our vessel steamed at high speed between low banks towards the Gulf of Finland. Suddenly a fresh breeze from the open sea brought us a heavy shower, but as suddenly the sun burst forth in his splendor. A few pearl-grey clouds, through which the sun's rays darted, hung here and there in the sky like sashes shot with gold. As far as the eye could reach, in a limpid flood of light the estuary of the Neva spread the immense sheet of its greenish, viscous, changing waters which always remind me of Venice.

At half-past eleven we stopped in the little harbor of Peterhof where the *Alexandria,* the Tsar's favorite yacht, was lying under steam.

Nicholas II, in the uniform of an admiral, arrived at the quay almost at once. We transferred to the *Alexandria.* Luncheon was served immediately. We had at least an hour and three-quarters before us until the arrival of the *France.* But the Tsar likes to linger over his meals. There are always long intervals between the courses in which he chats and smokes cigarettes.

I was on his right, Sazonov on his left and Count Fredericks, Minister of the Court, was opposite us.

After a few commonplaces the Tsar told me of his pleasure at receiving the President of the Republic.

"We shall have weighty matters to discuss," he said.

"I'm sure we shall agree on all points…But there's one question which is very much in my mind—our understanding with England. We must get her to come into our alliance. It would be such a guarantee of peace!"

"Yes, Sire, the Triple Entente cannot be too strong if it is to keep the peace."

"I've been told that you yourself are uneasy about Germany's intentions."

"Uneasy? Yes, Sire, I am uneasy although at the moment I have no particular reason to anticipate a war in the immediate future. But the Emperor William and his Government have let Germany get into a state of mind such that if some dispute arose, in Morocco, the East—anywhere—they could neither give way nor compromise. A success is essential at any price and to obtain it they risk some adventure."

The Tsar reflected a moment:

"I can't believe the Emperor wants war…If you knew him as I do! If you knew how much the-atricality there is in his posing…"

"Perhaps I am doing the Emperor William too much honour in thinking him capable of willing, or simply accepting the consequences of his acts. But if war threatened would he, and could he pre-vent it? No, Sire, I don't think so, honestly I don't."

The Tsar sat silent and puffed at his cigarette. Then he said in a resolute voice: "It's all the more important for us to be able to count on England in an emergency. Unless she has gone out of her mind altogether Germany will never attack Russia, France, and England combined."

Coffee had just arrived when the French squadron was signaled. The Tsar made me go up on the bridge with him.

It was a magnificent spectacle. In a quivering, silvery light the *France* slowly surged forward over the turquoise and emerald waves, leaving a long white furrow behind her. Then she stopped majes-tically. The mighty warship which has brought the head of the French State is well worthy of her name. She was indeed France coming to Russia. I felt my heart beating.

For a few minutes there was a prodigious din in the harbor; the guns of the ships and the shore batteries firing, the crews cheering, the *Marseillaise* answering the Russian national anthem, the cheers of thousands of spectators who had come from St. Petersburg on pleasure boats and so forth.

At length the President of the Republic stepped on board the *Alexandria*. The Tsar received him at the gangway.

As soon as the presentations were over the imperial yacht steered for Peterhof. Seated in the stern the Tsar and the President immediately entered into conversation, I should perhaps say a discussion, for it was obvious that they were talking business, firing questions at each other and arguing. As was proper it was Poincaré who had the initiative. Before long he was doing all the talking, the Tsar simply nodded acquiescence, but his whole appearance showed his sincere approval. It radiated confidence and sympathy.

Before long we were at Peterhof. Through its magnificent trees and sparkling fountains, Catherine II's favorite residence appeared above a long terrace from which a foaming cascade poured its majestic waters.

At a sharp trot our carriages ascended the drive leading to the palace entrance. At every bend we had a fleeting glimpse of some fresh vista, a line of statues, fountains or terraces. Though the detail is somewhat meretricious one scents something of the keen and delicious atmosphere of Versailles in the balmy, sunlit air.

At half-past seven, there was a banquet in the Empress Elizabeth room.

Thanks to the brilliance of the uniforms, superb toilettes, elaborate liveries, magnificent furnish-ings, and fittings, in short the whole panoply of pomp and power, the spectacle was such as no court in the world can rival. I shall long remember the dazzling display of jewels on the women's shoulders. It was simply a fantastic shower of diamonds, pearls, rubies, sapphires, emeralds, topaz, beryls—a blaze of fire and flame.

In this fairy milieu Poincare's black coat was a drab touch. But the wide, sky-blue ribbon of St. Andrew across his breast increased his importance in the eyes of the Russians. And then it was soon seen that the Tsar was listening to him with the closest and most sympathetic attention.

During dinner I kept an eye on the Tsarists Alexandra Feodorovna opposite whom I was sitting. Although long ceremonies are a very great trial to her she was anxious to be present this evening to do honour to the President of the allied Republic. She was a beautiful sight with her low brocade gown and a diamond tiara on her head. Her forty-two years have left her face and figure still pleasant to look upon. After the first course she entered into conversation with Poincaré who was on her right. Before long, however, her smile became set and the veins stood out in her cheeks. She bit her lips every minute. Her labored breathing made the network of diamonds sparkle on her bosom. Until the end of dinner, which was very long, the poor woman was obviously struggling with hysteria. Her features suddenly relaxed when the Tsar rose to propose his toast.

The imperial speech was received in a composed silence, for it was the reply which was most eagerly awaited. Poincaré spoke without notes instead of reading his speech as the Tsar had done. Never had his diction been more clear, lucid, and pointed. What he said was only the stale and formal official verbiage, but in his mouth the words acquired a remarkable wealth of meaning and authority. The effect was quite marked on that audience, brought up as it was in the traditions of despotism and the discipline of courts. I'm sure that of those decorated functionaries more than one thought: "That's how an autocrat should talk."

After dinner the Tsar held a levee. The general eagerness to be presented to Poincaré showed he had been a success. Even the German clique, the ultra-reactionary group, sought the honour of an introduction to the President.

At eleven o'clock a procession was formed. The Tsar conducted the President of the Republic to his room.

There Poincaré kept me in conversation a few minutes. We exchanged impressions, and very good they were.

When I returned to St. Petersburg by rail at a quarter to one in the morning, I heard that this afternoon the principal factories went on strike—for no reason and on a signal from no one knows where. There have been collisions with the police at several points. My informant knows the working-class quarters well and tells me that the movement has been instigated by German agents.

In fact, these movements were started by Russian Military Intelligence units under orders from Sazonov.

Chapter Twenty-Two
July 21, 1914

No. 28.
Russian Chargé d'Affaires at Paris to Russian Minister for Foreign Affairs.
Paris, July 21, 1914.
(Telegram)

THE German Ambassador again visited the Acting Minister for Foreign Affairs to-day, and made to him the following declarations:

"L'Autriche a déclaré à la Russie qu'elle ne récherche pas des acquisitions territoriales et qu'elle ne menace pas l'intégrit, de la Serbie. Son but unique est d'assurer sa propre tranquillité. Par conséquent il dépend de la Russie d'éviter la guerre. L'Allemagne se sent solidaire avec la France dans le désir ardent de conserver la pais et espère fermement quc la France usera de son influence à Pétersbourg dans un sens modérateur."

Translation: "Austria has declared to Russia that she does not desire territorial acquisitions, and that she harbors no designs against the integrity of Serbia. Her sole object is to secure her own peace and quiet, and consequently it rests with Russia to prevent war. Germany is at one with France in her ardent desire to preserve peace, and she sincerely hopes that France will exercise a moderating influence at St. Petersburg." The Minister pointed out that Germany on her part might well act on similar lines at Vienna, especially in view of the conciliatory spirit displayed by Serbia. The Ambassador replied that such a course was not possible, owing to the decision not to intervene in the Austro-Serbian dispute. The Minister then asked whether the four Powers Great Britain, Germany, Italy, and France could not make representations at St. Petersburg and Vienna, for that the matter amounted, in effect, to a dispute between Austria and Russia. The Ambassador alleged that he had no instructions. Finally, the Minister refused to agree to the German proposal.

July 21, 1914

Colonel House sailed and arrived in Boston eight days later. Immediately before he left, word was carried to him that the British Foreign Office had awakened to the serious character of the international situation.

No. 29.
Russian Chargé d'Affaires at Paris to Russian Minister for Foreign Affairs.
Paris, July 21, 1914.
(Telegram)

THE Director of the Political Department has expressed the personal opinion that the series of representations made by Germany at Paris aim at intimidating France and at securing her intervention at St. Petersburg.

M. Jules Cambon, French Ambassador at Berlin, to M. Bienvenu-Martin, Acting Minister for Foreign Affairs.
Berlin, July 21, 1914.

It has come to my knowledge that the Serbian representative at Berlin declared, at the Wilhelmstrasse, yesterday, that his Government was ready to entertain Austria's requirements arising out of the outrage at Sarajevo, provided that she asked only for judicial co-operation in the punishment and prevention of political crimes but that he was charged to warn the German Government that it would be dangerous to attempt. Through that investigation, to lower the prestige of Serbia.

In confidence I may also inform your Excellency that the Russian Chargé d'Affaires at the diplomatic audience to-day mentioned this subject to Herr von Jagow. He said that he supposed the German Government now had full knowledge of the note prepared by Austria, and were therefore willing to give the assurance that the Austro-Serbian difficulties would be localized.

The Secretary of State protested that he was in complete ignorance of the contents of that note, and expressed himself in the same way to me. I could not help showing my astonishment at a statement which agreed so little with what circumstances lead one to expect. I have also been assured that, from now on, the preliminary notices for mobilization, the object of which is to place Germany in a kind of "attention" attitude in times of tension, have been sent out here to those classes, which would receive them in similar circumstances. That is a measure to which the Germans, constituted as they are, can have recourse without indiscretion and without exciting the people. It is not a sensational measure, and is not necessarily followed by full mobilization, as we have already seen, but it is nonetheless significant.

JULES CAMBON.

M. Bienvenu-Martin, Acting Minister for Foreign Affairs, to London, St. Petersburgh, Vienna, Rome.
Paris, July 21, 1914.

I specially draw your attention to information of which I am in receipt from Berlin; the French Ambassador notifies the extreme weakness of the Berlin Bourse yesterday, and attributes it to the anxiety, which has begm to be aroused by the Serbian question. M. Jules Cambon has very grave reason for believing that when Austria makes the démarche at Belgrade which she judges necessary in consequence of the crime of Sarajevo, Germany will support her with her authority without seeking to play the part of mediator.

"An Ambassador's Memoirs"
By Maurice Paléologue
Day 2 with French President in Russia
Tuesday, July 21, 1914.

The President of the Republic has spent to-day visiting St. Petersburg.

Before leaving Peterhof he was in conference with the Tsar. They discussed *seriatim* all the questions on the diplomatic *tapis* at the moment: the strained relations between Greece and Turkey; the intrigues of the Bulgarian Government in the Balkans; the Prince of Wied's arrival in Albania; the application of the Anglo-Russian Agreements in Persia; the political orientation of the Scandinavian States, etc. They concluded their review with the problem of the Austro-Serbian dispute, a problem which becomes more worrying every day owing to the arrogant and mysterious attitude of Austria. Poincaré has insisted with great force that the only way of saving the peace of the world is an open discussion between all the Great Powers, taking care that one group is not opposed to another. "It's the method that served us so well in 1913," he said. "Let's try it again...!" Nicholas II entirely agreed.

At half-past one I attended the President at the imperial quay near to Nicholas Bridge. The Naval Minister, the Prefect of Police, the Commander of the Fortress and the municipal authorities were there to receive him.

In accordance with the old Slav rites Count Ivan Tolstoy, the Mayor of the capital, offered him bread and salt.

Then we mounted our carriages to visit the Fortress of SS. Peter and Paul which is the Bastille and the St. Denis of the Romanovs. As tradition decrees the President laid a wreath on the tomb of Alexander III, father of the alliance.

Escorted by the Guard Cossacks, whose scarlet tunics flamed in the sunshine, our carriages passed along the Neva at a smart trot.

A few days ago, when I was settling with Sazonov the final details of the President's visit, he had said to me with a smile: "The Guard Cossacks have been told off to escort the President. You see what a fine figure they'll cut! They're splendid fellows, fearful fellows. Besides they're dressed in red. I rather think Monsieur Viviani does not dislike that color."

I had replied, "No, he doesn't dislike it but his artistic eye doesn't enjoy it thoroughly except when it's next to white and blue."

In their scarlet tunics these long-haired, bearded and bristly Cossacks are certainly a formidable sight. When our carriages disappeared with them through the gateway of the fortress a spectator with a turn for irony, or a lover of historical antitheses, might well have asked whether it was not to the State Prison that they were conducting these two certificated and avowed "revolutionaries," Poincaré and Viviani, not to mention myself, their accomplice. The moral contradiction in terms, the tacit paradox in the background of the Franco-Russian Alliance, has never struck me more forcibly.

At three o'clock the President received the deputations of the French colonies in St. Petersburg and throughout Russia. Some of them had come from Moscow, Kharkov, Odessa, Kiev, Rostov, Tiflis. In presenting them to Poincaré I could say with perfect sincerity: "Their eagerness to come and greet you in no way surprises me. Every day I see practical proofs of the fervent and pious love of the French colonies in Russia for their distant homeland. In no province of our old France, Monsieur le Président, will you find better Frenchmen than those here before you."

At four o'clock the procession was reformed to take the President to the Winter Palace where a diplomatic levee was to be held.

We received an enthusiastic welcome all along the route. The police had arranged it all. At every street corner a group of poor wretches cheered loudly under the eye of a policeman.

At the Winter Palace it was a full-dress occasion.

Etiquette required that the Ambassadors should be introduced one by one to the President who had Viviani on his left.

It was my function to present my foreign colleagues.

The first to enter was the German Ambassador, Count Pourtalès, *doyen* of the Corps Diplomatique. The President received him with the greatest affability. He asked him about the French origin of his family, his wife's relationship to the Castellanes, a motor tour which the Count and

Countess were proposing to make through Provence and particularly Castellan, etc. Not a word of politics.

I next presented my Japanese colleague, Baron Motono, whom Poincaré knew in Paris in the old days. Their conversation was short but not without importance. In a few words the principle of the accession of Japan to the Triple Entente was formulated and virtually agreed.

After Motono I introduced my English colleague, Sir George Buchanan. Poincaré assured him that the Tsar was determined to show himself most conciliatory in the Persian question and added that the British Government must ultimately realize the necessity of transforming the Triple Entente into a Triple Alliance.

His conversation with the ambassadors of Italy and Spain was merely superficial.

At last there appeared my Austro-Hungarian colleague, Count Szapary, a typical Hungarian nobleman, dressed to perfection. For two months he has been away from St. Petersburg at the bedside of his invalid wife and son. He came back unexpectedly yesterday. I inferred from his sudden return that the Austro-Serbian difference is getting more acute; there is going to be a rupture and the ambassador must be at his post to play his part in the dispute and take his share of responsibility.

I told Poincaré what I thought and he replied: "I'll try and clear up this business."

After a few words of sympathy on the assassination of the Archduke Francis Ferdinand, the President asked Szapary: "Have you any news of Serbia?"

"The judicial enquiry is proceeding," Szapary replied coldly.

Poincaré continued: "Of course I'm anxious about the results of this enquiry, *Monsieur l'Ambassadeur.* I can remember two previous enquiries which did not improve your relations with Serbia...Don't you remember...the Friedjung affair and the Prochaska affair?"

Szapary replied in a dry tone: "Monsieur le Président, we cannot suffer a foreign government to allow plots against our sovereignty to be hatched on its territory!"

In a more than conciliatory tone Poincaré endeavored to point out that in the present state of public feeling in Europe every government should be twice as cautious as usual.

"With a little good will this Serbian business is easy to settle. But it can just as easily become acute. Serbia has some very warm friends in the Russian people. And Russia has an ally, France. There are plenty of complications to be feared!"

Then he thanked the ambassador for his call. Szapary bowed and went out without a word. When we three were alone again Poincaré said: "I'm not satisfied with this conversation. The ambassador had obviously been instructed to say nothing...Austria has a *coup de théâtre* in store for us. Sazonov must be firm and we must back him up...."

We then went to the next room where the ministers of the minor powers were in line in order of seniority.

As he was pressed for time, Poincaré passed swiftly down the line shaking hands with each minister in turn. Their disappointment could be read in their faces. Each was hoping he would make some substantial and veiled observation on which he could make a long report to his government. The President only stopped to speak to the Serbian minister, Spalaikovitch, for whom he had a few words of sympathy.

At six o'clock a visit to the French Hospital where the President laid the first stone of a public dispensary.

At eight o'clock banquet at the Embassy. Ninety-six covers. The Embassy has been entirely renovated and looks very fine. The *Garde-Meuble National* has let me have a splendid series of gobelins, including Natoire's *Triumph of Mark Antony* and the *Triumph of Mardocheus*—superb decoration for my banqueting-hall. Last, but not least, the Embassy was carpeted with roses and orchids.

The guests arrived, each more resplendent than the last. Their selection has put me on the rack owing to all the rivalries and jealousies life at Court involves. The question of seating has been an even more difficult problem. But I've received such excellent assistance from my secretaries that dinner and the evening passed off without a hitch.

Promptly at eleven o'clock the President withdrew. I accompanied him to the City Hall where the Petersburg Duma was giving a soirée to the officers of the French squadron. It is the first time that the head of a foreign state has honored a Municipal Council's reception with his presence so his reception was exceedingly warm.

At midnight the President returned to Peterhof by water.

The violent demonstrations continued to-day in the industrial quarters of St. Petersburg. This evening the Prefect of Police assured me that the agitation had been stopped and that work will resume to-morrow. He has also confirmed the fact that among the arrested leaders several notorious agents in the German espionage service have been identified. From the point of view of the Alliance the incident gives one food for thought.

Chapter Twenty-Three
July 22, 1914

M. Bienvenu-Martin, Acting Minister for Foreign Affairs, to the French Ambassadors at London, St. Petersburgh, Vienna, Rome.
Paris, July 22, 1914.

M. Jules Cambon having questioned Herr von Jagow on the tenure of the Austrian note at Belgrade, the latter replied that he knew nothing of the text; our Ambassador expressed his great astonishment at this. He emphasizes that the weakness of the Berlin Bourse continues, and that pessimistic rumors are current. M. Barrère also discussed the same question with the Marquis di San Giuliano, who appears disturbed by it, and gives the assurance that he is working at Vienna in order that Serbia may not be asked for anything beyond what is practicable, for instance, the dissolution of the Bosnian Club, and not a judicial inquiry into the causes of the crime of Sarajevo. In present circumstances, the most favorable presumption one can make is that the Cabinet at Vienna, finding itself carried away by the press and the military party, is trying to obtain the maximum from Serbia by starting to intimidate her, directly and indirectly, and looks to Germany for support in this. I have asked the French Ambassador at Vienna to use all his influence with Count Berchtold and to represent to him, in a friendly conversation, how much Europe would appreciate moderation on the part of the Austrian Government, and what consequences would be likely to be entailed by violent pressure on Serbia.

BIENVENU-MARTIN.

No. 2.
Sir H. Humbold, British Charg'e d` Affaires at Berlin to Sir Edward Grey.
Berlin, July 22, 1914.
(Telegraphic)

Last night I met Secretary of State for Foreign Affairs, and the forthcoming Austrian demarche at Belgrade was alluded to by his Excellency in the conversation that ensued. His Excellency was evidently of opinion that this step on Austria's part would have been made ere this. He insisted that questions at issue was one for settlement between Serbia and Austria alone, that there should be no interference from outside in the discussion between those two countries. He had therefore considered it inadvisable that the Austro-Hungarian Government should be approached by the German Government on the matter. He had, however, on several occasions in conversations with the Serbian

Minister, emphasized the extreme importance that Austro-Hungarian relations should be put on a proper footing.

Finally, his Excellency observed to me that for a long time past the attitude adopted towards Serbia by Austria had, in his opinion, been one of great forbearance.

No. 18.
M. Dumaine, French Ambassador at Vienna, to M. Bienvenu-Martin, Acting Minister for Foreign Affairs.
Vienna, July 22, 1914.

Nothing is known as to the decision which Count Berchtold, who is prolonging his stay at Ischl, is trying to obtain from the Emperor. The intention of proceeding against Serbia with the greatest severity, of having done with her, of "treating her like another Poland," is attributed to the Government. Eight army corps are said to be ready to start on the campaign, but M. Tisza, who is very disturbed about the excitement in Croatia, is said to have intervened actively in order to exercise a moderating influence. In any case it is believed that the démarche will be made at Belgrade this week. The requirements of the Austro-Hungarian Government with regard to the punishment of the outrage, and to guarantees of control and police supervisions seem to be acceptable to the dignity of the Serbians; M. Yovanovich believes they will be accepted. M. Pashitch wishes for a peaceful solution, but says that he is ready for a full resistance. He has confidence in the strength of the Serbian army; besides, he counts on the union of all the Slavs in the Monarchy to paralyze the effort directed against his country. Unless people are absolutely blinded, it must be recognized here that a violent blow has every chance of being fatal both to the Austro-Hungarian army and to the cohesion of the nationalities governed by the Emperor, which has already been so much compromised.

Herr von Tschirscky, the German Ambassador, is showing himself a supporter of violent measures, while at the same tome he is willing to let it be understood that the Imperial chancery would not be in entire agreement with him on this point. The Russian Ambassador, who left yesterday for the country in consequence to reassume explanations made to him at the Ministry for Foreign Affairs, has confided to me that his Government will not raise any objection to steps directed towards the punishment of the guilty and the dissolution of the societies which are notoriously revolutionary, but could not accept requirements which would humiliate Serbian national feeling.

DUMAINE.

No. 19.
M. Paul Cambon, French Ambassador at London, to M. Bienvenu-Martin, Acting Minister for Foreign Affairs.
London, July 22, 1914.

Your Excellency has been good enough to communicate to me the impressions which have been collected by our Ambassador at Berlin with regard to the démarche which the Austro-Hungarian Minister is proposing to make at Belgrade. These impressions have been confirmed by a conversation, which I had yesterday with the Secretary of State for Foreign Affairs. Sir Edward Grey told me that he had seen the German Ambassador, who stated to him that at Berlin a démarche of the Austro-Hungarian Government to the Serbian Government was expected. Prince Lichnowsky assured him that the German Government were endeavoring to hold back and moderate the Cabinet of Vienna, but that up to the present time they had not been successful in this, and that he was not without anxiety as to the results of a démarche of this kind. Sir Edward Grey answered Prince Lichnowsky that he would like to believe that, before intervening at Belgrade, the Austro-Hungarian Government had fully informed themselves as to the circumstances of the conspiracy to which the Hereditary Archduke and the Duchess of Hohenburg had fallen victims, and had assured themselves that the Serbian Government had been cognizant of it and had not done all that lay in their power to prevent the consequences. For if it could not be proved that the Serbian Government were responsible and implicated to a certain degree, the intervention of Austria-Hungary would not be justified and would arouse against them the opinion of Europe.

The communication of Prince Lichnowsky had left Sir Edward Grey with an impression of anxiety which he did not conceal from me. The Italian Ambassador, who also fears the possibility of fresh tension in Austro-Serbian relations, gave me the same impression. This morning the Serbian Minister came to see me, and he shares the apprehensions of Sir Edward Grey. He fears that Austria may make of the Serbian Government demands, which their dignity, and above all the susceptibility of public opinion, will not allow them to accept without a protest. When I pointed out to him the quiet which appears to reign at Vienna, and to which all the Ambassadors accredited to that Court bear testimony, he answered that this official quiet was only apparent and concealed feelings which were most fundamentally hostile to Serbia. But, he added, if these feelings take a public form (démarche) which lacks the moderation that is desirable, it will be necessary to take account of Serbian public opinion, which has been inflamed by the harsh treatment to which the Austrian Government have constantly subjected that country, and which has been made less patient by the memory of two victorious wars which is still quite fresh. Notwithstanding the sacrifices which Serbia has made for her recent victories she can still put 400,000 men in the field, and public opinion, which knows this, is not inclined to put up with any humiliation. Sir Edward Grey, in an interview with the Austro-Hungarian Ambassador, asked him to recommend his Government not to depart from the prudence and moderation necessary for avoiding new complications, not to demand from Serbia any measures to which she could not reasonably submit, and not to allow themselves to be carried away too far.

PAUL CAMBON.

No. 8.
Count Berchtold to the Imperial and Royal Ambassadors in Berlin, Rome, Paris, London, St. Petersburgh and Constantinople.
Vienna, July 22, 1914. (Translated from the French)

The Imperial and Royal Government felt compelled to address the following note to the Royal Serbian Government on Thursday, the 23rd instant, through the medium of the Imperial and Royal Minister at Belgrade (see instructions to the Imperial and Royal Envoy in Belgrade of July 22nd, 1914).

On the 31st March 1909, the Royal Serbian Government addressed to Austria-Hungary the declaration of which the text is reproduced above.

On the very day after this declaration Serbia embarked on a policy of instilling revolutionary ideas into the Serb subjects of the Austro-Hungarian Monarchy, and so preparing for the separation of the Austro-Hungarian territory on the Serbian frontier.

Serbia became the centre of a criminal agitation.

No time was lost in the formation of societies and groups, whose object, either avowed or secret, was the creation of disorders on Austro-Hungarian territory. These societies and groups count among their members generals and diplomatists, Government officials, and judges—in short, men at the top of official and unofficial society in the kingdom. Serbian journalism is almost entirely at the service of this propaganda, which is directed against Austria-Hungary, and not a day passes without the organs of the Serbian press stirring up their readers to hatred or contempt for the neighboring Monarchy, or to outrages directed more or less openly against its security and integrity.

A large number of agents are employed in carrying on by every means the agitation against Austria-Hungary and corrupting the youth in the frontier provinces. Since the recent Balkan crisis there has been a recrudescence of the spirit of conspiracy inherent in Serbian politicians, which has left such sanguinary imprints on the history of the kingdom; individuals belonging formerly to bands employed in Macedonia have come to place themselves at the disposal of the terrorist propaganda against Austria-Hungary. In the presence of these doings, to which Austria-Hungary has been exposed for years, the Serbian Government have not thought it incumbent on them to take the slightest step. The Serbian Government have thus failed in the duty imposed on them by the solemn declaration of the 31st March, 1909, and acted in opposition to the will of Europe and the undertaking given to Austria-Hungary. The patience of the Imperial and Royal Government in the face of the provocative attitude of Serbia was inspired by the territorial disinterestedness of the Austro-Hungarian Monarchy and the hope that the Serbian Government would end in spite of everything by appreciating Austria-Hungary's friendship at its true value.

By observing a benevolent attitude towards the political interests of Serbia, the Imperial and Royal Government hoped that the kingdom would finally decide to follow an analogous line of conduct on its own side. In particular, Austria-Hungary expected a development of this kind in the political ideas of Serbia, when, after the events of 1912, the Imperial and Royal Government, by its disinterested and ungrudging attitude, made such a considerable aggrandizement, of Serbia possible.

The benevolence which Austria-Hungary showed towards the neighboring state had no restraining effect on the proceedings of the kingdom, which continued to tolerate on its territory a propaganda of which the fatal consequences were demonstrated to the whole world on the 28th June last, when the Heir Presumptive to the Monarchy and his illustrious consort fell victims to a plot hatched at Belgrade.

In the presence of this state of things the Imperial and Royal Government have felt compelled to take new and urgent steps at Belgrade with a view to inducing the Serbian Government to stop the incendiary movement that is threatening the security and integrity of the Austro-Hungarian Monarchy. The Imperial and Royal Government are convinced that in taking this step they will find themselves in full agreement with the sentiments of all civilized nations, who cannot permit regicide to become a weapon that can be employed with impunity in political, strife, and the peace of Europe to be continually disturbed by movements emanating from Belgrade. In support of the above the Imperial and Royal Government hold at the disposal of the British Government a *dossier* elucidating the Serbian intrigues and the connection between these intrigues and the murder of the 28th June.

An identical communication has been addressed to the Imperial and Royal representatives accredited to the other signatory Powers.

You are authorized to leave a copy of this dispatch in the hands of the Minister for Foreign Affairs.

"An Ambassador's Memoirs"
By Maurice Paléologue
Day 3 with French President in Russia
Wednesday, July 22, 1914.

At midday the Tsar gave a luncheon in Peterhof Palace to the President of the Republic and the officers of the French squadron. No ladies were present, not even the Tsaritsa. We sat down at small tables for ten to twelve covers. It was very hot outside but cool, sweet breezes wafted through the open windows from the leafy shade and fountains and cascades of the park.

I was at the same table as the Tsar and the President with Viviani, Admiral Le Bris (commanding the French squadron), Goremykin, President of the Council, Count Fredericks, Minister of the Court, Sazonov, and Isvolsky. I was on Viviani's left and he had Count Fredericks on his right. Count Fredericks, who will soon be seventy-seven, is the very personification of court life. Of all the subjects of the Tsar none has received more honors and titles. He is Minister of the Imperial Court and household, aide-de-camp to the Tsar, cavalry general, member of the Council of Empire, Chancellor of the Imperial Orders, Head of his Majesty's Cabinet and military establishment, etc. He has passed the whole of his long life in palaces and ceremonies, in carriages and processions, under gold lace and decorations. In virtue of his functions he takes precedence of the highest dignitaries of the empire and he knows all the secrets of the imperial family. In the Tsar's name he dispenses all the favors and gifts, all the reproofs and punishments.

The grand dukes and grand duchesses overwhelm him with attentions for he it is who controls their households, hushes up their scandals, and pays their debts. For all the difficulties of his task he is not known to have an enemy, such is his charm of manner and tact. He was also one of the handsomest men of his generation, one of the finest horsemen, and his successes with women were past counting. He has kept his lithe figure, his fine drooping moustache, and his charming manners. From a physical and moral point of view he is the ideal type for his office, the supreme arbiter of the rites and precedence's, conventions and traditions, manners and etiquette.

At half-past three we left by the imperial train for the camp at Krasnoïe Selo. A blazing sun lit up the vast plain, a tawny and undulating plain bounded on the horizon by wooded hills. While the Tsar, the Tsaritsa, the President of the Republic, the grand dukes, grand duchesses, and the entire imperial staff were inspecting the cantonments of the troops, I waited for them with the ministers and civil functionaries on an eminence on which tents had been pitched. The élite of Petersburg society were crowded into some stands. The light toilettes of the women, their white hats and parasols made the stands look like azalea beds. Before long the imperial party arrived.

In a four-horse *calèche* was the Tsaritsa with the President of the Republic on her right and her two elder daughters opposite her. The Tsar was galloping by the side of the carriage, followed by a brilliant escort of the grand dukes and aides-de-camp. They all dismounted and assembled on the low hill dominating the plain. The troops, without arms, were drawn up in serried ranks as far as the eye could reach before the row of tents. The front line ran along the very foot of the hill.

The sun was dropping towards the horizon in a sky of purple and gold. On a sign from the Tsar an artillery salvo signaled evening prayer. The bands played a hymn. Everyone uncovered. A non-commissioned officer recited the *Pater* in a loud voice. All those men, thousands upon thousands, prayed for the Tsar and Holy Russia. The silence and composure of that multitude in that great plain, the magic poetry of the hour, the vision of the alliance which sanctified everything, gave the ceremony a touching majesty. From the camps we returned to the village of Krasnoïe-Selo, where the Grand Duke Nicholas Nicholaïevitch, Commander of the Imperial Guard, G.O.C. the St. Petersburg military area and subsequently generalissimo of the Russian armies, gave a dinner to the President of the Republic and the sovereigns. Three long tables were set in half-open tents around a garden which was in full flower. The beds had just been watered and from them the fresh scent of flowers—a delicious change after the baking day—rose into the warm air.

I was one of the first to arrive. The Grand Duchess Anastasia and her sister, the Grand Duchess Militza, gave me a boisterous welcome. The two Montenegrins burst out, talking both at once: "Do you realize that we're passing through historic days, fateful days!…At the review tomorrow the bands will play nothing but the *Marche Lorraine* and *Sambre et Meuse*. I've had a telegram (in pre-arranged code) from my father to-day. He tells me we shall have war before the end of the month….What a hero my father is!…He's worthy of the Iliad! Just look at this little box I always take about with me. It's got some Lorraine soil in it, real Lorraine soil I picked up over the frontier when I was in France with my husband two years ago. Look there, at the table of honour: it's covered with thistles. I didn't want to have any other flowers there. They're Lorraine thistles, don't you see! I gathered several plants on the annexed territory, brought them here and had the seeds sown in my garden…Militza, go on talking to the ambassador. Tell him all to-day means to us while I go and receive the Tsar…."

At dinner I was on the left of the Grand Duchess Anastasia and the rhapsody continued, interspersed with prophecies. "There's going to be war…There'll be nothing left of Austria….You're going to get back Alsace and Lorraine….Our armies will meet in Berlin….Germany will be destroyed…." Then suddenly: "I must restrain myself. The Emperor has his eye on me."

Under the Tsar's stern gaze the Montenegrin sybil suddenly lapsed into silence.

Quite funny how the French and Russians are calling for peace and a resolution to the current crisis, but Grand Duchess Anastasia and her sister know of Nicholas II's plans for war with not only Austria but Germany as well. These plans are taking place while Wilhelm II is still on vacation.

Chapter Twenty-Four

July 23, 1914

No. 9.
Count Berchtold to Count Mensdorff at London.
(Telegraphic)
Vienna, July 23, 1914.

As among the Entente Powers, Great Britain might be most easily led to form an impartial judgment on the step which we are to-day taking at Belgrade, I request Your Excellency in the conversation which you will have on the 24th instant on the occasion when you hand in our circular note at the Foreign Office, to point out among other matters that it would have been within the power of Serbia to render less acute the serious steps which she must expect from us, by spontaneously doing what is necessary in order to start an inquiry on Serbian soil against the Serbian accomplices in the crime of 28th June, and by bringing to light the threads, which, as has been proved, lead from Belgrade to Serbia. Up to the present time, although a number of notorious indications point to Belgrade, the Serbian Government have not taken any steps in this direction; on the contrary, they have attempted to wipe out the existing traces. Thus, from a telegraphic dispatch from our Legation at Belgrade, it is to be gathered that the Serbian civil servant Ciganovic, who is compromised by the independent testimony of the affidavits of both criminals, on the day of the outrage was still in Belgrade, and three days afterwards, when his name was mentioned in the papers, had already left the town. As is well known also, the director of the Serbian press declared that Ciganovic is completely unknown in Belgrade. With regard to the short time-limit attached to our demand, this must be attributed to our long experience of the dilatory arts of Serbia. The requirements which we demand that Serbia should fulfill, and which indeed contain nothing which is not a matter of course in the intercourse between States which are to live in peace and friendship, cannot be made the subject of negotiations and compromise; and, having regard to our economic interests, we cannot take the risk of a method of political action by which it would be open to Serbia at pleasure to prolong the crisis which has arisen.

No. 3.
Sir Edward Grey to Sir M. de Bunsen, British Ambassador at Vienna.
Foreign Office.
July 23, 1914.

Sir,

Count Mensdorff told me today that he would be able tomorrow morning to let me have officially the communication that he understood was being made to Serbia today by Austria. He then explained privately what the nature of the demands would be. As he told me that the facts would all be set out in the paper that he would give me tomorrow, it is unnecessary to record them now. I gathered that they would include proof of the complicity of some Serbian officials in the plot to murder the Archduke Franz Ferdinand, and a long list of demands consequently made by Austria on Serbia.

As regards all this, I said that it was not a matter on which I would make any comment until I received an official communication, and it seemed to me probably a matter on which I should not be able to make any comment at first sight.

But, when Count Mensdorff told me that he supposed there would be something in the nature of a time limit, which was in effect akin to an ultimatum, I said that I regretted this very much. To begin with a time limit might inflame opinion in Russia, and give more time, and it would make it difficult, if not impossible, to give more time, even if a few days it appeared that by giving more time there would be a prospect of securing a peaceful settlement and getting a satisfactory reply from Serbia. I admitted that, if there was no time limit, the proceedings might be unduly protracted, but I urged that a time limit could always be introduced afterwards; that, if the demands were made without a time limit in the first instance, Russian public opinion might be less excited, after a week it might have cooled down, and if the Austrian case was very strong it might be apparent the Russian Government would be in a position to use there influence in favor of a satisfactory reply from Serbia. A time limit was generally a thing to be used only in a last resort, after other means had been tried and failed.

Count Mensdorff said that if Serbia, in the interval that had elapsed since the murder of the Archduke, had voluntarily instituted an enquiry on her own territory, all this might have been avoided. In 1909, Serbia had said in a note that she intended to live on terms of good neighbor with Austria; but she never kept her promises, she stirred up agitation the object of which was to disintegrate Austria, and was absolutely necessary for Austria to protect herself.

I said that I would not comment upon or criticize what Count Mensdorff had told me this afternoon, but I could not help dwelling upon the awful consequence involved in the situation. Great apprehension had been expressed to me, not especially by M. Cambon and Count Benckendorff, but also by others, as to what might happen, and it had been represented to me that it would be very desirable that those who have influence in St. Petersburg should use it on behalf of patience and moderation. I had replied that the amount of influence that could be used in this sense would depend upon how reasonable were the Austrian demands and how strong the justification that Austria might have discovered for making her demands. The possible consequences of the present situation were terrible. If as many as Four Great Powers of Europe—let us say, Austria, France, Russia, and Germany—were engaged in war, it seemed to me that it must involve the expenditure of so vast a sum of money, and such an interference with trade, that war would be accompanied or followed by a complete collapse of European credit and industry. In these days, in great industrial states, this would mean a state of things worse than 1848, and irrespective of who were victors in the war, many things might be completely swept away.

Count Mensdorff did not demur to his statement of the possible consequences of the present situation, but he said that all would depend upon Russia.

I made the remark that in a time of difficulties such as this, it was just as true to say that it required two to keep the peace as it was to say, ordinarily, that it took two to make a quarrel. I hope very much that, if there were difficulties, Austria and Russia would be able in the first instances to discuss them directly with each other.

Count Mensdorff said that he hoped this would be possible, but he was under the impression that the attitude in St. Petersburg had not been very favorable recently.

I am, and &tc

E. Grey

Both Sir Grey and Count Mensdorff are very right. At this very moment France and Russia are meeting in St. Petersburg to plan how this war will start.

No. 20.
M. Bienvenu-Martin, Acting Minister for Foreign Affairs, to London, Berlin, St. Petersburgh, and Rome.
Paris, July 23, 1914.

According to information collected by the French Ambassador at Vienna, the first intention of the Austro-Hungarian Government had been to proceed with the greatest severity against Serbia while keeping eight army corps ready to start operations. The disposition at this moment was more conciliatory; in answer to a question put to him by M. Dumaine, whom I instructed to call the attention of the Austro-Hungarian Government to the anxiety aroused in Europe, Baron Macchio stated to our Ambassador that the tone of the Austrian note, and the demands which would be formulated in it, allow us to count on a peaceful result. In view of the customary procedure of the Imperial Chancery I do not know what confidence ought to be placed in these assurances. In any case the Austrian note will be presented in a very short space of time. The Serbian Minister holds that as M. Pashitch wishes to come to an understanding, he will accept those demands, which relate to the punishment of the outrage and to the guarantees for control and police supervision, but that he will resist everything, which might affect the sovereignty and sovereignty and dignity of his country. In diplomatic circles at Vienna the German Ambassador is in favor of violent measures, while at the same time confesses that the Imperial Chancery is perhaps not entirely in agreement with him on this point; the Russian Ambassador, trusting to assurances which have been given him, has left Vienna, and before his departure confided to M. Dumaine that his Government will not raise any objection to the punishment of the guilty and the dissolution of the revolutionary associations, but that they could not accept requirements which were humiliating to the national sentiment of Serbia.

BIENVENU-MARTIN.

No. 21.
M. Allizé, French Minister at Munich, to M. Bienvenu-Martin, Acting Minister for Foreign Affairs, Paris.
Munich, July 23, 1914.

The Bavarian press seems to believe that a peaceful solution of the Austro-Serbian incident is not only possible but also even probable; on the other hand, official circles have for some time been assuming with more or less sincerity an air of real pessimism.

In particular the President of the Council said to me to-day that the Austrian note the contents of which were known to him *(dont il avait connaissance)* was in his opinion drawn up in terms which could he accepted by Serbia, but that nonetheless the existing situation appeared to him to be very serious.

1914 July 23—Tsar told England to declare war on Germany.

No. 38.
Sir R. Rodd, British Ambassador at Rome, to Sir Edward Grey.
Rome, Italy.
July 23, 1914.

Sir,

I gather that the Italian government have been made cognizant of the terms of the communication which will be addressed to Serbia. Secretary General, whom I saw this morning at the Italian Foreign Office, took the view that the gravity of the situation lay in the conviction of the Austro-Hungarian Government that it was absolutely necessary for their prestige, after the many disillusions which the turn of events in the Balkans has occasioned, to score a definite success.

I have, and &tc
Rennell Rodd

This telegram was finally delivered to Sir Edward Grey on July 27. With this crisis, a telegram being sent even one day late could change the course of events.

Primary Documents: Explanatory Letter to Austria's Ultimatum to Serbia, 23 July 1914

The Austro-Hungarian government waited three weeks following the assassination of Archduke Franz Ferdinand—heir to the Austro-Hungarian throne currently held by Franz Josef—before issuing its formal response to Serbia, which dispatched on 23 July 1914.

Aware that the terms of the ultimatum might appear designed to prompt an inevitable Serbian rejection—and thus provide a plausible excuse to go to war against Serbia—an explanatory letter from the Austro-Hungarian government was dispatched to each of the major European powers and was sent attached to a copy of the ultimatum.

Letter of Explanation Transmitted to the Various European Powers

On the thirty-first of March, 1909, the Royal Serbian Government addressed to Austria-Hungary the declaration of which the text is reproduced above. On the very day after this declaration, Serbia embarked on a policy of instilling revolutionary ideas into the Serb subjects of the Austro-Hungarian Monarchy and so preparing for the separation of the Austro-Hungarian territory on the Serbian frontier. Serbia became the center of a criminal agitation. No time was lost in the formation of societies and groups whose object, either avowed or secret, was the creation of disorders on Austro-Hungarian territory. These societies and groups count among their members' generals and diplomatists, Government officials and judges-in short, men at the top of official and unofficial society in the kingdom. Serbian journalism is almost entirely at the service of this propaganda, which is directed against Austria-Hungary, and not a day passes without the organs of the Serbian press stirring up their readers to hatred or contempt for the neighboring monarchy or to outrages directed more or less openly against its security and integrity.

A large number of agents are employed in carrying on by every means the agitation against Austria-Hungary and corrupting the youth in the frontier provinces.

Since the recent Balkan crisis there has been a recrudescence of the spirit of conspiracy inherent in Serbian politicians, which has left such sanguinary imprints on the history of the kingdom; individuals belonging formerly to bands employed in Macedonia have come to place themselves at the disposal of the terrorist propaganda against Austria-Hungary. In the presence of these doings, to which Austria-Hungary has been exposed for years, the Serbian Government has not thought it incumbent on them to take the slightest step. The Serbian Government has thus failed in the duty imposed on them by the solemn declaration of the 31st of March, 1909, and acted in opposition to the will of Europe and the undertaking given to Austria-Hungary.

The patience of the Imperial and Royal Government in the face of the provocative attitude of Serbia was inspired by the territorial disinterestedness of the Austro-Hungarian Monarchy and the hope that the Serbian Government would end in spite of everything by appreciating Austria-Hungary's friendship at its true value. By observing a benevolent attitude towards the political interests of Serbia, the Imperial and Royal Government hoped that the kingdom would finally decide to follow an analogous line of conduct on its own side. In particular, Austria-Hungary expected a development of this kind in the political ideas of Serbia, when, after the events of 1912, the Imperial and Royal Government, by its disinterested and ungrudging attitude, made such a considerable aggrandizement of Serbia possible. The benevolence which Austria-Hungary showed towards the neighboring State had no restraining effect on the proceedings of the kingdom, which continued to tolerate on its territory a propaganda of which the fatal consequences were demonstrated to the whole world on the 28th of June last, when the Heir Presumptive to the Monarchy and his illustrious consort fell victims to a plot hatched at Belgrade. In the presence of this state of things the Imperial and Royal Government have felt compelled to take new and urgent steps at Belgrade with a view to inducing the Serbian Government to stop the incendiary movement that is threatening the security and integrity of the Austro-Hungarian Monarchy. The Imperial and Royal Government are convinced that in taking this step they will find themselves in full agreement with the sentiments of all civilized nations, who cannot permit regicide to become a weapon that can be employed with impunity in political strife, and the peace of Europe to be continually disturbed by movements emanating from Belgrade.

Source: *Source Records of the Great War, Vol. I, ed. Charles F. Horne, National Alumni, 1923.*

THE ORIGINAL TELEGRAMS AND NOTES
The Note of Austria-Hungary to Serbia
Presented July 23rd in Belgrade

"On March 31st, 1909, the Royal Serbian Minister to the Court of Vienna made the following statement, by order of his Government:

"Serbia declares that she is not affected in her rights by the situation established in *Bosnia,* and that she will therefore adapt herself to the decisions which the Powers are going to arrive at in reference to Art. 25 of the Berlin Treaty. By following the councils of the Powers, Serbia binds herself to Cease the attitude of protest and resistance, which she has assumed since last October, relative to the annexation, and she binds herself further to change the direction of her present policies towards Austria-Hungary, and, in the Future, to live with the latter in friendly and neighborly relations.

"The history of the last years, and especially the painful events of June 28th, have demonstrated the existence of a subversive movement in Serbia whose aim it is to separate certain territories from the Austro-Hungarian monarchy. This movement, which developed under the eyes of the Serbian Government, has found expression subsequently beyond the territory of the kingdom, in acts of terrorism, a series of assassinations and murders."

Far from fulfilling the formal obligations contained in the declaration of March 31st, 1909, the Royal Serbian Government has done nothing to suppress this movement. She suffered the criminal doings of the various societies and associations directed against the monarchy, the unbridled language of the Press, the glorification of the originators of assassinations, the participation of officers and officials in subversive intrigues; she suffered the unwholesome propaganda in public education, and lastly permitted all manifestations which would mislead the Serbian people into hatred of the monarchy and into contempt for its institutions. This sufferance, of which the Royal Serbian Government made itself guilty, has lasted up to the moment in which the events of June 28th demonstrated to the entire world the ghastly consequences of such sufferance.

"It becomes plain from the evidence and confessions of the criminal authors of the outrage of June 28th, that the murder at Sarajevo was conceived in Belgrade, that the murderers received the arms and bombs with which they were equipped, from Serbian officers and officials who belonged to the Narodna Odbrana, and that, lastly, the transportation of the criminals and their arms to Bosnia was arranged and carried out by leading Serbian frontier officials."

"The cited results of the investigation do not permit the Imperial and Royal Government to observe any longer the attitude of waiting, which it has assumed for years towards those agitations which have their centre in Belgrade, and which from there radiate into the territory of the monarchy. These results, on the contrary, impose upon the Imperial and Royal Government the duty to terminate intrigues which constitute a permanent menace for the peace of the monarchy." In order to obtain this purpose, the Imperial and Royal Government is forced to demand official assurance from the Serbian Government that it condemns the propaganda directed against Austria-Hungary, *i.e.,* the entirety of the machinations whose aim it is to separate parts from the monarchy which belong to it, and that she binds herself to suppress with all means this criminal and terrorizing propaganda. In order to give to these obligations a solemn character, the Royal Serbian Government will publish on the first page of its official organ of July 26th, 1914, the following declaration:

"The Royal Serbian Government condemns the propaganda" directed against Austria-Hungary, *i.e.,* the entirety of those machinations whose aim it is to separate from the Austro-Hungarian monarchy territories belonging thereto and she regrets sincerely the ghastly consequences of these criminal actions." The Royal Serbian Government regrets that Serbian officers and officials have participated in the propaganda, cited above, and have thus threatened the friendly and neighborly relations, which the Royal Government was solemnly bound to cultivate by its declaration of March 31st, 1909. "The Royal Government, which disapproves and rejects every thought or every attempt at influencing the destinations of the inhabitants of any part of Austria-Hungary, considers it its duty to call most emphatically to the attention of its officers and officials, and of the entire population of the kingdom, that it will henceforward proceed with the utmost severity against any persons guilty of similar actions to prevent and suppress which it will make every effort."

"This explanation is to be brought simultaneously to the cognizance of the Royal Army through an order of H.M. the King, and it is to be published in the official organ of the Army." The Royal Serbian Government binds itself, in addition, as follows:

1. To suppress any publication which fosters hatred of, and contempt for, the Austro-Hungarian monarchy, and whose general tendency is directed against the latter's territorial integrity;

74

2. To proceed at once with the dissolution of the society Narodna Odbrana, to confiscate their entire means of propaganda, and to proceed in the same manner against the other societies and associations in Serbia, which occupy themselves with the propaganda against Austria-Hungary. The Royal Government will take the necessary measures, so that the dissolved Societies may not continue their activities under another name or in another form;

3. To eliminate without delay from the instruction in Serbia, so fair as the corps of instructors, as well as the means of instruction are concerned, that which serves, or may serve, to foster the propaganda against Austria-Hungary;

4. To remove from military service and the administration in general all officers and officials who are guilty of propaganda against Austria-Hungary, and whose names, with a communication of the material which the Imperial and Royal Government possesses against them, the Imperial and Royal Government reserves the right to communicate to the Royal Government;

5. To consent that in Serbia officials of the Imperial and Royal Government co-operate in the suppression of a movement directed against the territorial integrity of the monarchy;

6. To commence a judicial investigation against the participants of the conspiracy of June 28th who are on Serbian territory. Officials, delegated by the Imperial and Royal Government will participate in the examinations;

7. To proceed at once with all severity to arrest Major Voja Tankosic and a certain Milan Ciganowic, Serbian State officials, who have been compromised through the result of the investigation;

8. To prevent through effective measures the participation of the Serbian authorities in the smuggling of arms and explosives across the frontier and to dismiss those officials of Shabatz and Loznica who assisted the originators of the crime of Sarajevo in crossing the frontier;

9. To give to the Imperial and Royal Government explanations in regard to the unjustifiable remarks of high Serbian functionaries in Serbia and abroad who have not hesitated, in spite of their official position, to express themselves in interviews in a hostile manner against Austria-Hungary after the outrage of June 28th.

10. The Imperial and Royal Government expects a reply from the Royal Government at the latest until Saturday, 25th inst., at 6 P.M. A memoir concerning the results of the investigations at Sarajevo, so far as they concern points 7 and 8, is enclosed with this note."

Enclosure.

The investigation carried on against Gabrilo Princip and accomplices in the Court of Sarajevo, on account of the assassination on June 28th has, so far, yielded the following results:

1. The plan to murder Archduke Franz Ferdinand during his stay in Sarajevo was conceived in Belgrade by Gabrilo Princip, Nedeljko, Gabrinowic, and a certain Milan Ciganowic and Trifko Grabez, with the aid of Major Voja Tankosic.

2. The six bombs and four Browning pistols which were used by the criminals were obtained by Milan Ciganowic and Major Tankosic, and presented to Princip Gabrinowic in Belgrade.

3. The bombs are hand grenades, manufactured at the arsenal of the Serbian Army in Kragujevac.

4. To insure the success of the assassination, Milan Ciganowic instructed Princip Gabrinowic in the use of the grenades and gave instructions in shooting with Browning pistols to Princip Grabez in a forest near the target practice field of Topshider (outside Belgrade).

5. In order to enable the crossing of the frontier of Bosnia and Herzegovina Princip Gabrinowic and Grabez, and the smuggling of their arms organized a secret system of transportation organized by Ciganowic. The entry of the criminals with their arms into Bosnia and Herzegovina was effected by the frontier captains of Shabatz (Rade Popowic) and of Loznica, as well as by the custom house official Rudivoy Grbic of Loznica with the aid of several other persons.

The Chancellor to the Imperial Ambassadors at Paris, London, and St. Petersburg, on July 23, 1914.

The publications of the Austro-Hungarian Government concerning the circumstances under which the Assassination of the Austrian successor to the throne and his consort took place, disclose clearly the aims which the pan Serb propaganda has set itself and the means which it utilizes for their realization. Through the published facts, the last doubt must disappear that the centre of action of the efforts for the separation of the south Slavic provinces from the Austro-Hungarian Monarchy and their union with the Serbian Kingdom must be sought in Belgrade where it displays its activity with the connivance of members of the Government and of the Army. The Serb intrigues may be traced back through a series of years.

In a specially marked manner the pan Serb chauvinism showed itself during the Bosnian crisis. Only to the far reaching self-restraint and moderation of the Austro-Hungarian Government and the energetic intercession of the Powers is it to be ascribed that the provocations to which at that time Austria-Hungary was exposed on the part of Serbia, did not lead to a conflict. The assurance of future behavior, which the Serbian Government gave at that time, it has not kept. Under the very eyes, at least with the tacit sufferance of official Serbia, the pan Serb propaganda has meanwhile increased in scope and intensity; at its door is to be laid the latest crime the threads of which lead to Belgrade. It has become evident that it is compatible neither with the dignity nor with the self-preservation of the Austro-Hungarian Monarchy to view any longer idly the doings across the border through which the safety and the integrity of the Monarchy are permanently threatened. With this state of affairs, the action as well as the demands of the Austro-Hungarian Government can be viewed only as justifiable. Nevertheless, the attitude assumed by public opinion as well as by the Government in Serbia does not preclude the fear that the Serbian Government will decline to meet these demands and that it will allow itself to be carried away into a provocative attitude toward Austria-Hungary. Nothing would remain for the Austro-Hungarian Government, unless it renounced definitely its position as a great Power, but to press its demands with the Serbian Government, and, if need be, enforce the same by appeal to military measures, in regard to which the choice of means must be left with it. I have the honor to request you to express yourself in the sense indicated above to (the present representative of M. Viviani), (Sir Edward Grey), (M. Sasonof) and therewith give special emphasis to the view that in this question there is concerned an affair which should be settled solely between Austria-Hungary and Serbia, the limitation to which it must be the earnest endeavor of the powers to insure. We anxiously desire the localization of the conflict because every intercession of another power on account of the various treaty-alliances would precipitate inconceivable consequences.

I shall look forward with interest to a telegraphic report about the course of your interview.

The text of the ultimatum follows, as does the Serbian response, which virtually conceded all demands made by the Austro-Hungarians' bar one or two minor clauses. Nonetheless, war was declared by Austria-Hungary shortly afterwards.

Austria-Hungary's Ultimatum to Serbia

On the thirty-first of March, 1909, the Serbian Minister in Vienna, on the instructions of the Serbian Government, made the following declaration to the Imperial and Royal Government:

> "Serbia recognizes that the fait accompli regarding Bosnia has not affected her rights and consequently she will conform to the decisions that the Powers may take in conformity with Article 25 of the Treaty of Berlin. In deference to the advice of the Great Powers, Serbia undertakes to renounce from now onwards the attitude of protest and opposition which she has adopted with regard to the annexation since last autumn. She undertakes, moreover, to modify the direction of her policy with regard to Austria-Hungary and to live in future on good neighborly terms with the latter."

The history of recent years, and in particular the painful events of the 28th of June last, have shown the existence of a subversive movement with the object of detaching a part of the territories of Austria-Hungary from the Monarchy. The movement, which had its birth under the eye of the Serbian Government, has gone so far as to make itself manifest on both sides of the Serbian frontier in the shape of acts of terrorism and a series of outrages and murders. Far from carrying out the formal undertakings contained in the declaration of the 31st of March, 1909, the Royal Serbian Government has done nothing to repress these movements. It has permitted the criminal machinations of various societies and associations directed against the Monarchy, and have tolerated unrestrained language on the part of the press, the glorification of the perpetrators of outrages, and the participation of officers and functionaries in subversive agitation. It has permitted an unwholesome propaganda in public instruction; in short, it has permitted all manifestations of a nature to incite the Serbian population to hatred of the Monarchy and contempt of its institutions. This culpable tolerance of the Royal Serbian Government had not ceased at the moment when the events of the 28th of June last proved its fatal consequences to the whole world. It results from the depositions and confessions of the criminal perpetrators of the outrage of the 28th of June that the Sarajevo assassinations were planned in Belgrade; that the arms and explosives with which the murderers were provided had been given to them by Serbian officers and functionaries belonging to the Narodna Odbrana; and finally, that the passage into Bosnia of the criminals and their arms was organized and effected by the chiefs of the Serbian frontier service. The above-mentioned results of the magisterial investigation do not permit the Austro-Hungarian Government to pursue any longer the attitude of expectant forbearance which they have maintained for years in face of the machinations hatched in Belgrade, and thence propagated in the territories of the Monarchy. The results, on the contrary, impose on them the duty of putting an end to the intrigues, which form a perpetual menace to the tranquility of the Monarchy. To achieve this end the Imperial and Royal Government see themselves compelled to demand from the Royal Serbian Government a formal assurance that they condemn this dangerous propaganda against the Monarchy; in other words the whole series of tendencies, the ultimate aim of which is to detach from the Monarchy territories belonging to it and that they undertake to suppress by every means this criminal and terrorist propaganda. In order to give a formal character to this undertaking the Royal Serbian Government shall publish on the front page of their "Official Journal" of the 13–26 of July the following declaration: "The Royal Government of Serbia condemn the propaganda directed against Austria-Hungary, i.e., the general tendency of which the final aim is to detach from the Austro-Hungarian Monarchy territories belonging to it, and they sincerely deplore the fatal consequences of these criminal proceedings. The Royal Government regret that Serbian officers and functionaries participated in the above-mentioned propaganda and thus compromised the good neighborly relations to which the Royal Government were solemnly pledged by their declaration of the 31st of March, 1909. The Royal Government, who disapprove and repudiate all idea of interfering or attempting to interfere with the destinies of the inhabitants of any part whatsoever of Austria-Hungary, consider it their duty formally to warn officers and functionaries, and the whole population of the Kingdom, that henceforward they will proceed with the utmost rigor against persons who may be guilty of such machinations, which they will use all their efforts to anticipate and suppress." This declaration shall simultaneously be communicated to the Royal army as an order of the day by His Majesty the King and shall be published in the "Official Bulletin" of the army.

The Royal Serbian Government shall further undertake:

(1) To suppress any publication which incites to hatred and contempt of the Austro-Hungarian Monarchy and the general tendency of which is directed against its territorial integrity;

(2) To dissolve immediately the society styled "Narodna Odbrana," to confiscate all its means of propaganda, and to proceed in the same manner against other societies and their branches in Serbia which engage in propaganda against the Austro-Hungarian Monarchy. The Royal Government shall take the necessary measures to prevent the societies dissolved from continuing their activity under another name and form;

(3) To eliminate without delay from public instruction in Serbia, both as regards the teaching body and also as regards the methods of instruction, everything that serves, or might serve, to foment the propaganda against Austria-Hungary;

(4) To remove from the military service and from the administration in general, all officers and functionaries guilty of propaganda against the Austro-Hungarian Monarchy whose names and deeds the Austro-Hungarian Government reserve to themselves the right of communicating to the Royal Government;

(5) To accept the collaboration in Serbia of representatives of the Austro-Hungarian Government for the suppression of the subversive movement directed against the territorial integrity of the Monarchy;

(6) To take judicial proceedings against accessories to the plot of the 28th of June who are on Serbian territory; delegates of the Austro-Hungarian Government will take part in the investigation relating thereto;

(7) To proceed without delay to the arrest of Major Voija Tankositch and of the individual named Milan Ciganovitch, a Serbian State employee, who have been compromised by the results of the magisterial inquiry at Sarajevo;

(8) To prevent by effective measures the cooperation of the Serbian authorities in the illicit traffic in arms and explosives across the frontier, to dismiss and punish severely the officials of the frontier service at Shabatz Loznica guilty of having assisted the perpetrators of the Sarajevo crime by facilitating their passage across the frontier;

(9) To furnish the Imperial and Royal Government with explanations regarding the unjustifiable utterances of high Serbian officials, both in Serbia and abroad, who, notwithstanding their official position, have not hesitated since the crime of the 28th of June to express themselves in interviews in terms of hostility to the Austro-Hungarian Government; and, finally,

(10) To notify the Imperial and Royal Government without delay of the execution of the measures comprised under the preceding heads.

The Austro-Hungarian Government expects the reply of the Royal Government at the latest by 5 o'clock on Saturday evening the 25th of July. (See Note 1)

(Note 1) The Austro-Hungarian Ambassador in a private letter on the 24th of July sent to the French Minister for Foreign Affairs the following correction:

"In the copy of the dispatch which I had the honor to send to your Excellency this morning, it was said that my Government expected an answer from the Cabinet at Belgrade at latest by 5 o'clock on the evening of Saturday the 25th of this month. As our Minister at Belgrade did not deliver his note yesterday until 6 o'clock in the evening, the time allowed for the answer has in consequence been prolonged to 6 o'clock to-morrow, Saturday evening. I consider it my duty to inform your Excellency of this slight alteration in the termination of the period fixed for the answer to the Serbian Government."

The Serbian Reply: (Preamble) …[Serbia] cannot be held responsible for manifestations of a private character, such as articles in the press and the peaceable work of societies … [The Serbian government] have been pained and surprised at the statements, according to which members of the Kingdom of Serbia are supposed to have participated in the preparations of the crime…[However, Serbia is] prepared to hand over for trial any Serbian subject of whose complicity in the crime of Sarajevo proofs are forthcoming [as well as officially condemn all propaganda against A–H].

[Serbia will] introduce…a provision into the press law providing for the most severe punishment of incitement to hatred and contempt of the [A-H] Monarchy…

[The Serbian government] possesses no proof…that the Narodna Odbrana and other similar societies have committed up to the present any criminal act of this nature…Nevertheless, [Serbia] will…dissolve the Narodna Obrana and every other society which…[Serbia will] eliminate without delay from public instruction…everything that serves or might serve to foment the propaganda against [A–H], whenever [Austria] furnish them with facts and proofs…[Serbia] also agree to remove from the military service all such persons as the judicial inquiry may have proved to be guilty of acts directed against the integrity of the territory of [A–H], and they expect [Austria] to communicate…the names and acts of these officers for the purpose of the proceedings which are to be taken against them.

[The Serbian government does] not clearly grasp the meaning or the scope of the demand…that Serbia shall undertake to accept the collaboration of the representatives of [A–H], but they declare that they will admit such collaboration as agrees with the principle of international law, with criminal procedure, and with good neighborly relations.

…As regards the participation in this inquiry [which Serbia intends to hold] of Austro-Hungarian agents… [Serbia] cannot accept such an arrangement, as it would be a violation of the Constitution.…

[States it has not yet been possible to arrest one of the persons named; request proofs of guilt from Austria.]

[Agrees to reinforce measures against illegal trafficking of arms and explosives across the frontier with Bosnia-Herzegovina.]

[Offers explanations of anti-Austrian comments by Serb officials if Austria sends examples of their actually having been made.]

[Serbia will duly notify the measures taken, but if Austria is not satisfied with the reply] the Serbian government…is ready…to accept a pacific understanding, either by referring this question to the decision of the International Tribunal of the Hague [i.e., the World Court], or to the Great Powers.…

No. 32.
From: **Baron Giesl von Gieslingen, Austro-Hungarian Minister at Belgrade.**
To: **Dr. Laza Patchou, Acting Prime Minister and Minister for Foreign Affairs.**
Belgrade, July 23, 1914.

Sir,

I have the honour to transmit to Your Excellency herewith the enclosed Note which I have received from my Government, addressed to the Royal Serbian Government.

Handed personally at 6 P.M.

No. 33.
From: **Dr. Laza Patchou, Acting Prime Minister and Minister for Foreign Affairs.**
To: **All the Serbian Legations abroad.**
Belgrade, July 23, 19 14.
(Telegraphic)

The Austro-Hungarian Minister handed me this afternoon at 6 P.M. a note in regard to the Sarajevo outrage embodying the demands of the Austro-Hungarian Government, and insisting on a reply from the Serbian Government within two days, i.e., by Saturday, at 6 P.M. He informed me orally that he and his staff would leave Belgrade unless a favorable answer were forthcoming within the stipulated time.

Some of the Ministers being absent from Belgrade the Serbian Government have not as yet come to any decision, but I am in a position to state now that the demands are such that no Serbian Government could accept them in their entirety.

No. 34.
From: **Minister at Belgrade.**
To: **Dr. Laza Patchou, Acting Prime Minister and Minister for Foreign Affairs.**
Belgrade, July 23, 1914.

Sir,
I have the honor to transmit to Your Excellency herewith the enclosed Note, which I have received from my Government, addressed to the Royal Serbian Government.

I have, &tc.
Handed personally at 6 P.M.

Russian Chargé d'Affaires at Belgrade to Russian Minister for Foreign Affairs.
Belgrade, July 23, 1914.
(Telegraphic)

The Austrian Minister, at 6 o'clock this evening, presented an ultimatum from his Government to the Minister of Finance, Patchou, in the absence of Pashitch, requiring the acceptance of the demands contained therein within forty-eight hours. Giesl added verbally that, in the event of failure to accept the note integrally within forty-eight hours, he was under instructions to leave Belgrade with the staff of the legation. Pashitch and the other Ministers, who are away electioneering, have been recalled and are expected at Belgrade tomorrow, Friday, at 10 A.M. Patchou, who communicated to me the contents of the note, solicits the help of Russia and declares that no Serbian Government could accept the demands of Austria.

TEXT of the note presented to the Serbian Government by the Austro-Hungarian Minister today. Here follows the text of the note, for which see No. 4 in British Correspondence, page 3.

"An Ambassador's Memoirs"
By Maurice Paléologue
Day 4 with French President in Russia
Thursday, July 23, 1914.

Review at Krasnoïe-Selo this morning. Sixty thousand men took part. A magnificent pageant of might and majesty. The infantry marched past to the strains of the *Marche de Sambre et Meuse* and the *Marche Lorraine.*

What a wealth of suggestion in this military machine set in motion by the Tsar of all the Russians before the President of the allied republic, himself a son of Lorraine!

The Tsar was mounted at the foot of the mound upon which was the imperial tent. Poincaré was seated on the Tsaritsa's right in front of the tent. The few glances he exchanged with me showed me that our thoughts were the same.

This evening we had a farewell dinner on the *France*. The moment it was over the French squadron was to prepare to leave for Stockholm.

The Tsaritsa had made a point of coming with the Tsar. All the grand dukes and grand duchesses were there.

About seven o'clock a momentary squall did some slight damage to the floral decorations of the deck but the table looked very fine all the same. It had indeed a kind of terrifying grandeur with the four gigantic 30 mm. gun raising their huge muzzles above the heads of the guests. The sky was soon clear again; a light breeze kissed the waves; the moon rose above the horizon.

Conversation between the Tsar and the President never ceased.

In the distance the Grand Duchess Anastasia raised her champagne glass towards me more than once, indicating with a sweep of her arm the warlike tackle all about us.

As the second entrée was about to be served a servant brought me a note from Viviani, scribbled on a menu: "Be quick and prepare a communiqué for the press."

Admiral Grigorovitch, Naval Minister, who was next to me, whispered in my ear: "It seems to me you're not left in peace for a minute!"

I took my own and my neighbor's menus and hastily drew up a note for Havas Agency, using the neutral and empty phraseology suitable for documents of this kind. But to end up I alluded to Serbia in the following terms:

The two governments have discovered that their views and intentions for the maintenance of the European balance of power, especially in the Balkan Peninsula, are absolutely identical. I sent my note to Viviani who read it and then shook his head at me across the table.

At length the toasts were reached. Poincaré delivered his concluding phrase like a trumpet call: The two countries have the same ideal of peace in strength, honour and self-respect.

These last words—words to be heard really to be appreciated—were followed by thunderous applause. The Grand Duke Nicholas, the Grand Duchess Anastasia, and the Grand Duke Nicholas Michaïlovitch turned flaming eyes upon me.

As we were rising from the table Viviani came up to me: "I don't much like the last sentence of your note: I think it involves us a little too much in Russia's Balkan policy…Wouldn't it be better to leave it out?"

"But you can't publish an official report of your voyage and pretend not to know that there are serious differences, a threat of open conflict between Austria and Serbia. It might even be thought that you were engaged in some scheme here which you dare not mention."

"That's true. Well, give me another draft."

A few minutes later I brought him this version: The visit which the President of the Republic has just paid to H.M. the Emperor of Russia has given the two friendly and allied governments an opportunity of discovering that they are in entire agreement in their views on the various problems which concern for peace and the balance of power in Europe has laid before the Powers, particularly in the East.

"Excellent!" said Viviani.

We immediately went to discuss the matter with the President of the Republic, the Tsar, Sazonov and Isvolsky. All four unreservedly approved the new draft and I sent it at once to the Havas Agency.

The time for departure was approaching. The Tsar told Poincaré he would like to continue the discussion a few minutes longer.

"Suppose we go on the bridge, Monsieur le President?… It will be quieter."

Thus I found myself alone with the Tsaritsa who asked me to take a chair on her left. The poor lady seemed worn out. With a forced smile she said in a tired tone: "I'm glad I came tonight...I was afraid there would be a storm...The decorations on the boat are magnificent...The President will have lovely weather for his voyage..."

But suddenly she put her hands to her ears. Then with a pained and pleading glance she timidly pointed to the ship's band quite near to us which had just started on a furious allegro with a full battery of brass and big drums. "Couldn't you?" she murmured.

I guessed the cause of her trouble and signaled sharply to the conductor who did not understand but stopped his band at once.

"Thank you, thank you!" sighed the Tsaritsa.

The young Grand Duchess Olga, who was sitting at the other end of the ship with the rest of the imperial family and the members of the French mission, had been observing us for some minutes with an anxious eye. She suddenly rose, glided towards her mother with graceful ease, and whispered two or three words in her ear. Then addressing me, she continued: "The Empress is rather tired, but she asks you to stay with her, *Monsieur l'Ambassadeur,* and to go on talking to her."

I resumed our conversation as she went off with quick, light steps. At that very moment the moon appeared in an archipelago of flaky, slow-moving clouds. The whole Gulf of Finland was lit up. My subject was found for me. I enlarged on the charm of sea voyages. The Tsaritsa listened to me in silence, her gaze vacant and strained, her cheeks livid, her lips motionless and swollen. After ten minutes or so which seemed to me an eternity the Tsar and the President of the Republic came down from the bridge.

It was eleven o'clock. Preparations for the departure were in progress. The guard shouldered arms. Sharp commands rang out. The *Alexandria's* launch greeted the *France*. The farewells were said to the strains of the Russian national anthem and the *Marseillaise*. The Tsar spoke very warmly to the President of the Republic. I myself said goodbye to Poincaré who kindly asked me to call on him in Paris in a fortnight's time.

As I was bowing to the Tsar at the top of the gangway he said to me: "Will you come with me, *Monsieur l'Ambassadeur?* We can talk undisturbed on my yacht. You'll be taken straight back to Petersburg."

From the *France* we transferred to the *Alexandria*. Only the imperial family accompanied their majesties. The ministers, functionaries, military staffs and my personal staff returned direct to Petersburg in an Admiralty yacht.

It was a splendid night. The milky way stretched, a pure band of silver, into unending space. Not a breath of wind. The *France* and her escorting division sped rapidly towards the west, leaving behind them long ribbons of foam which glistened in the moonlight like silvery streams.

When the imperial suite was on board Admiral Niloff came to the Tsar for orders. The latter said to me: "It's a wonderful night. Suppose we go for a sail."

The *Alexandria* steered for the coast of Finland.

The Tsar made me sit behind him in the stern of the yacht and told me of the conversation he had just had with Poincaré: "I'm delighted with my talk with the President. We see absolutely eye to eye. I am not less peace-loving than he, and he is not less determined than I to do everything necessary to prevent the cause of peace being compromised. He fears some Austro-German maneuver against Serbia and thinks we should reply with the united front of a common diplomatic policy. I think the same. We must show ourselves firm and united in our efforts to find possible solutions and the necessary adjustments. The more difficult the situation becomes the more important will unity and firmness become."

"That policy seems to me the essence of wisdom; I'm afraid we shall have to resort to it before long."

"You are still uneasy?"

"Yes, sire."

"Have you any fresh reason for your apprehension?"

"I have at least one—the unexpected return of my colleague Szapary, and the air of cold and hostile reserve he adopted towards the President of the Republic the day before yesterday. Germany and Austria are preparing a shock for us."

"What can they want? A diplomatic success at the expense of Serbia? To score a point off the Triple Entente?...No, no; notwithstanding appearances the Emperor William is too cautious to launch his country on some wild adventure, and the Emperor Francis Joseph's only wish is to die in peace."

For a minute he sat in silence, lost in thought as if he were following up some vague line of thought. Then he rose and paced the deck.

Around us the grand dukes were standing waiting for the moment to approach their master who grudgingly dispensed a few commonplaces among them. He called them up in turn and seemed to show them an unrestrained frankness, an affectionate familiarity, as if he wanted them to forget that he usually kept them at a distance and made it a rule never to talk politics with them.

The Grand Duke Nicholas Nicholaïevitch, the Grand Duke Nicholas Michaïlovitch, the Grand Duke Paul Alexandrovitch, and the Grand Duchess Marie Pavlovna came up to me, congratulating themselves and me that the presidential visit had been so supreme a success. In the court code that meant that the sovereign was satisfied.

The Grand Duchesses Anastasia and Militza, "the two Montenegrins," got me in a corner: "What a glorious speech the President made. It was just what wanted saying, just what we've been waiting for so long! Peace *in strength, honour, and self-respect*. Remember those words, *Monsieur l'Ambassadeur;* they will mark a date in the history of the world...."

At a quarter to one the *Alexandria* dropped anchor in Peterhof bay.

After leaving the Tsar and Tsaritsa I transferred to the escort yacht, *Strela,* and was taken to Petersburg which I reached at half-past two in the morning. As we sailed up the Neva I was thinking of the eager prophecy of the Montenegrin sybils.

Chapter Twenty-Five
July 24, 1914

Official Report by Sir Maurice de Bunsen,
British Ambassador in Vienna in 1914

The delivery at Belgrade on the 23rd of July of the Austrian note to Serbia was preceded by a period of absolute silence at the Ballplatz (note: Office of the Austrian Ministry of State). Except Herr von Tschirschky (note: German Ambassador at Vienna), who must have been aware of the tenor, if not of the actual words of the note, none of my colleagues were allowed to see through the veil. On the 22nd and 23rd of July, M. Dumaine, French Ambassador, had long interviews with Baron Macchio, one of the Under-Secretaries of State for Foreign Affairs, by whom he was left under the impression that the words of warning he had been instructed to speak to the Austro-Hungarian Government had not been unavailing, and that the note which was being drawn up would be found to contain nothing with which a self-respecting State need hesitate to comply.

At the second of these interviews he was not even informed that the note was at that very moment being presented at Belgrade, or that it would be published in Vienna on the following morning. Count Forgach, the other Under-Secretary of State, had indeed been good enough to confide to me on the same day the true character of the note, and the fact of its presentation about the time we were speaking.

So little had the Russian Ambassador been made aware of what was preparing that he actually left Vienna on a fortnight's leave of absence about the 20th of July. He had only been absent a few days when events compelled him to return. It might have been supposed that Duke Avarna, Ambassador of the allied Italian Kingdom, which was bound to be so closely affected by fresh complications in the Balkans, would have been taken fully into the confidence of Count Berchtold during this critical time.

In point of fact his Excellency was left completely in the dark. As for myself, no indication was given me by Count Berchtold of the impending storm, and it was from a private source that I received on the 15th of July the forecast of what was about to happen which I telegraphed to you the following day.

It is true that during all this time the *Neue Freie Presse* and other leading Viennese newspapers were using language which pointed unmistakably to war with Serbia. The official *Fremdenblatt,* however, was more cautious, and till the note was published, the prevailing opinion among my colleagues was that Austria would shrink from courses calculated to involve her in grave European complications.

On the 24th of July the note was published in the newspapers. By common consent it was at once styled an ultimatum. Its integral acceptance by Serbia was neither expected nor desired, and when, on the following afternoon, it was at first rumored in Vienna that it had been unconditionally accepted, there was a moment of keen disappointment.

The mistake was quickly corrected, and as soon as it was known later in the evening that the Serbian reply had been rejected and that Baron Giesl (note: Austro-Hungarian Minister at Belgrade) had broken off relations at Belgrade, Vienna burst into a frenzy of delight, vast crowds parading the streets and singing patriotic songs till the small hours of the morning.

The demonstrations were perfectly orderly, consisting for the most part of organized processions through the principal streets ending up at the Ministry of War. One or two attempts to make hostile manifestations against the Russian Embassy were frustrated by the strong guard of police which held the approaches to the principal embassies during those days.

The demeanor of the people at Vienna and, as I was informed, in many other principal cities of the Monarchy, showed plainly the popularity of the idea of war with Serbia, and there can be no doubt that the small body of Austrian and Hungarian statesmen by whom this momentous step was adopted gauged rightly the sense, and it may even be said the determination, of the people, except presumably in portions of the provinces inhabited by the Slav races.

There had been much disappointment in many quarters at the avoidance of war with Serbia during the annexation crisis in 1908 and again in connection with the recent Balkan War. Count Berchtold's peace policy had met with little sympathy in the Delegation. Now the floodgates were opened, and the entire people and press clamored impatiently for immediate and condign punishment of the hated Serbian race.

The country certainly believed that it had before it only the alternative of subduing Serbia or of submitting sooner or later to mutilation at her hands. But a peaceful solution should first have been attempted. Few seemed to reflect that the forcible intervention of a Great Power in the Balkans must inevitably call other Great Powers into the field.

So just was the cause of Austria held to be, that it seemed to her people inconceivable that any country should place itself in her path, or that questions of mere policy or prestige should be regarded anywhere as superseding the necessity which had arisen to exact summary vengeance for the crime of Sarajevo.

The conviction had been expressed to me by the German Ambassador on the 24th of July that Russia would stand aside. This feeling, which was also held at the Ballplatz, influenced no doubt the course of events, and it is deplorable that no effort should have been made to secure by means of diplomatic negotiations the acquiescence of Russia and Europe as a whole in some peaceful compromise of the Serbian question by which Austrian fears of Serbian aggression and intrigue might have been removed for the future.

Instead of adopting this course the Austro-Hungarian Government resolved upon war.

Source: *Source Records of the Great War, Vol. I, ed. Charles F. Horne, National Alumni, 1923.*

No. 4.
Count Berchtold, Austrian Minister for Foreign Affairs, to Count Mensdorff, Austrian ambassador in London.
(communicated by Count Mensdorff to Sir E. Grey)
Vienna.
July 24, 1914.

The Austro-Hungarian Government felt compelled to address the following note to the Serbian Government on the 23rd July, through the medium of the Austro-Hungarian Minister at Belgrade:

"On the 31ˢᵗ March, 1909, the Serbian Minister in Vienna, on the instructions of the Serbian Government, made the following declaration to the Imperial and Royal Government:

'Serbia recognizes that the fait accompli regarding Bosnia has not affected her rights, and consequently she will conform to the decisions that the Powers may take in conformity with article 25 of the Treaty of Berlin. In deference to the advice of the Great Powers, Serbia undertakes to renounce from now onwards the attitude of protest and opposition which she has adopted with regard to the annexation since last autumn. She undertakes, moreover, to modify the direction of her policy with regard to Austria-Hungary and to live in future on good neighborly terms with the latter.'

"The history of recent years, and in particular the painful events of the 28ᵗʰ June last, have shown the existence of a subversive movement with the object of detaching a part of the territories of Austria-Hungary from the Monarchy. The movement, which had its birth under the eye of the Serbian Government, has gone so far as to make itself manifest on both sides of the Serbian frontier in the shape of acts of terrorism and a series of outrages and murders.

"Far from carrying out the formal undertakings contained in the declaration of the 31ˢᵗ March, 1909, the Royal Serbian Government has done nothing to repress these movements. It has permitted the criminal machinations of various societies and associations directed against the Monarchy, and has tolerated unrestrained language on the part of the press the glorification and the participation of officers and functionaries in subversive agitation. It has permitted an unwholesome propaganda in public instruction, in short, it has permitted all manifestations of a nature to incite the Serbian population to hatred of the Monarchy and contempt of its institutions.

"This culpable tolerance of the Royal Serbian Government had not ceased at the moment when the events of the 28ᵗʰ June last proved its fatal consequences to the whole world.

"It results from the depositions and confessions of the criminal perpetrators of the outrage of the 28ᵗʰ June that the Sarajevo assassinations were planned in Belgrade; that the arms and explosives with which the murderers were provided had been given to them by Serbian officers and functionaries belonging to the Narodna Odbrana; and finally, that the passage into Bosnia of the criminals and their arms was organized and effected by the chiefs of the Serbian frontier service.

"The above-mentioned results of the magisterial investigation do not permit the Austro-Hungarian Government to pursue any longer the attitude of expectant forbearance which they have maintained for years in face of the machinations hatched in Belgrade, and thence propagated in the territories of the Monarchy. The results, on the contrary, impose on them the duty of putting an end to the intrigues which form a perpetual menace to the tranquility of the Monarchy.

"To achieve this end the Imperial and Royal Government see themselves compelled to demand from the Royal Serbian Government a formal assurance that they condemn this dangerous propaganda against the Monarchy; in other words, the whole series of tendencies, the ultimate aim of which is to detach from the Monarchy territories belonging to it, and that they undertake to suppress by every means this criminal and terrorist propaganda.

"In order to give a formal character to this undertaking the Royal Serbian Government shall publish on the front page of their 'Official Journal' of the 13/26 July the following declaration:

"'The Royal Government of Serbia condemn the propaganda directed against Austria-Hungary, i.e., the general tendency of which the final aim is to detach from the Austro-Hungarian Monarchy territories belonging to it, and they sincerely deplore the fatal consequences of these criminal proceedings.

"'The Royal Government regrets that Serbian officers and functionaries participated in the above-mentioned propaganda and thus compromised the good neighborly relations to which the Royal Government were solemnly pledged by their declaration of the 31ˢᵗ March, 1909.

"'The royal Government, who disapproves and repudiates all idea of interfering or attempting to interfere with the destinies of the inhabitants of any part whatsoever of Austria-Hungary, considers it their duty formally to warn officers and functionaries, and whole population of the kingdom, that henceforward they will proceed with the utmost rigor against persons who may be guilty of such machinations, which they will use all their effort to anticipate and suppress.'

"This declaration shall simultaneously be communicated to the Royal army as an order of the day by His Majest the King and shall be published in the 'Official Bulletin' of the Army.

"The Royal Serbian Government further undertakes:

"1. To suppress any publication which incites to hatred and contempt of the Austro-Hungarian Monarchy and the general tendency of which is directed against its territorial integrity;

"2. To dissolve immediately the society styled 'Narodna Odbrana,' to confiscate all its means of propaganda, and to proceed in the same manner against other societies dissolved from continuing their activity under another name and form;

"3. To eliminate without delay from public instruction in Serbia, both as regards the teaching body and also as regards the methods of instruction, everything that serves, or might serve, to foment the propaganda against Austria-Hungary;

"4. To remove from the military service, and from the administration in general, all officers and functionaries guilty of propaganda against the Austro-Hungarian Monarchy whose names and deeds the Austro-Hungarian Government reserve to themselves the right of communicating to the Royal Government;

"5. To accept the collaboration in Serbia of representatives of the Austro-Hungarian Government for the suppression of the Subversive movement directed against the territorial integrity of the Monarchy;

"6. To take judicial proceedings against accessories to the plot of the 28th June who are on Serbian territory; delegates of the Austro-Hungarian Government will take part in the investigation relating thereto;

"7. To proceed without delay to the arrest of Major Voija Tankositch and of the individual named Milan Ciganovitch, a Serbian State employee, who have been compromised by the results of the magisterial enquiry at Sarajevo;

"8. To prevent by effective measures the co-operation of the Serbian authorities in the illicit traffic in arms and explosives across the frontier, to dismiss and punish severely the officials of the frontier service at Schabatz and Loznica guilty of having assisted the perpetrators of the Sarajevo crime by facilitating their passage across the frontier;

"9. To furnish the Imperial and Royal Government with explanations regarding the unjustifiable utterances of high Serbian officials, both in Serbia and abroad, who, notwithstanding their official position, have not hesitated since the crime of the 28th June to express themselves in interviews in terms of hostility to the Austro-Hungarian Government; and, finally,

"10. To notify the Imperial and Royal Government without delay of the execution of the measures comprised under the preceding heads.

"The Austro-Hungarian Government expect the reply of the Royal Government at the latest by 6 o'clock on Saturday evening, the 25th July.

"A memorandum dealing with the results of the magisterial enquiry at Sarajevo with regard to the officials mentioned under heads (7) and (8) is attached to this note."

I have the honor to request your Excellency to bring the contents of this note to the knowledge of the Government to which you are accredited, accompanying your communication with the following observation:

On the 31st March, 1909, the Royal Serbian Government addressed to Austria-Hungary the declaration of which the text is reproduced above.

On the very day after this declaration Serbia embarked on a policy of instilling revolutionary ideas into the Serb subjects of the Austro-Hungarian Monarchy, and so preparing for the separation of the Austro-Hungarian territory on the Serbian frontier.

Serbia became the centre of a criminal agitation.

No time was lost in the formation of societies and groups, whose object, either avowed or secret, was the creation of disorders on Austro-Hungarian territory. These societies and groups count among their members generals and diplomatists, Government officials and judges—in short, men at the top of official and unofficial society in the kingdom.

Serbian journalism is almost entirely at the service of this propaganda, which is directed against Austria-Hungary, and not a day passes without the organs of the Serbian press stirring up their readers to hatred or contempt for the neighboring Monarchy, or to outrages directed more or less openly against its security and integrity.

A large number of agents are employed in carrying on by every means the agitation against Austria-Hungary and corrupting the youth in the frontier provinces.

Since the recent Balkan crisis there has been a recrudescence of the spirit of conspiracy inherent in Serbian politicians, which has left such sanguinary imprints on the history of the kingdom; individuals belonging formerly to bands employed in Macedonia have come to place themselves at the disposal of the terrorist propaganda against Austria-Hungary.

In the presence of these doings, to which Austria-Hungary has been exposed for years, the Serbian government have not thought it incumbent on them to take the slightest step. The Serbian Government have thus failed in the duty imposed on them by the solemn declaration of the 31st March, 1909, and acted in opposition to the will of Europe and the undertaking given to Austria-Hungary.

The patience of the Imperial and Royal government in the face of the provocative attitude of Serbia was inspired by the territorial disinterestedness of the Austro-Hungarian Monarchy and the hope that the Serbian Government would end in spite of everything by appreciating Austria-Hungarian Monarchy and the hope that the Serbian Government would end in spite of everything by appreciating Austria-Hungary's friendship at its true value. By observing a benevolent attitude toward the political interests of Serbia, the Imperial and Royal Government hoped the kingdom would finally decide to follow an analogous line of conduct on its own side. In particular, Austria-Hungary expected a development of this kind in the political ideas of Serbia when, after the events of 1912, the Imperial and Royal Government, by its disinterested and ungrudging attitude, made such a considerable aggrandizement of Serbia possible.

The benevolence which Austria-Hungary showed towards the neighboring State had no restraining effect on the Proceedings of the kingdom, which continued to tolerate on its territory a propaganda of which the fatal consequences were demonstrated to the whole world on the 28th June last, when the Heir Presumptive to the Monarchy and his illustrious consort fell victims to a plot hatched at Belgrade.

In the presence of this state of things the Imperial and Royal Government have felt compelled to take new and urgent steps at Belgrade with a view to inducing the Serbian Government to stop the incendiary movement that is threatening the security and integrity of the Austro-Hungarian Monarchy.

The Imperial and Royal Governments are convinced that in taking this step they will find themselves in full agreement with the sentiments of all civilized nations, who cannot permit regicide to become a weapon that can be employed with impunity in political stripe, and the peace of Europe to be continually disturbed by movements emanating from Belgrade.

In support of the above the Imperial and Royal Government hold at the disposal of the British Government a *dossier* elucidating the Serbian intrigues and the connection between these intrigues and the murder of the 28th June.

An identical communication has been Addressed to the Imperial and Royal representatives accredited to the other signatory Powers.

You are authorized to leave a copy of this dispatch in the hands of the Minister for Foreign Affairs.

Vienna, July 24, 1914.

ANNEX.

The criminal enquiry opened by the Court of Sarajevo against Gavrilo Princip and his accessories in and before the act of assassination committed by them on the 28th June last has up to the present led to the following conclusions:

1. The plot, having as its object the assassination of the Archduke Francis Ferdinand at the time of his visit to Sarajevo, was formed at Belgrade by Gavrilo Princip, Nedeljko Cabrinovic', one Milan Ciganovic', and Trifko Grabez, with the assistance of Commander Voija Tankosic'.
2. The six bombs and the four Browning pistols and ammunition with which the guilty parties committed the act were delivered to Princip, Cabrinovic', and Grabez by the man Milan Ciganovic' and Commander Voija Tankosic' at Belgrade.
3. The bombs are hand-grenades coming from the arms depot of the Serbian army at kragujevac'.
4. In order to ensure the success of the act, Ciganovic' taught Princip, Cabrinovic, and Grabez how to use the bombs, and gave lessons in firing Browning pistols to Princip and Grabez in a forest near the shooting ground at Topschider.
5. To enable Princip, Cabrinovic' and Grabez to cross the frontier of Bosnia-Herzegovina smuggle in their contraband of arms secretly, a secret system of transport was organized by Ciganovic'.

By this arrangement the introduction into Bosnia-Herzegovina of criminals and their arms was effected by the officials controlling the frontiers at Chabac' (Rade Popovic') and Loznica, as well as by the customs officer Rudivoj Grbie', of Loznica, with the assistance of various individuals.

No. 10.
Count Mensdorff to Count Berchtold.
London
July 24, 1914.
(Telegraphic)

Have just handed the circular note to Sir Edward Grey, who read it carefully. At the fifth heading, he asked what it meant; to introduce officials of our Government in Serbia would be equivalent to the end of Serbian political independence. I answered that co-operation of, e.g., police officials, in no way affected the sovereignty of the State.

He regretted the time-limit, as in this way we should be deprived of the possibility of quieting the first outbreak of excitement and bringing pressure to bear upon Belgrade to give us a satisfactory answer. It was always possible to send an ultimatum if answer not satisfactory.

I developed our point of view at length. (Necessity of defense against continued revolutionary undertakings which threaten the; territory of the Monarchy, protection of our most vital interests, complete failure of the conciliatory attitude which we had hitherto often shown to Serbia, who had had more than three weeks to set on foot of her own accord investigations as to accomplices in outrage, &tc.)

The Secretary of State repeated his objections to the short time limit, but recognized that what was said as to complicity in the crime of Sarajevo, as well as many of our other requirements, was justified.

He would be quite ready to look on the affair as one which only concerned Austria-Hungary and Serbia. He is, however, very "apprehensive" that several Great Powers might be involved in a war. Speaking of Russia, Germany, and France, he observed that the terms of the Franco-Russian Alliance might be more or less to the same effect as those of the Triple Alliance.

I fully explained to him our point of view, and repeated with emphasis that in this case we must stand firm so as to gain for ourselves some sort of guarantees, as hitherto Serbian promises have never been kept. I understood that in the first place he considered the question only as it influences the position of Europe. He must, however, in order to be fair to our point of view, put himself in our situation.

He would not go into any more detailed discussion on this subject, said he must have time to study the note more carefully. He was to see the German and the French Ambassadors, as he must first of all exchange ideas with the Powers who are allies of Austria-Hungary and Russia respectively, but have themselves no direct interest in Serbia.

No. 5.
Sir Edward Grey to Sir M. de Bunsen, British ambassador at Vienna.
Foreign Office
July 24, 1914
(Telegraphic)

Note addressed to Serbia, together with an explanation of the reasons leading up to it, has been communicated to me by Count Mensdorff.

In the ensuing conversation with his conversation with his Excellency, I remarked that it seemed to me a matter for great regret that a time limit, and such a short one at that, had been insisted upon at this stage of the proceedings. The murder of the archduke and some of the circumstances respecting Serbia quoted in the note aroused sympathy with Austria, as was but natural, but at the same time I had never before seen one addressed to another independent state a document of so formidable a character. Demand no. 5 would be hardly consistent with the maintenance of Serbia's independent sovereignty if it were to mean, as it seemed that it might, that Austria-Hungary was to be invested with the right to appoint officials who would have authority within the frontiers of Serbia. I added that I felt great apprehension, and that I should concern myself with the matter simply and solely from the point of view of the peace of Europe. The merits of the dispute between Austria and Serbia were not the concern of his Majesty's Government, and such comments as I had made above were not made in order to discuss those merits.

I ended by saying that doubtless we should enter into an exchange of views with the other powers, and I must await their views as to what could be done to mitigate the difficulties of the situation.

Count Mensdorff[1] replied that the present situation might never have arisen if Serbia had held out a hand after the murder of the Archduke; Serbia had, however, shown no sign of sympathy or help, though some weeks had already elapsed since the murder; a time limit, said his Excellency, was essential, owing to the procrastination on Serbia's part.

I said that if Serbia had procrastinated in reply, a time limit could have been introduced later; but, as things now stood, the terms of the Serbian reply had been dictated by Austria, who had not been content to limit herself to a demand for a reply within a limit of forty eight hours from its presentation.

I am, &tc.
E. Grey

Austria has every right to make any demands it wants in this case. International law states that if a country assassinates another countries leader or heir to the throne. That country has for all practical purpose as declared war on that country.

Line no. 5 in the ultimatum states to accept collaboration in Serbia of representatives of the Austro-Hungarian Government. Not Austria being able to pick the officials for the suppression subversive movement directed at Austria.

No. 11.
Count Szécsen to Count Berchtold.
Paris
July 24, 1914.
(Telegraphic)

I have just read instructions of the 22nd instant to the Minister of Justice, who is entrusted with the representation of the Minister for Foreign Affairs in his absence, and left copy.

M. Bienvenu-Martin, who had received information as to the contents of our *démarche* at Belgrade through this morning's papers, seemed to be considerably impressed by my communication. Without entering on any more detailed discussion of the text, he readily agreed that recent events and the attitude of the Serbian Government made energetic action on our side quite comprehensible.

Point 5 in the note handed in at Belgrade seemed to make a special impression on the Minister as he asked me to read it to him twice.

The Minister thanked me for my communication which, he said, would be carefully examined. I took the opportunity to impress on him that the question was one which must be brought to an issue directly between Serbia and us, but that it was in the general interests of Europe that the trouble which for years past had been kept up by Serbian intrigues against us should at last make way for a clear situation.

All friends of peace and order, and I placed France in the first rank of these, should therefore give serious advice to Serbia completely to change her attitude, and to satisfy our just demands. The Minister said that it was the duty of Serbia to proceed energetically against any accomplices of the murderers of Sarajevo, a duty which she could not escape. While laying special stress on the sympathy of France for Austria-Hungary, and on the good relations which existed between our two countries, he expressed the hope that the controversy would be brought to an end peacefully in a manner corresponding to our wishes.

---

[1] Austro-Hungarian Ambassador in London.

The Minister avoided every attempt to palliate or to defend in any way the attitude of Serbia.

No. 6.
Sir G. Buchanan, British Ambassador at St. Petersburg, to Sir Edward Grey.
St. Petersburg
July 24, 1914
(Telegraphic)

I had a telephone message this mourning from M. Sazonof* to the effect that the text of the Austrian ultimatum had just reached him.

His Excellency added that a reply within forty-eight hours was demanded, and he begged me to meet him at the French Embassy to discuss matters, as Austria step clearly meant that war was imminent.

Minister for Foreign Affairs said that Austria's conduct was both provocative and immoral; she would never have taken such action unless Germany had first been consulted[2]; some of her demands were quite impossible of acceptance. He hoped that his Majesty's Government would not fail to proclaim their solidarity with Russia and France.

The French Ambassador gave me to understand that France would fulfill all the obligations entailed by her alliance with Russia, if necessity arose, besides supporting Russia strongly in any diplomatic negotiations.

I said that I would telegraph a full report to you of what their Excellencies had just said to me. I could not, of course, speak in the name of his Majesty's Government, but personally I saw no reason to expect any declaration of solidarity from his Majesty's Government that would entail an unconditional engagement on their part to support Russia and France by force of arms. Direct British interests in Serbia were nil, and war on behalf of that country would never be sanctioned by British public opinion. To this M. Sazonof replied that we must not forget that the general European question was involved, the Serbian question being but a part of the former, and that Great Britain could not afford to efface from the problems now at issue.

In reply to these remarks, I observed that I gathered from what he said that his Excellency was suggesting that Great Britain should join in making a communication to Austria to the effect that active intervention by her in the internal affairs of Serbia could not be tolerated. But supposing Austria nevertheless proceeded to embark on military measures against Serbia in spite of our representations was in the intention of the Russian Government forthwith to declare war on Austria.

M. Sazonof said that he himself thought that Russian mobilization would at any rate have to be carried out; but council of Ministers was being held this afternoon to consider the whole question. A further council would be held, probably tomorrow, at which the Emperor would preside, when a decision would come to.

I said that it seemed to me that the important point was to induce Austria to extent the time limit and that the first thing to do was to bring an influence to bear on Austria with that end in view; French Ambassador, however, thought that either Austria had made up her mind to act at once or that she was bluffing. Which ever it might be, our only chance of averting war was for us to adopt a firm and united attitude. He did not think there was time to carry out my suggestion. Thereupon I said that it seemed to me desirable that we should know just how far Serbia was prepared to go to meet the demands formulated by Austria in her note. M Sazonof replied that he must first consult his colleagues on this point, but that doubtless some of Austrian demands could be accepted by Serbia.

---

[2] See No. 2.

French Ambassador and M. Sazonof both continued to press me for a declaration of complete solidarity of his Majesty's Government with French and Russian Governments, and I therefore said that it seemed to me possible that you might perhaps be willing to make strong representations to both German and Austrian Governments, urging upon them that an attack by Austria upon Serbia would endanger the whole peace of Europe. Perhaps you might see your way to saying to them that such an action on the part of Austria would probably mean Russian intervention, which would involve France and Germany, and that it would be difficult for Great Britain to keep out if the war were to become to general. M. Sazonof answered that we would sooner or later be dragged into war if it did not break out; we should render war more likely if we did not from the outset make common cause with his country and with France; at any rate, he hoped his majesty's Government would express strong reprobation of action taken by Austria.

President of French Republic and President of the Council cannot reach France, on their return from Russia, for four or five days, and it looks as though Austria purposely chose this moment to present their ultimatum.

It seems to me, from the language held by the French ambassador, that, even if we decline to join them, France and Russia are determined to make a strong stand.

This telegram clearly shows that France and Russia have made plans for war against not only Austria but Germany as well. By Great Britain not joining them, the war is not started that much sooner. Here it is also shows that Austria has no rights to seek justice against the perpetrators of the murder of the archduke. That is because the perpetrators who started this incident are Russia at this time. The French president does not leave for another twenty-four hours. So Russia and France can both see where England stands during this crisis. They can also plan accordingly on how to force Austria and Germany to war. The French and Russian decisions were being made while Wilhelm II of Germany was on vacation. Therefore, Germany is unable to converse with both France and Russia with the guidance of their leader.

No. 12.
Count Szécsen to Count Berchtold.
July 24, 1914.
Paris
(Telegraphic)

Baron Schoen will, in accordance with instructions, make a communication here to-day that according to the view of the Berlin Cabinet, our controversy with Serbia is a matter which concerns only Austria-Hungary and Serbia.

In this connection, he would give them to understand that in case third States should wish to intervene, Germany, true to the obligations of her alliance, would be on our side.

No. 7.
Sir M. de Bunsen, British Ambassador at Vienna, to Sir Edward Grey.
Vienna
July 24, 1914.
(Telegraphic)

Before departing on leave of absence, I was assured by Russian ambassador that any action taken by Austria to humiliate Serbia could not leave Russia indifferent.

Russian Charg`e d` affaires was received this morning by minister for Foreign affairs, and said to him, as his own personal view, that Austrian note was drawn up in a form rendering it impossible of acceptance as it stood, and that it was both unusual and peremptory in its terms. Minister for Foreign Affairs replied that Austrian Minister was under instructions to leave Belgrade unless Austrian demands were accepted integrally by 4 P.M. tomorrow. His Excellency added that Dual monarchy felt that its very existence was at stake; and that step taken had caused great satisfaction throughout the country. He did not think that objections to what had been done could be raised by any Power.

Russia and France both are trying to convince anybody who will listen that this crisis is really Austria's fault, and that Serbia was reacting to Austrian action.

No. 13.
Count Szécsen to Count Berchtold.
Paris
July 24, 1914.
(Telegraphic)

Baron Schoen has just made the *démarche* as he was instructed.

M. Bienvenu-Martin said to him he could not yet express himself definitely. He could, however, already say this, that the French Government is also of opinion that our controversy with Servia concerns Belgrade and Vienna alone, and that it was hoped here that the question would find a direct and peaceful solution.

The Serbian Minister here had already been advised that his Government should give way in every point so far as it was possible, with the limitation, however, "so far as their sovereign rights were not affected."

Baron Schoen laid stress on the European necessity that the focus of constant disturbance at Belgrade must at last be done away with.

No. 8.
Mr. Crackanthorpe, British Charg`e d` Affaires at Belgrade, to Sir Edward Grey.
Belgrade
July 24, 1914.
(Telegraphic)

Austrian demands are considered absolutely unacceptable by Serbian Government, who earnestly trusts that his Majesty's Government may see their way to induce Austrian government to moderate them.

This request was conveyed to me by Serbian Prime minister, who returned early this morning to Belgrade. His Excellency is dejected, and is clearly very anxious as to developments that may arise.

He should be anxious, since his orders are coming from Russia and France.

No. 14.
Count Száp´ry to Count Berchtold.
St. Petersburgh
July 24, 1914.
(Telegraphic)

The Minister for Foreign Affairs on receiving me, said that he knew what brought me to him, and he would at once explain to me that he could not take up any definite attitude towards my *démarche*.

I began by reading out my instructions. The Minister interrupted me for the first time on the mention of the series of outrages, and, on my explanation, asked if then it had been proved that they all had originated at Belgrade. I laid stress on the fact that they all sprang from Serbian instigation. In the further course of the reading he said that he knew what it was all about: we wanted to make war on Serbia, and this was to serve as a pretext. I replied that our attitude during recent years was a sufficient proof that we neither sought nor required pretexts against Serbia. The formal declaration which is required did not elicit any objection from the Minister; he only continued to maintain that Pasic had already expressed himself to this effect. This I corrected. *"Il dira cela 25 fois si vous voulez,"* said he. I said to him that no one among us was attacking the integrity of Serbia or the dynasty. M. Sazonof expressed himself most vigorously against the dissolution of the Narodna Odbrana, which Serbia would never undertake. The participation of Imperial and Royal officials in the suppression of the revolutionary movements elicited further protest on the part of the Minister. Serbia then will no longer be master in her own house. "You will always be wanting to intervene again, and what a life you will lead Europe." I answered that if Serbia shows goodwill it will be a quieter life than hitherto. The commentary added to the communication of the note was listened to by the Minister with fair composure; at the passage that our feelings were shared by those of all civilized nations, he observed that this was a mistake. With all the emphasis I could command, I pointed out how regrettable it would be if we could not come to an understanding with Russia on this question, in which everything which is most sacred to us was at stake and, whatever the Minister might say, everything which is sacred in Russia. The Minister attempted to minimize the Monarchical side of the question. With regard to the dossier which was put at the disposal of the Governments, M. Sazonof wanted to know why we had given ourselves this trouble, as we had already delivered the ultimatum. This was the best proof that we did not really desire an impartial examination of the matter. I said to him that the results which had been attained by our own investigations were quite sufficient for our procedure in this matter, which had to do with Austria-Hungary and Serbia, and that we were only ready to give the Powers further information if it interested them, as we had nothing to keep secret. M. Sazonof said that now that the ultimatum had been issued he was not in the least curious. He represented the matter as if we only wanted to make war with Serbia whatever happened. I answered that we were the most peace-loving Power in the world, but what we wanted was security for our territory from foreign revolutionary intrigues, and the protection of our dynasty from bombs.

In the course of the further discussion, M. Sazonof again made the observation that we certainly had created a serious situation.

In spite of his relative calm, the attitude of the Minister was throughout unaccommodating and hostile.

No. 15.
Communiqué of the Russian official Gazette.
St. Petersburgh
July 24, 1914.

The St. Petersburgh telegraphic agency announces:

The official journal publishes the following communiqué:

Recent events and the dispatch of an ultimatum to Serbia by Austria-Hungary are causing the Russian Government the greatest anxiety. The Government is closely following the course of the dispute between the two countries, to which Russia cannot remain indifferent.

No. 9.
Note communicated by German Ambassador.
July 24, 1914.

"The publication of the Austro-Hungarian Government concerning the circumstances under which the assassination of the Austrian heir presumptive and his consort has taken place disclose unmistakably the aims which the Great Serbian propaganda has set itself, and the means it employs to realize them. The facts now made known must also do away with the last doubts that the centre of activity of all those tendencies which are directed towards the detachment of the southern Slavic provinces from Austro-Hungarian Monarchy and their incorporation into the Serbian Kingdom is to be found in Belgrade, and is at work with at least the connivance of members of the Government and army.

The Serbian intrigues have been going on for many years. In an especially marked from the Great Serbian chauvinism manifested itself during the Bosnian crisis. It was only owing to the far, reaching self-restraint and moderation of the Austria-Hungarian Government and to the energetic interference of the Great Powers that the Serbian provocation to which Austria-Hungary was then exposed did not lead to conflict. The assurance of good conduct in the future which was given by the Serbian government at that time has not been kept. Under the eyes, at least with the tacit permission of official Serbian, the Great Serbian propaganda has continuously increased in extension and intensity; to its account must be set the recent crime, the threads of which lead to Belgrade. It as become clearly evident that it would not be consistent either with the dignity or with self-preservation of the Austro-Hungarian Monarchy still longer to remain inactive of this movement on the other side of the frontier, by which the security and the integrity of her territories are constantly menaced. Under these circumstances, the course of procedure and demands of the Austro-Hungarian Government can only be regarded as equitable and moderate. In spite of that, the attitude which public opinion as well as the government in Serbia have recently adopted does not exclude the apprehension that the Serbian government might refuse to comply with those demands and might allow themselves to be carried away into a provocative attitude against Austria-Hungary. The Austro-Hungarian Government, if it does not wish definitely to abandon Austria's position as a great Power, would then have no choice but to obtain the fulfillment of their demands from Serbian Government by strong pressure and, if necessary by using military measures, the choice of the means having to be left to them.

The Imperial Government wants to emphasis their opinion that in the present case there is only a question of a matter to be settled exclusively between Austria-Hungary and Serbia, and that the Great Powers ought to seriously to endeavor to reserve it to those two immediately concerned. The Imperial Government desire urgently the localization of the conflict, because every interference of another Power would, owing to the different treaty obligations, be followed by incalculable consequences.

No. 16.
Count Szápáry to Count Berchtold.
St. Petersburgh
July 24, 1914.
(Telegraphic)

After a Council of Ministers which lasted for five hours, M. Sazonof this evening received the German Ambassador, and had a long conversation with him.

The Minister took the point of view, which is probably to be considered as the outcome of the Council of Ministers, that the Austro-Hungarian-Serbian conduct was not a matter confined to these States, but a European affair, as the settlement arrived at in the year 1909 by the Serbian declaration had been made under the auspices of the whole of Europe. The Minister pointed out particularly that he had been disagreeably affected by the circumstance that Austria-Hungary had offered a dossier for investigation when an ultimatum had already been presented. Russia would require an international investigation off the dossier, which had been put at her disposal. My German colleague at once brought to M. Sazonof's notice that Austria-Hungary would not accept interference in her difference with Serbia, and that Germany also on her side could not accept a suggestion which would be contrary to the dignity of her ally as a Great Power.

In the further course of the conversation, the Minister explained that that which Russia could not accept with indifference was the eventual intention of Austria-Hungary *"de deévorer la Serbie."*

Count Pourtaleès answered that he did not accept any such intention on the part of Austria-Hungary, as this would be contrary to the most special interest of the Monarchy. The only object of Austria-Hungary was *"d'infliger à la Serbie le châtiment justement meériteé."* M. Sazonof on this expressed his doubts whether Austria-Hungary would allow herself to be contented with this, even if explanations on this point had been made.

The interview concluded with an appeal by M. Sazonof that Germany should work with Russia at the maintenance of peace. The German Ambassador assured the Russian Minister that Germany certainly had no wish to bring about a war, but that she naturally fully represented the interests of her ally.

No. 10.
Sir Edward Grey to Sir F. Bertie, Ambassador at Paris.
Foreign Office.
July 24, 1914.

Sir,

After telling M. Cambon today of the Austrian communication to Serbia, which I had received this morning, and of the comment I had made to Count Mensdorff upon it yesterday, I told M. Cambon that this afternoon I was to see the German Ambassador, who some days ago had asked me privately to exercise moderating influence in St. Petersburg. I would say to the Ambassador that, of course, if the presentation of this ultimatum to Serbia did not lead to trouble between Austria and Russia, we need not concern ourselves about it; but, if Russia took the view of the Austrian ultimatum, which it seemed to me that any Power interested in Serbia would take, I should be quite powerless, in face of the terms of the ultimatum, to exercise any moderating influence. I would say that I thought the only chance of any mediating or moderating influence being exercised was that of Germany, France, Italy, and ourselves, who had not direct interests in Serbia, should act together for the sake of peace, simultaneously in Vienna and St. Petersburg.

M. Cambon said that if there was a chance of mediation by the Four Powers, he had no doubt that his Government would be glad to join in it; but he pointed out that we could not say anything in St. Petersburg till Russia had expressed some opinion or taken some action. But, when two days were over, Austria would march into Serbia, for the Serbians could not possibly accept the Austrian demand. Russia would be compelled by her public opinion to take action as soon as Austria attacked Serbia, and therefore, once the Austrians had attacked Serbia, it would be too late for any mediation.

I said that I had not contemplated anything being said in St. Petersburg until after it was clear that there must be trouble between Austria and Russia. I had thought that if Austria did move into Serbia, and Russia then mobilized, it would be possible for the Four Powers to urge Austria to stop her advance, and Russia also to stop hers, pending mediation. But it would be essential for any chance of success for such a step that Germany should participate in it.

M. Cambon said that it would be too late after Austria had once moved against Serbia. The important thing was to gain time by mediation in Vienna. The best chance of this being accepted would be that Germany should propose it to the other Powers.

I said that by this: he meant a mediation between Austria and Serbia.

He said that it was so.

I said that I would like talk to the German Ambassador this afternoon on the subject.

I am, &tc.
Edward Grey

Here the French are playing both sides of the fence, hoping to buy time for Russia to mobilize on both the Austrian and German frontiers. As long as the French President is in Russia, mediation between the Powers will still be stalled.

No. 17.
Count Berchtold to Count Mensdorff at London.
Vienna
July 24, 1914.
(Telegraphic)

In answer to Your Excellency's telegram of yesterday:

I beg you to explain at once to Sir Edward Grey that our *démarche* of yesterday at Belgrade is not to be considered as a formal ultimatum, but that it is merely a *démarche* with a time-limit, which, as Your Excellency will be good enough to explain to Sir Edward Grey in strict confidence will—if the time-limit expires without result—for the time be followed only by the breaking off of diplomatic relations and by the beginning of the necessary military preparations, as we are absolutely resolved to carry through our just demands.

Your Excellency is empowered to add that if Serbia, after the expiration of the time-limit, were only to give way under the pressure of our military preparations, we should indeed have to demand that she should make good the expenses which we had incurred; as is well known, we have already had twice (1908 and 1912) to mobilize because of Serbia.

No. 18.
Count Berchtold to Count Szápáry at St. Petersburgh.
Vienna
July 24, 1914.

I received the Russian Chargé d'Affaires on the morning of the 24th, and assured him that I attached special importance to bringing to his knowledge as soon as possible the steps we were taking in Belgrade, and explaining to him our point of view as regards them.

Prince Koudacheff, while thanking me for this courtesy, did not hide his anxiety as to our categorical procedure against Serbia, and he observed that there had always been apprehension at St. Petersburgh: that our *deémarche* might take the form of a humiliation of Serbia, which must have an echo in Russia.

I took the opportunity of re-assuring the Russian Chargeé d'Affaires as to this. Our aim was to clear up the untenable position of Serbia as regards the Monarchy, and with this object to cause the Government of that State on the one hand publicly to disavow the tendencies directed against the present position of the Monarchy, and to suppress them by administrative measures, and on the other hand to, make it possible for us to satisfy ourselves that these measures were honestly carried out. I explained at greater length the danger, not only to the integrity of the Monarchy, but also to the balance of power and the peace of Europe, which would be involved in giving further scope to the Great-Serbian propaganda, and how all the dynasties and, not least, the Russian, would apparently be threatened, if the idea took root that a movement which made use of murder as a national weapon could be continued with impunity. In conclusion, I pointed out that we did not aim at any increase of territory but only at the maintenance of what we possess, a point of view which could not fail to be understood by the Russian government. Prince Koudacheff remarked on this that he did not know the view of his own Government, and also did not know what position Serbia would take towards individual demands. At the conclusion of our interview the Chargeé d'Affaires expressly said that he would not fail to bring to the notice of his Government the explanation which I had given him of the step we had taken, especially to the effect that no humiliation of Serbia was intended by us.

No. 1.
Count Errembault de Dudzeele, Belgian Minister at Vienna, to M. Davignon, Belgian Minister for Foreign Affairs.
Vienna
July 24, 1914.

Sir,
I have the honour to enclose herewith the text of the Austro-Hungarian ultimatum to Serbia.
Enclosure in No. 1.
(Text of Austro-Hungarian note, for which see British Correspondence, No. 4, page 3.)

No. 2.
M. Davignon, Belgian Minister for Foreign Affairs, to the Belgian Ministers at Paris, Berlin, London, Vienna, and St. Petersburg.
Brussels
July 24, 1914.

Sir,
The Belgian Government has had under their consideration whether, in present circumstances, it would not be advisable to address to the Powers who guarantee Belgian independence and neutrality a communication assuring them of Belgium's determination to fulfill the international obligations imposed upon her by treaty in the event of a war breaking out on her frontiers.

The Government has come to the conclusion that such a communication would be premature at present, but that events might move rapidly and not leave sufficient time to forward suitable instructions at the desired moment to the Belgian representatives abroad.

In these circumstances I have proposed to the King and to my colleagues in the Cabinet, who have concurred, to give you now exact instructions as to the steps to be taken by you if the prospect of a Franco-German war became more threatening.

I enclose herewith a note, signed but not dated, which you should read to the Minister for Foreign Affairs and of which you should give him a copy, if circumstances render such a communication necessary.

I will inform you by telegram when you are to act on these instructions.

This telegram will be dispatched when the order is given for the mobilisation of the Belgian army if, contrary to our earnest hope and to the apparent prospect of a peaceful settlement, our information leads us to take this extreme measure of precaution.

Enclosure in No. 2.

Sir,

The international situation is serious, and the possibility of a war between several Powers naturally preoccupies the Belgian Government.

Belgium has most scrupulously observed the duties of a neutral State imposed upon her by the treaties of April 19, 1839; and those duties she will strive unflinchingly to fulfill, whatever the circumstances may be.

The friendly feelings of the Powers towards her have been so often reaffirmed that Belgium confidently expects that her territory will remain free from any attack, should hostilities break out upon her frontiers.

All necessary steps to ensure respect of Belgian neutrality have nevertheless been taken by the Government. The Belgian army has been mobilized and is taking up such strategic positions as have been chosen to secure the defense of the country and the respect of its neutrality. The forts of Antwerp and on the Meuse have been put in a state of defense.

It is scarcely necessary to dwell upon the nature of these measures. They are intended solely to enable Belgium to fulfill her international obligations; and it is obvious that they neither have been nor can have been undertaken with any intention of taking part in an armed struggle between the Powers or from any feeling of distrust of any of those Powers.

In accordance with my instructions, I have the honour to communicate to your Excellency a copy of the declaration by the Belgian Government, and to request that you will be good enough to take note of it.

A similar communication has been made to the other Powers guaranteeing Belgian neutrality.

No. 12.
Sir Edward Grey to Mr. Crackanthrope, British Charge' D' Affaires at Belgrade.
British Foreign Office.
July 24, 1914.
(Telegraphic)

Serbia ought to promise that, if it is proved that Serbian officials, however subordinate they may be, were accomplices in the murder of the Archduke at Sarajevo, she will give Austria the fullest satisfaction. She certainly ought to express concern and regret. For the rest, Serbian Government must reply to Austrian demands as they consider best in Serbian interests.

It is impossible to say whether military action by Austria when time is limit expires can be averted by anything but unconditional acceptance of her demands, but only chance appears to lie in avoiding an absolute refusal and replying favorably to as many points as the time limit allows.

Serbian Minister here has begged that His Majesty's Government will express their views, but I cannot undertake responsibility of saying more than I have said, above and I do not like to say even that without knowing what is being said at Belgrade by the French and Russian Governments. You should therefore consult your French and Russian colleagues as to repeating what my views are, as expressed above, to Serbian Government.

I have urged upon the German Ambassador that Austria should not precipitate military action.

This telegram by Sir Edward Grey is hoping that some kind of pressure can be brought about by this ambassador on the Serbian Government by delaying or ending any military action by Austria on Serbian and by getting Serbia to meet all of Austria's demands in the investigation of the murder of the archduke.

No. 22.

M. René Viviani, President of the Council, to M. Bienvenu-Martin, Acting Minister for Foreign Affairs.

I should be obliged if you would urgently send on to M. Dumaine the following information and instructions.

Reval, July 24, 1914, 1 A.M.

In the course of my conversation with the Russian Minister for Foreign Affairs, we had to take into consideration the dangers, which might result from any step taken by Austria-Hungary in relation to Serbia in connection with the crime of which the Hereditary Archduke has been a victim. We found ourselves in agreement in thinking that we should not leave anything undone to prevent a request for an explanation or some *mise en demeure,* which would be equivalent to intervention in the internal affairs of Serbia, of such a kind that Serbia might consider it as an attack on her sovereignty and independence. We have in consequence come to the opinion that we might, by means of a friendly conversation with Count Berchtold, give him counsels of moderation, of such a kind as to make him understand how undesirable would be any intervention at Belgrade which would appear to be a threat on the part of the Cabinet at Vienna.

The British Ambassador, who was kept informed by M. Sazonof, expressed the idea that his Government would doubtless associate itself with a démarche for removing any danger which might threaten general peace, and he has telegraphed to his Government to this effect. M. Sazonof has addressed instructions to this effect to M. Schebeko. While there is no question in this of collective or concerted action at Vienna on the part of the representatives of the Triple Entente, I ask you to discuss the matter with the Russian and British Ambassadors, and to come to an agreement with them as to the best means by which each of you can make Count Berchtold understand without delay the moderation that the present situation appears to us to require. Further, it would be desirable to ask M. Paul Cambon to bring the advantages of this procedure to the notice of Sir Edward Grey, and to support the suggestion that the British Ambassador in Russia will have made to this effect to the Foreign Office. Count Benckendorif is instructed to make a similar recommendation.

RENÉ VIVIANI.

No. 23.

M. Bienvenu-Martin, Acting Minister for Foreign Affairs, to M. René Viviani, President of the Council, on board the *France*.
Paris
July 24, 1914.

I have sent on your instructions to Vienna as urgent, but from information contained in this morning's papers it appears that the Austrian note was presented at Belgrade at 6 o'clock yesterday evening.

This note, the official text of which has not yet been handed to us by the Austro-Hungarian Ambassador, appears to be very sharp; it appears to aim not only at obtaining the prosecution of the Serbs who were directly implicated in the outrage of Sarajevo but to require the immediate suppression of the whole of the anti-Austrian propaganda in the Serbian press and army. It is said to give Serbia till 6 o'clock on Saturday evening to make her submission. In sending your instructions to M. Dumaine, I requested him to come to an agreement with his British and Russian colleagues as to his action.

BIENVENU-MARTIN.

No. 25.

M. Bienvenu-Martin, Acting Minister for Foreign Affairs, to M. René Viviani, President of the Council, on board the *France*, and to London, Berlin, Vienna, St. Petersburgh, Rome, Belgrade.

Paris

July 24, 1914.

I have the honor to inform you that the Austro-Hungarian Ambassador this morning left me a copy of the Austrian note, which was handed in at Belgrade on Thursday evening. Count Scézsen informs me that the Austro-Hungarian Government gives the Serbian Government up to 5 o'clock on the evening of Saturday the 26th for their answer.* The note is based on the undertaking made by Serbia on the 31st March 1909, to recognize the annexation of Bosnia and Herzegovina, and reproaches the Serbian Government with having tolerated an anti-Austrian propaganda in which officials, the army, and the press have taken part, a propaganda which threatens the security and integrity of Austria, and the danger of which has been shown by the crime of the 28th June which, according to the facts established during the investigation, was planned at Belgrade.

*The Austro-Hungarian Ambassador in a private letter on the 24th July sent to the Minister for Foreign Affairs the following correction:

> "In the copy of the dispatch which I had the honor to send to your Excellency this morning, it was said that my Government expected an answer from the Cabinet at Belgrade at latest by 5 o'clock on the evening of Saturday the 25th of this month. As our Minister at Belgrade did not deliver his note yesterday until 6 o'clock in the evening, the time allowed for the answer has in consequence been prolonged to 6 o'clock to-morrow, Saturday evening.
>
> "I consider it my duty to inform your Excellency of this slight alteration in the termination of the period fixed for the answer to the Serbian Government."

The Austrian Government explains that they are compelled to put an end to a propaganda which forms a permanent danger to their tranquility, and to require from the Serbian Government an official pronouncement of their determination to condemn and suppress it, by publishing in the Official Gazette of the 26th a declaration, the terms of which are given, condemning it, stating their regret, and threatening to crush it. A general order of the King to the Serbian army is at the same time to make these declarations known to the army. In addition to this, the Serbian Government are to undertake to suppress publications, to dissolve the societies, to dismiss those officers and civil servants whose names would be communicated to them by the Austrian Government, to accept the co-operation of Austrian officials in suppressing the subversive acts to which their attention has been directed, as well as for the investigation into the crime of Sarajevo, and finally to proceed to the immediate arrest of a Serbian officer and an official who were concerned in it. Annexed to the Austrian memorandum is a note which sums up the facts established by the investigation into the crime of Sarajevo, and declares that it was planned at Belgrade; that the bombs were provided for the murderers, and came from a depot of the Serbian army; finally that the murderers were drilled and helped by Serbian officers and officials.

On visiting the Acting Political Director immediately after making this communication, Count Scézsen without any observations informed him that the note had been presented. M. Berthelot, on my instructions, confined himself to pointing out to the Austro-Hungarian Ambassador the feeling of anxiety which had been aroused by the information available this morning as to the contents of the Austrian note, and the painful feeling which could not fail to be aroused in French public opinion by the time chosen for so categorical a démarche with so short a time limit; that is to say, a time when the President of the Republic and the President of the Council and Minister for Foreign Affairs of the Republic had left St. Petersburgh and were at sea, and consequently were not able to exert, in agreement with those Powers which were not directly interested, that soothing influence on Serbia and Austria which was so desirable in the interest of general peace. The Serbian Minister has not yet received any information as to the intentions of his Government. The German Ambassador has asked me to receive him at 5 o'clock this afternoon.

BIENVENU-MARTIN.

No. 26.
M. Bienvenu-Martin, Acting Minister for Foreign Affairs to M. Thiébaut, French Minister at Stockholm (for the President of the Council), and to Belgrade, Vienna, London, Berlin, Rome, St. Petersburgh.
Paris
July 24, 1914.

M. Vesnitch was this morning still without any telegram from his Government informing him as to their intentions, and did not know the contents of the Austrian note.

To a request for advice which he made to the Political Director, M. Berthelot said to him, speaking personally and for himself alone, that Serbia must try to gain time, as the limit of forty-eight hours perhaps formed rather a *"mise en demeure"* than an ultimatum in the proper sense of the term; that there might, for instance, be an opportunity of offering satisfaction on all those points which were not inconsistent with the dignity and sovereignty of Serbia; he was advised to draw attention to the fact that statements based on the Austrian investigations at Sarajevo were one sided, and that Serbia, while she was quite ready to take measures against all the accomplices of a crime which she most strongly condemned, required full information as to the evidence in order to be able to verify it with all speed; above all to attempt to escape from the direct grip of Austria by declaring herself ready to submit to the arbitration of Europe. I have asked at London and St. Petersburgh for the views and intentions of the British and Russian Governments. It appears on the other hand from our information that the Austrian note was not communicated to Italy until to-day, and that Italy had neither been consulted nor even informed of it.

BIENVENU-MARTIN.

No. 27.
M. Bienvenu-Martin, Acting Minister for Foreign Affairs to Stockholm (for the President of the Council), and to Belgrade, London, St. Petersburgh, Berlin, Rome.
Paris
July 24, 1914.

The French Ambassador at Vienna informs me that opinion has been startled by the sudden and exaggerated nature of the Austrian demands, but that the chief fear of the military party appears to be that Serbia may give way. The Serbian Minister in Austria thinks that his Government will show themselves very conciliatory in all that concerns the punishment of the accomplices of the crime, and the guarantees to be given as to the suppression of the anti-Austrian propaganda, but that they could not accept a general order to the army dictated to the King, nor the dismissal of officers who were suspected by Austria, nor the interference of foreign officials in Serbia. M. Yovanovitch considers that, if it were possible to start a discussion, a settlement of the dispute might still be arranged, with the assistance of the Powers. Our Ambassador at Berlin gives an account of the excitement aroused by the Austrian note, and of the state of feeling of the Russian Chargé d'Affaires, who thinks that a large part of opinion in Germany would desire war. The tone of the press is threatening and appears to have as its object the intimidation of Russia. Our Ambassador is to see Herr von Jagow this evening, M. Barrìre informs us that Italy is exercising moderating influence at Vienna and is trying to avoid complications.

BIENVENU-MARTIN.

No. 28.
M. Bienvenu-Martin, Acting Minister for Foreign Affairs, to Stockholm (for the President of the Council), and to Belgrade, London, St. Petersburgh, Berlin, Vienna, Rome.
Paris
July 24, 1914.

Herr von Schoen came to inform me of a note from his Government, of which he would not leave me a copy, but at my request he read it twice over to me. The Note was almost word for word as follows:

> "The statements of the Austro-Hungarian newspapers concerning the circumstances under which the assassination of the Austrian heir presumptive and his consort has taken place disclose unmistakably the aims which the Pan-Serbian propaganda has set itself, and the means it employs to realize them. The facts made known must also do away with all doubt that the centre of activity of all those tendencies which are directed towards the detachment of the Southern Slav provinces from the Austro-Hungarian Monarchy and their incorporation into the Serbian Kingdom is to be found in Belgrade, and is, at any rate, at work there, with the connivance of members of the Government and the army.
>
> The German Ambassador particularly called my attention to the last two paragraphs of his note before reading it, pressing the point that this was the important matter. I noted down the text literally; it is as follows: "The German Government consider that in the present case there is only question of a matter to be settled exclusively between Austria-Hungary and Serbia, and that the Great Powers ought seriously to endeavor to restrict it to those two immediately concerned.
>
> "The German Government desire urgently the localization of the dispute, because every interference of another Power would, owing to the natural play of alliances is followed by incalculable consequences."

I called the German Ambassador's attention to the fact that while it might appear legitimate to demand the punishment of all those who were implicated in the crime of Sarajevo, on the other hand it seemed difficult to require measures which could not be accepted, having regard to the dignity and sovereignty of Serbia; the Serbian Government, even if it was willing to submit to them, would risk being carried away by a revolution.

I also pointed out to Herr von Schoen that his note only took into account two hypotheses: that of a pure and simple refusal or that of a provocative attitude on the part of Serbia. The third hypothesis (which would leave the door open for an arrangement) should also be taken into consideration; that of Serbia's acceptance and of her agreeing at once to give full satisfaction for the punishment of the accomplices and full guarantees for the suppression of the anti-Austrian propaganda so far as they were compatible with her sovereignty and dignity. I added that if within these limits the satisfaction desired by Austria could be admitted, the means of obtaining it could be examined; if Serbia gave obvious proof of goodwill it could not be thought that Austria would refuse to take part in the conversation. Perhaps they should not make it too difficult for third Powers, who could not either morally or sentimentally cease to take interest in Serbia, to take an attitude, which was in accord with the wishes of Germans to localize the dispute. Herr von Schoen recognized the justice of these considerations and vaguely stated that hope was always possible. When I asked him if we should give to the Austrian note the character of a simple *mise en demeure,* which permitted a discussion, or an ultimatum, he answered that personally he had no views.

BIENVENU-MARTIN.

No. 29.
M. Jules Cambon, French Ambassador at Berlin, to M. Bienvenu-Martin, Acting Minister for Foreign Affairs.
Berlin
July 24, 1914.

The delivery of the Austrian note to Serbia has made a deep impression.

The Austrian Ambassador declares that his Government could not abate any of their demands. At the Wilhelmstrasse, as well as in the press, the same view is expressed. Most of the Chargés d'Affaires present in Berlin came to see me this morning. They show little hope of a peaceful issue. The Russian Chargé d'Affaires bitterly remarked that Austria has presented her note at the very moment that the President of the Republic and the President of the Council had left St. Petersburgh. He is inclined to think that a considerable section of opinion in Germany desires war and would like to seize this opportunity, in which Austria will no doubt be found more united than in the past, and in which the German Emperor, influenced by a desire to give support to the monarchic principle *(par un sentiment de solidarité monarchique)* and by horror at the crime, is less inclined to show a conciliatory attitude.

Herr von Jagow is going to receive me late in the afternoon.

JULES CAMBON.

No. 30.
M. Jules Cambon, French Ambassadorat Berlin, to M. Bienvenu-Martin, Acting Minister for Foreign Affairs.
Berlin
July 24, 1914.

I asked the Secretary of State to-day, in the interview which I had with him, if it was correct, as announced in the newspapers, that Austria had presented a note to the Powers on her dispute with Serbia; if he had received it; and what view he took of it. Herr von Jagow answered me in the affirmative, adding that the note was forcible, and that he approved it, the Serbian Government having for a long time past wearied the patience of Austria. Moreover, he considers this question to be a domestic one for Austria, and he hopes that it will be localized.

I then said to him that not having as yet received any instructions, the views which I wished to exchange with him were strictly personal. Thereupon I asked him if the Berlin Cabinet had really been entirely ignorant of Austria's requirements before they were communicated to Belgrade, and as he told me that that was so, I showed him my surprise at seeing him thus undertake to support claims, of whose limit and scope he was ignorant. Herr von Jagow interrupted me, and said, It is only because we are having a personal conversation that I allow you to say that to me. "Certainly," I replied, "but if Peter I humiliates himself, domestic trouble will probably break out in Serbia; that will open the door to fresh possibilities, and do you know where you will be led by Vienna?" I added that the language of the German newspapers was not the language of persons who were indifferent to, and unacquainted with, the question, but betokened an active support.

Finally, I remarked that the shortness of the time limit given to Serbia for submission should make an unpleasant impression in Europe. Herr von Jagow answered that he quite expected a little excitement (*un peu d'émotion*) on the part of Serbia's friends, but that he was counting on their giving her wise advice. "I have no doubt," I then said to him, "that Russia would endeavor to persuade the Cabinet of Belgrade to make acceptable concessions; but why not ask from one what is being asked from the other, and if reliance is being placed on advice being given at Belgrade, is it not also legitimate to rely on advice being given at Vienna from another quarter?" The Secretary of State went so far as to say that that depended on circumstances; but immediately checked himself; he repeated that the difficulty must be localized. He asked me if I really thought the situation serious. "Certainly," I answered, "because if what is happening is the result of due reflection, I do not understand why all means of retreat have been cut off."

All the evidence shows that Germany is ready to support Austria's attitude with unusual energy. The weakness, which her Austro-Hungarian ally has shown for some years past, has weakened the confidence that was placed in her here. She was found heavy to drag along. Mischievous legal proceedings, such as the Agram and the Friedjung affairs, brought odium on her police and covered them with ridicule. All that was asked of the police was that they should be strong; the conviction is that they were violent.

An article which appeared in the *Lokal Anzeiger* this evening shows also that at the German Chancery there exists a state of mind to which we in Paris are naturally not inclined to pay sufficient attention, I mean the feeling that Monarchies must stand together (*sentiment de la solidarité monarchique*). I am convinced that great weight must be attached to this point of view in order to appreciate the attitude of the Emperor William, whose impressionable nature must have been affected by the assassination of a prince whose guest he had been a few days previously.

It is not less striking to notice the pains with which Herr von Jagow, and all the officials placed under his orders, pretend to everyone that they were ignorant of the scope of the note sent by Austria to Serbia.

JULES CAMBON.

No. 31.
M. Paléologue, French Ambassador at St. Petersburgh, to M. Bienvenu-Martin, Acting Minister for Foreign Affairs.
St. Petersburgh
July 24, 1914.

THE Austro-Hungarian Ambassador has communicated to M. Sazonof a threatening note to Serbia. The intentions of the Emperor of Russia and his Ministers could not be more pacific, a fact of which the President of the Republic and the President of the Council have been able to satisfy themselves directly; but the ultimatum which the Austro-Hungarian Government has just delivered to the Cabinet at Belgrade introduces a new and disquieting element into the situation. Public opinion in Russia would not allow Austria to offer violence to Serbia. The shortness of the time limit fixed by the ultimatum renders still more difficult the moderating influence that the Powers of the Triple Entente might exercise at Vienna. On the other hand, M. Sazonof assumes that Germany will desire to support her ally and I am afraid that this impression is correct. Nothing but the assurance of the solidarity of the Triple Entente can prevent the German Powers from emphasizing their provocative attitude.

PALÉOLOGUE.

No. 32.
M. Paul Cambon, French Ambassador at London, to M. Bienvenu-Martin, Acting Minister for Foreign Affairs.
London
July 24, 1914.

Sir Edward Grey, having discussed with me his desire to leave no stone unturned to avert the crisis, we agreed in thinking that the British Cabinet might ask the German Government to take the initiative in approaching Vienna with the object of offering the mediation, between Austria and Serbia, of the four Powers which are not directly interested. If Germany agrees, tome will be gained, and this is the essential point. Sir Edward Grey told me that he would discuss with Prince Lichnowsky the proposal I have just explained. I mentioned the matter to my Russian colleague, who is afraid of a surprise from Germany, and who imagines that Austria would not have dispatched her ultimatum without previous agreement with Berlin.

Count Benckendorff told me that Prince Lichnowsky, when he returned from leave about a month ago, had intimated that he held pessimistic views regarding the relations between St. Petersburgh and Berlin. He had observed the uneasiness caused in this latter capital by the rumors of a naval entente between Russia and Great Britain, by the Tsar's visit to Bucharest, and by the strengthening of the Russian army. Count Benckendorff had concluded from this that a war with Russia would be looked upon without disfavor in Germany. The Under-Secretary to State has been struck, as all of us have been, by the anxious looks of Prince Lichnowsky since his return from Berlin, and he considers that if Germany had wished to do so she could have stopped the dispatch of the ultimatum. The situation, therefore, is as grave as it can be, and we see no way of arresting the course of events. However, Count Benckendorff thinks it right to attempt the démarche upon which I have agreed with Sir Edward Grey.

PAUL CAMBON.

No. 33.
M. Paul Cambon, French Ambassador at London, to M. Bienvenu-Martin, Acting Minister for Foreign Affairs.
London
July 24, 1914.

The Serbian Minister received to-night from M. Pashitch a telegram saying that the Austro-Hungarian Government had sent him their ultimatum, the time limit of which expires at 6 o'clock to-morrow, Saturday evening, M. Pashitch does not give the terms of the Austrian communication, but if it is of the nature reported in to-day's *Times,* it seems impossible for the Serbian Government to accept it. In consultation with my Russian colleague, who thinks it extremely difficult for his Government not to support Serbia, we have been asking ourselves what intervention could avert the conflict. Sir Edward Grey having summoned me for this afternoon, I propose to suggest that he should ask for the semi-official intervention of the German Government at Vienna to prevent a sudden attack.

PAUL CAMBON.

No. 34.

M. Bienvenu-Martin, Acting Minister for Foreign Affairs, to Stockholm (for the President of the Council), Belgrade, St. Petersburgh, Berlin, Vienna, Rome.

Paris

July 24, 1914.

THE Austrian Ambassador having communicated his Government's note to Sir Edward Grey, the latter observed that no such formidable declaration had ever been addressed by one Government to another; he drew Count Mensdorff's attention to the responsibility assumed by Austria. With the possibility of a conflict between Austria and Russia before him, Sir Edward Grey proposes to ask for the co-operation of the German Government with a view to the mediation of the four powers who are not directly interested in the Serbian question, namely, England, France, Italy, and Germany; this mediation to be exercised simultaneously at Vienna and at St. Petersburgh. I advised the Serbian Minister to act cautiously, and I am willing to co-operate in any conciliatory action at Vienna, in the hope that Austria will not insist on the acceptance of all her demands as against a small State, if the latter shows herself ready to give every satisfaction which is considered compatible with her independence and her sovereignty.

BIENVENU-MARTIN.

Count Errembault de Dudzeele, Belgian Minister at Vienna, to M. Davignon, Belgian Minister for Foreign Affairs.

Vienna

July 24, 1914.

Sir,

I have the honor to enclose herewith the text of the Austro-Hungarian ultimatum to Serbia.

Primary Documents: Serbia's Appeal for Russian Assistance, 24 July 1914

Updated: Saturday, 24 May, 2003

Reproduced below is the text of the telegram dispatched by the Serbian regent, Alexander, to Russian Tsar Nicholas II in the midst of the so-called July Crisis of 1914. One day earlier, the Austro-Hungarian government had dispatched to Serbia a harsh ultimatum in response to the assassination of Austrian Archduke Franz Ferdinand a month earlier.

In the letter, Alexander appealed to the Tsar for assistance in dealing with Austria-Hungary's increasingly menacing stance against Serbia. Although Russia proved willing to help Serbia, it was to no avail; Austria-Hungary declared war against Serbia on 28 July 1914, sparking off the onset of the First World War.

Telegram from Alexander, Prince Regent of Serbia to the Tsar of Russia.

Belgrade

July 24, 1914.

The Austro-Hungarian Government yesterday evening handed to the Serbian Government a note concerning the *"attentat"* of Sarajevo. Conscious of its international duties, Serbia from the first days of the horrible crime declared that she condemned it, and that she was ready to open an inquiry on her territory if the complicity of certain of her subjects were proved in the investigation begun by the Austro-Hungarian authorities. However, the demands contained in the Austro-Hungarian note are unnecessarily humiliating for Serbia and incompatible with her dignity as an independent State.

Thus we are called upon in peremptory tones for a declaration of the Government in the "Official journal and an order from the Sovereign to the army wherein we should repress the spirit of hostility against Austria by reproaching ourselves for criminal weakness in regard to our perfidious actions. Then we have to admit Austro-Hungarian functionaries into Serbia to participate with our own in the investigation and to superintend the execution of the other conditions indicated in the note.

We have received a time-limit of forty-eight hours to accept everything, in default of which the legation of Austria-Hungary will leave Belgrade. We are ready to accept the Austro-Hungarian conditions which are compatible with the position of an independent State as well as those whose acceptance shall be advised us by your Majesty. All persons whose participation in the *"attentat"* shall be proved will be severely punished by us. Certain of these demands cannot be carried out without changes in our legislation, which require time. We have been given too short a limit. We can be attacked after the expiration of the time-limit by the Austro-Hungarian Army which is concentrating on our frontier. It is impossible for us to defend ourselves, and we supplicate your Majesty to give us your aid as soon as possible. The highly prized good will of your Majesty, which has so often shown itself toward us, makes us hope firmly that this time again our appeal will be heard by his generous Slav heart. In these difficult moments, I voice the sentiments of the Serbian people, who supplicate your Majesty to interest himself in the lot of the Kingdom of Serbia.

ALEXANDER.

Source: *Source Records of the Great War, Vol. I, ed. Charles F. Horne, National Alumni, 1923.*

24 July, 1914
Russian Memorandum of Advice to Serbia
Special Journal of the Council of Ministers
24 July, 1914

[The date, July 11, corresponds to July 24. The Russians at that time were using the Julian calendar, then thirteen days behind the Gregorian calendar, used by the West.]
Subsequent to the declaration made by the Minister of Foreign Affairs, regarding the most recent measures taken by the Austro-Hungarian Government against Serbia.

The Minister of Foreign Affairs informed the Council of Ministers that, according to information received by him and according to the announcement made by the Austro-Hungarian Ambassador to the Imperial Court, the Austro-Hungarian Government had turned upon the Serbian Government with demands which appeared, in fact, to be quite unacceptable to the Serbian Government as a sovereign State, and which were drawn up in the form of an ultimatum calling for a reply within a definite time, expiring tomorrow, July 12, at 6 o'clock in the evening.

Therefore, foreseeing that Serbia would turn to us for advice, and perhaps also for aid, there arose a need to prepare an answer which might be given to Serbia.

Having considered the declaration made by Marshal Sazonov in its relation to the information reported by the Ministers of War, Marine, and Finance concerning the political and military situation, the Council of Ministers decreed:

1: To approve the proposal of the Minister of Foreign Affairs to get in touch with the Cabinets of the Great Powers in order to induce the Austro-Hungarian Government to grant a postponement in the matter of the answer to the ultimatum demands presented by the Austro-Hungarian Government, so that it might be possible for the Governments of the Great Powers to become acquainted with and to investigate the documents on the Sarajevo crime which are in the hands of the Austro-Hungarian Government, and which, according to the declaration of the Austro-Hungarian Ambassador, it is willing to communicate to the Russian Government.

2: To approve the proposal of the Minister of Foreign Affairs to advise the Serbian Government, in case the situation of Serbia should be such that she could not with her own strength protect herself against the possible armed invasion by Austro-Hungary, not to offer armed resistance to the invasion of Serbian territory, if such all invasion should occur, but to announce that Serbia yields to force and that she entrusts her fate to the judgment of the Great Powers.

3: To authorize the Ministers of War and of Marine, in accordance with the duties of their offices, to beg your Imperial Majesty to consent, according to the progress of events, to order the mobilization of the four military districts of Kiev, Odessa, Moscow, and Kazan, and the Baltic and Black Sea fleets. (Note by the Acting Secretary of the Council: "In the original the word 'Baltic' has been added by his Imperial Majesty's own hand and the word 'fleet' corrected to read 'fleets.'")

4: To authorize the War Minister to proceed immediately to gather stores of war material.

5: To authorize the Minister of Finance to take measures instantly to diminish the funds of the Ministry of Finance, which may be at present in Germany or Austria.

The Council of Ministers considers it its loyal duty to inform your Imperial Majesty of these decisions which it has made.

> Countersigned: President of the Council of Ministers,
> STATE SECRETARY GOREMYKIN.
> [Names of Members of the Council follow.]

1914 July 24 tsar told Austria declared war on Russia.

Telegram of the Imperial Ambassador at Vienna
to the Chancellor on July 24th, 1914.

Count Berchtold has asked today for the Russian Chargé d'affaires in order to explain to him thoroughly and cordially Austria-Hungary's point of view toward Serbia. After recapitulation of the historical development of the past few years, he emphasized that the Monarchy entertained no thought of conquest toward Serbia. Austria-Hungary would not claim Serbian territory. It insisted merely that this step was meant as a definite means of checking the Serb intrigues.

Impelled by force of circumstances, Austria-Hungary must have a guaranty for continued amicable relations with Serbia. It was far from him to intend to bring about a change in the balance of powers in the Balkan. The Chargé d'affaires, who had received no instructions from St. Petersburg, took the discussion of the Secretary "ad referendum with the promise to submit it immediately to Sasonof.

Exhibit 4.
Telegram of the Imperial Ambassador at St. Petersburg to the Chancellor
on July 24th, 1914.

I have just utilized the contents of Order 592 in a prolonged interview with Sasonof. The Secretary (Sasonof) indulged in unmeasured accusations toward Austria-Hungary and he was very much agitated. He declared most positively that Russia could not permit under any circumstances that the Serbia-Austrian difficulty be settled alone between the parties concerned.

Primary Documents: Belgian Reaction to Austria's Ultimatum, 24–26 July 1914
Updated: Saturday, 31 May, 2003

Reproduced below is the text of a series of letters dispatched from Berlin during the period 24–26 July 1914 by the Belgian ambassador to Germany, Baron Beyens. In his letters, Beyens demonstrates increasing anxiety over the prospect of an apparently engineered war against Serbia by both Austria-Hungary and Germany. Beyens, as with the other European powers, expressed shock at the strict terms of the Austro-Hungarian ultimatum to Serbia of 23 July 1914, the latter comprising Vienna's response to the assassination of Archduke Franz Ferdinand the previous month.

Two days following Beyens' last letter—on 28 July 1914—Austria-Hungary duly declared war on Serbia, setting in train events that led to the First World War.

Official Report by Baron Beyens
Belgian Minister at Berlin in 1914
Berlin, July 24, 1914

The publication of the ultimatum addressed yesterday by the Cabinet of Vienna to that of Belgrade goes far beyond anything that the most pessimistic anticipations of which I informed you in my report of the 16th of this month had anticipated. Evidently Count Berchtold and Count Tisza, the responsible authors of this sudden blow, have come under the influence of the military party and the Austro-Hungarian General Staff. The result of such a lack of moderation and discretion will inevitably be to attract the sympathies of the great mass of European public opinion to Serbia, in spite of the horror caused by the murders of Sarajevo. Even at Berlin, to judge by the Liberal papers, one has the impression that the Austro-Hungarian demands are considered excessive. "Austro-Hungary," says the *Vossische Zeitung* this morning, "will have to prove the grave accusations which she brings against Serbia and her Government by publishing the results of the judicial inquiry held at Sarajevo." Her von Jagow and Herr Zimmermannn (note: the German Secretary of State and Under-Secretary) had assured us last week that they did not know the decisions taken by the Vienna Cabinet, nor the extent of the Austro-Hungarian demands. How can we believe in this ignorance to-day?

It is improbable that the Austro-Hungarian statesmen should have made up their minds to such a step, the most dangerous stroke which their diplomacy has ever ventured against a Balkan State, without having consulted their colleagues at Berlin, and without having obtained the assent of the Emperor William. The fact that the Emperor has given a free hand to his allies in spite of the risk of bringing on a European conflict is explained by the fear and horror, which he has of regicides. "What is Serbia going to do?" was the question which the majority of my colleagues were asking this morning; "Will she turn to Russia and beg for her support by telegram?" If she does so, she cannot receive any reply before the expiration of the time limit in the Austrian ultimatum. Russia will be obliged as a preliminary to concert measures with France and, very astutely, the Cabinet of Vienna has postponed the outbreak of the storm until the moment when M. Poincare and M. Viviani (note: the French President and Prime Minister) are on their voyage between St. Petersburg and Stockholm. The threatening tone in which the Austro-Hungarian note is couched is all the more unfortunate because the Russian Ambassador at Vienna, I learn, had recently informed Count Berchtold that his Government would support the Austro-Hungarian demands with the Pashitch Cabinet if those demands were moderate. To-day a new crisis has begun, recalling the crisis of 1909 after the annexation of Bosnia and Herzegovina. The best we can hope is that it will not develop in a more tragic manner, in spite of the bellicose wishes of the Austrian General Staff, which are perhaps shared by that at Berlin. The best advice to give to Serbia would be to invite the mediation and intervention of the Great Powers.

M. Davignon, Belgian Minister for Foreign Affairs, to the Belgian Ministers at Paris, Berlin, London, Vienna, and St. Petersburg.
Brussels
July 24, 1914.

Sir,

The Belgian Government have had under their consideration whether, in present circumstances, it would not be advisable to address to the Powers who guarantee Belgian independence and neutrality a communication assuring them of Belgium's determination to fulfill the international obligations imposed upon her by treaty in the event of a war breaking out on her frontiers. The Government has come to the conclusion that such a communication would be premature at present, but that events might move rapidly and not leave sufficient time to forward suitable instructions at the desired moment to the Belgian representatives abroad. In these circumstances, I have proposed to the King and to my colleagues in the Cabinet, who have concurred, to give you now exact instructions as to the steps to be taken by you if the prospect of a Franco-German war became more threatening. I enclose herewith a note, signed but not dated, which you should read to the Minister for Foreign Affairs and of which you should give him a copy, if circumstances render such a communication necessary. I will inform you by telegram when you are to act on these instructions.

This telegram will be dispatched when the order is given for the mobilization of the Belgian army if, contrary to our earnest hope and to the apparent prospect of a peaceful settlement, our information leads us to take this extreme measure of precaution.

"An Ambassador's Memoris"
By Maurice Paléologue
Day 5 with French President in Russia
Friday, July 24, 1914.

Tired by these four days of continuous high pressure I was hoping for a little rest and had told my servant to let me sleep on this morning. At seven o'clock, however, the telephone bell woke me with a start: I was informed that Austria had presented an ultimatum to Serbia yesterday evening.

As I was half asleep the news at first produced a curious impression of amazement and authority.

The occurrence seemed to me unreal and yet definite, imaginary but authentic. I seemed to be continuing my conversation of yesterday with the Tsar, putting forward my theories and conjectures. At the same time I had a sensation, a potent, positive, and compelling sensation, that I was in the presence of a *fait accompli*.

During the morning details of what had happened in Belgrade began to come in.

At half-past twelve, Sazonov and Buchanan came to the Embassy to confer on the situation. Our discussion was interrupted by lunch but we resumed immediately afterwards. Taking my stand on the toasts exchanged between the Tsar and the President, the declarations of the two Foreign Ministers and the communiqué to the Havas Agency yesterday, I had no hesitation in advocating a Policy of firmness.

"But suppose that policy is bound to lead to war?" said Sazonov.

"It will only lead to war if the Germanic powers have already made up their minds to resort to force to secure the hegemony of the East. Firmness does not exclude conciliation. But it is essential for the other side to be prepared to negotiate and compromise. You know my own views as to Germany's designs. The Austrian ultimatum seems to me to provoke the dangerous crisis I have anticipated for a long time. Henceforth we must recognize that war may break out at any moment. That prospect must govern all our diplomatic action."

Buchanan assumed that his government would desire to remain neutral and was therefore apprehensive that France and Russia would be crushed by the Triple Alliance.

Sazonov protested: "At the present juncture England's neutrality would be tantamount to her suicide!"

"I'm certain of that," Sir George replied sadly. "But I'm afraid public opinion with us is still far from realizing what our national interests so imperiously require."

I emphasized the decisive part England could play in quenching Germany's warlike ardour; I cited the view the Tsar Nicholas expressed to me four days ago—"Unless Germany has lost her reason altogether, she will never dare to attack Russia, France, and England combined." Thus it was urgently necessary for the British Government to announce its adhesion to our cause, which was the cause of peace. Sazonov warmly advocated the same course.

Buchanan promised to make strong representations to Sir Edward Grey in favour of the policy of resistance to Germanic arrogance.

At three o'clock, Sazonov left us to go to Ielaguin Island to which Goremykin, the President of the Council, had summoned the ministers.

At eight o'clock in the evening I went to the Foreign Office where Sazonov was closeted with my German colleague.

A few minutes later I saw Pourtalès come out, his face purple and his eyes flashing. The discussion must have been lively. He furtively shook my hand as I entered the minister's room.

Sazonov was still agitated over the dispute in which he had just been engaged. He has quick, nervous movements and his voice is dry and jerky.

"What's happened?" I said.

"As I anticipated, Germany wholeheartedly supports the Austrian cause. Not the slightest suggestion of conciliation. So I told Pourtalès quite bluntly that we should not leave Serbia to settle her differences with Austria alone. Our talk ended in a very acrimonious tone."

"Really?"

"Yes…Can you imagine what he had the audacity to tell me? He reproached me, me and all other Russians, with disliking Austria and having no scruples about troubling the last years of her aged Emperor. I retorted: 'No, of course we don't like Austria…Why should we like her? She has never done us anything but harm. As for her aged Emperor, he owes it to us that he still has his crown on his head. Just remember how he showed his gratitude in 1855, 1878, and 1908…What! Reproach us with not liking Austria! That's a bit too much!'"

"It's a bad business, Minister. If conversations between Petersburg and Berlin are to continue in this strain they won't last long. Very soon we shall see the Emperor William rise in his 'shining armour.' Please be calm. Exhaust every possibility of compromise! Don't forget that my government is a government based on public opinion and can only support you effectively if it has public opinion behind it. And think of English opinion also."

"I shall do everything possible to avoid war. But like you I am very uneasy about the turn events are taking."

"Can I give my government an assurance that you have not yet ordered any military preparations?"

"None whatsoever. All we have decided is privately to withdraw the eighty million roubles we have on deposit in the German banks."

He added that he would endeavour to obtain from Count Berchtold an extension of the time fixed for the Serbian reply in the ultimatum so that the powers might have an opportunity of forming an opinion on the legal aspect of the dispute and finding some peaceful solution.

The Russian ministers are to meet again to-morrow with the Tsar presiding. I recommended to Sazonov the greatest caution as to the advice he is to give.

Our conversation was enough to soothe his nerves. He continued with calm deliberation: "You needn't fear! Besides you know the Tsar's caution. Berchtold has put himself in the wrong. It's our business to make him solely responsible for everything that comes. I even consider that if the Vienna cabinet resorts to action the Serbians ought to let their territory be invaded and confine themselves to denouncing Austria's infamy to the civilized world.

Chapter Twenty-Six
July 25, 1914

No. 19.
Count Berchtold to the Imperial and Royal Ambassadors at Berlin, Rome, Paris, London, St. Petersburgh and Constantinople.
Vienna
July 25, 1914.

Your Excellency will find herewith the dossier mentioned in the circular note to the Powers with reference to the Great-Servian propaganda, and its connection with the Sarajevo murder.

Your Excellency is instructed to bring this dossier to the notice of the Government to which you are accredited.

Enclosure.

The Servian agitation, which has as its object the separation from the Austrian Monarchy of the Southern Slav districts in order to unite them with the Servian State, dates from far back. This propaganda on Servian soil, always the same in its ultimate object, although varying in its means and intensity, reached one of its culminating points at the time of the annexation crisis. Throwing off the protecting cloak of secrecy, it then revealed its purpose openly and undisguised, and attempted, under the patronage of the Servian Government, to attain its ends by every means in its power.

While the whole of the Servian press was calling for war against the Monarchy by malicious invectives in which facts were perverted, apart from other means of propaganda, associations were being formed to prepare for this war.

The Narodna Odbrana stood out as the most important of these associations. Having its origin in an already existing revolutionary committee, it was constituted as a private society, although in fact it took the form of an organization of Servian military and civil officials wholly dependent on the Foreign Office at Belgrade. Amongst its founders one may mention: General Bozo Jankovic, ex-ministers Ljuba Jovanovio, Ljuba Davidovic, and Velislav Vulovic, Zivojin Dacic (Director of the Government printing establishment), and Majors (then Captains) Voja Tankosic and Milan Pribicevic. This association aimed at the creation and equipment of free companies for use in the impending war against the Austro-Hungarian Monarchy. (See Appendix 2.)

A convincing description of the activity at that time of the Narodna Odbrana will be found amongst others in the deposition of Trifko Krstanovic, a Bosnia-Herzegovinian subject, in the course of his evidence before the district court at Sarajevo; he was then at Belgrade, and had been accepted by the Narodna Odbrana, with other subjects of the Monarchy as a komitadji. At the beginning of 1909, Krstanovic had arrived with about 140 fellow-members at a school established for the formation of new bands at Cuprija (in the district of Jagodina), managed by Captains Voja Tankosic and Dusan Putnik. The only instructors at this school were Servian officers. General Bozo Jankovic and Captain Milan Pribicevic inspected the three monthly courses of these bands at regular intervals.

The new komitadjis received their training in musketry, bomb throwing, mine laying, blowing up of railways, tunnels and bridges, and the destruction of telegraph wires. According to the instructions of their leaders, it was their duty to put into practice in Bosnia and Herzegovina the knowledge they had recently acquired.

By this action, carried on in the most open manner and encouraged by the Servian Government, the Narodna Odbrana was thus prepared for guerilla warfare against Austria-Hungary. In this way, subjects of the Monarchy were led into treason against their country, and induced, as Servian emissaries, systematically to practice underhand attacks against the means of defense of their country.

This period of aggressive aspirations ended with the declaration made by the Servian Government on the 31st March, 1909, in which the Government of Belgrade announced that they were prepared to accept the new situation created in municipal and international law by the annexation of Bosnia and Herzegovina, and solemnly promised to maintain in future friendly relations with the Austro-Hungarian Monarchy.

With this declaration, the agitation, which constituted a source of constant trouble to Austria-Hungary, seemed to have come to an end and the road to an amicable *rapprochement* between Serbia and the Monarchy to have been entered on. Deprived of the encouragement of the Servian Government, and combated by that Government in accordance with their engagements, the propaganda hostile to the Monarchy could only have continued a shadowy existence and would have been condemned to early destruction. On the other hand, the ties of language, race, and culture existing between the Southern Slav districts of the Monarchy and Serbia ought to have resulted in the realization of a task of common development inspired by mutual friendship and parallel interests.

These hopes, however, have not been realized.

Aspirations hostile to the Monarchy have continued, and under the eyes of the Servian Government, who has done nothing to suppress this movement, the anti-Austro-Hungarian propaganda has only increased in extent and volume. Hatred against the Monarchy has been fanned and kindled into an irreconcilable feeling. The Servian people alike by adapting their former course of action to the new situation and by supplementing it by fresh methods were summoned to the "inevitable death struggle" against Austria-Hungary. Secret ramifications have been systematically spread towards the Slav districts in the south of the Monarchy whose subjects have been incited to treason against their country.

Above all, the Servian press has since then worked incessantly in this spirit.

Up to the present time no fewer than eighty-one newspapers appearing in Serbia have had to forfeit their right to delivery through the post on account of their contents falling within the scope of the penal law. There is hardly a clause in the penal code protecting the sacred person of the Monarch and the members of the Imperial Family, or the integrity of the State, that has not been violated by Servian papers.

A few examples of these press views, selected from the great mass of material published by the press at various dates, are contained in Appendix I.

Without entering into a detailed account of these expressions of Servian public opinion, it is necessary to note that in spite of the formal recognition accorded by Serbia, it has never ceased to consider the annexation of Bosnia and Herzegovina, both before and after the event, as a robbery committed against Serbia for which reparation is due. This idea not only constantly recurs with every modulation of its coarse language in the papers professing most advanced views, but also finds expression in hardly veiled terms in the "Samouprava," which is in such close touch with the Foreign Office of Belgrade. (See Appendix I (*b*).)

Nor can one omit to draw attention to the manner in which the attempt made on the 15th June, 1910, at Sarajevo, by Bogdan Zerajic against the Feldzeugmeister von Varesanin, Governor of Bosnia and Herzegovina, was turned to account by the press.

As is known, Zerajic had killed himself immediately after his deed, and before committing, it had burnt all his papers. Under these circumstances, it was impossible to throw full light upon the motives of his crime. It could, however, be inferred from a document found on his person that he was a follower of the views of Krapotkin. Evidence collected leads likewise to the conclusion that the crime was of an anarchist type.

This, however, did not prevent the Servian press from celebrating the criminal as a national Servian hero and from glorifying his deed. Indeed, the "Politika" protested strongly against the idea that Zerajic was an anarchist, and declared him "a Serbian hero whose name all Servians will repeat with respect and grief."

The "Politika" considers the 18th August[3] of the same year as a suitable opportunity on which to return to the crime of Zerajic, "whose name will be sacred to the people," and to celebrate the outrage in verse. (See Appendix I (*a*).)

In this way, this crime, which had nothing to do with the territorial aspirations against the Monarchy, was exploited for the furtherance of these ideas and by the glorifying of Zerajic, murder was hailed in the most explicit way as a glorious means toward the realisation of this aim and one worthy to be imitated in the struggle. This approbation of murder as a weapon fully admissible in the struggle against the Monarchy reappears later in the press in discussing the attempt made by Jukic against the Royal Commissioner von Cuvaj. (See Appendix I (*c*).)

These newspapers, which were circulated not only in Serbia but also, as we shall show later, illicitly smuggled into the Monarchy by well-organized secret methods, have awakened and kept alive this mood in the masses, a mood that has provided a fruitful field for the activities of the associations hostile to the Monarchy. The Narodna Odbrana became the center of the agitation carried on by the associations. The same persons who were at its head at the time of the annexation still control it. Now as then, they still control it in the capacity of the most active and energetic organizers, the most violent opponents of the Monarchy; General Bozo Jankovic, Zivojin Dacic (Director of the Government printing establishment), and Majors Milan Pribicevic and Voja Tankosic. Organized on a broad and far-reaching scale and constituted on a strict hierarchical basis (see Appendix 2, "Organization"), the Narodna Odbrana counted soon some 400 committees, which developed a very active agitation.

Moreover, the Narodna Odbrana became closely allied with the "shooting federation" (*Schützenbund*), (762 societies), the great Sokol[4] Association "Dusan" (2,500 members), the Olympian Club, the association of horsemen (*Reiterverein*), "Prince Michael," the society of sportsmen (*Jägerbund*), and the league of development (*Kulturliga*), as well as numerous other associations all of which, subordinate to it, were under the guidance and protection of the Narodna Odbrana, and worked on the same lines. Becoming more and more closely intermingled, these associations arrived at a complete amalgamation in such a way that to-day they are nothing but members of the single body of the Narodna Odbrana.

Thus, the Narodna Odbrana has set up all over Serbia a close network of agitation, and has attracted to its principles all those who were receptive of its ideas.

---

[3] Birthday of His Imperial and Apostolic Majesty.

[4] Sokol falcon. The name given to gymnastic associations throughout Slav countries, which have adopted the falcon as their emblem.

The official publications of the Narodna Odbrana demonstrate sufficiently clearly the spirit, which animates it.

While in its statutes, it represents itself as an "educational society" *(Kulturverein)* concerning itself only with the spiritual and physical improvement of the Servian population and its material progress, the Narodna Odbrana discloses in its official publication (see Appendix 2) the true and single motive of its existence in that which it calls its "re-organized programmed": to preach to the Servian people the sacred truth by "fanatical and indefatigable work" under the pretense that the Monarchy wishes to "take away Servian liberty and language and even to destroy her"; that it is an essential necessity to wage against Austria-Hungary, her "first and greatest enemy," "a war of extermination with rifle and cannon," and "by every means" to prepare the people for this war, which is "to liberate the con-quered territories," in which "seven million brothers are suffering in bondage." All the efforts "at an educational programmed" *(Kulturbestrebungen)* of the Narodna Odbrana are exclusively concerned with this idea simply as a means for the organization and education of the people for the longed-for death struggle against the Monarchy.

All the associations affiliated to the Narodna Odbrana work in the same spirit; the Sokol Association at Kragujevac will serve as an example (see Appendix 3).

As in the case of the Narodna Odbrana, officers, professors, and civil servants are at its head. The speech in which its President, Major Kovacevic, opened the annual meeting of 1914, made absolutely no mention of physical training, which is supposed to be the real object of a Sokol association, and confined itself solely to "the preparations for war" against the "dangerous, heartless, grasping, odious, and greedy enemy in the north" who "robs millions of Servian brothers of their liberty and rights, and holds them in bondage and chains."

In the administrative reports of this association the technical work is placed entirely in the back-ground, and only serves as headlines for the avowal of the real "objects of the activities of the ad-ministration," namely, the preparation of national development and the strengthening of the "oppressed nation" with the object of enabling it to carry out its "incomplete programmed and its un-finished task," and to accomplish that "great action" "which is to be carried out in the near future," "the liberation of those brothers who live across the Drina, who are suffering the martyrdom of the crucified."

Even the treasurer makes use of his financial reports to send forth the appeal that "falcons must be reared 'capable' of bringing freedom to the brothers still in bondage."

As in the case of the "educational programmed" of the Narodna Odbrana, the gymnastic activity of the Sokols is not the real object but merely a means at the service of the same propaganda carried on in the same spirit, and even with the very same words.

When the Narodna Odbrana appeals to the "people" for a death struggle against the Monarchy, it does not address itself only to the Servian people, but to all Southern Slav nationalities. In the eyes of the Narodna Odbrana, the Slav regions in the south of the Monarchy are regarded as "our subjected Servian territories" (see Appendix 4). The Southern Slav subjects of the Monarchy are further also ex-pected to take part in this "national work." This "healthy and necessary work "is, therefore, to be car-ried on beyond the Servian frontier. The Narodna Odbrana recruits its "heroes for this holy war" even on the soil of the Monarchy, and among them Obilic, the murderer of Murad, is to light them on their way as an example of sacrifice for one's country worthy of imitation.

But in order to incite "brothers outside Serbia 'to share in' the work of private effort," the Narodna Odbrana keeps in close touch with the "brothers beyond the frontier." It is not said in the publica-tions of the society, how this intimate association is carried out, no doubt because it appertains to that part of the "common work which for many reasons cannot, or ought not to be divulged."

How comprehensive this branch of its activity is, can be seen by the fact that not only the central committee of the Narodna Odbrana, but also certain of its local committees contain special sections for "foreign affairs."

This "foreign" activity of the Narodna Odbrana and its affiliated branches is extremely varied. What is relatively less dangerous inasmuch as it can be officially controlled, consists of lecture tours undertaken by distinguished members of the Narodna Odbrana in the south-eastern parts of the Monarchy where they speak before various societies on national or educational subjects. These tours give the speakers the desired opportunity, which is indeed the chief object of these journeys, of explaining the true aims of the associations in language more or less veiled, which is intelligible to those who are already initiated.

Amongst these emissaries, one of the best known is Zivojin Dacic (Director of the Government printing establishment), already several times alluded to; it was he who, on the 8th August, 1909, issued an "appeal" to the Servian people in which he called Austria-Hungary the enemy of Serbia, and exhorted them to prepare for the war against the Monarchy. On numerous occasions, Dacic undertook tours of this nature in the southeastern districts of the Austro-Hungarian Monarchy. During one of these lectures at Karlovoi in 1912, he flung his accustomed prudence to the winds and spoke openly of the "union of all Serbs against the common foe," by which he designated Austria-Hungary in unmistakable language.

More dangerous are the relations with associations in the Monarchy formed by Servian associations imbued with the spirit of the Narodna Odbrana under the cloak of community of interests and of culture; for the mutual visits of these associations, whether by delegates or in bodies, which escape all official control, are utilized by the Servians for all sorts of plots against the Monarchy.

Thus, for instance, at the well-known feast of the Prosvjeta Association at Sarajevo, in September 1912, an envoy of the Narodna Odbrana had the effrontery secretly to recruit Bosnian adherents to his society (see Appendix 6). The message which the representative of the Sokol Association at Kragujevac brought to the "brothers in Bosnia" at this feast was: "We have not forgotten you; the wings of the falcon of Sumadija are still powerful"—a thought which in confidential intercourse would no doubt have found quite a different expression and one better corresponding to the tendencies of this society which we have already explained (see Appendix 3). As to the events that take place at meetings of the same kind in Serbia the Imperial and Royal authorities cannot have any information founded on unimpeachable authority, as they only possess on this matter confidential information which it is difficult to check. In this connection, one may mention the visit of Agram students to Serbia in April, 1912, who received from the Servians an official military reception accompanied even by a review of troops in their honour, and that in a manner so suggestive that the administrative report of the Sokol Association at Kragujevac could say, "This event marks the beginning and germ of a great deed which will be accomplished in the near future, it is a germ which will ripen when the soul of the people bursts its bonds and until there is no barrier that has not been destroyed."

It is only recently that it has come to the knowledge of the Austro-Hungarian authorities that the Servian Sokol associations have succeeded in inducing similar societies into the Monarchy to establish a connection with them which is up to the present secret, and the character of which is not yet quite clear, for the inquiries on this point are still in progress. Up to the present, however, the information obtained permits the conclusion that traces have been discovered of one of the ways by which the subversive aims of the Servian Sokols and their friends have poisoned the minds of certain groups of mistaken and misled persons in the Monarchy.

This propaganda which is aimed at wider circles, and is rather of a preparatory nature, assumes minor importance compared with that of the "foreign work" which is conducted by the Narodna Odbrana and its friends in the form of personal agitation among individuals. It is in this field that the most melancholy results are shown.

By means of confidential and secret emissaries, it carries the poison of rebellion to the circles of men of mature age as well as those of irresponsible youth.

It is thus, for example, that the late officers of the Honved V.B., D.K., V.M., and the lieutenant of Croatian-Slavonia Gendarmerie V.K., led astray by Milan Privicevic, left the service of the army of the Monarchy under most suspicious circumstances and turned to Serbia; they have seen in the meanwhile most of their dreams unrealized and some of them, at any rate, are thinking of returning to the Fatherland they have betrayed.

The agitation introduced from Serbia into the middle schools of Croatia and Bosnia as unhappily too well known to need illustration; what is less known is that people who have been expelled from Croatian and Bosnian schools owing to grave breaches of discipline, are received in Serbia with open arms, and often even protected by the State and educated as enemies of the Monarchy. The Servian schools with their anti-Austrian staffs, and their large number of professors and teachers who are members of the Narodna Odbrana, are clearly establishments thoroughly adapted for training experts of this kind, a very notable case of this sort may be quoted here.

In March 1914, several pupils of the Training College of Pakrac (Croatia) were dismissed on account of a strike. They went to Serbia, where some of them immediately obtained situations as schoolmasters, while others were admitted to a college for teachers. One of those who had been thus dismissed, and who was connected with anti-Austrian circles, declared publicly that he and his people would give a proof, during the sojourn of the hereditary Archduke in Bosnia, that this province was Servian territory. It is, as we may add, highly significant that during the stay of the Archduke Franz Ferdinand in Bosnia, the Royal Servian Prefect of the district of Krajna gave to the three training college students, who were thus gravely implicated, Servian passports in which he falsely described them as Servian subjects, although he must have known that they were Croatians. With these passports, the three agitators were able to enter the Monarchy without being noticed, where, however, they were eventually recognized and arrested.

All this is not, by a long way, enough to give a complete representation of the "foreign" activity of the Narodna Odbrana.

The Imperial and Royal Government had been informed for a long time past by confidential reports that the Narodna Odbrana had made military preparations for the war which it desired to make against the Monarchy, inasmuch as it kept emissaries in Austria-Hungary, who, as soon as hostilities broke out, would attempt in the usual guerilla manner to destroy means of transport and equipment and stir up revolt or panic (see Appendix 7).

The criminal proceedings taken in 1913 by the District Court at Sarajevo against Jovo Jaglicic and his associates for espionage (Appendix 6) confirm this confidential information. As at the time of its foundation, the preparation for guerilla warfare still figures in the programmed of the Narodna Odbrana, to which must now be further added a complete system of espionage.

It is for this reason that the programmed of the Narodna Odbrana, described as "re-organized," is in reality an extended programmed which includes the preparation for a "war of extermination" against the Monarchy, and even its realization, and finally the unfurling of the "ancient red flag of the Narodna Odbrana."

Acts of terrorism must finally result from this atmosphere of hatred against the Monarchy, which is publicly and secretly provoked, and from an agitation, which considers itself free from all responsibility; in order to bring them about, all means are regarded as permissible in the struggle against Austria-Hungary, including even without any sense of shame common acts of murder. On the 8th June, 1912, a man named Lukas Jukic shot Von Cuvaj, the Royal Commissioner at Agram, with the result that the Councilor *(Banalrat)* Von Hervoic, who was seated in the same carriage was mortally wounded. Jukic, in his flight, shot a policeman who was pursuing him, and wounded two others.

From the subsequent public investigation it appeared that Jukic was saturated with the ideas and plans propagated by the Narodna Odbrana, and that although Jukic had for some time past been devoting himself to criminal schemes, these schemes were only matured after he had made an excursion to Belgrade, together with the Agram students on the 18th of April, 1912. At the noisy celebrations in honour of the visitors, Jukic had entered into relations with several people belonging to the circle of the Narodna Odbrana, with whom he had had political discussions. A few days afterwards he returned to Belgrade, and there received from a Servian major a bomb, and from a comrade the Browning pistol with which he carried out his crime.

In the opinion of experts, the bomb found at Agram was made in an arsenal for military purposes.

Jukic's attempt had not been forgotten, when on the 18th of August, 1913, Stephen Dojcic, who had returned from America, made an attempt on the life of the Royal Commissioner, Baron Skerleez, at Agram—an attempt which was the outcome of action organized by the Servians among the Southern Slavs living in America, and which was also the work of the "foreign" propaganda of the Narodna Odbrana and its confederates.

A pamphlet by the Servian, T. Dimitrijevic, printed in Chicago, and entitled "Natrag u staro ognjiste vase," with its unbridled attacks against His Imperial and Royal Apostolic Majesty, and its appeal to the Servians of the Monarchy with reference to their impending "deliverance," and urging them to migrate home to Serbia, demonstrates the fact that the propaganda carried out unchecked in America from Serbia, and that carried on from Serbia in the territory of the Monarchy, worked on parallel lines.

And again, scarcely a year later, Agram was the scene of a new outrage, this time unsuccessful. On the 20th of May, 1914, Jakob Schafer made an attempt at the Agram Theatre on the life of the Ban, Freiherr von Skerlecz, an attempt which was frustrated at the last moment by a police official. The subsequent investigation revealed the existence of a plot inspired by Rudolf Hercigonja. From the depositions of Hercigonja and his five accomplices, it is manifest that this crime also originated in Serbia.

Having taken part in an unsuccessful attempt to liberate Jukic, Hercigonja fled to Serbia (October 1912), where, together with his accomplice Marojan Jaksic, he consorted with the komitadjis and members of the Narodna Odbrana. As frequently happens when immature minds are excited by occupying themselves too early with political questions, the result of this corrupting company was here also disastrous. Hercigonja returned home impressed by the dogma learnt in Belgrade that the Southern Slav territories of Austria-Hungary must be separated from it and re-united to the Servian kingdom. He had further been persuaded by the teachings of the friends with whom he associated there, that this object should be pursued by means of attempts on the lives of persons holding high office and leading politicians of the Monarchy as the only means of obtaining this end.

This is the spirit in which Hercigonja influenced his friends at Agram and converted some of them to his ideas. Foremost among his plans was the carrying out of an attempt on the life of the heir to the throne, the Archduke Franz Ferdinand.

A few months before proceedings had been taken against Luka Aljinovic for treasonable agitation. In the course of these proceedings, three witnesses declared that Aljinovic had told him that in the year 1913 he had received at Belgrade 100 dinar from the Narodna Odbrana, and a similar sum from a secret association of students, for purposes of agitation, but especially to carry out an attempt on the life of the Archduke Franz Ferdinand.

It is clear how far the criminal agitation of the Narodna Odbrana and those who shared in its views, has of late been primarily directed against the person of the hereditary Archduke. From these facts, the conclusion may be drawn that the Narodna Odbrana, as well as the associations hostile to the monarchy in Serbia, which were grouped 'round it, recently decided that the hour had struck to translate theory into practice.

It is noteworthy, however, that the Narodna limits itself in this way to inciting, and where the incitement has fallen on fertile soil to providing means of material assistance for the realization of its plans, but that it has confided the only dangerous part of this propaganda of action to the youth of the Monarchy, which it has excited and corrupted, and which alone has to bear the burden of this miserable "heroism."

All the characteristics of this procedure are found in the history and origin of the profoundly regrettable outrage of the 28th of June (see Appendix 8).

Princip and Grabez are characteristic examples of young men who have been poisoned from their school days by the doctrines of the Narodna Odbrana.

At Belgrade, where he frequented the society of students imbued with these ideas, Princip busied himself with criminal plans against the Archduke Franz Ferdinand, against whom the hatred of the Servian element hostile to the Monarchy was particularly acute on the occasion of his tour in the annexed territories.

He was joined by Cabrinovic, who moved in the same circles, and whose shifting and radically revolutionary views, as he himself admits, as well as the influence of his surroundings in Belgrade and the reading of the Servian papers, inspired him with the same sense of hostility to the Monarchy, and brought him into the propaganda of action.

Thanks to the state of mind in which he already was, Grabez succumbed very quickly to this milieu, which he now entered.

But however far this plot may have prospered, and however determined the conspirators may have been to carry out the attempt, it would never have been elected, if people had not been found, as in the case of Jukic, to provide the accomplices with means of committing their crime. For, as Princip and Cabrinovic have expressly admitted, they lacked the necessary arms, as well as the money to purchase them.

It is interesting to see where the accomplices tried to procure their arms. Milan Pribicevic and Zivojin Dacic, the two principal men in the Narodna Odbrana, were the first accomplices thought of as a sure source of help in their need, doubtless because it had already become a tradition amongst those ready to commit crimes, that they could obtain instruments for murder from these representatives of the Narodna Odbrana. The accidental circumstance that these two men were not at Belgrade at the critical moment doubtless baulked this plan. However, Princip and Cabrinovic were not at a loss in finding other help, that of Milan Ciganovic, an ex-komitadji, and now a railway official at Belgrade, and at the same time an active member of the Narodna Odbrana, who, in 1909, first appeared as a pupil at the school *(Bandenschule)* at Cuprija (see Appendix 5). Princip and Cabrinonc were not deceived in their expectations, as they at once received the necessary help from Ciganovic.

The latter, and at his instigation, his friend Major Voja Tankosic, of the Royal Servian Army, also one of the leaders of the Narodna Odbrana, who has already been mentioned several times, and who, in 1908, was at the head of the school of armed bands at Cuprija (see Appendix 5), now appear as moving spirits and active furthered in the plot; the repulsive manner in which they approved as a matter of course, is significant of the moral qualities of the whole anti-Austrian movement. They had at first only one doubt, and that but a fleeting one, as to whether the three conspirators were really resolved to commit this act. This doubt, however, soon disappeared, thanks to their insidious counsels. Thenceforth they were prepared to give every assistance.

Tankosic produced four Browning pistols, ammunition and money for the journey; six hand-grenades from the Servian army supplies completed the equipment, of which the composition and origin recalls the case of Jukic. Anxious about the success of the attempt, Tankosic had the conspirators instructed in shooting, a task which Ciganovic carried out with a success which has since been fully proved. Tankosic and Ciganovic were further anxious to ensure secrecy for the plot by special means, which had not been bargained for by the assassins. They therefore supplied cyanide of potassium, telling the two culprits to commit suicide after the crime, a precaution which was to be specially advantageous to themselves, as secrecy would thus relieve them of the slight danger which they were incurring in the enterprise. Sure, death for the victims of their corruption, perfect security for themselves, this is the motto of the Narodna Odbrana, as was already known.

In order to render the execution of the crime possible, it was necessary that the bombs and arms should be secretly smuggled into Bosnia. There again Ciganovic gave all the assistance in his power;

he wrote out for the conspirators the exact route to be followed, and assured them of the collusion of the Servian Customs officials for getting them into Bosnia. The way in which this journey, described by Princip as "mysterious," was organized and carried out can leave no doubt but that this route was a secret one, prepared in advance, and already often used for the mysterious designs of the Narodna Odbrana. With an assurance and a certainty, which could only result from long habit, the frontier guards at Sabac and Loœnica lent their administrative organization for the purpose. The secret transport with its complicated system of ever-changing guides, who were summoned as if by magic, and who were always on the spot when wanted, was effected without a hitch. Without inquiring into the object of this strange journey of some immature students, the Servian authorities set this smooth machinery into motion at a word from the ex-komitadji and minor railway official, Ciganovic. However, they had no need to ask any questions, as from the instructions they had received, it was perfectly clear that a new "mission" of the Narodna Odbrana was being carried out. The sight of the arsenal of bombs and revolvers caused the exciseman Grbic merely to smile good-naturedly and approvingly sufficient proof of how accustomed they were on this "route" to find contraband of this nature.

The Royal Servian Government has taken a grave responsibility on their shoulders, in allowing all this to take place.

Though bound to cultivate neighborly relations with Austria-Hungary, they have allowed their press to disseminate hatred against the Monarchy; they have allowed associations established on their own territory under the leadership of high officers, of public officials, of professors and of judges, to carry on openly a campaign against the Monarchy, with the ultimate object of inciting its citizens to revolution; they have not prevented men devoid of all moral scruples, who share in the direction of its military and civil administration from poisoning the public conscience, so that in this struggle low murder appears as the best weapon.

APPENDIX 1.
OPINIONS OF THE SERBIAN PRESS.

(A) The "Politika," on the 18th August, 1910, on the occasion of the eightieth birthday of His Imperial and Royal Apostolic Majesty, published a large portrait of Bogdan Zerajic, who, two months earlier, had made a murderous attack on the Governor of Bosnia, Freiherr Von Varesanin. In the article dealing with this, the following observations were made: "Two months ago, on the 2nd of June (old style), on the opening day of the Diet of Bosnia and Herzegovina, a young Servian, the student Bogdan Zerajic, made an attempt in Sarajevo to kill the Governor of Bosnia and Herzegovina, General Marian Varesanin. Zerajic fired five shots at this renegade, who had assured his career by pouring out the blood of his brothers in the famous insurrection in Rakovica, but, owing to a remarkable accident, did not succeed in killing him. Whereon the brave and composed Zerajic fired the sixth and last bullet through his own head, and immediately fell dead. In Vienna, they knew very well that it was not the reading of Russian and revolutionary writings which had induced Zerajic to make his attempt, but that he acted thus as the noble scion of a race which wished to protest against foreign rule in this bloody way. Therefore, they sought to hush up the whole matter as quickly as possible, and contrary to their custom to avoid an affair, which would have, still more compromised the Austrian Government in Bosnia and Herzegovina. In Vienna, it was desired that every memory of Zerajic should be extinguished, and that no importance should be attached to his attempt; but just this fear of the dead Zerajic, and the prohibition against mentioning his name throughout Bosnia and Herzegovina, brought it about that his name is spoken among the people as something sacred to-day, on the 18th of August, perhaps more than ever.

'Today, we too light a candle at his grave and cry, "Honour to Zerajic!"'

To this is added a poem, the translation of which is as follows:

> "Bosnia lives and is not dead yet,
> In vain have you buried her corpse;
> still the chained victim spits fire,
> Nor is it yet time to sing the dirge.
> With devil's hand have scratched a grave for her
> But the living dead will not descend into the vault;
> Emperor, dost thou hear?
> In the flash of the revolver, the leaden bullets hiss about
> thy throne!
> These are not slaves; this is glorious freedom
> Which flashes from the bold hand of the oppressed!
> Why does this horrible Golgotha shudder?
> Peter drew the sword in Christ's defense,
> His hand fell, but out of the blood
> A thousand brave hands will rise;
> that shot was only the first herald
> of the glorious Easter after Golgotha's torments."

(B) On the 8th October, 1910. On the occasion of the anniversary of the annexation of Bosnia and Herzegovina, the "Politika": and the "Mali Journal," the last of which appeared with a black border, published articles in which they indulged in violent attacks against Austria-Hungary. Europe must convince herself that the Servian people still think always of the *"revanche"* The day of the *"revanche"* must come; for this the feverish exertions of Serbia to organize her military power as well as the feeling of the Servian people and their hatred of the neighboring kingdom were a guarantee.

On the same, occasion the "Samouprava" wrote on the 9th October, 1910, "Abuse and excesses are no fit means to express true patriotism; quiet, steady and honest work alone leads to the goal."

(C) On the 18th April, 1911, the "Politika" said: "Except for a few cynics, no one in Serbia would be glad to see Icing Peter proceeding to Vienna or Budapest. By the annexation of Bosnia and Herzegovina, the possibility of friendship between Serbia and Austria-Hungary was once for all destroyed. Every Servian feels that."

(D) The "Beogradske Novine" wrote on the 18th April. 1911: "Even in Government circles the projected journey of King Peter to the Emperor Francis Joseph is disapproved. The storm of indignation which has seized the whole of the Servian race on account of the King's proposed journey is entirely comprehensible."

(E) The "Mali Journal" of the 19th April, 1911, says: "A visit of King Peter to the ruler of Austria-Hungary would be an insult to all Serbs. By this visit, Serbia would forfeit the right to play the part of Piedmont. The interests of Serbia can never coincide with the interests of Austria."

(F) On the 23rd April, 1911, the "Politika," the "Mali Journal," the "Tribuna," the "Beogradske Novine," and the "Vecernje Novosti," commented on the projected visit of King Peter to the Court of Vienna: "Between Serbia and Austria, friendship can never exist. The projected visit of King Peter would, therefore, be for Serbia a 'shameful capitulation,' 'a humiliation of Serbia,' 'a solemn sanctioning of all the crimes and misdeeds that Austria-Hungary has committed against Serbia and the Servian people.'"

(G) On the 18th April, 1912, the "Trgovinski Glasnik" wrote in an article headed, "The decay of Austria":

"In Austria-Hungary decay prevails on all sides. What is now happening beyond the Danube and the Save is no longer a German, Magyar, Bohemian, or Croatian crisis, it is a universal Austrian crisis, a crisis of the dynasty itself. We Servians can observe such a development of affairs in Austria with satisfaction."

(H) The "Balkan," in an article entitled "The Borders of Albania," in attacking Austria-Hungary, expressed itself to this effect: "If Europe is too weak to call a halt to Austria-Hungary, Montenegro and Serbia will do it, saying to Austria, 'Halt! No further!' A war between Austria-Hungary and Serbia is inevitable. We have dismembered the Turkish Empire, we will dismember Austria too. We have finished one war; we are now facing a second."

(I) The "Vecernje Novosti," of the 22nd April, 1913, appeals to the Servian travelling public and to Servian traders to boycott the *Donau Dampfschiffahrts-Gesellschaft* (The Danube Steam Navigation Company). "No one should travel or consign goods by ships of this Austrian Company. All who do this should be punished with fines by a committee. The monies would fiow to the funds of the komitadjis which are to be applied for the purpose of the coming war with Austria."

(J) The "Tribuna" of the 26th May, 1913, on the occasion of the seizure of Ada Kaleh by Austria, writes: "The criminal black and yellow Austria has again carried out a piratical trick. It is a thief who, when he cannot steal a whole sack of gold, contents himself with one dinar."

(K) On the 10th June, 1913, on the occasion of the recurrence of the anniversary of the murderous attack on the Royal Commissary in Agram by the student Luka Jukic, the Servian newspapers published memorial articles. An article in the "Pragda" stated that: "It must grieve us to the bottom of our hearts that everyone has not acted like our Jukic. We have no longer a Jukic, but we have the hatred, we have the anger, we have to-day ten million Jukics. We are convinced that soon Jukic, through his prison window, will hear the last cannon shot of freedom."

(L) The "Mali Journal" of the 7th October, 1913, gives a leading place to an article in which Austria-Hungary is denied the right of existence, and the Slavonic peoples are invited to support the offensive campaign contemplated by Serbia.

(M) The "Piemont" writes on the commemoration day of the annexation: "Five years ago to-day an imperial decree extended the sovereignty of the Hapsburg sceptre over Bosnia and Herzegovina. The

Servian people will feel for decades yet the grief which was that day inflicted on them. Shamed and shattered, the Servian people groaned in despair. The people vow to take vengeance in attaining freedom by an heroic step. This day has aroused the energy which had already sunk to sleep, and soon the refreshed hero will strive for freedom. To-day when Servian graves adorn the ancient Servian territories, when the Servian cavalry has trod the battlefields of Macedonia and old Serbia the Servian people having ended their task in the South turn to the other side, whence the groans and tears of the Servian brother are heard, and where the gallows has its home. The Servian soldiers who to-day in Dusan's kingdom fight those Albanians who were provoked against us by the state which took Bosnia and Herzegovina from us, vowed to march against the 'second Turkey' even as with God's help they had marched against the Balkan Turkey. Then make this vow and hope that the day of revenge is drawing near. One Turkey vanished. The good Servian God will grant that the 'second Turkey' will vanish too."

(N) The "Mali Journal" of the 4th November, 1913, writes: "Every effort towards a *rapprochement* with Austria-Hungary is equivalent to a betrayal of the Servian people. Serbia must understand the facts and always hold before her eyes that she has in Austria-Hungary her most dangerous enemy, and that it must be the sacred obligation of every Servian Government to fight this enemy."

(O) On the 14th January, 1914, the "Pragda" said: "Our new year's wishes are first of all for our still unfreed brothers sighing under a foreign yoke. Let the Servians endure; after Kosovo came Kumanovo, and our victorious career is not yet ended."

(P) The "Novosti" of the 18th January, 1914, published a picture of "The Blessing of the Water in Bosnia" with the following text: "Even in places which lie under the foreign yoke, the Servians preserve their customs against the day when in glorious joy the day of freedom dawns."

(Q) The "Zastava" confesses in January 1914: "Serbia incites the Austro-Hungarian Servians to revolution."

(R) The "Mali Journal" of the 9th March, 1914, writes: "Serbia can ever forget Franz Ferdinand's saber-rattling in the Skutari affair."

(S) On the 4th April, 1914, the "Zastava" writes: "The Austrian statesmen who only conduct a policy of hatred, a bureaucratic policy, not a policy inspired by broad vision, are themselves preparing the ruin of their State."

(T) The "Pravda" of the 8th April, 1914, says: "Austria has now lost her right to exist."

(U) In their Easter numbers (April 1914) all the Servian newspapers expressed the hope that soon their unfreed, oppressed brothers under the yoke would celebrate a joyous resurrection.

(V) In the "Tribune" of the 23rd April, 1914, it is stated that: "The pacifists have invented a new catchword, that of the 'patriotism of Europe.' This programmed can only be realized, however, when Austria is partitioned."

(W) The "Mali Journal" of the 12th May, 1914, writes: "What are called crimes in private life are called, in Austria, politics. History knows, a monster, and that monster is called Austria."

APPENDIX 2.

Extract from the "Narodna Odbrana, an Organ Published by the Central Committee of the Narodna Odbrana Society" (Narodna Odbrana Izdanje Stredisnog Odbora Narodne Odbrane. Beograd, 1911. "Nova Stamparija" Davidovic, Decanska Ulica Br. 14, Ljub. Davidovica).

In a short introduction, it is first of all remarked that this pamphlet "does not completely or exhaustively reproduce the whole work of the Narodna Odbrana because, for many reasons, it is neither permissible nor possible to do this."

The document is divided into three parts of which the first consists of fourteen chapters and is in the nature of a programmed, while the second contains a report of the activities of the society, and in the third examples are given for the organization of similar societies abroad.

In the first chapter, "Origin and Activity of the First Narodna Odbrana," it is remarked that the society was founded as a consequence of the popular movement arising in Serbia on the annexation of Bosnia and Herzegovina and that it had the following objects:

(1) Raising, inspiring, and strengthening the sentiment of nationality.
(2) Registration and enlistment of volunteers.
(3) Formation of volunteer units and their preparation for armed action.
(4) Collection of voluntary contributions, including money and other things necessary for the realization of its task.
(5) Organization, equipment, and training of a special revolutionary band (Komitee), destined for special and independent military action.
(6) Development of activity for the defense of the Servian people in all other directions. In this connection, it is remarked that owing to the recognition of the annexation by the Great Powers an end had been made to all this work of the Society on which, while retaining its existing constitution, the Society had taken measures to reorganize its programmed and to undertake new work, so that, on the recurrence of a similar occasion, "the old red War Flag of the Narodna Odbrana would again be unfurled."

At the beginning of the second chapter, "The New Narodna Odbrana of To-day," it is stated that "at the time of the annexation, experience had shown that Serbia was not ready for the struggle which circumstances imposed upon her, and that this struggle, which Serbia must take up, is much more serious and more difficult than it was thought to be; the annexation was only one of the blows which the enemies of Serbia have aimed at this land, many blows have preceded it, and many will follow it. Work and preparation are necessary so that a new attack may not find Serbia equally unprepared." The object assigned to the work to be done by people of every class is stated to be "the preparation of the people for war in all forms of national work, corresponding to the requirements of the present day," and the means suggested to effect this object are "strengthening of the national consciousness, bodily exercises, increase of material and bodily well-being, cultural improvement, &tc.... So far as individuals and societies can and should assist the State in these spheres."

The third chapter, "The Three Principal Tasks," begins with a hint that the annexation has taught that national consciousness in Serbia is not so strong as it should be in a country which, as a small fraction of three millions, forms a hope of support for seven millions of the oppressed Servian people. The first task of the society therefore consists in strengthening the national consciousness. The second task is the cultivation of bodily exercises, the third the proper utilization of these activities learned in the field of sport.

In the fourth chapter, "Musketry," prominence is given to the value of good training in musketry, especially having regard to the circumstances of Serbia, where the military training only lasts six months. These observations conclude with the sentence: "A new blow, like that of the annexation, must be met by a new Serbia, in which every Servian,' from child to greybeard, is a rifleman.""

The fifth chapter, which treats of "The Relations of the Narodna Odbrana to the Sokol Societies," begins with a social and political excursus as to the conditions on which the powers of States depend. In this connection, the fall of Turkey is referred to, and it is said: "The old Turks of the South gradually disappear and only a part of our people suffers under their rule. But new Turks come from the North. More fearful and dangerous than the old; stronger in civilization and more advanced economically, our northern enemies come against us. They want to take our freedom and our language from us and to crush us. We can already feel the presages of the struggle which approaches in that quarter. The Servian people are faced by the question 'to be or not to be?'"

"What Is the Object of the Lectures?" is the title of the seventh chapter, the principal contents of which are covered by the following sentences: "The Narodna Odbrana instituted lectures which were largely propaganda lectures. The programmed of our new work was developed. Every lecture referred to the annexation, the work of the old Narodna Odbrana and the task of the new. The lectures will never cease to be propaganda lectures but they will develop special branches more and more and concern themselves with all questions of our social and national life."

In the eighth chapter, "Women's Activities in the Narodna Odbrana," the ninth, "Detail and Lesser Work," and the tenth, "Renaissance of the Society," the preparation and deepening of the society's work and the necessity of a regeneration of the individual, the nation, and the state are treated in reference to the tasks of the Narodna Odbrana.

The introduction to the eleventh chapter, "New Obilice and Singjelice,"* runs as follows:

> * Milos Obilice (or Kobilic) crept—according to Servian tradition—into the Turkish Camp, after the battle on the Amselveld, and there murdered the Sultan Murad (Von Kallay "Geschichte Der Serben," Vol. I). Stephan Singjelic, Prince of Resara, played a part during the Servian Revolution, 1807–1810. In 1809, Singjelic defended the redoubt of Tschagar against the Turks, and is said to hare blown himself into the air, with some of his followers and many Turks, when outnumbered. (Von Kallay; "Die Geschichte des serbischen Aufstandes.")

"It is an error to assert that Kosovo is past and gone. We find ourselves in the midst of Kosovo. Our Kosovo of to-day is the gloom and ignorance in which our people live. The other causes of the new Kosovo live on the frontiers to the North and West: the Germans, Austrians, and 'Schwabas,' with their onward pressure against 'our Servian and Slavonic South.' In conjunction with the reference, too the heroic deeds of Obilice and Singjelice, the necessity of sacrifice in the service of the nation is alluded to, and it is declared that 'national work is interwoven with sacrifice, particularly in Turkey and in Austria, where such workers are persecuted by the authorities and dragged to prison and the gallows.' For this struggle, also, against gloom and ignorance there is need of such heroes. The Narodna Odbrana does not doubt that in the fight with gun and cannon against the 'Schwabas' and the other enemies with whom we stand face to face. Our people will provide a succession of heroes. However, the Narodna Odbrana is not content with this, for it regards the so-called peaceful present-day conditions as war, and demands heroes too for this struggle of to-day which we are carving on in Serbia and beyond the frontier."

The twelfth chapter treats of "Union with Our Brothers and Friends," and its principal contents are concentrated in the following sentences: "The maintenance of union with our brothers near and far across the frontier, and our other friends in the world, is one of the chief tasks of the Narodna Odbrana. In using, the word 'people' the Narodna Odbrana means our whole people, not only those in Serbia. It hopes that the work done by it in Serbia will spur the brothers outside Serbia to take a more energetic share in the work of private initiative, so that the new present-day movement for the creation of a powerful Servian Narodna Odbrana will go forward in unison in all Servian territories."

The thirteenth chapter, which is headed "Two Important Tasks," proceeds as follows: "As we take up the standpoint that the annexation of Bosnia and Herzegovina has completely brought into the light of day the pressure against our countries from the North, the Narodna Odbrana proclaims to the people that Austria is our first and greatest enemy." This work (that is to say, to depict Austria to the Servian people as their greatest enemy) is regarded by the society, according to the following expressions of opinion, as a healthy and necessary task, in fact, as its principal obligation. For the pamphlet goes on as follows: "Just as once the Turks attacked us from the south, so Austria attacks us to-day from the north. If the Narodna Odbrana preaches the necessity of fighting Austria, she preaches a sacred truth of our national position."

The hatred against Austria brought about by this propaganda is, of course, not the aim but the natural consequence of this work, the object of which is independence and freedom. If on this account hatred of Austria germinates, it is Austria who sows it by her advance, which conduct "makes obligatory a war of extermination against Austria."

After some praise of the modern conception of nationalism the remark is made that in speaking of "freedom and unity," too much is mere talk. The people must be told that "For the sake of bread and room, for the sake of the fundamental essentials of culture and trade, the freeing of the conquered Servian territories and their union with Serbia is necessary to gentlemen, tradesmen and peasants alike." Perceiving this the people will tackle the national work with greater self-sacrifice. Our people must be told that the freedom of Bosnia is necessary for her, not only out of pity for the brothers suffering there, but also for the sake of trade and the connection with the sea.

The "two tasks" of the Narodna Odbrana are then again brought together in the following concluding sentence: "In addition to the task of explaining to the people the danger threatening it from Austria, the Narodna Odbrana has the important duty, while preserving intact the sacred national memories, of giving to the people this new, wholesome and, in its consequences, mighty conception of nationalism and of work in the cause of freedom and union."

The fourteenth and final chapter begins with an appeal to the Government and people of Serbia to prepare themselves in all ways for the struggle "which the annexation has foreshadowed." Hereon the activities of the Narodna Odbrana are again recapitulated in the following sentences: "While the Narodna Odbrana works in conformity with the times according to the altered conditions, it also maintains all the connections made at the time of the annexation; today therefore it is the same as it was at the time of the annexation. To-day, too, it is Odbrana (defense); to-day, too, Narodna (of the people); to-day, too, it gathers under its standard the citizens of Serbia as it gathered them at the time of the annexation. Then the cry was for war, now the cry is for work. Then meetings demonstrations, voluntary clubs (Komitees), weapons and bombs were asked for; to-day steady, fanatical, tireless work and again work is required to fulfill the tasks and duties to which we have drawn attention by way of present preparation for the fight with gun and cannon which will come."

The pamphlet and the annual report contain the following information as to the organization of the Narodna Odbrana: "A Central Committee at Belgrade directs all proceedings of the Narodna Odbrana. All other committees of the Narodna Odbrana are subject to this. The Central Committee is divided into four sections: for cultural work, for bodily training, for financial policy, and for foreign affairs. District Committees, with their centre at the seat of the offices of the District Government, conduct the affairs of the Society in the corresponding districts. Every District Committee divides itself into sections for culture (the President being the Chairman of the local branch of the "Culture League"), for bodily training (the President being a local member of the Riflemen's, Sokol, Sportsmen's, and Horsemen's clubs) and for financial affairs; some District Committees have also a section for Foreign Affairs."

Divisional Committees located at the seat of the local authorities conduct the affairs of the Society in the various divisions.

Local Committees conduct the Society's affairs in the various towns and villages.

Confidential men are located in those places in the interior of the country where the constitution of a Committee is not necessary.

Societies "which work in close connection with the organization of the Narodna Odbrana" and are supported by the latter in every respect are the following: The Riflemen's Association with 762 societies, the Sokol Association "Dusan the Strong" with 2,500 members, the Olympic Club, the Horsemen's Society "Prince Michael," the Sportsmen's Association, and the Culture League.

All these societies are organized on similar lines to those of the Narodna Odbrana and use their premises, including clubhouses, libraries, &tc. Distinguished members of these societies are chairmen of sections in the Committees of the Narodna Odbrana.

No. 13.
Note communicated by Russian Ambassador
M. Sazonof to Russian Charg'e d' Affaires, Vienna.
July 25, 1914.

"The communication made by Austria-Hungary to the Powers the day after the presentation of the ultimatum at Belgrade leaves a period to the Powers which is quite insufficient to enable them to take any steps which might help to smooth away the difficulties that have arisen.

"In order to prevent the consequences, equally incalculable and fatal to all the powers, which may result from the course of action followed by the Austro-Hungarian Government, it seems to us to be above all essential, that the period allowed for the Serbian reply should be extended. Austria-Hungary, having declared her readiness to inform the Powers of the results of the enquiry upon which the Imperial and Royal Government base their accusations, should equally allow them sufficient time to study them.

"In this case, if the powers were convinced that certain of Austria demands were well founded, they would be in a position to offer advice to the Serbian Government.

"A refusal to prolong the term of the ultimatum would render nugatory the proposals made by the Austro-Hungary Government to the Powers, and would be in contradiction to the very bases of international relations.

"Prince Kudachef is instructed to communicate the above to the cabinet of Vienna."

M. Sazonof hopes that His Britannic Majesty's Government will adhere to the point of view set forth, and he trusts that Sir Edward Grey will see his way to furnish similar instructions to the British Ambassador at Vienna.

No. 14.
Sir Edward Grey to Sir F. Bertie, British Ambassador at Paris, and to Sir G. Buchanan, British Ambassador at St. Petersburg.
July 25, 1914.
(Telegraphic)

Austrian Ambassador has been authorized to explain to me that the step taken at Belgrade was not an ultimatum, but a de'marche with a time limit, and that if the Austrian demands were not complied with within a the time limit the Austro–Hungarian Government would break off diplomatic relations and begin military preparations, not operations.

In case Austro-Hungarian Government has not given the same information at Paris and St. Petersburg, you should inform Minister of Foreign affairs as soon as possible; it makes the immediate situation rather less acute.

No. 3.
M. Davignon, Belgian Minister for Foreign Affairs, to the Belgian Ministers at Rome, The Hague, and Luxemburg.
Brussels
July 25, 1914.

Sir,

I have addressed an undated circular note, a copy of which is enclosed, to the Belgian representatives accredited to the Powers guaranteeing the independence and neutrality of Belgium.

Should the danger of a war between France and Germany become imminent, this circular note will be communicated to the Governments of the guaranteeing Powers, in order to inform them of our fixed determination to fulfill those international obligations that are imposed upon us by the treaties of 1839.

The communications in question would only be made upon telegraphic instructions from me. If circumstances lead me to issue such instructions, I shall request you also, by telegram, to notify the Government to which you are accredited of the step we have taken, and to communicate to them a copy of the enclosed circular note for their information, and without any request that they should take note thereof.

My telegram will inform you of the date to be given to the circular note; which you should be careful to fill in on the copy which you hand to the Minister for Foreign Affairs.

It is unnecessary to point out that this dispatch and its enclosure should be treated as strictly confidential until the receipt of fresh instructions from me.

No. 15.
Sir F. Bertie, British Ambassador at Paris, to Sir Edward Grey.
(Received July 25)
Paris, France
July 25, 1914.
(Telegraphic)

I learned from the acting Political Director that the French Government has not received the explanation from the Austrian Government contained in your telegram of today.[5] They have, however, through the Serbian Minister here, given similar advice to Serbia as was contained in your telegram to Belgrade of yesterday.[6]

---

[5] See telegram No. 14.
[6] See telegram No. 12.

No. 4.
M. Michotte de Welle, Belgian Minister at Belgrade, to M. Davignon, Belgian Minister for Foreign Affairs.
Belgrade
July 25, 1914.

Sir,

I have the honour to transmit to you herewith the text of the reply returned by the Servian Government to the Austro-Hungarian note of the 10 (23) July.

No. 16.
Sir F. Bertie, British Ambassador at Paris, to Sir Edward Grey.
(Received July 25)
Paris, France
July 25, 1914.
(Telegraphic)

Acting Minister for Foreign affairs has no suggestion to make except that moderating advice might be given to Vienna as well as Belgrade. He hopes that the Serbian government's answer to the Austrian ultimatum will sufficiently favorable to obviate extreme measures being taken by the Austrian Government. He says, however, that there would be a revolution in Serbia if she were to accept the Austrian demands in their entirely.3

No. 17.
Sir G. Buchanan, British Ambassador at St. Petersburg, to Sir Edward Grey,
St. Petersburg
July 25, 1914.
(Telegraphic)

I saw the Minister for Foreign Affairs this morning and communicated to his Excellency the substance of your telegram of today to Paris[7] and this afternoon I discussed with him the communication which the French Ambassador suggested should be made to the Serbian Government, as recorded in your telegram of yesterday to Belgrade.[8]

The Minister for Foreign Affairs said, as regards the former, that the explanations of the Austrian Ambassador did not quite correspond with the information which had reached him from German quarters. As regards the latter both his Excellency and the French Ambassador agree that it is too late to make such a communication, as the time limit expires this evening. The minister for Foreign Affairs said that Serbia was quite ready to do as you had suggested and to punish those who proved to be guilty, but that no independent state could be expected to accept the political demands which had been put forward. The minister for Foreign Affairs thought, from a conversation which he had with the Serbian Minister yesterday, that in the event of the Austrians attacking Serbia, the Serbian Government would abandon Belgrade, and withdraw their forces into the interior, while they would at the same time appeal to the Powers to help them. His Excellency was in favor of their making this appeal. He would like to see the question placed on an international footing, as the obligation taken by Serbia

---

[7] See No. 14.
[8] See No. 12.

in 1908, to which reference is made in the Austrian ultimatum, were given not to Austria, but to the powers.

If Serbia should appeal to the Powers, Russia would be quite ready to stand aside and leave the question in the hands of England, France, Germany, and Italy. It was possible, in his opinion that Serbia might propose to submit the question to arbitration.

On my expressing the earnest hope that Russia would not precipitate war by mobilizing until you had time to use your influence in favor of peace, his Excellency assured me that Russia had no aggressive intentions, and she would take no action until it was forced upon her. Austria's action was in reality directed against Russia. She aimed at overthrowing the present *status quo* in the Balkans, and establishing her own hegemony there. He did not believe Germany really wanted war, but her attitude was decided by ours. If we took our stand firmly with France and Russia there would be no war. If we failed them now, rivers of blood would flow, and we would in the end be dragged into war.

I said that England could play the role of mediator at Berlin and Vienna to better purpose as friend who, if her counsels of moderation were disregarded, might one day be converted into an ally, than if she were to declare herself Russia's ally at once. His Excellency said unfortunately Germany was convinced that she could count upon our neutrality.

I said all I could to impress prudence on the Minister for Foreign affairs, and warned him that if Russia mobilized, Germany would not be content with mere mobilization, or give Russia time to carryout hers, but would declare war at once. His Excellency replied that Russia could not allow Austria to crush Serbia and become the predominate Power in the Balkans, and if she feels secure of the support of France, she will face all the risks of war. He assured me once more that he did not wish to precipitate a conflict, but that unless Germany could restrain Austria I could regard the situation as desperate.

This telegram is saying that Russia is buying time to completely mobilize and get her military ready to attack both Austria and Germany, and that if Austria does not stop itself from seeking justice, she will be at war with France. Russia is also saying that unless Austria stops, Germany will be at fault for the current crisis getting out of hand and of general war in Europe.

No. 18.
Sir H. Humbold, British charg`e d' Affaires at Berlin, to Sir Edward Grey.
Berlin
July 25, 1914.
(Telegraphic)

Your telegram of the 24th July[9] acted on. Secretary of State says that on receipt of a telegram at 10 this morning from German Ambassador at London, he immediately instructed German Ambassador at Vienna to pass on to Austrian Minister for Foreign Affairs your suggestion for an extension of the time limit, and to speak to his Excellency about it. Unfortunately it appeared from the press that Count Berchtold[10] is at Ischl, and Secretary of State thought that in these circumstances there would be a delay and difficulty in getting the time limit extended. Secretary of State said that he did not know what Austria-Hungary had ready on the spot, but he admitted quite freely that Austro-Hungarian Government wished to give Serbia a lesson and that meant military action. He also admitted that Serbian Government could not swallow certain of the Austro-Hungarian demands.

Secretary of State said that a reassuring feature of the situation was that Count Berchtold had sent for Russian representative at Vienna and told him that Austria-Hungary had no intention of seizing

---

[9] See No. 11.
[10] Austro-Hungarian Minister for Foreign Affairs.

Serbian territory. This step should, in his opinion, exercise a calming influence in St. Petersburg. I asked whether it was not to be feared that taking military action against Serbia, Austria would dangerously excite public opinion in Russia. He said he thought not. He remained of the opinion that the crisis could be localized. I said that telegrams from Russia in this mornings papers did not look very reassuring, but he maintained his optimistic view with regard to Russia. He said that he had given the Russian Government to understand that the last thing Germany wanted was a general war, and he would do all in his power to prevent such a calamity. If the relations between Austria and Russia became threatening, he was quite ready to fall in with your suggestion as to the Four Powers working in favor of moderation at Vienna and St. Petersburg.

Secretary of State confessed privately that he thought the note left much to desire as a diplomatic document. He repeated very earnestly that, though he had been accused of knowing all about the contents of that note, he had in fact no such knowledge.

No. 19.
Sir R. Rodd, British Ambassador at Rome, Italy, to Sir Edward Grey.
Rome, Italy
July 25, 1914.
(Telegraphic)

I saw the Secretary General this morning and found that he knew of the suggestion that France, Italy, Germany, and ourselves should work at Vienna and St. Petersburg in favor of moderation, if the relations between Austria and Serbia become menacing.

In his opinion, Austria will only be restrained by the unconditional acceptance by the Serbian Government of her note. There is reliable information that Austria intends to seize the Salonica Railway.

No. 20.
Sir M. De Bunsen, British Ambassador at Vienna, to Sir Edward Grey.
Vienna, Austria
July 25, 1914.
(Telegraphic)

Language of the press this morning leaves the impression that the surrender of Serbia is neither expected nor really desired. It is officially announced that the legation failing unconditional acceptance of the note at 6 P.M. today.

Minister of Foreign Affairs goes to Ischl today to communicate personally to the Emperor Serbian reply when it comes.

No. 21.
Mr. Crackanthrope, British Charge' D' Affaires at Belgrade, to Sir Edward Grey.
Belgrade
July 25, 1914.
(Telegraphic)

The Council is now drawing up their reply to the Austrian note. I'm informed by the Under Secretary of the State for foreign affaires that it will be most conciliatory and will meet the Austrian demands in as large a measure as is possible.

The following is a brief summary of the projected reply:

The Serbian Government consents to the publication of a declaration in the "Official Gazette." The ten points are accepted with reservation. The Serbian Government declares itself ready to agree to a mix commission of inquiry so long as the appointment of the commission can be shown to be in accordance with international usage. They consent to dismiss and prosecute those officers who can be clearly proven to be guilty, and they have already arrested the officer referred to in the Austrian note. They are ready to suppress the Narodna Odbrana.

The Serbian Government consider that, unless the Austrian Government want war at any cost, they cannot but be content with the full satisfaction offered in the Serbian reply.

Telegram of the Imperial Ambassador at St. Petersburg, to the Chancellor
on July 25th, 1914.

Message to H.M. from General von Chelius (German honorary aide de camp to the Czar).

The maneuvers of the troops in the Krasnoe camp were suddenly interrupted and the regiments returned to their garrisons at once. The maneuvers have been cancelled. The military pupils were raised to-day to the rank of officers instead of next fall. At headquarters there obtains great excitement over the procedure of Austria. I have the impression that complete preparations for mobilization against Austria are being made.

No. 22.
Mr. Crackanthrope, British Charge' D' Affaires at Belgrade, to Sir Edward Grey.
Belgrade
July 25, 1914.
(Telegraphic)

I have seen the new French Minister, who has just arrived from Constantinople, and my Russian colleague, and informed them of your views.

They have not yet received instruction from their governments, and in view of this and of the proposed conciliatory terms of the Serbian reply, I have up to now abstained from offering advice to the Serbian government.

I think it is highly possible that the Russian Government has urged the utmost moderation on the Serbian Government.

The French and Russian envoys would not have heard anything just yet because the French President is not back from meeting Nicholas II, and their meeting was deferred to what Austria was demanding in their note to Serbia. Not matter what the note said, Russia and France were going to tell Serbia that their reply was to be very vague and open ended as to what the Austrian government wanted.

No. 39.
Reply of Serbian Government to the Austro-Hungarian Note.
Belgrade
July 25, 1914.
The Serbian Answer
Presented at Vienna,
July 25, 1914.
(With Austria's commentaries [in italics].)

The Royal Government has received the communication of the Imperial and Royal Government of the 23rd inst and is convinced that its reply will dissipate any misunderstanding, which threatens to destroy the friendly and neighborly relations between the Austrian monarchy and the kingdom of Serbia. The Royal Government is conscious that nowhere there have been renewed protests against the great neighborly monarchy like those which at one time were expressed in the Skuptchina, as well as in the declaration and actions of the responsible representatives of the state at that time, and which were terminated by the Serbian declaration of March 31st, 1909; furthermore that since that time neither the different corporations of the kingdom, nor the officials have made an attempt to alter the political and judicial condition created in Bosnia and the Herzegovina. The Royal Government states that the I. and R. Government has made no protestation in this sense excepting in the case of a textbook, in regard to which the I. and R. Government has received an entirely satisfactory explanation. Serbia has given during the time of the Balkan crisis in numerous cases evidence of her pacific and moderate policy, and it is only owing to Serbia and the sacrifices, which she has brought in the interest of the peace of Europe that this peace has been preserved.

The Royal Serbian Government limits itself to establishing that since the declaration of March 31st, 1909, there has been no attempt on the part of the Serbian Government to alter the position of Bosnia and the Herzegovinian.

With this, she deliberately shifts the foundation of our note, as we have not insisted that she and her officials have undertaken anything official in this direction. Our gravamen is that in spite of the obligation assumed in the cited note, she has omitted to suppress the movement directed against the territorial integrity of the monarchy.

Her obligation consisted in charging her attitude and the entire direction of her policies, and in entering into friendly and neighborly relations with the Austro-Hungarian monarchy, and not only not to interfere with the possession of Bosnia.

The Royal Government cannot be made responsible for expressions of a private character, as for instance newspaper articles and the peaceable work of societies, expressions which are of very common appearance in other countries, and which ordinarily are not under the control of the state. This, all the less, as the Royal Government has shown great courtesy in the solution of a whole series of questions which have arisen between Serbia and Austria-Hungary, whereby it has succeeded to solve the greater number thereof, in favor of the progress of both countries.

The assertion of the Royal Serbian Government that the expressions of the press and the activity of Serbian associations possess a private character and thus escape governmental control, stands in full contrast with the institutions of modern states and even the most liberal of press and society laws, which nearly everywhere subject the press and the societies to a certain control of the state. This is also provided for by the Serbian institutions. The rebuke against the Serbian Government consists in the fact that it has totally omitted to supervise its press and its societies, in so far as it knew their direction to be hostile to the monarchy.

The Royal Government was therefore painfully surprised by the assertions that citizens of Serbia had participated in the preparations of the outrage in Sarajevo. The Government expected to be invited to co-operate in the investigation of the crime, and it was ready, in order to prove its complete correctness, to proceed against all persons in regard to whom it would receive information.

This assertion is incorrect. The Serbian Government was accurately informed about the suspicion resting upon quite definite personalities and not only in the position, but also obliged by its own laws to institute investigations spontaneously. The Serbian Government has done nothing in this direction.

According to the wishes of the I. and R. Government, the Royal Government is prepared to surrender to the court, without regard to position and rank, every Serbian citizen for whose participation in the crime of Sarajevo it should have received proof. It binds itself particularly on the first page of the official organ of the 26th of July to publish the following enunciation:

"The Royal Serbian Government condemns every propaganda which should be directed against Austria-Hungary, *i.e.,* 'the entirety of such activities as aim towards the separation of certain territories from the Austro-Hungarian monarchy,' and it regrets sincerely the lamentable consequences of these criminal machinations."

The Austrian demand reads:

> *"The Royal Serbian Government condemns the propaganda against Austria-Hungary..."*

Tile alteration of the declaration as demanded by us, which has been made by the Royal Serbian Government, is meant to imply that a propaganda directed against Austria-Hungary does not exist, and that it is not aware of such. This formula is insincere, and the Serbian Government reserves itself the subterfuge for later occasions that it had not disavowed by this declaration the existing propaganda, nor recognized the same as hostile to the monarchy, whence it could deduce further that it is not obliged to suppress in the future a propaganda similar to the present one.

The Royal Government regrets that according to a communication of the I. and R. Government certain Serbian officers and functionaries have participated in the propaganda just referred to, and that these have therefore endangered the amicable relations for the observation of which the Royal Government had solemnly obliged itself through the declaration of March 31st, 1909. The Government...identical with the demanded text.

The formula as demanded by Austria reads:

> *"The Royal Government regrets that Serbian officers and functionaries...have participated..."*

Also with this formula and the further addition "according to the declaration of the I. and R. Government," the Serbian Government pursues the object, already indicated above, to preserve a free hand for the future.

The Royal Government binds itself further:

1. During the next regular meeting of the Skuptchina to embody in the press laws a clause, to wit, that the incitement to hatred of, and contempt for, the monarchy is to be most severely punished, as well as every publication whose general tendency is directed against the territorial integrity of Austria-Hungary. It binds itself in view of the coming revision of the constitution to embody an amendment into Art. 22 of the constitutional law which permits the confiscation of such publications as is at present impossible according to the clear definition of Art. 22 of the constitution.

Austria had demanded:

1. *"To suppress every publication which incites to hatred and contempt for the monarchy, and whose tendency is directed against the territorial integrity of the monarchy."*

    We wanted to bring about the obligation for Serbia to take care that such attacks of the press would cease in the future. Instead, Serbia offers to pass certain laws, which are meant as means towards this end, viz.:

    (a) *A law according to which the expressions of the press hostile to the Monarchy can be individually punished, a matter which is immaterial to us, all the more so, as the individual prosecution of press intrigues is very rarely possible and as, with a lax enforcement of such laws, the few cases of this nature would not be punished. The proposition, therefore, does not meet our demand in any way, and it offers not the least guarantee for the desired success.*

    (b) *An amendment to Art. 22 of the constitution, which would permit confiscation, a proposal which does not satisfy us, as the existence of such a law in Serbia is of no use to us. For we want the obligation of the Government to enforce it and that has not been promised us.*

    These proposals are therefore entirely unsatisfactory and evasive as we are not told within what time these laws will be passed, and as in the event of the not passing of these laws by the Skuptchina everything would remain as it is, excepting the event of a possible resignation of the Government.

2. The Government possesses no proofs and the note of the I. and R. Government does not submit them that the society Narodna Odbrana and other similar societies have committed, up to the present, any criminal actions of this manner through any one of their members.

Notwithstanding this, the Royal Government will accept the demand of the I. and R. Government and dissolve the society Narodna Odbrana, as well as every society which should act against Austria-Hungary.

The propaganda of the Narodna Odbrana and affiliated societies hostile to the monarchy; fills the entire public life of Serbia; it is therefore an entirely inacceptable reserve if the Serbian Government asserts that it knows nothing about it. Aside from this, our demand is not completely fulfilled, as we have asked besides:

"To confiscate the means of propaganda of these societies to prevent the reformation of the dissolved societies under another name and in another form."

In these two directions the Belgrade Cabinet is perfectly silent, so that through this semi-concession there is offered us no guarantee for putting an end to the agitation of the associations hostile to the Monarchy, especially the Narodna Odbrana.

3. The Royal Serbian Government binds itself without delay to eliminate from the public instruction in Serbia anything which might further the propaganda directed against Austria-Hungary provided the I. and R. Government furnishes actual proofs.

Also in this case the Serbian Government first demands proofs for a propaganda hostile to the Monarchy in the public instruction of Serbia while it must know that the textbooks introduced in the Serbian schools contain objectionable matter in this direction and that a large portion of the teachers are in the camp of the Narodna Odbrana and affiliated societies. Furthermore the Serbian Government has not fulfilled a part of our demands, as we have requested, as it omitted in its text the addition desired by us: "...as far as the body of instructors is concerned, as well as the means of instruction," a sentence which shows clearly where the propaganda hostile to the Monarchy is to be found in the Serbian schools.

4. The Royal Government is also ready to dismiss those officers and officials from the military and civil services in regard to whom it has been proved by judicial investigation that they have been guilty of actions against the territorial integrity of the Monarchy: It expects that the I. and R. Government communicate to it for the purpose of starting the investigation the names of these officers and officials, and the facts with which they have been charged.

By promising the dismissal from the military and civil services of those officers and officials who are found guilty by judicial procedure, the Serbian Government limits its assent to those cases, in which these persons have been charged with a crime according to the statutory code. As, however, we demand the removal of such officers and officials as indulge in a propaganda hostile to the Monarchy, which is generally not punishable in Serbia, our demands have not been fulfilled in this point.

5. The Royal Government confesses that it is not clear about the sense and the scope of that demand of the I. and R. Government which concerns the obligation on the part of the Royal Serbian Government to permit the co-operation of officials of the I. and R. Government on Serbian territory, but it declares that it is willing to accept every co-operation which does not run counter to international law and criminal law, as well as to the friendly and neighborly relations.

The international law, as well as the criminal law, has nothing to do with this question; it is purely a matter of the nature of state police which is to be solved by way of a special agreement. The reserved attitude of Serbia is therefore incomprehensible and on account of its vague general form it would lead to unbridgeable difficulties.

6. The Royal Government considers it its duty as a matter of course to begin an investigation against all those persons who have participated in the outrage of June 28th and who are in its terri-

tory. As far as the co-operation in this investigation of specially delegated officials of the T. and R. Government is concerned, this cannot he accept, as this is a violation of the constitution and of criminal procedure. Yet in some cases, the result of the investigation might be communicated to the Austro-Hungarian officials.

The Austrian demand was clear and unmistakable:

A. *To institute a criminal procedure against the participants in the outrage.*

B. *Participation by I. and R. Government officials in the examinations ("Recherche" in contrast with "enquête judiciaire").*

C. *It did not occur to us to let I. and R. Government officials participate in the Serbian court procedure; they were to co-operate only in the police researches, which had to furnish and fix the material for the investigation. If the Serbian Government misunderstands us here, this is done deliberately, for it must be familiar with the difference between "enquête judiciaire" and simple police researches. As it desired to escape from every control of the investigation which would yield, if correctly carried out, highly undesirable results for it, and as it possesses no means to refuse in a plausible manner the co-operation, of our officials (precedents for such police intervention exist in great numbers) it tries to justify its refusal by showing up our demands as impossible.*

7. The Royal Government has ordered on the evening of the day on which the note was received the arrest of Major Voislar Tankosic. However, as far as Milan Ciganowic is concerned, who is a citizen of the Austro-Hungarian Monarchy and who has been employed till June 28th with the Railroad Department, it has as yet been impossible to locate him, wherefore a warrant has been issued against him. The I. and R. Government is asked to make known, as soon as possible, for the purpose of conducting, the investigation, the existing grounds for suspicion and the proofs of guilt, obtained in the investigation at Sarajevo.

This reply is disingenuous. According to our investigation, Ciganowic, by order of the police prefect in Belgrade, left three days after the outrage for Ribari, after it had become known that Ciganowic had participated in the outrage. In the first place, it is therefore incorrect that Ciganowic left the Serbian service on June 28th. In the second place, we add that the prefect of police at Belgrade, who had himself caused the departure of this Ciganowic and who knew his whereabouts, declared in an interview that a man by the name of Milan Ciganowic did not exist in Belgrade.

8. The Serbian Government will amplify and render more severe the existing measures against the suppression of smuggling of arms and explosives. It is a matter of course that it will proceed at once against, and punish severely, those officials of the frontier service on the line Shabatz-Loznica who violated their duty and who have permitted the perpetrators of the crime to cross the frontier.

9. The Royal Government is ready to give explanations about the expressions, which its officials in Serbia and abroad have made in interviews after the outrage and which, according to the assertion of the I. and R. Government, were hostile to the Monarchy. As soon as the I. and R. Government points out in detail where those expressions were made and succeeds in proving that the functionaries concerned have actually made those expressions, the Royal Government itself will take care that the necessary evidences and proofs are collected therefore.

The Royal Serbian Government must be aware of the interviews in question. If it demands of the I. and R. Government that it should furnish all kinds of detail about the said interviews and if is reserves for itself the right of a formal investigation it shows that it is not its intention seriously to fulfill the demand.

10. The Royal Government will notify the I. and R. Government, so far as this has not been already done by the present note, of the execution of the measures in question as soon as one of those measures has been ordered and put into execution. The Royal Serbian Government believes it to be to the common interest not to rush the solution of this affair and it is therefore, in case the I. and R. Government should not consider itself satisfied with this answer, ready, as ever, to accept a peaceable

solution, be it by referring the decision of this question to the International Court at the Hague or by leaving it to the decision of the Great Powers who have participated in the working out of the declaration given by the Serbian government on March 31st, 1909.

The Serbian Note, therefore, is entirely a play for time.

This reply contradicts everything that is involved with the murder of the archduke, and Serbia is only trying to buy time so as to know where Russia and France stand with the impending demands of the murdered archduke by Serbian citizens and government officials.

No. 23.
Mr. Crackanthorpe, British Charge' D' Affaires at Belgrade, to Sir Edward Grey
Belgrade
July 25, 1914.
(Telegraphic)

The Austrian minister left at 1830.

The government has left for Nish, where Skuptchina[11] will meet on Monday. I am leaving with my other colleagues, but the Vice Consul is remaining in charge of the archives.

No. 24.
Sir Edward Grey, to Sir G. Buchanan, British Ambassador at St. Petersburg.
Foreign office, England
July 25, 1914.
(Telegraphic)

You spoke quite rightly in a very difficult circumstances as to the attitude of His Majesty's Government. I entirely approve of what you said, as reported in your telegram of yesterday,[12] and I cannot promise more on behalf of the government.

I do not consider that public opinion here would or ought to sanction our going to war over a Serbian quarrel. If, however, war does take place, the development of other issues may draw us into it, and therefore anxious to prevent it.

The sudden brusque, and peremptory character of the Austrian de`marche makes it almost inevitable that in a very short time both Russia and Austria will have mobilized against each other. In this event, the only chance of peace, in my opinion, is for the other four Powers to join in asking the Austrian and Russian Government not to cross the frontier, and to give time for the four Powers acting at Vienna and St. Petersburg to try and arrange matters. If Germany will adopt this view, I feel strongly that France and ourselves should act upon it. Italy would no doubt gladly co-operate.

No diplomatic intervention or mediation would be tolerated by either Russia or Austria unless it was clearly impartial and included the allies or friends of both. The co-operation of Germany would, therefore, be essential.

---

[11] The Serbian Parliament.
[12] See telegram No. 6.

No. 25.
Sir Edward Grey to Sir H. Rumbold, British Charge' D' Affaires at Berlin.
Foreign Office
July 25, 1914.
(Telegraphic)

The Austrian Ambassador has been authorized to inform me that the Austrian method of procedure on expiry of time limit would be to break off diplomatic relations and commence with military preparations, but not military operations. In informing the German Ambassador of this, I said that it interposed a stage of mobilization before the frontier was actually crossed, which I had urged yesterday should be delayed.

Apparently, we should now soon be face to face with the mobilization Austria and Russia. The only chance of peace, if this did happen, would be for Germany, France, Russia,[13] and ourselves to keep together, and join in asking Austria and Russia not to cross the frontier till we had time to try and arrange matters between them.

The German Ambassador read me a telegram from German Foreign Office saying that his Government had not known beforehand and had no more that the other Powers to do with the stiff terms of the Austrian note to Serbia, but once she had launched that note, Austria could not draw back. Prince Lichnowsky[14] said, however, that if what I contemplated was mediation between Austria and Russia, Austria might be able with dignity to accept it. He expressed himself as personally favorable to this suggestion.

I concurred in his observation, and said that I felt I had no title to intervene between Austria and Serbia. The peace of Europe was affected, in which we must all take a hand.

I impressed upon the ambassador that, in the event of Russian and Austrian mobilization, the participation of Germany would be essential to any diplomatic action for peace. Alone we could do nothing. The French Government was traveling at the moment, and I had no time to consult them, and could not therefore be sure of there views, but I was prepared, if the German Government agreed with my suggestion, to tell the French Government that I thought it was the right thing to act upon it.

No. 35.
M. Jules Cambon, French Minister at Berlin, to M. Bienvenu-Martin, Acting Minister for Foreign Affairs.
Berlin
July 25, 1914.

The Belgian Minister appears very anxious about the course of events. He is of opinion that Austria and Germany have desired to take advantage of the fact that, owing to a combination of circumstances at the present moment, Russia and England appear to them to be threatened by domestic troubles, while in France the state of the army is under discussion. Moreover, he does not believe in the pretended ignorance of the Government of Berlin on the subject of Austria's *démarche*.

He thinks that if the form of it has not been submitted to the cabinet at Berlin, the moment of its dispatch has been cleverly chosen in consultation with that Cabinet in order to surprise the Triple Entente at a moment of disorganization.

He has seen the Italian Ambassador, who has just interrupted his holiday in order to return. It looks as if Italy would be surprised, to put it no higher, at having been kept out of the whole affair by her two allies.

JULES CAMBON.

---

[13] Should be Italy.
[14] German Ambassador in London.

No. 36.

M. Bienvenu-Martin, Acting Minister for Foreign Affairs, to Stockholm (for the President of the Council), and to London, Berlin, St. Petersburgh, Vienna.

Paris

July 25, 1914.

The German Ambassador came at 12 o'clock to protest against an article in the *Echo de Paris* which applied the term "German threat" (*menace allemande*) to his I démarche of yesterday. Herr von Schoen told a certain number of journalists, and came to state at the *Direction Politique,* that there has been no "concert" between Austria and Germany in connection with the Austrian note, and that the German Government had no knowledge of this note when it was communicated to them at the same time as to the other Powers, though they had approved it subsequently. Baron von Schoen added, moreover, that there was no "threat"; the German Government had merely indicated that they thought it desirable to localize the dispute, and that the intervention of other Powers ran the risk of aggravating it. The Acting Political Director took note of Baron von Schoen's *démarche*. Having asked him to repeat the actual terms of the last two paragraphs of his note, he remarked to him that the terms showed the willingness of Germany to act as intermediary between the Powers and Austria. M. Berthelot added that, as no private information had been given to any journalist, the information in the *Echo de Paris* involved this newspaper alone and merely showed that the German *démarche* appeared to have been known elsewhere than at the Quai d'Orsay, and apart from any action on his part. The German Ambassador did not take up the allusion. On the other hand, the Austrian Ambassador at London also came to reassure Sir Edward Grey, telling him that the Austrian note did not constitute an "ultimatum" but "a demand for a reply with a time limit"; which meant that if the Australian demands are not accepted by 6 o'clock this evening, the Austrian Minister will leave Belgrade and the Austro-Hungarian Government will begin military "preparations" but not military "operations."

The Cabinet of London, like those of Paris and St. Petersburgh, has advised Belgrade to express regret for any complicity, which might be established in the crime of Sarajevo, and to promise the most complete satisfaction in this respect. The Cabinet added that in any case it was Serbia's business to reply in terms, which the interests of the country appeared to call for. The British Minister at Belgrade is to consult his French and Russian colleagues, and, if these have had corresponding instructions in the matter, advise the Serbian Government to give satisfaction on all the points on which they shall decide that they are able to do so. Sir Edward Grey told Prince Lichnowsky (who, up to the present, has made no communication to him similar to that of Herr von Schoen at Paris) that if the Austrian note caused no difficulty between Austria and Russia, the British Government would not have to concern themselves with it, but that it was to be feared that the stiffness of the note and the shortness of the time limit would bring about a state of tension. Under these conditions the only chance that could be seen of avoiding a conflict would consist in the mediation of France, Germany, Italy, and England, Germany alone being able to influence the Government at Vienna in this direction. The German Ambassador replied that he would transmit this suggestion to Berlin, but he gave the Russian Ambassador, who is a relative of his, to understand that Germany would not lend herself to any *démarche* at Vienna.

BIENVENU-MARTIN.

No. 37.

M. de Fleuriau, French Chargé d'Aftaires at London, to M. Bienvenu-Martin, Acting Minister for Foreign Affairs.

London

July 25, 1914.

The German Ambassador came to the Foreign Office to state that his Government would refuse to interfere in the dispute between Austria and Serbia. Sir Edward Grey replied that without co-operation of Germany at Vienna, England would not be able to take action at St. Petersburgh. If, however, both Austria and Russia mobilized, that would certainly be the occasion for the four other Powers to intervene. Would the German Government then maintain its passive attitude, and would it refuse to join with England, France, and Italy? Prince Lichnowsky does not think so, since the question would no longer be one of difficulties between Vienna and Belgrade, but of a conflict between Vienna and St. Petersburgh. Sir Edward Grey added this observation that if war eventually broke out, no Power in Europe would be able to take up a detached attitude (*pourrait s'en désintéresser*).

DE FLEURIAU.

No. 38.

M. Paléologue, French Ambassador at St, Petersburgh, to M. Bienvenu-Martin, Acting Minister for Foreign Affairs.

St. Petersburgh

July 25, 1914.

THE Russian Government is about to endeavor to obtain from the Austro-Hungarian Government an extension of the time limit fixed by the ultimatum, in order that the Powers may be able to form an opinion on the judicial, I dossier, the communication of which is offered to them.

M. Sazonof has asked the German Ambassador to point out to his Government the danger of the situation, but he refrained from alluding to the measures, which Russia would no doubt be led to take, if either the national independence or the territorial integrity of Serbia were threatened. The evasive replies and the recriminations of Count de Pourtalès left an unfavorable impression on M. Sazonof. The Ministers will hold a Council to-morrow with the Emperor presiding. M. Sazonof preserves complete moderation. "We must avoid," he said to me, "everything which might precipitate the crisis. I am of opinion that even if the Austro-Hungarian Government comes to blows with Serbia; we ought not to break off negotiations."

PALÈLOGUE.

No. 39.

M. Bienvenu-Martin, Acting Minister for Foreign Affairs, to M. Dumaine, French Ambassador at Vienna.

Paris

July 25, 1914.

The Russian Government has instructed its representative at Vienna to ask the Austrian Government for an extension of the time limit fixed for Serbia, so as to enable the Powers to form an opinion on the *dossier* which Austria has offered to communicate to them, and with a view to avoiding regrettable consequences for everyone. A refusal of this demand by Austria-Hungary would deprive of all meaning the *démarche* which she made to the Powers by communicating her note to them, and would place her in a position of conflict with international ethics. The Russian Government has asked that you should make a corresponding and urgent *démarche* to Count Berchtold. I beg you to support the request of your colleague. The Russian Government has sent the same request to London, Rome, Berlin, and Bucharest.

BIENVENU-MARTIN.

No. 40.
M. de Fleuriau, French Chargé d'Affaires at London, to M. Bienvenu-Martin, Acting Minister for Foreign Affairs.
London
July 25, 1914.

Sir Edward Grey has had communicated to him this morning the instructions which require the Russian Arnbassador at Vienna to ask for an extension of the time limit given to Serbia by Austria's note of the day before yesterday. M. Sazonof asked that the Russian *démarche* should be supported by the British Embassy. Sir Edward Grey telegraphed to Sir M. de Bunsen to take the same action as his Russian colleague, and to refer to Austria's communication which was made to him late last night by Count Mensdorff, according to the terms of which the failure of Serbia to comply with the conditions of the ultimatum would only result, as from to-day, in a diplomatic rupture and not in immediate military operations. Sir Edward Grey inferred from this action that time would be left for the Powers to intervene and find means for averting the crisis.

DF FLEURIAU.

No. 41.
M. Jules Cambon, French Ambassador at Berlin, to M. Bienvenu-Martin, Acting Minister for Foreign Affairs.
Berlin
July 25, 1914.

This morning the British Chargé d'Affaires, acting under instructions from his Government, asked Herr von Jagow if Germany was willing to join with Great Britain, France, and Italy with the object of intervening between Austria and Russia, to prevent a conflict and, in the first instance, to ask Vienna to grant an extension of the time limit imposed on Serbia by the Ultimatum. The Secretary of State for Foreign Affairs replied that directly after the receipt of Prince Lichnowsky's dispatch informing him of the intentions of Sir Edward Grey, he had already telegraphed this very morning to the German[1515]In French text by an obvious error, "de la Grande-Bretagne" is printed. Ambassador at Vienna to the effect that he should ask Count Berchtold for this extension. Unfortunately Count Berchtold is at Ischl. In any case Herr von Jagow does not think that this request would be granted. The British Chargé d'Affaires also enquired of Herr von Jagow, as I had done yesterday, if Germany had had no knowledge of the Austrian note before it was dispatched, and he received so clear a reply in the negative that he was not able to carry the matter further; but he could not refrain from expressing his surprise at the blank cheque given by Germany to Austria. Herr von Jagow having replied to him that the matter was a domestic one for Austria, he remarked that it had become essentially an international one.

JULES CAMBON.

Berlin, July 25, 1914

The situation has grown no worse since yesterday, but this does not mean that it has grown any better.

As unfavorable symptoms, mention must first be made of the language used at the Wilhelmstrasse to the members of the diplomatic body: The Imperial Government approves the *demarche* made by the Austro-Hungarian Government at Belgrade, and does not consider it excessive in form. An end must be made of the murder plots and revolutionary intrigues which are hatched in Serbia. Herr von Jagow and Herr Zimmermannn would not talk in this way if they had not received orders to this effect from the Emperor, who has determined in the interests of dynastic friendship to support Austria-Hungary to the last, and who is susceptible to the very legitimate fears inspired by outrages against Royal personages. It should, further, be remarked that the German press, with the exception of course of the socialist papers, appears to have recovered from the first astonishment caused by the Austro-Hungarian note. It plays the part of chorus to the press of Vienna and Budapest, and contemplates coolly the contingency of war while expressing the hope that it will remain localized. Finally, the view gains ground more and more among my colleagues—and I believe it to be well founded—that it is not so much a desire to avenge the death of the Hereditary Archduke and to put an end to the pan-Serbian propaganda, as an anxiety for a personal rehabilitation as a statesman which has induced Count Berchtold to send to Belgrade this incredible and unprecedented note. From the moment when his personal feelings and reputation are at stake it will be very difficult for him to draw back, to temporize and not to put his threats into execution. The favorable signs are less evident. However, they deserve to be pointed out. Not to mention European public opinion, which would not understand the necessity for taking up arms to determine a dispute whose settlement is undoubtedly within the sphere of diplomacy, it appears impossible not to notice the general movement of reaction and disapproval, which manifests itself outside Germany and Austro-Hungary against the terms of Count Berchtold's ultimatum? The Vienna Cabinet, which was right in substance, is wrong in form. The demand for satisfaction is just; the procedure employed to obtain it is indefensible. Although Count Berchtold has skillfully chosen his moment to act—the British Cabinet being absorbed in the question of Home Rule and Ulster, the head of the French State and his Prime Minister being on a journey, and the Russian Government being obliged to put down important strikes—the fact that the Austrian Minister has thought himself bound to send to the Great Powers an explanatory memorandum, gives to those Powers, and particularly those of the Triple Entente, the right to reply, that is to say, to open a discussion and intervene in favor of Serbia, and enter into negotiation with the Cabinet of Vienna. If it is done at the earliest moment possible, a great gain in favor of the maintenance of European peace will result. Even a hasty military demonstration by the Austro-Hungarian army against Belgrade, after the refusal of the Serbian Government to accept the ultimatum, might, perhaps, not produce irremediable consequences. Lastly, the three members of the Triple Alliance are not in perfect agreement in the present dispute. It would not be surprising if the Italian Government should determine to play a separate part and seek to intervene in the interests of peace.

London
on July 25th, 1914.

The distinction made by Sir Edward Grey between an Austro-Serbian and an Austro-Russian conflict is perfectly correct. We do not wish to interpose in the former any more than England, and as heretofore, we take the position that this question must be localized by virtue of all powers refraining from intervention. It is therefore our hope that Russia will refrain from any action in view of her responsibility and the seriousness of the situation. We are prepared, in the event of an Austro-Russian controversy, quite apart from our known duties as allies, to intercede between Russia and Austria jointly with the other powers.

No. 4.
M. Michotte de Welle, Belgian Minister at Belgrade, to M. Davignon, Belgian Minister for Foreign Affairs
Belgrade
July 25, 1914.

Sir,
I have the honor to transmit to you herewith the text of the reply returned by the Serbian Government to the Austro-Hungarian note of the 10 (23) July.

No. 38.
From: **M. N. Pashitch, Prime Minister and Minister for Foreign Affairs.**
To: **All the Serbian Legations abroad.**
Belgrade
July 25, 1914.
(Telegraphic)

A brief Summary of the reply of the Royal Government was communicated to the representatives of the allied Governments at the Ministry for Foreign Affairs to-day. They were informed that the reply would be quite conciliatory on all points, and that the Serbian Government would accept the Austro-Hungarian demands as far as possible. The Serbian Government trust that the Austro-Hungarian Government, unless they are determined to make war at all costs, will see their way to accept the full satisfaction offered in the Serbian reply.

No. 40.
From: **Baron Giesl von Gieslingen, Austro-Hungarian Minister at Belgrade.**
To: **M. N. Pashitch, Prime Minister and Minister for Foreign Affairs.**
Belgrade
July 25, 1914.

Sir,
As the time limit stipulated in the note, which, by order of my Government, I handed to His Excellency M. Patchou, on Thursday, the day before yesterday, at 6 P.M., has now expired, and as I have received no satisfactory reply, I have the honour to inform Your Excellency that I am leaving Belgrade to-night together with the staff of the Imperial and Royal Legation.

The protection of the Imperial and Royal Legation, together with all its appurtenances, annexes, and archives, as well as the care of the subjects and interests of Austria-Hungary in Serbia, is entrusted to the Imperial German Legation.

Finally, I desire to state formally that from the moment this letter reaches Your Excellency the rupture in the diplomatic relations between Serbia and Austria-Hungary will have the character of a fait accompli.

No. 41.
From: **M. N. Pashitch, Prime Minister and Minister for Foreign Affairs.**
To: **All the Serbian legations abroad.**
Belgrade
July 25, 1914.

I communicated the reply to the Austro-Hungarian note to-day at 5.45 P.M. You will receive the full text of the reply to-night. From it you will see that we have gone as far as was possible. When I handed the note to the Austro-Hungarian Minister he stated that he would have to compare it with his instructions, and that he would then give an immediate answer. As soon as I returned to the Ministry, I was informed in a note from the Austro-Hungarian Minister that he was not satisfied with our reply, and that he was leaving Belgrade the same evening, with the entire staff of the Legation. The protection of the Legation and its archives, and the care of Austrian and Hungarian interests had been entrusted by him to the German Legation. He stated finally that on receipt of the note diplomatic relations between Serbia and Austria-Hungary must be considered as definitely broken off.

The Royal Serbian Government has summoned the Skupshtina to meet on July 14/27 at Nish, whither all the Ministries with their staffs are proceeding this evening. The Crown Prince has issued, in the name of the King, an order for the mobilisation of the army, while to-morrow or the day after a proclamation will be made in which it will be announced that civilians who are not liable to military service should remain peaceably at home, while soldiers should proceed to their appointed posts and defend the country to the best of their ability, in the event of Serbia being attacked.

No. 42.

From: **Count Leopold Berchtold, Austro-Hungarian Minister for Foreign Affairs.**
To: **M. Yov. M. Yovanovitch, Serbian Minister at Vienna.**
Vienna
July 25, 1914.

Sir,

As no satisfactory reply has been given to the note which the Imperial and Royal Minister Extraordinary and Plenipotentiary handed to the Royal Government on the 10/23 instant, I have been compelled to instruct Baron Giesl to leave the Serbian capital and to entrust the protection of the subjects of His Imperial and Royal Apostolic Majesty to the German Legation.

I regret that the relations, which I have had the honour to maintain with you, M. le Ministre, are thus terminated, and I avail myself of this opportunity to place at your disposal the enclosed passports for your return to Serbia, as well as for the return of the staff of the Royal Legation.

No. 11.

Russian Chargé d'Affaires at Vienna to Russian Minister for Foreign Affairs.
Vienna
July 25, 1914.
(Telegraphic)

COUNT BERCHTOLD is at Ischl. In view of the impossibility of arriving there in time, I have telegraphed to him our proposal to extend the time limit of the ultimatum, and I have repeated this proposal verbally to Baron Macchio. The latter promised to communicate it in time to the Minister for Foreign Affairs but added that he had no hesitation in predicting a categorical refusal.

No. 26.

Sir Edward Grey to Sir M. de Bunsen, British Ambassador at Vienna.
British Foreign Office
July 25, 1914.
(Telegraphic)

The Russian Ambassador has communicated to me the following telegram which his Government have sent to the Russian Ambassador at Vienna, with the instruction to communicate it to the Austrian Minister for Foreign Affaires:

"The delay given to Serbia for a reply is sop limited that the Powers are prevented from taking any steps to avert the complications which are threatening. The Russian Government trust that the Austrian Government will prolong the time limit, and as the latter have declared their willingness to inform the Powers of the data on which they base their demands on Serbia, the Russian Government hope that these particulars will be furnished in order that the Powers may examine the matter. If they found that some of the Austrian requests were well founded, they would be in a position to advise the Serbian Government accordingly. If the Austrian Government were indisposed to prolong the time limit, not only would they be acting against international ethics, but they would deprive their communication to the Powers of any practical meaning."

You may support in general terms the step taken by your Russian colleague.

Since the telegram to the Russian Ambassador at Vienna was sent, it has been a relief to hear that the steps which the Austrian Government were taking to be limited for the moment to the rupture of relations and military preparations, and not operation. I trust, therefore, that if the Austro-Hungarian Government considers it too late to prolong the time limit, they will at any rate give time in the sense and for the reason desired by the Russia before taking any irretrievable steps.

No. 27.
Sir Edward Grey to Sir F. Bertie, British Ambassador at Paris, Sir H. Rumbold, British Charge' D' Affaires at Berlin, and Sir G. Buchanan, British Ambassador at St. Petersburg.
British Foreign Office
July 25, 1914.
(Telegraphic)

I have communicated to the German Ambassador the forecast of the Serbian reply contained in Mr. Crackanthorpe's telegram of today. I have said that, if Serbian reply, when received at Vienna, corresponds to this forecast, I hope the German Government will feel able to influence the Austrian Government to take favorable view of it.

No. 28.
NIL

No. 12.
Russian Chargé d'Affaires at Vienna to Russian Minister for Foreign Affaires.
Vienna
July 25, 1914.
(Telegraphic)

In continuation of my telegram of to-day, I have just heard from Macchio that the Austro-Hungarian Government refuses our proposal to extend the time limit of the note.

No. 29.
Sir Edward Grey to Mr. Crackanthorpe, British Charge' D' Affaires at Belgrade.
British Foreign Office
July 25, 1914.
Sir,
The Italian Ambassador came to see me today. I told him in general terms what I said to the German Ambassador this morning.

The Italian Ambassador cordially approved of this. He made no secret of the fact that Italy was most desirous to see war avoided.

E. Grey

No. 13.
Russian Chargé d'Affaires at Belgrade to Russian Minister for Foreign Affairs.
Belgrade
July 25, 1914.
(Delayed in transmission, received July 14, 1914.)
(Telegraphic)

FOLLOWING is the reply, which the President of the Serbian Cabinet to-day handed to the Austro-Hungarian Minister at Belgrade before the expiration of the time limit of the ultimatum. [Here follows the text of the Serbian reply, for which see No. 39 in British Correspondence, page 31.]

No. 15.
Russian Chargé d'Affaires at Paris to Russian Minister for Foreign Affairs.
Paris
July 25, 1914.
(Telegraphic)

I HAVE received your telegram of the 11th (24th) July respecting the extension of the time limit of the Austrian ultimatum, and I have made the communication in accordance with your instructions. The French Representative at Vienna has been furnished with similar instructions.

No. 16.
Russian Ambassador at London to Russian Minister for Foreign Affairs.
London
July 25, 1914.
(Telegraphic)

I HAVE received your telegram of the 11th July. Grey has instructed the British Ambassador at Vienna to support our action for the extension of the time limit of the ultimatum. At the same time, he explained to me that the Austrian Ambassador had come to see him, and had explained that the Austrian note should not be regarded as an ultimatum. It should be regarded as a step, which, in the event of no reply, or in the event of an unsatisfactory reply within the time fixed would be followed by a rupture of diplomatic relations and the immediate departure of the Austro-Hungarian Minister from Belgrade; without, however, entailing the immediate opening of hostilities. Grey added that as a result of this explanation he had told the British Ambassador at Vienna that, should it be too late to raise the question of extending the time limit of the ultimatum, the question of preventing hostilities might perhaps serve as a basis for discussion.

No. 17.
Russian Minister for Foreign Affairs to Russian Ambassador at London.
St. Petersburg
July 25, 1914.
(Telegraphic)

IN the event of a change for the worse in the situation which might lead to joint action by the Great Powers, we count upon it that England will at once side definitely with Russia and France, in order to maintain the European balance of power, for which she has constantly intervened in the past, and which would certainly be compromised in the event of the triumph of Austria.

No. 18.
Note verbale handed to Russian Minister for Foreign Affairs by the German Ambassador at St. Petersburg.
July 25, 1914.

IL NOUS revient de source autoritative que la nouvelle répandue par quelques journaux d'après laquelle la démarche du Gouvernement d'Autrich-Hongrie à Belgrade aurait éte faite à l'instigation de l'Allemagne EST absolument fausse. Le Gouvernement allemand n'a pas eu conaissance du texte de la note autrichienne avant qu'elle ait été remise, ET n'a exercé aucune influence sur son contenu. C'est à tort qu'on attribue à l'Allemagne une attitude comminatoire.

L'Allemagne appuie naturellement comme allié de l'Autriche les revendications à son avis légitimes du Cabinet de Vienne contre la Serbie.

Avant tout elle désireé comme elle l'a déja déclaré dès le commencement du différend austro-serbe, que ce conflit reste localisé.

(Translation)

WE learn from an authoritative source that the news spread by certain newspapers, to the effect that the action of the Austro-Hungarian Government at Belgrade was instigated by Germany, is absolutely false. The German Government had no knowledge of the text of the Austrian note before it was presented, and exercised no influence upon its contents. A threatening attitude is wrongly attributed to Germany.

Germany, as the ally of Austria, naturally supports the claims made by the Vienna Cabinet against Serbia, which she considers justified.

Above all Germany wishes, as she has already declared from the very beginning of the Austro-Serbian dispute, that this conflict should be localized.

No. 19.
Russian Chargé d'Affaires at Paris to Russian Minister for Foreign Affairs.
Paris
July 25, 1914.
(Telegraphic)

PLEASE refer to my telegram of the 11th (24th) July.

A morning paper has to-day published, in a not altogether correct form, the declarations made yesterday by the German Ambassador, and has added comments in which it characterizes these utterances as being in the nature of threats. The German Ambassador, who is much upset by these disclosures, to-day visited the Acting Head of the Political Department, and explained to him that his words in no wise bore the threatening character attributed to them. He stated that Austria had presented her note to Serbia without any definite understanding with Berlin, but that Germany nevertheless approved of the Austrian point of view, and that undoubtedly "the bolt once fired" (these were his own words), Germany could only be guided by her duties as an ally.

No. 20.
Russian Ambassador at London to Russian Minister for Foreign Affairs.
London
July 25, 1914.
(Telegraphic)

GREY has told me that the German Ambassador has declared to him that the German Government was not informed of the text of the Austrian note, but that they entirely supported Austria's action. The Ambassador at the same time asked if Great Britain could see her way to bring conciliatory pressure to bear at St. Petersburg. Grey replied that this was quite impossible. He added that, as long as complications existed between Austria and Serbia alone, British interests were only indirectly affected; but he had to look ahead to the fact that Austrian mobilization would lead to Russian mobilization, and that from that moment a situation would exist in which the interests of all the Powers would be involved. In that event Great Britain reserved to herself full liberty of action.

No. 21.
Russian Chargé d'Affaires at Belgrade to Russian Minister for Foreign Affairs.
Belgrade
July 25, 1914.
(Telegraphic)

IN spite of the extremely conciliatory nature of the Serbian reply to the ultimatum, the Austrian Minister has just informed the Serbian Government, in a note handed in at 6.30 P.M. this evening, that, not having received a satisfactory answer within the time limit fixed, he was leaving Belgrade with the entire staff of the legation. The Skupchtina is convoked for the 14th (27th) July at Nish. The Serbian Government and the Diplomatic Body are leaving this evening for that town.

No. 22.
*Russian Ambassador at London to the Russian Minister for Foreign Affairs.*London
July 25, 1914.
(Telegraphic)

GREY has told the German Ambassador that in his opinion Austrian mobilization must lead to Russian mobilization, that grave danger of a general war will thereupon arise, and that he sees only one means of reaching a peaceful settlement, namely, that, in view of the Austrian and Russian mobilizations, Germany, France, Italy, and Great Britain should abstain from immediate mobilization, and should at once offer their good offices. Grey told me that the first essential of this plan was the consent of Germany and her promise not to mobilize. He has therefore, as a first step, made an enquiry on this point at Berlin.

July 25, 1914
Jaures' speech for local election was more about Serbian reply than local politics.

Citizens, the note which Austria has sent to Serbia is full of threats; and if Austria invades Slavic territory, if the Austrians attack the Serbs…we can foresee Russia's entry into the war; and if Russia intervenes, Austria, confronted by two enemies, will invoke her treaty of alliance with Germany; and Germany has in-

formed the powers through her ambassadors that she will come to the aid of Austria....But then, it is not only the Austro-German Alliance which will come into play, but also the secret treaty between Russia and France.

No. 30.
Sir Edward Grey to Mr. Crackanthorpe, British Charg`e d' Affaires at Belgrade.
Foreign Office
July 25, 1914.

Sir,

The Serbian Minister called on the 23rd instantly and spoke to Sir A. Nicholas[16] on the present strained relations between Serbia and Austria-Hungary.

He said that his government were most anxious and disquieted. They were perfectly ready to meet any reasonable demands of Austria-Hungary so long as such demands were kept on the "terrain juridique." If the results of the enquiry at Sarajevo—an enquiry conducted with so much mystery and secrecy—disclosed the fact that there were any individual conspiring or organizing plots on Serbian territory, the Serbian Government would be quite ready to take the necessary steps to give satisfaction; but if Austria transported the question on to the political ground, and said that Serbian policy, being inconveniently to her, must undergo a radical change, and that Serbia must abandon certain political ideals; no independent state would, or could, submit to such dictation....

He mentioned that both assassins of the Archduke were Austrian subjects—Bosnian; that one of them had been in Serbia and that the Serbian authorities, considering him suspect and dangerous, had desired to expel him but on applying to the Austrian authorities found that the latter protected him, and said that he was an innocent and harmless individual. Sir A. Nicholas, on being asked by M. Boschkovitch[17] his opinion on the whole question, observed that there were no data on which to base one, though it was to be hoped that the Serbian government would endeavor to meet the Austrian demands in a conciliatory and moderate spirit.

"An Ambassador's Memoirs"
By Maurice Paléologue
Day 6 with French President in Russia
Saturday, July 25, 1914.

Yesterday the German ambassadors in Paris and London read to the French and British governments a note to the effect that the Austro-Serbian dispute must be settled by Vienna and Belgrade alone. The note ended thus: *The German Government is extremely anxious that the conflict shall be localized as any intervention by a third power may, by the natural operation of alliances, have incalculable consequences.*

The policy of threats is already beginning.

At three o'clock in the afternoon Sazonov received me with Buchanan. He told us that an extraordinary council was held this morning at Krasnoïe-Selo, with the Tsar presiding, and that His Majesty has decided *in principle* to mobilize the thirteen army corps, which are ultimately earmarked for operations against Austria-Hungary.

Then he turned to Buchanan very gravely and pleaded with all his might that England should hesitate no longer to range herself on the side of Russia and France in a crisis in which the stake is not merely the European balance of power but the very liberties of Europe itself.

I backed up Sazonov and concluded with an argument *ad hominem*, pointing to the portrait of the great Chancellor Gortchakoff which adorns the room in which we were talking: "In July, 1870, on

---

[16] British—Under-secretary of State for Foreign Affairs.
[17] Serbian Minister in London.

this very spot, my dear Sir George, Prince Gortchakoff said to your father (1) who was warning him of the danger of German ambition: 'There's nothing to worry Russia in the increase of German power.' Don't let England make the same mistake to-day which cost Russia so dear then!"

"You know you're preaching to the converted," said Buchanan with a weary smile.

Public feeling is rising every hour. The following note has been communicated to the Press: The Imperial Government is closely following the development of the Austro-Serbian conflict, which cannot leave Russia indifferent.

Almost simultaneously Pourtalès informed Sazonov that as Austria's ally she naturally supported the legitimate claims of the Vienna cabinet against Serbia.

Sazonov on his part has advised the Serbian government immediately to invite the mediation of the British Government.

At seven o'clock this evening, I went to the Warsaw station to say goodbye to Isvolsky who is returning to his post in hot haste. There was a great bustle on the platforms. The trains were packed with officers and men. This looked like mobilization. We rapidly exchanged impressions and came to the same conclusion:

"It's war this time."

When I returned to the embassy, I was informed that the Tsar had just ordered the measures preliminary to mobilization in the military areas of Kiev, Odessa, Kazan, and Moscow. Further, the cities and Governments of St. Petersburg and Moscow have been declared in a state of siege. Lastly, the camp at Krasnoïe-Selo has been broken up and from this evening, the troops are being sent back to their usual garrisons.

At half-past eight my military attaché, General de Laguiche, was summoned to Krasnoïe-Selo to confer with the Grand Duke Nicholas Nicholaïevitch and General Sukhomlinov, the War Minister.

Chapter Twenty-Seven
July 26, 1914

No. 31.
Sir M. de Bunsen, British Ambassador at Vienna, to Sir Edward Grey.
Vienna
July 26, 1914.
(Telegraphic)

Serbian reply to the Austro-Hungarian demands is not considered satisfactory, and the Austro-Hungarian Minister has left Belgrade. War is thought to be imminent.

No. 32.
Sir M. de Bunsen, British Ambassador at Vienna, to Sir Edward Grey.
Vienna
July 26, 1914.
(Telegraphic)

According to confident belief of German Ambassador, Russia will keep quiet during chastisement of Serbia, which Austria-Hungary is resolved to inflict, having received assurances that no Serbian territory will be annexed by Austria-Hungary. In my reply to my question whether Russia Government might not be compelled by public opinion to intervene on behalf of kindred nationality, he said that everything depended on the personality of the Russian Minister for Foreign Affairs, who could resist easily, if he chose, the pressure of a few newspapers. He pointed out that the days of Pan-Slav agitation in Russia were over and that Moscow was perfectly quiet. The Russian Minister for Foreign Affairs would not, his Excellency though, be so imprudent as to take a step which would probably result in many frontier questions in which Russia is interested, such as Swedish, Polish, Ruthene, Romanian, and Persian questions being brought into the melting. France, too, was not at all in a condition for facing war.

I replied that matters had, I thought, been made a little difficult for other Powers by the tone of Austro-Hungarian Governments ultimatum to Serbia. One naturally sympathized with many of the requirements of the ultimatum, if only the manner of expressing them had been more temperate. It was however, impossible, according to the German Ambassador, to speak effectively in any other way to Serbia. Serbia was not about top receive a lesson which she required; the quarrel, however, ought not be extended in any way to Foreign countries. He doubted Russia, who had no right to assume a protectorate over Serbia, acting as if she made any such claim. As for Germany, she knew very well what she was about in backing up Austria-Hungary in this matter.

The German Ambassador had heard of a letter addressed by you yesterday to the German Ambassador in London in which you expressed the hope that the Serbian concessions would be regarded as satisfactory. He asked whether I had been informed that a pretence of giving way at the last moment had been made by the Serbian Government. I had, I said heard that on practically every point Serbia had been willing to give in. His Excellency replied that Serbian concessions were a sham. Serbia proved that she well knew that they were insufficient to satisfy the legitimate demands of Austria-Hungary by the fact that before making her offer she had ordered mobilization and retirement of Government from Belgrade.

With Russia being the deciding factor and telling Serbia what to do in this situation, Serbia is only acting on advice from her protectorate. But Russia's decisions are being based on what was decided when the Russian and French president's were having their meeting.

No. 33.
Sir H. Humbold, British Charg'e d' Affaires at Berlin, to Sir Edward Grey.
Berlin
July 26, 1914.
(Telegraphic)

Emperor returns suddenly tonight, and undersecretary of State says that Foreign Office regret this step, which was taken on his Majesty's own initiative. They fear that his Majesty's sudden return may cause speculation and excitement. Under-Secretary of State likewise told me that German Ambassador at St. Petersburg had reported that, in conversation with Russian Minister for Foreign Affairs, latter had said that if Austria annexed bits of Serbian territory Russia would not remain indifferent. Under-Secretary of State drew a conclusion that Russia would not act if Austria did not annex territory.

Of course, the Russian minister would say this. This is, of course, what was discussed with the French president. Russia and France have a plan, a plan that will bring Germany into a war these two countries want, so France can get her revenge on Germany for her defeat in the Franco-Prussia War of 1870.

No. 34.
Sir H. Humbold, British Charg'e d' Affaires at Berlin, to Sir Edward Grey.
Berlin
July 26, 1914.
(Telegraphic)

Under-Secretary of State has just telephoned me to say that German Ambassador at Vienna has been instructed to pass on to Austro-Hungarian Government your hopes that they may take a more favorable view of Serbian reply if it corresponds to the forecast contained in Belgrade telegram of July 25[th*]

Under-Secretary of State considers very fact of their making this communication to Austro-Hungarian Government implies that they associate themselves to a certain extent with your hope. German Government do not see their way to going beyond this.

---

* See no. 21.

No. 35.
Sir R. Rodd, British Ambassador at Rome, to Sir Edward Grey.
Rome
July 26, 1914.
(Telegraphic)

Minister for Foreign Affairs welcomes your proposal for a conference, and will instruct Italian Ambassador tonight accordingly.

Austrian Ambassador has informed Italian Government this evening that Minister in Belgrade had been recalled, but that this did not imply declaration of war.

No. 30.
Russian Chargé d'Affaires at Berlin to Russian Minister for Foreign Affairs.
Berlin
July 26, 1914.
(Telegraphic)

ON the news reaching Berlin that, the Austrian army had mobilized against Serbia, a large crowd, in which the papers report the presence of an Austrian element, gave vent to a series of noisy demonstrations in favor of Austria Late in the evening the crowd several times collected before the Imperial Russian Embassy and some anti-Russian shouting occurred. Hardly any police were present and no precautions were taken.

No. 31.
Russian Minister for Foreign Affairs to Russian Ambassador at Rome.
St. Petersburg
July 26, 1914.
(Telegraphic)

ITALY might play a part of the first importance in favor of preserving peace, by bringing the necessary influence to bear upon Austria, and by adopting a definitely unfavorable attitude towards the dispute on the ground that it could not be localized. You should express your conviction that Russia cannot possibly avoid coming to the help of Serbia.

1914 July 26: Russia recalls youngest reservist.

No. 24.
Acting Russian Consul at Prague to Russian Minister for Foreign Affairs.
Prague
July 26, 1914.
(Telegraphic)

SERBIAN army mobilization as been ordered.

No. 36.
Sir Edward Grey to Sir F. Bertie, British Ambassador at Paris, Sir H. Rumbold, British Charge'
D' Affaires at Berlin, and Sir R. Rodd, British Ambassador at Rome.
British Foreign Office
July 26, 1914.
(Telegraphic)

Would Minister of Foreign Affairs be disposed to instruct Ambassador here to join with representatives of France, Italy, and Germany, and myself to meet here in conference immediately for the purpose of discovering an issue which would prevent complications? You should ask Minister for Foreign Affaires whether he would do this. If so, when bringing the above suggestion to the notice of the Governments to which they are accredited, representatives at Belgrade, Vienna, and St. Petersburg should be authorized to request that all active military operations should be suspended pending results of the conference.

This telegram would be in reference to Russia's order for military mobilization. And some of their units are moving at this time to the Austrian and Russian frontier.

No. 25.
Russian Minister for Foreign Affairs to Russian Ambassador at Vienna.
St. Petersburg
July 26, 1914.
(Telegraphic)

I HAD a long and friendly conversation to-day with the Austro-Hungarian Ambassador. After discussing the ten demands addressed to Serbia, I drew his attention to the fact that, quite apart from the clumsy form in which they were presented some of them were quite impracticable, even if the Serbian Government agreed to accept them. Thus, for example, points 1 and 2 could not be carried out without recasting the Serbian press law and association's law, and to that, it might be difficult to obtain the consent of the Skupchtina. As for enforcing points 4 and 5, this might lead to most dangerous consequences, and even to the risk of acts of terrorism directed against the Royal Family and against Pashitch, which clearly could not be the intention of Austria. With regard to the other points, it seemed to me that, with certain changes of detail, it would not be difficult to find a basis of mutual agreement, if the accusations contained in them were confirmed by sufficient proof. In the interest of the maintenance of peace, which, according to the statements of Szapary, is as much desired by Austria, as by all the Powers, it was necessary to end the tension of the present moment as soon as possible. With this object in view it seemed to me most desirable that the Austro-Hungarian Ambassador should be authorized to enter into a private exchange of views in order to redraft certain articles of the Austrian note of the 10th (23rd) July in consultation with me. This method of procedure would perhaps enable us to find a formula, which would prove acceptable to Serbia, while giving satisfaction to Austria in respect of the chief of her demands. Please convey the substance of this telegram to the Minister for Foreign Affairs in a judicious and friendly manner.

Communicated to Russian Ambassadors in Germany, France, Great Britain, and Italy.

No. 26.
Russian Minister for Foreign Affairs to Russian Ambassador at Berlin.
St. Petersburg
July 26, 1914.
(Telegraphic)

PLEASE communicate the contents of my telegram to Vienna of to-day to the German Minister for Foreign Affairs, and express to him the hope that he, on his part, will be able to advise Vienna to meet Russia's proposal in a friendly spirit.

No. 37.
Sir Edward Grey to Sir F. Bertie, British Ambassador at Paris.
British Foreign Office
July 26, 1914.
(Telegraphic)
(Berlin telegram of 25 July.[18])

It is important to know if France will agree to suggest action by the Four Powers if necessary.

No. 27.
Russian Chargé d'Affaires at Paris to Russian Minister for Foreign Affairs.
Paris
July 26, 1914.
(Telegraphic)

THE Director of the Political Department informs me that upon his informing the Austro-Hungarian Ambassador of the contents of the Serbian reply to the ultimatum, the Ambassador did not conceal his surprise that it had failed to satisfy Giesl. In the opinion of the Director of the Political Department, Serbia's conciliatory attitude should produce the best impression in Europe.

No. 5.
Communication made on July 26, 1914, by the Austro-Hungarian Legation at Brussels to the Belgian Minister for Foreign Affairs.

M. Pashitch gave the reply of the Servian Government to the Austro-Hungarian note before 6 o'clock yesterday. This reply not having been considered satisfactory, diplomatic relations have been broken off and the Minister and staff of the Austrian Legation have left Belgrade. Servian mobilisation had already been ordered before 3 o'clock.

Berlin, July 26, 1914

What I have to tell you on the subject of the crisis is so serious that I have decided to send you this report by special messenger. Yesterday's reports which I have committed to the post, with a fear lest they should be read by the German *cabinet noir*, necessarily contained opinions of a much more optimistic nature. Repeated conversations, which I had yesterday with the French Ambassador, the Dutch and Greek Ministers, and the British Charge d'Affaires, raise in my mind the presumption that the ultimatum to Serbia is a blow prepared by Vienna and Berlin, or rather designed here and exe-

---

[18] See No. 18.

cuted at Vienna. It is this fact, which creates the great danger. The vengeance to be taken for the murder of the hereditary Archduke, and the pan-Serbian propaganda would only serve as a pretext. The object sought, in addition to the annihilation of Serbia and of the aspirations of the Jugo-Slavs, would be to strike a mortal blow at Russia and France, in the hope that England would remain aloof from the struggle. To justify these conclusions I must remind you of the opinion which prevails in the German General Staff that war with France and Russia is unavoidable and near—an opinion which the Emperor has been induced to share. Such a war, warmly desired by the military and pan-German party, might be undertaken to-day, as this party think, in circumstances which are extremely favorable to Germany, and which probably will not again present themselves for some time: Germany has finished the strengthening of her army which was decreed by the law of 1912, and on the other hand she feels that she cannot carry on indefinitely a race in armaments with Russia and France which would end by her ruin.

The *Wehrbeitrag* has been a disappointment for the Imperial Government, to whom it has demonstrated the limits of the national wealth. Russia has made the mistake of making a display of her strength before having finished her military reorganization. That strength will not be formidable for several years; at the present moment it lacks the railway lines necessary for its deployment.

As to France, M. Charles Humbert has revealed her deficiency in guns of large calibre; and apparently, it is this arm that will decide the fate of battles. For the rest, England, which during the last two years Germany has been trying, not without some success, to detach from France and Russia, is paralyzed by internal dissensions and her Irish quarrels. In the eyes of my colleagues as well as in my own, the existence of a plan concerted between Berlin and Vienna is proved by the obstinacy with which the Wilhelmstrasse (note: Offices of the German Ministry) denies having had knowledge of the tenor of the Austrian note prior to Thursday last. It was also only on Thursday last that it was known at Rome, from which circumstance arises the vexation and dissatisfaction displayed here by the Italian Ambassador.

How can it be admitted that this note, which, owing to the excessive severity of its terms and the shortness of the period allowed to the Cabinet of Belgrade for their execution is destined to render war immediate and unavoidable, was drafted without consultation with and without the active collaboration of the German Government, seeing that it will involve the most serious consequences for that Government? An additional fact, which proves the intimate cooperation of the two Governments, is their simultaneous refusal to prolong the period allowed to Serbia. After the request for an extension formulated by the Russian Charge d'Affaires at Vienna had been refused yesterday at the Ballplatz, here, at the Wilhelmstrasse, Herr von Jagow evaded similar requests presented by the Russian and English Charges d'Affaires who, in the name of their respective Governments, claimed the support of the Berlin Cabinet for the purpose of inducing Austria to grant Serbia a longer interval in which to reply. Berlin and Vienna were at one in their desire for immediate and inevitable hostilities. The paternity of the scheme, as well as of the procedure employed, which is, because of their very cleverness, worthy of a Bismarck, is attributed here, in the diplomatic world, to a German rather than to an Austrian brain. The secret had been well guarded, and the execution of the scheme followed with marvelous rapidity. It should be observed that, even if the secret aim of the statesmen of the two empires is not to make the war general and force Russia and France to take part, but merely to destroy the power of Serbia and prevent her from carrying on her clandestine propaganda, the result is the same. It is impossible that that result has not been perceived by the far-seeing rulers of the German Empire. On either of these assumptions, the intervention of Russia would appear inevitable; they must have deliberately faced this complication, and prepared themselves to support their allies with vigor. The prospect of a European war has not caused them an instant's hesitation, if, indeed, the desire to evoke it has not been the motive of their actions. Diplomatic relations between Austria and Serbia have been broken off since yesterday evening. Events are developing rapidly. It is expected here that the Serbian King, together with his Government and the Army, will withdraw to the newly annexed territories, and allow the Austrian troops to occupy Belgrade and the country abutting on the Danube, without offering any resistance. Then, however, arises the painfully acute question: What will Russia do? We too must put this disquieting question to ourselves, and hold ourselves in readiness for the worst eventualities, for the European war, of which people were always talking on the agreeable assumption that it would never break out, has now become a threatening reality. The tone of the semi-official German press is more moderate this morning and suggests the possibility of a localization of the war, only however at the cost of the *desinteressement* of Russia, who is to content herself with the assurance that the territorial integrity of Serbia will be respected. Is not the aim of this language to give some satisfaction to England and also to German public opinion which, in spite of yesterday's Austrophile demonstrations in the streets of Berlin, is still pacific and alarmed? In any event, the denouement. Of the crisis, whatever it may be is apparently to be expected soon.

Source: *Source Records of the Great War, Vol. I, ed. Charles F. Horne, National Alumni, 1923.*

The Imperial Ambassador at St. Petersburg to the Chancellor.
Telegram of July 26th, 1914.

The Austro-Hungarian Ambassador had an extended interview with Sasonof this afternoon. Both parties had a satisfactory impression as they told me afterwards. The assurance of the Ambassador that Austria-Hungary had no idea of conquest but wished to obtain peace at last at her frontiers greatly pacified the Secretary.

Telegram of the Imperial Ambassador at St. Petersburg, to the Chancellor
on July 26th, 1914.

The military Attaché requests the following message to be sent; to the general staff: I deem it certain that mobilization has been ordered for Kiev and Odessa. It is doubtful at Warsaw and Moscow and improbable elsewhere.

Telegram of the Chancellor to the Imperial Ambassador at London.
Urgent. July 26th, 1914.

Austria-Hungary has declared in St. Petersburg officially and solemnly that it has no desire for territorial gain in Serbia; that it will not touch the existence of the Kingdom, but that it desires to establish peaceful conditions. According to news received here, the call for several classes of the reserves is expected immediately which is equivalent to mobilization. If this news proves correct, we shall be forced to countermeasures very much against our own wishes. Our desire to localize the conflict and to preserve the peace of Europe remains unchanged. We ask to act in this sense at St. Petersburg with all possible emphasis.

Telegram of the Imperial Chancellor to the Imperial Ambassador at Paris.
July 26th, 1914.

After officially declaring to Russia that Austria-Hungary has no intention to acquire territorial gain and to touch the existence of the Kingdom, the decision whether there is to be a European war rests solely with Russia, which has to bear the entire responsibility. We depend upon France with which we are at one in the desire for the preservation of the peace of Europe that it will exercise its influence at St. Petersburg in favor of peace.

Telegram of the Chancellor to the Imperial Ambassador at St. Petersburg on July 26th, 1914.

After Austria's solemn declaration of its territorial disinterestedness, the responsibility for a possible disturbance of the peace of Europe through a Russian intervention rests solely upon Russia. We trust still that Russia will undertake no steps, which will threaten seriously the peace of Europe.

No. 40.
Sir M. de Bunsen, British Ambassador at Vienna, to Sir Edward Grey.
Vienna
July 26, 1914.
(Telegraphic)

Russian Ambassador just return from leave thinks that Austro-Hungary Government is determined on war, and that it is impossible for Russia to remain indifferent. He does not propose a press for more time in the sense of your telegram of the 25[19] instant (last paragraph).

When the repetition of your telegram of the 26[20] instant to Paris arrived, I had the French and Russian Ambassador both with me. They expressed great satisfaction with its content, which I communicated to them. They doubted, however, whether the principle of Russia being an interested party entitled to have a say in the settlement of a purely Austro-Serbian dispute would be accepted by either the Austro-Hungarian or the German Government.

Instructions were also given to the Italian Ambassador to support the request of the Russian government at that the time limit should be postponed. They arrived, however, too late for any useful action to be taken.

---

[19] See No. 26.
[20] See No. 36.

Chapter Twenty-Eight
July 27, 1914

No. 43.
From: His Imperial Majesty, the Emperor of Russia.
To: His Royal Highness, the Crown Prince of Serbia.
Petrograd
July 27, 1914
(Telegraphic)

When Your Royal Highness applied to me at a time of especial stress, you were not mistaken in the sentiments which I entertain for you, or in my cordial sympathy with the Servian people.

The existing situation is engaging my most serious attention, and my Government is using its utmost endeavor to smooth away the present difficulties. I have no doubt that your Highness and the Royal Servian Government wish to render that task easy by neglecting no step which might lead to a settlement, and thus both prevent the horrors of a new war and safeguard the dignity of Serbia.

So long as the slightest hope exists of avoiding bloodshed, all our efforts must be directed to that end; but if in spite of our earnest wish we are not successful, your Highness may rest assured that Russia will in no case disinterest herself in the fate of Serbia.

No. 41.
Sir M. de Bunsen, ambassador at Vienna, to Sir Edward Grey.
Vienna
July 27, 1914
(Telegraphic)

I have had conversations with all my colleagues representing the Great Powers. The impression left on my mind is that Austro-Hungarian note was so drawn up as to make war inevitable; that the Austro-Hungarian Government is fully resolved to have war with Serbia; that they consider their position as a Great Power to be at stake; and that until punishment has been administered to Serbia it is unlikely that they will listen to proposals of mediation. This country has gone wild with joy at the prospect of war with Serbia, and its postponement or prevention would undoubtedly be a great disappointment be a great disappointment.

I propose, subject to any special directions you desire to send me, to express to the Austrian Minister for Foreign affairs the hope of His Majesty's Government that it may yet be possible to avoid war, and to ask his Excellency whether he cannot suggest a way out even now.

The murder of the Archduke is an act of war. The Austrian Government is acting accordingly to this. Now they want Serbia to admit the fact and take full responsibility. When Serbia refutes Austria's demands then Austria acted accordingly.

No. 32.
Russian Ambassador at London to Russian Minister for Foreign Affairs.
London
July 27, 1914.
(Telegraphic)

I HAVE received your telegram of the 26th July. Please inform me by telegraph whether you consider that your direct discussions with the Vienna Cabinet harmonize with Grey's scheme for mediation by the four Governments. Having heard from the British Ambassador at St. Petersburg that you would be prepared to accept such a combination, Grey decided to turn it into an official proposal, which he communicated yesterday to Berlin, Paris, and Rome.

This Ambassador is either hiding the fact or does not know that Russian as called a general recall of all the reservist.

No. 33.
Russian Minister for Foreign Affairs to Russian Ambassadors at Paris, London, Berlin, Vienna, and Rome.
St. Petersburg
July 27, 1914.
(Telegraphic)

I HAVE taken note of the reply returned by the Serbian Government to Baron Giesl. It exceeds all our expectations in its moderation, and in its desire to afford the fullest satisfaction to Austria. We do not see what further I demands could be made by Austria, unless the Vienna Cabinet is seeking for a pretext for war with Serbia.

Read the reply more carefully and the Serbs don't want a joint investigation with Austria, because of the Serbian Government involvement of the murders.

No. 34.
Russian Chargé d'Affaires at Paris to Russian Minister for Foreign Affairs.
Paris
July 27, 1914.
(Telegraphic)

The German Ambassador discussed the situation again to-day at great length with the Director of the Political Department. The Ambassador laid great stress on the utter impossibility of any mediation or conference.

No. 35.
Russian Ambassador at Paris to Russian Minister for Foreign Affairs.
Paris
July 27, 1914.
(Telegraphic)

I DISCUSSED the situation with the Acting Minister for Foreign Affairs, in the presence of Berthelot, directly after my return to Paris. They both confirmed the information respecting the action taken by the German Ambassador, which Sevastopoulo has already telegraphed to you. This morning Baron von Schoen confirmed his declaration of yesterday in writing, i.e.:

1. That Austria has declared to Russia that she seeks no territorial acquisitions and that she harbors no designs against the integrity of Serbia. Her sole object is to secure her own peace and quiet.
2. That consequently it rests with Russia to avoid war.
3. That Germany and France, entirely at one in their ardent desire to preserve peace, should exercise their moderating influence upon Russia. Baron von Schoen laid special emphasis on the expression of solidarity of Germany and France. The Minister of Justice is convinced that these steps on the part of Germany are taken with the evident object of alienating Russia and France, of inducing the French Government to make representations at St. Petersburg, and of thus compromising our ally in our eyes; and finally, in the event of war, of throwing the responsibility not on Germany, who is ostensibly making every effort to maintain peace, but on Russia and France.

No. 42.
Sir F. Bertie, British Ambassador at Paris, to Sir Edward Grey.
Vienna
July 27, 1914.
(Telegraphic)

Your proposal, as stated in you two telegrams of yesterday,[21] is accepted by the French Government. French Ambassador in London who returns there this evening has been instructed accordingly. Instructions have been sent to the French Ambassador at Berlin to concert with his British colleague as to the advisability of their speaking jointly to the German Government. Necessary instructions have also been sent to the French representatives at Belgrade, Vienna, and St. Petersburg, but until it is known that the Germans have spoken at Vienna with some success, it would, in the opinion of the Ministry of Foreign affairs, be dangerous for the French, Russia, and British Ambassadors to do so.

No. 36.
Russian Ambassador at Paris to Russian Minister for Foreign Affairs.
Paris
July 27, 1914.
(Telegraphic)

IT is clear from your telegrams of the 13th (26) July that you were not then aware of the reply of the Serbian Government. The telegram from Belgrade informing me of it also took twenty hours to reach us. The telegram from the French Minister for Foreign Affairs, sent the day before yesterday at 11

---

[21] nos. 36 and 37.

o'clock in the morning, at the special urgent rate, which contained instructions to support our representations only reached its destination at 6 o'clock. There is no doubt I that this telegram was intentionally delayed by the Austrian telegraph office.

No. 43.
Sir E. Goshen, British Ambassador at Berlin, to Sir Edward Grey.
Paris, France
July 27, 1914.
(Telegraphic)
YOUR telegram of 26 July.[22]

Secretary of State says that the conference you suggest would be practically amount to a court of arbitration and could not, in his opinion be called together except at the request of Austria and Russia.

He was to co-operate for the maintenance of peace. I said I was sure that your idea had nothing to do with arbitration, but meant that representatives of the four nations not directly interested should discuss and suggest means for avoiding a dangerous situation. He maintained, however, that such a conference as you proposed was not practicable. He added that news he had just received from St. Petersburg showed that there was an intention on the part of M. de Sazonof to exchange views with Count Berchtold. He thought that this method of procedure might lead to a satisfactory result, and that it would be best, before doing anything else, to await the out come of the exchange of views between the Austrian and Russia Government.

In the course of a short conversation, the secretary of State said that as yet Austria was only partially mobilizing, but that if Russia mobilized against Germany the latter would have to follow suit. I asked him what he meant by "mobilizing against Germany." He said that if Russia only mobilized in south, Germany would not mobilize, but if she mobilized in the north, Germany would have to do so too, and Russian system of mobilization was so complicated that it might be difficult exactly to locate her mobilization. Germany would therefore have to be very careful not to be taken by surprise.

Finally, Secretary of State said that the news from St. Petersburg had caused him to take a more hopeful view of the general situation.

Austria is still not aware that the Russian military is now going to full mobilization at the encouragement of the French president. France wants war with Germany, as does Russia. This is their excuse to make this happen. By this time, most of the concerns are between Austria and Russia. Now they are trying to make it look like it is all of Germany's fault here. In this telegram, the German government is telling the British what will happen on the part as they react to the Russians.

No. 44.
Sir G. Buchanan, British Ambassador at St. Petersburg, to Sir Edward Grey.
St. Petersburg
July 27, 1914.
(Telegraphic)
Austrian Ambassador tried, in a long conversation, which he had yesterday with the Minister for Foreign Affairs, to explain away objectionable features of the recent action taken by the Austro-Hungarian Government. Minister for Foreign Affairs pointed out that, although he perfectly under-

---

[22] See No. 6.

stood Austria's motives, the ultimatum had been so drafted that it could not possibly be accepted as a whole by the Serbian Government. Although the demands were reasonable enough in some cases, others not only could not possibly be put into immediate execution seeing that they entailed revision of existing Serbian laws, but were, moreover, incompatible with Serbia's dignity as an independent State. It would be useless for Russia to offer her good offices at Belgrade, in view of the fact that she was the object of such suspicion in Austria. The Austrian Ambassador undertook to communicate his Excellency's remarks to his government.

On the Minister for Foreign Affairs questioning me, I told him that I had correctly defined the attitude of his Majesty's government in my conversation with him, which I reported in my telegram of the 24th instant*. I added that you could not promise to do anything more, and that his Excellency was mistaken if he believed that the cause of peace could be promoted by our telling the German Government that they would have to deal with us as well as with Russia and France if they supported Austria by force of arms. Their attitude would merely stiffened by such a menace, and we could only induce her to use her influence at Vienna to avert war by approaching her in the capacity of a friend who was anxious to preserve peace. His Excellency must not, if our efforts were to be successful, do anything to precipitate a conflict. In these circumstances, I trusted that the Russian Government would defer mobilization ukase for as long as possible, and that troops would not be allowed to cross the frontier even when it was issued.

In reply, the minister for Foreign Affairs told me that until the issue of the imperial ukase, no effective steps towards mobilization could be taken and the Austro-Hungarian government would profit by delay in order to complete her military preparations if it was deferred too long.

No. 45.
Sir G. Buchanan, British Ambassador at St. Petersburg, to Sir Edward Grey.
St. Petersburg, Russia
July 27, 1914.
(Telegraphic)

Since my conversation with the Minister For Foreign Affairs, as reported in my telegram of today,* I understand that his Excellency has proposed that a modification to be introduced into Austrian demands should be the subject of direct conversation between Vienna and St. Petersburg.

No. 37.
Russian Ambassador at Paris to Russian Minister for Foreign Affairs.
Paris
July 27, 1914.
(Telegraphic)

ON the instructions of his Government, the Austrian Ambassador has informed the Acting Minister for Foreign Affairs that Serbia's answer has not been considered satisfactory in Vienna, and that tomorrow, Tuesday, Austria will proceed to take "energetic action" with the object of forcing Serbia to give the necessary guarantees. The Minister having asked what form such action would take, the Ambassador replied that he had no exact information on the subject, but it might mean either the crossing of the Serbian frontier, or an ultimatum, or even a declaration of war.

No. 46.
Sir Edward Grey to Sir E. Goschen, British Ambassador at Berlin.
Foreign Office
July 27, 1914.
(Telegraphic)

German Ambassador has informed me that German Government accepts in principle mediation between Austria and Russia by the Four Powers, reserving, of course, their right as an ally to help Austria if attacked. He has also been instructed to request me to use influence in St. Petersburg to localize the war and to keep up the peace of Europe.

I have replied that the Serbian reply went farther than could have been expected to meet Austrian demands. German secretary of State has himself said that there were some things in the Austrian note that Serbia could hardly be expected to accept. I assumed that Serbian reply could not have gone as far as it did unless Russia had exercised conciliatory influence at Belgrade, and it was really at Vienna that moderating influence was now required. If Austria put the Serbian reply aside as being worth nothing and marched into Serbia, it meant that she was determined to crush Serbia at all cost, being reckless of the consequences that might be involved. Serbian reply should at least be treated as a basis for discussion and pause. I said German Government should urge this at Vienna.

I recalled what German government had said as to the gravity of the situation if the war could not be localized, and observed that if Germany assisted Austria against Russia it would because, without any reference to the merits of the dispute, Germany could not afford to see Austria crushed. Just so other issues might be raised that would supersede the dispute between Austria and Serbia, and would bring other Powers in, and the war would be the biggest ever known; but as long as Germany would work to keep the peace I would keep closely in touch. I repeated that after the Serbian reply it was at Vienna that some moderation must be urged.

No. 47.
Sir Edward Grey to Sir G. Buchanan, British Ambassador at St. Petersburg.
British Foreign office
July 27, 1914.
(Telegraphic)

SEE my telegram of today to Sir E. Goschen.

I have been told by the Russian Ambassador that in German and Austria circles impression prevails that in any event we would stand aside. His Excellency deplored the effect that such an impression must produce.

This impression ought, as I have pointed out, to be dispelled by the orders we have given to the First Fleet, which is concentrated, as it happens, at Portland, not to dispose for maneuvers leave. But I explained to the Russian Ambassador that my reference to it must not be taken to mean anything more than diplomatic action that was promised.

We hear from German and Austrian sources that they believe Russia will take no action so long as Austria agrees not to take Serbian territory. I pointed this out, and added that it would be absurd if we were to appear more Serbian than the Russians in our dealings with the German and Austrian Governments.

No. 38.
Russian Chargé d'Affaires at Berlin to Russian Minister for Foreign Affairs.
Berlin
July 27, 1914.
(Telegraphic)

I BEGGED the Minister for Foreign Affairs to support your proposal in Vienna that Szapary should be authorized to draw up, by means of a private exchange of views with you, a wording of the Austro-Hungarian demands, which would be acceptable to both parties. Jagow answered that he was aware of this proposal and that he agreed with Pourtals that, as Szapary had begun this conversation, he might as well go on with it. He will telegraph in this sense to the German Ambassador at Vienna. I begged him to press Vienna with greater insistence to adopt this conciliatory line; Jagow answered that he could not advise Austria to give way.

No. 39.
Russian Chargé d'Affaires at Berlin to Russian Minister for Foreign Affairs.
Berlin
July 27, 1914.
(Telegraphic)

BEFORE my visit to the Minister for Foreign Affairs today, his Excellency had received the French Ambassador, who endeavored to induce him to accept the British proposal for action in favor of peace, such action to be taken simultaneously at St. Petersburg and at Vienna by Great Britain, Germany, Italy, and France. Cambon suggested that these Powers should give their advice to Vienna in the following terms: "To abstain from all action which might aggravate the existing situation." (*S'abstenir de touts acte qui pourrait aggraver la situation de l'heure actuelle.*) By adopting this vague formula, all mention of the necessity of refraining from invading Serbia might be avoided. Jagow refused pointblank to accept this suggestion in spite of the entreaties of the Ambassador, who emphasized, as a good feature of the suggestion, the mixed grouping of the Powers, thanks to which the opposition between the Alliance and the Entente a matter of which Jagow himself had often complained was avoided.

No. 57.
Sir R. Rodd, British Ambassador at Rome, to Sir Edward Grey.
(received July 28th)
Rome
July 27, 1914.
(Telegraphic)

Minister for Foreign Affairs greatly doubts whether Germany will be willing to invite Austria to suspend military action pending the conference, but he had hopes that military action may be practically deferred by the fact of the conference meeting at once. As at present informed, he sees no possibility of Austria, receding from any point laid down in her note to Serbia, but believes that if Serbia will even now accept it. Austria will be satisfied and if she had reason to think that such will be the advice of the Powers, Austria may defer action. Serbia may be induced to accept the note in its entirely on the advice of the four Powers invited to the conference, and this would enable her to say that she had yielded to Europe and not to Austria-Hungary alone.

Telegrams from Vienna to the press here stating that Austria is favorably impressed with the declaration of the Italian Government have, the Minister for Foreign Affairs assures me, no foundation.

He said he as expressed no opinion to Austria with regard to the note. He assured me both before and after communication of the note, again today, that Austria Government has given him assurances that they demand no territorial sacrifices from Serbia.

No. 40.
Telegram from His Imperial Majesty the Emperor of Russia to His Royal Highness Prince Alexander of Serbia.
July 27, 1914.

WHEN your Royal Highness applied to me at a time of especial stress, you were not mistaken in the sentiments, which I entertain for you or in my cordial sympathy with the Serbian people. The existing situation is engaging my most serious attention, and my Government is using its utmost endeavor to smooth away the present difficulties. I have no doubt that your Highness and the Royal Serbian Government wish to render that task easy by neglecting no step which might lead to a settlement, and thus both prevent the horrors of a new war and satisfy the dignity of Serbia. So long as the slightest hope exists of avoiding bloodshed, all our efforts must be directed to that end; but if in spite of our earnest wish we are not successful, your Highness may rest assured that Russia will in no case disinterest herself in the fate of Serbia.

No. 41.
Russian Ambassador at Vienna to Russian Minister for Foreign Affairs.
Vienna
July 27, 1914.
(Telegraphic)

THE Minister for Foreign Affairs is away. During a long conversation which I had with Macchio today I drew his attention, in a perfectly friendly way, to the unfavorable impression produced in Russia by the presentation of demands by Austria to Serbia, which it was quite impossible for any independent State, however small, to accept. I added that this method of procedure might lead to the most undesirable complications, and that it had aroused profound surprise and general condemnation in Russia. We can only suppose that Austria, influenced by the assurances given by the German Representative at Vienna, who has egged her on throughout this crisis, has counted on the probable localization of the dispute with Serbia, and on the possibility of inflicting with impunity a serious blow upon that country. The declaration by the Russian Government that Russia could not possibly remain indifferent in the face of such conduct has caused a great sensation here.

No. 42.
Russian Ambassador at London to Russian Minister for Foreign Affairs.
London
July 27, 1914.
(Telegraphic)

GREY has just informed the German Ambassador, who came to question him as to the possibility of taking action at St. Petersburg, that such action ought rather to be taken at Vienna, and that the Berlin Cabinet were the best qualified to do so. Grey also pointed out that the Serbian reply to the Austrian note had exceeded anything that could have been expected in moderation and in its spirit of conciliation. Grey added that he had therefore come to the conclusion that Russia must have advised

Belgrade to return a moderate reply, and that he thought the Serbian reply could form the basis of a peaceful and acceptable solution of the question.

In these circumstances, continued Grey, if Austria were to begin hostilities in spite of that reply, she would prove her intention of crushing Serbia. Looked at in this light, the question might give rise to a situation, which might lead to a war in which all the Powers would be involved. Grey finally declared that the British Government was sincerely anxious to act with the German Government as long as the preservation of peace was in question; but, in the contrary event, Great Britain reserved to herself full liberty of action.

No. 6.
Baron Beyers, Belgian Minister at Berlin, to M. Davignon, Belgian Minister for Foreign Affairs.
Berlin
July 27, 1914.
(Telegraphic)

According to a telegram from the British Chargé d'Affaires at Belgrade, the Servian Government has given way on all the points of the Austrian note. They even allow the intervention of Austrian officials if such a proceeding is in conformity with the usages of international law. The British Chargé d'Affaires considers that this reply should satisfy Austria if she is not desirous of war. Nevertheless, a more hopeful atmosphere prevails here to-day, more particularly because hostilities against Serbia have not begun. The British Government suggests mediation by Great Britain, Germany, France, and Italy at St. Petersburg and Vienna in order to find some basis for compromise. Germany alone has not yet replied. The decision rests with the Emperor.

By this time, Russia and France want a war with Germany and are stopping at nothing to make it happen. To hide their true ambitions both countries are playing the mediator against Austria, even though both know the Serbian government was at fault for the crisis being started in the first place!

The murder of any European royal family is a declaration of war!

Telegram of the Imperial Ambassador at St. Petersburg to the Chancellor on July 27th, 1914.

Military Attaché reports a conversation with the Secretary of War.

Sasonof has requested the latter to enlighten me on the situation. The Secretary of War has given me his word of honor that no order to mobilize has as yet been issued. Though general preparations are being made, no reserves were called and no horses mustered. If Austria crossed the Serbian frontier, such military districts as are directed toward Austria, viz., Kiev, Odessa, Moscow, Kazan, are to be mobilized. Under no circumstances those on the German frontier, Warsaw, Vilni, St. Petersburg. Peace with Germany was desired very much. Upon my inquiry into the object of mobilization against Austria, he shrugged his shoulders and referred to the diplomats. I told the Secretary that we appreciated the friendly intentions, but considered mobilization even against Austria as very menacing.

Sazonof is misleading in this telegram. General mobilization has just been ordered.

Telegram of the Chancellor to the Imperial Ambassador at London on July 27th, 1914.

We know as yet nothing of a suggestion of Sir Edward Grey's to hold a quadruple conference in London. It is impossible for us to place our ally in his dispute with Serbia before a European tribunal. Our mediation must be limited to the danger of an Austro-Russian conflict.

**Telegram of the Imperial Consulate at Kovno to the Chancellor
on July 27th, 1914.**

Kovno has been declared to be in a state of war.

**Telegram of the Imperial Minister at Berne to the Chancellor
on July 27th, 1914.**

I have learned reliably that French XIVth corps has discontinued maneuvers.

This French Corp has just been put on mobilization alert and is pulling back for resupplying and refitting.

**Primary Documents: British Reaction to Austria's Ultimatum, 27 July 1914
No. 48.**

Reproduced below is the text of the reaction of Sir Edward Grey, British Foreign Secretary, to news that the Austro-Hungarian government regarded Serbia's reply to their ultimatum of 23 July 1914 unsatisfactory.

Grey stated to Count Mensdorff—the Austro-Hungarian ambassador to Britain—that he felt Serbia's response sufficient and was consequently disappointed at Austria-Hungary's apparent lack of patience in seeking a diplomatic solution.

The day following Grey's statement—on 28 July 1914—Austria-Hungary declared war on Serbia.

**Official Statement by Sir Edward Grey
British Secretary of State for Foreign Affairs
Foreign Office
July 27, 1914.**

Count Mensdorff told me by instruction to-day that the Serbian Government had not accepted the demands which the Austrian Government was obliged to address to them in order to secure permanently the most vital Austrian interests. Serbia showed that she did not intend to abandon her subversive aims, tending towards continuous disorder in the Austrian frontier territories and their final disruption from the Austrian Monarchy. Very reluctantly, and against their wish, the Austrian Government was compelled to take more severe measures to enforce a fundamental change of the attitude of enmity pursued up to now by Serbia. As the British Government knew, the Austrian Government had for many years endeavored to find a way to get on with their turbulent neighbor, though this had been made very difficult for them by the continuous provocations of Serbia. The Sarajevo murder had made clear to everyone what appalling consequences the Serbian propaganda had already produced and what a permanent threat to Austria it involved. We would understand that the Austrian Government must consider that the moment had arrived to obtain, by means of the strongest pressure, guarantees for the definite suppression of the Serbian aspirations and for the security of peace and order on the southeastern frontier of Austria.

As the peaceable means to this effect were exhausted, the Austrian Government must at last appeal to force. They had not taken this decision without reluctance. Their action, which had no sort of aggressive tendency, could not be represented otherwise than as an act of self-defense. Also they thought that they would serve a European interest if they prevented Serbia from being henceforth an element of general unrest such as she had been for the last ten years.

The high sense of justice of the British nation and of British statesmen could not blame the Austrian Government if the latter defended by the sword what was theirs, and cleared up their position with a country whose hostile policy had forced upon them for years measures so costly as to have gravely injured Austrian national prosperity.

Finally, the Austrian Government, confiding in their amicable relations with us, felt that they could count on our sympathy in a fight that was forced on them, and on our assistance in localizing the fight, if necessary.

Count Mensdorff added on his own account that, as long as Serbia was confronted with Turkey, Austria never took very severe measures because of her adherence to the policy of the free development of the Balkan States. Now that Serbia had doubled her territory and population without any Austrian interference, the repression of Serbian subversive aims was a matter of self-defense and self-preservation on Austria's part. He reiterated that Austria had no intention of taking Serbian territory or aggressive designs against Serbian territory.

I said that I could not understand the construction put by the Austrian Government upon the Serbian reply, and I told Count Mensdorff the substance of the conversation that I had had with the German Ambassador this morning about that reply.

Count Mensdorff admitted that, on paper, the Serbian reply might seem to be satisfactory; but the Serbians had refused the one thing—the cooperation of Austrian officials and police—which would be a real guarantee that in practice the Serbians would not carry on their subversive campaign against Austria.

I said that it seemed to me as if the Austrian Government believed that, even after the Serbian reply, they could make war upon Serbia anyhow, without risk of bringing Russia into the dispute. If they could make war on Serbia and at the same, time satisfies Russia, well and good; but if not, the consequences would be incalculable.

I pointed out to him that I quoted this phrase from an expression of the views of the German Government. I feared that it would be expected in St. Petersburg that the Serbian reply would diminish the tension, and now, when Russia found that there was increased tension, the situation would become increasingly serious. Already the effect on Europe was one of anxiety. I pointed out that our fleet was to have dispersed to-day, but we had felt unable to let it disperse. We should not think of calling up reserves at this moment, and there was no menace in what we had done about our fleet; but, owing to the possibility of a European conflagration, it was impossible for us to disperse our forces at this moment. I gave this as an illustration of the anxiety that was felt. It seemed to me that the Serbian reply already involved the greatest humiliation to Serbia that I had ever seen a country undergo, and it was very disappointing to me that the reply was treated by the Austrian Government as if it were as unsatisfactory as a blank negative.

Source: *Source Records of the Great War*, *Vol. I*, ed. *Charles F. Horne*, *National Alumni, 1923*.

1914 July 27: France pressured Russia to achieve highest state of readiness.

Primary Documents: British Ambassador's Reaction in Vienna to Austria's Ultimatum, 27 July 1914
Updated: Saturday, 31 May 2003.

Reproduced below is the text of the official report to Sir Edward Grey (the British Foreign Secretary) made by the British Ambassador in Vienna, Sir Maurice de Bunsen.

In his report, de Bunsen made clear his belief that the Austro-Hungarian government was set upon war with Serbia from the outset, crafting their ultimatum to Serbia in such a manner as to make war inevitable.

Primary Documents: French Reaction to Austria's Ultimatum, 27 July 1914
Updated: Saturday, 24 May 2003.

Reproduced below is the text of the reaction of Jules Cambon, French ambassador to Germany, to news that the Austro-Hungarian government regarded Serbia's reply to their ultimatum of 23 July 1914 unsatisfactory.

Cambon reported that a meeting with von Jagow in Berlin led him to believe that Germany, like Austria-Hungary, appeared not to desire a peaceful settlement with Serbia—this in spite of protestations to the contrary by von Jagow.

The day following Cambon's report—on 28 July 1914—Austria-Hungary declared war on Serbia.

Official Report by Jules Cambon,
French Ambassador at Berlin in 1914.
Berlin
July 27, 1914.

I had a conversation yesterday with the Secretary of State and gave support to the *demarche* which Sir E. Goschen (British ambassador to Germany) had just made.

Herr von Jagow replied to me, as he had to the English Ambassador, that he could not accept the proposal that the Italian, French, and German Ambassadors should be instructed to Endeavour to find with Sir Edward Grey a method of resolving the present difficulties, because that would be to set up a real conference to deal with the affairs of Austria and Russia.

I replied to Herr von Jagow that I regretted his answer, but that the great object which Sir Edward Grey had in view went beyond any question of form; that what was important was the cooperation of England and France with Germany and Italy in a work of peace; that this cooperation could take effect through common *demarches* at St. Petersburg and at Vienna; that he had often expressed to me his regret at seeing the two allied groups always opposed to one another in Europe; that there was here an opportunity of proving that there was a European spirit, by showing four Powers belonging to the two groups acting in common agreement to prevent a conflict.

Herr von Jagow evaded the point by saying that Germany had engagements with Austria. I observed to him that the relations of Germany with Vienna were no closer than those of France with Russia, and that it was he himself who actually was putting the two groups of allies in opposition.

The Secretary of State then said to me that he was not refusing to act so as to keep off an Austro-Russian dispute, but that he could not intervene in the Austro-Serbian dispute. "The one is the consequence of the other," I said, "and it is a question of preventing the appearance of a new factor of such a nature as to lead to intervention by Russia."

As the Secretary of State persisted in saying that he was obliged to keep his engagements towards Austria, I asked him if he was bound to follow her everywhere with his eyes blindfolded, and if he had taken note of the reply of Serbia to Austria which the Serbian Charge d'Affaires had delivered to him this morning.

"I have not yet had time," he said. "I regret it. You would see that except on some points of detail Serbia has yielded entirely. It appears then, that, since Austria has obtained the satisfaction which your support has procured for her, you might to-day advise her to be content or to examine with Serbia the terms of her reply."

As Herr von Jagow gave me no clear reply, I asked him whether Germany wished for war. He protested energetically, saying that he knew what was in my mind, but that it was wholly incorrect. "You must then," I replied, "act consistently. When you read the Serbian reply, I entreat you in the name of humanity to weigh the terms in your conscience, and do not personally assume a part of the responsibility for the catastrophe which you are allowing to be prepared."

Herr von Jagow protested anew, adding that he was ready to join England and France in a common effort, but that it was necessary to find a form for this intervention, which he could accept, and that the Cabinets must come to an understanding on this point.

"For the rest," he added, "direct conversations between Vienna and St. Petersburg have been entered upon and are in progress. I expect very good results from them and I am hopeful."

As I was leaving, I told him that this morning I had had the impression that the hour of *detente* had struck, but I now saw clearly that there was nothing in it. He replied that I was mistaken; that he hoped that matters were on the right road and would perhaps rapidly reach a favorable conclusion. I asked him to take such action in Vienna as would hasten the progress of events, because it was a matter of importance not to allow time for the development in Russia of one of those currents of opinion, which carry all before them.

In my opinion it would be well to ask Sir Edward Grey, who must have been warned by Sir Edward Goschen of the refusal to his proposal in the form in which it was made, to renew it under another form, so that Germany would have no pretext for refusing to associate herself with it, and would have to assume the responsibilities that belong to her in the eyes of England.

Source: *Source Records of the Great War, Vol. I, ed. Charles F. Horne, National Alumni, 1923.*

Primary Documents: U.S. Ambassador's Reaction to Austria's Ultimatum, July 1914
Updated: Saturday, 31 May, 2003.

Reproduced below are portions of the memoirs, published as *Ambassador Morgenthau's Story* in 1918 by Doubleday & Page, of the wartime U.S. Ambassador to Turkey, Henry Morgenthau. In the following extract from his memoirs, Morgenthau offers thoughts on both his and others' reaction to news of Archduke Franz Ferdinand's assassination in late June 1914.

More interestingly, Morgenthau also avers that the German government, in tandem with Vienna, definitively resolved to go to war with both France and Russia in early July and that the archduke's assassination merely gave Austria-Hungary a pretext for doing so.

Memoirs of Henry Morgenthau
U.S. Ambassador to Constantinople in 1914.

On June 29th we heard of the assassination of the Grand Duke of Austria and his consort. Everybody received the news calmly; there was, indeed, a stunned feeling that something momentous had happened, but there was practically no excitement.

A day or two after this tragedy I had a long talk with Talaat (note: Talaat Bey, the Turkish Minister of the Interior, was the chief leader of the "Young Turks" and the real ruler of the country) on diplomatic matters; he made no reference at all to this event. I think now that we were all affected by a kind of emotional paralysis—as we were nearer the centre than most people, we certainly realized the dangers in the situation.

In a day or two, our tongues seemed to have been loosened, for we began to talk—and to talk war. When I saw Von Mutius, the German charge, and Weitz, the diplomat-correspondent of the *Frankfurter Zeitung,* they also discussed the impending conflict, and again they gave their forecast a characteristically Germanic touch; when war came, they said, of course the United States would take advantage of it to get all the Mexican and South American trade!

When I called upon Pallavicini (note: the Austrian Ambassador at Constantinople) to express my condolences over the Grand Duke's death, he received me with the most stately solemnity. He was conscious that he was representing the imperial family, and his grief seemed to be personal; one would think that he had lost his own son. I expressed my abhorrence and that of my nation for the deed, and our sympathy with the aged emperor.

"Ja, ja, es ist sehr schrecklich" (yes, yes, it is very terrible), he answered, almost in a whisper. "Serbia will be condemned for her conduct," he added. "She will be compelled to make reparation."

A few days later, when Pallavicini called upon me, he spoke of the nationalistic societies that Serbia had permitted to exist and of her determination to annex Bosnia and Herzegovina. He said that his government would insist on the abandonment of these societies and these pretensions, and that probably a punitive expedition into Serbia would be necessary to prevent such outrages as the murder of the Grand Duke. Herein I had my first intimation of the famous ultimatum of July 23rd.

The entire diplomatic corps attended the requiem mass for the Grand Duke and Duchess, celebrated at the Church of Sainte Marie on July 4th. The church is located in the Grande Rue de Pera, not far from the Austrian Embassy; to reach it we had to descend a flight of forty stone steps. At the top of these stairs representatives of the Austrian Embassy, dressed in full uniform, with crepe on the left arm, met us, and escorted us to our seats.

All the ambassadors sat in the front pew; I recall this with strange emotions now, for it was the last time that, we ever sat together. The service was dignified and beautiful; I remember it with especial vividness because of the contrasting scene that immediately followed.

When the stately, gorgeously robed priests had finished, we all shook hands with the Austrian Ambassador, returned to our automobiles, and started on our eight-mile ride along the Bosphorus to the American Embassy. For this day was not only the day when we paid our tribute to the murdered heir of this medieval autocracy; it was also the Fourth of July.

The very setting of the two scenes symbolized these two national ideals. I always think of this ambassadorial group going down those stone steps to the church, to pay their respect to the Grand Duke, and then going up to the gaily decorated American Embassy, to pay their respect to the Declaration of Independence....

In glancing at the ambassadorial group at the church and, afterward, at our reception, I was surprised to note that one familiar figure was missing. Wangenheim, Austria's ally, was not present. This somewhat puzzled me at the time, but afterward I had the explanation from Wangenheim's own lips. He had left some days before for Berlin. The Kaiser had summoned him to an imperial council, which met on July 5th, and which decided to plunge Europe into war. *(The author fully describes Baron von Wangenheim, the German Ambassador, as being the most important figure in Constantinople, dictating the Turkish policies, and later almost intoxicated by the early German victories.)*

The good fortune of the German armies so excited him that he was sometimes led into indiscretions, and his exuberance one day caused him to tell me certain facts, which, I think, will always have great historical value.

He disclosed precisely how and when Germany had precipitated this war. To-day his revelation of this secret looks like a most monstrous indiscretion, but we must remember Wangenheim's state of mind at the time. The whole world then believed that Paris was doomed and Wangenheim reflected this attitude in his frequent declarations that the war would be over in two or three months. The whole German enterprise was evidently progressing according to program. I have already mentioned that the German Ambassador had left for Berlin soon after the assassination of the Grand Duke, and he now revealed the cause of his sudden disappearance.

The Kaiser, he told me, had summoned him to Berlin for an imperial conference. This meeting took place at Potsdam on July 5th. The Kaiser presided and nearly all the important ambassadors attended.

Wangenheim himself was summoned to give assurance about Turkey and enlighten his associates generally on the situation in Constantinople, which was then regarded as almost the pivotal point in the impending war.

In telling me who attended this conference Wangenheim used no names, though he specifically said that among them were—the facts are so important that I quote his exact words in the German which he used—"die Haupter des Generalstabs und der Marine" (The heads of the general staff and of the navy) by which I have assumed that he meant Von Moltke and Von Tirpitz.

The great bankers, railroad directors, and the captains of German industry, all of whom were as necessary to German war preparations as the army itself, also attended.

Wangenheim now told me that the Kaiser solemnly put the question to each man in turn: "Are you ready for war?" All replied "yes" except the financiers. They said that they must have two weeks to sell their foreign securities and to make loans. At that time, few people had looked upon the Sarajevo tragedy as something that would inevitably lead to war.

This conference, Wangenheim told me, took all precautions that no such suspicion should be aroused. It decided to give the bankers time to readjust their finances for the coming war, and then the several members went quietly back to their work or started on vacations. The Kaiser went to Norway on his yacht, Von Bethmann-Hollweg left for a rest, and Wangenheim returned to Constantinople.

In telling me about this conference Wangenheim, of course, admitted that Germany had precipitated the war. I think that he was rather proud of the whole performance, proud that Germany had gone about the matter in so methodical and farseeing a way, and especially proud that he himself had been invited to participate in so epoch-making a gathering.

I have often wondered why he revealed to me so momentous a secret, and I think that perhaps the real reason was his excessive vanity—his desire to show me how close he stood to the inner counsels of his emperor and the part that he had played in bringing on this conflict.

Whatever the motive, this indiscretion certainly had the effect of showing me who the guilty parties were really in this monstrous crime. The several blue, red, and yellow books which flooded Europe during the few months following the outbreak, and the hundreds of documents which were issued by German propagandists attempting to establish Germany's innocence, have never made the slightest impression on me. For my conclusions as to the responsibility are not based on suspicions or belief or the study of circumstantial data. I do not have to reason or argue about the matter. I know.

The conspiracy that has caused this greatest of human tragedies was hatched by the Kaiser and his imperial crew at this Potsdam conference of July 5, 1914. One of the chief participants, flushed with his triumph at the apparent success of the plot, told me the details with his own mouth.

Whenever I hear people arguing about the responsibility for this war or read the clumsy and lying excuses put forth by Germany, I simply recall the burly figure of Wangenheim, as he appeared that August afternoon, puffing away at a huge black cigar, and giving me his account of this historic meeting. Why waste any time discussing the matter after that?

This imperial conference took place July 5th and the Serbian ultimatum was sent on July 23d. That is just about the two weeks' interval, which the financiers had demanded to complete their plans. All the great stock exchanges of the world show that the German bankers profitably used this interval. Their records disclose that stocks were being sold in large quantities and that prices declined rapidly.

At that time, the markets were somewhat puzzled at this movement but Wangenheim's explanation clears up any doubts that may still remain. Germany was changing her securities into cash for war purposes. If any one wishes to verify Wangenheim, I would suggest that he examine the quotations of the New York stock market for these two historic weeks.

He will find that there were astonishing slumps in prices, especially on the stocks that had an international market. Between July 5th and July 22nd, Union Pacific dropped from 155.5 to 127.5, Baltimore and Ohio from 91.5 to 81, United States Steel from 61 to 50.5, Canadian Pacific from 194 to 185.5, and Northern Pacific from 111 to 108.

At that time, the high protectionists were blaming the Simmons-Underwood Tariff Act as responsible for this fall in values, while other critics of the Administration attributed it to the Federal

Reserve Act—which had not yet been put into effect. How little the Wall Street brokers and the financial experts realized that an imperial conference, which had been held in Potsdam and presided over by the Kaiser, was the real force that was then depressing the market!

Wangenheim not only gave me the details of this Potsdam conference, but he disclosed the same secret to the Marquis Garroni, the Italian Ambassador at Constantinople. Italy was at that time technically Germany's ally.

The Austrian Ambassador, the Marquis Pallavicini, also practically admitted that the Central Powers had anticipated the war. On August 18th, Francis Joseph's birthday, I made the usual ambassadorial visit of congratulation. Quite naturally, the conversation turned upon the Emperor, who had that day passed his 84th year.

Pallavicini spoke about him with the utmost pride and veneration. He told me how keen-minded and clear-headed the aged emperor was how he had the most complete understanding of international affairs, and how he gave everything his personal supervision.

To illustrate the Austrian Kaiser's grasp of public events, Pallavicini instanced the present war. The previous May, Pallavicini had had an audience with Francis Joseph in Vienna. At that time, Pallavicini now told me, the Emperor had said that a European war was unavoidable. The Central Powers would not accept the Treaty of Bucharest as a settlement of the Balkan question, and only a general war, the Emperor had told Pallavicini, could ever settle that problem.

The Treaty of Bucharest, I may recall, was the settlement that ended the second Balkan War. This divided the European dominions of Turkey, excepting Constantinople and a small piece of adjoining territory, among the Balkan nations, chiefly Serbia and Greece. That treaty strengthened Serbia greatly; so much did it increase Serbia's resources, indeed, that Austria feared that it had laid the beginning of a new European state, which might grow sufficiently strong to resist her own plans of aggrandizement.

Austria held a large Serbian population under her yoke in Bosnia and Herzegovina, and these Serbians desired, above everything else, annexation to their own country. Moreover, the Pan-German plans in the East necessitated the destruction of Serbia, the state which, so long as it stood intact, blocked the Germanic road to the Orient.

It had been the Austro-German expectation that the Balkan War would destroy Serbia as a nation that Turkey would, simply annihilate King Peter's forces. This was precisely what the Germanic plans demanded, and for this reason, Austria and Germany did nothing to prevent the Balkan wars. However, the result was exactly the reverse, for out of the conflict arose a stronger Serbia than ever, standing firm like a breakwater against the Germanic flood.

Most historians agree that the Treaty of Bucharest made inevitable this war. I have the Marquis Pallavicini's evidence that this was likewise the opinion of Francis Joseph himself. The audience at which the Emperor made this statement was held in May, more than a month before the assassination of the Grand Duke. Clearly, therefore, we have the Austrian Emperor's assurances that the war would have come irrespective of the assassination at Sarajevo.

Source: *Source Records of the Great War, Vol. I, ed. Charles F. Horne, National Alumni, 1923*

Henry Morgenthau has it wrong! It is France and Russia who wanted war in July; Germany was doing all it could to avoid a general European conflict. Russia and France are giving the orders for general mobilization, while Germany is still seeking a peaceful resolution. It was the French president who was in Russia to encourage the Russian tsar to tell the Serbian government to accept parts of Austrian demands while French and Russian leaders work out a plan of action.

1914 July 27: Russia drew up the order for full mobilization.

Telegram of the Chancellor to the Imperial Ambassador in London
on July 27th, 1914.

We have at once started the mediation proposal in Vienna in the sense as desired by Sir Edward Grey. We have communicated besides to Count Berchtold's the desire of M. Sasonof for a direct parley with Vienna.

No. 49.
Sir Edward Grey to Sir R. Rodd, British Ambassador at Rome.
British Foreign Office
July 27, 1914.

Sir,

The Italian Ambassador informed Sir A. Nicolson today that the Italian Minister of Foreign Affairs agreed entirely with my proposal for a conference of the Four Powers to be held in London.

As regards the question of asking Russia, Austria-Hungary, and Serbia to suspend military operations pending the results of the conference, the Marquis di San Giuliano would recommend the suggestion warmly to the German Government, and would enquire what procedures they would propose should be followed at Vienna.

I am, &tc.
Sir E. Grey

No. 50.
Sir M. Bunsen, British Ambassador at Vienna, to Sir Edward Grey.
(received July 31)
Vienna
July 28, 1914.

Sir,

I have the honor to transmit to you herewith the text of the Austro-Hungarian note announcing the declaration of war against Serbia.

Enclosure in No. 50

Copy of note verbal, dated Vienna, July 28, 1914

In order to bring to an end the subversive intrigues originating from Belgrade and aimed at the territorial integrity of the Austro-Hungarian Monarchy, the Imperial and Royal Government has delivered to the Royal Serbian government a note, dated July 23, 1914, in which a series of demands were formulated, for the acceptance of which a delay of forty-eight hours has been granted to the Royal Government. The Royal Serbian Government not having answered this note in a satisfactory manner, the Imperial and Royal government are themselves compelled to see to the safeguarding of their rights and interests, and, with this object, to have recourse to force of arms.

Austria-Hungary, who has just addressed to Serbia, a formal declaration, in conformity with article 1 of the convention of the 18th October, 1907, relative to the opening of hostilities, consider herself henceforward in a state of war with Serbia.

In bringing the above to notice of his Britannic Majesty's Embassy, the Minister for Foreign Affairs has the honor to declare that Austria-Hungary will act during the hostilities in conformity with the terms of the Conventions of the Hague of the 18th October, 1907, as also with those declarations of London of the 28th February, 1909, provided an analogous procedure is adopted by Serbia.

The Embassy is requested to be so good as to communicate the present notification as soon as possible to the British government.

No. 51.
Sir F. Bertie, British Ambassador at Paris, Sir Edward Grey.
(received July 28)
Paris
July 27, 1914.
Sir
I have the honor to transmit to you herewith copy of a memorandum from acting Minister for Foreign Affairs as to the steps to be taken to prevent an out break of hostilities between Austria and Serbia.

I have, &tc.
Francis Bertie

Enclosure in No. 51

Note communicated to Sir F. Bertie by M. Bienvenu-Martin

In a note of the 25th of this month, his Excellency the British Ambassador informed the Government of the Republic that, in Sir E. Grey's opinion, the only possible way of assuring the maintenance of peace in the case of the relations between Russia and Austria becoming more strained would be if the representatives of the Great Britain, France, Germany, and Italy in Austria and Russia were to take joint action at Vienna and at St. Petersburg; and he expressed the wish to know if the Government of the Republic were disposed to welcome such a suggestion.

The Minister for Foreign Affairs *ad interim* has the honor to inform his Excellency Sir F. Bertie that he as requested M. Jules Cambon to concert with the British Ambassador in Germany and to support any representation which may the may consider it advisable to make to the Berlin Cabinet.

In accordance with the desire expressed by the British Government and conveyed to them by Sir F. Bertie in his note of the 26th of this month, the Government of the Republic has also authorized M. Paul Cambon* to take part in the conference which Sir E. Grey has proposed with a view to discovering in consultation with himself and the German and Italian Ambassadors in London a means of settling the present difficulties.

The Government of the Republic is likewise ready to instruct the French representatives at St. Petersburg, Vienna, and Belgrade to induce the Russian, Austrian, and Serbian Governments to abstain from all military operations pending the results of this conference. He considers, however, that the chance of Sir E. Grey's proposal of being successful depends essentially on the action, which the Berlin Government would be willing to take at Vienna. Representations made to the Austrian-Hungarian Government for the purpose of bringing about a suspension of military operations would seem bound to fail unless the German Government do not before hand exercise their influence on the Vienna cabinet.

The President of the Council *ad interim* takes the opportunity, &tc.

---

* French Ambassador in London

No. 52.
Note communicated by French Embassy.
(received July 28, 1914)

The Government of the Republic accepts Sir Edward Grey's proposal in regard to intervention by Great Britain, France, Germany, and Italy with a view to avoiding military operations on the frontiers of Austria, Russia, and Serbia; and they have authorized M. P. Cambon* to take part in the deliberations of the four representative at the meeting which is to be held in London.

The French Ambassador in Berlin has received instructions to consult first the British Ambassador in Berlin, and then to support the action taken by the latter in such a manner and degree as may be considered appropriate.

M. Viviani^ is ready to send to the representatives of France in Vienna, St. Petersburg, and Belgrade instructions in the sense suggested by the British Government.

French Embassy
July 27, 1914

The key phrase in this telegram is "in a sense," which tells me that France will do as they seem appropriate as far as the plan they have with Russia. It also says that Sir E. Grey's proposal will only be used if it fits in with what the French representatives find out in Vienna, Russia, and Belgrade. They will, of course, communicate with Russia and Belgrade first.

No. 53.
M. Sazonof, Russian Minister for Foreign affairs, to Count Benckendorff, Russian Ambassador in London.
(communicated by Count Benckendorff)
(received July 28, 1914)
St. Petersburg
July 27, 1914.
(Telegraphic)

The British Ambassador came to ascertain whether we think it is desirable that Great Britain should take the initiative in convoking a conference in London of the representatives of Great Britain, France, Germany, and Italy to examine the possibility of a way out of the present situation.

I replied to the Ambassador that I have begun conversations with the Austro-Hungarian Ambassador under conditions which, I hope, may be favorable. I have not, however, received yet any reply to the proposal made by me for revising the note between the two Cabinets.

If direct explanations with the Vienna Cabinet were to prove impossible, I am ready to accept the British proposal, or any other proposal of a kind that would bring about a favorable solution of the conflict.

I wish, however, to put an end from this day forth to a misunderstanding which might arise from the answer given by the French minister of justice to the German Ambassador, regarding counsels of moderation to be given to the imperial Cabinet.

The Russian Minister for Foreign Affairs, M. Sazonof, knows already what Austria's reply will be to his proposal. He is not to keen to the idea that Britain has possibly stopped another Balkan crisis in which he wants to happen and possibly help start. Why would he bring up the fact that the French Minister of Justice is involved with this when he knows that legal matters are used to finish political

---

^ French minister of Foreign Affairs.

negotiations for legal purposes? He also knows that Germany won't decide how this will end, though he does know that Germany is trying to get Austria to settle this crisis while not going back on their demands to Serbia.

No. 55.
Sir G. Buchanan, British Ambassador at St. Petersburg, to Sir Edward Grey.
St. Petersburg
July 27, 1914.
(Telegraphic)

With reference to my telegram of yesterday,[24] I saw the minister for Foreign affairs this afternoon and found him very conciliatory and more optimistic.

He would, he said use all his influence at Belgrade to induce the Serbian Government to go as far as possible in giving satisfaction to Austria, but her territorial integrity must be guaranteed and her right as a sovereign State respected, so that she should not become Austria's vassal. He did not know whether Austria would accept friendly exchange of views, which he had proposed, but, if she did, he wished to keep in close contact with the other Powers throughout the conversation that would ensue.

He again referred to the fact that the obligations undertaken by Serbia in 1908, alluded to in the Austrian ultimatum, were given to the Powers.

I asked if he had heard of your proposal with regard to conference of the Four Powers, and on his replying in the affirmative, I told him confidentially of your instructions to me, and enquired whether instead of such a conference he would prefer a direct exchange of views would be more agreeable to Austria-Hungary.

His Excellency said he was perfectly ready to stand aside if the Powers accepted the proposal for a conference, but he trusted that you would keep in touch with the Russian Ambassador in the event of its taking place

No. 56.
Sir M. de Bunsen Ambassador at Vienna, to Sir Edward Grey.
(received July 28, 1914)
Vienna
(Telegraphic)

The Russian Ambassador had today a long and earnest conversation with Baron Macchio, the Under-Secretary of State For Foreign Affairs. He told him that, having just come back from St. Petersburg, he was well acquainted with the views of the Russian Government and the state of Russian public opinion. He could assure him that if actual war broke out with Serbia it would be impossible to localize it. Russia was not prepared to give away again, as she had done on previous occasions, and especially during the annexation crisis of 1909. He earnestly hoped that something would be done before Serbia was actually invaded. Baron Macchio replied that this would now be difficult, as a skirmish had already taken place on the Danube, in which the Serbians had been the aggressors.

The Russians ambassador said that he would do all he could to keep the Serbians quiet pending any discussions that might yet take place, and he told me that he would advise his government to induce the Serbian Government to avoid any conflict as long as possible, and to fall back before an

---

[23] See No. 44.

Austrian advance. Time so gained should suffice to enable a settlement to be reached. He had just heard of a satisfactory conversation, which the Russian Minister for Foreign Affairs had yesterday with the Austrian Ambassador at St. Petersburg. The former had agreed that much of the Austro-Hungary note to Serbia had been perfectly reasonable, and in fact, they had practically reached an understanding as to the guarantees, which Serbia might reasonably be asked to give to Austria-Hungary for her future good behavior.

The Russian Ambassador urged that the Austrian Ambassador at St. Petersburg should be furnished with full powers to continue discussion with the Russian Minister for Foreign Affairs, who was very willing to advise Serbia to yield all that could be fairly asked of her as an independent Power. Baron Macchio promised to submit this suggestion to the minister for Foreign Affairs.

The only way the Serbs would act as the aggressors would be with the Russian Foreign Affairs telling them to act in a matter that would send a message to Austria that we are willing to go further in this crisis.

Chapter Twenty-Nine
July 28, 1914

28 July 1914: Austria declares war on Serbia.

Primary Documents: Austria-Hungary's Declaration of War with Serbia, 28 July 1914
Updated: Thursday, 3 January 2002.

The following telegram sent by Count Leopold von Berchtold's (Austro-Hungarian Foreign Minister) at 11.10 A.M. to M. N. Pashitch (Serbian Prime Minister and Foreign Minister), who received it at 12.30 P.M.

Sent by telegram (the first such declaration of war).

Vienna
28 July 1914

The Royal Serbian Government not having answered in a satisfactory manner the note of July 23, 1914, presented by the Austro-Hungarian Minister at Belgrade, the Imperial and Royal Government are themselves compelled to see to the safeguarding of their rights and interests, and, with this object, to have recourse to force of arms.

Austria-Hungary consequently considers herself henceforward in state of war with Serbia.

Count Berchtold's Russian Consul General at Fiume to Russian Minister for Foreign Affairs.
Fiume
July 28, 1914.
(Telegraphic)

STATE of siege has been proclaimed in Slavonia, in Croatia, and at Fiume, and the reservists of all classes have also been called up.

No. 58.
Sir F. Bertie, British Ambassador at Paris, to Sir Edward Grey.
Paris, France
July 28, 1914.
(Telegraphic)

I communicated to the acting minister for Foreign Affairs this afternoon the substance of your conversation with the German Ambassador, recorded in your telegram[24] to Berlin of July 27.

His Excellency is grateful for the communication. He said that it confirms what he heard of your attitude, and feels confident that your observations to the German Ambassador will have a good effect in the interest of peace.

No. 46.
Russian Chargé d'Affaires at Berlin to Russian Minister for Foreign Affairs.
Berlin
July 28, 1914.
(Telegraphic)

THE Wolff Bureau has not published the text of the Serbian reply, although it was communicated to them. Up to the present, this note has not appeared in extensor in any of the local papers, which, to all appearances, do not wish to publish it in their columns, being well aware of the calming effect, which it would have on German readers.

No. 54.
M. Sazonof, Russian Minister for Foreign affairs, to Count Benckendorff, Russian Ambassador in London.
(communicated by Count Benckendorff)
St. Petersburg
July 28, 1914.
(Telegraphic)

My interviews with the German Ambassador confirm my impression that Germany is, if anything in favor of the uncompromising attitude adopted by Austria. The Berlin Cabinet, who could have prevented the whole crisis developing, appears to be exerting no influence on their ally.

The Ambassador considers that the Serbian reply is insufficient.

This attitude of the German government is most alarming.

It seems to me that Great Britain is in a better position than any other Power to make another attempt at Berlin to induce the German Government to take the necessary action. There is no doubt that the key of the situation is to be found at Berlin.

M. Sazonof is being quite foolish right here. It was Serbian citizens who murdered the archduke and not German citizens. This crisis is a product of Russian influence by French desires to disrupt Europe. So M. Sazonof should be putting a lot of pressure on Serbia to come to terms with Austria. After all, this murder is an act of war and Austria is treating it as such now.

---

[24] See No. 46 of British telegrams.

No. 47.
Russian Ambassador at Vienna to Russian Minister for Foreign Affairs.
Vienna
July 28, 1914.
(Telegraphic)

THE order for general mobilization has been signed.

No. 48.
Russian Minister for Foreign Affairs to Russian Ambassador at London.
St. Petersburg
July 28, 1914.
(Telegraphic)

In face of the hostilities between Austria-Hungary and Serbia, it is necessary that Great Britain should take instant mediatory action, and that the military measures undertaken by Austria against Serbia should be immediately suspended. Otherwise mediation will only serve as an excuse to make the question drag on, and will meanwhile make it possible for Austria to crush Serbia completely and to acquire a dominant position in the Balkans. Sent to Paris, Berlin Vienna, and Rome.

From: **Count Leopold Berchtold, Austro-Hungarian Minister for Foreign Affairs.**
To: **M. N. Pashitch, Prime Minister and Minister for Foreign Affairs.**
Vienna
July 28, 1914.
(Telegraphic)

THE Royal Serbian Government not having answered in a satisfactory manner the note of July 23, 1914, presented by the Austro-Hungarian Minister at Belgrade, the Imperial and Royal Government are themselves compelled to see to the safeguarding of their rights and interests, and, with this object, to have recourse to force of arms. Austria-Hungary consequently considers herself henceforward in state of war with Serbia.

No. 46.
From: **M. N. Pashitch, Prime Minister and Minister for Foreign Affairs.**
To: **All the Serbian Legations abroad.**
Nish
July 28, 1914.
(Telegraphic)

The Austro-Hungarian Government declared war on Serbia at noon to-day by an open telegram to the Serbian Government.

No. 59.
Sir F. Bertie Ambassador at Paris, to Sir Edward Grey.
Paris, France
July 28, 1914.
(Telegraphic)

I informed the acting Minister for Foreign Affairs today of your conversation with the Russian Ambassador, as recorded in your telegram of yesterday[25] to St. Petersburg.

He is grateful for the communication, and quite appreciates the impossibility for His Majesty's Government to declare themselves with solidarity with Russia on a question between Austria and Serbia, which in its present condition is not one affecting England. He also sees that you cannot take up an attitude at Berlin and Vienna more Serbian thane that attributed in German and Austrian sources to the Russian Government.

German Ambassador has stated that Austria would respect the integrity of Serbia, but when asked whether her independence also would be respected, he gave no assurance.

Why should he give an assurance to Serbia's independence? Twice now Serbia as committed an act of war against Austria. With this being said Austria has every right to invade Serbia.

No. 47.
From: **Dr. M. Spalaikovitch, Minister at Petrograd.**
To: **M. Sazonof, Russian Minister for Foreign Affairs.**
Petrograd
July 28, 1914.

Your Excellency,
I have the honor to inform Your Excellency that I have received from M. Pashitch the following urgent telegram dispatched from Nish at 2.10 P.M.

"The Austro-Hungarian Government declared war on Serbia to-day at noon by an open telegram to the Serbian Governments." I have the honor to inform Your Excellency of this regrettable act, which a Great Power had the courage to commit against a small Slav country which only recently emerged from a long series of heroic, but exhausting battles, and I beg leave on this occasion of deep gravity for my country, to express the hope that this act, which disturbs the peace of Europe and revolts her conscience, will be condemned by the whole civilized world and severely punished by Russia, the protector of Serbia. I beg Your Excellency to be so kind as to lay this petition from the whole Serbian nation before the throne of His Majesty. I take this opportunity to assure Your Excellency of my loyalty and respect. I have, &tc.

This telegram is showing that the murder of the Royal Austrian family is okay and that Serbia was in its legal right to assassinate the archduke and his pregnant wife.

---

[25] See No. 47.

No. 46.
From: M. N. Pashitch, Prime Minister and Minister for Foreign Affairs.
To: All the Serbian Legations abroad.
Nish
July 28, 1914.
(Telegraphic)

The Austro-Hungarian Government declared war on Serbia at noon to-day by an open telegram to the Serbian Government.

No. 60.
Sir E. Goschen, British Ambassador at Berlin, to Sir Edward Grey.
Berlin
July 28, 1914.
(Telegraphic)

Secretary of State Spoke yesterday in the same sense as that reported in my telegram of yesterday[26] to my French and Italian colleagues respecting your proposal. I discussed with my two colleagues this morning his reply, and we found that, while refusing the proposed conference, he had said to all of us that nevertheless he desired to work with us for the maintenance of general peace. We therefore deduced that if he is sincere in this wish he can only be objecting to the form of your proposal. Perhaps he himself could be induced to suggest lines on which he would find it possible to work with us.

No. 47.
From: Dr. M. Spalaikovitch, Minister at Petrograd.
To: M. Sazonof, Russian Minister for Foreign Affairs.
Petrograd
July 28, 1914.

Your Excellency,

I have the honour to inform Your Excellency that I have received from M. Pashitch the following urgent telegram dispatched from Nish at 2.10 P.M. "The Austro-Hungarian Government declared war on Serbia to-day at noon by an open telegram to the Serbian Governments."

I have the honour to inform Your Excellency of this regrettable act, which a Great Power had the courage to commit against a small Slav country which only recently emerged from a long series of heroic, but exhausting battles, and I beg leave on this occasion of deep gravity for my country, to express the hope that this act, which disturbs the peace of Europe and revolts her conscience, will be condemned by the whole civilized world and severely punished by Russia, the protector of Serbia.

I beg Your Excellency to be so kind as to lay this petition from the whole Serbian nation before the throne of His Majesty.

I take this opportunity to assure Your Excellency of my loyalty and respect.

---

[26] See No. 43.

No. 7.
Count Errembault de Dudzeele, Belgian Minister at Vienna, to M. Davignon, Belgian Minister for Foreign Affairs.
Vienna
July 28, 1914.
(Telegraphic)

The Minister for Foreign Affairs has notified me of the declaration of war by Austria-Hungary against Serbia.

Telegram of the Chancellor to the Imperial Ambassador at St. Petersburg
On July 28th, 1914.

We continue in our endeavor to induce Vienna to elucidate in St. Petersburg the object and scope of the Austrian action in Serbia in a manner both convincing and satisfactory to Russia. The declaration of war, which has meanwhile ensued, alters nothing in this matter.

The Chancellor to the Governments of Germany.
Confidential. Berlin, July 28, 1914.

You will make the following report to the Government to which you are accredited:

In view of the facts which the Austrian Government has published in its note to the Serbian Government, the last doubt must disappear that the outrage to which the Austro-Hungarian successor to the throne has fallen a victim, was prepared in Serbia, to say the least with the connivance of members of the Serbian Government and army. It is a product of the pan-Serb intrigues, which for a series of years have become a source of permanent disturbance for the Austro-Hungarian Monarchy and for the whole of Europe.

The pan-Serb chauvinism appeared especially marked during the Bosnian crisis. Only to the far-reaching self-restraint and moderation of the Austro-Hungarian Government and the energetic intercession of the Powers is it to be ascribed that the provocations to which Austro-Hungary was exposed at that time, did not lead to a conflict. The assurance of future behavior, which the Serbian Government gave at that time, it has not kept. Under the very eyes, at least with the tacit sufferance of official Serbia, the pan-Serb propaganda has meanwhile continued to increase in scope and intensity. It would be compatible neither with its dignity nor with its right to self-preservation if the Austro-Hungarian Government persisted to view idly any longer the intrigues beyond the frontier, through which are the safeties and the integrity of the Monarchy permanently threatened. With this state of affairs, the action as well as the demands of the Austro-Hungarian Government can be viewed only as justifiable.

The reply of the Serbian Government to the demands, which the Austro-Hungarian Government put on the 23rd inst., through its representative in Belgrade, shows that the dominating factors in Serbia are not inclined to cease their former policies and agitation. There will remain nothing else for the Austro-Hungarian Government than to press its demands, if need be, through military action, unless it renounces for good its position as a great Power.

Some Russian personalities deem it their right as a matter of course and a task of Russia's, to actively become a party to Serbia in the conflict between Austria-Hungary and Serbia. For the European conflagration, which would result from a similar step by Russia, the "Nowoje Wremja" believes itself justified in making Germany responsible in so far as it does not induce Austria-Hungary to yield.

The Russian press thus turns conditions upside down. It is not Austria-Hungary, which has called forth the conflict with Serbia, but it is Serbia, which, through unscrupulous favor toward pan-Serb aspirations, even in parts of the Austro-Hungarian Monarchy, threatens the same in her existence and creates conditions, which eventually found expression in the wanton outrage at Sarajevo. If Russia believes that it must champion the cause of Serbia in this matter, it certainly has the right to do so. However, it must realize that it makes the Serb activities its own, to undermine the conditions of existence of the Austro-Hungarian Monarchy, and that thus it bears the sole responsibility if out of the Serbian affair, which all other Great Powers desire to localize, and there arises a European war. This responsibility of Russia's is evident and it weighs the more heavily as Count Berchtold has officially declared to Russia that Austria-Hungary has no intention to acquire Serbian territory or to touch the existence of the Serbian Kingdom, but only desires peace against the Serbian intrigues threatening its existence. The attitude of the Imperial Government in this question is clearly indicated. The agitation conducted by the pan-Slavs in Austria-Hungary has for its goal, with the destruction of the Austro-Hungarian Monarchy, the scattering or weakening of the Triple Alliance with a complete isolation of the German Empire in consequence. Our own interest therefore calls us to the side of Austria-Hungary. The duty, if at all possible, to guard Europe against a universal war, points to the support by ourselves of those endeavors which aim at the localization of the conflict, faithful to the course of those policies which we have carried out successfully for forty-four years in the interest of the preservation of the peace of Europe.

Should, however, against our hope, through the interference of Russia the fire be spread, we should have to support, faithful to our duty as allies, the neighbor with all the power at our command. We shall take the sword only if forced to it, but then in the clear consciousness that we are not guilty of the calamity which war will bring upon the peoples of Europe.

Telegram of the Imperial Ambassador at Vienna to the Chancellor on July 28th, 1914.

Count Berchtold requests me to express to Your Excellency his thanks for the communication of the English mediation proposal. He states, however, that after the opening of hostilities by Serbia and the subsequent declaration of war, the step appears belated.

No. 61.
Sir M. de Bunsen, British Ambassador at Vienna, to Sir Edward Grey.
Vienna
July 28, 1914.
(Telegraphic)

I saw Minister for Foreign Affairs this morning.

His Excellency declared that Austria-Hungary cannot delay warlike proceedings against Serbia, and would have to decline any suggestion of negotiations on basis of Serbian reply.

Prestige of Dual Monarchy was engaged, and nothing could now prevent conflict.

No. 62.
Sir M. de Bunsen, British Ambassador at Vienna, to Sir Edward Grey.
Vienna
July 28, 1914.
(Telegraphic)

I spoke to Minister of Foreign affairs today in the sense of your telegram of 27 July to Berlin. I avoided the word "mediation," but said that, as mentioned in your speech, which he had just read to me, you had hopes that conversations in London between the Four Powers less interested might yet lead to an arrangement, which Austro-Hungary Government would accept as satisfactory and as rendering actual hostilities unnecessary. I added that you had regarded Serbian reply as having gone far to meet just demands of Austria-Hungary; that you thought it constituted a fair basis of discussion during which warlike operations might remain in abeyance, and that Austrian Ambassador in Berlin was speaking in this sense. Minister for Foreign Affairs said quietly, but firmly, that no discussion could be accepted on basis of Serbian note; that war would be declared today, and that well-known pacific character of Emperor, as well as, he might add, his own, might be accepted as a guarantee that war was both just and inevitable. This was a matter that must be settled directly between the two parties immediately concerned. I said that you would hear with regret that hostilities could not now be arrested, as you fear that they may lead to complications threatening the peace of Europe.

In taking leave of His Excellency, I begged him to believe that, if in the course of present crisis our point of view should sometimes differ from his, this would arise, not from want of sympathy with many just complaints, which Austria-Hungary put first her quarrel with Serbia, you were anxious in the first instance for peace of Europe. I trusted this larger aspect of the question would appeal with equal force to his Excellency. He said he had it also in those impending which did not aim at territorial aggrandizement and which could no longer be postponed.

No. 63.
Sir R. Rodd, British Ambassador at Rome, to Sir Edward Grey.
Rome
July 28, 1914.
(Telegraphic)

Your telegram of 25 July to Paris.[27]

I have communicated substance to Minister for Foreign Affairs, who immediately telegraphed in precisely in similar terms to Berlin and Vienna.

No. 64.
Sir R. Rodd, British Ambassador at Rome, to Sir Edward Grey.
Rome
July 28, 1914.
(Telegraphic)

At the request of the Minister for Foreign Affairs, I submit the following to you

In a long conversation this mourning Serbian Charge` d'Affaires had said he thought that if some explanation were given regarding mode in which Austrian agents would require to intervene under article 5 and article 6, Serbia might still accept the whole Austrian note.

As it was not to be anticipated that Austria would give such explanations to Serbia, they might be given to Powers engaged in discussions, who might then advise Serbia to accept without conditions.

The Austro-Hungary Government had in the meantime published a long official explanation of grounds on which Serbian reply was considered inadequate, Minister for Foreign Affairs considered many points besides explanation—such as slight verbal difference in sentence regarding renunciation of propaganda—quite childish, but there was a passage which might prove useful in facilitating such a course as was considered practicable by the Serbian Charge` d'Affaires. It was stated that co-operation of Austrian agents in Serbia was to be only in investigation, not in judicial or administration measures. Serbia was said to have willfully misinterpreted this. He thought, therefore, that ground might be cleared here.

I can only reproduce from memory, as I had not yet received text of Austrian declaration.

---

[27] See No. 27.

Minister impressed upon me, above all, his anxiety for the immediate beginning of discussion. A wide general latitude to accept at once every point or suggestion on which he could be in agreement with ourselves and Germany had been given to Italian Ambassador.

No. 65.
Mr. Crackanthorpe, British Charge` d'Affaires at Belgrade, to Sir Edward Grey.
Nish
July 28, 1914.
(Telegraphic)

I have urged on the Serbian Government the greatest moderation pending efforts being made towards a peaceful resolution.

Two Serbian steamers fired on and damaged, two Serbian merchant vessels have been captured by a Hungarian monitor at Orsova.

No. 66.
Mr. Crackanthorpe, British Charge` d' Affaires at Belgrade, to Sir Edward Grey.
July 28, 1914.
(Telegraphic)

Telegram received here that war declared by Austria.

28 July 1914:
The Pledge Plan
Telegram from the Imperial Chancellor, von Bethmann-Hollweg, to the German Ambassador at Vienna, Tschirschky, July 28, 1914:
Telegram 174
Berlin
July 28, 1914.

Urgent;

The Austro-Hungarian government has distinctly informed Russia that it is not considering any territorial acquisitions in Serbia. This agrees with Your Excellency's report to the effect that neither the Austrian nor the Hungarian statesmen consider the increase of the Slavic element in the monarchy to be desirable. On the other hand, the Austro-Hungarian government has left us in the dark concerning its intentions, despite repeated interrogations. The reply of the Serbian government to the Austrian ultimatum, which has now been received, makes it clear that Serbia has agreed to the Austrian demands to so great an extent that, in case of a completely uncompromising attitude on the part of the Austro-Hungarian government, it will become necessary to reckon upon the gradual defection from its cause of public opinion throughout all Europe.

According to the statements of the Austrian General Staff, an active military movement against Serbia will not be possible before the 12th of August. As a result, the Imperial government is placed in the extraordinarily difficult position of being exposed in the meantime to the mediation and conference proposals of the other cabinets and if it continues to maintain its previous aloofness in the face of such proposals, it will incur the odium of having been responsible for a world war, even, finally, among the German people themselves. A successful war on three fronts cannot be commenced and carried on any such basis. It is imperative that the responsibility for the eventual extension of the war among those nations not originally immediately concerned should, under all circumstances, fall on

Russia. At Mr. Sazonof's last conversation with Count Pourtals, the Minister already conceded that Serbia would have to receive her "deserved lesson." At any rate, the Minister was no longer opposed to the Austrian point of view, as he had been earlier. From this fact it is not difficult to draw the conclusion that the Russian government might even realize that, once the mobilization of the Austro-Hungarian Army had begun, the very honor of its arms demanded an invasion of Serbia. But it will be all the better able to compromise with this idea if the Vienna Cabinet repeats at Petersburg its distinct declaration that she is far from wishing to make any territorial acquisitions in Serbia, and that her military preparations are solely for the purpose of a temporary occupation of Belgrade and certain other localities on Serbian territory in order to force the Serbian government to the complete fulfillment of her demands, and for the creation of guarantees of future good behavior—to which Austria-Hungary has an unquestionable claim after the experiences she has had with Serbia. An occupation like the German occupation of French territory after the Peace of Frankfort, for the purpose of securing compliance with the demands for war indemnity, is suggested. As soon as the Austrian demands are complied with, evacuation would follow. Should the Russian government fail to recognize the justice of this point of view, it would have against it the public opinion of all Europe, which is now in the process of turning away from Austria. As a further result, the general diplomatic, and probably the military, situation would undergo material alteration in favor of Austria-Hungary and her allies.

Your Excellency will kindly discuss the matter along these lines thoroughly and impressively with Count Berchtold's, and instigate an appropriate move at St. Petersburg. You will have to avoid very carefully giving rise to the impression that we wish to hold Austria back. The case is solely one of finding a way to realize Austria's desired aim, that of cutting the vital cord of the Greater-Serbia propaganda without at the same time bringing on a world war, and, if the latter cannot be avoided in the end, of improving the conditions under which we shall have to wage it, insofar as is possible.
Wire report.

BETHMANN-HOLLWEG.

No. 67.
Foreign Office
July 28, 1914.
(Telegraphic)
Explanation given in your telegram of the 27th of July of what was my idea in proposing a conference is quite right. It would not be an arbitration, but a private and informal discussion to ascertain what suggestion could be made for a settlement. No suggestion would be put forward that had not previously been ascertained to be accepted to Austria and Russia, with whom the mediating Powers could easily keep in touch through their respective allies.

But as long as there is a prospect of a direct exchange of views between Austria and Russia, I would suspend every other suggestion, as I entirely agree that it is most preferable method of all.

I understand that the Russian Minister for Foreign Affairs has proposed a friendly exchange of views to the Austrian Government, and, if the latter accepts, it will no doubt relieve the tension and make the situation less critical.
It is very satisfactory to hear from the German Ambassador here that the German Government have taken action at Vienna in the sense of the conversation recorded in my telegram of yesterday to you[28]

---

[28] See No. 46.

No. 68.
Sir Edward Grey to Sir E. Goschen, British Ambassador at Berlin.
Foreign Office
July 28, 1914.
(Telegraphic)

German Government having accepted principle of mediation between Austria and Russia by the Four Powers, if necessary, I am ready to propose that the German Secretary of State should suggest the lines on which this principle should be applied. I will, however, keep the idea in reserve until we see how the conversation between Austria and Russia progresses.

Count Errembault de Dudzeele, Belgian Minister at Vienna, to M. Davignon, Belgian Minister for Foreign Affairs.
Vienna
July 28, 1914.
(Telegraphic)

The Minister for Foreign Affairs has notified me of the declaration of war by Austria-Hungary against Serbia.

No. 52.
Communicated by the French Embassy to British Foreign Affairs.
July 28, 1914.
(Note)

The Government of the Republic accept Sir Edward Grey's proposal in regard to intervention by Great Britain, France, Germany, and Italy with a view to avoiding active military operations on the frontiers of Austria, Russia, and Serbia; and they have authorized M. P. Cambon to take part in the deliberations of the four representatives at the meeting which is to be held in London.

The French Ambassador in Berlin has received instruction to consult first the British Ambassador in Berlin, and then to support the action taken by the latter in such a manner and degree as may be considered appropriate.

M. Viviana is ready to send to the representatives of France in Vienna, St. Petersburg, and Belgrade instructions in the sense suggested by the British Government.

His Majesty to the Czar.
July 28th, 10.45 P.M.

I have heard with the greatest anxiety of the impression, which caused by the action of Austria-Hungary against Serbia. The unscrupulous agitation, which has been going on for years in Serbia, has led to the revolting crime of which Archduke Franz Ferdinand has become at victim. The spirit, which made the Serbians murder their own King and his consort, still dominates that country. Doubtless, you will agree with me that both of us, you as well as I, and all other sovereigns, have a common interest to insist that all those who are responsible for this horrible murder shall suffer their deserved punishment.

On the other hand, I by no means overlook the difficulty encountered by you and Your Government to stem the tide of public opinion. In view of the cordial friendship, which has joined us both for a long time with firm ties, I shall use my entire influence to induce Austria-Hungary to obtain a frank and satisfactory understanding with Russia. I hope confidently that you will support me in my efforts to overcome all difficulties, which may yet arise.
You are a most sincere and devoted friend and cousin.

(Signed)
WILHELM.

No. 69.
Sir Edward Grey to Sir G. Buchanan, British Ambassador at St. Petersburgh.
Foreign Office
July 28, 1914.
(Telegraphic)

It is most satisfactory that there is a prospect of direct exchange of views between the Russian and Austrian Governments, as reported in your telegram of July 27.*

I am ready to put forward any practical proposal that would facilitate this, but I am not quite clear as to what the Russian Minister for Foreign Affairs proposes the Ministries at Belgrade should do. Could he not first mention in an exchange of views with Austria his willingness to co-operate in some such scheme? It might then take more concrete shape.

No. 74.
Sir M. de Bunsen, British Ambassador at Vienna, to Sir Edward Grey.
(received July 29)
Vienna
July 28, 1914.
(Telegraphic)

I am informed by the Russian Ambassador that the Russian Government's suggestion has been declined by the Austro-Hungarian Government. The suggestion was to the effect that the means of settling the Austro-Serbian conflict should be discussed directly between Russian Minister for Foreign Affairs and the Austrian Ambassador at St. Petersburg, who should be authorized accordingly.

The Russian Ambassador thinks that a conference in London of the less interested Powers, such as you have proposed, offers now the only prospect of preserving peace of Europe, l and he is sure that the Russian Government will acquiesce willingly come in contact, all hope need not be abandoned.

---

* See no. 55

Chapter Thirty

July 29, 1914

Russian Chargé d'Affaires at Berlin to Russian Minister for Foreign Affairs.
Berlin
July 29, 1914.
(Telegraphic)

On my enquiry whether he had received from Vienna, a reply respecting your proposal for private discussions at St. Petersburg the Secretary of State answered in the negative. He declares that it is very difficult for him to produce any effect at Vienna, especially openly. He even added, in speaking to Cambon, that were pressure brought to bear too obviously Austria would hasten to face Germany with a fait accompli. The Secretary of State tells me that he received a telegram to-day from Pourtalès, stating that you seemed more inclined than you previously were to find a compromise acceptable to all parties. I replied that presumably you had been in favor of a compromise from the outset, provided always that it were acceptable, not only to Austria, but equally to Russia. He then said that it appeared that Russia had begun to mobilize on the Austrian frontier, and that he feared that this would make it more difficult for Austria to come to an understanding with us, all the more so as Austria was mobilizing against Serbia alone, and was making no preparations upon our frontier. I replied that, according to the information in my possession, Austria was mobilizing upon the Russian frontier also, and that consequently we had to take similar steps. I added that whatever measures we might, perhaps have taken on our side were in no wise directed against Germany.

No. 70.
Telegrams communicated by Count Benckendorff, Russian Ambassador in London.
July 29, 1914.

(1.) Telegram From M. Sazonof to Russian Ambassador at Berlin.
(July 28, 1914)

In consequence of the declaration of war by Austria against Serbia, the Imperial Government will announce tomorrow (29th) the mobilization in the military conscriptions of Odessa, Kyeff, Moscow, and Kazan. Please inform German Government, confirming the absence in Russia of any aggressive intention against Germany.

The Russian Ambassador at Vienna has not bee recalled from his post.

(2.) Telegram to Count Benckendorff[29]

The Austrian declaration for war puts an end to the idea of direct communication between Austria and Russia. Action by London cabinet in order to set on foot mediation with a view to suspension of military operations of Austria against Serbia is now most urgent.

Unless military operations are stopped, mediation would only allow matters to drag on and give Austria time to crush Serbia.

No. 52.
Russian Chargé d'Affaires to Russian Minister for Foreign Affairs.
Nish
July 29, 1914.
(Telegraphic)

'The Bulgarian Minister to-day declared to Pashitch, ill the name of his Government, that Bulgaria would remain neutral.

No. 71.
Sir E. Goschen, British Ambassador at Berlin, to Sir Edward Grey.
(received July 29th)
Berlin
July 28, 1914.
(Telegraphic)

At the invitation of Imperial Chancellor, I called upon his Excellency this evening. He said that he wished me to tell you that he was most anxious that Germany should work together with England for maintenance of general peace, as they had done successfully in the last European crisis. He had not been able to accept your proposal for a conference of representatives of the Great Powers, because he did not think that it would be effective, and because he would in his opinion have had appearance of an "Areopagus" consisting of two Powers of each group sitting in judgment upon the two remaining Powers; but his inability to accept proposed conference must not be regarded as militating against his strong desire for effective co-operation. You could be assured that he was doing his very best both at Vienna and St. Petersburg to get the two Governments to discuss the situation directly with each other and in a friendly way. He had great hopes that such discussions would take place and lead to a satisfactory results, but if the news were true which he had just read in the papers, that Russia had mobilized fourteen army corps in the south. He thought the situation was very serious and he himself would be in a very difficult position, as in these circumstances it would be out of his power to continue to preach moderation at Vienna. He added that Austria, who as yet was only partially mobilizing, would have to take similar measures, and if war were a result, Russia would be entirely responsible. I venture to say that if Austria refused to take any notice of Serbian note, which, to my mind, gave way nearly every point demanded by Austria, and which in any case offered a basis for discussion, surely a certain portion of responsibility would rest with her. His Excellency said that he did not wish to discuss the Serbian note, but that Austria's standpoint, and in this agreed, was that her quarrel with Serbia was a purely Austrian concern with which Russia had nothing to do; he reiterated his desire to co-operate with England and his intention to do his utmost to maintain general peace. "A war between the Great Powers must be avoided" were his last words.

---

[29] Russian Ambassador in London.

Austrian colleagues said to me today that a general war was most unlikely, as Russia neither wanted nor was in a position to make war. I think that, that opinion is shared by many people here.

No. 53.
Russian Ambassador at Paris to Russian Minister for Foreign Affairs.
Paris
July 29, 1914.
(Telegraphic)

FOR the information of the President of the French Republic on his return, the French Minister for Foreign Affairs had prepared a short summary of the present political situation, approximately in the following terms: Austria, fearing internal disintegration, seized upon the assassination of the Archduke as an excuse for an attempt to obtain guarantees, which may assume the form of an occupation of Serbian military lines or even Serbian territory. Germany is supporting Austria. The preservation of peace depends upon Russia alone, for the question at issue must be "localized" between Austria and Serbia; that question is the punishment of Serbia for her previous policy and the obtaining of guarantees for the future. Germany concludes from this that a moderating influence should be exerted at St. Petersburg. This sophism has been refuted both in Paris and in London. In Paris, Baron von Schoen vainly endeavored to induce France to adopt joint action with Germany towards Russia for the preservation of peace. The same attempts were made in London. In both capitals, the answer was given that any action taken should be at Vienna, as it was Austria's inordinate demands, her refusal to discuss Serbia's few reservations, and her declaration of war, that threatened to provoke a general war. France and England are unable to bring any moderating pressure to bear upon Russia, as, so far, that Power has shown the greatest moderation, more particularly in her advice to Serbia to accept as much as was possible of the Austrian note. Apparently, Germany has now given up the idea of pressure upon Russia only and inclines towards mediatory action both at St. Petersburg and at Vienna, but at the same time both Germany and Austria are endeavoring to cause the question to drag on. Germany is opposing the conference without suggesting any other practical course of action. Austria is continuing discussions at St. Petersburg, which are manifestly of a procrastinating nature. At the same time she is taking active steps, and if these steps are tolerated, her. Claims will increase proportionately. It is highly desirable that Russia should lend all her support to the proposal for mediation, which will be made by Sir E. Grey. In the contrary event, Austria, on the plea of "guarantees," will be able, in effect, to alter the territorial status of Eastern Europe.

The events described in this telegram are the events that are influenced by the French government. It is the French telling the Russian delegates to stall any efforts for peace and to mobilize their military to push Germany into war so the two governments can take possession of German economic properties.

No. 72.
Sir G. Buchanan, British Ambassador at St. Petersburg, to Sir Edward Grey.
St. Petersburg
July 29, 1914.
(Telegraphic)

Minister for Foreign Affairs begged me to thank you for the language you had held to the German Ambassador, as reported in your telegram[30] to Berlin, substance of which I communicated to his

---

[30] See No. 46

Excellency. He took a pessimistic view of the situation, having received the same disquieting news from Vienna as had reached his Majesty's Government. I said it was important that we should know the real intentions of the Imperial Government, and ask him whether he would be satisfied with the assurance, which the Austrian Ambassador had; I understood, been instructed to give in respect of Serbia's integrity and independence. I added that I was sure any arrangement for averting a European war would be welcomed by his Majesty's government. In reply, his Excellency stated that if Serbia were attacked. Russia would not be satisfied with any engagement, which Austria might take on these two points, and that order for mobilization against Austria would be issued on the day that Austria crossed Serbian Frontier.

I told the German Ambassador, who appealed to me to give moderating counsels to the Minister for Foreign Affairs, that from the beginning I had not ceased to do so, and that the German Ambassador at Vienna should now in his turn use his restraining influence. I made it clear to his Excellency that, Russia being thoroughly in earnest, a general war could not be averted if Serbia were attacked by Austria.

As regards the suggestion of conference, the Ambassador had received no instructions, and before acting with me the French and Italian Ambassadors are still waiting for their final instructions

No. 54.
Russian Ambassador at London Russian Minister for Foreign Affairs.
London
July 29, 1914.
(Telegraphic)

I HAVE communicated the contents of your telegrams of the 28th July to Grey. He informed the German Ambassador to-day that the direct discussions between Russia and Austria had been fruitless, and that press correspondents were reporting from St. Petersburg that Russia was mobilizing against Austria in consequence of the latter's mobilization. Grey said that, in principle, the German Government had declared themselves in favor of mediation, but that he was experiencing difficulties in the form it should take. Grey has urged that the German Government should indicate the form which in their opinion, would enable the four Powers to have recourse to mediation to prevent war, France, Italy, and Great Britain having consented, mediation could only come into play if Germany consented to range herself on the side of peace.

No. 73.
Sir M. de Bunsen, British Ambassador at Vienna, to Sir Edward Grey.
(received July 29)
Vienna
July 28, 1914.
(Telegraphic)

I have received a note *verbale* from Ministry for Foreign Affairs, stating that the Serbian Government not having replied to note of 23rd July[31] in a satisfactory manner, Imperial and Royal Government is compelled itself to provide for protection of its rights, and to have recourse for that object to force of arms. Austria-Hungary has addressed to Serbia Formal declaration according to article 1 of convention of 18th October, 1907, relative to opening hostilities, and considers herself from today in state of war with Serbia.

---

[31] See No. 4

Austria-Hungary will conform, provided Serbia does so, to stipulations of Hague convention of 18th October, 1907, and to Declaration of London of 26th February, 1909

No. 55.
Russian Ambassador at Paris Russian Minister for Foreign Affairs.
Paris
July 29, 1914.
(Telegraphic)

VIVIANI has just confirmed to me the French Government's firm determination to act in concert with Russia. This determination is upheld by all classes of society and by the political parties, including the Radical Socialists who have just addressed a resolution to the Government expressing the absolute confidence and the patriotic sentiments of their party. Since his return to Paris, Viviani has telegraphed an urgent message to London that, direct discussions between St. Petersburg and Vienna having ended, the London Cabinet should again put forward their proposal for mediation by the Powers as soon as possible under one form or another. Before seeing me to-day Viviani saw the German Ambassador, and the latter again assured him of the peaceful intentions of Germany. Viviani having pointed out that if Germany wished for peace she should hasten to give her support to the British proposal for mediation, Baron von Schoen replied that the words "conference" or "arbitration" alarmed Austria. Viviani retorted that it was not a question of words, and that it would be easy to find some other form for mediation. In the opinion of Baron von Schoen, it was necessary for the success of the negotiations between the Powers to know what Austria intended to demand from Serbia. Viviani answered that the Berlin Cabinet could quite easily make this enquiry of Austria, but that, meanwhile, the Serbian reply might well form the basis of discussion; he added that France sincerely desired peace, but that she was determined at the same time to act in complete harmony with her allies and friends, and that he, Baron von Schoen, might have convinced himself that this determination met with the warmest approval of the country.

No. 75.
Sir E. Goschen, British Ambassador at Berlin, to Sir Edward Grey.
(received July 29)
Berlin
July 29, 1914.
(Telegraphic)

I was sent for again today by the Imperial Chancellor, who told me that he regretted to state that the Austro-Hungarian Government to whom he had at once communicated your opinion, had answered that events had marched too rapidly and that it was therefore too late to act upon your suggestion that the Serbian reply might form the basis of discussion. His Excellency had, on receiving their reply, dispatched a message to Vienna, in which he explained that, although a certain desire had, in his opinion, been shown in the Serbian reply to meet the demands of Austria, he understood entirely that, without some sure guarantees that Serbia would carry out their entirety the demands made upon her, the Austro-Hungarian Government could not rest satisfied in view of their past experience. He had then gone on to say that the hostilities which were about to be undertaken against Serbia had presumably the exclusive object of securing such guarantees, seeing that the Austrian Government already assured the Russian Government that they had no territorial designs.

He advised the Austro-Hungarian Government, should this view be correct, to speak openly in the sense. The holding of such language would, he hoped, eliminate all possible misunderstandings.

As yet, he told me, he had not received a reply from Vienna.

From the fact that he had gone so far in the matter of giving advice at Vienna, his Excellency hoped that you would realize that he was sincerely doing all in his power to prevent the danger of European complications.

The fact of his communicating this information to you was proof of the confidence, which he felt in you, and evidence of his anxiety that you should know he was doing his best to support your efforts in the cause of general peace, efforts which he sincerely appreciated.

No. 56.
Telegram from His Royal Highness, Alexander of Serbia, to His Majesty the Emperor of Russia.
July 29, 1914.

DEEPLY touched by the telegram, which your Majesty was pleased to address to me yesterday, I hasten to thank you with all my heart. Your Majesty may rest assured that the cordial sympathy, which your Majesty feels towards my country, is especially valued by us, and fills our hearts with the belief that the future of Serbia is secure now that it is the object of your Majesty's gracious solicitude. These painful moments cannot but strengthen the bonds of deep attachment, which bind Serbia to Holy Slav Russia, and the sentiments of everlasting gratitude, which we feel for the help, and protection afforded to us by your Majesty will ever be cherished in the hearts of all the Serbs.

No. 57.
Russian Chargé d'Affaires in Serbia Russian Minister for Foreign Affairs
Nish
July 29, 1914.
(Telegraphic)

I HAVE communicated to Pashitch the text of the telegraphic reply returned by His Majesty the Emperor to Prince Alexander. On reading it, Pashitch crossed himself and exclaimed: "The Czar is great and merciful!" He then embraced me and was overcome with emotion. The heir-apparent is expected at Nish late to-night.

No. 76.
Sir E. Goschen, British Ambassador at Berlin, to Sir Edward Grey.
(received July 29)
Berlin
July 29, 1914.
(Telegraphic)

I found Secretary of State very depressed today. He reminded me that he had told me the other day that he had to be very careful in giving advice to Austria, as any idea that they were being pressed would be likely to cause them to precipitate matters and present a *fait accompli*. This had in fact, now happened, and he was not sure that his communication of your suggestion that Serbia's reply offered a basis for discussion had not hastened declaration of war. He was much troubled by reports of mobilization in Russia, and of certain military measures, which he did not specify, being taken in France. He subsequently spoke of these measures to my French colleague, who informed him that the French Government had done nothing more than the German Government had done, namely recalled officers on leave. His Excellency denied German Government had done this, but as a matter of fact it is true. My French Colleague said to under-Secretary of State, in course of conversation, that it seemed to him that when Austria had entered Serbia, and so satisfied her military prestige, the moment might then be favorable for four disinterested Powers to discuss the situation and come forward with suggestions for preventing graver complications. Under-Secretary of State seemed to think the idea worthy of consideration, as he replied that would be a different matter from conference proposed by you.

Russian Ambassador returned today, and had informed imperial Government that Russia is mobilizing in four Southern governments.

No. 58.
Russian Minister for Foreign Affairs to Russian Ambassador at Paris.
St. Petersburg
July 29, 1914.
(Telegraphic)

THE German Ambassador to-day informed me of the decision of his Government to mobilize, if Russia did not stop her military preparations. Now, in fact, we only began these preparations in consequence of the mobilization already undertaken by Austria, and owing to her evident unwillingness to accept, any means of arriving at a peaceful settlement of her dispute with Serbia. As we cannot comply with the wishes of Germany, we have no alternative but to hasten on our own military preparations and to assume that war is probably inevitable. Please inform the French Government of this, and add that we are sincerely grateful to them for the declaration, which the French Ambassador made to me on their behalf, to the effect that we could count fully upon the assistance of our ally, France. In the existing circumstances, that declaration is especially valuable to us. Communicated to the Russian Ambassadors in Great Britain, Austria-Hungary, Italy, and Germany.

Here again it is seen that Russia and France are desiring war and are doing everything but firing the first shot to achieve it.

No. 77.
Sir Edward Grey to Sir E. Goschen, British Ambassador at Berlin.
Foreign Office
July 29, 1914.
(Telegraphic)

I much appreciate the language of the Chancellor, as reported in your telegram of today.[32] His Excellency may rely upon it that this country will continue, as theretofore, to strain every effort to secure peace and to avert the calamity we all fear. If he can induce Austria to satisfy Russia and to abstain from going so far as to come into a collision with her, we shall all join in deep gratitude to his Excellency for having saved the peace of Europe.
Sir Edward Grey's Speech before Parliament
From: *Great Britain, Parliamentary Debates, Commons, Fifth Series, Vol. LXV, 1914, pp. 1809.*
ff. [with House comments as found in original]

Last week I stated that, we were working for peace not only for this country, but to preserve the peace of Europe. To-day events move so rapidly that it is exceedingly difficult to state with technical

---

[32] See No. 75.

accuracy the actual state of affairs, but it is clear that the peace of Europe cannot be preserved. Russia and Germany, at any rate, have declared war upon each other.

Before I proceed to state the position of his Majesty's Government I would like to clear the ground so that, before I come to state to the House what our attitude is with regard to the present crisis, the House may know exactly under what obligations the government is, or the House can be said to be, in coming to a decision on the matter. First of all, let me say, very shortly, that we have consistently worked with a single mind, with all the earnestness in our power, to preserve peace. The House may be satisfied on that point. We have always done it. During these last years, as far as his Majesty's Government is concerned, we would have no difficulty in proving that we have done so. Throughout the Balkan crisis, by general admission, we worked for peace. The cooperation of the great powers of Europe was successful in working for peace in the Balkan crisis. It is true that some of the powers had great difficulty in adjusting their points of view. It took much time, labour, and discussion before they could settle their differences, but peace was secured, because peace was their main object, and they were willing to give time and trouble rather than accentuate differences rapidly.

In the present crisis it has not been possible to secure the peace of Europe: because there has been little time, and there has been a disposition—at any rate in some quarters on which I will not dwell—to force things rapidly to an issue, at any rate to the great risk of peace, and, as we now know, the result of that is that the policy of peace as far as the great powers generally are concerned is in danger. I do not want to dwell on that, and to comment on it, and to say where the blame seems to us lie, which powers were most in favour of peace, which were most disposed to risk war or endanger peace, because I would like the House to approach this crisis in which we are now from the point of view of British interests, British honour, and British obligations, free from all passion as to why peace has not yet been preserved....

The crisis is not precisely the same as it was in the Morocco question....It has originated in a dispute between Austria and Serbia. I can say this with the most absolute confidence—no government and no country has less desire to be involved in war over a dispute with Austria than the country of France. They are involved in it because of their obligation of honour under a definite alliance with Russia. Well, it is only fair to say to the House that that obligation of honour cannot apply in the same way to us. We are not parties to the Franco-Russian alliance. We do not even know the terms of the alliance. So far, I have, I think, faithfully and completely cleared the ground with regard to the question of obligation.

I now come to what we think the situation requires of us. For many years, we have had a long-standing friendship with France [An HON. MEMBER: "And with Germany!"]. I remember well the feeling in the House and my own feeling—for I spoke on the subject, I think, when the late Government made their agreement with France—the warm and cordial feeling resulting from the fact that these two nations, who had had perpetual differences in the past, had cleared these differences away; I remember saying, I think, that it seemed to me that some benign influence had been at work to produce the cordial atmosphere that had made that possible. But how far that friendship entails obligation—it has been a friendship between the nations and ratified by the nations—how far that entails an obligation, let every man look into his own heart, and his own feelings, and construe the extent of the obligation for himself. I construe it myself as I feel it, but I do not wish to urge upon anyone else more than their feelings dictate as to what they should feel about the obligation. The House, individually and collectively, may judge for itself. I speak my personal view, and I have given the House my own feeling in the matter.

The French fleet is now in the Mediterranean, and the northern and western coasts of France are undefended. The French fleet is now in the Mediterranean, and the northern and western coasts of France are undefended. The French fleet being concentrated in the Mediterranean, the situation is very different from what it used to be, because the friendship which has grown up between the two countries has given them a sense of security that there was nothing to be feared from us. My own feeling is that if a foreign fleet, engaged in a war which France had not sought, and in which she had not been the aggressor, came down the English Channel and bombarded and battered the undefended coasts of France, we could not stand aside [*Cheers*] and see this going on practically within sight of our eyes, with our arms folded, looking on dispassionately, doing nothing. I believe that would be the feeling of this country. There are times when one feels that if these circumstances actually did arise, it would be a feeling, which would spread with irresistible force throughout the land.

However, I also want to look at the matter without sentiment, and from the point of view of British interests, and it is on that that I am going to base and justify what I am presently going to say to the House. If we say nothing at this moment, what is France to do with her fleet in the Mediterranean? If she leaves it there, with no statement from us as to what we will do, she leaves her northern and western coasts absolutely undefended, at the mercy of a German fleet coming down the Channel to do as it pleases in a war, which is a war of life and death between them. If we say nothing, it may be that the French fleet is withdrawn from the Mediterranean. We are in the presence of a European conflagration; can anybody set limits to the consequences that may arise out of it? Let us assume that to-day we stand aside in an attitude of neutrality, saying, "No, we cannot undertake and engage to help either party in this conflict." Let us suppose the French fleet is withdrawn from the Mediterranean; and let us assume that the consequences—which are already tremendous in what has happened in Europe even to countries which are at peace—in fact, equally whether countries are at peace or at war—let us assume that out of that come consequences unforeseen, which make it necessary at a sudden moment that, in defense of vital British interests, we should go to war; and let us assume which is quite possible—that Italy, who is now neutral [HON. MEMBERS: "Hear, hear!"]—because, as I understand, she considers that this war is an aggressive war, and the Triple Alliance being a defensive alliance her obligation did not arise—let us assume that consequences which are not yet foreseen and which, perfectly legitimately consulting her own interests—make Italy depart from her attitude of neutrality at a time when we are forced in defense of vital British interest ourselves to fight—what then will be the position in the Mediterranean? It might be that at some critical moment those consequences would be forced upon us because our trade routes in the Mediterranean might be vital to this country.

Nobody can say that in the course of the next few weeks there is any particular trade route the keeping open of which may not be vital to this country. What will be our position then? We have not kept a fleet in the Mediterranean, which is equal to dealing alone with a combination of other fleet in the Mediterranean. It would be the very moment when we could not detach more ships to the Mediterranean, and we might have exposed this country from our negative attitude at the present moment to the most appalling risk. I say that from the point of view of British interest. We feel strongly that France was entitled to know—and to know at once!—Whether or not in the event of attack upon her unprotected northern and western coast she could depend upon British support. In that emergency and in these compelling circumstances, yesterday afternoon I gave to the French Ambassador the following statement:

> "*I am authorized to give an assurance that if the German fleet comes into the Channel or through the North Sea to undertake hostile operations against the French coasts or shipping, the British fleet will give all the protection in its power. This assurance is, of course, subject to the policy of his Majesty's Government receiving the support of Parliament, and must not be taken as binding his Majesty's Government to take any action until the above contingency of action by the German fleet takes place.*"

I read that to the House, not as a declaration of war on our part, not as entailing immediate aggressive action on our part, but as binding us to take aggressive action should that contingency arise. Things move very hurriedly from hour to hour. French news comes in, and I cannot give this in any very formal way; but I understand that the German Government would be prepared, if we would pledge ourselves to neutrality, to agree that its fleet would not attack the northern coast of France. I have only heard that shortly before I came to the House, but it is far too narrow an engagement for us. And, Sir, there is the more serious consideration—becoming more serious every hour—there is the question of the neutrality of Belgium....

I will read to the House what took place last week on this subject. When mobilisation was beginning, I knew that this question must be a most important element in our policy—a most important subject for the House of Commons. I telegraphed at the same time in similar terms to both Paris and Berlin to say that it was essential for us to know whether the French and German Governments, respectively, were prepared to undertake an engagement to respect the neutrality of Belgium. These are the replies. I got from the French Government this reply:

> *"The French Government is resolved to respect the neutrality of Belgium, and it would only be in the event of some other power violating that neutrality that France might find herself under the necessity, in order to assure the defense of her security, to act otherwise. This assurance has been given several times. The President of the Republic spoke of it to the King of the Belgians, and the French Minister at Brussels has spontaneously renewed the assurance to the Belgian Minister of Foreign Affairs to-day."*

From the German Government the reply was:

> *"The Secretary of State for Foreign Affairs could not possibly give an answer before consulting the Emperor and the Imperial Chancellor."*

Sir Edward Goschen, to whom I had said it was important to have an answer soon, said he hoped the answer would not be too long delayed. The German Minister for Foreign Affairs then gave Sir Edward Goschen to understand that he rather doubted whether they could answer at all, as any reply they might give could not fail, in the event of war, to have the undesirable effect of disclosing, to a certain extent, part of their plan of campaign. I telegraphed at the same time to Brussels to the Belgian Government, and I got the following reply from Sir Francis Villiers:

> *"The Minister for Foreign Affairs thanks me for the communication and replies that Belgium will, to the utmost of her power, maintain neutrality, and Belgium expects and desires other powers to observe and uphold it. He begged me to add that the relations between Belgium and the neighboring Powers were excellent, and there was no reason to suspect their intentions, but that the Belgian Government believe, in the case of violence, they were in a position to defend the neutrality of their country."*

It now appears from the news I have received to-day—which has come quite recently, and I am not yet quite sure how far it has reached me in an accurate form—that an ultimatum has been given to Belgium by Germany, the object of which was to offer Belgium friendly relations with Germany on condition that she would facilitate the passage of German troops through Belgium. [*Ironical laughter*]. Well, Sir, until one has these things absolutely definite, up to the last moment I do not wish to say all that one would say if one were in a position to give the House full, complete, and absolute information upon the point. We were sounded in the course of last week as to whether, if a guarantee were given that, after the war, Belgian integrity would be preserved, that would content us. We replied that we could not bargain away whatever interests or obligations we had in Belgian neutrality. [*Cheers.*]

Shortly before I reached the House, I was informed that the following telegram had been received from the King of the Belgians by our King—King George:

> "Remembering the numerous proofs of your Majesty's friendship and that of your prede-cessors, and the friendly attitude of England in 1870, and the proof of friendship she has just given us again, I make a supreme appeal to the diplomatic intervention of your Majesty's Government to safeguard the integrity of Belgium."

Diplomatic intervention took place last week on our part. What can diplomatic intervention do now? We have great and vital interests in the independence—and integrity is the least part—of Belgium... [*Loud cheers*]. If Belgium is compelled to submit to allow her neutrality to be violated, of course the situation is clear. Even if by agreement she admitted the violation of her neutrality, it is clear she could only do so under duress. The smaller States in that region of Europe ask but one thing. Their one desire is that they should be left alone and independent. The one thing they fear is, I think, not so much that their integrity but that their independence should be interfered with. If in this war, which is before Europe, the neutrality of those countries is violated, if the troops of one of the com-batants violate its neutrality and no action be taken to resent it, at the end of war, whatever the in-tegrity may be, the independence will be gone...[*Cheers*].

No, Sir, if it be the case that there has been anything in the nature of an ultimatum to Belgium, asking her to compromise or violate her neutrality, whatever may have been offered to her in return, her independence is gone if that holds. If her independence goes, the independence of Holland will follow. I ask the House from the point of view of British interests to consider what may be at stake. If France is beaten in a struggle of life and death, beaten to her knees, loses her position as a great power, becomes subordinate to the will and power of one greater than herself—consequences which I do not anticipate, because I am sure that France has the power to defend herself with all the energy and ability and patriotism which she has shown so often [*Loud cheers.*]—still, if that were to happen and if Belgium fell under the same dominating influence, and then Holland, and then Denmark, then would not Mr. Gladstone's words come true, that just opposite to us there would be a common in-terest against the unmeasured aggrandizement of any power? [*Loud cheers.*]

It may be said, I suppose, that we might stand aside, husband our strength, and that, whatever happened in the course of this war, at the end of it intervene with effect to put things right, and to adjust them to our own point of view. If, in a crisis like this, we run away [*Loud cheers*] from those obligations of honour and interest as regards the Belgian treaty, I doubt whether, whatever material force we might have at the end, it would be of very much value in face of the respect that we should have lost. And I do not believe, whether a great power stands outside this war or not, it is going to be in a position at the end of it to exert its superior strength. For us, with a powerful fleet, which we believe able to protect our commerce, to protect our shores, and to protect our interests, if we are en-gaged in war, we shall suffer but little more than we shall suffer even if we stand aside.

We are going to suffer, I am afraid, terribly in this war, whether we are in it or whether we stand aside. Foreign trade is going to stop, not because the trade routes are closed, but because there is no trade at the other end. Continental nations engaged in war all their populations, all their energies, all their wealth, engaged in a desperate struggle they cannot carry on the trade with us that they are car-rying on in times of peace, whether we are parties to the war or whether we are not. I do not believe for a moment that at the end of this war, even if we stood aside and remained aside, we should be in a position, a material position, to use our force decisively to undo what had happened in the course of the war, to prevent the whole of the west of Europe opposite to us—if that had been the result of the war—falling under the domination of a single power, and I am quite sure that our moral posi-tion would be such as—[*the rest of the sentence—"to have lost us all respect."—was lost in a loud outburst of cheering*]. I can only say that I have put the question of Belgium somewhat hypothetically, because

I am not yet sure of all the facts, but, if the facts turn out to be as they have reached us at present, it is quite clear that there is an obligation on this country to do its utmost to prevent the consequences to which those facts will lead if they are undisputed....

One thing I would say. The one bright spot in the whole of this terrible situation is Ireland. [*Prolonged cheers.*] The general feeling throughout Ireland, and I would like this to be clearly understood abroad, does not make that a consideration that we feel we have to take into account [*Cheers*]. I have told the House how far we have at present gone in commitments, and the conditions, which influence our policy; and I have put and dealt at length to the House upon how vital the condition of the neutrality of Belgium is.

What other policy is there before the House? There is but one way in which the Government could make certain at the present moment of keeping outside this war, and that would be that it should immediately issue a proclamation of unconditional neutrality. We cannot do that. [*Cheers.*] We have made the commitment to France that I have read to the House, which prevents us doing that. We have got the consideration of Belgium which prevents us also from any unconditional neutrality, and, without these conditions absolutely satisfied and satisfactory, we are bound not to shrink from proceeding to the use of all the forces in our power. If we did take that line by saying, "We will have nothing whatever to do with this matter," under no conditions—the Belgian treaty obligations, the possible position in the Mediterranean, with damage to British interests, and what may happen to France from our failure to support France—if we were to say that all those things matter nothing, were as nothing, and to say we would stand aside, we should, I believe, sacrifice our respect and good name and reputation before the world, and should not escape the most serious and grave economic consequences. [*Cheers and a voice, "No."*]

My object has been to explain the view of the government, and to place before the House the issue and the choice. I do not for a moment conceal, after what I have said, and after the information, incomplete as it is, that I have given to the House with regard to Belgium, that we must be prepared, and we are prepared, for the consequences of having to use all the strength we have at any moment—we know not how soon—to defend ourselves and to take our part. We know, if the facts all be as I have stated them, though I have announced no intending aggressive action on our part, no final decision to resort to force at a moment's notice, until we know the whole of the case, that the use of it may be forced upon us. As far as the forces of the Crown are concerned, we are ready. I believe the Prime Minister and my right hon. Friend, the First Lord of the Admiralty have no doubt whatever that the readiness and the efficiency of those forces were never at a higher mark than they are to-day, and never was there a time when confidence was more justified in the power of the Navy to protect our commerce and to protect our shores. The thought is with us always of the suffering and misery entailed, from which no country in Europe will escape, and from which no abdication or neutrality will save us. The amount of harm that can be done by an enemy ship to our trade is infinitesimal, compared with the amount of harm that must be done by the economic condition that is caused on the Continent.

The most awful responsibility is resting upon the Government in deciding what to advise the House of Commons to do. We have disclosed our minds to the House of Commons. We have disclosed the issue, the information which we have, and made clear to the House, I trust, that we are prepared to face that situation, and that should it develop, as probably it may develop, we will face it. We worked for peace up to the last moment, and beyond the last moment. How hard, how persistently, and how earnestly we strove for peace last week the House will see from the papers that will be before it.

But that is over, as far as the peace of Europe is concerned. We are now face to face with a situation and all the consequences, which it may yet have to unfold. We believe we shall have the support of the House at large in proceeding to whatever the consequences may be and whatever measures may be forced upon us by the development of facts or action taken by others. I believe the country, so quickly has the situation been forced upon it, has not had time to realize the issue. It perhaps is still thinking of the quarrel between Austria and Serbia, and not the complications of this matter, which have grown out of the quarrel between Austria and Serbia. Russia and Germany we know are at war. We do not yet know officially that Austria, the ally whom Germany is to support, is yet at war with Russia. We know that a good deal has been happening on the French frontier. We do not know that the German Ambassador has left Paris. The situation has developed so rapidly that technically, as regards the condition of the war, it is most difficult to describe what has actually happened. I wanted to bring out the underlying issues, which would affect our own conduct, and our own policy, and to put them clearly. I have now put the vital facts before the House, and if, as seems not improbable, we are forced, and rapidly forced, to take our stand upon those issues, then I believe, when the country realizes what is at stake, what the real issues are, the magnitude of the impending dangers in the west of Europe, which I have endeavored to describe to the House, we shall be supported throughout, not only by the House of Commons, but by the determination, the resolution, the courage, and the endurance of the whole country.

[Later in the day, Sir Edward added the following words:]

I want to give the House some information, which I have received, and which was not in my possession when I made my statement this afternoon. It is information I have received from the Belgian Legation in London, and is to the following effect:

> *"Germany sent yesterday evening at seven o'clock a note proposing to Belgium friendly neutrality, covering free passage on Belgian territory, and promising maintenance of independence of the kingdom and possession at the conclusion of peace, and threatening, in case of refusal, to treat Belgium as an enemy. A time limit of twelve hours was fixed for the reply. The Belgians have answered that an attack on their neutrality would be a flagrant violation of the rights of nations, and that to accept the German proposal would be to sacrifice the honour of a nation. Conscious of its duty, Belgium is finally resolved to repel aggression by all possible means."*

Of course, I can only say that the Government is prepared to take into grave consideration the information which they have received. I make no further comment upon it.

The letter that Germany sends to Belgium has not been sent at this time. So how can Sir Edward Grey make an announcement that has not yet taken place? The only reason for this is that Russia, through a spy in 1908, acquired the Schefflien Plan and is making an assumption of what is said in the so-called letter at this time. Belgium at this time is conveying a problem at the Port of Antwerp with German merchant ships.

No. 78.
Sir G. Buchanan, British Ambassador at St. Petersburg, to Sir Edward Grey.
St. Petersburg
July 29, 1914.
(Telegraphic)

Partial mobilization was ordered today.

I communicated the substance of your telegram of the 28th[33] to Berlin to the minister of Foreign Affairs in accordance with your instructions, and informed him confidentially of remarks as to mobilization which the German Secretary of state had made to the British Ambassador at Berlin. This had already reached his Excellency from another source. The mobilization, he explained, would only be directed against Austria.

---

[33] See No. 67

Austrian government had now definitely declined direct conversation between Vienna and St. Petersburg. The Minister for Foreign Affairs said he had proposed such an exchange of views on advice of German ambassador. He proposed, when informing German ambassador of this refusal of Austria's, to urge that a return should be made to your proposal for a conference of the four Ambassadors, or, at all events, for an exchange of views between the three ambassadors less directly interested, yourself and also the Austrian Ambassador if you thought it advisable. Any arrangement approved by France and England would be acceptable to him, and he did not care what form such conversation took. No time was to be lost, and the only way to avert war was for you to succeed in arriving, by mean of conversation with Ambassadors either collectively or individually, at some formula which Austria could be induced to accept.

Throughout the Russian Government had been perfectly frank and conciliatory, and had done all in their power to maintain peace.

In their efforts to maintain peace failed, he trusted that it would be realized by the British public that it was not the fault of the Russian Government.

I asked him whether he would raise objections if the suggestion made in Rome telegram of the 27th July,[34] which I mentioned to him, were carried out. In reply, his Excellency said that he would agree to anything arranged by the Four Powers provided it was acceptable to Serbia; he could not, he said, be more Serbian than Serbia. Some supplementary statement or explanation would, however, have to be made in order to tone down the sharpness of the ultimatum.

Minister for Foreign Affairs said that the proposal referred to in your telegram of the 28th[35].was one of secondary importance under which altered circumstances of the situation he did not attach weight to it. Further, the German Ambassador had informed his Excellency, so the latter told me, that his government was continuing at Vienna to exert friendly influence. I fear that the German ambassador will not help to smooth matters over, if he uses to his own Government the same language as he did to me today. He accused the Russian government of endangering the peace of Europe by their mobilization, and said when I referred to all that had been recently done by Austria, that he could not discuss such matters. I called his attention to the fact that Austrian consuls had warned all Austrian subjects liable to military service to join the colors, that Austria had already partially mobilized, and now had declared war on Serbia. From what had passed during the Balkan crisis, she knew that this act was one, which it was impossible without humiliation for Russia to submit to. Had not Russia by mobilizing shown that she was in earnest; Austria would have traded on Russia's desire for peace, and would have believed that she could go to any lengths. Minister for Foreign Affairs had given me to understand that Russia would not precipitate war by crossing the frontier immediately, and a week or more would, in any case, elapse before mobilization was complete. In order to find issue out of a dangerous situation it was necessary that we should in the meanwhile all work together.

No. 8.
M. Davignon, Belgian Minister for Foreign Affairs, to the Belgian Ministers at Berlin, Paris, London, Vienna, St. Petersburg, Rome, The Hague, and Luxemburg.
Brussels
July 29, 1914.

Sir,
The Belgian Government has decided to place the army upon a strengthened peace footing. This step should in no way be confused with mobilisation.

---

[34] See No. 57
[35] See No. 69

Owing to the small extent of her territory, all Belgium consists, in some degree, of a frontier zone. Her army on the ordinary peace footing consists of only one class of armed militia; on the strengthened peace footing, owing to the recall of three classes, her army divisions and her cavalry division comprise effective units of the same strength as those of the corps permanently maintained in the frontier zones of the neighboring Powers.

This information will enable you to reply to any questions, which may be addressed to you.

No. 79.
Sir M. de Bunsen, British Ambassador at Vienna, to Sir Edward Grey.
Vienna
July 29, 1914.
(Telegraphic)

There is at present no step which we could usefully take to stop war with Austria, to which the Austro-Hungarian Government is now fully committed by the emperor's appeal to his people which has been fully published this morning, and by the declaration of war. French and Italian ambassadors agree with me in this view. If the Austro-Hungarian Government would convert into a binding engagement to Europe the declaration which as been made at St. Petersburg to the effect that she desires neither to destroy the independence of Serbia nor to acquire Serbian territory, the Italians Ambassador thinks that Russia might be induced to remain quiet. This, however, the Italian Ambassador is convinced the Austrian government would refuse to do.

This idea sounds like it was proposed to Austria already, but Austria did not give an immediate answer, so there is some doubt. With the French involved, it could be a double deal on France's part to lure the fighting to start sooner. Then there is the possibility that Austria sees what France has planned with Russia without knowing if this idea was presented to Austria already or even if it is an Austrian plan. It is too difficult to tell.

II. The Czar to His Majesty.
Peterhof Palace, July 29, 1 P.M.

I am glad that you are back in Germany. In this serious moment, I ask you earnestly to help me. An ignominious war has been declared against a weak country and in Russia; the indignation, which I fully share, is tremendous. I fear that very soon I shall be unable to resist the pressure exercised upon me and that I shall be forced to take measures which will lead to war. To prevent a calamity as a European war would be, I urge you in the name of our old friendship to do all in your power to restrain your ally from going too far.

(Signed)
NICOLAS.

No. 80.
Sir. Rodd, British Ambassador at Rome, to Sir Edward Grey.
Rome
July 29, 1914.
(Telegraphic)

In your telegram of the 27th instant[36] instant to Berlin, German Ambassador was reported to have accepted in principle the idea of a conference. This is in contradiction with the telegram of the 27th ^ instant from Berlin.

Information received by the Italian government from Berlin shows that German view is correctly represented in Sir E. Goshen's telegram of the 27th[37] July, but what creates difficulty is rather the "conference," so the Minister for Foreign Affairs understands, than the principle. He is going to urge, in a telegram, which he is sending to Berlin tonight, adherence to the idea of an exchange of views in London. He suggests that the German Secretary of State might propose a formula acceptable to his Government. Minister for Foreign Affairs is of opinion that this exchange of views would keep the door open if direct communication between Vienna and St. Petersburg fails to have any result. He thinks that this exchange of views might be concomitant with such direct communication.

III. His Majesty to the Czar.
July 29th, 6.30 P.M.

I have received your telegram and I share your desire for the conservation of peace. However: I cannot as I told you in my first telegram consider the action of Austria-Hungary as an "ignominious war." Austria-Hungary knows from experience that the promises of Serbia as long as they are merely on paper are entirely unreliable.

According to my opinion, the action of Austria-Hungary is to be considered as an attempt to receive full guaranty that the promises of Serbia are effectively translated into deeds. In this opinion, I am strengthened by the explanation of the Austrian Cabinet that Austria-Hungary intended no territorial gain at the expense of Serbia. I am therefore of opinion that it is perfectly possible for Russia to remain a spectator in the Serbian war without drawing Europe into the most terrible war it has ever seen. I believe that a direct understanding is possible and desirable between Your Government and Vienna, an understanding which as I have already telegraphed you my Government endeavors' to aid with all possible effort. Naturally military measures by Russia, which might be construed as menace by Austria-Hungary, would accelerate a calamity, which both of us desire to avoid, and would undermine my position as mediator which upon Your appeal to my friendship and aide willingly accepted.

(Signed)
WILHELM.

No. 81.
Sir Edward Grey to Sir R. Rodd, British Ambassador at Rome.
Foreign Office
July 29, 1914.
(Telegraphic)

With reference to your telegram of yesterday.[38]

---

[36]See No. 46.
[37]See No. 43.
[38]See No. 64.

It is impossible for me to initiate discussions with Ambassadors here, as I understand from Austrian Minister for Foreign Affairs that Austria will not accept any discussion on a basis of the Serbian note, and the interference of all I have heard from Vienna and Berlin is that Austria will not accept any form of mediation by the Powers as between Austria and Serbia. Italian Minister for Foreign Affairs must therefore speak at Berlin and Vienna. I shall be glad if a favorable reception is given to any suggestions he can make there.

Austria wants to keep this crisis local at Germany's recommendation. The problem is that Russia wants to make it everyone's problem by getting into foreign politics of their ally even though their ally is clearly at fault for the current crisis. Russia is starting to recognize that Serbia had every right to assassinate the archduke and murder his wife and unborn child.

No. 82.
Mr. Beaumont, British charge` d' Affaires at Constantinople, to Sir Edward Grey.
Constantinople
July 29, 1914.
(Telegraphic)

I understand that the designs of Austria may extend considerably beyond the Sanjak and a punitive occupation of Serbia territory. I gather this from a remark let fall by the Austrian Ambassador here, who spoke of the deplorable economic situation of Salonica under Greek administration and of the assistance on which the Austrian army could count from Mussulman population discontented with Serbian rule.

Though Austria did want to occupy Serbian territory to get the justice they sought from the murders, they had no desire to keep it. They would pull out just as soon as justice was served for all those involved with the murder of the archduke and his wife.

No. 83.
Mr. Crackanthorpe, British charge` d' Affaires at Belgrade, to Sir Edward Grey.
Nish
July 29, 1914.
(Telegraphic)

I have been requested by Prime Minister to convey to your expression of his deep gratitude for the statement, which you made on the 27th instant to the House of Commons.

Telegram of the Chancellor to the Imperial Ambassador at Paris
on July 29th, 1914.
News received here regarding French preparations of war multiplies from hour to hour. I request that you call the attention of the French Government to this and accentuate that such measures would call forth counter-measures on our part. We should have to proclaim threatening state of war (*drohende Kriegsgefahr*), and while this would not mean a call for the reserves or mobilization, yet the tension would be aggravated. We continue to hope for the preservation of peace.

No. 84.
Sir Edward Grey to Sir E. Goschen, British Ambassador at Berlin.
Foreign Office
July 29, 1914.
(Telegraphic)

The German Ambassador has been instructed by the German Chancellor to inform me that he is endeavoring to mediate between Vienna and St. Petersburg, and hopes with good success. Austria and Russia seem to be in constant touch and he is endeavoring to make Vienna explain in a satisfactory form at St. Petersburg the scope and extension of Austrian proceedings in Serbia. I told the German Ambassador that an agreement arrived at direct between Austria and Russia would be the best possible solution. I would press no proposal as long as there was a prospect of that, but my information this morning was that the Austrian Government has declined the suggestion of the Russian government that the Austrian Ambassador at St. Petersburg should be authorized to discuss directly with the Russian Minister for Foreign Affairs the means of settling the Austro-Serbian conflict. The press correspondents at St. Petersburg had been told that the Russian Government mobilizes. The German Government had said that they were favorable in principle to mediation between Russia and Austria if necessary. They seemed to think the particular method of conference, consultation or discussion, or even conversations a' quatre inn London too formal a method. I urged that the German Government should accept any method by which the influences of the Four Powers could be used together to prevent war between Austria and Russia. France agreed, Italy agreed. The whole idea of mediation or mediating influence was ready to be put into operation by any method that Germany could suggest if mine was not acceptable. In fact mediation was ready to come into operation by any method that Germany though possible if only Germany would "press the button" in the interest of peace.

What Sir Goschen does not realize is that France and Russia already have a plan put together and are in action to make sure that looks as if Germany started the war.

Primary Documents: The "Willy-Nicky" Telegrams
Updated: Saturday, 27 October, 2001.

This page lists the succession of telegrams sent, in the original English, between the German Emperor, Wilhelm II, and the Russian Tsar, Nicholas II, in the immediate run-up to the outbreak of war between 29 July 1914 and 1 August 1914.

The original source for the telegrams is *The Kaiser's Letters to the Tsar, Copied from the Government Archives in Petrograd and Brought from Russia*, edited by Isaac Don Levine, published by Hodder and Stoughton (London, 1920).

Tsar to Kaiser
29 July 1914, 1 A.M.
Peter's Court Palais, 29 July 1914.
Sa Majesté l'Empereur
Neues Palais

Am glad you are back. In this serious moment, I appeal to you to help me. An ignoble war has been declared to a weak country. The indignation in Russia shared fully by me is enormous. I foresee that very soon I shall be overwhelmed by the pressure forced upon me and be forced to take extreme measures which will lead to war. To try and avoid such a calamity as a European war I beg you in the name of our old friendship to do what you can to stop your allies from going too far.

Kaiser to Tsar

29 July 1914, 1.45 A.M. (this and the previous telegraph crossed)
28 July 1914.

It is with the gravest concern that I hear of the impression which the action of Austria against Serbia is creating in your country.

The unscrupulous agitation that has been going on in Serbia for years has resulted in the outrageous crime, to which Archduke Francis Ferdinand fell a victim. The spirit that led Serbians to murder their own king and his wife still dominates the country.

You will doubtless agree with me that we both, you and me, have a common interest as well as all Sovereigns to insist that all the persons morally responsible for the dastardly murder should receive their deserved punishment. In this case politics plays no part at all.

On the other hand, I fully understand how difficult it is for you and your Government to face the drift of your public opinion. Therefore, with regard to the hearty and tender friendship which binds us both from long ago with firm ties, I am exerting my utmost influence to induce the Austrians to deal straightly to arrive to a satisfactory understanding with you. I confidently hope that you will help me in my efforts to smooth over difficulties that may still arise.

Your very sincere and devoted friend and cousin,
Willy

No. 85.
Sir E. Goschen, British Ambassador at Berlin, to Edward Grey.
Berlin
July 29, 1914.
(Telegraphic)

I was asked to call upon the Chancellor tonight. His Excellency had just returned from Potsdam.

He said that should Austria be attacked by Russia a European conflagration might, he feared, become inevitable, owing to Germany's obligations as Austria's ally, in spite of his continue efforts to maintain peace. He then proceeded to make the following strong bid for British neutrality. He said that it was clear, so far as he was able to judge the main principle which governed British policy, that Great Britain would never stand by and allow France to be crushed in any conflict there might be. That, however, was not the object at which Germany aimed. Provided that neutrality of Great Britain were certain, every assurance would be given to the British Government that the Imperial aimed at no territorial acquisitions at the expense of France should they prove victorious in any war that might ensue.

I questioned his Excellency about French colonies, and he said that he was unable to give a similar undertaking in that respect. As regards Holland, however, his Excellency said that, so long as Germany's adversaries respected the integrity and neutrality of the Netherlands, Germany was ready to give His Majesty's Government an assurance that she would do likewise. It depended upon the action of France what operations Germany might be forced to enter upon Belgium, but when the war was over, Belgium integrity would be respected if she had not sided against Germany.

His Excellency ended by saying that ever since he had been Chancellor the object of his policy had been, as you were aware to bring about an understanding with England; he trusted that these assurances might form the basis of that understanding which he so much desired. He had in mind a general neutrality agreement between England and Germany, though it was of course at the present moment too early to discuss details, and assurance of British neutrality in the conflict which present crisis might possibly produce, would enable him to look forward to realization of his desire.

In reply to his Excellency's enquiry how I thought his request would appeal to you, I said that I did not think it probable that at this stage of events, you would care to bind yourself to any course of action and that I was opinion that you would desire to retain full liberty.

Our conversation upon this subject having come to an end, I communicated the contents of your telegram of today[39] to his Excellency, who expressed his best thanks to you.

Kaiser to Tsar
29 July 1914, 6.30 P.M.
Berlin
29 July 1914.
I received your telegram and share your wish that peace should be maintained.

However, as I told you in my first telegram, I cannot consider Austria's action against Serbia an "ignoble" war. Austria knows by experience that Serbian promises one paper is wholly unreliable. I understand its action must be judged as trending to get full guarantee that the Serbian promises shall become real facts. This reasoning is borne out by the statement of the Austrian cabinet that Austria does not want to make any territorial conquests at the expense of Serbia.

I therefore suggest that it would be quite possible for Russia to remain a spectator of the Austro-Serbian conflict without involving Europe in the most horrible war she ever witnessed. I think a direct understanding between your Government and Vienna possible and desirable, and as I already telegraphed to you, my Government is continuing its exercises to promote it.

Of course, military measures on the part of Russia would be looked upon by Austria as a calamity we both wish to avoid and jeopardize my position as mediator, which I readily accepted on your appeal to my friendship and my help.

Willy

Tsar to Kaiser
29 July 1914, 8.20 P.M.
Peter's Court Palace, 29 July 1914.
Thanks for your telegram conciliatory and friendly. Whereas official message presented today by your ambassador to my minister was conveyed in a very different tone. Beg you to explain this divergence! It would be right to give over the Austro-Serbian problem to the Hague conference.

Trust in your wisdom and friendship.
Your love, Nicky

On July 29th, the German Military Attaché at St. Petersburg wired the following report on a conversation with the Chief of the General Staff of the Russian army:

"The Chief of the General Staff has asked me to call on him, and he has told me that he has just come from His Majesty. He has been requested by The Secretary of War to reiterate once more that everything had remained as the Secretary had informed me two days ago. He offered confirmation in writing and gave me his word of honor in the most solemn manner that nowhere there had been a mobilization, viz., calling in of a single man or Horse up to the present time, *i.e.,* 3 o'clock in the afternoon. He could not assume a guarantee for the future, but he could emphasize that in the fronts directed towards our frontiers His Majesty desired no Mobilization. "As, however, I had received here many pieces of news concerning the calling in of the reserves in different parts of the country also in Warsaw and in Vilna, I told the general that his statements placed me before a riddle. On his officer's Word of honor, he replied that such news was wrong, but that possibly here In addition, there a false alarm might have been

---

[39] See No. 77.

given." I must consider this conversation as an attempt to mislead us as to the extent of the Measures hitherto taken in view of the abundant and positive information about the calling in of reserves.

In reply to various inquiries concerning reasons for its threatening attitude, the Russian Government repeatedly pointed out that Austria-Hungary had commenced no conversation in St. Petersburg. The Austro-Hungarian Ambassador in St. Petersburg was therefore instructed on July 29th, at our suggestion, to enter into such conversation with Sasonof. Count Szapary was empowered to explain to the Russian minister the note to Serbia, though it had been overtaken by the state of war, and to accept any suggestion on the part of Russia as well as to discuss with Sasonof all questions touching directly upon the Austro-Russian relations. Shoulder to shoulder with England we labored incessantly and supported every proposal in Vienna from which we hoped to gain the possibility of a peaceable solution of the conflict. [*See exhibit 19.*] We even as late as 30 July forwarded the English proposal to Vienna, as basis for negotiations that Austria-Hungary should dictate her conditions in Serbia, *i.e.,* after her march into Serbia. We thought that Russia would accept this basis.

During the interval from July 29th to July 31ˢᵗ there appeared renewed and cumulative news concerning Russian measures of mobilization. Accumulation of troops on the East Prussian frontier and the declaration of the state of war over all important parts of the Russian west frontier allowed no further doubt that the Russian mobilization was in full swing against us, while simultaneously all such cures were denied to our representative in St. Petersburg on word of honor. Nay, even before the reply from Vienna regarding the Anglo-German mediation whose tendencies and basis must have been known in St. Petersburg could possibly have been received in Berlin, Russia ordered a general mobilization. During the same days, there took place between His Majesty the Kaiser and Czar Nicolas an exchange of telegrams in which His Majesty called the attention of the Czar to the menacing, character of the Russian mobilization during the continuance of his own mediating activities. [*See exhibits 18, 20, 21, 22, 23, 23a.*]

No. 86.
Sir R. Rodd, British Ambassador at Rome, to Sir Edward Grey.
Rome
July 29, 1914.
Rome
(Telegraphic)

Minister for Foreign Affairs thinks that the moment is past for any further discussions on a basis of the Serbian note, in view of communication made today by Russia at Berlin regarding partial mobilization. The utmost he now hopes for is that Germany may use her influence at Vienna to prevent or moderate any further demands on Serbia.

Up to this point, Austria has had no desire to change what they have put in the note to Serbia.

No. 87.
Sir Edward Grey to Sir F. Bertie, British Ambassador at Paris.
Foreign Office
July 29, 1914.

Sir,

After telling M. Cambon[40] today how grave the situation seemed to be, I told him that I meant to tell the German Ambassador today that he must not be misled by the friendly tone of our conversations into any sense of false security that we should stand aside if all the efforts to preserve the peace, which we are now making in common with Germany, failed. But I went on to say to Cambon[40] that I thought it necessary to tell him also that public opinion here approached the present difficulty from a quite different point of view from that taken during the difficulty as to Morocco a few years ago. In the case of Morocco, the dispute was one in which France was primarily interested, and in which it appeared that Germany, in an attempt to crush France, was fastening a quarrel on France on a question that was the subject of a special agreement between France and us. In the present case the dispute between Austria and Serbia was not one in which we felt called to take a hand. Even if the question became one between Austria and Russia we should not feel called upon to take a hand in it. It would then be a question of the supremacy of Teuton or Slav struggle for supremacy in the Balkans; and our idea had always been to avoid being drawn into a war over a Balkan question. If Germany became involved and France became involved, we had not made up our minds what we should do; it has been a case that we should have to consider. France would then have been drawn into a quarrel, which was not hers, but in which owing to her alliance, her honor and interest obliged her to engage we were free from engagements and we should have to decide what British interests require us to do. I thought it necessary to say that, because, as he knew, we were taking all precautions with regard to our fleet, and I was about to warn Prince Lichnowsky[40] not to count on our standing aside, but it would not be fair that I should let Mr. Cambon be misled into supposing that this meant that we had decided what to do in a contingency that I still hope might not arise.

Sounds like M. Cambon was seeking to confirm that Britain would support France when Russia attacked both Austria and Germany. This also follows the treaty signed by France and Britain for mutual support in all military actions against Germany.

No. 88.
Sir Edward Grey to Sir E. Goschen, British Ambassador at Berlin.
Foreign Office
July 29, 1914.

Sir,

I told the German ambassador this afternoon of the information that I had received that Russia had informed Germany respecting her mobilization. I also told him of the communication made by Count Benckendorff, that Austrian declaration of war manifestly rendered vain any direct conversation between Russia and Austria. I said that the hop built upon those direct conversations by the German Government yesterday had disappeared today. Today the German Chancellor was working in the interest of mediation in Vienna and St. Petersburg. If he succeeded, well and good. If not, it was more important than ever that Germany should up what I had suggested to the German Ambassador this morning, and propose some method buy which the Four Powers should be able to work together to keep the peace of Europe. I pointed out, however, that the Russian Government, while desirous of mediation, regarded it as a condition that the military operations against Serbia should be suspended,

---

[40] German Ambassador in London.

as otherwise a mediation would only drag on matters, and give Austria time to crush Serbia. It was, of course, too late for all military operations against Serbia to be suspended. In a short time, I suppose, the Austrian forces would be in Belgrade, and in occupation of some Serbian territory. But even then might be possible to bring mediation into existence, if Austria, while saying that she must hold the occupied territory until she had complete satisfaction from Serbia, stated she would not advance further, pending an effort of the Powers to mediate between her and Russia.

The German ambassador said that he had already telegraphed to Berlin what I had said to him this morning

E. Grey

No. 89.
Sir Edward Grey to Sir E. Goschen, British Ambassador at Berlin.
Foreign Office
July 29, 1914.

Sir,

After speaking to the German Ambassador this afternoon about the European situation, I said that I wished to say to him, in quiet private and friendly way, something that was on my mind. The situation was very grave. While it was restricted to the issues at present actually involved, we had no thought of interfering in it. But if Germany became involved in it, and then France, the issue might be so great that it would involve all European interest; and I did not wish him to be misled by the friendly tone of our conversation—which I hoped would continue—into thinking that we should stand aside.

He said that he quite understood this, but he asked whether I meant that we should, under certain circumstances, intervene?

I replied that I did not wish to say that, or to use anything that was like a threat or an attempt to apply pressure by saying that, if things became worse, we should intervene. There would be no question of our intervening if Germany was not involved, or even if France was not involved. But we knew very well, that if the issue did become such that we thought British interest required us to intervene, we must intervene at once, and the decision would have to be very rapid, just has the decision of the other Powers had to be. I hoped that the friendly of our conversation would continue as at present, and that I should be able to keep as closely in touch as at the present, and that I should be able to keep as closely in touch with the German Government in working for peace. But if we fail in our efforts to keep the peace, and if the issue spread so that it involved practically every European interest, I did not wish to be open to any reproach from him that the friendly tone of all our conversations had misled him or his government into supposing that we should not take action, and to the reproach that, if they had not been so misled, the course of things might have been different.

The German ambassador took no exception to what I had said; indeed, he told me that it accorded with what he had already given in Berlin as his view of the situation.

E. Grey

No. 90.
Sir Edward Grey to Sir E. Goschen, British Ambassador at Berlin.
Foreign Office
July 29, 1914.

Sir,

In addition to what passed with the German Ambassador this morning, as recorded in my telegram of the 29[41] to your Excellency, I gave the Ambassador a copy of Sir Rennell Rodd's[42] telegram of the 28[42] and my reply to it[43] I said I had begun to doubt whether even a complete acceptance of the Austrian demands by Serbia would now satisfy Austria. But there appealed, from what the Marquis di San Giuliano` had to say, to be a method by which, if Powers were allowed to have any say in the matter, they might bring about complete satisfaction for Austria, if only the latter would give them an opportunity. I could, however, make no proposal, for the reason I have given in my telegram to you, and could only give what the Italian minister for Foreign Affairs had said to the German ambassador for information, as long as it was understood that Austria would accept no discussion with the Powers over her dispute with Serbia. As to mediation between Austria and Russia, I said it could not take the form simply of urging Russia to stand to one side while Austria had a free hand to go to any length as she pleased. That would not be mediation; it would simply be putting pressure upon Russia in the interest of Austria. The German Ambassador said the view of the German government was that Austria could not be forced to be humiliated, and could not abdicate her position as a Great Power. I said I entirely agree, but it was not a question of humiliating Austria, it was a question of how far Austria meant to push the humiliation of others. There must, of course, be some humiliation of Serbia; Austria might press things so far as to involve the humiliation of Russia.

The German Ambassador said that Austria would not take Serbian territory, as to which I observed that, by taking territory while leaving nominal Serbian independence, Austria might turn Serbia into a vassal state, and this would affect the whole position of Russia in the Balkans.

I observed that when there was danger of a European conflict it was impossible to say who would not be drawn into it. Even the Netherlands apparently were taking precautions.

The German Ambassador said empathically that some means must be found of preserving the peace of Europe.

E. Grey

No. 91.
Sir Edward Grey to Sir E. Bunsen, British Ambassador at Vienna.
Foreign Office
July 29, 1914.

Sir,

The Austrian Ambassador told me today he had ready a long memorandum, which he proposed to leave, and which he said gave an account of the conduct of Serbia towards Austria, an explanation of how necessary the Austrian action was.

I said that I did not wish to discuss the merits of the question between Austria and Serbia. The news today seemed to me very bad for the peace of Europe. The Powers were not allowed to help in getting satisfaction for Austria, which they might get if they were given an opportunity, and European peace was at stake.

---

[41] See No. 84
[42] See No. 64
[43] See No. 81

Count Mensdorff said that the war with Serbia must proceed. Austria could not continue to be exposed to the necessity of mobilizing again and again, as she had been obliged to do in recent years. She had no idea of territorial aggrandizement, and all she wished was to make sure that her interests were safeguarded.

I said that it would be quite possible, without nominally interfering with the independence Serbia or taking away any of her territory, to turn her into a sort of vassal state.

Count Mensdorff deprecated this.

In reply to some further remarks of mine, as to the effect that the Austrian action might have upon the Russian position in the Balkans, he said that, before the Balkan war, Serbia had always been regarded as being in the Austrian sphere on influence.

E. Grey

No. 92.
Sir Edward Grey to Sir R. Rodd, British Ambassador at Rome.
Foreign Office
July 29, 1914.

Sir,

The Italian Ambassador made to me today a communication from the Marquis di San Giuliano suggesting that the German objections to mediation of the Four Powers, a mediation that was strongly favored by Italy, might be removed by some change in the form of procedure.

I said that I had already anticipated this by asking the German Government to suggest any form of procedure under which the idea of mediation between Austria and Russia, already accepted by the German Government in principle, could be applied.

E. Grey

No. 93.
Telegrams communicated by Count Benckendorff, Russian ambassador in London.
London
July 30, 1914.

1. **Russian Ambassador at Vienna to M. Sazonof**
   Vienna
   July 28, 1914.
   (Telegraphic)

I spoke to Count Berchtold today in the sense of your Excellency's instructions. I brought to his notice, in the most friendly manner, how desirable it was to find a solution which, while consolidating good relations between Austria-Hungary and Russia, would give to the Austro-Hungarian Monarchy genuine guarantees for its future relations with Serbia.

I drew count Berchtold's attention to all the dangers to the peace of Europe which would be involved by an armed conflict between Austria-Hungary and Serbia.

Count Berchtold replied that he was well aware of the gravity of the situation and of the advantages of a frank explanation with the St. Petersburg Cabinet. He told me that, on the other hand, the Austro-Hungarian Government, who had only decided much against their will on the energetic measures, which they had taken against Serbia, could no longer recede, nor enter into any discussion about the terms of the Austro-Hungarian note. Count Berchtold added that the crisis had become so acute, and that public opinion had risen to such a pitch of excitement, that the government, even if they wished it, could no longer consent to such a course. This was all the more impossible, he said, inasmuch as the Serbian reply itself furnished proof of the insincerity of Serbia's promise for the future.

2. **M. Sazonof, Russian Minister for Foreign affairs, to count Benckendorff, Russian Ambassador in London.**
St. Petersburg
July 29, 1914.
(Telegraphic)

The German Ambassador informs me, in the name of the Chancellor, that Germany has not ceased to exercise a moderating influence at Vienna, and that she will continue to do so even after the declaration of war. Up to this morning there has been no news that the Austrian army has crossed the Serbian frontier. I have begged the Ambassador to express my thanks to the Chancellor for the friendly tenure of this communication. I have informed the military measures taken by Russia, none of which, I told him, were directed against Germany; I added that neither should they be taken as aggressive measures against Austria-Hungarian army.

The Ambassador said that he was in favor of direct explanation between the Austrian Government and ourselves, and quite willing, provided that the advice of the German government, to which he had referred, found an echo at.

I said at that time that we were quite ready to accept the proposal for a conference of the Four Powers, a proposal with which apparently, Germany was not entire sympathy.

I told him that, in my opinion, the best manner of turning to account the most suitable methods of finding a peaceful resolution would be by arranging for parallel discussions to be carried on by a conference of the Four Powers—Germany, France, Great Britain, and Italy—and by a direct exchange of views between Austria-Hungary and Russia on much the same lines as occurred during the most critical moments of last year's crisis.

I told the Ambassador that, after the concessions, which had been made by Serbia, it should not be very difficult to find a compromise to settle the other questions which remained out standing, provided that Austria showed some good will and that all the Powers used their entire influence in the direction of conciliation.

3. **M. Sazonof, Russian Minister for Foreign Affairs, to count Benckendorff, Russian Ambassador in London.**
St. Petersburg
July 29, 1914.
(Telegraphic)

At the time of my interview with the German Ambassador, dealt with in my proceeding telegram, I had not received M. Sche`beko's[44] of the 28th of July.

The contents of this telegram constitute a refusal of the Vienna cabinet to agree to a direct exchange of views with the Imperial government.

From now on, nothing remains for us to do but to rely entirely on the British government to take the initiative in any steps, which they may consider advisable.

---

[44] Russian Ambassador at Vienna

No. 94.
Sir M. de Bunsen, British Ambassador at Vienna, to Sir Edward Grey.
(received July 30, 1914)
Vienna
July 29, 1914.
(Telegraphic)

I learned that mobilization of Russian corps destined to carry out operations on the Austrian frontier has been ordered. My informant is the Russian Ambassador. Minister for Foreign Affairs here has realized, though somewhat late in the day that Russia will not remain indifferent in present crisis. I believe that the news of Russian mobilization will not be a surprise to the Ministry, but so far, it is not generally known in Vienna this evening. Unless mediation, which German government declared themselves ready to offer in concert with three other Great Powers not immediately interested in the Austro-Serbian dispute, be brought to bear forthwith, irrevocable steps may be taken in present temper of this country. German Ambassador Feigns surprise that the Serbian affairs should be of such interest to Russia. Both my Russian and French colleagues have spoken to him today. Russian Ambassador expressed the hope that it might still be possible to arrange matters, and explained that it was possible for Russia to do otherwise than take an interest in the present dispute. Russia, he said, had done what she could already in Belgrade to induce Serbian Government to meet principle Austrian demands in a favorable spirit; if approached in a proper manner, he thought she would probably go still further in this direction. But she was justly offended at having been completely ignored, and she could not consent to be excluded from the settlement. German Ambassador said that if proposal were put forward which opened any prospect of possible acceptance by both sides, he personally thought that Germany might consent to act as mediator in concert with the three other Powers.

I gather from what Russian Ambassador said to me that he is much afraid of the effect that any serious engagement may have upon Russian public opinion. I gathered, however, that Russia would go a long way to meet Austrian demands on Serbia.

Chapter Thirty-One
July 30, 1914

No. 95.
Sir M. de Bunsen, British Ambassador at Vienna, to Sir Edward Grey.
Vienna
July 30, 1914.
(Telegraphic)

Russian Ambassador hopes Russian mobilization will be regarded by Austria as what it is, viz., a clear intimation that Russia must be consulted regarding the fate of Serbia, but he does not know how the Austrian Government is taking it. He says that Russia must have assurance that Serbia will not be crushed, but she would understand that Austria-Hungary is compelled to exact from Serbia measures, which will secure her Slavic provinces from the continuance of hostile propaganda from Serbian territory.

The French Ambassador hears from Berlin that the German Ambassador at Vienna is instructed to speak seriously to the Austro-Hungarian Government against acting in a manner calculated to provoke a European war.

Unfortunately, the German Ambassador is himself so identified with extreme anti-Russian and anti-Serbian feeling prevalent in Vienna that he is unlikely to plead the cause of peace with entire sincerity.

Although I am not able to verify it, I have a private information that the German Ambassador knew the text of the Austrian ultimatum to Serbia before it was dispatched and telegraphed it to the German Emperor. I know from the German Ambassador himself that he endorses every line of it.

This telegram does not confirm anything. All it says is that Austria went to Germany for their view on the Serbian ultimatum. Germany was in a position to endorse or revoke the note. They saw the murder of the Archduke as an act of war against Austria.

The past few days of telegrams has been geared for the appeasement of Russia and not the justice that Austria seeks. Serbia has been following Russian orders during this whole time, and Russia as been following French instructions to escalate the current crisis for their own agenda against Germany.

No. 96.
Sir M. de Bunsen, British Ambassador at Vienna, to Sir Edward Grey.
Vienna
July 30, 1914.
(Telegraphic)

The Russian Ambassador gave the French Ambassador and myself this afternoon at the French embassy, where I happened to be, account of his interview with the Minister of Foreign Affairs, which he said was quite friendly. The Minister for Foreign Affairs had told him that as Russia had mobilized, Austria must, of course, do the same. This, however, should not be regarded as a threat, but merely as the adoption of military precautions similar to those, which had been taken across the frontier. He said he had no objection to the Russian Minister for Foreign Affairs and the Austrian Ambassador at St. Petersburg continuing their conversations, although he did not say that they could be resumed on the basis of the Serbian reply.

On the whole, the Russian Ambassador is not dissatisfied. He had begun to make his preparations for his departure on the strength of a rumor that Austria would declare war in reply to mobilization. He now hopes that something may yet be done to prevent war with Austria.

Germany would play a part in stopping Austria from declaring war on Russia.

No. 97.
Sir G. Buchanan, British Ambassador at St. Petersburg, to Sir Edward Grey.
St. Petersburg
July 30, 1914.
(Telegraphic)

French Ambassador and I visited Minister for Foreign Affairs this morning. His Excellency said that German Ambassador had told him yesterday afternoon that the German Government were willing to guarantee that Serbian integrity would be respected by Austria. To this, he had replied that this might be so, but nevertheless Serbia would become an Austrian vassal, just as, in similar circumstances, Bokhara had become a Russian vassal. There would be revolution in Russia if she were tolerate such a state of affairs.

M. Sazonof[45] told us that absolute proof was in the possession of the Russian government that Germany was making military and naval preparations against Russia, more particularly in the direction of the Gulf of Finland.

German Ambassador had a second interview with the Minister for Foreign Affairs at 2 A.M., when the former completely broke down on see that war was inevitable. He appealed to M. Sazonof to make some suggestion which he could telegraph to German Government as a last hope. M. Sazonof accordingly drew up and handed to German Ambassador a formula in French, of which is the following translation:

"If Austria, recognizing that her conflict with Serbia has assumed character of question of European interest, declares herself ready to eliminate from her ultimatum points which violate principle of sovereignty of Serbia, Russia engages to stop all military preparations."

Preparations for general mobilization will be proceeded with, if this proposal is rejected by Austria, and inevitable result will be a European war. Excitement here as reached such a pitch that, if Austria refuses to make a concession, Russia cannot hold back, and now that she knows that Germany is arming, she can hardly postpone, for strategic reasons, converting partial into general mobilization.

---

[45] Russian Minister for Foreign Affairs.

This telegram taken at face value says Russia is getting tough. But by reading the undertone and attitude of the contents of this letter, Russia unofficially declared war on not only Austria but Germany as well. The mention of Finland is just that—German ships, whether they be merchant men or naval fleet, have to go by that country because of where German ports are. Germany gave the order to mobilize only after Russia and France gave the order to mobilize. Germany is still trying to find a peaceful resolution to the Austrian and Serbian crises. The formula that was translated was possibly written beforehand and given to Sazonof when the French president was in Russia from July 20 to July 25, 1914.

No. 98.
Sir E. Goschen, British Ambassador at Berlin, to Sir Edward Grey.
Berlin
July 30, 1914.
(Telegraphic)

Secretary of State informs me that immediately on receipt of Prince Lichnowsky's telegram[46] recording his last conversation with you he asked Austro-Hungarian Government whether they would be willing to accept mediation on basis of occupation by Austrian troops of Belgrade or some other point and issue their condition from here. He has up till now received no reply, but fears Russian mobilization against Austria will have increased difficulties, as Austria-Hungary who has yet only mobilized against Serbia, will probably find it necessary also against Russia. Secretary of State says if you can succeed in getting Russia to agree to above basis for an arrangement and in persuading her in the meantime to take no steps, which might be regarded as an act of aggression against Austria he still sees some chance that European peace may be preserved.

He begged me to impress on your difficulty of Germany's position in view of Russian mobilization and military measures, which he hears, are being taken in France. Beyond recall of officers on leave—a measure, which had been officially taken after, and not before, visit of French Ambassador yesterday—imperial Government, had done nothing special in way of military preparations. Something, however, would have soon to be done, for it might be too late, and when they mobilize, they would have to mobilize on three sides. He regretted this, as he knew France did not desire war, but it would be a military necessity.

His Excellency added that telegram[47] received from Prince Lichnowsky last night contains matter which he had heard with regret, not exactly with surprise, and all events he thoroughly appreciated frankness and loyalty with which you had spoken.

He also told me that this telegram had only reached Berlin very late last night; had it been received earlier Chancellor would, of course, not have spoken to me in the way he had done.

This telegram is now saying that Russia holds the decision for war or peace now with Austria.

Russia is being difficult in negotiations with Austria, Germany, and Great Britain. What is Russia trying to hide, their involvement with the murder of the archduke or France's desire to get revenge for the Franco-Prussia War?

---

[46] See No. 102
[47] German Ambassador in London.

No. 44.
From: **His Royal Highness the Crown Prince Alexander.**
To: **His Imperial Majesty the Emperor of Russia.**
Nish
July 30, 1914.
(Telegraphic)

Deeply touched by the telegram, which your Majesty was pleased to address to me yesterday, I hasten to thank you with all my heart. Your Majesty may rest assured that the cordial sympathy which your Majesty feels towards my country is especially valued by us, and fills our hearts with the belief that the future of Serbia is secure now that it is the object of your Majesty's gracious solicitude. These painful moments cannot but strengthen the bonds of deep attachment which bind Serbia to Holy Slav Russia, and the sentiments of everlasting gratitude which we feel for the help and protection afforded to us by your Majesty will ever be cherished in the hearts of all the Serbs.

No. 99.
Sir F. Bertie, British Ambassador at Paris, to Sir Edward Grey.
Paris
July 30, 1914.
(Telegraphic)

President of the Republic tells me that the Russian government has been informed by the German Government that unless Russia stops her mobilization Germany would mobilize. But a further report, since received from St. Petersburg, states that the German communication had been modified, and was now a request to be informed on what conditions Russia would consent to demobilization. The answer given is that she agrees to do so on condition that Austria-Hungary gives an assurance that she will respect the sovereignty of Serbia and submit certain of the demands of the Austrian note, which Serbia has not accepted, to an international discussion. President thinks that these conditions will not be accepted by Austria. He is convinced that peace between the powers is in the hands of Great Britain. If his Majesty's Government announced that England would come to the aid of France in the event of a conflict between France and Germany as a result of the present Differences between Austria and Serbia, there would be no war, for Germany would at once modify her attitude.

I explained to him how difficult it would be for his Majesty's Government to make such an announcement, but he said that he must maintain that it would be in the interest of peace. France he said is specific. She does not desire war, and all that she has done at present is to make preparations for mobilization so as not to be taken unaware.

The French Government will keep his Majesty's government informed of everything that may be done in that way. They have reliable information that German troops are concentrated around Thionville and Metz ready for war. If there were a general war on the continent, it would inevitably draw England into it for her protection of her vital interest. A declaration now of her intention to support France, whose desire it is that peace should be maintained, would almost certainly prevent Germany from going to war.

France is trying to force Germany into make the first move of aggression against Russia and France, or France is in the process of fabricating a lie of German aggression so England will mobilize against Germany. Germany and Great Britain up to this point are still trying to come up with an agreement that both Austria and Serbia will accept.

No. 100.
Sir R. Rodd, British Ambassador at Rome, to Sir Edward Grey.
Rome
July 30, 1914.
(Telegraphic)

German Ambassador told me last night that he thought Germany would be able to prevent Austria from making any exorbitant demands if Serbia could be induced to submit, and to ask for peace early, say, as soon as the occupation of Belgrade had been accomplished.

I made to his Excellency the personal suggestion that some formula might be devised by Germany, which might be acceptable for an exchange of views.

I see that you have already made this suggestion.

This telegram still shows that Germany wants peace, as does England.

From: M. Sazonof, Russian Minister for Foreign Affairs.
To: Dr. M. Spalaikovitch, Minister at Petrograd.
Petrograd
July 30, 1914.

Sir,

I had the honor to receive your note of July 28, No. 527, in which you communicated to me the contents of the telegram received by you from His Excellency, M. Pashitch, in regard to the declaration of war on Serbia by Austria-Hungary. I sincerely regret this sad event, and will not fail to lay before His Majesty the petition by the Serbian nation, whose interpreter you are.

No. 101.
Sir Edward Grey to Sir E. Goschen, British Ambassador at Berlin.
Foreign Affairs
July 30, 1914.
(Telegraphic)

Your telegram of July 29th.[48]

His Majesty's Government cannot for a moment entertain the Chancellors proposal that they should bind themselves to neutrality on such terms.

What he asks us in effect is to engage to stand by while French colonies are taken and France is beaten so long as Germany does not take French territory as distinct from the colonies.

From the material point of view such a proposal is unacceptable for France, without further territory in Europe being taken from her, could so be crushed as to lose her position as a Great Power, and become subordinate to Germany policy.

Altogether apart from that, it would be a disgrace for us to make this bargain with Germany at the expense of France, a disgrace from which the good name of this country would never recover.

The Chancellor also in effect asks us to bargain away whatever obligations or interest we have as regards to the neutrality of Belgium.

We could not entertain that bargain either.

---

[48] German Ambassador in London.

Having said so much it is unnecessary to examine whether the prospect of a future general neutrality agreement between England and Germany offered positive advantages sufficient to compensate us for tying our hands now. We must preserve our full freedom to act, as circumstances may seem to us to require in any such unfavorable and regrettable development of the present crisis as the Chancellor contemplates.

You should speak to the Chancellor in the above sense, and add most earnestly that the one way of maintaining the good relations between England and Germany is that they should continue to work together to preserve the peace of Europe; if we succeed in this object, the mutual relations of Germany and England will, I believe, be *ipso facto* improved and strengthen. For that object, his Majesty's government will work in that way with all sincerity and good will.

And I will say this: if peace of Europe can be preserved and the present crisis safely passed, my own endeavor will be to promote some arrangement to which Germany could be a party by which she could be assured that no aggrieve or hostile policy would be pursued against her or her allies by France and Russia, and ourselves, jointly or separately. I have desired this and worked for it, as far as I could, through the last Balkan crisis, and, Germany having corresponding object, our relations sensibly improved. The idea has hitherto been to utopia to form the subject of definite proposals, but if this present crisis, so much more acute than any that Europe has gone through for generations, be safely passed, I am hopeful that the relief and reaction which will follow may make possible some more definite rapprochement between the Powers than has been possible hitherto.

Russian Chargé d'Affaires in Serbia to Russian Minister for Foreign Affairs.
Nish
July 30, 1914.
(Telegraphic)

THE Prince Regent yesterday published a manifesto, signed by all the Serbian Ministers, on the declaration of war by Austria against Serbia. The manifesto ends with the following words: "Defend your homes and Serbia with all your might." At the solemn opening of the Skupchtina, the Regent read the speech from the Throne in his own name. At the beginning of his speech, he pointed out that the place of their convocation showed the importance of present events. He followed this with a summary of recent events the Austrian ultimatum, the Serbian reply, the efforts of the Serbian Government to do their utmost to avoid war that was compatible with the dignity of the State, and, finally, the armed aggression of their most powerful neighbor against Serbia, at whose side stood Montenegro. Passing in review the attitude of the Powers towards the dispute, the Prince emphasized in the first place the sentiments, which animated Russia, and the gracious communication from His Majesty the Emperor that Russia would in no case abandon Serbia. At each mention of His Majesty the Czar and of Russia, the hall resounded with loud bursts of wild cheering. The sympathy shown by France and England was also touched upon in turn, and called forth approving plaudits from the members. The speech from the throne ended by declaring the Skupchtina open, and by expressing the hope that everything possible would be done to lighten the task before the Government.

No. 102.
Sir Edward Grey to Sir E. Goschen, British Ambassador at Berlin.
Foreign Office
July 30, 1914.
(Telegraphic)

I have warned Prince Lichnowsky* that Germany must not count upon our standing aside in all circumstances. This is doubtless the substance of your telegram from Prince Lichnowsky* to German Chancellor, to which reference is made in the last two paragraphs of your telegram of July 30[th49]. So accordingly to this telegram, if Austria is attacked by Russia, Britain will let it happen because of France's close relations with England. This would include Germany, too.

No. 60.
Russian Minister for Foreign Affairs to Russian Ambassadors at Berlin, Vienna, Paris, London, and Rome.
St. Petersburg, July 30, 1914.
(Telegraphic)

THE German Ambassador, who has just left me, has asked whether Russia would not be satisfied with the promise which Austria might give that she would not violate the integrity of the Kingdom of Serbia and whether we could not indicate upon what conditioned we would agree to suspend our military preparations. I dictated to him the following declaration to be forwarded to Berlin for immediate action: *"Si l'Autriche, reconnaissant que la question austro-serbe a assume le caractère d'une question européenneé se déclare prête à éliminer de son ultimatum les points qui portent atteinte aux droits souverains de la Serbie, la Russie s'engage à cesser ses préparatifs militaires."*

If Austria, recognising that the Austro-Serbian question has assumed the character of a question of European interest, declares herself ready to eliminate from her ultimatum points which violate the sovereign rights of Serbia, Russia engages to stop her military preparations. Please inform me at once by telegraph what attitude the German Government will adopt in face of this fresh proof of our desire to do the utmost possible for a peaceful settlement of the question, for we cannot allow such discussions to continue solely in order that Germany and Austria may gain time for their military preparations

No.103.
Sir Edward Grey to Sir G. Buchanan, British Ambassador at St. Petersburg.
Foreign Office
July 30, 1914.
(Telegraphic)

German Ambassador informs me that the German Government would endeavor to influence Austria, after taking Belgrade and Serbian territory in region of frontier, to promise not to advance further, while Powers endeavored to arrange that Serbia should give satisfaction sufficient to pacify Austria. Territory occupied would of course be evacuated when Austria was satisfied. I suggested this yesterday as a possible relief to the situation, and, if it can be obtained, I would earnestly hope that it might be agreed to suspend further military preparations on all sides.

---

[49] See No. 98

Russian Ambassador has told me of condition laid down by M. Sazonof,[50] as quoted in your telegram of July 30th[51], and fears it cannot be modified; but if Austria advance were stopped after occupation of Belgrade, I think the Russian Minister for Foreign Affairs formula might be changed to read that the Powers would examine how Serbia could fully satisfy Austria without impairing Serbian sovereign rights or independence.

If Austria, having occupied Belgrade and neighboring Serbian territory, declares herself ready, in the interest of European peace, to cease her advance and to discuss how a complete settlement can be arrived at, I hope that Russia would also consent to discussions and suspension of further military preparation, provided that other Powers did the same. It is a slender chance of preserving peace, but the only one I can suggest if Russian Minister for Foreign Affairs can come to no agreement at Berlin. You should inform Minister for Foreign Affairs.

This telegram sounds like this was Austria's idea or Germany already presented it to Austria and they agreed to it.

No. 61.
Russian Ambassador at Berlin to Russian Minister for Foreign Affairs.
Berlin
July 30, 1914.
(Telegraphic)

I learn that the order for the mobilization of the German army and navy has just been issued.

No. 104.
Sir Edward Grey to Sir Bertie, British Ambassador at Paris.
Foreign Office
July 30, 1914.
(Telegraphic)

You should inform the Minister for Foreign Affairs of my telegram to Sir G. Buchanan[52] of today,[53] and say that I know that he as been urging Russia not to participate a crisis. I hope he may be able to support this last suggestion at St. Petersburg.

No. 62.
Russian Ambassador at Berlin to Russian Minister for Foreign Affairs.
Berlin
July 30, 1914.
(Telegraphic)

The Minister for Foreign Affairs has just telephoned that the news of the mobilization of the German army and fleet, which has just been announced, is false; that the news sheets had been printed in advance so as to be ready for all eventualities, and that they were put on sale in the afternoon, but that they have now been confiscated.

---

[50] Russian Minister for Foreign Affairs
[51] See No. 97
[52] British Ambassador at St Petersburg.
[53] See No. 103

No. 105.
Sir Edward Grey to Sir F. Bertie, British Ambassador at Paris.
Foreign Office
July 30, 1914.
(Telegraphic)

Sir,

M. Cambon reminded me today of the letter I had written to him two years ago, in which we agreed that, if the peace of Europe was seriously threatened, we would discuss what we were prepared to do. I enclosed for convenience of reference copies of the letter in question and of M. Cambon's reply. He said that the peace of was never more seriously threatened that it was now. He did not wish to ask me to say directly that we would intervene, but he would like me to say what we should do if certain circumstances arose. The particular hypothesis he had in mind was an aggression by Germany on France. He gave me a paper, of which a copy is also enclosed, showing that the German military preparations were more advanced and more the offensive upon the frontier than anything France had yet done. He anticipated that the aggression would take the form of either a demand that France should cease her preparations, or demand that she should engage to remain neutral if there was war between Germany and Russia. Neither of these things could France admit.

I said that the cabinet was to meet tomorrow morning, and I would see him again tomorrow afternoon.

E. Grey

Enclosure 1 in No 105

Sir Edward Grey to M. Cambon, French Ambassador in London.
Foreign Office
November 22, 1912.

My Dear Ambassador,

From time to time in recent years, the French and British naval and military experts have consulted together. It has always been understood that such consultation does not restrict the freedom of either Government to decide at any future time whether or not to assist the other by armed force. We have agreed that consultation between experts is not, and ought not to be regarded as, an engagement that commits either Government to action in a contingency that has not arisen and may never arise. The disposition, for instance, of the French and British fleets respectively at the present moment is not based upon an engagement to co-operate in war.

You have, however, pointed out that, if either Government had grave reason to expect an unprovoked attack by a third Power, it might become essential to know whether it could in that event depend upon the armed assistance of the other.

I agree that, if either Government had grave reason to expect an unprovoked attack by a third Power, or something that threatened the general peace, it should immediately discuss with the other whether both governments should act together to prevent aggression and to preserve peace, and, if so what measures involved would be prepared to take in common. If these measures involved action, the plans of the general staff would at once be taken into consideration, and the Governments would then decide what effect should be given to them.

E. Grey

M. Cambon, French Ambassador in London, to Sir Edward Grey.
French Embassy London
November 23, 1912.

Dear Sir Edward,

You reminded me in your letter of yesterday, November 22, that during the last few years the military and naval authorities of France and Great Britain had consulted with each other from time to time; that it had always been understood that these consultations should not restrict the liberty of either Government to decide in the future whether they should lend each other the support of their armed forces; that on either side, these consultations between experts were not and should not be considered as engagements binding our governments to take action in certain eventualities; that, however, I had remarked to you that, if one or the other of the two Governments had grave reasons to fear an unprovoked attacked on the part of a third Power, it would become essential to know whether it could count on the armed support of the other.

Your letter answers that point, and I am authorized to state that, in the event of one of our two Governments having grave reason to fear either an act of aggression from a third Power, or some event threatening the general peace, that Government would immediately examine with the other the question whether both Governments should act together in order to prevent the act of aggression or preserve the peace. If so, the two Governments would deliberate as to the measures, which they would be prepared to take in common; if those measures involved action, the two Governments would take into immediate consideration the plans of their general staffs and would then decide as to the effect to be given to those plan.

Yours,
Paul Cambon

Enclosure 3 in 105

French Minister for Foreign Affairs to M. Cambon, French ambassador in London.

The German Army had its advance post on our frontiers yesterday; German patrols twice penetrated on to our territory. Our advance posts are withdrawn to a distance of ten kilometers from the frontier. The local population is protesting against being thus abandoned to the attacked of the enemy's army, but the government wishes to make it clear to public opinion and to the British Government that in no case will France be the aggressor. The whole 16th corp from Metz, reinforced by a part of the 8th from Tre'ves and Cologne, is occupying the frontier at the Metz on the Luxemburg side. The 15th army corps from Strasburg has closed up the on the frontier. The inhabitants of Alsace-Lorraine are being prevented by the threat of being shot from crossing the frontier. Reservist have been called to Germany by tens of thousands. This is the last stage before mobilization, whereas we have not called back a single reservist.

As you see, Germany has done so. I would add that all my information goes to show that the German preparations began on Saturday, the very day on which the Austrian note was handed in.

These facts, added to those contained in my telegram of yesterday, will enable you to prove to the British Government the pacific intentions of the one party and the aggressive intentions of the other.

This act that France talks about is a pure propaganda act. The only thing Germany has done up to this point is recalled her troops from the field and officers on leave. Germany will only react as France and Russia act.

No. 63.
Russian Ambassador at Berlin to Russian Minister for Foreign Affairs.
Berlin
July 30, 1914.
(Telegraphic.)

I HAVE received your telegram of 16th (29th) July, and have communicated the text of your proposal to the Minister for Foreign Affairs, whom I have just seen. He told me that he had received an identic telegram from the German Ambassador at St. Petersburg, and he then declared that he considered it impossible for Austria to accept our proposal.

No. 64.
Russian Ambassador at London Russian Minister for Foreign Affairs.
London
July 30, 1914.
(Telegraphic.)

I HAVE communicated the substance of your telegrams of the 29th and 30th July to Grey, who looks upon the situation as most serious, but wishes to continue the discussions. I pointed out to Grey that since you agreed with him to accept whatever proposal he might make in order to preserve peace, provided that Austria did not profit by any ensuing delays to crush Serbia the situation in which you were placed had apparently been modified. At that time, our relations with Germany had not been compromised. After the declaration made by the German Ambassador at St. Petersburg regarding German mobilization, those relations had changed, and you had returned the only reply to his request that was possible from a Great Power. When the German Ambassador again visited you, and enquired what your conditions were, you had formulated them in altogether special circumstances. I also again emphasized to Grey the necessity of taking into consideration the new situation brought about by the fault of Germany in consequence of the German Ambassador's action. Grey replied that he fully understood this, and that he would remember these arguments.

No. 65.
Russian Ambassador at London to Russian Minister for Foreign Affairs.
London
July 30, 1914.
(Telegraphic)

THE German Ambassador has asked Grey why Great Britain was taking military measures on both land and sea. Grey replied that these measures had no aggressive character, but that the situation was such that each Power must be ready.

When you look at the situation of Europe at this time, you can see every country is mobilizing. But only Germany is questioned as being the aggressors for war. When other leaders are asked about their country mobilizing, they use the mandated statement that it is a precaution. So if Russia, France, and Great Britain are mobilizing as a precaution, then Germany is also doing so. By this time, Europe is full of double standards when it comes to foreign policy, but it still comes down to who mobilized first and who encouraged it.

No. 48.
From: M. Sazonof, Russian Minister for Foreign Affairs.
To: Dr. M. Spalaikovitch, Minister at Petrograd.
Petrograd
July 30, 1914.

Sir,

I had the honour to receive your note of July 28, No. 527, in which you communicated to me the contents of the telegram received by you from His Excellency, M. Pashitch, in regard to the declaration of war on Serbia by Austria-Hungary. I sincerely regret this sad event, and will not fail to lay before His Majesty the petition by the Serbian nation, whose interpreter you are.

Telegram of the Military Attaché at St. Petersburg to H.M. the Kaiser
on July 30th, 1914.

Prince Troubetzki said to me yesterday, after causing Your Majesty's telegram to be delivered at once to Czar Nicolas: Thank God that a telegram of Your Emperor has come. He has just told me the telegram has made a deep impression upon the Czar but as the mobilization against Austria had already been ordered and Sasonof had convinced His Majesty that it was no longer possible to retreat. His Majesty was sorry he could not change it any more. I then told him that the guilt for the measureless consequences lay at the door of premature mobilization against Austria-Hungary, which after all was involved merely in a local war with Serbia, for Germany's answer, was clear and the responsibility rested upon Russia, which ignored Austria-Hungary's assurance that it had no intentions of territorial gain in Serbia. Austria-Hungary mobilized against Serbia and not against Russia and there was no ground for an immediate action on the part of Russia. I further added that in Germany I could not understand any more Russia's phrase that "she could not desert her brethren in Serbia," after the horrible crime of Sarajevo. I told him finally he need not wonder if Germany's army were to be mobilized.

IV. His Majesty to the Czar.
July 30th, 1 A.M.

My Ambassador has instructions to direct the attention of Your Government to the dangers and serious consequences of a mobilization. I have told you the same in my last telegram. Austria-Hungary has mobilized only against Serbia, and only a part of her army. If Russia, as seems to be the case, according to your advice and that of Your Government, mobilizes against Austria-Hungary, the part of the mediator with which you have entrusted me in such friendly manner and which I have accepted upon your express desire is threatened if not made impossible. The entire weight of decision now rests upon your shoulders; you have to bear the responsibility for war or peace.

(Signed)
Willy

No. 106.
Sir R. Rodd, British Ambassador at Rome, to Sir Edward Grey.
(received July 31, 1914)
Rome
July 30, 1914.
(Telegraphic)

I learned from the Minister for Foreign Affairs, who sent for me this evening, that the Austrian Government had declined to continue the direct exchange of views with the Russian Government. But he had reason to believe that Germany was now disposed to give more reconciliatory advice to Austria, as she seemed convinced that we should act with France and Russia, and was more anxious to avoid issues with us.

He said he was telegraphing to the Italian Ambassador at Berlin to ask the German Government to suggest that the idea of an exchange of views between the Four Powers should be resumed in any form, which Austria would consider acceptable. It seemed to him that Germany might invite Austria to state exactly the terms which she would demand from Serbia, and give a guarantee that she would neither deprived her independence nor annex territory. It would be useless to ask for anything less than was contained in the Austrian ultimatum and Germany would support no proposal that might imply nonsuccess for Austria. We might, on the other hand, ascertain from Russia what she would accept, and, once we knew the standpoints of these two countries, discussions could be commenced at once. There was still time so long as Austria had received no check. He in any case was in favor of containing an exchange of views with his Majesty's Government if the idea of discussions between the Four Powers was impossible.

V. The Czar to His Majesty.
Peterhof, July 30, 1914, 1.20 P.M.

I thank you from my heart for your quick reply. I am sending to-night Tatisheff (Russian honorary aide to the Kaiser) with instructions. The military measures now taking form were decided upon five days ago, and for the reason of defense against the preparations of Austria. I hope with all my heart that these measures will not influence in any manner your position as mediator, which I apprise very highly. We need your strong pressure upon Austria so that an understanding can be arrived at with us.
NICOLAS.

Tsar to Kaiser
30 July 1914, 1.20 A.M.
Peter's Court Palais, 30 July 1914.

Thank you heartily for your quick answer. Am sending Tatischev this evening with instructions. The military measures, which have now come into force, were decided five days ago for reasons of defense because of Austria's preparations.

I hope from all my heart that these measures won't in any way interfere with your part as mediator which I greatly value. We need your strong pressure on Austria to come to an understanding with us.

Nicky

Kaiser to Tsar
30 July 1914, 1.20 A.M.
Berlin
30 July 1914.

Best thanks for telegram. It is quite out of the question that my ambassador's language could have been in contradiction with the tenor of my telegram. Count Pourtalès was instructed to draw the attention of your government to the danger & grave consequences involved by a mobilization; I said the same in my telegram to you. Austria has only mobilized against Serbia & only a part of her army. If, as it is now the case, according to the communication by you & your Government, Russia mobilizes against Austria, my rôle as mediator you kindly entrusted me with, & which I accepted at you[r] express prayer, will be endangered if not ruined. The whole weight of the decision lies solely on you[r] shoulders now, who have to bear the responsibility for Peace or War.

Willy

No. 107.
Sir E. Goschen, British Ambassador at Berlin, to Sir Edward Grey.
(received July 31, 1914)
Berlin
July 30, 1914.

I do not know whether you have received a reply from the German Government to the communication[54] which you made to them through the German Ambassador in London asking whether they could suggest any method by which the Four Powers could use their mediating influence between Russia and Austria. I was informed last night that they had not had time to send an answer yet. Today, in reply to an enquiry from the French Ambassador as to whether the Imperial Government had proposed any course of action, the Secretary of State said that he felt that time would be saved by communicating with Vienna directly, and that he had asked the Austro-Hungarian Government what would satisfy them. No answer had, however, yet been returned.

The Chancellor told me last night that he was "pressing the button" as hard as he could and that he was not sure whether he had gone so far in urging moderation at Vienna that matters had been precipitated rather than otherwise.

---

[54] See No. 84.

Chapter Thirty-Two
July 31, 1914

Belgium port authorities seize German merchant ships with grain that is headed for Germany. This a direct violation of 1839 Treaty of London.

No. 108.
Sir E. Goschen, British Ambassador at Berlin, to Sir Edward Grey.
Berlin
July 31, 1914.
(Telegraphic)

Chancellor informs me that his efforts to preach peace and moderation at Vienna have been seriously handicapped by the Russian mobilization against Austria. He has done everything possible to attain this object at Vienna, perhaps even rather more than was altogether palatable at the Ballplatz. He could not, however, leave his country defenseless while time was being utilized by other Powers; And if, as he learns is the case, military measures are now being taken by Russia against Germany also, it would be impossible for him to remain quiet. He wished to tell me that it was quite possible that in a very short time, today perhaps, the German Government would take some very serious steps; he was in fact, just on the point of going to have an audience with the Emperor.

His Excellency added that the news of the active preparation on the Russo-German frontier had reached him just when the Czar had appealed to the Emperor, in the name of their old friendship, to mediate at Vienna, and when the emperor was actually conforming to that request.

Here the British ambassador sees that Russia is causing the German government to react at the Russian actions on their frontier. If this ambassador only knew that France was behind this all along....

No. 66.
Russian Ambassador at Vienna to Russian Minister for Foreign Affairs.
Vienna
July 31, 1914.
(Telegraphic)

IN spite of the general mobilization, my exchange of views with Count Berchtold and his colleagues continues. They all dwell upon the absence on Austria's part of any hostile intentions whatsoever against Russia, and of any designs of conquest at the expense of Serbia, but they are all equally insistent that Austria is bound to carry through the action which she has begun and to give Serbia a serious lesson, which would constitute a sure guarantee for the future.

No. 109.
Sir E. Goschen, British Ambassador at Berlin, to Sir Edward Grey.
Berlin
July 31, 1914.
(Telegraphic)

I read to the Chancellor this morning your answer to his appeal for British neutrality in the event of war, as contained in your telegram of yesterday[55]. His Excellency was so taken up with the news of Russian measures along the frontier, referred to in my immediately proceeding telegram, that he received your communication without comment. He asked me to let him have the message that I just read to him as a memorandum, as he would like to reflect upon it before giving an answer, and his mind was so full of grave matters that he could not be certain of remembering all its points. I therefore handed to him the text of your message on the understanding that it should be regarded merely as a record of conversation, and not as an official document.

His Excellency agreed.

No. 67.
Russian Minister for Foreign Affairs to Russian Ambassadors at Berlin, Vienna, Paris, London, and Rome.
St. Petersburg
July 31, 1914.
(Telegraphic)

PLEASE refer to my telegram of 30 July. The British Ambassador, on the instructions of his Government, has informed me of the wish of the London Cabinet to make certain modifications in the formula, which I suggested, yesterday to the German Ambassador. I replied that I accepted the British suggestion. I accordingly send you the text of the modified formula, which is as follows:

> *"Si l'Autriche consent à arrêter la marche de ses armées sur le territoire serbe et si, reconnaissant que le conflit austro-serbe a assumé le caractère d'une question d'intérêt européen, elle admet que les Grandes Puissances examinent la satisfaction que la Serbie pourrait accorder au Gouvernement d'Autriche-Hongrie sans laisser porter atteinte à ses droits d'état souverain et à son indépendance, la Russie s'engage à conserver son attitude expectante."*

"If Austria consents to stay the march of her troops on Serbian territory; and if, recognizing that the Austro-Serbian conflict has assumed the character of a question of European interest. She admits that the Great Powers may examine the satisfaction which Serbia can accord to the Austro-Hungarian Government without injury to her rights as a sovereign State or her independence, Russia undertakes to maintain her waiting attitude."

---

[55] See No. 101.

Russia say's that Austria has rights accorded them, but Russia is trying to deny these rights because it involves Serbia and has French influence to stop Austria, while Austria seeks justice for the murder of the archduke.

No. 110.
Sir Edward Grey to Sir G. Buchanan, British Ambassador at St. Petersburg.
Foreign Office
July 31, 1914.
(Telegraphic)

I learned from the German Ambassador that, as a result of suggestions by the German Government, a conversation has taken place at Vienna between the Austrian Minister for Foreign Affairs and the Russian Ambassador. The Austrian Ambassador at St. Petersburg has also been instructed that he may converse with the Russian Minister for Foreign Affairs, and that he should give explanations about the Austrian ultimatum to Serbia, and discusses suggestions and any questions directly affecting Austro-Russian relations. If the Russian Government objects to the Austrians mobilizing eight army corps, it might be point out that this is not too great a number against 400,000 Serbians.

The German Ambassador asked me to urge the Russian Government to show goodwill in the discussions and to suspend their military preparations.

It is with great satisfaction that I have learned that discussions are being resumed between Austria and Russia, and should express this to the Minister for Foreign Affairs and tell him that I earnestly hope he will encourage them.

I informed the German Ambassador that, as regards to military preparations, I did not see how Russia could be urged to suspend them unless some limits were put by Austria to the advance of troops into Serbia.

No. 68.
Russian Ambassador at Berlin to Russian Minister for Foreign Affairs.
Berlin
July 31, 1914.
(Telegraphic)

THE Minister for Foreign Affairs has just told me that our discussions, which were already difficult enough on account of the mobilization against Austria, were becoming even more so in view of the serious military measures that we were taking against Germany. He said that information on this subject was reaching Berlin from all sides, and this must inevitably provoke similar measures on the part of Germany. To this, I replied that, according to sure information in my possession, which was confirmed by all our compatriots arriving from Berlin, Germany also, was very actively engaged in taking military measures against Russia. In spite of this, the Minister for Foreign Affairs asserts that the only step taken in Germany has been the recall of officers from leave and of the troops from maneuvers.

No. 111.
Sir Edward Grey to Sir E. Goschen, British Ambassador at Berlin.
Foreign Office
July 31, 1914.
(Telegraphic)

I hope that the conversations, which are now proceeding between Austria and Russia, may lead to a satisfactory result. The stumbling block hitherto has been Austrian mistrust of Serbian assurances, and Russian mistrust of Austrian intentions with regard to the independence and integrity of Serbia. It as occurred to me that, in the event of this mistrust preventing a solution being found by Vienna and St. Petersburg, Germany might sound Vienna and I would undertake to sound St. Petersburg, whether it would be possible for the four disinterested Powers to offer Austria that they would undertake to see that she obtained full satisfaction of her demands on Serbia, provided that they did not impair Serbian sovereignty and the integrity of Serbian territory. As your Excellency is aware, Austria has already declared her willingness to respect them. Russia might be informed by the four Powers that they would undertake to prevent Austria demands going the length of impairing Serbian sovereignty and integrity. All Powers would of course suspend further military operations or preparations.

You may sound the Secretary of State about this proposal.

I said to German Ambassador this morning that if Germany could get any reasonable proposal put forward which made it clear that Germany and Austria were striving to preserve European peace, and that Russia and France would be unreasonable if they rejected it, I would support it at St. Petersburg and Paris, and go the length of saying that if Russia and France would not accept it His Majesty's Government would have nothing more to do with the consequences; but, otherwise, I told the German Ambassador that if France became involved we would be drawn in.

You can add this when sounding chancellor or Secretary of state as to proposal above.

If this telegram was the British's new attitude in this crisis, then all Germany and Austria had to do was be firm in their negotiating with Serbia and Russia, then Britain would have been either neutral or allies with Germany so Germany could not be accused of being impatient.

No. 69.
Russian Minister for Foreign Affairs to Russian Ambassador at London.
St. Petersburg
July 31, 1914.
(Telegraphic)

I HAVE requested the British Ambassador to express to Grey my deep gratitude for the firm and friendly tone which he has adopted in the discussions with Germany and Austria, thanks to which the hope of finding a peaceful issue to the present situation need not yet be abandoned. I also requested him to inform the British Minister that in my opinion it was only in London that the discussions might still have some faint chance of success and of rendering the necessary compromise easier for Austria.

Communicated to Russian Ambassador in France.

No. 112.
Sir E. Goschen, British Ambassador at Berlin, to Sir Edward Grey.
Berlin
July 31, 1914.
(Telegraphic)

According to information just received by German Government from their Ambassador at St. Petersburg, the whole Russian army and fleet is being mobilized. Chancellor tells me that "kriegsgefahr" will be proclaimed at once by German Government, as it can only be against Germany that Russia general mobilization is directed. Mobilization would follow almost immediately. His Excellency added in explanation "kriegsgefahr" signifies the taking of certain precautionary measures consequent upon strained relations with a foreign country.

This news from St. Petersburg, added his Excellency, seemed to him to put an end to all hope of a peaceful solution of the crisis. Germany must certainly prepare for all emergencies.

I asked him whether he could not still put pressure on the authorizes at Vienna to do something in general interests to reassure Russia and to show themselves disposed to continue discussions on a friendly basis. He replied that last night he had begged Austria to reply to your last proposal, and that he had received a reply to the effect that Austrian Minister for Foreign Affairs would take wishes of the Emperor this morning in the matter.

France lied to Britain that day, and now Russia goes to full mobilization. The meeting the French president had with the tsar from July 20 to 25 had a lot to do with making Germany make a mistake so Russia and France could eliminate Germany from Europe.

No. 9.
M. Davignon, Belgian Minister for Foreign Affairs, to the Belgian Ministers at Berlin, Paris, and London.
Brussels
July 31, 1914.

Sir,
The French Minister came to show me a telegram from the Agency Havas reporting a state of war in Germany, and said:

> *I seize this opportunity to declare that no incursion of French troops into Belgium will take place, even if considerable forces are massed upon the frontiers of your country. France does not wish to incur the responsibility, so far as Belgium is concerned, of taking the first hostile act. Instructions in this sense will be given to the French authorities."*

I thanked M. Klobukowski for his communication, and I felt bound to observe that we had always had the greatest confidence in the loyal observance by both our neighboring States of their engagements towards us. We have also every reason to believe that the attitude of the German Government will be the same as that of the Government of the French Republic.

No. 10.

M. Davignon, Belgian Minister for Foreign Affairs to all Heads of Belgian Missions abroad.

Brussels

July 31, 1914.

(Telegraphic)

The Minister of War informs me that mobilisation has been ordered, and that Saturday, the 1st August, will be the first day.

No. 113.

Sir G. Buchanan, British Ambassador at St. Petersburg to Sir Edward Grey.

St. Petersburg

July 31, 1914.

(Telegraphic)

It has been decided to issue orders for general mobilization.

This decision was taken in consequence of reports received from Russian Ambassador in Vienna to the effect that Austria is determined not to yield to intervention of Powers, and that she is moving troops against Russia as well as against Serbia.

Russia has also reason to believe that Germany is making active military preparations, and she cannot afford to let get a start.

No. 11.

M. Davignon, Belgian Minister for Foreign Affairs, to the Belgian Ministers at Berlin, London, and Paris.

Brussels

July 31, 1914.

Sir,

The British Minister asked to see me on urgent business, and made the following communication, which he had hoped for some days to be able to present to me: Owing to the possibility of a European war, Sir Edward Grey has asked the French and German Governments separately if they were each of them ready to respect Belgian neutrality provide that no other Power violated it:

"In view of existing treaties, I am instructed to inform the Belgian Minister for Foreign Affairs of the above, and to say that Sir Edward Grey presumes that Belgium will do her utmost to maintain her neutrality, and that she desires and expects that the other Powers will respect and maintain it."

I hastened to thank Sir Francis Villiers for this communication, which the Belgian Government particularly appreciates, and I added that Great Britain and the other nations guaranteeing our independence could rest assured that we would neglect no effort to maintain our neutrality, and that we were convinced that the other Powers, in view of the excellent relations of friendship and confidence which had always existed between us, would respect and maintain that neutrality. I did not fail to state that our military forces, which had been considerably developed in consequence of our recent re-organization, were sufficient to enable us to defend ourselves energetically in the event of the violation of our territory.

In the course of the ensuing conversation, Sir Francis seemed to me somewhat surprised at the speed with which we had decided to mobilize our army. I pointed out to him that the Netherlands, had come to a similar decision before we had done so, and that, moreover, the recent date of our new military system, and the temporary nature of the measures upon which we then had to decide, made it necessary for us to take immediate and thorough precautions. Our neighbors and guarantors should see in this decision our strong desire to uphold our neutrality ourselves.

Sir Francis seemed to be satisfied with my reply, and stated that his Government was awaiting this reply before continuing negotiations with France and Germany, the result of which would be communicated to me.

No. 114.
Sir Edward Grey to Sir F. Bertie, British ambassador at Paris, and Sir E. Goschen, British Ambassador at Berlin.
Foreign Office
July 31, 1914.
(Telegraphic)

I still trust the situation is not irretrievable, but in view of prospect of mobilization in Germany it becomes essential to his majesty's Government, in view of existing treaties to ask whether French (German) Government is prepared to engage to respect neutrality of Belgium so long no other Power violates it.

Similar request is being addressed to German (French) government. It is important to have an early answer.

The German government does not reply right away because of the possibility that Belgium has violated international maritime treaties, and Germany is trying to get this crisis straightened out before they reply to the British government.

No. 12.
M. Davignon, Belgian Minister for Foreign Affairs, to the Belgian Ministers at Berlin, London, and Paris.
Brussels
July 31, 1914.

Sir,

In the course of the conversation which the Secretary-General of my Department had with Herr von Below this morning, he explained to the German Minister the scope of the military measures which we had taken, and said to him that they were a consequence of our desire to fulfill our international obligations, and that they in no wise implied an attitude of distrust towards our neighbors.

The Secretary-General then asked the German Minister if he knew of the conversation, which he had had with his predecessor, Herr von Flotow, and of the reply, which the Imperial Chancellor had instructed the latter to give.

In the course of the controversy, which arose in 1911 as a consequence of the Dutch scheme for the fortification of Flushing, certain newspapers had maintained that in the case of a Franco-German war Belgian neutrality would be violated by Germany.

The Department of Foreign Affairs had suggested that a declaration in the German Parliament during a debate on foreign affairs would serve to calm public opinion, and to dispel the mistrust, which was so regrettable from the point of view of the relations between the two countries.

Herr von Bethmann-Hollweg replied that he had fully appreciated the feelings, which had inspired our representations. He declared that Germany had no intention of violating Belgian neutrality, but he considered that in making a public declaration Germany would weaken her military position in regard to France, who, secured on the northern side, would concentrate all her energies on the east.

Baron van der Elst, continuing, said that he perfectly understood the objections raised by Herr von Bethmann-Hollweg to the proposed public declaration, and he recalled the fact that since then, in 1913, Herr von Jagow had made reassuring declarations to the Budget Commission of the Reichstag respecting the maintenance of Belgian neutrality.

Herr von Below replied that he knew of the conversation with Herr von Flotow, and that he was certain that the sentiments expressed at that time had not changed.

No. 115.
Sir Edward Grey to Sir F. Villiers, British Minister at Brussels.
Foreign Office
July 31, 1914.
(Telegraphic)

In view of existing treaties, you should inform Minister for Foreign Affairs that, in consideration of the possibility of a European war, I have asked French and German governments whether each is prepared to respect the neutrality of Belgium provided it is violated by no other Power.

You should say that I assume that the Belgian government will maintain to the utmost of their power their neutrality, which I desire and expect other Powers to uphold and observe.

You should inform the Belgian government that an early reply is desired.

The Belgian government has just violated article 9.3 of the 1839 Treaty of London. It reads as follows:

In order that the said vessels may not be, subject to any visit, nor to any delay or hindrance whatever within Dutch waters, either in ascending the Scheldt from the high seas or in descending the Scheldt in order to reach the high seas.

Telegram of the Chancellor to the Imperial Ambassador at St. Petersburg on July 31st, 1914. Urgent.

In spite of negotiations still pending and although we have up to this hour made no preparations for mobilization, Russia has mobilized her *entire* army and navy, hence also against us. Because of these Russian measures, we have been forced, for the safety of the country, to proclaim the threatening state of war, which does not yet imply mobilization. Mobilization, however, is bound to follow if Russia does not stop every measure of war against us and against Austria-Hungary within 12 hours, and notifies us definitely to this effect. Please to communicate this at once to M. Sasonof and wire hour of communication.

Here again Germany is trying to keep the Austro-Serbian problem localized between the two countries by the secret treaty between Russia and France, which says any military mobilization against them or their allies is considered an act of war. Germany has yet to mobilize, but Russia and France have ordered military mobilization. If Germany knew the contents of this treaty, then his Majesty Wilhelm II could show to England and rest of world that she was acting in self-defense.

Telegram of the Chancellor to the Imperial Ambassador in Paris on July 31st, 1914. Urgent.

Russia has ordered mobilization of her entire army and fleet, therefore also against us in spite of our still pending mediation. We have therefore declared the threatening state of war, which is bound to be followed by mobilization unless Russia stops within 12 hours all measures of war against Austria and us. Mobilizations inevitably imply war. Please ask French Government whether it intends to remain neutral in a Russo-German war. Reply must be made in 18 hours. Wire at once hour of inquiry. Utmost speed necessary.

France is ready to give the order for mobilization of the whole military. The order is being drawn up and being ready for French Parliament vote.

No. 116.
Sir Edward Grey to Sir F. Bertie, British Ambassador at Paris.
Foreign office
July 31, 1914.
(Telegraphic)

I have received your telegram of yesterday's date[56].

Nobody here feels that in this dispute, so far as it has yet gone, British treaties or obligations are involved. Feeling is quite different from what it was during the Morocco question. That crisis involved a dispute directly involving France, whereas in this case France is being drawn into a dispute, which is not hers.

I believe it to be quite untrue that our attitude has been a decisive factor in the situation. The German Government does not expect our neutrality.

We cannot undertake a definite pledge to intervene in a war. I have so told the French Ambassador, who has urged his Majesty's Government to reconsider this decision.

I have told him that we should not being justified in giving any pledge at the present moment, but that we will certainly consider the situation again directly when there is a new development.

No. 9.
M. Davignon, Belgian Minister for Foreign Affairs, to the Belgian Ministers at Berlin, Paris, and London.
Brussels
July 31, 1914.

Sir,

The French Minister came to show me a telegram from the Agency Havas reporting a state of war in Germany, and said:

"I seize this opportunity to declare that no incursion of French troops into Belgium will take place, even if considerable forces are massed upon the frontiers of your country. France does not wish to incur the responsibility, so far as Belgium is concerned, of taking the first hostile act. Instructions in this sense will be given to the French authorities."

I thanked M. Klobukowski for his communication, and I felt bound to observe that we had always had the greatest confidence in the loyal observance by both our neighboring States of their engagements towards us. We have also every reason to believe that the attitude of the German Government will be the same as that of the Government of the French Republic.

---

[56] See No. 99.

Telegram of the Chancellor to the Imperial Ambassador at Rom
on July 31st, 1914.

We have continued to negotiate between Russia and Austria-Hungary through a direct exchange of telegrams between His Majesty the Kaiser and His Majesty the Czar, as well as in conjunction with Sir Edward Grey. Through the mobilization of Russia all our efforts have been greatly handicapped if they have not become impossible. In spite of pacifying assurances, Russia is taking such far-reaching measures against us that the situation is becoming continually more menacing.

No. 10.
M. Davignon, Belgian Minister for Foreign Affairs to all Heads of Belgian Missions abroad.
Brussels
July 31, 1914.
(Telegraphic)

The Minister of War informs me that mobilization has been ordered, and that Saturday, 1 August, will be the first day.

This telegram does not say who orders mobilization. But from records, it is France who orders this mobilization.

No. 11.
M. Davignon, Belgian Minister for Foreign Affairs, to the Belgian Ministers at Berlin, London, and Paris.
Brussels
July 31, 1914.

Sir,

The British Minister asked to see me on urgent business, and made the following communication, which he had hoped for some days to be able to present to me: Owing to the possibility of a European war, Sir Edward Grey has asked the French and German Governments separately if they were each of them ready to respect Belgian neutrality provides that no other Power violated it:

"In view of existing treaties, I am instructed to inform the Belgian Minister for Foreign Affairs of the above, and to say that Sir Edward Grey presumes that Belgium will do her utmost to maintain her neutrality, and that she desires and expects that the other Powers will respect and maintain it."

I hastened to thank Sir Francis Villiers for this communication, which the Belgian Government particularly appreciates, and I added that Great Britain and the other nations guaranteeing our independence could rest assured that we would neglect no effort to maintain our neutrality, and that we were convinced that the other Powers, in view of the excellent relations of friendship and confidence which had always existed between us, would respect and maintain that neutrality.

I did not fail to state that our military forces, which had been considerably developed in consequence of our recent re-organization, were sufficient to enable us to defend ourselves energetically in the event of the violation of our territory.

In the course of the ensuing conversation, Sir Francis seemed to me somewhat surprised at the speed with which we had decided to mobilize our army. I pointed out to him that the Netherlands, had come to a similar decision before we had done so, and that, moreover, the recent date of our new military system, and the temporary nature of the measures upon which we then had to decide, made it necessary for us to take immediate and thorough precautions. Our neighbors and guarantors should see in this decision our strong desire to uphold our neutrality ourselves.

Sir Francis seemed to be satisfied with my reply, and stated that his Government was awaiting this reply before continuing negotiations with France and Germany, the result of which would be communicated to me.

No. 117.
Sir F. Bertie, British Ambassador at Paris, to Sir Edward Grey.
Paris
July 31, 1914.
(Telegraphic)

At 7 o'clock this evening I was sent for by the Minister for Foreign Affairs. When I arrived, the German Ambassador was leaving his Excellency.

The German Ambassador had informed his Excellency that in view of the fact that orders had been given for the total mobilization of Russian army and fleet, German Government has in an ultimatum, which they addressed to the Russian Government, required that Russian forces should be demobilized.

The Minister for Foreign Affairs asked me to communicate this to you and enquires what, in these circumstances, will be the attitude of England.

The German Ambassador could not say the twelve hours terminates. He is going to call at the Ministry for Foreign Affairs tomorrow (Saturday) at 1 P.M. in order to receive the French Governments answer as to the attitude they will adopt in the circumstances.

He is intimated the possibility of his Passports.

I am informed by the Russian Ambassador that he is not aware of any general mobilization of the Russian forces having taken place.

No. 12.
M. Davignon, Belgian Minister for Foreign Affairs, to the Belgian Ministers at Berlin, London, and Paris.
Brussels
July 31, 1914.

Sir,

In the course of the conversation which the Secretary-General of my Department had with Herr von Below this morning, he explained to the German Minister the scope of the military measures which we had taken, and said to him that they were a consequence of our desire to fulfill our international obligations, and that they in no wise implied an attitude of distrust towards our neighbors.

The Secretary-General then asked the German Minister if he knew of the conversation, which he had had with his predecessor, Herr von Flotow, and of the reply, which the Imperial Chancellor had instructed the latter to give.

In the course of the controversy, which arose in 1911 as a consequence of the Dutch scheme for the fortification of Flushing, certain newspapers had maintained that in the case of a Franco-German war Belgian neutrality would be violated by Germany.

The Department of Foreign Affairs had suggested that a declaration in the German Parliament during a debate on foreign affairs would serve to calm public opinion, and to dispel the mistrust, which was so regrettable from the point of view of the relations between the two countries. Herr von Bethmann-Hollweg replied that he had fully appreciated the feelings, which had inspired our representations. He declared that Germany had no intention of violating Belgian neutrality, but he considered that in making a public declaration Germany would weaken her military position in regard to France, who, secured on the northern side, would concentrate all her energies on the east.

Baron van der Elst, continuing, said that he perfectly understood the objections raised by Herr von Bethmann-Hollweg to the proposed public declaration, and he recalled the fact that since then, in 1913, Herr von Jagow had made reassuring declarations to the Budget Commission of the Reichstag respecting the maintenance of Belgian neutrality.

Herr von below replied that he knew of the conversation with Herr von Flotow, and that he was certain that the sentiments expressed at that time had not changed.

No. 118.
Sir M. de Bunsen, British Ambassador at Vienna, to Sir Edward Grey.
Vienna
July 31, 1914.
(Telegraphic)

I am informed by Count Forgach, Under-Secretary of State, that although Austria was compelled to respond to Russian mobilization, which he deplored, the Austrian Ambassador in London has received instructions to inform you that mobilization was not regarded as a necessarily hostile act on either side. Telegrams were being exchanged between the Emperor of Russia and the German Emperor, and conversation were proceeding between Austrian Ambassador at St. Petersburg and Russian Minister for Foreign Affairs. A general war might, he seriously hoped, be staved off by these efforts. On my expressing my fear that Germany would mobilize, he said that Germany must do something, in his opinion to secure her position. As regards to Russian intervention on behalf of Serbia, Austria-Hungary found it difficult to recognize such a claim. I called his attention to the fact that during the discussion of the Albanian frontier at the London Conference of Ambassadors the Russian government had stood behind Serbia. And that a compromise between the views of Russia and Austria-Hungary resulted with accepted frontier line. Although he spoke in a conciliatory tone, and did not regard the situation as desperate, I could not get from him any suggestion for a similar comprises in the present case. Count Forgach is going this afternoon to see the Russian Ambassador, whom I have informed of the above conversation.

The Russian Ambassador has explained that Russia has no desire to interfere unduly with Serbia; that, as compared with the late Russian Minister, the present Minister at Belgrade is a man of very moderate views; and that, as regards Austria demands, Russia had counseled Serbia to yield to them as far as she could possibly could without sacrificing her independence. His Excellency is exerting himself strongly in the interest of peace.

The Russian government still fails to see the fact that Serbia declared war on Austria by the murder of the archduke.

Kaiser to Tsar.
Berlin
31 July 1914.

On your appeal to my friendship and your call for assistance began to mediate between your and the Austro-Hungarian Government. While this action was preceding your troops were mobilized against Austro-Hungary, my ally. Thereby, as I have already pointed out to you, my mediation has been made almost illusory.

I have nevertheless continued my action.

I now receive authentic news of serious preparations for war on my Eastern frontier. Responsibility for the safety of my empire forces preventive measures of defense upon me. In my endeavors to maintain the peace of the world, I have gone to the utmost limit possible. The responsibility for the disaster which is now threatening the whole civilized world will not be laid at my door. In this moment, it still lies in your power to avert it. Nobody is threatening the honor or power of Russia who can well afford to await the result of my mediation. My friendship for you and your empire, transmitted to me by my grandfather on his deathbed, has always been sacred to me and I have honestly often backed up Russia when she was in serious trouble, especially in her last war.

You may still maintain the peace of Europe, if Russia will agree to stop the military. Measures, which must threaten Germany and Austro-Hungary.

Willy

Tsar to Kaiser
31 July 1914 (this and the previous telegram crossed)
Petersburg Palace, 31 July 1914.
Sa Majesté l'Empereur, Neues Palais.

I thank you heartily for your mediation which begins to give one hope that all may yet end peacefully.

It is *technically* impossible to stop our military preparations, which were obligatory owing to Austria's mobilization. We are far from wishing war. As long as the negotiations with Austria on Serbia's account are taking place, my troops shall not make any provocative action. I give you my solemn word for this. I put all my trust in God's mercy and hope in your successful mediation in Vienna for the welfare of our countries and for the peace of Europe.

You are affectionate,
Nicky

Sir Edward Grey's Indecisiveness

No. 119.
Sir Edward Grey to British Ambassador to France, Sir F. Bertie.
Foreign Office
July 31, 1914.

Sir,

M. Cambon[57] referred today to a telegram that had been shown to Sir Arthur Nicolson this morning from the French Ambassador in Berlin saying that it was the uncertainty with regard to whether we would intervene which was the encouraging element in Berlin, and that, if we would only declare definitely on the side of Russia and France, it would decide the German attitude in favor of peace.

I said that it was quite wrong to suppose that we had left Germany under the impression that we would not intervene. I had refused overtures to promise that we should remain neutral. I had not only definitely declined to say that we would remain neutral; I had even gone so far this morning as to say to the German Ambassador that, if France and Germany became involved in war, we should be drawn into it. That, of course, was not the same thing as taking an engagement to France, and I told M. Cambon of it only to show that we had not left Germany under the impression that we would stand aside.

M. Cambon then asked for my reply to what he had said yesterday.

---

[57] French Ambassador in London.

I said that we had come to the conclusion, in the Cabinet today, that we could not give any pledge at the present time. The commercial and financial situation was exceedingly serious; there was danger of a complete collapse that would involve us and everyone else in ruin; and it was possible that our standing aside might be the only means of preventing a complete collapse of European credit, in which we should be involved. This might be a paramount consideration in deciding our attitude.

I went on to say to M. Cambon that though we should have to put our policy before Parliament, we could not pledge Parliament in advance. Up to the present moment, we did not feel, and public opinion did not feel, that any treaties or obligations of this country were involved. Further developments might alter this situation and cause the Government and Parliament to take the view that intervention was justified. The preservation of the neutrality of Belgium might be, I would not say a decisive, but an important factor, in determining our attitude. Whether we proposed to Parliament to intervene or not to intervene in a war, Parliament would wish to know how we stood with regard to the neutrality of Belgium, and it might be that I should ask both France and Germany whether each was prepared to undertake an engagement that she would not be the first to violate the neutrality of Belgium. M. Cambon expressed great disappointment at my reply. He repeated his question of whether we would help France if Germany made an attack on her.

I said that I could only adhere to the answer that, as far as things had gone at present, we could not take any engagement the latest news was that Russia had ordered a complete mobilization of her fleet and army. This, it seemed to me, would precipitate a crisis, and would make it appear that German mobilization was being forced by Russia.

M. Cambon urged that Germany had from the beginning rejected proposals that might have made for peace. It could not be to England's interest that France should be crushed by Germany. We should then be in a much-diminished position with regard to Germany. In 1870, we had made a great mistake in allowing an enormous increase in German strength; and we should now be repeating the mistake. He asked me whether I could not submit his question to the Cabinet again.

I said that the Cabinet would certainly be summoned as soon as there was some new development, but at the present moment the only answer I could give was that we could not undertake any definite engagement.

I am, etc.
E. GREY

Sir Grey is trying to negotiate with both Germany and Russia for a peaceful resolution with the Austro-Serbian crisis. He is unsure what the Parliament would do in case of war. Sir Grey is fully aware of the Russian and French mutual defense treaty and also sees the fact that a Russian mobilization on the German frontier will cause Germany to call for a general mobilization. Sir Grey at this time is unaware that Belgium authorities have seized German merchant ships. So all he can do is refer to the 1839 Treaty of London as one possibility that will draw England into war if it is violated. Sir Grey shows that he does not have the full scope of what is actually happening in Europe at this time.

No. 111.
M. Mollard, French Minister at Luxemburg, to M. René Viviani, President of the Council, Minister for Foreign Affairs.
Luxemburg
July 31, 1914.

The Minister of State has just left the Legation; he has just told me that the Germans have closed the bridges over the Moselle at Schengen and at Rennich with vehicles and the bridge at Wormeldange with ropes. The bridges at Wasserbillig and at D'Echternach over the Sûre have not been closed, but the Germans no longer allow the export from Prussia of corn, cattle, or motor cars.

M. Eyschen requested me—and this was the real object of his visit—to ask you for an official declaration to the effect that France will, in case of war, respect the neutrality of Luxemburg. When I asked him if he had received a similar declaration from the German Government, he told me that he was going to the German Minister to get the same declaration.

Postscript.—Up to the present no special measure has been taken by the Cabinet of Luxemburg. M. Eyschen has returned from the German Legation. He complained of the measures showing suspicion which were taken against a neutral neighbor. The Minister of State has asked the German Minister for an official declaration from his Government undertaking to respect the neutrality. Herr Von Buch is stated to have replied, "That is a matter of course, but it would be necessary for the French Government to give the same undertaking."

MOLLARD.

No. 112.
M. René Viviani, President of the Council, Minister for Foreign Affairs, to the French Ambassadors at London, St. Petersburgh, Berlin, Vienna, and Rome.
Paris
July 31, 1914.

The British Ambassador has handed me a note from his Government asking the French Government to support a proposal at St. Petersburgh for the peaceful solution of the Austro-Serbian conflict.

This note shows that the German Ambassador has informed Sir E. Grey of the intention of his Government to try to exercise influence on the Austro-Hungarian Government after the capture of Belgrade and the occupation of the districts bordering on the frontier, in order to obtain a promise not to advance further, while the Powers endeavored to secure that Serbia should give sufficient satisfaction to Austria; the occupied territory would be evacuated as soon as she had received satisfaction.

Sir E. Grey made this suggestion on the 29th July, and expressed the hope that military preparations would be suspended on all sides. Although the Russian Ambassador at London has informed the Secretary of State that he fears that the Russian condition (*if Austria, recognizing that her conflict with Serbia has assumed the character of a question of European interest, declares herself ready to eliminate from her ultimatum the points which endanger the principle of Serbian sovereignty, Russia undertakes to stop all military preparations*) cannot be modified, Sir E. Grey thinks that, if Austria stops her advance after the occupation of Belgrade, the Russian Government could agree to change their formula in the following way:

That the Powers would examine how Serbia should give complete satisfaction to Austria without endangering the sovereignty or independence of the Kingdom. In case Austria after occupying Belgrade and the neighboring Serbian territory should declare she ready, in the interests of Europe, to stop her advance and to discuss how an arrangement might be arrived at, Russia could also consent to the discussion and suspend her military preparations, if the other Powers acted in the same way.

In accordance with the request of Sir E. Grey, the French Government joined in the British suggestion, and in the following terms asked their Ambassador at St. Petersburgh to try to obtain, without delay, the assent of the Russian Government:

"Please inform M. Sazonof urgently that the suggestion of Sir E. Grey appears to me to furnish a useful basis for conversation between the Powers, who are equally desirous of working for an honorable arrangement of the Austro-Serbian conflict, and of averting in this manner the dangers which threaten general peace.

"The plan proposed by the Secretary of State for Foreign Affairs, by stopping the advance of the Austrian army and by entrusting to the Powers the duty of examining how Serbia could give full satisfaction to Austria without endangering the sovereign rights and the independence of the Kingdom, by thus affording Russia a means of suspending all military preparations, while the other Powers are to act in the same way, is calculated equally to give satisfaction to Russia and to Austria and to provide for Serbia an acceptable means of issue from the present difficulty.

"I would ask you carefully to be guided by the foregoing considerations in earnestly pressing M. Sazonof to give his adherence without delay to the proposal of Sir E. Grey, of which he will have been himself informed."

RENÉ VIVIANI.

No. 120.
Sir G. Buchanan, British Ambassador at St. Petersburg, to Sir Edward Grey.
St. Petersburg
July 31, 1914.
(Telegraphic)

Minister for Foreign Affairs sent for me and the French Ambassador and asked us to telegraph to our respective Governments to subjoined a formula as best calculated to amalgamate proposal made by you in your telegram of July 30[58] with formula recorded in my telegram of July 30th[59]. He trusted it would meet with your approval.

His Excellency then alluded to the telegram sent to the German Emperor by Emperor of Russia in reply to the former's telegram. He said that Emperor Nicholas II had begun by thanking William for his telegram and for the hopes of a peaceful resolution, which it held out. His Majesty had then proceeded to assure Emperor William that no intention whatever of an aggressive character was concealed behind Russian military preparations. So long as conversation with Austria continued, his Imperial Majesty undertook that not a single man should be moved across the frontier; it was, however of course impossible, for reasons explained, to stop a mobilization which was already in progress.

M. Sazonof said undoubtedly there would be a better prospect of a peaceful resolution if the suggested conversation were to take place in London, where the atmosphere was far more favorable, and he therefore hoped that you would see your way to agreeing to this.

His Excellency ended by expressing his deep gratitude to his Majesty's Government, who had done so much to save the situation. It would be largely due to them if war were prevented. The Emperor, the Russian Government, and the Russian people would never forget the firm attitude adopted by Great Britain.

No. 113.
M. Paléologue, French Ambassador at St. Petersburgh, to M. René Viviani, President of the Council, Minister on Foreign Affairs.
St. Petersburgh
July 31, 1914.

The news of the bombardment of Belgrade during the night and morning of yesterday has provoked very deep feeling in Russia. One cannot understand the attitude of Austria, whose provocations since the beginning of the crisis have regularly followed Russia's attempts at conciliation and the satisfac-

---

[58] See No. 103.
[59] See No. 97.

tory conversations exchanged between St. Peterburgh and Vienna. Nevertheless, desirous of leaving nothing undone in order to prove his sincere desire to safeguard peace, M. Sazonof informs me that he has modified his formula, as requested by the British Ambassador, in the following way:

"If Austria consents to stay the march of her troops on Serbian territory, and if, recognizing that the Austro-Serbian conflict has assumed the character of a question of European interest, she admits that the great Powers may examine the satisfaction which Serbia can accord to the Austro-Hungarian Government, without injury to her sovereign rights as a State and to her independence, Russia undertakes to preserve her waiting attitude.

PALÉOLOGUE.

No. 121.
Sir E. Goschen, British Ambassador at Berlin, to Sir Edward Grey.
(received August 1)
Berlin
July 31, 1914.
(Telegraphic)

Your telegram of July 31st[60]. I spent an hour with Secretary of State urging him most earnestly to accept your proposal and make another effort to prevent terrible catastrophe of a European war. He expressed himself very sympathetically towards your proposal, and appreciated your continued efforts to maintain peace, but said it was impossible for the Imperial Government to considered any proposal until they had received an answer from Russia to their communication of today; this communication, which he admitted had the form of an ultimatum, being that, unless Russia could inform the Imperial Government within twelve hours that she would immediately countermand her mobilization against Germany and Austria, Germany would be obliged on her side to mobilize at once.

I asked his Excellency why they had made their demand even more difficult for Russia to accept by asking them to demobilize in the south as well. He replied that it was in order to prevent Russia from saying all her mobilization was only directed against Austria.

His Excellency said that if the answer from Russia was satisfactory he thought personally that your proposal merited favorable consideration, and in any case, he would lay it before the Emperor and Chancellor, but he repeated that it was no use discussing it until the Russian Government had sent in their answer to the German demand.

He again assured me both that Emperor William, at the request of the Emperor of Russia, and the German Foreign Office had even up till last night been urging Austria to show willingness to continue discussions and telegraphic and telephonic communications from Vienna had been of a promising nature, but Russia's mobilization had spoiled everything.

The German secretary of state is trying to avoid a first-strike capability for any nation except that which concerns Austria and Serbia.

---

[60] See No. 111.

No. 114.

M. René Viviani, President of the Council, Minister for Foreign Affairs, to the French Ambassadors at London, St. Petersburgh, Berlin, Vienna, Rome, and Constantinople.
Paris
July 31, 1914.

The efforts made up till now concurrently by Great Britain and Russia with the earnest support of France (obtained in advance for every peaceful effort) with the object of a direct understanding between Vienna and St. Petersburgh, or of the mediation of the four Powers in the most appropriate form, are being united to-day; Russia, giving a fresh proof of her desire for an understanding, has hastened to reply to the first appearance of an overture made by Germany since the beginning of the crisis (as to the conditions on which Russia would stop her military preparations) by indicating a formula, and then modifying it in accordance with the request of Great Britain; there ought to be hope, therefore, negotiations having also been begun again between the Russian and Austrian Ambassadors, that British mediation will complete at London that which is being attempted by direct negotiations at Vienna and St. Petersburgh.

Nevertheless, the constant attitude of Germany who, since the beginning of the conflict, while ceaselessly protesting to each Power her peaceful intentions, has actually, by her dilatory or negative attitude, caused the failure of all attempts at agreement, and has not ceased to encourage through her Ambassador the uncompromising attitude of Vienna; the German military preparations begun since the 25th July and subsequently continued without cessation; the immediate opposition of Germany to the Russian formula, declared at Berlin inacceptable for Austria before that Power had even been consulted; in conclusion, all the impressions derived from Berlin bring conviction that Germany has sought to humiliate Russia, to disintegrate the Triple Entente, and if these results could not be obtained, to make war.

RENÉ VIVIANI.

No. 122.
Sir E. Goschen, British Ambassador at Berlin, to Sir Edward Grey.
(received August 1)
Berlin
July 31, 1914.
(Telegraphic)

Neutrality of Belgium, referred to in your telegram of 31st July to Sir F. Bertie.*

I have seen Secretary of State, who informs me that he must consult the Emperor and the Chancellor before he could possibly answer. I gather from what he said that he thought any reply they might give could not but disclose a certain amount of their plan of campaign in the event of war ensuring, and he was therefore very doubtful whether they would return any answer at all. His Excellency, nevertheless, took note of your request.

It appears from what he said that the German government considers that certain hostile acts already been committed by Belgium. As an instance of this, he alleged that a consignment of corn for Germany had been placed under an embargo already.

I hope to see his Excellency tomorrow again to discuss the matter further, but the prospect of obtaining a definite answer seems to me remote.

In speaking to me, today the Chancellor made it clear that Germany would in any case desire to know the reply returned to you by the French Government.

No. 115.
M. Dumaine, French Ambassador at Vienna, to M. René, Viviani President of the Council, Minister for Foreign Affairs.
Vienna
July 31, 1914.

General mobilization for all men from 19 to 42 years of age was declared by the Austro-Hungarian Government this morning at 1 o'clock.

My Russian colleague still thinks that this step is not entirely in contradiction to the declaration made yesterday by Count Berchtold.

DUMAINE.

No. 123.
Sir Edward Grey to Sir E. Goschen, British Ambassador at Berlin.
Foreign Office
August 1, 1914.

Sir,

I told the German Ambassador today that the reply[61] of the German Government with regard to the neutrality of Belgium affected the feeling of this country. If Germany could see her way to give the same assurance as that which have been given by France it would materially contribute to relieve anxiety and tension here. On the other hand, if there were a violation of the neutrality of Belgium by one combatant while the other respected it, it would be extremely difficult to restrain public feeling in this country. I said that we had been discussing this question at a Cabinet meeting, and as I was authorized to tell him this, I gave him a memorandum of it.

He asked me whether, if Germany gave a promise not to violate Belgium neutrality we would engage to remain neutral.

I replied that I could not say that; our hands were still free and we would considering what our attitude would be determined largely by public opinion here, and that neutrality of Belgium would appeal very strongly to public opinion here. I did not think that we could give a promise of neutrality on that condition alone.

The Ambassador on which we would remain neutral. He even suggested that the integrity of France and her colonies might be guaranteed.

I said that I felt obliged to refuse definitely any promise to remain neutral on similar terms, and I could only say that we must keep our hands free.

I am, &tc.
E. Grey

This telegram could be Britain's biggest mistake to date, though their stand on Belgium's neutrality is not of question. But the mistake is in reference to telegram No. 123, and there is no mention that Germany is investigating whether Belgium has seized control of food shipments bound for Germany. Sir Grey could have at least mentioned that they would see if there was any truth to this and see why this had happened.

---

[61] See No. 122.

No. 116.
M. Jules Cambon, French Ambassador at Berlin, to M René Viviani, President of the Council, Minister for Foreign Affairs.
Berlin
July 31, 1914.

Herr von Jagow sent for me and has just told me that he was very sorry to inform me that in face of the total mobilization of the Russian army, Germany, in the interest of the security of the Empire, found herself obliged to take serious precautionary measures. What is called "Kriegsgefahrzustand" (the state of danger of war) has been declared, and this allows the authorities to proclaim if they deem it expedient, a state of siege, to suspend some of the public services, and to close the frontier.

At the same time, a demand is being made at St. Petersburgh that they should demobilize, as well on the Austrian as on the German side, otherwise Germany would be obliged to mobilize on her side. Herr von Jagow told me that Herr von Schoen had been instructed to inform the French Government of the resolution of the Berlin Cabinet and to ask them what attitude they intended to adopt.

JULES CAMBON.

No. 124.
Sir F. Bertie, British Ambassador at Paris, to Sir Edward Grey.
(received August 1)
Paris
July 31, 1914.
(Telegraphic)

On the receipt at 8:30 tonight of your telegram of this afternoon,[62] I sent a message to Minister of Foreign Affairs requesting to see him. He received me at 10:30 tonight at the Elysee, were a Cabinet Council was being held. He took a note of the enquiry as to the respecting by France of the neutrality of Belgium, which you instructed me to make.

He told me that a communication had been made to you by the German Ambassador in London of the intention of Germany to order a general mobilization of her army if Russia did not demobilize at once. He is urgently anxious as to what the attitude of England will be in the circumstances, and begs an answer may be made by his Majesty's government at the earliest moment possible.

Minister for Foreign Affairs also told me that the German Embassy is packing up.

Though France does not reveal it just yet, she has just ordered full mobilization of her military at this same Cabinet Council meeting.

No. 117.
M. René Viviani, President of the Council, Minister for Foreign Affairs, to M. Paléologue, French Ambassador at St. Petersburgh.
Paris
July 31, 1914.

The German Government decided at mid-day to take at military measures implied by the state called "state of danger of war."

---

[62] See No. 114.

In communicating this decision to me at 7 o'clock this evening, Baron von Schoen added that the Government required at the same time that Russia should demobilize. If the Russian Government has not given, a satisfactory reply within twelve hours Germany will mobilize in her turn. I replied to the German Ambassador that I had no information at all about an alleged total mobilization of the Russian army and navy, which the German Government invoked as the reason for the new military measures, which they are taking to-day.

Baron von Schoen finally asked me, in the name of his Government, what the attitude of France would be in case of war between Germany and Russia. He told me that he would come for my reply to-morrow (Saturday) at 1 o'clock. I have no intention of making any statement to him on this subject, and I shall confine myself to telling him that France will have regard to her interests. The Government of the Republic need not indeed give any account of her intentions except to her ally.

I ask you to inform M. Sazonof of this immediately. As I have already told you, I have no doubt that the Imperial Government, in the highest interests of peace, will do everything on their part to avoid anything that might render inevitable or precipitate the crisis.

RENÉ VIVIANI.

The secret treaty France has with Russia will not be revealed at this time, though Germany does suspect a treaty does exist. Shortly after this meeting, France will give the order for full mobilization. Viviani knows this is going to happen. Hence, he is showing his resolve that France and Russia want war with Germany and are going to great lengths to make sure Germany is shown as the aggressor in this current crisis.

No. 125.
Sir F. Bertie, British Ambassador at Paris, to Sir Edward Grey.
(received August 1)
Paris
July 31, 1914.
(Telegraphic)

My immediately proceeding telegram.[63]

Political Director has brought me the reply of the Minister for Foreign Affairs to your enquiry respecting the neutrality of Belgium. It is as follows.

The French government is resolved to respect the neutrality of Belgium and it would only be in the event of some other Power violating that neutrality that France might find herself under the necessity, in order to assure defense of her own security, to act otherwise. This assurance has been given several times. President of the Republic spoke of it to the King of the Belgians, and the French Minister for Foreign Affairs today.

No. 118.
M. Paléologue, French Ambassador at St. Petersburgh, to M. René Viviani, President of Council, Minister for Foreign Affairs.
St. Petersburgh
July 31, 1914.

As a result of the general mobilization of Austria and of the measures for mobilization taken secretly, but continuously, by Germany for the last six days, the order for the general mobilization of the

---

[63] See No. 124.

Russian army has been given, Russia not being able, without most serious danger, to allow herself to be further out-distanced; really she is only taking military measures corresponding to those taken by Germany.

For imperative reasons of strategy the Russian Government, knowing that Germany was arming, could no longer delay the conversion of her partial mobilization into a general mobilization:

PALÉOLOGUE.

Here the reference is to Germany recalling officers off leave and cancelling current field maneuvers for her troops. By this time, Russia is mobilizing troops on both the Austrian and German frontiers.

No. 119.
M. Klobukowski, French Minister at Brussels, to M.René Viviani, President of the Council, Minister for Foreign Affairs.
Brussels
July 31, 1914.

L'agence Havas having announced that the state "of danger of war" had been declared in Germany, I told M. Davignon that I could assure him that the Government of the Republic would respect the neutrality of Belgium. The Minister for Foreign Affairs replied that the Government of the King had always thought that this would be so, and thanked me. The Russian Minister and the British Minister, whom I saw subsequently, appeared much pleased that in the circumstances I gave this assurance, which further, as the British Minister told me, was in accordance with the declaration of Sir E. Grey.

KLOBUKOWSKI.

You are cordially devoted,
NICOLAS.

This telegram of the Czar crossed with the following, sent by H.M. the Kaiser, also on July 31st, at 2 p.m.:

Upon Your appeal to my friendship and your request for my aid I have Engaged in mediation between Your Government and the Government of Austria-Hungary. While this action was taking Place, your troops were being mobilizes against my ally Austria-Hungary, whereby, as I have l already communicated to you, my mediation has become almost illusory. In spite of this, I have continued it, and now I receive reliable news that serious preparations for war are going on my eastern frontier. The responsibility for the security of my country forces me to measures of defense. I have gone to the extreme limit of the possible in my efforts for the preservation of the peace of the world. It is not I who bear the responsibility for the misfortune which now threatens the entire civilized world. It rests in your hand to avert it. No one threatens the honor and peace of Russia which might well have awaited the success of my mediation. The friendship for you and your country, bequeathed to me by my grandfather on his deathbed, has always been sacred to me, and I have stood faithfully by Russia while it was in serious affliction, especially during its last war. The peace of Europe can still be preserved by you if Russia decides to discontinue those military preparations, which menace Germany and Austria-Hungary. Before this telegram reached its destination, the mobilization of all the Russian forces, obviously directed against us and already ordered during the afternoon of the 31st of July, was in full swing. Notwithstanding, the telegram of the Czar was sent at 2 o'clock that same afternoon. After the Russian general mobilization became known in Berlin, the Imperial Ambassador at St. Petersburg was instructed on the afternoon of July 31st to explain to the Russian Government that Germany declared the state of war as counter-measure against the general mobilization of the Russian army and navy which must be followed by mobilization if Russia did not cease its military measures against Germany and Austria-Hungary within 12 hours, and notified Germany thereof. [*See exhibit 24.*]

At the same time, the Imperial Ambassador in Paris was instructed to demand from the French Government a declaration within 18 hours whether it would remain neutral in a Russo-German war. [*See exhibit 25.*]

The Russian Government destroyed through its mobilization, menacing the security of our country, the laborious action at mediation of the European cabinets. The Russian mobilization about the seriousness of which the Russian Government was never allowed by us to entertain a doubt, in connection with its continued denial, shows clearly that Russia wanted war.

The Imperial Ambassador at St. Petersburg delivered his note to M. Sasonof on July 31st at 12 o'clock midnight.

The reply of the Russian Government has never reached us.

Two hours after the expiration of the time limit, the Czar telegraphed to H.M. the Kaiser, as follows:

"I have received your telegram. I comprehend that you are forced to mobilize; However, I should like to have from you the same guarantee, which I have given your viz., that these measures do not mean war, and that we shall continue to negotiate for the welfare of our two countries and the Universal peace, which is so dear to our hearts. With the aid of God, it must be possible to our long tried friendship to prevent the shedding of Blood. I expect with full confidence your urgent reply."

Colonel House to President Wilson.
Prides Crossing, Massachusetts

July 31, 1914.

Dear Governor:

When I was in Germany, it seem clear to me that the situation, as far as a continuation of peace was concerned, was in a very precarious condition; and you will recall my first letter to you telling of the high tension that Germany and southern Europe were under.

I tried to convey this feeling to Sir Edward Grey and other members of the British Government. They seemed astonished at my pessimistic view and thought that the conditions were better than they had been for a long time. While I shook their confidence, at the same time I did not do it sufficiently to make them feel that a quick action was necessary; consequently, they let matters drag until after the Kaiser had gone into the Norwegian waters for his vacation, before giving me any definite ward to send to him.

It was my purpose to go back to Germany and see the Emperor, but the conservative delay of Sir Edward Grey and his confreres made that impossible.

The night before I sailed, Sir Edward sent me word that he was worried over conditions, but he did not anticipate what has followed. I have a feeling that if general war is finally averted, it will be because of the better feeling that has been brought between England and Germany. England is exerting a restraining hand upon France and, as far as possible, upon Russia; but her influence with the latter is slight.

If the matter could have been pushed a little further, Germany would have laid a heavy hand upon Austria and possibly peace could have been continued until a better understanding could have been brought about.

Russia has a feeling, so I was told in England, that Germany was trying to project Austrian and German influence deep into the Balkan states in order to check her. She has evidently been preparing for some decisive action since the Kaiser threw several hundred thousand German troops on his eastern frontier two years ago, thereby compelling Russia to relinquish the demands that she made in regard to a settlement of the Balkan matters....

Your faithful and affectionate,
E. M. House

Halls of the Palais Bourbon
31 July 1914
1930 hrs

French Socialist journalist Jean Jaures accompanied by Cachin, Longuet, and Bedouce being unable to see the French Premier, carried the socialist case to Abel Ferry, the Under Secretary of State for Foreign Affairs. Neither ministries nor deputies, even the most conservative among them, could afford to ignore Jaures; more than any other socialist in the parliaments of Europe, he was a moral and political force, hated by some, feared by more, but universally respected. When Ferry received the socialist delegates, he offered them little comfort and less information; but what he revealed something of the government's anxiety when asked what the socialist if events took another turn for the worse. Without hesitation, Jaures replied: "We will clear our party of any guilt; to the very end, we will continue to struggle against war." To which ferry answered prophetically: "No, you won't be able to continue. You will be assassinated on the nearest street corner." As the socialist was leaving, the Under Secretary, who couldn't bear to compound Jaures suffering, pulled Bedouce aside and told him the bitter truth: "Everything is finished. There is nothing left to do." If Jaures didn't hear Ferry, he undoubtedly divined his meaning. "He looked as though he had been hit with a sledge hammer; all that day, his friends had seen him weighted down by the impending tragedy. But at this moment, his moral suffering seemed to be transformed into genuine physical suffering. It was after 8 P.M. when Jaures and party returned to the offices of *L'humanite* at 142 Rue Montemartre. His gait was heavy and his face deeply lined, but when he spoke, he betrayed neither resignation nor despair: "Tonight I'm going to write a new *l'accuse!* I will expose everyone responsible for this crisis." He would reveal the government's ineptitude, Russia's militarism, Ivolsky's influence; he would identify all the male factors of Poincare's France. Like Zola before him, Jaures would appeal to the public to turn the of history.

At 9 P.M., the group broke for dinner before composing the August 1 issue. At Jaures' suggestion, they went to the Croissant, a café popular with journalist, which was closer to the office and generally more sedated. While looking at the picture of the daughter for Rene Dolie. Raoul Villain pulled the screen aside from the street and fired two shots. Jaures friend grabbed a bottle and subdued the assassin.

France has just secured their participation in what would be known as World War I.

Chapter Thirty-Three
August 1, 1914

Russian' plan No. 19, a prompt attack on East Prussia to save France, meant abandoning fortresses on the frontiers and instead building up the field army. Chief of Staff Sukhomlinov was an old guard praetorian conservative who sought army reforms for more artillery and a modern navy, opposed old fortresses as obsolete, and created thirty-five reserve divisions for the seventy-five first line divisions, opposed by Grand Duke Nicholas's General HQ, the Stavka who favored traditional cavalry and traditional fortresses. The Stavka was able to keep the fortresses, and only two of the four armies were put in the field in East Prussia. As a result, Russia would be defeated early in the war. The two armies under Rennenkampf and Samsonov were large but unprepared for the high rate of shells required by rapid firing weapons (infantry rifles fired fifteen rounds per minute; French seventy-five fired fifteen shells per minute) for high casualties that required more field hospitals and wagons and trains for the vast distances that required special reconnaisance. Both Russians and Germans had cavalry, but the internal combustion engine was too new to completely replace the horse.

Germans had only eighty-three trucks, and most broke down in the Ardennes. The Russian second army had only ten autos, four motorcycles, and forty-two airplanes, and most had mechanical problems. By 1914 Russia had raised a standing army of two million, which was three times the size of the German army, had built 8358 field guns, and had greatly improved the railroads. Russia mobilized with 360 trains per day, up from only 250 in 1910. "War by timetable" put great emphasis on schedules; one Russian colonel ordered 200 watches for his regiment from the American Waltham Watch Co., which had made a profit selling low-cost pocket watches to Union soldiers in the Civil War, but in 1914, most Russians did not have watches. The Russian army was not aristocratic like the Germans but had many low-and middle-class officers. They were paid less than half what the German officers were paid. The czar had appointed Grand Duke Nicholas to be commander in chief, and the duke appointed Danilov as quartermaster general of the Stavka to direct military operations. The Stavka was confident of a quick victory; Russian officers agreed no drink and no women until victory because all thought it would be a short six-week war. On August 2, Russian patrols fired on German advance pickets near Schwidden in preparation for the Russian second army invasion of East Prussia.

Secret Telegram to Russian Representatives abroad.
August 1, 1914.
(Telegraphic)

AT midnight the German Ambassador announced to me, on the instruction of his Government, that if within 12 hours that is by midnight on Saturday, we had not begun to demobilize, not only against Germany, but also against Austria the German Government would be compelled to give the order for mobilization. To my enquiry whether this meant war, the Ambassador replied in the negative, but added that we were very near it.

No. 71.
Russian Ambassador at London Russian Minister for Foreign Affairs.
London
August 1, 1914.
(Telegraphic)

GREY tells me that he has telegraphed to Berlin that in his opinion the last formula accepted by the Russian Government offers the best prospect as a basis of negotiations for a peaceful settlement of the dispute. At the same time, he expressed the hope that no Great Power would open hostilities before this formula had been considered.

No. 72.
Russian Ambassador at London Russian Minister for Foreign Affairs.
London
August 1, 1914.
(Telegraphic)

THE British Government has enquired of the French and German Governments whether they will respect the neutrality of Belgium.

France answered in the affirmative, but the German Government stated that they could not give any definite answer to the question.

By this time, the crew of seized German merchant ships had been ordered home by the Belgium government.

No. 127.
Sir M. de Bunsen, British Ambassador at Vienna, to Sir Edward Grey.
Vienna
August 1, 1914.
(Telegraphic)

General mobilization of the Army and the Fleet.

On July 31st, the Czar directed the following telegram to His Majesty the Kaiser:

"I thank you cordially for your mediation which permits the hope that everything may yet end peaceably. It is technically impossible to discontinue our military preparations, which have been made necessary by the Austrian mobilization. It is far from us to want war. As long as the negotiations between Austria and Serbia continue, my troops will undertake no provocative action. I give you my solemn word thereon. I confide with all my faith in the grace of God, and I hope for the success of your mediation in Vienna for the welfare of our countries and the peace of Europe."

No. 126.
Sir F. Bertie, British Ambassador at Paris, to Sir Edward Grey.
Paris
August 1, 1914.
(Telegraphic)

I have had a conversation with the Political Director, who states that the German Ambassador was informed on calling at the Ministry for Foreign Affairs the morning that the French Government failed to comprehend the reason, which prompted his communication of yesterday evening. It was pointed out to his Excellency that general mobilization in Russia had not been ordered until after Austria had decreed a general mobilization, and that the Russian Government was ready to demobilize if all Powers did likewise. It seemed strange to the French Government that in view of this and of the fact that Russia and Austria were ready to converse, the German Government should have at that moment presented an ultimatum at St. Petersburg requiring immediate demobilization by Russia. There were no differences at issue between France and Germany, but the German Ambassador had made a menacing communication to the French Government and had requested an answer the next day, intimating that he would have to break off relations and leave Paris if the reply were not satisfactory. The Ambassador was informed that the French Government considered that this was an extraordinary proceeding.

The German Ambassador, who is to see the Minister for Foreign Affairs again this evening, said nothing about demanding his passports, but he stated that he had packed up.

The German ambassador probably just found out that Russia and France were planning this whole thing or France was behind all the decisions Russia was making.

No. 73.
Russian Ambassador at Paris to Russian Minister for Foreign Affairs.
Paris
August 1, 1914.
(Telegraphic)

THE Austrian Ambassador yesterday visited Viviani and declared to him that Austria, far from harboring any designs against the integrity of Serbia, was in fact ready to discuss the grounds of her grievances against Serbia with the other Powers. The French Government is much exercised at Germany's extraordinary military activity on the French frontier, for they are convinced that, under the guise of Kriegszustand, mobilization is in reality being carried out.

No. 128.
Sir F. Villiers, British Minister at Brussels, to Sir Edward Grey.
Brussels
August 1, 1914.
(Telegraphic)
Belgium neutrality.
The instructions conveyed in your telegram of yesterday[64] have been acted upon.

Belgium expects and desires that other Powers will observe and uphold her neutrality, which she intends to maintain to the utmost of her Power. In so informing me, Minister for Foreign Affairs said

---

[64] See No. 115.

that, in the event of the violation of neutrality of their territory, they believe that they were in a position to defend themselves against intrusions. The relations between Belgium and her neighbors were excellent, and there was no reason to suspect their intentions; but he thought it well, nevertheless, to be prepared against emergencies.

No. 74.
Russian Ambassador at Paris to Russian Minister for Foreign Affairs.
Paris
August 1, 1914.
(Telegraphic)

ON the receipt in Paris of the telegram from the French Ambassador at St. Petersburg, reporting the communication made to you by the German Ambassador respecting Germany's decision to order general mobilization to-day, the President of the French Republic signed the order for mobilization. Lists of the reservists recalled to the colours are being posted up in the streets. The German Ambassador has just visited Viviani, but told him nothing fresh, alleging the impossibility of deciphering the telegrams he has received. Viviani informed him of the signature of the order for mobilization issued in reply to that of Germany, and expressed to him his amazement that Germany should have taken such a step at a moment when a friendly exchange of views was still in progress between Russia, Austria, and the Powers. He added that mobilization did not necessarily entail war, and that the German Ambassador might stay in Paris as the Russian Ambassador had remained in Vienna and the Austrian Ambassador in St. Petersburg.

No. 130.
Sir Edward Grey to Sir E. Goschen, British Ambassador at Berlin.
Foreign Office
August 1, 1914.
(Telegraphic)

We are informed that authorities at Hamburg have forcibly detained steamers belonging to the Great Central Company and other British merchant ships.

I cannot ascertain what grounds the detention of British ships has been ordered.

You should request German Government to send immediate orders that they should be allowed to proceed without delay. The effect on public opinion here will be deplorable unless this is done. His Majesty's Government on their side are most anxious to avoid any incident of an aggressive nature, and the German Government will I hope, be equally careful not to take any steps which would make the situation between us impossible.

No. 75.
Russian Ambassador at Paris to Russian Minister for Foreign Affairs.
Paris
August 1, 1914.
(Telegraphic)

I HEAR from the President that during the last few days the Austrian Ambassador emphatically assured both the President of the Council of Ministers and him that Austria had declared to Russia that she was ready to respect both the territorial integrity of Serbia and also her sovereign rights, but that Russia had intentionally received this declaration in silence. I contradicted this flatly.

No. 131.
Sir Edward Grey to Sir E. Goschen, British Ambassador at Berlin.
Foreign Office
August 1, 1914.
(Telegraphic)

I still believe that it might be possible to secure peace if only a little respite in time can be gained before any Great Power begins war.

The Russian Government has communicated to me the readiness of Austria to discuss with Russia and the readiness of Austria to accept a basis of mediation, which is not open to the objections raised in regard to the formula which Russia originally suggested.

Things ought not to be hopeless so long as Austria and Russia are ready to converse, and I hope that the German Government may be able to make use of the Russian communications referred to above, in order to avoid tension. His Majesty's Government is carefully abstaining from any act which may precipitate matters.

No. 76.
Note presented by the German Ambassador at
St. Petersburg.
August 1 at 7:10 P.M.

LE Gouvernement Impérial s'est efforcé dès les débuts de la crise de la mener à une solution pacifique. Se ren-dant à un désir qui lui en avait été exprimé par Sa Majesté l'Empereur de Russie, Sa Majest, l'Empereur d'Allemagne d'accord avec l'Angleterre s'était appliqué à accomplir un rôle médiateur auprès des Cabinets de Vienne et de Saint-Pétersbourg, lorsque la Russie, sans en attendre le résultat, procéda à la mobilization de la totalité de ses forces de terre et de mer. A la suite de cette mesure menaçante ne motivée par aucun presage militaire de la part de l'Allemagne, l'Empire allemand s'est trouvé vis-à-vis d'un danger grave et im-minent. Si le Gouvernement Impérial eût manquè de parer à ce péril, il aurait compromis la sécurit, et l'ex-istence même de l'Allemagne. Par conséquent le Gouvernement allemand se vit forcé de s'adresser au Gouvernement de Sa Majesté l'Empereur de Toutes les Russies en insistant sur la cessation desdits actes mil-itaires. La Russie avant refusé de faire droit à (n'ayant pas cru devoir répondre à[65]) cette demande et ayant manifesté par ce refils (cette attitude[65]) que son action était dirigée contre l'Allemagne, j'ai l'honneur, d'ordre de mon Gouvernement, de faire savoir à votre Excellence ce qui suit: Sa Majesté l'Empereur, mon auguste Souverain. au nom de l'Empire, relevant le défié se considère en état de guerre avec la Russie.[65] Les mots placés entre parenthèses se trouvent dans l' original. Il faut supposer que deus variantes avaient été préparees d'avanee et que par erreur elles ont été insérées toutes les deux dans la note.

(Translation)

THE Imperial German Government has used every effort since the beginning of the crisis to bring about a peaceful settlement. In compliance with a wish expressed to him by His Majesty the Emperor of Russia, the German Emperor had undertaken, in concert with Great Britain, the part of mediator between the Cabinets of Vienna and St. Petersburg; but Russia, without waiting for any result, proceeded to a general mobilization of her forces both on land and sea. Ill consequence of this threatening step, which was not justified by any military proceedings on the part of Germany, the German Empire was faced by a grave and imminent danger. If the German Government had failed to guard against this peril, they would have compromised the safety and the very existence of Germany. The German Government were, therefore, obliged to make representations to the Government of His Majesty the Emperor of All the Russia and to insist upon a cessation of the afore-said military acts. Russia having refused to comply with (not having considered it necessary to answer[65] this demand. In addition, having shown by this refusal (this attitude[65] that her action was

---

[65] The words in brackets occur in the original. It must be supposed that two variations had been prepared in advance, and that, by mistake, they were both inserted in the note.

directed against Germany, have the honor, on the instructions of my Government, to inform y our Excellency as follows:

His Majesty the Emperor, my august Sovereign, in the name of the German Empire, accepts the challenge, and considers himself at war with Russia.

No. 132.
Sir Edward Grey to Sir E. Goschen, British Ambassador at Berlin.
Foreign Office
August 1, 1914.
(Telegraphic)

Following the telegraph from M. Sazonof to Count Benckendorff of July 31ˢᵗ communicated to me today:

"(urgent.)

"Formula amended in accordance with the English proposal: if Austria consents to stay the march of her troops on Serbian territory, and if recognizing that the Austro-Serbian conflict has assumed the character of a question of European interest, she admits that the Great Powers may examine the satisfaction which Serbia can accord to the Austro-Hungarian Government without injury to her sovereign rights as a state and her independence, Russia undertakes to preserve her waiting attitude.

No. 13.
Count de Lalaing, Belgian Minister at London, to M. Davignon, Belgian Minister for Foreign Affairs.
London
August 1, 1914.
(Telegraphic)

Great Britain has asked France and Germany separately if they intend to respect Belgian territory in the event of its not being violated by their adversary. Germany's reply is awaited. France has replied in the affirmative.

No. 133.
Sir Edward Grey to Sir E. Goschen, British Ambassador at Berlin
Foreign Office
August 1, 1914
(Telegraphic)

M. de Etter* came today to communicate the contents of a telegram from M. Sazonof^, dated the 31ˢᵗ July, which are as follows:

"The Austro-Hungarian Ambassador declared the readiness of his government to discuss the substances of the Austrian ultimatum to Serbia. M. Sazonof replied by expressing his satisfaction, and said it was desirable that the discussions should take place in London with the participation of the Great Powers.

"M. Sazonof hoped that the British Government would assume the direction of these discussions. The whole of Europe would be thankful to them. It would be very important that Austria should mean while put a stop provisionally to her military action on Serbian territory."

(The above has been communicated to the Six Powers.)

No. 14.
Baron Beyerns, Belgian Minister at Berlin, to M. Davignon, Belgian Minister for Foreign Affairs.
Berlin
August 1, 1914.
(Telegraphic)

The British Ambassador has been instructed to inquire of the Minister for Foreign Affairs whether, in the event of war, Germany would respect Belgian neutrality, and I understand that the Minister replied that he was unable to answer the question.

No. 134.
Sir F. Bertie, British Ambassador at Paris, to Sir Edward Grey.
Paris
August 1, 1914.
(Telegraphic)

President of the Republic has informed me that German government was trying to saddle Russia with the responsibility; that it was only after a decree of general mobilization had been issued in Austria that the Emperor of Russia ordered a general mobilization; that, although the measures which the German Government have already taken are in effect a general mobilization, they are not so designated; that a French general mobilization will become necessary in self-defense, and that France is already forty-eight hours behind Germany as regards German preparations; that the French troops have orders not to go nearer to the German frontier than a distance of 10 kilometers so has to avoid any grounds for accusation of provocation to Germany, whereas the German troops, on the other hand, are actually on the French frontier and have made incursions on it; that notwithstanding mobilization, the Emperor of Russia has expressed himself ready to continue his conversation with the German Ambassador with a view to preserving peace; that French government, whose wishes are markedly pacific, sincerely desire the preservation of peace and do not quite despair, even now, of its being possible to avoid war.

No. 15.
M. Davignon, Belgian Minister for Foreign Affairs, to the Belgian Ministers at Berlin, Paris, and London.
Brussels
August 1, 1914.
Sir,
I have the honour to inform you that the French Minister has made the following verbal communication to me:
(Translation.)

"I am authorized to declare that, in the event of an international war, the French Government, in accordance with the declarations they have always made will respect the neutrality of Belgium. In the event of this neutrality not being respected by another Power, the French Government, to secure their own defense, might find it necessary to modify their attitude."

I thanked his Excellency and added that we on our side had taken without delay all the measures necessary, to ensure that our independence and our frontiers should be respected.

No. 135.
Sir Edward Grey to Sir G. Buchanan, British Ambassador at St. Petersburg.
Foreign Office
August 1, 1914.
(Telegraphic)

Information reaches me from a most reliable source that Austrian Government has informed German Government that though the situation has been changed by the mobilization of Russia they would in full appreciation of the efforts of England for the preservation of peace be ready to consider favorably my proposal for mediation between Austria and Serbia. The effect of this acceptance would naturally be that the Austrian military against Serbia would continue for the present, and that the British Government would urge upon Russian Government to stop mobilization of troops directed against Austria, in which case Austria would naturally cancel those defensive military counter-measures in Galicia, which have been forced upon Austria by Russian mobilization.

You should inform Minister for Foreign Affairs and say that if, in the consideration of the acceptance of mediation by Austria, Russia can agree to stop mobilization, it appears still to be possible to preserve peace. Presumably the matter should be discussed with German Government also by Russian Government.

This telegram must be the last proposal Germany made to Austria, and they had to wait until morning to get the reply from the Austrian government.

No. 16.
M. Davignon, Belgian Minister for Foreign Affairs to Belgian Ministers at Paris, Berlin, London, Vienna, and St. Petersburg.
Brussels
August 1, 1914.
(Telegraphic)

Carry out instructions contained in my dispatch of the 24th July.

No. 136.
Sir F. Bertie, British Ambassador at Paris, to Sir Edward Grey.
Paris
August 1, 1914.
(Telegraphic)

Minister of War informed military attaché this afternoon that orders had been given at 3:40 P.M. for a general mobilization of the French Army. This became necessary because Minister of War knows that, under the system of "Kriegszunstand",* the Germans have called up six classes. Three classes are sufficient to bring their covering troops up to war strength, the remaining three being the reserve. This he says, being tantamount to mobilization, is mobilization under another name.

The French forces on the frontier have opposed to them eight army corps on a war footing, and an attack is expected at any moment. It is therefore of the utmost importance to guard against this. A zone of 10 kilometers has been left between the French troops and German frontier. The French troops will not attack, and the Minister of War is anxious that it should be explained that this act of mobilization is one for purely defensive purpose.

Still the German government has not called for mobilization. What they have been doing is re-organizing available troops just in case the crisis crosses over to German frontier.

No. 137.
Sir Edward Grey to Sir M. de Bunsen, British Ambassador at Vienna.
Foreign Office
August 1, 1914.
(Telegraphic)

I saw the Austro-Hungarian Ambassador this morning. He supplied me with the substance of a telegram, which Austro-Hungarian Minister for Foreign Affairs had sent to the Austrian Ambassador in Paris. In this telegram, his Excellency was given instructions to assure the French Minister for Foreign Affairs that there was no intention in the minds of the Austro-Hungarian government to impair the sovereign rights of Serbia or to obtain territorial aggrandizement. The Ambassador added that he was further instructed to inform the French Minister for Foreign Affairs that there was no truth in the report, which had been published in Paris to the effect that Austria-Hungary intended to Sanjak.

Count Mensdorff called again later at the Foreign Office. He informed me of a telegram sent yesterday to the Austro-Hungarian Ambassador at St. Petersburg by Count Berchtold, and gave me the substance.

It states that Count Berchtold begged the Russian Ambassador, whom he sent for yesterday, to do his best to remove wholly erroneous impression in St. Petersburg that the "door had been banged" by Austria-Hungary on all further conversations. The Russian Ambassador promised to do this. Count Berchtold repeated on this occasion to the Russian Ambassador the assurance, which had already been given in St. Petersburg, to the effect that neither an infraction of Serbian sovereign rights nor the acquisition of Serbian territory was being contemplated by Austria-Hungary.

Special attention was called by count Mensdorff to the fact that this telegram contains a statement to the effect that conversations at St. Petersburg had not been broken off by Austria-Hungary.

No. 17.
M. Davignon, Belgian Minister for Foreign Affairs to Belgian Ministers at Rome, The Hague, Luxemburg.
Brussels
August 1, 1914.
(Telegraphic)

Carry out instructions contained in my dispatch of the 20th July.

(See No. 3)
Prince Lichownowsky's Reply to Sir Edward Gray.
August 1, 1914.

Sir Edward Grey [the British Secretary for Foreign Affairs] begged us to come forward with a proposal of our own. We insisted on war….The impression grew continually stronger that we desired war under any circumstances. In no other way was it possible to interpret our attitude…. Then, on July 29 [1914], Sir Edward decided to give his famous warning. I replied that I had invariably reported that we should have to reckon with English opposition if it came to a war with France. Repeatedly the Minister said to me: "If war breaks out, it will be the greatest catastrophe the world has ever seen."

Soon after this events were precipitated. Until this time, following the directions he received from Berlin, Count Berchtold had played the part of the strong man. When at last he decided to change his course, and after Russia had negotiated and waited a whole week in vain, we answered the Russian mobilization with the ultimatum and the declaration of war....

It is shown by all official publications and is not disproved by our White Book, which, owing to the poverty of its contents and to its omissions, constitutes a grave indictment against ourselves, that:

1. We encouraged Count Berchtold to attack Serbia, although no German interest was involved and the danger of a World War must have been known to us. Whether we were acquainted with the wording of the ultimatum is completely immaterial.

2. During the period between the 23rd and the 30th of July, 1914, when M. Sazonof emphatically declared that he could not tolerate an attack on Serbia, we rejected the British proposals of mediation, although Serbia, under Russian and British pressure, had accepted almost the whole of the ultimatum, and although an agreement about the two points at issue could easily have been reached and Count Berchtold was even prepared to content himself with the Serbian reply.

3. On the 30th of July, when Count Berchtold showed a disposition to change his course, we sent an ultimatum to St. Petersbourg merely because of the Russian mobilization and though Austria had not been attacked; and on the 31st of July we declared war against the Russians, although the Czar pledged his word that he would not permit a single man to march as long as negotiations were still going on. Thus, we deliberately destroyed the possibility of a peaceful settlement. In view of these incontestable facts, it is no wonder that the whole civilized world outside of Germany places the sole responsibility for the World War upon our shoulders.

No. 138.
Sir E. Goschen, British Ambassador ay Berlin, to Sir Edward Grey.
(received August 2, 1914)
Berlin
August 1, 1914.
(Telegraphic)

Your telegram of today.

I have communicated the substance of the above telegram to the Secretary of State, and spent a long time arguing with him that the chief dispute was between Austria and Russia, and that Germany was only drawn in as Austria's ally. If therefore Austria and Russia were, as evident, ready to discuss matters and Germany did not desire war on her own account, it seemed to me only logical that Germany should hold her hand and continue to work for a peaceful settlement. Secretary of State said Austria's readiness to discuss was the result of German influence at Vienna, and not Russia mobilized against Germany, all would have been well. But Russia by abstaining from answering Germany's demand that she should demobilize, had caused Germany to mobilize also. Russia had said that her mobilization did not necessarily imply war, and that she could perfectly well remain mobilized for months without waging war. This was not the case with Germany. She had speed and Russia had the numbers, and the safety of the German Empire forbade that Germany should allow Russia time to bring up masses of troops from all parts of her wide dominions. The situation now was that, though the imperial Government had allowed her several hours beyond the specific time, Russia had sent no answer. Germany had therefore ordered mobilization, and the German representative at St. Petersburg had been instructed within a certain time to inform the Russian Government that the Imperial Government must regard their refusal to an answer as creating a state of war.

This telegram gives an inside look at how Russia and France were going to start this war. They were trying to make it look like Germany was doing all that it could to start a war on both her western and eastern fronts. Sir E. Goschen is trying to show Sir E. Grey that in fact, Russia is the one being the aggressor for wanting this war to start while France sits back, fat and happy that all is going to plan.

No. 139.
Sir G. Buchanan, British Ambassador at St. Petersburg, to Sir Edward Grey.
(received August 2, 1914)
St. Petersburg
August 1, 1914.
(Telegraphic)

My telegram of July 31st.

The Emperor of Russia read this telegram to the German Emperor and to the German Ambassador at the audience given to his Excellency yesterday. No progress whatever was made.

In the evening M. Sazonof had an interview with the Austrian Ambassador who, not being definitely instructed by his Government, did his best to deflect the conversation towards a general discussion of the relations between Austria-Hungary and Russia instead of keeping to the question of Serbia. In reply the Minister for Foreign Affairs expressed his desire that these relations should remain friendly, and said that, taken in general, they were perfectly satisfactory; but the real question which they had to resolve at this moment was whether Austria was to crush Serbia and to reduce her to the status of a vassal, or whether to leave Serbia a free and independent state. In these circumstances, while the Serbian question was unsolved, the abstract discussion of the relations between Austria-Hungary and Russia was a waste of time. The only place where a successful discussion of this question could be expected was London, and any such discussion was being made impossible by the action of Austria-Hungary is subjecting Belgrade, a virtually unfortified town, to bombardment.

M. Sazonof informed the French Ambassador and myself this morning of his conversation with Austrian Ambassador. He went on to say that during the Balkan crisis, he had made it, clear to the Austrian Government that war with Russia must inevitably follow an attack on Serbia. It was clear that Austrian domination of Serbia was as intolerable for Russia as the dependence of the Netherlands on Germany would be to Great Britain. It was in fact, for Russia a question of life and death. The policy of Austria had throughout been both tortuous and immoral, and she thought that she could treat Russia with defiance, secure in the support of her German ally. Similarly, the policy of Germany had been an equivocal and double-faced policy, and it mattered little whether the German Government knew or did not know the terms of the Austrian ultimatum; what matter was that her intervention with the Austrian Government had been postponed until the moment had passed when its influence would have been felt. Germany was unfortunate in her representatives in Vienna and St. Petersburg: the former was a violent Russophobe who had urged Austria on, the latter had reported to his government that Russia would never go to war. M. Sazonof was completely weary of the ceaseless endeavors he had made to avoid a war. No suggestion held out to him had been refused. He had accepted the proposal for a conference of four, for mediation by Great Britain and Italy, for direct conversation between Austria and Russia; but Germany and Austria-Hungary had either rendered these attempts for peace ineffective by evasive replies or had refused them altogether. The action of the

Austro-Hungarian Government and the German preparations had forced the Russian Government to order mobilization, and the mobilization of Germany had created a desperate situation.

M. Sazonof added that the formula, of which the text is contained in my telegram of July 31st, had been forwarded by the Russian Government to Vienna, and he would adhere to it if you could obtain its acceptance before the frontier was crossed by German troops. In no case would Russia begin hostilities first.

I now see no possibility of a general war being avoided unless the agreement of France and Germany can obtain to keep their armies mobilized on their own sides of the frontier, as Russia has expressed her readiness to do, pending a last attempt to reach a settlement of the present crisis.

M. Sazonof makes a strong case for lying. He fails to tell this group of diplomats what he had told the German Ambassador in St. Petersburg. See British telegram No. 97. At this point, someone should have stood up and said it was a Serbian conspiracy to assassinate the archduke, which had Serbian Government involvement.

No. 14.
Baron Beyerns, Belgian Minister at Berlin, to M. Davignon, Belgian Minister for Foreign Affairs.
Berlin
August 1, 1914.
(Telegraphic)

The British Ambassador has been instructed to inquire of the Minister for Foreign Affairs whether, in the event of war, Germany would respect Belgian neutrality, and I understand that the Minister replied that he was unable to answer the question.

No. 140.
Sir F. Bertie, British Ambassador at Paris, to Sir Edward Grey.
Paris
August 1, 1914.
(Telegraphic)

The Minister of War again sent for the military attaché this evening, as he said he wished to keep me inform of the situation. He laid great stress on the fact that the zone of 10 kilometers, which he had arranged between French troops and the German frontier, and which was still occupied by peasants, was a proof of the French endeavors to commit no provocative act.

No. 15.
M. Davignon, Belgian Minister for Foreign Affairs, to the Belgian Ministers at Berlin, Paris, and London.
Brussels
August 1, 1914.
Sir,
I have the honor to inform you that the French Minister has made the following verbal communication to me:

"I am authorized to declare that, in the event of an international war, the French Government, in accordance with the declarations they have always made will respect the neutrality of Belgium. In the event of this neutrality not being respected by another Power, the French Government, to secure their own defense, might find it necessary to modify their attitude."

I thanked his Excellency and added that we on our side had taken without delay all the measures necessary, to ensure that our independence and our frontiers should be respected.

No. 141.
Sir M. Bunsen, British Ambassador at Vienna, to Sir Edward Grey.
Vienna
August 1, 1914.
(Telegraphic)

I am to be received tomorrow by Minister for Foreign Affairs. This afternoon he is to see the French and Russian Ambassadors. I have just been informed by Russian Ambassador to German ultimatum requiring that Russia should demobilize within twelve hours. On being asked by the Russian Minister for Foreign Affairs whether the inevitable refusal of Russia to yield to this curt summons meant war, the German Ambassador replied that Germany would be forced to mobilize if Russia refuses. Russian Ambassador at Vienna thinks that war is almost inevitable, and that as mobilization is too expensive to be kept for long, Germany will attack Russia at once. He says that so-called mobilization of Russia amounted to nothing more than that Russia had taken military measures corresponding to those taken by Germany. There seems to be even greater tension between Germany and Russia than there is between Austria and Russia. Russia would according to the Russian Ambassador, be satisfied even now with assurance respecting Serbian integrity and independence. He says that Russia had no intention to attack Austria. He is going again today to point out to the Minister for Foreign Affairs that most terrific consequences must ensue from refusal to make this slight concession. This time Russia would fight to the last extremity. I agree with his Excellency that the German Ambassador at Vienna desired war from the first, at that his strong personnel bias probably colored his action here. The Russian Ambassador is convinced that the German government also desired war from the first.

It is the intention of the French Ambassador to speak earnestly to the Minister for Foreign Affairs today on the extreme danger of the situation, and to ask whether proposals to serve as a basis of mediation from any quarter are being considered. There is great anxiety to know what England will do. I fear that nothing can alter the determination of Austro-Hungarian Government to proceed on there present course, if they have made up their mind with the approval of Germany.

No. 16.
M. Davignon, Belgian Minister for Foreign Affairs to Belgian Ministers at Paris, Berlin, London, Vienna, and St. Petersburg.
Brussels
August 1, 1914.
(Telegraphic)

Carry out instructions contained in my dispatch of 24 July.

No. 142.
Sir E. Goschen, British Ambassador at Berlin, to Sir Edward Grey.
Berlin
August 1, 1914.
(Telegraphic)

Orders have just been issued for the general mobilization of army and navy, the first day of mobilization to be August 2, 1914.

This mobilization was finally happening after France ordered her military to full mobilization.

No. 17.
M. Davignon, Belgian Minister for Foreign Affairs to Belgian Ministers at Rome, The Hague, Luxemburg.
Brussels
August 1, 1914.
(Telegraphic)

Carry out instructions contained in my dispatch of 20 July.
(See No. 3.)

No. 143.
Sir E. Goschen, British Ambassador at Berlin, to Sir Edward Grey.
Berlin
August 1, 1914.
(Telegraphic)

Detention of British merchant ships at Hamburg.
Your telegram of Aug. 1st[66] acted on.

Secretary of State, who expressed the greatest surprise and annoyance, has promised to send orders at once to allow steamers to proceed with out delay.

Telegram of the Chancellor to the Imperial Ambassador in St. Petersburg on August 1, 12:62 P.M. Urgent.

If the Russian Government gives no satisfactory reply to our demand, Your Excellency will please transmit this afternoon 5 o'clock (mid European time) the following statement:

"The Imperial Government endeavored as of the beginnings of the crisis to lead it to a peaceful solution. Going to a desire that him had been expressed by it by Its Majesty the Emperor of Russia, Its Majesty the Emperor of Germany of agreement with England was applied to achieve a mediator role near the Cabinets of Vienna and St Petersbourg, when Russia, without expecting the result from it, carried out the mobilization of the totality of its forces of ground and sea. Following this threatening measurement moved by any préparatif soldier on behalf of Germany, the German Empire was with respect to a serious and imminent danger. If the Imperial Government had missed countering this danger, it would have compromised safety and the mâme existence of Germany. Consequently, the German Government was seen forced to apply to the Government of Its Majesty the Emperor of all Russies while insisting on the suspension of the known as military acts. Russia having refused to

---

[66] See No. 130.

grant this request and having expressed by this refusal, that its action was directed against Germany, I have the honor of order of my Government to let know with Your Excellency what follows: Its Majesty the Emperor, my majestic Souverain in the name of the Empire takes up the challenge and is considered in a state of war with Russia."

Please wire urgent receipt and time of carrying out this instruction by Russian time.

Please ask for your passports and turn over protection and affairs to the American Embassy.

Telegram of the Imperial Ambassador in Paris to the Chancellor on August 1, 1:05 P.M.

Upon my repeated definite inquiry whether France would remain neutral in the event of a Russo-German war, the Prime Minister declared that France would do that which her interests dictated.

Tsar to Kaiser.
1 August 1914.
Peter's Court, Palace, 1 August 1914
Sa Majesté l'Empereur
Berlin

I received your telegram. Understand you are obliged to mobilize but wish to have the same guarantee from you as I gave you, that these measures do not mean war and that we shall continue negotiating for the benefit of our countries and universal peace deal to all our hearts. Our long proved friendship must succeed, with God's help, in avoiding bloodshed. Anxiously, full of confidence await your answer.

Nicky

Kaiser to Tsar
1 August 1914.
Berlin, 1 August 1914

Thanks for your telegram. I yesterday pointed out to your government the way by which alone war may be avoided.

Although I requested an answer for noon today, no telegram from my ambassador conveying an answer from your Government has reached me as yet. I therefore have been obliged to mobilize my army.

Immediate affirmative clear and unmistakable answer from your government is the only way to avoid endless misery. Until I have received this answer alas, I am unable to discuss the subject of your telegram. In fact, I must request you to immediately [sic] order your troops on no account to commit the slightest act of trespassing over our frontiers.

Willy

No. 120.
René Viviani, President of the Council, Minister for Foreign Affairs, to the French Ambassadors at London, St. Petersburgh, Berlin, Vienna, Rome.
Paris
August 1, 1914.

Two *démarches* were made yesterday evening by the Austrian Ambassadors—the one at Paris, which was rather vague, the other at St. Petersburgh, precise and conciliatory. Count Scézsen came to explain to me that the Austro-Hungarian Government had officially informed Russia that it had no territorial ambition, and would not touch the sovereignty of Serbia; that it also repudiates any intention of occupying the Sandjak; but that these explanations of disinterestedness only retain their force if the war remains localized to Austria and Serbia, as a European war would open out eventualities which it was impossible to foresee. The Austrian Ambassador, in commenting on these explanations, gave me to understand that if his Government could not answer the questions of the Powers speaking in their own name, they would certainly answer Serbia, or any single Power asking for these conditions in the name of Serbia. He added that a step in this direction was perhaps still possible.

At St. Petersburgh, the Austrian Ambassador called on M. Sazonof and explained to him that his Government was willing to begin a discussion as to the basis of the ultimatum addressed to Serbia. The Russian Minister declared he satisfied with this declaration, and proposed that the *pourparlers* should take place in London with the participation of the Powers. M. Sazonof will have requested the British Government to take the lead in the discussion; he pointed out that it would be very important that Austria should stop her operations in Serbia. The deduction from these facts is that Austria would at last show she ready to come to an agreement, just as the Russian Government is ready to enter into negotiations based on the British proposal.

Unfortunately these arrangements, which allowed one to hope for a peaceful solution, appear, in fact, to have been rendered useless by the attitude of Germany. This Power has in fact presented an ultimatum giving the Russian Government twelve hours in which to agree to the demobilization of their forces not only as against Germany, but also as against Austria; this time limit expires at noon. The ultimatum is not justified, for Russia has accepted the British proposal, which implies a cessation of military preparation by all the Powers. The attitude of Germany proves that she wishes for war. And she wishes for it against France. Yesterday when Herr von Schoen came to the Quai d'Orsay to ask what attitude France proposed to take in case of a Russo-German conflict, the German Ambassador, although there has been no direct dispute between France and Germany, and although from the beginning of the crisis we have used all our efforts for a peaceful solution and are still continuing to do so, added that he asked me to present his respects and thanks to the President of the Republic, and asked that we would be good enough to make arrangements as to him personally *(des dispositions pour sa propre personne)*; we know also that he has already put the archives of the Embassy in safety. This attitude of breaking off diplomatic relations without any direct dispute, and although he has not received any definitely negative answer, is characteristic of the determination of Germany to make war against France. The want of sincerity in her peaceful protestations is shown by the rupture, which she is forcing upon Europe at a time when Austria had at last agreed with Russia to begin negotiations.

RENÉ VIVIANI.

No. 121.
M. Jules Cambon, French Ambassador at Berlin, to M. René Viviani, President of the Council, Minister for Foreign Affairs.
Berlin
August 1, 1914.

My Russian colleague received yesterday evening two 2 telegrams from M. Sazonof advising him that the Austrian Ambassador at St. Petersburgh had explained that his Government was ready to discuss the note to Serbia with the Russian Government even as to its basis; M. Sazonof answered that in his opinion these conversations should take place in London.

The ultimatum to Russia can only do away with the last chances of peace, which these conversations still seemed to leave. The question may be asked whether in such circumstances the acceptance by Austria was serious, and had not the object of throwing the responsibility of the conflict on to Russia.

My British colleague during the night made a pressing appeal to Herr von Jagow's feelings of humanity. The latter answered that the matter had gone too far and that they must wait for the Russian answer to the German ultimatum. But he told Sir Edward Goschen that the ultimatum required that the Russians should countermand their mobilization, not only as against Germany but also as against Austria; my British colleague was much astonished at this, and said that it did not seem possible for Russia to accept this last point.

Germany's ultimatum coming at the very moment when an agreement seemed about to be established between Vienna and St. Petersburgh, is characteristic of her warlike policy. In truth the conflict was between Russia and Austria only, and Germany could only intervene as an ally of Austria; in these circumstances, as the two Powers which were interested as principals were prepared for conversations, it is impossible to understand why Germany should send an ultimatum to Russia instead of continuing like all the other Powers to work for a peaceful solution, unless she desired war on her own account.

J. CAMBON.

No. 122.
M. René Viviani, President of the Council, Minister for Foreign Affairs, to the French Ambassadors at London, Berlin, and to French Minister at Brussels.
Paris
August 1, 1914.

The British Ambassador, under the instructions to his Government, came to ask me what would be the attitude of the French Government as regards Belgium in case of conflict with Germany. I stated that, in accordance with the assurance, which we had repeatedly given Belgian Government, we intended to respect their neutrality.

It would only be in the event of some other Power violating that neutrality that France might find herself brought to enter Belgian territory, to fulfilling her obligations as a guaranteeing Power.

RENÉ VIVIANI.

No. 123.
M. Jules Cambon, French Ambassador at Berlin, to M. René Viviani, President of the Council, Minister for Foreign Affairs.
Berlin
August 1, 1914.

The British Ambassador has been instructed by his Government to make to the German Government a communication identical with that which he made to you on the subject of the neutrality of Belgium.

Herr von Jagow answered that he would take the instructions of the Emperor and the Chancellor, but that he did not think an answer could be given, for Germany could not disclose her military plans in this way. The British Ambassador will see Herr von Jagow to-morrow afternoon.

J. CAMBON.

No. 124.
M. Barrère, French Ambassador at Rome, to M. René Viviani, President of the Council, Minister for Foreign Affairs.
Rome
August 1, 1914.

I went to see the Marquis di San Giuliano this morning at half-past eight, in order to get precise information from him as to the attitude of Italy in view of the provocative acts of Germany and the results, which they may have.

The Minister for Foreign Affairs answered that he had seen the German Ambassador yesterday evening. Herr von Flotow had said to him that Germany had requested the Russian Government to suspend mobilization, and the French Government to inform them as to their intentions; Germany had given France a time limit of eighteen hours and Russia a time limit of twelve hours.

Herr von Flotow as a result of this communication asked what were the intentions of the Italian Government.

The Marquis di San Giuliano answered that as the war undertaken by Austria was aggressive and did not fall within the purely defensive character of the Triple Alliance, particularly in view of the consequences, which might result from it according to the declaration of the German Ambassador, Italy could not take part in the war.

BARRÈRS.

No. 125.
M. René Viviani, President of the Council, Minister for Foreign Affairs, to the French Ambassadors at London, St. Petersburgh, Berlin, Vienna, Rome, Madrid, Constantinople.
Paris
August 1, 1914.

The German Ambassador came to see me again at 11 o'clock this morning. After having recalled to his memory all the efforts made by France towards an honorable settlement of the Austro-Serbian conflict and the difficulty between Austria and Russia which has resulted from it, I put him in possession of the facts as to the *pourparlers* which have been carried on since yesterday:

(1) A British compromise, proposing, besides other suggestions, suspension of military preparations on the part of Russia, on condition that the other Powers should act in the same way; adherence of Russia to this proposal.

(2) Communications from the Austrian Government declaring that they did not desire any aggrandizement in Serbia, nor even to advance into the Sandjak, and stating that they were ready to discuss *even the basis* of the Austro-Serbian question at London with the other Powers.

I drew attention to the attitude of Germany who, abandoning all *pourparlers,* presented an ultimatum to Russia at the very moment when this Power had just accepted the British formula (which implies the cessation of military preparations by all the countries which have mobilized) and regarded as imminent a diplomatic rupture with France.

Baron von Schoen answered that he did not know the developments which had taken place in this matter for the last twenty-four hours, that there was perhaps in them a "glimmer of hope" for some arrangement, that he had not received any fresh communication from his Government, and that he was going to get information. He gave renewed protestations of his sincere desire to unite his efforts to those of France for arriving at a solution of the conflict. I laid stress on the serious responsibility, which the Imperial Government would assume if, in circumstances such as these, they took an initiative, which was not justified, and of a kind, which would irremediably compromise peace.

Baron von Schoen did not allude to his immediate departure and did not make any fresh request for an answer to his question concerning the attitude of France in case of an Austro-Russian conflict. He confined himself to saying of his own accord that the attitude of France was not doubtful.

It would not do to exaggerate the possibilities, which may result from my conversation with the German Ambassador for, on their side, the Imperial Government continues the most dangerous preparations on our frontier. However, we must not neglect the possibilities, and we should not cease to work towards an agreement. On her side, France is taking all military measures required for protection against too great an advance in German military preparations. She considers that her attempts at solution will only have a chance of success so far as it is felt that she will be ready and resolute if the conflict is forced on her.

RENÉ VIVIANI.

No. 126.
M. Paul Cambon, French Ambassador at London, to M. René Viviani, President of the Council, Minister for Foreign Affairs.
Paris
August 1, 1914.

Sir Edward Grey said to me that, at a meeting this morning, the Cabinet had again considered the situation. As Germany had asked Great Britain to give a declaration of neutrality and had not obtained it, the British Government remained masters of their action; this could shape itself in accordance with different hypotheses.

In the first place, Belgian neutrality is of great importance to Great Britain. France has immediately renewed her engagement to respect it. Germany has explained, "That she was not in a position to reply." Sir Edward Grey will put the Cabinet in possession of this answer and will ask to be authorized to state on Monday in the House of Commons, that the British Government will not permit a violation of Belgian neutrality.

In the second place, the British fleet is mobilized and Sir Edward Grey will propose to his colleagues that he should state that it will oppose the passage of the Straits of Dover by the German fleet, or, if the German fleet should pass through (*venaient à le passer*), will oppose any demonstration on the French coasts. These two questions will be dealt with at the meeting on Monday. I drew the attention of the Secretary of State to the point that, if during this intervening period any incident took place, it was necessary not to allow a surprise, and that it would be desirable to think of intervening in time.

PAUL CAMBON.

No. 127.
M. René Viviani, President of the Council, Minister for Foreign Affairs, to M. Paul Cambon, French Ambassador at London.
Paris
August 1, 1914.

We are warned through several channels that the German and the Austrian Governments are trying at this moment to influence England by making her believe that the responsibility for war, if it breaks out, will fall on Russia. Efforts are being made to obtain the neutrality of England by disguising the truth.

France has not ceased in co-operation with England to advise moderation at St. Petersburgh; this advice has been listened to.

From the beginning, M. Sazonof has exercised pressure on Serbia to make her accept all those clauses of the ultimatum, which were not incompatible with her sovereignty.

He then engaged in a direct conversation with Austria; this was fresh evidence of his conciliatory spirit. Finally he has agreed to allow those Powers which are less interested to seek for means of composing the dispute.

In accordance with the wish expressed to him by Sir George Buchanan, M. Sazonof consented to modify the first formula, which he had put forward, and he has drawn up a second, which is shown not to differ materially from the declaration, which Count Scézsen made yesterday to M. de Margerie. Count Scézsen affirms that Austria does not intend to seek territorial aggrandizement and does not wish to touch the sovereignty of Serbia. He expressly adds that Austria has no designs on the Sandjak of Novi-Bazar.

It would then seem that an agreement between Sir Edward Grey's suggestion, M.Sazonof's formula and the Austrian declarations could easily be reconciled.

France is determined, in co-operation with England, to work to the very end for the realization of this.

However, while these negotiations were going on, and while Russia in the negotiations showed a goodwill, which cannot be disputed, Austria was the first to proceed to a general mobilization. Russia has found herself obliged to imitate Austria, so as not to be left in an unfavorable position, but all the time she has continued ready to negotiate.

It is not necessary for me to repeat that, so far as we are concerned, we will, in co-operation with England, continue to work for the success of these *pourparlers*.

But the attitude of Germany has made it absolutely compulsory for us to make out the order for mobilization to-day.

Last Wednesday, well in advance of Russian mobilization, as I have already telegraphed to you, Herr von Schoen announced to me the impending publication of *Kriegsgefahrzustand*. This measure has been taken by Germany, and under the protection of this screen, she immediately began a mobilization in the proper sense of the word.

To-day M. Paléologue telegraphed that Count Pourtalès had notified the Russian Government of German mobilization.

Information, which has been received by the Ministry of War, confirms the fact that this mobilization is really in full execution.

Our decree of mobilization is then an essential measure of protection. The Government has accompanied it by a proclamation signed by the President of the Republic and by all the Ministers, in which they explain that mobilization is not war, and that in the present state of affairs it is the best means for France of safeguarding peace, and that the Government of the Republic will redouble their efforts to bring the negotiations to a conclusion.

Will you be good enough to bring all these points urgently to the notice of Sir Edward Grey, and to point out to him that we have throughout been governed by the determination not to commit any act of provocation?

I am persuaded that in case war were to break out, British opinion would see clearly from which side aggression comes, and that it would realize the strong reasons which we have given to Sir Edward Grey for asking for armed intervention on the part of England in the interest of the future of the European balance of power.

RENÉ VIVIANI.

No. 128.
M. Bollard, French Minister at Luxemburg, to M. René Viviani, President of the Council, Minister for Foreign Affairs.
Luxemburg
August 1, 1914.

The Minister of State instructs me to ask from the French Government an assurance of neutrality similar to that, which has been given to Belgium. M. Eyschen has stated that at present, as the declaration in question was made to the President of the Council of the Belgian Government by the French Minister at Brussels, he thought that the same procedure would be most suitable with regard to the Grand Duchy.

This is the reason why he has abstained from making a request direct to the Government of the Republic. As the Chamber of Deputies meets on Monday, M. Eyschen wishes to have the answer by that date; a similar *démarche* is being made at the same time with the German Minister at Luxemburg.
MOLLARD.

No. 129.
M. René Viviani, President of the Council, Minister for Foreign Affairs, to M. Mollard, French Minister at Luxemburg.
Paris
August 1, 1914.

Be good enough to state to the President of the Council that in conformity with the Treaty of London, 1867, the Government of the Republic intends to respect the neutrality of the Grand Duchy of Luxemburg, as they have shown by their attitude.

The violation of this neutrality by Germany would, however, be an act of a kind, which would compel France from that time to be guided in this matter by care for her defense and her interests.
RENÉ VIVIANI.

No. 130.
M. Jules Cambon, French Ambassador at Berlin, to M. René Viviani, President of the Council, Minister for Foreign Affairs.
Berlin
August 1, 1914.

Special editions of newspapers are being distributed in the streets of Berlin announcing that the general mobilization of the army and the navy has been decreed and that the first day of the mobilization is Sunday, 2nd August.
JULES CAMBON.

Primary Documents: Germany's Declaration of War with Russia, 1 August 1914
Presented by the German Ambassador to St. Petersburg

The Imperial German Government has used every effort since the beginning of the crisis to bring about a peaceful settlement. In compliance with a wish expressed to him by His Majesty the Emperor of Russia, the German Emperor had undertaken, in concert with Great Britain, the part of mediator between the Cabinets of Vienna and St. Petersburg; but Russia, without waiting for any result, proceeded to a general mobilization of her forces both on land and sea.

In consequence of this threatening step, which was not justified by any military proceedings on the part of Germany, the German Empire was faced by a grave and imminent danger. If the German

Government had failed to guard against this peril, they would have compromised the safety and the very existence of Germany.

The German Government was, therefore, obliged to make representations to the Government of His Majesty the Emperor of All the Russia and to insist upon a cessation of the previously mentioned military acts. Russia having refused to comply with this demand, and having shown by this refusal that her action was directed against Germany, I have the honor, on the instructions of my Government, to inform your Excellency as follows:

His Majesty the Emperor, my august Sovereign, in the name of the German Empire, accepts the challenge, and considers himself at war with Russia.

Colonel House to President Wilson
Prides Crossing, Massachusetts
August 1, 1914.

Dear Governor:

There are one or two things that would perhaps be of interest to you at this time and which I shall tell you now and not wait until I see you. Sir Edward Grey told me that England had no written agreement with either Russia or France, or any formal alliance; that the situation was brought about by a mutual desire for protection and that they discussed international mattered with as much freedom with one another as if they had an actual written alliance.

The great danger is that some overt act may occur which will get the situation out of control. Germany is exceedingly nervous and at high tension, and she knows that her best chance of success is to strike quickly and hard; therefore her very alarm might cause her to precipitate action as a means of safety.

Please let me suggest to you do not let Mr. Bryan make any overtures to any of the powers involved. They look upon him, as absolutely visionary, and it would lessen the weight of your influence if you desire to use it yourself later....

If I thought I could live through the heat, I would go to Washington to see you; but I am afraid if I reached there, I would be utterly helpless. I wish you could get time to take the *Mayflower* and cruise for a few days in these waters so that I might join you.

Your faithful and affectionate,
E.M. House

Here one can see the British absolutely lied to a representative to the President of the United States. In fact, Britain was a signatory of the Triple Entente of 1907. And since 1891, France has put together a military plan to not only destroy Germany but divide Germany up between France, Russia, and England. This plan was formalized in 1913. There was other secrets dealing with France and Russia that England is not telling E.M. House.

Herr Zimmerman to Colonel House

Berlin
August 1, 1914.

My dear Colonel;
I beg to inform you that I laid the letter which you addressed to his Majesty the Emperor from London before his Majesty. I'm directed to convey to you his Majesty's sincere thanks, the Emperor

took note of its content with the greatest interest. Alas, all his strong and sincere efforts to conserve peace have entirely failed. I'm afraid that the Russians procedure will force the old world and especially my country in the most terrible war! There is no chance now to discuss the possibility of an understanding, so much desired, which would lay the foundation for permanent peace and security.

With assurances of my high regard, I remain, my dear colonel.

Sincerely Yours,
Zimmerman

Chapter Thirty-Four
August 2, 1914

No. 144.
Sir E. Goschen, British Ambassador at Berlin, to Sir Edward Grey.
Berlin
August 2, 1914.
(Telegraphic)
Secretary of State has just informed me that, owing to certain Russian Troops having crossed Frontier, Germany and Russia are now in a State of War.

No. 145.
Sir E. Goschen, British Ambassador at Berlin, to Sir Edward Grey.
Berlin
August 2, 1914.
(Telegraphic)
My telegram of August 1st.

Secretary of State informs me that orders were sent last night to allow British ships in Hamburg to proceed on their way. He says that this must be regarded as a special favor to His Majesty's Government, as no other foreign ships have been allowed to leave. Reason of detention was that mines were being laid and other precautions being taken.

Announcement by the Russian Minister for Foreign Affairs respecting Recent Events.
August 2, 1914.
A GARBLED version of the events of the last few days having appeared in the foreign press, the Russian Minister for Foreign Affairs considers it his duty to publish the following brief account of the diplomatic discussions during the period under review:

On the 23rd July, 1914, the Austro-Hungarian Minister at Belgrade presented a note to the Prime Minister of Serbia, in which the Serbian Government was accused of having fostered the pan-Serb movement, which had led to the assassination of the heir to the Austro-Hungarian throne. Austria-Hungary, therefore, demanded of the Serbian Government, not only the condemnation in the most formal manner of the above-mentioned propaganda, but also the adoption, under Austrian supervision, of a series of measures for the discovery of the plot, for the punishment of any Serbian subjects who had taken part in it, and for the prevention of any future attempts at assassination upon Austrian soil A time limit of forty-eight hours was given to the Serbian Government within which to reply to this note. The Russian Government, to whom the Austro-Hungarian Ambassador at St. Petersburg had communicated the text of the note seventeen hours after its presentation at Belgrade having taken note of the demands contained therein, could not but perceive that some of these demands were impossible of execution as regards their substance, whilst others were presented in a form which was incompatible with the dignity of an independent State. Russia considered that the humiliation of Serbia, involved in these demands, and equally the evident intention of Austria-Hungary to secure her own hegemony in the Balkans, which underlay her conditions, were inadmissible. The Russian Government, therefore, pointed out to Austria-Hungary in the most friendly manner that it would be desirable to re-examine the points contained in the Austro-Hungarian note. The Austro-Hungarian Government did not see their way to agree to a discussion of the note. The moderating influence of the four Powers at Vienna was equally unsuccessful. Despite the fact that Serbia had reprobated the crime, and had shown herself ready to give Austria satisfaction to an extent beyond the expectations, not only of Russia, but also of the other Powers despite these facts, the Austro-Hungarian Minister at Belgrade considered the Serbian reply insufficient and left the town. Recognising the exaggerated nature of the demands made by Austria, Russia had previously declared that she could not remain indifferent, while not desisting from doing her utmost to find a peaceful issue which might prove acceptable to Austria, and spare the latter's self-respect as a Great Power. At the same time, Russia let it be clearly understood that she could accept a peaceful settlement of the question only so far as it involved no humiliation of Serbia as an independent State. Unhappily, all the efforts of the Russian Government to this end were fruitless. The Austro-Hungarian Government, which had shunned any attempt at conciliatory intervention by the Powers in the Austrian dispute with Serbia, proceeded to mobilize and declared war officially against Serbia, and the following day Belgrade was bombarded. The manifesto, which accompanied the declaration of war openly, accuses Serbia of having prepared and carried out the crime of Sarajevo. Such an accusation of a crime at common law, launched against a whole people and a whole State, aroused, by its evident inanity, widespread sympathy for Serbia throughout all classes of European society. In consequence of this behavior of the Austro-Hungarian Government, in spite of Russia's declaration that she could not remain indifferent to the fate of Serbia, the Russian Government considered it necessary to order mobilization in the military districts of Kieff, Odessa, Moscow, and Kazan. This decision was rendered necessary by the fact that since the date when the Austro-Hungarian note was communicated to the Serbian Government, and since the first steps taken by Russia, five days had elapsed, and yet the Vienna Cabinet had not taken one step to meet Russia halfway in her efforts towards peace. Indeed, quite the contrary; for the mobilization of half of the Austro-Hungarian army had been ordered. The German Government was kept informed of the steps taken by Russia. At the same time, it was explained to them that these steps were only the result of the Austrian preparations, and that they were not in any way aimed at Germany.

Simultaneously, the Russian Government declared that Russia was ready to continue discussions with a view to a peaceful settlement of the dispute, either in the form of direct negotiations with Vienna or, as suggested by Great Britain, in the form of a conference of the four Great Powers not directly interested, that is to say, Great Britain, France, Germany, and Italy.

This attempt on the part of Russia was, however, equally unsuccessful. Austria-Hungary declined a further exchange of views with Russia, and the Vienna Cabinet was unwilling to join the proposed conference of the Powers.

Nevertheless, Russia did not abandon her efforts for peace.

When questioned by the German Ambassador as to the conditions on which we would still agree to suspend our preparations, the Minister for Foreign Affairs declared that these conditions were Austria's recognition that the Austro-Serbian question had assumed a European character, and a declaration by her that she agreed not to insist upon such of her demands as were incompatible with the sovereign rights of Serbia. Germany considered this Russian proposal unacceptable to Austria-Hungary. At that, very moment news of the proclamation of general mobilization by Austria-Hungary reached St. Petersburg. All this time hostilities were continuing on Serbian territory, and Belgrade was bombarded afresh. The failure of our proposals for peace compelled us to extend the scope of our precautionary military measures. The Berlin Cabinet questioned us on this, and we replied that Russia was compelled to begin preparations so as to be ready for every emergency. But while taking this precautionary step, Russia did not on that account abandon her strenuous efforts to find some solution of the situation, and she announced that she was ready to accept any proposed settlement of the problem that might be put forward, provided it complied with the conditions laid down by her.

In spite of this conciliatory communication, the German Government on the 31st July demanded of the Russian Government that they should suspend their military measures by midday on the 1st August, and threatened, should they fall to comply, to proceed to general mobilization. On the following day, the 1st August, the German Ambassador, on behalf of his Government, forwarded a declaration of war to the Minister for Foreign Affairs.

No. 146.
Sir F. Villiers, British Minister at Brussels, to Sir Edward Grey.
Brussels
August 2, 1914.
(Telegraphic)

The news that a German force has entered Grand Duchy of Luxemburg has been officially confirmed to the Belgian government.

No. 129.
Minister of State, Luxemburg, to Sir Edward Grey.
Luxemburg
August 2, 1914.

(Telegraphic)

The Luxemburg Minister of State, Eyshen, has just received through the German Minister in Luxemburg, M. de Buch, a telegram from the Chancellor of the German Empire, Bethmann-Hollweg, to the effect that the military measures taken in Luxemburg, do not constitute a hostile act against Luxemburg, but are only intended to insure against a possible of the French army. Full compensation will be paid to Luxemburg for any damages caused by using the railways, which are leased to the Empire.

No. 147.
Minister of State, Luxemburg, to Sir Edward Grey.
Luxemburg
August 2, 1914.
(Telegraphic)

I have the honor to bring to your Excellency's notice the following note:

On Sunday, the 2nd August, very early, the German troops, according to the information which has up to now reached the Grand Ducal Government, penetrated into Luxemburg territory by bridges of Wasserbillig and Remich, and proceeded particularly towards the south and in the direction

Luxemburg, the Capital of the Grand Duchy. A certain number of armored trains with troops and ammunition have been sent along the railway line from Wasserbillig to Luxemburg, where their arrival is expected. These occurrences constitute acts, which are manifestly contrary to the neutrality of the Grand Duchy as guaranteed by the Treaty of London of 1867. The Luxemburg Government has not failed to address an energetic protest against this aggression to the representatives of his Majesty's the German Emperor at Luxemburg. An identical protest will be sent by telegraph to the Secretary of State for Foreign Affairs at Berlin.

This incursion by Germany into Luxemburg could be the result of doing an end round military maneuver to get behind French forces that have penetrated the German frontier to blow up and destroy railway tunnels and tracks that led from Germany straight into France. Due to the heavy region of mountains, military maneuver is very limited between Germany and France. At the same time this incursion is taking place, Russian troops are trying to blow up and destroy the same kind of targets in eastern Germany as well.

No. 78.
Russian Minister for Foreign Affairs to Russian Representatives Abroad.
St. Petersburg
August 2, 1914.
(Telegraphic)

IT is quite evident that Germany is now doing her utmost to foist upon us the responsibility for the rupture. We were forced to mobilize by the immense responsibility, which would have fallen upon our shoulders if we had not taken: all possible precautionary measures at a time when Austria, while confining herself to discussions of a dilatory nature, was bombarding Belgrade and was undertaking general mobilization. The Emperor of Russia had promised the German Emperor that he would take no aggressive action as long as the discussions with Austria continued. With such a guarantee, and after so many proofs of Russia's desire for peace, Germany neither could, nor had the right to, doubt our declaration that we would joyfully accept any peaceful settlement compatible with the dignity and independence of Serbia. Any other solution, besides being entirely incompatible with our own dignity, would assuredly have upset the European balance of power by securing the hegemony of Germany. The European nay, the worldwide character of this dispute is infinitely more important than the pretext from which it springs. By her decision to declare war upon us, at a moment when negotiations were in progress between the Powers, Germany has assumed a heavy responsibility.

No. 148.
Sir Edward Grey to Sir F. Bertie, British Ambassador at Paris.
Foreign office
August 2, 1914.
(Telegraphic)

After the Cabinet this morning, I gave M. Cambon the following memorandum:

I am authorized to give an assurance that, if the German Fleet comes into the Channel or through the North Sea to undertake hostile operations against French coasts or shipping, the British Fleet will give all the protection in its power.

This assurance is of course subject to the policy of his Majesty's Government receiving support of the Parliament, and must not be taken as binding His Majesty's Government to take any action until the above contingency of action by the German fleet takes place.

I pointed out that we had a very large question and most difficult issue to consider, and that government felt that they could not bind themselves to declare war upon Germany necessarily if war broke out between France and Germany tomorrow, but it was essential to the French Government, whose fleet had long been concentrated in the Mediterranean, to know how to make their dispositions with their north coast entirely undefended. We therefore thought it necessary to give them this assurance. It did not bind us to go to war with Germany unless German fleet took action indicated, but it did give a security to France that would enable her to settle the disposition of her own Mediterranean fleet.

M. Cambon asked me about violation of Luxemburg. I told him the doctrine on that point laid down by Lord Derby and Lord Clarendon in 1867. He asked me what we should say about the violation of the neutrality of Belgium. I said that was a much more important matter; we were considering what statement we should make in Parliament tomorrow—in effect, whether we should declare violation of Belgian neutrality to be *casus belli*. I told him what had been said to the German Ambassador on this point.

Though it was Belgium who violated the Treaty of London of 1839 by seizing German merchant ships and their cargo, Germany makes a mistake by not bringing this up.

No. 19.
M. Davignon, Belgian Minister for Foreign Affairs, to Belgian Ministers at Paris, Berlin, London, Vienna, and St. Petersburg.
Brussels
August 2, 1914.

Sir,
I was careful to warn the German Minister through M. de Bassompierre that an announcement in the Brussels press by M. Klobukowski, French Minister, would make public the formal declaration, which the latter had made to me on the 1st August. When I next met Herr von Below, he thanked me for this attention, and added that up to the present he had not been instructed to make us an official communication, but that we knew his personal opinion as to the feelings of security, which we had the right to entertain towards our eastern neighbors. I at once replied that all that we knew of their intentions, as indicated in numerous previous conversations, did not allow us to doubt their perfect correctness towards Belgium. I added, however, that we should attach the greatest importance to the possession of a formal declaration, which the Belgian nation would hear of with joy and gratitude.

No. 149.
Sir Edward Grey to Sir Goschen, British Ambassador at Berlin.
Foreign Office
August 2, 1914.
(Telegraphic)

Your telegram of August 1st.
I regret to learn that 100 tons of sugar was compulsorily unloaded from British Steamships "Sappho" at Hamburg and detained.
Similar action appears to have taken with regard to other British vessels loaded with sugar.
You should inform secretary of state that, for reasons stated in my telegram of Aug 1st[67], I most earnestly trust that the orders already sent to Hamburg to allow the clearance of British ships covers also the release of their cargoes, the detention of which cannot be justified.

---

[67] See No. 130.

No. 20.
Note presented by Herr von Below Saleske, German Minister at Brussels, to M. Davignon, Belgian Minister for Foreign Affairs.
Kaiserlich Deutsche Gesandtschaft in Belgien-Brüssel, den 2. August 1914.
Imperial German Legation in Belgium-Brussels, August 2, 1914.

(Translation. Very Confidential.)

Reliable information has been received by the Imperial Government to the effect that French forces intend to march on the line of the Meuse by Givet and Namur. This information leaves no doubt as to the intention of France to march through Belgian territory against Germany.

The Imperial Government cannot but fear that Belgium, in spite of the utmost goodwill, will be unable, without assistance, to repel so considerable a French invasion with sufficient prospect of success to afford an adequate guarantee against danger to Germany. It is essential for the self-defense of Germany that she should anticipate any such hostile attack. The German Government would, however, feel the deepest regret if Belgium regarded as an act of hostility against herself the fact that the measures of Germany's opponents force Germany, for her own protection, to enter Belgian territory.

In order to exclude any possibility of misunderstanding, the German Government makes the following declaration:

1. Germany has in view no act of hostility against Belgium. In the event of Belgium being prepared in the coming war to maintain an attitude of friendly neutrality towards Germany, the German Government binds themselves, at the conclusion of peace, to guarantee the possessions and independence of the Belgian Kingdom in full.
2. Germany undertakes, under the above-mentioned condition, to evacuate Belgian territory on the conclusion of peace.
3. If Belgium adopts a friendly attitude, Germany is prepared, in co-operation with the Belgian authorities, to purchase all necessaries for her troops against a cash payment, and to pay an indemnity for any damage that may have been caused by German troops.
4. Should Belgium oppose the German troops, and in particular should she throw difficulties in the way of their march by a resistance of the fortresses on the Meuse, or by destroying railways, roads, tunnels, or other similar works, Germany will, to her regret, be compelled to consider Belgium as an enemy.

In this event, Germany can undertake no obligations towards Belgium, but the eventual adjustment of the relations between the two States must be left to the decision of arms.

The Imperial Government, however, entertains the distinct hope that this eventuality will not occur, and that the Belgian Government will know how to take the necessary measures to prevent the occurrence of incidents such as those mentioned. In this case, the friendly ties, which bind the two neighboring States, will grow stronger and more enduring.

No. 19.
M. Eyschen, Minister of State for Luxemburg, to M. René Viviani, President of the Council, Minister for Foreign Affairs.
Luxemburg
August 2, 1914.

I have the honor to bring to your Excellency's notice the following facts:

On Sunday, 2 August, very early, German troops. According to the information, which has up to now reached the Grand Ducal Government, penetrated into Luxemburg territory by the bridges of Wasserbillig and Remich, and preceded particularly towards the south and in the direction of Luxemburg, the capital of the Grand Duchy. A certain number of armored trains with troops and ammunition have been sent along the railway line from Wasserbillig to Lusemburg, where their arrival is expected. These occurrences constitute acts, which are manifestly contrary to the neutrality of the Grand Duchy as guaranteed by the Treaty of London of 1867. The Luxemburg Government has not failed to address an energetic protest against this aggression to the representatives of His Majesty the German Emperor at Luxemburg. An identical protest will be sent by telegraph to the Secretary of State for Foreign Affairs at Berlin.

The Minister of State,
President of the Government.
EYSCHEN.

No. 132.
M. Mollard, French Minister at Luxemburg, to M. René Viviani, President of the Council, Minister for Foreign Affairs.
Luxemburg
August 2, 1914.

The Minister of State for Luxemburg, M. Eyschen, has just received, through Herr von Buch, German Minister at Luxemburg, a telegram from Bethmann-Hollweg, Chancellor of the German Empire, saying that the military measures taken by Germany in Luxemburg do not constitute a hostile act against this country, but are solely measures tended to assure the use of the railways which have been leased to the Empire against the eventual attack of a French army. Luxemburg will receive a complete indemnity for any damage.
MOLLARD.

No. 133.
Note handed in by the German Ambassador.
Paris
August 2, 1914.

The German Ambassador has just been instructed, and hastens to inform the Minister for Foreign Affairs, that the Military measures taken by Germany in the Grand Duchy of Luxemburg do not constitute an act of hostility. They must be considered as purely preventive measures taken for the protection of the railways, which, under the treaties between Germany and the Grand Duchy of Luxemburg, are under German administration.
VON SCHOEN.

No. 134.
M. Paléologue, French Ambassador at St. Petersburgh, to M. René Viviani, President of the Council, Minister for Foreign Affairs.
St. Petersburgh
August 2, 1914.

Yesterday at ten minutes past seven in the evening the German Ambassador handed to M. Sazonof a declaration of war by his Government; he will leave St. Petersburgh to-day. The Austro-Hungarian Ambassador has not received any instructions from his Government as to the declaration of war.
PALÉOLOGUE.

No. 135.
M. René Viviani, President of the Council, Minister for Foreign Affairs, to the Representatives of France abroad.
Paris
August 2, 1914.

The Russian Ambassador informs me that Germany has just declared war on Russia, notwithstanding the negotiations, which are proceeding, and at a moment when Austria-Hungary was agreeing to discuss with the Powers even the basis of her conflict with Serbia.
RENÉ VIVIANI.

No. 136.
M. René Viviani, President of the Council, Minister for Foreign Affairs, to the French Ambassadors at London, St. Petersburgh, Berlin, Vienna, Rome, Madrid, and Constantinople.
Paris
August 2, 1914.

This morning, French territory was violated by German troops at Ciry and near Longwy. They are marching on the fort, which bears the latter name. Elsewhere the Custom House at Delle has twice been fired upon. Finally, German troops have also violated this morning the neutral territory of Luxemburg.

You will at once use this information to lay stress on the fact that the German Government is committing itself to acts of war against France without provocation on our part, or any previous declaration of war, whilst we have scrupulously respected the zone of ten kilometers which we have maintained, even since the mobilization, between our troops and the frontier.
RENÉ VIVIANI.

No. 137.
M. Paul Cambon, French Ambassador at London, to M. René Viviani, President of the Council, Minister for Foreign Affairs.
London
August 2, 1914.

After the meeting of the Cabinet held this morning, Sir Edward Grey made the following declaration to me:

"I am authorized to give an assurance that, if the German fleet come into the Channel or through the North Sea to undertake hostile operations against French coasts or shipping, the British fleet will give all the protection in its power.

"This assurance is of course subject to the policy of His Majesty's Government receiving the support of Parliament, and must not be taken as binding His Majesty's Government to take any action until the above contingency of action by the German fleet takes place."

Afterwards in speaking to me of the neutrality of Belgium and that of Luxemburg, the Secretary of State reminded me that the Convention of 1867, referring to the Grand Duchy, differed from the Treaty referring to Belgium, in that Great Britain was bound to require the observance of this latter (convention without the assistance of the other guaranteeing Powers, while with regard to Luxemburg all the guaranteeing Powers were to act in concert).

The protection of Belgian neutrality is here considered so important that Great Britain will regard its violation by Germany as a *casus belli*. It is an especially British interest and there is no doubt that the British Government, faithful to the traditions of their policy, will insist upon it, even if the business world in which German influence is making tenacious efforts, exercises pressure to prevent the Government committing itself against Germany.
PAUL CAMBON.

No. 138.
M. René Viviani, President of the Council, Minister for Foreign Affairs, to M. Paul Cambon, French Ambassador at London.
Paris
August 2, 1914.

I note the points contained in your telegrams of the 27th, 30th, 31st July and the 1st August, and in that which you have sent to me to-day.

In communicating to the Chambers the declaration, which Sir Edward Grey has made to you, the text of which is contained in your last telegram, I will add that in it we have obtained from Great Britain a first assistance, which is most valuable to us.

In addition, I propose to indicate that the help which Great Britain intends to give to France for the protection of the French coasts or the French merchant marine, will be used in such a way that our navy will also, in case of a Franco-German conflict, be supported by the British fleet in the Atlantic as well as in the North Sea and Channel. In addition, I would note that British ports could not serve as places for revictualling for the German fleet.
RENÉ VIVIANI.

No. 139.
M. René Viviani, President of the Council, Minister for Foreign Affairs, to M. Jules Cambon, French Ambassador at Berlin.
Paris
August 2, 1914.

German troops having to-day violated the eastern frontier at several points I request you immediately to protest in writing to the German Government. You will be good enough to take as your text the following note which, in the uncertainty of communications between Paris and Berlin, I have addressed directly to the German Ambassador:

"The French administrative and military authorities in the eastern district have just reported several acts which I have instructed the Ambassador of the Republic at Berlin to bring to the knowledge of the Imperial Government.

"The first has taken place at Delle in the district of Belfort; on two occasions the French Customs station in this locality has been fired upon by a detachment of German soldiers. North of Delle two

German patrols of the 5th mounted Jaegers crossed the frontier this morning and advanced to the villages of Joncherey and Baron, more than ten kilometers from the frontier. The officer who commanded the first has blown out the brains of a French soldier. The German cavalry carried off some horses, which the French mayor of Suarce was collecting and forced the inhabitants of the commune to lead the said horses.

"The Ambassador of the Republic at Berlin has been instructed to make a formal protest to the Imperial Government against acts which form a flagrant violation of the frontier by German troops in arms, and which are not justified by anything in the present situation. The Government of the Republic can only leave to the Imperial Government the entire responsibility for these acts."
RENÉ VIVIANI.

No. 20.
M. Eyschen, President of the Luxemburg Government, to M. Davignon, Belgian Minister for Foreign Affairs.
Luxemburg
August 2, 1914.
(Telegraphic)

I have the honor to acquaint your Excellency with the following facts: On Sunday, the 2nd August, very early, the German troops, according to the information which has up to now reached the Grand Ducal Government, penetrated into Luxemburg territory by the bridges of Wasserbillig and Remich and proceeded particularly towards the south and in the direction of Luxemburg, the capital of the Grand Duchy. A certain number of armored trains with troops and ammunition have been sent along the railway line from Wasserbillig to Luxemburg, where their arrival is expected. These occurrences constitute acts, which are manifestly contrary to the neutrality of the Grand Duchy as guaranteed by the Treaty of London of 1867. The Luxemburg Government has not failed to address an energetic protest against this aggression to the representatives of His Majesty the German Emperor at Luxemburg. An identical protest will be sent by telegraph to the Secretary of State for Foreign Affairs at Berlin.

No. 19.
M. Davignon, Belgian Minister for Foreign Affairs, to Belgian Ministers at Paris, Berlin, London, Vienna, and St. Petersburg.
Brussels
August 2, 1914.

Sir,

I was careful to warn the German Minister through M. de Bassompierre that an announcement in the Brussels press by M. Klobukowski, French Minister, would make public the formal declaration, which the latter had made to me on the 1st August. When I next met, Herr von Below he thanked me for this attention, and added that up to the present he had not been instructed to make us an official communication, but that we knew his personal opinion as to the feelings of security, which we had the right to entertain towards our eastern neighbors. I at once replied that all that we knew of their intentions, as indicated in numerous previous conversations, did not allow us to doubt their perfect correctness towards Belgium. I added, however, that we should attach the greatest importance to the possession of a formal declaration, which the Belgian nation would hear of with joy and gratitude.

Primary Documents: Turco-German Alliance, 2 August 1914

Reproduced below are the terms of the military alliance arrived at between Turkey and Germany on 2 August 1914. Details of the alliance remained a secret with the consequence that Turkey's eventual entrance into the war at the end of October 1914 proved something of a disappointment (if not entirely a surprise) to the .

Constantinople, August 2, 1914

1. The two contracting parties agree to observe strict neutrality in regard to the present conflict between Austria-Hungary and Serbia.
2. In case Russia should intervene with active military measures, and should thus bring about a *casus foederis* for Germany with relation to Austria-Hungary, this *casus foederis* would also come into existence for Turkey.
3. In case of war, Germany will leave her military mission at the disposal of Turkey. The latter, for her part, assures the said military mission an effective influence on the general conduct of the army, in accordance with the understanding arrived at directly between His Excellency the Minister of War and His Excellency the Chief of the Military Mission.
4. Germany obligates herself, if necessary by force of arms Ottoman territory in case it should be threatened.
5. This agreement which has been concluded for the purpose of protecting both Empires from international complications which may result from the present conflict goes into force as soon as it is signed by the above-mentioned plenipotentiaries, and shall remain valid, together with any similar mutual agreements, until December 31, 1918.
6. In case it shall not be denounced by one of the high contracting parties six months before the expiration of the term named above, this treaty shall remain in force for a further period of five years.
7. This present document shall be ratified by His Majesty the German Emperor, King of Prussia, and His Majesty shall exchange the Emperor of the Ottomans and the ratifications within a period of one month from the date of its signing.
8. The present treaty shall remain secret and can only be made public as a result of an agreement arrived at between the two high contracting parties.

> In testimony whereof, etc.
> Baron von Wangenheim (for Germany)
> Said Halim (for Turkey)

Primary Documents: German Request for Free Passage through Belgium, and the Belgian Response, 2–3 August 1914
Updated: Sunday, 14 April 2002

On 2 August 1914, the day before Germany declared war on France, the German government wrote to the Belgian government demanding the right of free passage across Belgium for its troops, so that the latter could most efficiently invade France and reach Paris.

Belgium's reply to what amounted to a German ultimatum (grant free passage or suffer occupation as an enemy of Germany) was delivered on 3 August 1914. It was a clear refusal of free passage.

On the same day as the Belgian reply Germany declared war on France; the former invaded Belgium the next day, which resulted in Britain's entry into the war to defend Belgian neutrality.

Germany to Belgium

Delivered by the German Ambassador at Brussels von Below Saleske, to M. Davignon, Belgian Minister for Foreign Affairs

2 August 1914.

Very Confidential

Reliable information has been received by the German Government to the effect that French forces intend to march on the line of the Meuse by Givet and Namur. This information leaves no doubt as to the intention of France to march through Belgian territory against Germany.

The German Government cannot but fear that Belgium, in spite of the utmost goodwill, will be unable, without assistance, to repel so considerable a French invasion with sufficient prospect of success to afford an adequate guarantee against danger to Germany.

It is essential for the self-defense of Germany that she should anticipate any such hostile attack. The German Government would, however, feel the deepest regret if Belgium regarded as an act of hostility against herself the fact that the measures of Germany's opponents force Germany, for her own protection, to enter Belgian territory.

In order to exclude any possibility of misunderstanding, the German Government makes the following declaration:

1. Germany has in view no act of hostility against Belgium. In the event of Belgium being prepared in the coming war to maintain an attitude of friendly neutrality towards Germany, the German Government binds themselves, at the conclusion of peace, to guarantee the possessions and independence of the Belgian Kingdom in full.
2. Germany undertakes, under the above-mentioned condition, to evacuate Belgian territory on the conclusion of peace.
3. If Belgium adopts a friendly attitude, Germany is prepared, in cooperation with the Belgian authorities, to purchase all necessaries for her troops against a cash payment, and to pay an indemnity for any damage that may have been caused by German troops.
4. Should Belgium oppose the German troops, and in particular should she throw difficulties in the way of their march by a resistance of the fortresses on the Meuse, or by destroying railways, roads, tunnels, or other similar works, Germany will, to her regret, be compelled to consider Belgium as an enemy.

In this event, Germany can undertake no obligations towards Belgium, but the eventual adjustment of the relations between the two States must be left to the decision of arms.
The German Government, however, entertain the distinct hope that this eventuality will not occur, and that the Belgian Government will know how to take the necessary measures to prevent the occurrence of incidents such as those mentioned. In this case, the friendly ties, which bind the two neighboring States, will grow stronger and more enduring.

Chapter Thirty-Five
August 3, 1914

No. 539.
German Embassy to Sir Wm. Tyrrell (Foreign Office).
(Received August 3, 1914)
London
August 3, 1914.

Dear Sir William,
I herewith beg to hand to you the translation of the two telegrams, which I had the pleasure of reading to you this morning.

Believe me,
Yours faithfully,
WESENDONK.

Enclosures in No. 539.
(1.)
German Embassy, London, August 2nd (1)
According to absolutely certain news, France has committed the following acts against Germany:

1. A patrol of French cavalry has passed this morning the frontier near Alt-Muensterol, in Alsatia.
2. A French aviator has been shot whilst flying over German territory.
3. Two Frenchmen have been shot whilst attempting to blow up the tunnel near Cochem on the Moselle Railway.
4. French infantry have passed the Alsatian frontier and have opened fire.

These incidents have occurred although the French Prime Minister has officially assured the Imperial Ambassador in Paris that the mobilisation of the French army had no aggressive character against Germany and the French troops had been instructed to respect a 10-kilom zone on the German boundary.

Please notify these facts to the British Government, who will surely understand, into what a perilous position Germany has been brought through such disloyal provocations and what serious decisions have been forced upon her.

Great Britain will no doubt recognize that Germany has done her utmost to preserve peace and the provocation of her enemies have forced her to take up the arms in order to maintain her existence.

(1) The telegram was however dispatched from Berlin at 12, 25 A.M. on August 3. (See DD No. 693.)

German Embassy (undated). (1)

During the negotiations for mediation Russia has mobilized her entire forces without notifying Germany officially of this step and without adding, that this measure was not directed against us, though Germany had previously declared in a friendly but utterly serious manner, that a mobilisation would force Germany to take grave counter steps and though Russia had repeatedly and most formally assured us that she had no intention against Germany.

It was only in the afternoon of the first day of the Russian mobilisation, that His Majesty the Tsar telegraphed to His Majesty the German Emperor, that he personally guaranteed that Russia would commit no hostile act against Germany. During the whole crisis the contrast between the undoubtedly sincere assurances of His Majesty the Tsar and the acts of the Government has been so clear, and the attitude taken by the Russian Government has been so openly unfriendly that notwithstanding the assurances of His Majesty the Tsar the mobilisation of the total Russian forces was bound to be a severe provocation to Germany. This appears to have been fully recognized by the Germanophile surroundings of His Majesty the Tsar.

The news of the Russian mobilisation has called forth such indignation in our public opinion, that the Russian refusal of our demand, to stop the mobilisation, had to be regarded as a hostile act involving the beginning of the state of war, if Germany did not want to abandon her national honour.

Moreover, the fact that Russian troops have opened fire on German soldiers on the frontier. Before Germany had made her last declarations, proves, that the so-called peaceful mobilisation is a state of affairs, which cannot be kept up.

(1) Dispatched from Berlin August 3, 12:55 A.M. (see DD No. 696).
These telegrams were communicated in English.

No. 150.
Sir E. Goschen, British Ambassador at Berlin, to Sir Edward Grey.
Berlin
August 3, 1914.
(Telegraphic)
Your telegram of August 2[nd68]: detention of British ships at Hamburg.
No information available.

No. 21.
Memorandum of an Interview asked for at 1.30 A.M., on August 3, by Herr von Below Saleske German Minister, with Baron van der Elst, Secretary-General to the Ministry for Foreign Affairs.

At 1.30 A.M., the German Minister asked to see Baron van der Elst. He told him that he had been instructed by his Government to inform the Belgian Government that French dirigibles had thrown

---

[68] See No. 149.

bombs, and that a French cavalry patrol had crossed the frontier in violation of international law, seeing that war had not been declared.

The Secretary-General asked Herr von Below where these incidents had happened, and was told that it was in Germany. Baron van der Elst then observed that in that case he could not understand the object of this communication. Herr von Below stated that these acts, which were contrary to international law, were calculated to lead to the supposition that other acts, contrary to international law, would be committed by France.

No. 22.
Note communicated by M. Davignon, Belgian Minister for Foreign Affairs, to Herr von Below Saleske, German Minister.
Brussels
August 3, 1914 (7 A.M.).

The German Government stated in their note of the 2nd August, 1914, that according to reliable information French forces intended to march on the Meuse via Givet and Namur, and that Belgium, in spite of the best intentions, would not be in a position to repulse, without assistance, an advance of French troops.

The German Government, therefore, considered themselves compelled to anticipate this attack and to violate Belgian territory. In these circumstances, Germany proposed to the Belgian Government to adopt a friendly attitude towards her, and undertook, on the conclusion of peace, to guarantee the integrity of the Kingdom and its possessions to their full extent. The note added that if Belgium put difficulties in the way of the advance of German troops, Germany would be compelled to consider her as an enemy, and to leave the ultimate adjustment of the relations between the two States to the decision of arms.

This note has made a deep and painful impression upon the Belgian Government. The intentions attributed to France by Germany are in contradiction to the formal declarations made to us on August 1, in the name of the French Government.

Moreover, if, contrary to our expectation, Belgian neutrality should be violated by France, Belgium intends to fulfill her international obligations and the Belgian army would offer the most vigorous resistance to the invader.

The treaties of 1839, confirmed by the treaties of 1870, vouch for the independence and neutrality of Belgium under the guarantee of the Powers, and notably of the Government of His Majesty the King of Prussia.

Belgium has always been faithful to her international obligations, she has carried out her duties in a spirit of loyal impartiality, and she has left nothing undone to maintain and enforce respect for her neutrality.

The attack upon her independence with which the German Government threaten her constitutes a flagrant violation of international law. No strategic interest justifies such a violation of law.

The Belgian Government, if they were to accept the proposals submitted to them, would sacrifice the honour of the nation and betray their duty towards Europe.

Conscious of the part, which Belgium has played for more than eighty years in the civilization of the world, they refuse to believe that the independence of Belgium can only be preserved at the price of the violation of her neutrality.

If this hope is disappointed the Belgian Government is firmly resolved to repel, by all the means in their power, every attack upon their rights.

No. 23.
M. Davignon, Belgian Minister for Foreign Affairs, to the Belgian Ministers at St. Petersburg, Berlin, London, Paris, Vienna, The Hague.
Brussels
August 3, 1914.
(Telegraphic)

At 7 P.M. last night, Germany presented a note proposing friendly neutrality. This entailed free passage through Belgian territory, while guaranteeing the maintenance of the independence of Belgium and of her possessions on the conclusion of peace, and threatened, in the event of refusal, to treat Belgium as an enemy a time limit of twelve hours was allowed within which to reply.

Our answer has been that this infringement of our neutrality would be a flagrant violation of international law. To accept the German proposal would be to sacrifice the honour of the nation. Conscious of her duty, Belgium is firmly resolved to repel any attack by all the means in her power.

No. 151.
Sir Villiers, British Minister at Brussels, to Sir Edward Grey.
Brussels
August 3, 1914.
(Telegraphic)

French Government has offered through military attaché the support of five French army corps to the Belgian Government. Following reply has been sent today:

"We are sincerely grateful to the French government for offering eventual support. In the actual circumstances, however, we do not propose to appeal to the guarantee of the Power. Belgian Government will decide later on the action, which they may think it necessary to take."

No. 24.
M. Davignon, Belgian Minister for Foreign Affairs, to the Belgian Ministers at Paris, Berlin, London, Vienna, St. Petersburg.
Brussels
August 3, 1914 (12 noon).

Sir,

As you are aware, Germany has delivered to Belgium an ultimatum which expires this morning, 3rd August, at 7 A.M. As no act of war has occurred up to the present, the Cabinet has decided that there is, for the moment, no need to appeal to the guaranteeing Powers.

The French Minister has made the following statement to me upon the subject:

> *"Sans être chargé d'une déclaration de mon Gouvernement, je crois cependant, m'inspirant de ses intentions connues, pouvoir dire que si le Gouvernement Royal faisait appel au Gouvernement francais, commep Puissance garante de sa neutralité, nous répondrions immédiatemeIlt à son appel; si cet appel n'était pas forrnulé, il est probable, à moins bien entendu que le souci de sa propre défense ne détermine des mesures exceptionnelles, qu'il attendra pour intervenir que la Belgique ait fait un acte de résistance effective."*

Translation:
"Although I have received no instructions to make a declaration from my Government, I feel justified, in view of their well-known intentions, in saying that if the Belgian Government were to appeal

to the French Government as one of the Powers guaranteeing their neutrality, the French Government would at once respond to Belgium's appeal; if such an appeal were not made it is probable, that—unless of course exceptional measures were rendered necessary in self-defense—the French Government would not intervene until Belgium had taken some effective measure of resistance."

I thanked M. Klobukowski for the support which the French Government had been good enough to offer us in case of need, and I informed him that the Belgian Government were making no appeal at present to the guarantee of the Powers, and that they would decide later what ought to be done.

No. 152.
Sir Edward Grey to Sir F Bertie, British Ambassador at Paris.
Foreign Office
August 3, 1914.

Sir,

On the first instant, the French Ambassador made the following communication.

"In my reply to the German Government's intimation of the fact that an ultimatum had been presented to France and Russia and to the question as to what were the intentions of Italy, the Marquis di San Giuliano replied:

"'The war undertaken by Austria, and the consequences which might result, had, in the words of the German Ambassador himself, an aggressive object. Both were therefore in conflict with the purely defensive character of the triple Alliance, and in such circumstances Italy would remain neutral."

In making this communication, M. Cambon was instructed to lay stress upon the Italian declaration that the present war was not a defensive but an aggressive war, and that, for this reason, the *casus foederis* under the terms of the Triple Alliance did not arise.

No. 25.
His Majesty the King of the Belgians to His Majesty King George.
Brussels
August 3, 1914.
(Telegraphic)

Remembering the numerous proofs of your Majesty's friendship and that of your predecessor, and the friendly attitude of England in 1870 and the proof of friendship you have just given us again, I make a supreme appeal to the diplomatic intervention of your Majesty's Government to safeguard the integrity of Belgium.

No. 26.
Count de Lalaing, Belgian Minister at London, to M. Davignon, Belgian Minister for Foreign Affairs.
London
August 3, 1914.
(Telegraphic)

I showed your telegram to the Minister for Foreign Affairs, who has laid it before the Cabinet. The Minister for Foreign Affairs has informed me that if our neutrality is violated it means war with Germany.

Belgium to Germany

No. 26.
Count de Lalaing, Belgian Minister at London, to M. Davignon, Belgian Minister for Foreign Affairs.
London
August 3, 1914.
(Telegraphic)

I showed your telegram to the Minister for Foreign Affairs, who has laid it before the Cabinet. The Minister for Foreign Affairs has informed me that if our neutrality is violated it means war with Germany.
(See No. 23.)

M. Marcelin Pellet, French Minister at The Hague, to M. René Viviani, President of the Council, Minister for Foreign Affairs.
The Hague
August 3, 1914.

The German Minister called yesterday on the Minister for Foreign Affairs to explain the necessity under which, as he said, Germany was placed of violating the neutral territory of Luxemburg, adding that he would have a fresh communication to make to him to-day. He has now this morning announced the entry of German troops into Belgium in order, as he has explained, to prevent an occupation of that country by France.

PELLET.

No. 141.
M.Klobukowski, French Minister at Brussels, to M. René Viviani, President of the Council, Minister for Foreign Affairs.
Brussels
August 3, 1914.

Yesterday evening the German Minister handed to the Belgian Government an ultimatum stating that his Government, having learnt that the French were preparing for operations in the districts of Givet and of Namur, were compelled to take steps, the first of which was to invite the Belgian Government to inform them, within seven hours, if they were disposed to facilitate military operations in Belgium against France. In case of refusal, the fortune of war would decide.
The Government of the King answered that the information as to the French movements appeared to them to be inaccurate in view of the formal assurances which had been given by France, and were still quite recent; that Belgium, which since the; establishment of her Kingdom, has taken every care to assure the protection of her dignity and of her interests, and has devoted all her efforts to peaceful development of progress, strongly protests against any violation of her territory from whatever quarter it may come: and that, supposing the violation takes place, she will know how to defend with energy her neutrality, which has been guaranteed by the Powers, and notably by the King of Prussia.
KLOBUKOWSKI.

No. 142.
M. Klobukowski, French Minister at Brussels, to M. René Viviani, President of the Council, Minister for Foreign Affairs.
Brussels
August 3, 1914.

To the assurance which I gave him that if Belgium appealed to the guarantee of the Powers against the violation of her neutrality by Germany, France would at once respond to her appeal, the Minister for Foreign Affairs answered:

"It is with great sincerity that we thank the Government of the Republic for the support which it would eventually be able to offer us, but under present conditions we do not appeal to the guarantee of the Powers. At a later date the Government of the King will weigh the measures which it may be necessary to take."

No. 143.
M. Paul Cambon, French Ambassador at London, to M. René, Viviani, President of the Council, Minister for Foreign Affairs.
London
August 3, 1914.

Sir Edward Grey has authorized me to inform you that you could state to Parliament that he was making explanations to the Commons as to the present attitude of the British Government, and that the chief of these declarations would be as follows:

"In case the German fleet came into the Channel or entered the North Sea in order to go 'round the British Isles with the object of attacking the French coasts or the French navy and of harassing French merchant shipping, the British fleet would intervene in order to give to French. Shipping its complete protection, in such a way that from that moment Great Britain and Germany would be in a state of war."

Sir Edward Grey explained to me that the notion of operation by way of the North Sea implied protection against a demonstration in the Atlantic Ocean.

The declaration concerning the intervention of the British fleet must be considered as binding the British Government. Sir Edward Grey has assured me of this and has added that the French Government was thereby authorized to inform the Chambers of this.

On my return to the Embassy I received your telephonic communication relating to the German ultimatum addressed to Belgium. I immediately communicated it to Sir Edward Grey.

PAUL CAMBON.

No. 144.
M. Paul Cambon, French Ambassador at London, to M. René Viviani, President of the Council, Minister for Foreign Affairs.
London
August 3, 1914.

Just as Sir Edward Grey was starting this morning for the meeting of the Cabinet, my German colleague, who had already seen him yesterday, came to press him to say that the neutrality of Great Britain did not depend upon respecting Belgian neutrality. Sir Edward Grey refused all conversation on this matter.

The German Ambassador has sent to the press a *communiqué* saying that if Great Britain remained neutral Germany would give up all naval operations and would not make use of the Belgian coast as a *point d'appui*. My answer is that respecting the coast is not respecting the neutrality of the territory, and that the German ultimatum is already a violation of this neutrality.

PAUL CAMBON.

No. 145.

M. Paul Cambon, French Ambassador at London, to M René Viviani, President of the Council, Minister for Foreign Affairs.
London
August 3, 1914.

Sir Edward Grey has made the statement regarding the intervention of the British fleet. He has explained, in considering the situation, what he proposed to do with regard to Belgian neutrality; and the reading of a letter from King Albert asking for the support of Great Britain has deeply stirred the House.

The House will this evening vote the credit, which is asked for; from this moment, its support is secured to the policy of the Government, and it follows public opinion, which is declaring itself more and more in our favor.

PAUL CAMBON.

No. 146.

M. René Viviani, President of the Council, Minister for Foreign Affairs, to M. Paul Cambon, French Ambassador at London.
Paris
August 3, 1914.

I am told that the German Ambassador is said to have stated to the Foreign Office that yesterday morning eighty French officers in Prussian uniform had attempted to cross the German frontier in twelve motor cars at Walbeck, to the west of Geldern, and that this formed a very serious violation of neutrality on the part of France.

Be good enough urgently to contradict this news, which is pure invention, and to draw the attention of the Foreign Office to the German campaign of false news, which is beginning.

RENÉ VIVIANI.

No. 147.

Letter handed by the German Ambassador to M. René Viviani, President of the Council, Minister for Foreign Affairs, during his farewell audience, August 3, 1914, at 6.45 P.M.

M. le Président,

The German administrative and military authorities have established a certain number of flagrantly hostile acts committed on German territory by French military aviators. Several of these have openly violated the neutrality of Belgium by flying over the territory of that country; one has attempted to destroy buildings near Wesel; others have been seen in the district of the Eifel, one has thrown bombs on the railway near Carlsruhe and Nuremberg.

I am instructed, and I have the honor to inform your Excellency, that in the presence of these acts of aggression the German Empire considers itself in a state of war with France in Consequence of the acts of this latter Power.

At the same time I have the honor to bring to the knowledge of your Excellency that the German authorities will detain French mercantile vessels in German ports, but they will release them if, within forty-eight hours, they are assured of complete reciprocity.

My diplomatic mission having thus come to an end it only remains for me to request your Excellency to be good enough to furnish me with my passports, and to take the steps you consider suitable to assure my return to Germany, with the staff of the Embassy, as well as with the staff of the Bavarian Legation and of the German Consulate General in Paris.

Be good enough, M. le Président, to receive the assurances of my deepest respect.
(Signed)

SCHOEN.

No. 148.
M. René Viviani, President of the Council, Minister for Foreign Affairs, to the French Representatives abroad.
Paris
August 3, 1914.

The German Ambassador has asked for his passports and is leaving this evening with the staffs of the Embassy, the German Consulate General, and the Bavarian Legation. Baron von Schoen has given as his reason the establishment by the German administrative and military authorities of acts of hostility, which are said to have been committed by French military aviators, accused of having flown over territory of the Empire and thrown bombs. The Ambassador adds that the aviators are said to have also violated the neutrality of Belgium by flying over Belgian territory.

"In the presence of these acts of aggression," says the letter of Baron von Schoen, "the German Empire considers itself in a state of war with France in consequence of the acts of this latter Power."

I formally challenged the inaccurate allegations of the Ambassador, and for my part, I reminded him that I had yesterday addressed to him a note protesting against the flagrant violations of the French frontier committed two days ago by detachments of German troops.

RENÉ VIVIANI.

No. 149.
M. René Viviani, President of the Council, Minister for Foreign Affairs, to M. Jules Cambon, French Ambassador at Berlin.
(Telegram communicated to French Representatives abroad.)
Paris
August 3, 1914.

I request you to ask for your passports and to leave Berlin at once with the staff of the Embassy, leaving the charge of French interests and the care of the archives to the Spanish Ambassador. I request you at the same time to protest in writing against the violation of the neutrality of Luxemburg by German troops, of which notice has been given by the Prime Minister of Luxemburg; against the ultimatum addressed to the Belgian Government by the German Minister at Brussels to force upon them the violation of Belgian neutrality and to require of that country that she should facilitate military operations against France on Belgian territory; finally against the false allegation of an alleged projected invasion of these two countries by French armies, by which he has attempted to justify the state of war which he declares henceforth exists between Germany and France.

RENÉ VIVIANI.

No. 150.

M. René Viviani, President of the Council, Minister for Foreign Affairs, to M. Allizé, French Minister at Munich.

Paris

August 3, 1914.

Be good enough to inform the Royal Bavarian Government that you have received instructions to adapt your attitude to that of our Ambassador at Berlin and to leave Munich.

RENÉ VIVIANI.

No. 151.

M. René Viviani, President of the Council, Minister for Foreign Affairs, to the French Representatives at London, St. Petersburgh, Vienna, Rome, Madrid, Berne, Constantinople, The Hague, Copenhagen, Christiania, Stockholm, Bucharest, Athens, Belgrade

Paris

August 3, 1914.

I learn from an official Belgian source that German troops have violated Belgian territory at Gemmerich in the district of Verviers.

RENÉ VIVIANI.

Primary Documents: Germany's Appeal to Americans, August 1914

Below do prominent politicians, industrialists, and bankers in Germany issue the text of a public appeal to the citizens of the then-neutral U.S....

Essentially a propaganda exercise, the appeal was designed to instill in the minds of its American readers the firm notion that Russia was chiefly responsible for the outbreak of war in Europe in 1914, aided and abetted by France and Britain.

German Appeal to Americans

Issued by an Imposing Committee of Leading German Statesmen, Scholars, Bankers, and Merchants, Including Prince von Bulow, Marshal von der Goltz, Matthias Erzerberger, Herr Ballin, Count von Reventlow, and the Head of the Imperial Bank.

Listen, All Ye People!

Try to realize, every one of you, what we are going through! Only a few weeks ago all of us were peacefully following our several vocations. The peasant was gathering in this summer's plentiful crop, the factory hand was working with accustomed vigor.

Not one human being among us dreamed of war. We are a nation that wishes to lead a quiet and industrious life. This need hardly be stated to you Americans. You, of all others, know the temper of the German who lives within your gates.

Our love of peace is so strong that we do not regard it in the light of a virtue; we simply know it to be an inborn and integral portion of ourselves. Since the foundation of the German Empire in the year 1871, we, living in the centre of Europe, have given an example of tranquility and peace, never once seeking to profit by any momentary difficulties of our neighbors.

Our commercial extension, our financial rise in the world, are far removed from any love of adventure, they are the fruit of painstaking and plodding labor.

We are not credited with this temper, because we are insufficiently known. Our situation and our way of thinking are not easily grasped.

Every one is aware that we have produced great philosophers and poets; we have preached the gospel of humanity with impassioned zeal. America fully appreciates Goethe and Kant, looks upon them as corner stones of elevated culture. Do you really believe that we have changed our natures, that our souls can be satisfied with military drill and servile obedience?

We are soldiers because we have to be soldiers, because otherwise Germany and German civilization would be swept away from the face of the earth. It has cost us long and weary struggles to attain our independence, and we know that, in order to preserve it, we must not content ourselves with building schools and factories; we must look to our garrisons and forts.

We and all our soldiers have remained, however, the same lovers of music and lovers of exalted thought. We have retained our old devotion to all peaceable sciences and arts; as the entire world knows, we work in the foremost rank of all those who strive to advance the exchange of commodities, who further useful, technical knowledge.

But we have been forced to become a nation of soldiers, in order to be free. And we are bound to follow our Kaiser, because he symbolizes and represents the unity of our nation. To-day, knowing no distinction of party, no difference of opinion, we rally around him, willing to shed the last drop of our blood.

For though it takes a great deal to rouse us Germans, when once aroused, our feelings run deep and strong. Every one is filled with this passion, with the soldier's ardor. But when the waters of the deluge shall have subsided, gladly will we return to the plow and to the anvil.

It deeply distresses us to see two highly civilized nations, England and France, joining the onslaught of autocratic Russia. That this could happen will remain one of the anomalies of history. It is not our fault: we firmly believed in the desirability of the great nations working together, we peaceably came to terms with France and England in sundry difficult African questions.

There was no cause for war between Western Europe and us, no reason why Western Europe should feel itself constrained to further the power of the Tsar.

The Tsar, as an individual, is most certainly not the instigator of the unspeakable horrors that are now inundating Europe. But he bears before God and Posterity the responsibility of having allowed himself to be terrorized by an unscrupulous military clique.

Ever since the weight of the crown has pressed upon him, lie has been the tool of others. He did not desire the brutalities in Finland, he did not approve of the iniquities of the Jewish Pogroms, but his hand was too weak to stop the fury of the reactionary party.

Why would he not permit Austria to pacify her southern frontier? It was inconceivable that Austria should calmly see her heir apparent murdered. How could she?

All the nationalities under her rule realized the impossibility of tamely allowing Serbia's only too evident and successful intrigues to be carried on under her very eyes.

The Austrians could not allow their venerable and sorely stricken monarch to be wounded and insulted any longer. This reasonable and honorable sentiment on the part of Austria has caused Russia to put itself forward as the patron of Serbia, as the enemy of European thought and civilization.

Russia has an important mission to fulfill in its own country and in Asia. It would do better in its own interest to leave the rest of the world in peace. But the die is cast, and all nations must decide whether they wish to further us by sentiments and by deeds, or the government of the Tsar.

This is the real significance of this appalling struggle, all the rest is immaterial. Russia's attitude alone has forced us to go to war with France and with their great ally.

The German nation is serious and conscientious. Never would a German Government dare to contemplate a war for the sake of dynastic interest, or for the sake of glory. This would be against the entire bent of our character.

Firmly believing in the justice of our cause, all parties, the conservatives and the clericals, the liberals and the socialists, have joined hands. All disputes are forgotten, one duty exists for all, the duty of defending our country and vanquishing the enemy.

Will not this calm, self-reliant and unanimous readiness to sacrifice all, to die or to win, appeal to other nations and force them to understand our real character and the situation in which we are placed?

The war has severed us from the rest of the world; all our cable communications are destroyed.

But the winds will carry the mighty voice of justice even across the ocean. We trust in God, we have confidence in the judgment of right-minded men. And through the roar of battle, we call to you all. Do not believe the mischievous lies that our enemies are spreading about!

We do not know if victory will be ours, the Lord alone knows. We have not chosen our path; we must continue doing our duty, even to the very end. We bear the misery of war, the death of our sons, believing in Germany, believing in duty.

And we know that Germany cannot be wiped from the face of the earth.

Photograph courtesy of Photos of the Great War website.

Source: *Source Records of the Great War, Vol. II, ed. Charles F. Horne, National Alumni. 1923.*

1914 Aug 3: Germany declares war on France and Russia.

Primary Documents: Germany's Declaration of War with France, 3 August 1914.
Updated: Saturday, 14 June 2003.
Presented by the German Ambassador to Paris.

M. le President,

The German administrative and military authorities have established a certain number of flagrantly hostile acts committed on German territory by French military aviators.

Several of these have openly violated the neutrality of Belgium by flying over the territory of that country; one has attempted to destroy buildings near Wesel; others have been seen in the district of the Eifel; one has thrown bombs on the railway near Carlsruhe and Nuremberg.

I am instructed, and I have the honor to inform your Excellency, that in the presence of these acts of aggression the German Empire considers itself in a state of war with France in consequence of the acts of this latter Power.

At the same time, I have the honor to bring to the knowledge of your Excellency that the German authorities will retain French mercantile vessels in German ports, but they will release them if, within forty-eight hours, they are assured of complete reciprocity.

My diplomatic mission having thus come to an end, it only remains for me to request your Excellency to be good enough to furnish me with my passports, and to take the steps you consider suitable to assure my return to Germany, with the staff of the Embassy, as well as, with the Staff of the Bavarian Legation and of the German Consulate General in Paris.

Be good enough, M. le President, to receive the assurances of my deepest respect.

(Signed)
SCHOEN.

Source: *Source Records of the Great War, Vol. II, ed. Charles F. Horne, National Alumni, 1923.*

Chapter Thirty-Six

August 4, 1914

1914 Aug 4: Germany marches into Belgium.

No. 153.
Sir Edward Grey to Sir E. Goschen, British Ambassador at Berlin.
Foreign Office
August 4, 1914.
(Telegraphic)

The King of the Belgians has made an appeal to his Majesty the King for diplomatic intervention on behalf in the following terms:

"Remembering the numerous proofs of your majesty's friendship and that of your predecessor and the friendly attitude of England in 1870 and the proof of friendship you have just given us again, I make a supreme appeal to the diplomatic intervention of your Majesty's Government to safeguard the integrity of Belgium."

His Majesty's Government is also informed that the German Government has delivered to the Belgian Government a note proposing friendly neutrality entailing free passage through Belgian territory, and promising to maintain the independence and integrity of the Kingdom and its possessions at the conclusion of peace, threatening in case of refusal to treat Belgium as an enemy. An answer was requested within twelve hours.

We also understand that Belgium has categorically refused this as a flagrant violation of the law of nations.

His Majesty's Government is bound to protest against this violation of a treaty to which Germany is a party in common with themselves, and must request an assurance that the demand made upon Belgium will not be proceeded with and that her neutrality will be respected by Germany. You should ask for an immediate reply.

No. 27.
Herr von Below Saleske, German Minister at Brussels, M. Davignon, Belgian Minister for Foreign Affairs.
(The original is in French.)
Brussels
August 4, 1914 (6 A.M.).

Sir,

In accordance with my instructions, I have the honour to inform your Excellency that in consequence of the refusal of the Belgian Government to entertain the well-intentioned proposals made to them by the German Government, the latter, to their deep regret, find themselves compelled to take—if necessary by force of arms—those measures of defense already foreshadowed as indispensable, in view of the menace of France.

No. 28.
Note communicated by Sir Francis H. Villiers, British Minister at Brussels, to M. Davignon, Belgian Minister for Foreign Affairs.
Brussels
August 4, 1914.

I am instructed to inform the Belgian Government that if Germany brings pressure to bear upon Belgium with the object of forcing her to abandon her attitude of neutrality, His Britannic Majesty's Government expect Belgium to resist with all the means at her disposal.

In that event, His Britannic Majesty's Government is prepared to join Russia and France, should Belgium so desire, in tendering at once joint assistance to the Belgian Government with a view to resisting any forcible measures adopted by Germany against Belgium, and also offering a guarantee for the maintenance of the future independence and integrity of Belgium.

No. 154.
Sir Villiers, British Minister at Brussels, to Sir Edward Grey.
Brussels
August 4, 1914.
(Telegraphic)

German Minister has this morning addressed note to minister for Foreign Affairs stating that as Belgian Government declined the well-intentioned proposals submitted to them by the imperial Government, the latter will, deeply to their regret, be compelled to carry out, if necessary by force of arms, the measures considered indispensable in view of the French menaces.

No. 29.
Baron Fallon, Belgian Minister at The Hague, to M. Davignon, Belgian Minister for Foreign Affairs.
The Hague
August 4, 1914.

Sir,

The Minister for Foreign Affairs told me yesterday evening that the Netherlands Government would perhaps be obliged, owing to the gravity of the present situation, to institute war buoying upon the Scheldt.

M. Loudon read me the draft of the note, which would announce this decision to me.

I have the honour to transmit to you herewith a copy of the note in question, which was communicated to me yesterday evening.

As you will observe, the Scheldt will only be closed at night. By day, navigation will be possible, but only with Dutch pilots who have been furnished with the necessary nautical instructions. In this way both Dutch interests in the defense of their territory, and Belgian interests in the navigation of Antwerp will be safeguarded.

You will note that the Netherlands Government further asks that in the event of the war buoying being carried out, we should cause the lightships *Wielingen* and *Wandelaar* to be withdrawn in order to facilitate the maintenance of the neutrality of Dutch territory.

I would point out that the phrase used in this note, "sailing up the Scheldt," is not sufficiently explicit; sailing down would be permitted under the same conditions. The Minister has, however, given me this assurance.

As soon as the Netherlands Government have decided upon this exceptional measure I shall be informed of it.

About six hours are necessarily to carry out war buoying.

I will at once telegraph to you.

Note enclosed in No. 29.

The Netherlands Government may be compelled, in order to maintain the neutrality of Dutch territory, to institute war buoying upon the Scheldt, that is to say, to move or modify a portion of the actual arrangement of buoys and lights.

At the same time, this special arrangement of buoys has been so drawn up that when it is brought into force it will still be possible to sail up the Scheldt as far as Antwerp by day, but only with Dutch pilots who have been furnished with the necessary nautical instructions. In thus acting the Netherlands Government are convinced that they will be able to serve equally both the Dutch interests in the defense of Netherlands territory and Belgian interests in the navigation of Antwerp. After the establishment of war buoying on the Scheldt, there would be no further reason to enter the tidal water of Flushing at night, and as the presence of the lightships *Wielingen* and *Wandelaar* is not indispensable to navigation by day, the Netherlands Government would be much obliged if the Belgian Government would be good enough, in the event of the establishment of war buoying, to withdraw these boats in order to facilitate the maintenance of the neutrality of Dutch territory.

No. 155.
Sir Edward Grey to Sir F. Villiers, British Minister at Brussels.
Foreign Office
August 4, 1914.
(Telegraphic)

You should inform Belgian Government that if pressure is applied to them by Germany to induce them to depart from neutrality, his Majesty's Government expect that they will resist by any means in their power, and that his Majesty's government in this event are prepared to join Russia and France, if desired, in offering to the Belgian Government at once common action for the purpose of resisting use of force by Germany against them, and a guarantee to maintain their independence and integrity in future years.

No. 30.

M. Davignon, Belgian Minister for Foreign Affairs, to Belgian Ministers at London and Paris.
Brussels
August 4, 1914.
(Telegraphic)

The General Staff announces that Belgian territory has been violated at Gemmenich.

No. 156.

Sir Edward Grey to Sir E. Goschen, British Ambassador at Berlin.
Foreign Office
August 4, 1914.
(Telegraphic)

I continue to receive numerous complaints from British firms as to the detention of their ships at Hamburg, Cuxhaven, and other German ports. This action on the part of the German authorities is totally unjustified. It is in direct contravention of international law and of the assurances given to your Excellency by the Imperial Chancellor. You should demand the immediate release of all British ships if such release has not yet been given.

No. 31.

M. Davignon, Belgian Minister for Foreign Affairs, to Herr von Below Saleske, German Minister at Brussels.
Brussels
August 4, 1914.

Sir,

I have the honour to inform your Excellency that from today the Belgian Government is unable to recognize your diplomatic status and cease to have official relations with you. Your Excellency will find enclosed the passports necessary for your departure with the staff of the legation.

No. 157.

German Foreign Secretary to Prince Lichnowsky, German Ambassador in London.
(Communicated by German Embassy)
Berlin
August 4, 1914.

Please dispel any mistrust that may subsist on the part of the British Government with regard to our intentions, by repeating most positively formal assurance that, even in the case of armed conflict with Belgium, Germany will, under no pretense whatever, annex Belgian territory. Sincerity of this declaration is borne out by fact that we solemnly pledge our word to Holland to strictly to respect her neutrality. It is obvious that we could not profitably annex Belgian territory without making at the same time territorial acquisition at expense of Holland.

Please impress upon Sir E. Grey that German army could not be exposed to French attack across Belgium, which was planned according to absolutely unimpeachable information. Germany had consequently to disregard Belgian neutrality, it being for her a question of life or death to prevent French advance.

No. 32.
Herr von Below Saleske, German Minister at Brussels, to M. Davignon, Belgian Minister for Foreign Affairs.
Brussels
August 4, 1914.

Sir,

I have the honour to acknowledge the receipt of your Excellency's note of the 4th August, and to inform you that I have entrusted the custody of the German Legation of Brussels to the care of my United States colleague.

No. 158.
Sir F. Villiers, British Minister at Brussels, to Sir Edward Grey.
Brussels
August 4, 1914.
(Telegraphic)

Military attaché has been informed at War office that German troops have entered Belgian territory, and that Liege has been summoned to surrender by small party of Germans who, however, were repulsed.

No. 33.
M. Davignon, Belgian Minister for Foreign Affairs, to Baron Grenier, Belgian Minister at Berlin.
Brussels
August 4, 1914
(Telegraphic)

Please ask the Spanish Government if they will be good enough to take charge of Belgian interests in Germany, and whether in that event they will issue the necessary instructions to their Ambassador at Berlin.

No. 159.
Sir Edward Grey to Sir E. Goschen, British Ambassador at Berlin.
Foreign Office
August 4, 1914.
(Telegraphic)

We hear that Germany has addressed a note to Belgian Minister for Foreign Affairs stating that German Government will be compelled to carry out, if necessary, by force of arms, the measures considered indispensable.

We are also informed that Belgian territory has been violated at Gemmenich.
In these circumstances, and in view of the fact that Germany declined to give same assurance respecting Belgium as France gave last week in reply to our request made simultaneously at Berlin and Paris, we must repeat that request, and ask that a satisfactory reply to it and to my telegram of this morning[69] be received here by 12 o'clock tonight. If not, you are instructed to ask for your passports,

---

[69] See No. 153.

311

and say that His Majesty's Government feel bound to take steps in their power to uphold the neutrality of Belgium and the observance of a treaty to which Germany is as much a party as ourselves.

No. 34.
M. Davignon, Belgian Minister for Foreign Affairs, to Baron Beyens, Belgian Minister at Berlin.
Brussels
August 4, 1914.
(Telegraphic)

The German Minister is leaving to-night; you should ask for your passports. We are requesting the Spanish Government to authorize the Spanish Ambassador to be good enough to take charge of Belgian interests in Germany.

No. 35.
Baron Beyens, Belgian Minister at Berlin, to M. Davignon, Belgian Minister for Foreign Affairs.
Berlin
August 4, 1914.

Sir,

I have the honour to transmit to you herewith a translation of part of the speech made to-day in the Reichstag by the Imperial Chancellor on the subject of the infamous violation of Belgian neutrality: "We are in a state of legitimate defense, and necessity knows no law.

"Our troops have occupied Luxemburg and have perhaps already entered Belgium. This is contrary to the dictates of international law. France has, it is true, declared at Brussels that she was prepared to respect the neutrality of Belgium so long as it was respected by her adversary. But we knew that France was ready to invade Belgium. France could wait; we could not. A French attack upon our flank in the region of the Lower Rhine might have been fatal. We were, therefore, compelled to ride roughshod over the legitimate protests of the Governments of Luxemburg and Belgium. For the wrong which we are thus doing, we will make reparation as soon as our military object is attained.

"Anyone in such grave danger as ourselves, and who is struggling for his supreme welfare, can only be concerned with the means of extricating himself; we stand side by side with Austria."

It is noteworthy that Herr von Bethmann-Hollweg recognizes, without the slightest disguise, that Germany is violating international law by her invasion of Belgian territory and that she is committing a wrong against us.

No. 36.
Count de Lalaing, Belgian Minister at London, to M. Davignon, Belgian Minister for Foreign Affairs.
London
August 4, 1914.

Sir,

I have the honour to inform you that in the House of Commons this afternoon the Prime Minister made a fresh statement with regard to the European crisis.

After recalling the principal points set forth yesterday by Sir E. Grey, the Prime Minister read:

1. A telegram received from Sir F. Villiers this morning, which gave the substance of the second ultimatum, presented to the Belgian Government by the German Government, which had been sent to you this morning (See No. 27).
2. Your telegram informing me of the violation of the frontier at Gemmenich, a copy of which I have given to Sir A. Nicolson.
3. A telegram, which the German Government addressed to its Ambassador in London this morning with the evident intention of misleading popular opinion as to its attitude. Here is the translation as published in one of this evening's newspapers:

"Please dispel any mistrust which may subsist on the part of the British Government with regard to our intentions, by repeating most positively the formal assurance that, even in the case of armed conflict with Belgium, Germany will, under no pretence whatever, annex Belgian territory.

"Sincerity of this declaration is borne out by fact that we solemnly pledged our word to Holland strictly to respect her neutrality.

"It is obvious that we could not profitably annex Belgian territory without making at the time territorial acquisitions at the expense of Holland.

"Please impress upon Sir E. Grey that German army could not be exposed to French attack across Belgium, which was planned according to absolutely unimpeachable information.

"Germany had consequently to disregard Belgian neutrality, it being for her a question of life or death to prevent French advance."

Mr. Asquith then informed the House that in answer to this note of the German Government the British Government had repeated their proposal of last week, namely, that the German Government should give the same assurances as to Belgian neutrality as France had given last week both to England and to Belgium. The British Cabinet allowed the Berlin Cabinet till midnight to reply.

No. 37.
Count de Lalaing, Belgian Minister at London, M. Davignon, Belgian Minister for Foreign Affairs.
London
August 4, 1914.
(Telegraphic)

The Minister for Foreign Affairs has informed the British Ministers in Norway, Holland, and Belgium, that Great Britain expects that these three kingdoms will resist German pressure and observe neutrality. Should they resist they will have the support of Great Britain, who is ready in that event, should the three above-mentioned Governments desire it, to join France and Prussia, in offering an alliance to the said Governments for the purpose of resisting the use of force by Germany against them, and a guarantee to maintain the future independence and integrity of the three kingdoms. I observed to him that Belgium was neutral in perpetuity. The Minister for Foreign Affairs answered: This is in case her neutrality is violated.

No. 38.
M. Davignon, Belgian Minister for Foreign Affairs, to Belgium Ministers at Paris, London, and St. Petersburg.
Brussels
August 4, 1914.

Sir,

I have the honour to inform you of the course of recent events as regards the relations of Belgium with certain of the Powers, which guarantee her neutrality and independence.

On the 31st July the British Minister made me a verbal communication according to which Sir E. Grey, in anticipation of a European war, had asked the German and French Governments separately if each of them were resolved to respect the neutrality of Belgium should that neutrality not be violated by any other Power.

In view of existing treaties, Sir E. Villiers was instructed to bring this step to the knowledge of the Belgian Government, adding that Sir E. Grey presumed that Belgium was resolved to maintain her neutrality, and that she expected other Powers to respect it.

I told the British Minister that we highly appreciated this communication, which was in accordance with our expectation, and I added that Great Britain, as well as the other Powers who had guaranteed our independence, might rest fully assured of our firm determination to maintain our neutrality; nor did it seem possible that our neutrality could be threatened by any of those States, with whom we enjoyed the most cordial and frank relations. The Belgian Government, I added, had given proof of this resolution by taking, from now on all such military measures as seemed to them to be necessitated by the situation.

In his turn the French Minister made a verbal communication on August 1st to the effect that he was authorized to inform the Belgian Government that in case of an international war the French Government, in conformity with their repeated declarations, would respect Belgian territory, and that they would not be induced to modify their attitude except in the event of the violation of Belgian neutrality by another power.

I thanked his Excellency, and added that we had already taken all the necessary precautions to ensure respect of our independence and our frontiers.

On the morning of the 9th August I had a fresh conversation with Sir F. Villiers, in the course of which he told me that he had lost no time in telegraphing our conversation to July 31st to his Government, and that he had been careful to quote accurately the solemn declaration which he had received of Belgium's intention to defend her frontiers from whichever side they might be invaded. He added: "We know that France has given you formal assurances, but Great Britain has received no reply from Berlin on this subject."

The latter fact did not particularly affect me, since a declaration from the German Government might appear superfluous in view of existing treaties. Moreover, the Secretary of State had reaffirmed, at the meeting of the committee of the Reichstag of April 29th, 1913, "that the neutrality of Belgium is established by treaty which Germany intends to respect."

The same day Herr von Below Saleske, the German Minister, called at the Ministry for Foreign Affairs at 7 o'clock, and handed to me the enclosed note (see No. 20). The German Government gave the Belgian Government a time limit of twelve hours within which to communicate their decision.

No hesitation was possible as to the reply called for by the amazing proposal of the German Government. You will find a copy enclosed. (See No. 22.)

The ultimatum expired at 7 A.M. on August 3rd. As at 10 o'clock no act of war had been committed, the Belgian Cabinet decided that there was no reason for the moment to appeal to the guaranteeing powers.

Towards mid-day the French Minister questioned me upon this point, and said:

"Although in view of the rapid march of events I have as yet received no instructions to make a declaration from my Government, I feel justified, in view of their well-known intentions, in saying that if the Belgian Government were to appeal to the French Government as one of the Powers guaranteeing their neutrality, the French Government would at once respond to Belgium's appeal; if such an appeal were not made it is probable that—unless, of course, exceptional measures were rendered necessary in self-defense—the French Government would not intervene until Belgium had taken some effective measure of resistance."

I thanked M. Klobukowski for the support which the French Government had been good enough to offer us in case of need, and I informed him that the Belgian Government were making no appeal at present to the guarantee of the Powers, and that they would decide later what ought to be done.

Finally, at 6 A.M. on August 4th, the German Minister made the following communication to me. (See No. 27.)

The Cabinet is at the present moment deliberating on the question of an appeal to the Powers guaranteeing our neutrality.

No. 39.
Count de Lalaing, Belgian Minister at London, to M. Davignon, Belgian Minister for Foreign Affairs.
London
August 4, 1914.
(Telegraphic)

Great Britain this morning called upon Germany to respect Belgian neutrality. The ultimatum says that whereas the note addressed by Germany to Belgium threatens the latter with an appeal to the force of arms if she opposes the passage of German troops; and whereas Belgian territory has been violated at Gemmenich; and whereas Germany has refused to give Great Britain a similar assurance to that given last week by France; therefore Great Britain must once again demand a satisfactory reply on the subject of the respect of Belgian neutrality and of the treaty to which Germany, no less than Great Britain, is a signatory. The ultimatum expires at midnight. In consequence of the British ultimatum to Germany, the British proposal, which I telegraphed to you, is cancelled for the time being. (See No. 37.)

No. 40.
M. Davignon, Belgian Minister for Foreign Affairs, to British, French, and Russian Ministers at Brussels.
Brussels
August 4, 1914.

Sir,

The Belgian Government regrets to have to announce to your Excellency that this morning the armed forces of Germany entered Belgian territory in violation of treaty engagements.

The Belgian Government is firmly determined to resist by all the means in their power.

Belgium appeals to Great Britain, France, and Russia to co-operate as guaranteeing Powers in the defense of her territory.

There should be concerted and joint action, to oppose the forcible measures taken by Germany against Belgium, and, at the same time, to guarantee the future maintenance of the independence and integrity of Belgium.

Belgium is happy to be able to declare that she will undertake the defense of her fortified places.

Primary Documents: Britain is Breaking off of Diplomatic Relations with Germany; 4 August 1914

Reproduced below is the official report prepared by the British ambassador to Germany, Sir Edward Goschen, which recounted the events of 4 August 1914.

In his report, Sir Edward documented the reaction of both von Jagow (the Foreign Minister) and Bethmann-Hollweg (the German Chancellor) to news that Britain was breaking off diplomatic relations with Germany and had issued an ultimatum requiring that Germany withdraw its troops from Belgium by midnight the same day.

Goschen concluded that neither von Jagow nor Bethmann-Hollweg had any intention of recalling German troops now situated in Belgium, and that war with Germany was inevitable.

Official Report of the Breaking of Diplomatic Relations and of the "Scrap of Paper" by Sir Edward Goschen, British Ambassador to Berlin.

In accordance with the instructions contained in your telegram of the 4th instant, I called upon the Secretary of State that afternoon and inquired, in the name of His Majesty's Government, whether the Imperial Government would refrain from violating Belgian neutrality.

Herr von Jagow at once replied that lie was sorry to say that his answer must be "No," as, in consequence of the German troops having crossed the frontier that morning, Belgian neutrality had been already violated.

Herr von Jagow again went into the reasons why the Imperial Government had been obliged to take this step, namely, that they had to advance into France by the quickest and easiest way, to be able to get well ahead with their operations and endeavor to strike some decisive blow as early as possible.

It was a matter of life and death for them, as if they had gone by the more southern route they could not have hoped, in view of the paucity of roads and the strength of the fortresses, to have got through without formidable opposition entailing great loss of time.

This loss of time would have meant time gained by the Russians for bringing up their troops to the German frontier. Rapidity of action was the great German asset, while that of Russia was an inexhaustible supply of troops.

I pointed out to Herr von Jagow that this fait accompli of the violation of the Belgian frontier rendered, as he would readily understand, the situation exceedingly grave, and I asked him whether there was not still time to draw back and avoid possible consequences, which both he and I would deplore. He replied that, for the reasons he had given me, it was now impossible for them to draw back.

During the afternoon I received your further telegram of the same date, and, in compliance with the instructions therein contained, I again proceeded to the Imperial Foreign Office and informed the Secretary of State that unless the Imperial Government could give the assurance by 12 o'clock that night that they would proceed no further with their violation of the Belgian frontier and stop their advance, I had been instructed to demand my passports and inform the Imperial Government that His Majesty's Government would have to take all steps in their power to uphold the neutrality of Belgium and the observance of a treaty to which Germany was as much a party as themselves.

Herr von Jagow replied that to his great regret he could give no other answer than that which he had given me earlier in the day, namely, that the safety of the Empire rendered it absolutely necessary that the Imperial troops should advance through Belgium.

I gave his Excellency a written summary of your telegram and, pointing out that you had mentioned 12 o'clock as the time when His Majesty's Government would expect an answer, asked him whether, in view of the terrible consequences which would necessarily ensue, it were not possible even at the last moment that their answer should be reconsidered.

He replied that if the time given were even twenty-four hours or more, his answer must be the same. I said that in that case I should have to demand my passports. This interview took place at about 7 o'clock. In a short conversation which ensued Herr von Jagow expressed his poignant regret at the crumbling of his entire policy and that of the Chancellor, which had been to make friends with Great Britain, and then, through Great Britain, to get closer to France.

I said that this sudden end to my work in Berlin was to me also a matter of deep regret and disappointment, but that he must understand that under the circumstances and in view of our engagements, His Majesty's Government could not possibly have acted otherwise than they had done.

I then said that I should like to go and see the Chancellor, as it might be, perhaps, the last time I should have an opportunity of seeing him. He begged me to do so. I found the Chancellor very agitated.

His Excellency at once began a harangue, which lasted for about twenty minutes. He said that the step taken by His Majesty's Government was terrible to a degree; just for a word—"neutrality," a word which in war time had so often been disregarded—just for a scrap of paper Great Britain was going to make war on a kindred nation who desired nothing better than to be friends with her.

All his efforts in that direction had been rendered useless by this last terrible step, and the policy to which, as I knew, he had devoted himself since his accession to office had tumbled down like a house of cards. What we had done was unthinkable; it was like striking a man from behind while he was fighting for his life against two assailants.

He held Great Britain responsible for all the terrible events that might happen. I protested strongly against that statement, and said that, in the same way as he and Herr von Jagow wished me to understand that for strategically reasons it was a matter of life and death to Germany to advance through Belgium and violate the latter's neutrality, so I would wish him to understand that it was, so to speak, a matter of "life and death" for the honor of Great Britain that she should keep her solemn engagement to do her utmost to defend Belgium's neutrality if attacked.

That solemn compact simply had to be kept, or what confidence could any one have in engagements given by Great Britain in the future? The Chancellor said, "But at what price will that compact have been kept? Has the British Government thought of that?"

I hinted to his Excellency as plainly as I could that fear of consequences could hardly be regarded as an excuse for breaking solemn engagements, but his Excellency was so excited, so evidently overcome by the news of our action, and so little disposed to hear reason that I refrained from adding fuel to the flame by further argument.

As I was leaving, he said that the blow of Great Britain joining Germany's enemies was all the greater that almost up to the last moment he and his Government had been working with us and supporting our efforts to maintain peace between Austria and Russia.

I said that this was part of the tragedy, which saw the two nations fall apart just at the moment when the relations between them had been more friendly and cordial than they had been for years. Unfortunately, notwithstanding our efforts to maintain peace between Russia and Austria, the war had spread and had brought us face to face with a situation which, if we held to our engagements, we could not possibly avoid, and which unfortunately entailed our separation from our late fellow workers. He would readily understand that no one regretted this more than I.

After this somewhat painful interview, I returned to the embassy and drew up a telegraphic report of what had passed. This telegram was handed in at the Central Telegraph Office a little before 9 P.M. It was accepted by that office, but apparently never dispatched.

At about 9.30 P.M. Herr von Zimmermannn, the Under-Secretary of State, came to see me. After expressing his deep regret that the very friendly official and personal relations between us were about to cease, he asked me casually whether a demand for passports was equivalent to a declaration of war.

I said that such an authority on international law as he was known to be must know as well or better than I what was usual in such cases. I added that there were many cases where diplomatic relations had been broken off, and, nevertheless, war had not ensued; but that in this case he would have seen from my instructions, of which I had given Herr von Jagow a written summary, that His Majesty's Government expected an answer to a definite question by 12 o'clock that night and that in default of a satisfactory answer they would be forced to take such steps as their engagements required.

Herr Zimmermann said that that was, in fact, a declaration of war, as the Imperial Government could not possibly give the assurance required either that night or any other night.
Source: *Source Records of the Great War, Vol. I, ed. Charles F. Horne, National Alumni, 1923.*

By Belgium violating Article 9.3 of the 1839 Treaty of London, they therefore nullify the treaty with Germany. In reaction to this violation of Article 9.3, the German government orders the army into Belgium to seize what is rightfully theirs by international maritime laws and the 1839 Treaty of London. Once they reclaim their merchant ships that are in port, the German army activates the Schieffel Plan. Just before Germany enters Belgium, France and Russian cross the frontier. France sends in small patrols, and Russia is making a full military push into Germany.

The Belgium port authorities sent the crew home off the German merchant ship on August 2. On the third, they confiscated the cargo. On the morning of the fourth, they sunk the ship in the mouth of the river leading to Germany. The exact time of the sinking is unclear.

Primary Documents: The Scrap of Paper, 4 August 1914
Updated: Saturday, 21 June 2003.

Reproduced below is the text of a published interview with the German Chancellor Theobald von Bethmann-Hollweg.

The interview conducted during wartime, Bethmann-Hollweg seized the opportunity to explain—and justify—his controversial description of Britain's treaty with Belgium—which guaranteed her neutrality—as "a scrap of paper."

The German Chancellor had so described the treaty in his final meeting with the British Ambassador to Germany, Sir Edward Goschen, on 4 August 1914. Within hours, Britain declared herself at war with Germany.

A published interview explaining the "Scrap of Paper" Phrase
by German Chancellor Theobald von Bethmann-Hollweg.

My conversation with Sir E. Goschen occurred on the 4th of August.

I had just declared in the Reichstag that only dire necessity, only the struggle for existence, compelled Germany to march through Belgium, but that Germany was ready to make compensation for the wrong committed.

When I spoke, I already had certain indications, but no absolute proof, on which to base a public accusation that Belgium had long before abandoned its neutrality in its relations with England. Nevertheless, I took Germany's responsibilities towards neutral States so seriously that I spoke frankly on the wrong committed by Germany.

What was the British attitude on the same question? The day before my conversation with the British Ambassador, Sir Edward Grey had delivered his well-known speech in Parliament, wherein, while he did not state expressly, that England would take part in the war; he left the matter in little doubt.

One needs only to read this speech through carefully to learn the reason of England's intervention in the war. Amid all his beautiful phrases about England's honor and England's obligations we find it over and over again expressed that England's interests—its own interests—called for participation in war, for it was not in England's interests that a victorious, and therefore stronger, Germany should emerge from the war.

This old principle of England's policy—to take as the sole criterion of its actions its private interests regardless of right, reason, or considerations of humanity—is expressed in that speech of Gladstone's in 1870 on Belgian neutrality from which Sir Edward quoted.

Mr. Gladstone then declared that he was unable to subscribe to the doctrine that the simple fact of the existence of a guarantee is binding upon every party thereto, irrespective altogether of the particular position in which it may find itself at the time when the occasion for action on the guarantee arrives, and he referred to such English statesmen as Aberdeen and Palmerston as supporters of his views.

England drew the sword only because she believed her own interests demanded it. Just for Belgian neutrality, she would never have entered the war. That is what I meant when I told Sir E. Goschen, in that last interview when we sat down to talk the matter over privately man to man, that among the reasons which had impelled England into war the Belgian neutrality treaty had for her only the value of a scrap of paper.

I may have been a bit excited and aroused. Who would not have been at seeing the hopes and work of the whole period of my Chancellorship going for naught?

I recalled to the Ambassador my efforts for years to bring about an understanding between England and Germany, an understanding which, I reminded him, would have made a general European war impossible, and have absolutely guaranteed the peace of Europe.

Such understanding would have formed the basis on which we could have approached the United States as a third partner.

However, England had not taken up this plan, and through its entry into the war had destroyed forever the hope of its fulfillment.

In comparison with such momentous consequences, was the treaty not a scrap of paper?

Source: *Source Records of the Great War, Vol. I, ed. Charles F. Horne, National Alumni, 1923.*

FOREIGN OFFICE
Berlin
August 1914.

On June 28 the Austro-Hungarian successor to the throne, a member of a band of Serbian conspirators assassinated Arch-Duke Franz Ferdinand, and his wife, the Duchess of Hohenberg. The investigation of the crime through the Austro-Hungarian authorities has yielded the fact that the conspiracy against the life of the Archduke and successor to the throne was prepared and abetted in Belgrade with the co-operation of Serbian officials, and executed with arms from the Serbian State arsenal. This crime must have opened the eyes of the entire civilized world, not only in regard to the aims of the Serbian policies directed against the conservation and integrity of the Austro-Hungarian monarchy, but also concerning the criminal means which the pan-Serb propaganda in Serbia had no hesitation in employing for the achievement of these aims.

The goal of these policies was the gradual revolutionizing and final separation of the southeasterly districts from the Austro-Hungarian monarchy and their union with Serbia. This direction of Serbia's policy has not been altered in the least in spite of the repeated and solemn declarations of Serbia in which it vouchsafed a change in these policies towards Austria-Hungary as well as the cultivation of good and neighborly relations.

In this manner for the third time in the course of the last 6 years, Serbia has led Europe to the brink of a world war.

It could only do this because it believed itself supported in its intentions by Russia. Russia, soon after the events brought about by the Turkish revolution of 1908, endeavored to found a union of the Balkan states under Russian patronage and directed against the existence of Turkey. This union which succeeded in 1911 in driving out Turkey from a greater part of her European possessions, collapsed over the question of the distribution of spoils. The Russian policies were not dismayed over this failure. According to the idea of the Russian statesmen a new Balkan union under Russian patronage should be called into existence, headed no longer against Turkey, now dislodged from the Balkan, but against the existence of the Austro-Hungarian monarchy. It was the idea that Serbia should cede to Bulgaria those parts of Macedonia, which it had received during the last Balkan war, in exchange for Bosnia, and the Herzegovina, which were to be taken from Austria. To oblige Bulgaria to fall in with this plan it was to be isolated, Romania attached to Russia with the aid of French propaganda, and Serbia promised Bosnia and the Herzegovina.

Under these circumstances, it was clear to Austria that it was not compatible with the dignity and the spirit of self-preservation of the monarchy to view idly any longer this agitation across the border. The Imperial and Royal Government appraised Germany of this conception and asked for our opinion. With all our heart we were able to agree with our ally's estimate of the situation, and assure him that any action considered necessary to end the movement in Serbia directed against the conservation of the monarchy would meet with our approval.

We were perfectly aware that a possible warlike attitude of Austria-Hungary against Serbia might bring Russia upon the field, and that it might therefore involve us in a war, in accordance with our duty as allies. We could not, however, in these vital interests of Austria-Hungary, which were at stake, advise our ally to take a yielding attitude not compatible with his dignity, nor deny him our assistance in these trying days. We could do this all the less as our own interests were menaced through the continued Serb agitation. If the Serbs continued with the aid of Russia and France to menace the existence of Austria-Hungary, the gradual collapse of Austria and the subjection of all the Slavs under one Russian sceptre would be the consequence, thus making untenable the position of the Teutonic race in Central Europe. A morally weakened Austria under the pressure of Russian pan-Slavism would be no longer an ally on whom we could count and in whom we could have confidence, as we must be able to have, in view of the ever more menacing attitude of our easterly and westerly neighbors. We, therefore, permitted Austria a completely free hand in her action towards Serbia, but have not, participated in her preparations. Austria chose the method of presenting to the Serbian Government a note, in which the direct connection between the murder at Sarajevo and the pan-Serb movement, as not only countenanced but also actively supported by the Serbian Government, was explained, and in which a complete cessation of this agitation, as well as a punishment of the guilty, was requested. At the same time, Austria-Hungary demanded as necessary guarantee for the accomplishment of her desire the participation of some Austrian officials in the preliminary examination on Serbian territory and the final dissolution of the pan-Serb societies agitating against Austria-Hungary. The Imperial and Royal Government gave a period of 48 hours for the unconditional acceptance of its demands.

The Serbian Government started the mobilization of its army one day after the transmission of the Austro-Hungarian note.

As after the stipulated date the Serbian Government rendered a reply which, though complying in some points with the conditions of Austria-Hungary, yet showed in all essentials the endeavor through procrastination and new negotiations to escape from the just demands of the monarchy, the latter discontinued her diplomatic relations with Serbia without indulging in further negotiations or accepting further Serbian assurances, whose value, to its loss, she had sufficiently experienced.

From this moment, Austria was in fact in a state of war with Serbia, which it proclaimed officially on 28 July by declaring war.

From the beginning of the conflict we assumed the position that there were here concerned the affairs of Austria alone, which it would have to settle with Serbia. We therefore directed our efforts toward the localizing of the war, and toward convincing the other powers that Austria-Hungary had to appeal to arms in justifiable self-defense, forced upon her by the conditions. We emphatically took the position that no civilized country possessed the right to stay the arm of Austria in this struggle with barbarism and political crime, and to shield the Serbians against their just punishment. In this sense, we instructed our representatives with the foreign powers. [*See exhibits 1 and 2.*]

Simultaneously the Austro-Hungarian Government communicated to the Russian Government that the step undertaken against Serbia implied merely a defensive measure against the Serb agitation but that Austria-Hungary must of necessity demand guarantees for a continued friendly behavior of Serbia towards the monarchy. Austria-Hungary had no intention whatsoever to shift the balance of power in the Balkan. [*See exhibit 3.*]

In answer to our declaration that the German Government desired, and aimed at, a localization of the conflict, both the French and the English Governments promised an action in the same direction. However, these endeavors did not succeed in preventing the interposition of Russia in the Austro-Serbian disagreement.

The Russian Government submitted an official communiqué on July 24th, according to which Russia could not possibly remain indifferent in the Servo-Austrian conflict. The same # was declared by the Russian Secretary of Foreign Affairs, M. Sasonof, to the German Ambassador, Count Pourtalès, in the afternoon of July 26th. [*See exhibit 4.*] The German Government declared again, through its Ambassador at St. Petersburg, that Austria-Hungary had no desire for conquest and only wished peace at her frontiers. After the official explanation [*See exhibit 5.*] by Austria-Hungary to Russia that it did not claim territorial gain in Serbia, the decision concerning the peace of the world rested exclusively with St. Petersburg.

The same day the first news of Russian mobilization reached Berlin in the evening. [*See exhibits 6. 7, 8, 9.*]

The German Ambassadors at London, Paris, and St. Petersburg were instructed to energetically point out the danger of this Russian mobilization. The Imperial Ambassador at St. Petersburg was also directed to make the following declaration to the Russian Government: # [*See exhibits 10, 10a, and 10b.*]

"Preparatory military measures by Russia will force us to counter-measures which must consist in mobilizing the army." But mobilization means war. "As we know the obligations of France towards Russia, this "mobilization would be directed against both Russia and France. We cannot assume that Russia desires to unchain such a European war. Since Austria-Hungary will not touch the existence of the Serbian kingdom we are of the opinion that Russia can afford to assume an attitude of waiting. We can all the more support the desire of Russia to protect the integrity of Serbia as Austria-Hungary does not intend to question the latter. It will be easy in the further development of the affair to find a basis for is understanding."

On July 27, the Russian Secretary of War, M. Ssuchomlinof, gave the German military attaché his word of honor that no order to mobilize had been issued, merely preparations were being made, but not a horse mustered, nor reserves called in. If Austria-Hungary crossed the Serbian frontier, the military districts directed towards Austria, *i.e.*, Kiev, Odessa, Moscow, Kazan, would be mobilized, under no circumstances those situated on the German frontier, *i.e.*, St. Petersburg, Vilna, and Warsaw. Upon inquiry into the object of the mobilization against Austria-Hungary, the Russian Minister of War replied by shrugging his shoulders and referring to the diplomats. [*See exhibit 11.*] The military attaché then pointed to these mobilization measures against Austria-Hungary as extremely menacing also for Germany. [*See exhibit 11.*]

In the succeeding days, news concerning Russian mobilization came at a rapid rate. Among it was also news about preparations on the German-Russian frontier, as for instance the announcement of the state of war in Kovno, the departure of the Warsaw garrison, and the strengthening of the Alexrandrovo garrison.

On July 27, the first information was received concerning preparatory measures taken by France: the 14th Corps discontinued the maneuvers and returned to its garrison.

In the meantime, we had endeavored to localize the conflict by most emphatic steps.

On July 26, Sir Edward Grey had made the proposal to submit the differences between Austria-Hungary and Serbia to a conference of the Ambassadors of Germany, France, and Italy under his chair. We declared about a proposal that we could not, however much we approved the idea, participate in such a conference, as we could not call Austria in her dispute with Serbia before a European tribunal. [*See exhibit 12.*]

France consented to the proposal of Sir Edward Grey, but it foundered upon Austria's declining it, as was to be expected.

Faithful to our principle that mediation should not extend to the Austro-Serbian conflict, which is to be considered as a purely Austro-Hungarian affair, but merely to the relations between Austria-Hungary and Russia, we continued our endeavors to bring about an understanding between these two powers. [See exhibit 13.]

We further declared ourselves ready [See exhibit 14.] after failure of the conference idea, to transmit a second proposal of Sir Edward Grey's to Vienna in which he suggested Austria-Hungary should decide that either the Serbian reply was sufficient, or that it be used as a basis for further negotiations. [See exhibit 15.] The Austro-Hungarian Government remarked with full appreciation of our action that it had come too late, the hostilities having already been opened. [See exhibit 16.]

In spite of this, we continued our attempts to the utmost, and we advised Vienna to show every possible advance compatible with the dignity of the monarchy.

Unfortunately, all these proposals were overtaken by the military preparations of Russia and France.

On July 29, the Russian Government made the official notification in Berlin that four army districts had been mobilized. At the same time, further news was received concerning rapidly progressing military preparations of France, both on water and on land. [*See exhibit 17.*]

On the same day, the Imperial Ambassador in St. Petersburg had an interview with the Russian Foreign Secretary, in regard to which he reported by telegraph, as follows:

"The Secretary tried to persuade me that I should urge my Government to Participate in a quadruple conference to find means to induce Austria-Hungary to give up those demands, which touch upon the sovereignty of Serbia. I could merely promise to report the conversation and took the position that, after Russia had decided upon the baneful step of mobilization every exchange of ideas appeared now extremely difficult, if not impossible. Besides, Russia now was demanding from us in regard to Austria-Hungary the same, which Austria-Hungary was being blamed for with regard to Serbia, *i.e.,* an infraction of sovereignty. Austria-Hungary having promised to consider the Russian interests by disclaiming any territorial aspiration great concession on the part of a state engaged in war should therefore be permitted to attend to its affairs with Serbia alone. There would be time at the peace conference to return to the matter of forbearance towards the sovereignty of Serbia.

"I added very solemnly that at this moment the entire Austro-Serbian affair was eclipsed by the danger of a general European conflagration, and I endeavored to present to the secretary the magnitude of this danger. It was impossible to dissuade Sasonof from the idea that Serbia could not now be deserted by Russia."

To this H.M. the Kaiser replied:

"I thank you for your telegram. I have shown yesterday to Your Government avert the way through which alone war may yet. Although I asked for a reply by to-day noon, no telegram from my Ambassador has reached me with the reply of Your Government. I therefore have been forced to mobilize my army. An immediate, clear, and unmistakable reply of your Government is the sole way to avoid endless misery. Until I receive this reply, I am unable, to my great grief, to enter upon the subject of your telegram. I must ask most earnestly that you, without delay, order Your troops to commit under no circumstances, the slightest violation of our Frontiers."

As the time limit given to Russia had expired without the receipt of a reply to our inquiry, H.M. the Kaiser ordered the mobilization of the entire German Army and Navy on August 1st at 5 P.M. The German Ambassador at St. Petersburg was instructed that, in the event of the Russian Government not giving a satisfactory reply within the stipulated time, he should declare that we considered ourselves in at state of war after the refusal of our demands. [*See exhibit 26.*] However, before a confirmation of the execution of this order had been received, that is to say, already in the afternoon of August 1st, i.e., the same afternoon on which the telegram of the Czar, cited above, was sent, Russian troops crossed our frontier and marched into German territory.

Thus, Russia began the war against us.

Meanwhile the Imperial Ambassador in Paris put our question to the French Cabinet on July 31st at 7 P.M.

The French Prime Minister gave an equivocal and unsatisfactory reply on August 1st at 1 P.M., which gave no clear idea of the position of France, as he limited himself to the explanation that France would do that which her interests demanded. A few hours later, at 5 P.M., the mobilization of the entire French Army and Navy was ordered. [*See exhibit 27.*]

On the morning of the next day, France opened hostilities.

Primary Documents: President Poincare's War Address, 4 August 1914.

With Germany's decision to declare war with France on 3 August 1914, the French government found itself swept along (and somewhat surprised) by a tide of popular enthusiasm, a jubilant mood evident throughout the European continent. Thus on the following day, 4 August 1914—the date Britain joined France and Russia in the war against Germany—the French President wrote the following speech (his first war address), which was read to the French parliament by the minister of justice. The text of his speech is reproduced below.

Men:

France has just been the object of a violent and premeditated attack, which is an insolent defiance of the law of nations. Before any declaration of war had been sent to us, even before the German Ambassador had asked for his passports, our territory has been violated. The German Empire has waited until yesterday evening to give at this late stage the true name to a state of things, which it had already created.

For more than forty years, the French, in sincere love of peace, have buried at the bottom of their heart the desire for legitimate reparation.

They have given to the world the example of a great nation, which, definitely raised from defeat by the exercise of will, patience, and labor, has only used its renewed and rejuvenated strength in the interest of progress and for the good of humanity.

Since the ultimatum of Austria opened a crisis, which threatened the whole of Europe, France has persisted in following and in recommending on all sides a policy of prudence, wisdom, and moderation.

To her there can be imputed no act, no movement, no word, which has not been peaceful and conciliatory.

At the hour when the struggle is beginning, she has the right, in justice to herself, of solemnly declaring that she has made, up to the last moment, supreme efforts to avert the war now about to break out, and the crushing responsibility for which the German Empire will have to bear before history. Our fine and courageous army, which France today accompanies with her maternal thought has raised eager to defend the honor of the flag and the soil of the country.

The President of the Republic interpreting the unanimous feeling of the country expresses to our troops by land and sea the admiration and confidence of every Frenchman.

Closely united in a common feeling, the nation will persevere with the cool self-restraint of which, since the beginning of the crisis, she has given daily proof. Now, as always, she will know how to harmonies the most noble daring and most ardent enthusiasm with that self-control which is the sign of enduring energy and is the best guarantee of victory. In the war, which is beginning, France will have Right on her side, the eternal power of which cannot be disregarded with impunity by nations any more than by individuals.

All her sons will heroically defend her; nothing will break their sacred union before the enemy; today they are joined together as brothers in a common indignation against the aggressor, and in a common patriotic faith.

She is faithfully helped by Russia, her ally; she is supported by the loyal friendship of Great Britain.

In addition, already from every part of the civilized world sympathy and good wishes are coming to her. For today, once again she stands before the universe for Liberty, Justice, and Reason. *"Haut les course et vive la France!"*

Primary Documents: French Prime Minister's Statement, 4 August 1914.

Reproduced below is the text of the official statement issued by the French Prime Minister Rene Viviani on 4 August 1914.

In it, he recounts the countdown to war, drawing particular attention to Germany's apparent determination to engineer conflict from the outset.

Viviani went on to praise those nations that had either declared neutrality, i.e., Italy, or had else indicated support for France, including Russia and Britain.

He concluded by declaring that France would defend her honor and liberty against German aggression.

Official Statement of Prime Minister Rene Viviani.
August 4, 1914.

The German Ambassador yesterday left Paris after notifying us of the existence of a state of war. The Government owe to Parliament a true account of the events which, in less than ten days, have unloosed a European war and compelled France, peaceful and valiant, to defend her frontier against an attack, the hateful injustice of which is emphasized by its calculated unexpectedness.

This attack, which has no excuse, and which began before we were notified of any declaration of war, is the last act of a plan, whose origin and object I propose to declare before our own Democracy and before the opinion of the civilized world.

Because of the abominable crime, which cost the Austro-Hungarian Heir-Apparent and the Duchess of Hohenburg their lives, difficulties arose between the Cabinets of Vienna and Belgrade.

The majority of the Powers were only semi-officially informed of these difficulties up until Friday, July 24th, the date on which the Austro-Hungarian Ambassadors communicated to them a circular which the press has published.

The object of this circular was to explain and justify an ultimatum delivered the evening before to Serbia by the Austro-Hungarian Minister at Belgrade.

This ultimatum, in alleging the complicity of numerous Serbian subjects and associations in the Sarajevo crime, hinted that the official Serbian authorities themselves were no strangers to it. It demanded a reply from Serbia by 6 o'clock on the evening of Saturday, July 25th.

The Austrian demands, or at any rate many of them, without doubt struck a blow at the rights of a sovereign State. Notwithstanding their excessive character, Serbia, on July 25th, declared that she submitted to them almost without reserve.

This submission, which constituted a success for Austria-Hungary, a guarantee for the peace of Europe, was not unconnected with the advice tendered to Belgrade from the first moment by France, Russia, and Great Britain.

The value of this advice was all the greater since the Austro-Hungarian demands had been concealed from the Chanceries of the Triple Entente, to whom in the three preceding weeks the Austro-Hungarian Government had on several occasions given an assurance that their claims would be extremely moderate.

It was, therefore, with natural astonishment that the Cabinets of Paris, St. Petersburg, and London learned on July 26th that the Austrian Minister at Belgrade, after a few minutes' examination, declared that the Serbian reply was unacceptable, and broke off diplomatic relations.

This astonishment was increased by the fact that on Friday, the 24th, the German Ambassador came and read to the French Minister for Foreign Affairs a *note verbal* asserting that the Austro-Serbian dispute must remain localized, without intervention by the great Powers, or otherwise "incalculable consequences" were to be feared. A similar *demarche* was made on Saturday, the 25th, at London and at St. Petersburg.

Need I, gentlemen, point out to you the contrast between the threatening expressions used by the German Ambassador at Paris and the conciliatory sentiments which the Powers of the Triple Entente had just manifested by the advice which they gave to Serbia to submit?

Nevertheless, in spite of the extraordinary character of the German *demarche*, we immediately, in agreement with our Allies and our friends, took a conciliatory course and invited Germany to join in it.

We have had from the first moment regretfully to recognize that our intentions and our efforts met with no response at Berlin.

Not only did Germany appear wholly unwilling to give to Austria-Hungary the friendly advice, which her position gave her the right to offer, but also from this moment and still more in the following clays, she seemed to intervene between the Cabinet at Vienna and the compromises suggested by the other Powers.

On Tuesday, July 28th, Austria-Hungary declared war on Serbia. This declaration of war, with its aggravation of the state of affairs brought about by the rupture of diplomatic relations three days before, gave ground for believing that there was a deliberate desire for war, and a systematic program for the enslavement of Serbia.

Thus there was now involved in the dispute not only the independence of a brave people, but the balance of power in the Balkan, embodied in the Treaty of Bucharest of 1913, and consecrated by the moral support of all the great Powers.

However, at the suggestion of the British Government with its constant and firm attachment to the maintenance of the peace of Europe, the negotiations were continued, or, to speak more accurately, the Powers of the Triple Entente tried to continue them.

From this common desire sprang the proposal for action by the four Powers, England, France, Germany, and Italy, which was intended, by assuring to Austria all legitimate satisfaction, to bring about an equitable adjustment of the dispute.

On Wednesday, the 29th, the Russian Government, noting the persistent failure of these efforts and faced by the Austrian mobilization and declaration of war, fearing the military destruction of Serbia, decided as a precautionary measure to mobilize the troops of four military districts, that is to say, the formations echeloned along the Austro-Hungarian frontier exclusively.

In taking this step, the Russian Government were careful to inform the German Government that their measures, restricted as they were and without any offensive character towards Austria, were not in any degree directed against Germany.

In a conversation with the Russian Ambassador at Berlin, the German Secretary of State for Foreign Affairs acknowledged this without demur.

On the other hand, all the efforts made by Great Britain with the adherence of Russia and the support of France, to bring Austria and Serbia into touch under the moral patronage of Europe, were encountered at Berlin with a predetermined negative of which the diplomatic dispatches afford the clearest proof.

This was a disquieting situation, which made it probable that there existed at Berlin intentions, which had not been disclosed. Some hours afterwards, this alarming suspicion was destined to become a certainty.

In fact, Germany's negative attitude gave place thirty-six hours later to positive steps, which were truly alarming. On July 31st, Germany, by proclaiming "a state of danger of war, cut the communications between herself and the rest of Europe, and obtained for herself complete freedom to pursue against France in absolute secrecy military preparations which, as you have seen, nothing could justify.

Already for some days, and in circumstances difficult to explain, Germany had prepared for the transition of her army from a peace footing to a war footing.

From the morning of July 25th, that is to say, even before the expiration of the time limit given to Serbia by Austria, she had confined to barracks the garrisons of Alsace-Lorraine. The same day she had placed the frontier works in a complete state of defense.

On the 26th, she had indicated to the railways the measures preparatory for concentration. On the 27th, she had completed requisitions and placed her covering troops in position.

On the 28th, the summons of individual reservists had begun and units, which were distant from the frontier, had been brought up to it.

Could all these measures, pursued with implacable method, leave us in doubt of Germany's intentions?

Such was the situation when, on the evening of July 31st, the German Government, which since the 24th had not participated by any active step in the conciliatory efforts of the Triple Entente, addressed an ultimatum to the Russian Government under the pretext that Russia had ordered a general mobilization of her armies, and demanded that this mobilization should be stopped within twelve hours.

This demand, which was all the more insulting in form because a few hours earlier the Emperor Nicholas II, with a movement at once confiding and spontaneous, had asked the German Emperor for his mediation, was put forward at a moment when, on the request of England and with the knowledge of Germany, the Russian Government was accepting a formula of such a nature as to lay the foundation for a friendly settlement of the Austro-Serbian dispute and of the

Austro-Russian difficulties by the simultaneous arrest of military operations and of military preparations.

The same day this unfriendly *demarche* towards Russia was supplemented by acts which were frankly hostile towards France; the rupture of communications by road, railway, telegraph and telephone, the seizure of French locomotives on their arrival at the frontier, the placing of machine guns in the middle of the permanent way which had been cut, and the concentration of troops on this frontier.

From this moment, we were no longer justified in believing in the sincerity of the pacific declaration, which the German representative continued to shower upon us.

We knew that Germany was mobilizing under the shelter of the "state of danger of war."

We learnt that six classes of reservists had been called up, and that transport was being collected even for those army corps, which was, stationed a considerable distance from the frontier.

As these events unfolded themselves, our government, watchful and vigilant, took from day to day, and even from hour to hour, the measures of precaution, which the situation required; the general mobilization of our forces on land and sea was ordered.

The same evening, at 7.30, Germany, without waiting for the acceptance by the Cabinet of St. Petersburg of the English proposal, which I have already mentioned, declared war on Russia. The next day, Sunday, August 2nd, without regard for the extreme moderation of France, in contradiction to the peaceful declarations of the German Ambassador at Paris, and in defiance of the rules of international law, German troops crossed our frontier at three different points.

At the same time, in violation of the Treaty of 1867, which guaranteed with the signature of Prussia the neutrality of Luxemburg, they invaded the territory of the Grand Duchy and so gave cause for a protest by the Luxemburg Government.

Finally, the neutrality of Belgium also was threatened. The German Minister, on the evening of August 2nd, presented to the Belgian Government an ultimatum requesting facilities in Belgium for military operations against France, under the lying pretext that Belgian neutrality was threatened by us; the Belgian Government refused, and declared that they were resolved to defend with vigor their neutrality, which was respected by France and guaranteed by treaties, and in particular by the King of Prussia.

Since then, gentlemen, the German attacks have been renewed, multiplied, and accentuated. At more than fifteen points, our frontier has been violated. Shots have been fired at our soldiers and Customs officers. Men have been killed and wounded. Yesterday a German military aviator dropped three bombs on Luneville.

The German Ambassador, to whom as well as to all the great Powers, we communicated these facts, did not deny them or express his regrets for them.

On the contrary, he came yesterday evening to ask me for his passports, and to notify us of the existence of a state of war, giving as his reason, in the teeth of all the facts, hostile acts committed by French aviators in German territory in the Eifel district, and even on the railway near Carlsruhe and near Nuremberg.

This is the letter, which he handed to me on the subject:

Letter of Baron Schoen Declaring War

M. le President

The German administrative and military authorities have established a certain number of flagrantly hostile acts committed on German territory by French military aviators.

Several of these have openly violated the neutrality of Belgium by flying over the territory of that country; one has attempted to destroy buildings near Wesel; others have been seen in the district of the Eifel; one has thrown bombs on the railway near Carlsruhe and Nuremberg.

I am instructed, and I have the honor to inform your Excellency, that in the presence of these acts of aggression the German Empire considers itself in a state of war with France in consequence of the acts of this latter Power.

At the same time, I have the honor to bring to the knowledge of your Excellency that the German authorities will retain French mercantile vessels in German ports, but they will release them if, within forty-eight hours, they are assured of complete reciprocity.

My diplomatic mission having thus come to an end, it only remains for me to request your Excellency to be good enough to furnish me with my passports, and to take the steps you consider suitable to assure my return to Germany, with the staff of the Embassy, as well as, with the Staff of the Bavarian Legation and of the German Consulate General in Paris.

Be good enough, M. le President, to receive the assurances of my deepest respect.

(Signed) SCHOEN.

Need I, gentlemen, lay stress on the absurdities of these pretexts which they put forward as grievances?

At no time has any French aviator penetrated into Belgium, nor has any French aviator committed in either Bavaria or any other part of Germany any hostile act. The opinion of Europe has already done justice to these wretched inventions.

Against these attacks, which violate all the laws of justice and all the principles of public law, we have now taken all the necessary steps; they are being carried out strictly, regularly, and with calmness.

The mobilization of the Russian army also continues with remarkable vigor and unrestrained enthusiasm. The Belgian army, mobilized with 250,000 men, prepares with a splendid passion and magnificent ardor to defend the neutrality and independence of their country.

The entire English fleet is mobilized and orders have been given to mobilize the land forces. Since 1912, pourparlers had taken place between English and French General Staffs and were concluded by an exchange of letters between Sir Edward Grey and M. Paul Cambon.

The Secretary of State for Foreign Affairs yesterday evening communicated these letters to the House of Commons, and spoke of France amidst the applause of the members in a noble and warm-hearted manner.

His language has already found an echo deep in the hearts of all Frenchmen. I wish in the name of the Government of the Republic to thank the English Government from this tribune for their cordial words and the Parliament of France will associate itself in this sentiment.

The Secretary of State for Foreign Affairs made in particular the following declaration: "In case the German fleet came into the Channel or entered the North Sea in order to go 'round the British Isles with the object of attacking the French coasts or the French navy and of harassing French merchant shipping, the English fleet would intervene in order to give to French shipping its complete protection in such a way that from that moment England and Germany would be in a state of war."

From now onwards, the English fleet protects our northern and western coasts against a German attack.

Gentlemen, these are the facts. I believe that the simple recital of them is sufficient to justify the acts of the Government of the Republic. I wish, however, to make clear the conclusion to be drawn from my story and to give its true meaning to the unheard—of attack of which France is the victim.

The victors of 1870 have, at different times, as you know, desired to repeat the blows, which they dealt us then.

In 1875, the war which was intended to complete the destruction of conquered France was only prevented by the intervention of the two Powers to whom we were to become united at a later date by ties of alliance and of friendship, by the intervention of Russia and of Great Britain.

Since then the French Republic, by the restoration of her national forces and the conclusion of diplomatic agreements unswervingly adhered to, has succeeded in liberating herself from the yoke, which even in a period of profound peace Bismarck was able to impose upon Europe.

She has re-established the balance of power in Europe, a guarantee of the liberty and dignity of all.

Gentlemen, I do not know if I am mistaken, but it seems to me that this work of peaceful reparation, of liberation and honor finally ratified in 1904 and 1907, with the genial co-operation of King Edward VII of England and the Government of the Crown, this is what the German Empire wishes to destroy to-day by one daring stroke.

Germany can reproach us with nothing.

Bearing in silence in our bosom for half a century the wound, which Germany dealt us, we have offered to peace an unprecedented sacrifice.

We have offered other sacrifices in all the discussions, which since 1904 German diplomacy has systematically provoked, whether in Morocco or elsewhere in 1905, in 1906, in 1908, in 1911.

Russia also has given proof of great moderation at the time of the events of 1908, as she has done in the present crisis.

She observed the same moderation and the Triple Entente with her, when in the Eastern crisis of 1912, Austria and Germany formulated demands, whether against Serbia or against Greece, which still were, as the event proved, capable of settlement by discussion.

Useless sacrifices, barren negotiations, empty efforts, since to-day in the very act of conciliation we, our allies and ourselves, are attacked by surprise.

No one can honestly believe that we are the aggressors. Vain is the desire to overthrow the sacred principles of right and of liberty to which nations, as well as individuals, are subject; Italy with that clarity of insight possessed by the Latin intellect, has notified us that she proposes to preserve neutrality.

This decision has found in all France an echo of sincerest joy.

I made myself the interpreter of this feeling to the Italian *Charge d'Affaires* when I told him how much I congratulated myself that the two Latin sisters, who have the same origin and the same ideal, a common and glorious past, are not now opposed to one another.

Gentlemen, we proclaim loudly the object of their attack—it is the independence, the honor, the safety, which the Triple Entente has regained in the balance of power for the service of peace. The object of attack is the liberties of Europe, which France, her allies, and her friends, are proud to defend.

We are going to defend these liberties, for it is they that are in dispute, and all the rest is but a pretext.

France, unjustly provoked, did not desire war; she has done everything to avert it.

Since it is forced upon her, she will defend herself against Germany and against every Power, which has not yet declared its intentions, but joins with the latter in a conflict between the two countries.

A free and valiant people that sustains an eternal ideal, and is wholly united to defend its existence; a Democracy which knows how to discipline its military strength, and was not afraid a year ago to increase its burden as an answer to the armaments of its neighbor; a nation armed, struggling for its own life and for the independence of Europe—here is a sight which we are proud to offer to the onlookers in this desperate struggle, that has for some days been preparing with the greatest calmness and method.

We are without reproach. We shall be without fear. France has often proved in less favorable circumstances that she is a most formidable adversary when she fights, as she does to-day, for liberty and for right.

In submitting our actions to you, gentlemen, who are our judges, we have, to help us in bearing the burden of our heavy responsibility, the comfort of a clear conscience and the conviction that we have done our duty.

Source: *Source Records of the Great War, Vol. II, ed. Charles F. Horne, National Alumni, 1923.*

Primary Documents: Address by King Albert to Belgian Parliament, 4 August 1914

Reproduced below is the text of the speech given by of Belgium to the Belgian parliament on 4 August 1914.

Having two days earlier across Belgium for its troops in the latter is war against France; Belgium prepared itself to defend its independence. Such was the background to the monarch's speech to parliament on 4 August 1914—the same day Britain entered the war in defense of Belgium.

Address by King Albert to the Belgian Parliament, 4 August 1914.

Gentlemen:

Never, since 1839, has a more solemn hour struck for Belgium: the integrity of our territory is threatened.

The very force of our righteous cause, the sympathy which Belgium, proud of her free institutions and her moral victories, has always received from other nations, and the necessity of our autonomous existence in respect of the equilibrium of Europe, make us still hopeful that the dreaded emergency will not be realized.

However, if our hopes are betrayed, if we are forced to resist the invasion of our soil, and to defend our threatened homes, this duty, however hard it may be, will find us armed and resolved upon the greatest sacrifices.

Even now, in readiness for any eventuality, our valiant youth is up in arms, firmly resolved, with the traditional tenacity and composure of the Belgians, to defend our threatened country.

In the name of the nation, I give it a brotherly greeting. Everywhere in Flanders and Wallonia, in the towns and in the countryside, one single feeling binds all hearts together: the sense of patriotism.

One single vision fills all minds: that of our independence endangered. One single duty imposes itself upon our wills: the duty of stubborn resistance.

In these solemn circumstances, two virtues are indispensable: a calm but unshaken courage, and the close union of all Belgians.

Both virtues have already asserted themselves, in a brilliant fashion, before the eyes of a nation full of enthusiasm.

The irreproachable mobilization of our army, the multitude of voluntary enlistments, the devotion of the civil population, the abnegation of our soldiers' families, have revealed in an unquestionable manner the reassuring courage which inspires the Belgian people.

It is the moment for action.

I have called you together, gentlemen, in order to enable the Legislative Chambers to associate themselves with the impulse of the people in one and the same sentiment of sacrifice.

You will understand, gentlemen, how to take all those immediate measures which the situation requires, in respect both of the war and of public order.

No one in this country will fail in his duty.

If the foreigner, in defiance of that neutrality whose demands we have always scrupulously observed, violates our territory, he will find all the Belgians gathered about their sovereign, who will never betray his constitutional oath, and their Government, invested with the absolute confidence of the entire nation.

I have faith in our destinies; a country, which is defending itself, conquers the respect of all; such a country does not perish!

Source: *Source Records of the Great War, Vol. II, ed. Charles F. Horne, National Alumni, 1923.*

Primary Documents: UK *Daily Mirror* News Report, 4 August 1914

With Britain's decision to enter the war on 4 August 1914 and its consequent declaration against Germany, popular enthusiasm for the government's stance (led by Prime Minister Herbert Asquith) was overwhelming.

Reproduced below is the text of the front page of the bestselling *Daily Mirror* newspaper for that date, 4 August 1914.

REPORT OF A SPEECH DELIVERED BY HERR VON BETHMANN HOLLWEG, GERMAN IMPERIAL CHANCELLOR, ON AUGUST 4th, 1914.

A stupendous fate is breaking over Europe. For forty-four years, since the time we fought for and won the German Empire and our position in the world, we have lived in peace and have protected the peace of Europe. In the works of peace we have become strong and powerful, and have thus aroused the envy of others. With patience, we have faced the fact that, under the pretence that Germany was desirous of war, enmity has been awakened against us in the East and the West, and chains have been fashioned for us. The wind then sown has brought forth the whirlwind which has now broken loose. We wished to continue our work of peace, and, like a silent vow, the feeling that animated everyone from the Emperor down to the youngest soldier was this: Only in defense of a just cause shall our sword fly from its scabbard.

The day has now come when we must draw it, against our wish, and in spite of our sincere endeavors. Russia has set fire to the building. We are at war with Russia and France war that has been forced upon us.

Gentlemen, a number of documents, composed during the pressure of these last eventful days, is before you. Allow me to emphasize the facts that determine our attitude.

From the first moment of the Serbian conflict, we declared that this question must be limited to Austria-Hungary and Serbia, and we worked with this end in view. All Governments especially that of Great Britain, took the same attitude. Russia alone asserted that she had to be heard in the settlement of this matter. Thus, the danger of a European crisis raised its threatening head. As soon as the first definite information regarding the military preparations in Russia reached us, we declared at St. Petersburgh in a friendly but emphatic manner that military measures against Austria would find us on the side of our ally, and that military preparations against ourselves would oblige us to take countermeasures; but that mobilization would come very near to actual war.

Russia assured us in the most solemn manner of her desire for peace, and declared that she was making no military preparations against us.

In the meantime, Great Britain, warmly supported by us, tried to mediate between Vienna and St. Petersburgh.

On July 28th the Emperor telegraphed to the Czar asking him to take into consideration the fact that it was both the duty and the right of Austria-Hungary to defend herself against the pan-Serb agitation, which threatened to undermine her existence. The Emperor drew the Czar's attention to the solidarity of the interests of all monarchs in face of the murder of Sarajevo. He asked for the latter's personal assistance in smoothing over the difficulties existing between Vienna and St. Petersburgh. About the same time, and before receipt of this telegram, the Czar asked the Emperor to come to his aid and to induce Vienna to moderate her demands. The Emperor accepted the role of mediator.

However, scarcely had active steps on these lines begun, when Russia mobilized all her forces directed against Austria, while Austria-Hungary had mobilized only those of her corps, which were directed against Serbia. To the north, she had mobilized only two of her corps, far from the Russian frontier. The Emperor immediately informed the Czar that this mobilization of Russian forces against Austria rendered the role of mediator, which he had accepted at the Czar's request, difficult, if not impossible.

In spite of this, we continued our task of mediation at Vienna and carried it to the utmost point, which was compatible with our position as an ally.

Meanwhile Russia of her own accord renewed her assurances that she was making no military preparations against us.

We come now to July 31st. The decision was to be taken at Vienna. Through our representations, we had already obtained the resumption of direct conversations between Vienna and St. Petersburg, after they had been for some time interrupted. But before the final decision was taken at Vienna, the news arrived that Russia had mobilized her entire forces and that her mobilization was therefore directed against us also. The Russian Government, who knew from our repeated statements what mobilization on our frontiers meant, did not notify us of this mobilization, nor did they even offer any explanation. It was not until the afternoon of July 31st that the Emperor received a telegram from the Czar in which he guaranteed that his army would not assume a provocative attitude towards us. But mobilization on our frontiers had been in full swing since the night of July 30th–31st.

While we were mediating at Vienna in compliance with Russia's request, Russian forces were appearing all along our extended and almost entirely open frontier, and France, though indeed not actually mobilizing, was admittedly making military preparations. What was our position? For the sake of the peace of Europe we had, up until then, deliberately refrained from calling up a single reservist.

Were we now to wait further in patience until the nations on either side of us chose the moment for their attack? It would have been a crime to expose Germany to such peril. Therefore, on July 31st we called upon Russia to demobilize as the only measure which could still preserve the peace of Europe. The Imperial Ambassador at St. Petersburgh was also instructed to inform the Russian Government that in case our demand met with a refusal, we should have to consider that a state of war (*Kriegszustand*) existed.

The Imperial Ambassador has executed these instructions. We have not yet learnt what Russia answered to our demand for demobilization. Telegraphic reports on this question have not reached us even though the wires still transmitted much less important information.

Therefore, the time limit having long since expired, the Emperor was obliged to mobilize our forces on the 1st August at 5 P.M.

At the same time, we had to make certain what attitude France would assume. To our direct question, whether she would remain neutral in the event of a Russo-German War, France replied that she would do what her interests demanded. That was an evasion, if not a refusal.

In spite of this, the Emperor ordered that the French frontier be to be unconditionally respected. This order, with one single exception, was strictly obeyed. France, who mobilized at the same time as we did, assured us that she would respect a zone of 10 kilometers on the frontier. What really happened? Aviators dropped bombs, and cavalry patrols and French infantry detachments appeared on the territory of the Empire! Though war had not been declared, France thus broke the peace and actually attacked us.

Regarding the one exception on our side which I mentioned, the Chief of the General Staff reports as follows:

"Only one of the French complaints about the crossing of their frontier from our side is justified. Against express orders, a patrol of the 14th Army Corps, apparently led by an officer, crossed the frontier on August 2nd. They seem to have been shot down, only one man having returned. But long before this isolated instance of crossing the frontier had occurred, French aviators had penetrated into Southern Germany and had thrown bombs on our railway lines. French troops had attacked our frontier guards on the Schlucht Pass. Our troops, in accordance with their orders, have remained strictly on the defensive." This is the report of the General Staff.

Gentlemen, we are now in a state of necessity (*Notwehr*), and necessity (*Not*) knows no law. Our troops have occupied Luxemburg and perhaps have already entered Belgian territory.

Gentlemen, that is a breach of international law. It is true that the French Government declared at Brussels that France would respect Belgian neutrality as long as her adversary respected it. We knew, however, that France stood ready for an invasion. France could wait, we could not. A French attack on our flank on the lower Rhine might have been disastrous. Thus, we were forced to ignore the rightful protests of the Governments of Luxemburg and Belgium. The wrong speak openly the wrong we thereby commit we will try to make good as soon as our military aims have been attained.

He who is menaced as we are and is fighting for his highest possession can only consider how he is to hack his way through (*durchhauen*).

Gentlemen, we stand shoulder to shoulder with Austria-Hungary.

As for Great Britain's attitude, the statements made by Sir Edward Grey in the House of Commons yesterday show the standpoint assumed by the British Government. We have informed the British Government that, as long as Great Britain remains neutral, our fleet will not attack the northern coast of France, and that we will not violate the territorial integrity and independence of Belgium. These assurances I now repeat before the world, and I may add that, as long as Great Britain remains neutral, we would also be willing, upon reciprocity being assured, to take no warlike measures against French commercial shipping.

Gentlemen, so much for the facts. I repeat the words of the Emperor: "With a clear conscience we enter the lists." We are fighting for the fruits of our works of peace, for the inheritance of a great past and for our future. The fifty years are not yet past during which Count Moltke said we should have to remain armed to defend the inheritance that we won in 1870. Now the great hour of trial has struck for our people. But with clear confidence we go forward to meet it. Our army is in the field; our navy is ready for battle—behind them stands the entire German nation united to the last man.

Gentlemen, you know your duty and all that it means. The proposed laws need no further explanations I ask you to pass them quickly.

DAILY MIRROR, NEWS HEADLINES, 4 AUGUST 1914.
Great Britain Declares War on Germany

Declaration last night after "unsatisfactory reply" to British ultimatum that Belgium must be kept neutral

The King's Message to his Navy

Government to take control of all railways Admiral Jellicoe to be in supreme command of the Home Fleets.
Huge Crowds Cheer Their Majesties at Palace.
£100,000,000 voted in Commons in five minutes German invasion of Belgium with airships.
Great Britain Declares War on Germany.

Great Britain is in a state of war with Germany. It was officially stated at the Foreign Office last night that Great Britain declared war against Germany at 7.00 PM. The British Ambassador in Berlin has been handed his passport.

War was Germany's reply to our request that she should respect the neutrality of Belgium, whose territories we were bound in honor and by treaty obligations to maintain inviolate.

Speaking in a crowded and hushed House the Premier yesterday afternoon made the following statement: "We have made a request to the German Government that we shall have a satisfactory assurance as to the Belgian neutrality before midnight tonight."

The German reply to our request, officially stated last night, was unsatisfactory.

The King and His Navy

The King has addressed the following message to Admiral Sir John Jellicoe: "At this grave moment in our national history I send to you and, through you, to the officers and men of the fleets, of which you have assumed command, the assurance of my confidence that under your direction they will revive and renew the old glories of the Royal Navy, and prove once again the sure shield of Britain and of her Empire in the hour of trial."

The above message has been communicated to the senior naval officers on all stations outside of home waters.

It was reported yesterday evening that Germany had taken the first hostile step by destroying a British minelayer.

At the present time Germany is in a state of war with: Great Britain, Russia, France, and Belgium.

It would seem as if Germany, in her ambition to control the destiny of the whole of Europe, were ready to embark on any grandiose scheme of adventure, however precarious her chances.

As far as Great Britain is concerned, her attitude has always been plain, straightforward and perfectly intelligible. She was prepared to stand aside from the conflict that has now involved practically the whole of Europe.

However, she insisted and had to insist on two things: these were that Belgium's neutrality should be respected; and that the German fleet should not bombard defenseless French towns.

Germany tried to bribe us with peace to desert our friends and duty. But Great Britain has preferred the path of honor.

Chief of the Fleets

Sir John R. Jellicoe has assumed the supreme command of the Home Fleets, with the acting rank of Admiral. Rear Admiral Charles E. Madden has been appointed to be his chief of staff. Field Marshal Sir John French, the famous cavalry leader, has been appointed Inspector General to the Forces.

Mr. Lloyd George subsequently announced in the House that the Government was engaged in preparing a scheme for the distribution of food, and hoped that it would be completed in the course of one or two days. The House unanimously passed in five minutes all outstanding votes, amounting to over £100,000,000.

An Order in Council has been issued declaring it expedient that Government should have control over the railroads of Great Britain.

Mr. Asquith's Statement

In a strained silence in every part of the House of Commons yesterday, the Prime Minister made his momentous statement.

He explained how the King of the Belgians had appealed to England for diplomatic intervention on behalf of his country—Germany having demanded free passage for her troops through Belgium, promising to maintain the integrity and independence of the kingdom. "Simultaneously," continued Mr. Asquith, "we received from the Belgian Legation in London the following telegram from the Belgian Minister for Foreign Affairs: 'The General Staff announce that territory has been violated at Verviers, near Aix-la-Chapelle. Subsequent information tends to show that a German force has penetrated still further into Belgian territory.'"

"We also received this morning from the German Ambassador here a telegram sent to him from the German Foreign Secretary: 'Please dispel any distrust that must exist on the part of the British Government with regard to our intentions by repeating, most positively, the formal assurance that, even in case of armed conflict with Belgium, Germany will not, under any pretence whatever, annex Belgian territory. Please impress upon Sir Edward Grey that the German Army could not be exposed to a French attack across Belgium, which was planned according to absolutely unimpeachable information.'"

"I have," continued Mr. Asquith, "to add this on behalf of the Government: we cannot regard this as in any sense a satisfactory communication."

"We have, in reply to it, repeated the request we made last week to the German Government that they should give us the same assurance with regard to Belgian neutrality as was given to us and to Belgium by France last week."

"We have asked that a reply to that request and a satisfactory answer to the telegram of this morning, which I have read to the House, should be given before midnight."

Roars of Cheers for the King

The King and Queen, accompanied by the Prince of Wales and Princess Mary, were hailed with wild, enthusiastic cheers when they appeared at about eight o'clock last night on the balcony of Buckingham Palace, before which a record crowd had assembled.

Seeing the orderliness of the crowd, the police did not attempt to force the people back and went away.

A little later the police passed the word around that silence was necessary as the King was holding a meeting in the Palace and except for a few spasmodic outbursts there was silence for a time.

Afterwards the cheering was renewed with increased vigor and soon after 11.00 P.M. the King and Queen and Prince of Wales made a further appearance on the balcony and the crown once more sang the National Anthem, following this with hearty clapping and cheering.

After the departure of the royal party some minutes later, many of the crowd dispersed. Several enthusiasts, however, stayed outside keeping up the demonstration by shouting and waving flags.

Why There Is War

The following statement was issued from the Foreign Office last night: Owing to the summary rejection by the German Government of the request made by his Majesty's Government for assurances that the neutrality of Belgium would be respected, his Majesty's Ambassador in Berlin has received his passport, and his Majesty's Government has declared to the German Government that a state of war exists between Great Britain and Germany as from 11.00 P.M. on August 4.

No. 49.
From: M. N. Pashitch, Prime Minister and Minister for Foreign Affairs.
To: Dr. M. Yovanovitch, Chargé d'Affaires at Berlin.
Nish
August 4, 1914.
(Telegraphic)

Please inform the Imperial Government that you have received instructions to leave Germany, together with the staffs of the Legation and Consulate. You should leave immediately.

Chapter Thirty-Seven
August 6, 1914

No. 51.

From: Dr. M. Yovanovitch, Chargé d'Affaires at Berlin.

To: M. N. Pashitch, Prime Minister and Minister for Foreign Affairs.

Berlin

August 6, 1914.

On the occasion of my visit to the Under-Secretary of State, M. Zimmermann, for the purpose of breaking off diplomatic relations, he stated, in the course of conversation, that Germany had always cherished friendly feelings towards Serbia, and that he regretted that owing to the political groupement our relations had to be broken off. He blames Russia only, as the instigator of Serbia, for the developments which have occurred, and which will have grave consequences for all nations. If Russia, at the last moment—just when it appeared possible that an armed convict might be avoided—had not ordered the mobilisation of her whole forces, there would have been no war, for Germany had used her whole influence in Austria-Hungary in order to bring about an understanding with Russia. Austria-Hungary would have probably been satisfied with the occupation of Belgrade, when negotiations would have begun with a view to regularizing the relations between Serbia and Austria.

Note presented by the Austro-Hungarian Ambassador at St. Petersburg to the Russian Minister for Foreign Affairs on August 6, 1914, at 6 P.M.

ON the instructions of his Government, the undersigned the Austro-Hungarian Ambassador, has the honor to inform his Excellency the Russian Minister for Foreign Affairs as follows: "*Vu latitude menaçante prise par la Russie dans le confit entre la Monarchie austrohongroise et la Serbie et en presence du fait qu'en suite de ce conflit la Russie d'après une communication du Cabinet de Berlin a cru devoir ouvrir les hostilités contre l'Allemagne et que celle-ci se trouve par conséquent en état de guerre avec ladite Puissance, l'Autriche-Hongrie se considère également en état de guerre avec la Russie à partir du present moment.*"

(Translation)

"In view of the threatening attitude adopted by Russia in the conflict between the Austro-Hungarian Monarchy and Serbia; and of the fact that, according to a communication from the Berlin Cabinet, Russia has seen fit, as a result of that conflict, to open hostilities against Germany; and whereas Germany is consequently at war with Russia; Austria-Hungary therefore considers herself also at war with Russia from the present moment."

From: **The Royal Serbian Ministry for Foreign Affairs.**
To: **The German legation at Nish.**
Nish
August 6, 1914.

The Royal Serbian Ministry for Foreign Affairs has the honor to inform the Imperial Legation that, in view of the state of war which now exists between Serbia and Austria-Hungary, and of that between Russia and Germany, the ally of Austria-Hungary, the Royal Serbian Government, in view of the solidarity of her interests with Russia and her allies, considers the mission of Baron Gieslingen, the Imperial German Minister Plenipotentiary and Envoy Extraordinary, to be at an end. The Royal Serbian Government requests His Excellency to leave Serbian territory with the staff of the Legations. The necessary passports are enclosed herewith.

Primary Documents: British Prime Minister's Address to Parliament, 6 August 1914

Reproduced below is the text of the speech given to the British Parliament by Prime Minister Herbert Asquith.

Given on 6 August 1914—two days after Britain entered the war against Germany in defense of Belgium—Asquith recounted the background to the outbreak of general war in Europe in July/August 1914, placing great emphasis on the efforts of the British Foreign Secretary, Sir Edward Grey, to secure continued peace in the face of German aggression.

Asquith finished his speech by stating that Britain would throw her entire Empire's resources into the struggle against Germany in order to ensure victory.

British Prime Minister Herbert Asquith's Address to Parliament, 6 August 1914

With the utmost reluctance and with infinite regret, His Majesty's Government has been compelled to put this country in a state of war with what for many years and indeed generations past has been a friendly Power.

The Papers which have since been presented to Parliament will, I think, show how strenuous, how unremitting, how persistent, even when the last glimmer of hope seemed to have faded away, were the efforts of my right hon. Friend the Foreign Secretary (note: Sir Edward Grey) to secure for Europe an honorable and a lasting peace.

Everyone knows in the great crisis which occurred last year in the East of Europe, it was largely, if not mainly, by the acknowledgment of all Europe, due to the steps taken by my right hon.

Friend that the area of the conflict was limited, and that so far as the great Powers are concerned, peace was maintained.

If his efforts upon this occasion have, unhappily, been less successful, I am certain that this House and the country—and I will add posterity and history—will accord to him what is, after all, the best tribute that can be paid to any statesman: that, never derogating for an instant or by an inch from the honor and interests of his own country, he has striven, as few men have striven, to maintain and preserve the greatest interest of all countries—universal peace.

The Papers, which are now in the hands of hon. members, show something more than that. They show what were the terms, which were offered to us in exchange for our neutrality. I trust that not only the Members of this House, but all our fellow-subjects everywhere will read the communications—will read, learn, and mark the communications which passed only a week ago to-day between Berlin and London in this matter.

The terms by which it was sought to buy our neutrality are contained in the communication made by the German Chancellor to Sir Edward Goschen on the 29th July. I think I must refer to them for a moment. After alluding to the state of things as between Austria and Russia, Sir Edward Goschen goes on:

"He [the German Chancellor] then proceeded to make the following strong bid for British neutrality. He said that it was clear, as far as he was able to judge the main principle, which governed British policy that Great Britain would never stand by and allow France to be crushed in any conflict there might be.

"That, however, was not the object at which Germany aimed. Provided that neutrality of Great Britain were certain, every assurance would be given to the British Government that the Imperial Government."

Let the Committee observe these words:

"Aimed at no territorial acquisition at the expense of France should they prove victorious in any war that might ensue?"

Sir Edward Goschen proceeded to put a very pertinent question: "I questioned His Excellency about the French colonies."

What are the French colonies? They mean every part of the dominions and possessions of France outside the geographical area of Europe—"and he said that he was unable to give a similar undertaking in that respect."

Let me cone to what, in my mind, personally has always been the crucial and almost the governing consideration, namely, the position of the small States:

"As regards Holland, however, His Excellency said that so long as Germany's adversaries respected the integrity and neutrality of the Netherlands, Germany was ready to give His Majesty's Government an assurance that she would do likewise."

Then we come to Belgium:

"It depended upon the action of France what operations Germany might he forced to enter upon in Belgium, but, when the war was over, Belgian integrity would be respected if she had not sided against Germany."

Let the Committee observe the distinction between those two cases. In regard to Holland it was not only independence and integrity, but also neutrality; but in regard to Belgium, there was no mention of neutrality at all, nothing but an assurance that after the war came to an end the integrity of Belgium would be respected.

Then His Excellency added: "Ever since he had been Chancellor the object of his policy had been to bring about an understanding with England. He trusted that these assurances"—the assurances I have read out to the House—"might form the basis of that understanding which he so much desired."

What does that amount to? Let me just ask the Committee. I do so, not with the object of inflaming passion, certainly not with the object of exciting feeling against Germany, but I do so to vindicate and make clear the position of the British Government in this matter.

What did that proposal amount to? In the first place, it meant this: That behind the back of France—they were not made a party to these communications—we should have given, if we had assented to that, a free license to Germany to annex, in the event of a successful war, the whole of the extra European dominions and possessions of France.

What did it mean as regards Belgium? When she addressed, as she has addressed in these last few days, her moving appeal to us to fulfill our solemn guarantee of her neutrality, what reply should we have given? What reply should we have given to that Belgian appeal?

We should have been obliged to say that, without her knowledge, we had bartered away to the Power threatening her our obligation to keep our plighted word.

The House has read, and the country has read, of course, in the last few hours, the most pathetic appeal addressed by the King of Belgium, and I do not envy the man who can read that appeal with an unmoved heart. Belgians are fighting and losing their lives. What would have been the position of Great Britain to-day, in the face of that spectacle, if we had assented to this infamous proposal?

Yes, and what are we to get in return for the betrayal of our friends and the dishonor of our obligations? What are we to get in return? A promise—nothing more; a promise as to what Germany would do in certain eventualities; a promise, be it observed—I am sorry to have to say it, but it must be put upon record—given by a Power which was at that very moment announcing its intention to violate its own treaty and inviting us to do the same.

I can only say, if we had dallied or temporized, we, as a Government, should have covered ourselves with dishonor, and we should have betrayed the interests of this country, of which we are trustees.

I am glad, and I think the country will be glad, to turn to the reply which my right hon. Friend made, and of which I will read to the Committee two of the more salient passages. This document, No. 101 of the Papers, puts on record a week ago the attitude of the British Government, and, as I believe, of the British people.

My right hon. Friend says:

"His Majesty's Government cannot for a moment entertain the Chancellor's proposal that they should bind themselves to neutrality on such terms. What he asks us in effect is to engage to stand by while French Colonies are taken if France is beaten, so long as Germany does not take French territory as distinct from the Colonies. From the material point of view—" My right lion. Friend, as he always does, used very temperate language:

"—Such a proposal is unacceptable, for France, without further territory in Europe being taken from her, could be so crushed as to lose her position as a Great Power, and become subordinate to German policy."

That is the material aspect. But he proceeded:

"Altogether, apart from that, it would be a disgrace for us to make this bargain with Germany at the expense of France, a disgrace from which the good name of this country would never recover. The Chancellor also in effect asks us to bargain away whatever obligation or interest we have as regards the neutrality of Belgium. We could not entertain that bargain either."

He then says:—"We must preserve our full freedom to act, as circumstances may seem to us to require."

And he added, I think in sentences which the Committee must appreciate:

"You should... add most earnestly that the one way of maintaining the good relations between England and Germany are that they should continue to work together to preserve the peace of Europe... For that object, this Government will work in that way with all sincerity and goodwill.

"If the peace of Europe can be preserved and the present crisis safely passed, my own endeavor will be to promote some arrangement to which Germany could be a party, by which she could be assured that no aggressive or hostile policy would be pursued against her or her allies by France, Russia, and ourselves, jointly or separately.

"I have desired this and worked for it"—the statement was never more true— "as far as I could, through the last Balkan crisis, and Germany having a corresponding object, our relations sensibly improved.

"The idea has hitherto been too Utopian to form the subject of definite proposals, but if this present crisis, so much more acute than any that Europe has gone through for generations, be safely passed, I am hopeful that the relief and reaction which will follow may make possible some more definite rapprochement between the Powers than has been possible hitherto."

That document, in my opinion, states clearly, in temperate and convincing language, the attitude of this Government.

Can anyone who reads it fail to appreciate the tone of obvious sincerity and earnestness which underlies it; can any one honestly doubt that the Government of this country in spite of great provocation—and I regard the proposals made to us as proposals which we might have thrown aside without consideration and almost without answer can any one doubt that in spite of great provocation the right hon. Gentleman, who had already earned the title and no one ever more deserved it—of "Peace Maker of Europe," persisted to the very last moment of the last hour in that beneficent but unhappily frustrated purpose?

I am entitled to say, and I do so on behalf of this country—I speak not for a party, I speak for the country as a whole—that we made every effort any Government could possibly make for peace. But this war has been forced upon us. What is it we are fighting for? Everyone knows, and no one knows better than the Government, the terrible, incalculable suffering, economic, social, personal and political, which war, and especially a war between the Great Powers of the world, must entail.

There is no man amongst us sitting upon this bench in these trying days—more trying perhaps than any body of statesmen for a hundred years have had to pass through—there is not a man amongst us who has not, during the whole of that time, had clearly before his vision the almost unequalled suffering which war, even in a just cause, must bring about, not only to the people who are for the moment living in this country and in the other countries of the world, but to posterity and to the whole prospects of European civilization.

Every step we took we took with that vision before our eyes, and with a sense of responsibility, which it is impossible to describe.

Unhappily, if in spite of all our efforts to keep the peace, and with that full and overpowering consciousness of the result, if the issue be decided in favor of war, we have, nevertheless, thought it to be the duty as well as the interest of this country to go to war, the House may be well assured it was because we believe, and I am certain the country will believe, that we are unsheathing our sword in a just cause.

If I am asked what we are fighting for I reply in two sentences: In the first place, to fulfill a solemn international obligation, an obligation which, if it had been entered into between private persons in the ordinary concerns of life, would have been regarded as an obligation not only of law but of honor, which no self-respecting man could possibly have repudiated.

I say, secondly, we are fighting to vindicate the principle which, in these days when force, material force, sometimes seems to be the dominant influence and factor in the development of mankind, we are fighting to vindicate the principle that small nationalities are not to be crushed, in defiance of international good faith, by the arbitrary will of a strong and overmastering Power. I do not believe any nation ever entered into a great controversy—and this is one of the greatest history will ever know—with a clearer conscience and a stronger conviction that it is fighting, not for aggression, not for the maintenance even of its own selfish interest, but that it is fighting in defense of principles the maintenance of which is vital to the civilization of the world.

With a full conviction, not only of the wisdom and justice, but also of the obligations, which lay upon us to challenge this great issue, we are entering into the struggle. Let us now make sure that all the resources, not only of this United Kingdom, but also of the vast Empire of which it is the centre, shall be thrown into the scale.

Source: *Source Records of the Great War, Vol. I, ed. Charles F. Horne, National Alumni, 1923.*

Kaiser Wilhelm is back from his vacation, believing the war against Russia is self-defense and hoping France will stay out of the war. But France sides with Russia and invades Germany. Germany launches an offensive against France, which goes through Belgium. The British stand by their military agreement with France and are opposed to Germany marching through Belgium, and they join the war against Germany.

Primary Documents: Official German Statement on the Outbreak of War in August 1914

Reproduced below is the text of the German government's official statement—published some months after war was initiated in July/August 1914—which attempted to lay blame for the outbreak of war on Russia.

In short, Germany argued that while Russia protested in public and via diplomatic dispatches—not least from the Russian Tsar to the German Kaiser—her intention to ensure continued peace in Europe, her real intent was to rapidly mobilize her army to gain a crucial initial advantage against Germany on the battlefield.

The official statement reproduced below was chiefly intended for consumption by those nations who had at that time adopted a neutral stance, e.g., America and Italy.

Official Statement of the German Government:
"How Russia Betrayed Germany's Confidence"

On June 28th the Austro-Hungarian successor to the throne, Archduke Franz Ferdinand, and his wife, the Duchess of Hohenberg, were assassinated by a member of a band of Serbian conspirators.

The investigation of the crime through the Austro-Hungarian authorities has yielded the fact that the conspiracy against the life of the Archduke and successor to the throne was prepared and abetted in Belgrade with the cooperation of Serbian officials, and executed with arms from the Serbian State arsenal.

This crime must have opened the eyes of the entire civilized world, not only in regard to the aims of the Serbian policies directed against the conservation and integrity of the Austro-Hungarian monarchy, but also concerning the criminal means which the pan-Serb propaganda in Serbia had no hesitation in employing for the achievement of these aims.

The goal of these policies was the gradual revolutionizing and final separation of the southeasterly districts from the Austro-Hungarian monarchy and their union with Serbia. This direction of Serbia's policy has not been altered in the least in spite of the repeated and solemn declarations of Serbia in which it vouchsafed a change in these policies towards Austria-Hungary as well as the cultivation of good and neighborly relations.

In this manner for the third time in the course of the last six years Serbia has led Europe to the brink of a world war.

It could only do this because it believed itself supported in its intentions by Russia. Russia, soon after the events brought about by the Turkish revolution of 1908, endeavored to found a union of the Balkan states under Russian patronage and directed against the existence of Turkey. This union, which succeeded in 1911 in driving out Turkey from a greater part of her European possessions, collapsed over the question of the distribution of spoils.

The Russian policies were not dismayed over this failure. According to the idea of the Russian statesmen a new Balkan union under Russian patronage should be called into existence, headed no longer against Turkey, now dislodged from the Balkans, but against the existence of the Austro-Hungarian monarchy.

It was the idea that Serbia should cede to Bulgaria those parts of Macedonia, which it had received during the last Balkan war, in exchange for Bosnia, and the Herzegovina, which were to be taken from Austria. To oblige Bulgaria to fall in with this plan it was to be isolated, Rumania attached to Russia with the aid of French propaganda, and Serbia promised Bosnia and the Herzegovina.

Under these circumstances, it was clear to Austria that it was not compatible with the dignity and the spirit of self-preservation of the monarchy to view idly any longer this agitation across the border.

The Imperial and Royal Government appraised Germany of this conception and asked for our opinion. With all our heart we were able to agree with our ally's estimate of the situation, and assure him that any action considered necessary to end the movement in Serbia directed against the conservation of the monarchy would meet with our approval.

We were perfectly aware that a possible warlike attitude of Austria-Hungary against Serbia might bring Russia upon the field, and that it might therefore involve us in a war, in accordance with our duty as allies. We could not, however, in these vital interests of Austria-Hungary, which were at stake, advise our ally to take a yielding attitude not compatible with his dignity, nor deny him our assistance in these trying days.

We could do this all the less as our own interests were menaced through the continued Serb agitation. If the Serbs continued with the aid of Russia and France to menace the existence of Austria-Hungary, the gradual collapse of Austria and the subjection of all the Slavs under one Russian sceptre would be the consequence, thus making untenable the position of the Teutonic race in Central Europe.

A morally weakened Austria under the pressure of Russian pan-Slavism would be no longer an ally on whom we could count and in whom we could have confidence, as we must be able to have, in view of the ever more menacing attitude of our easterly and westerly neighbors. We, therefore, permitted Austria a completely free hand in her action towards Serbia, but have not participated in her preparations.

Austria chose the method of presenting to the Serbian Government a note, in which the direct connection between the murder at Sarajevo and the pan-Serb movement, as not only countenanced but also actively supported by the Serbian Government, was explained, and in which a complete cessation of this agitation, as well as a punishment of the guilty, was requested.

At the same time, Austria-Hungary demanded as necessary guarantee for the accomplishment of her desire the participation of some Austrian officials in the preliminary examination of Serbian territory and the final dissolution of the pan-Serb societies agitating against Austria-Hungary.

The Imperial and Royal Government gave a period of 48 hours for the unconditional acceptance of its demands.

The Serbian Government started the mobilization of its army one day after the transmission of the Austro-Hungarian note.

As after the stipulated date the Serbian Government rendered a reply which, though complying in some points with the conditions of Austria-Hungary, yet showed in all essentials the endeavor through procrastination and new negotiations to escape from the just demands of the monarchy, the latter discontinued her diplomatic relations with Serbia without indulging in further negotiations or accepting further Serbian assurances, whose value, to her loss, she had sufficiently experienced.

From this moment, Austria was in fact in a state of war with Serbia, which it proclaimed officially on the 28th of July by declaring war.

From the beginning of the conflict we assumed the position that there were here concerned the affairs of Austria alone, which it would have to settle with Serbia. We therefore directed our efforts toward the localizing of the war, and toward convincing the other powers that Austria-Hungary had to appeal to arms in justifiable self-defense, forced upon her by the conditions. We emphatically took the position that no civilized country possessed the right to stay the arm of Austria in this struggle with barbarism and political crime, and to shield the Serbians against their just punishment. In this sense, we instructed our representatives with the foreign powers. Simultaneously the Austro-Hungarian Government communicated to the Russian Government that the step undertaken against Serbia implied merely a defensive measure against the Serb agitation, but that Austria-Hungary must of necessity demand guarantees for a continued friendly behavior of Serbia towards the monarchy.

Austria-Hungary had no intention whatsoever to shift the balance of power in the Balkans.

In answer to our declaration that the German Government desired, and aimed at, a localization of the conflict, both the French and the English Governments promised an action in the same direction. However, these endeavors did not succeed in preventing the interposition of Russia in the Austro-Serbian disagreement.

The Russian Government submitted an official communiqué on July 24, according to which Russia could not possibly remain indifferent in the Serb-Austrian conflict. The same was declared by the Russian Secretary of Foreign Affairs, M. Sazonof, to the German Ambassador, Count Pourtales, in the afternoon of July 26th.

The German Government declared again, through its Ambassador at St. Petersburg, that Austria-Hungary had no desire for conquest and only wished peace at her frontiers. After the official explanation by Austria-Hungary to Russia that it did not claim territorial gain in Serbia, the decision concerning the peace of the world rested exclusively with St. Petersburg.

The same day the first news of Russian mobilization reached Berlin in the evening.

The German Ambassadors at London, Paris, and St. Petersburg were instructed to point out energetically the danger of this Russian mobilization. The Imperial Ambassador at St. Petersburg was also directed to make the following declaration to the Russian Government:

"Preparatory military measures by Russia will force us to counter-measures which must consist in mobilizing the army.

"But mobilization means war.

"As we know the obligations of France towards Russia, this mobilization would be directed against both Russia and France. We cannot assume that Russia desires to unchain such a European war. Since Austria-Hungary will not touch the existence of the Serbian kingdom, we are of the opinion that Russia can afford to assume an attitude of waiting. We can all the more support the desire of Russia to protect the integrity of Serbia as Austria-Hungary does not intend to question the latter. It will be easy in the further development of the affair to find a basis for an understanding."

On July 27, the Russian Secretary of War, M. Suchomlinof, gave the German military attaché his word of honor that no order to mobilize had been issued, merely preparations were being made, but not a horse mustered, nor reserves called in.

If Austria-Hungary crossed the Serbian frontier, the military districts directed towards Austria, i.e., Kiev, Odessa, Moscow, Kazan, would be mobilized, under no circumstances those situated on the German frontier, i.e., St. Petersburg, Vilna, and Warsaw.

Upon inquiry into the object of the mobilization against Austria-Hungary, the Russian Minister of War replied by shrugging his shoulders and referring to the diplomats. The military attaché then pointed to these mobilization measures against Austria-Hungary as extremely menacing also for Germany.

In the succeeding days, news concerning Russian mobilization came at a rapid rate. Among it was also news about preparations on the German-Russian frontier, as for instance the announcement of the state of war in Kovno, the departure of the Warsaw garrison, and the strengthening of the Alexandrovo garrison.

On July 27, the first information was received concerning preparatory measures taken by France: the 14th Corps discontinued the maneuvers and returned to its garrison.

In the meantime, we had endeavored to localize the conflict by most emphatic steps.

On July 26th, Sir Edward Grey had made the proposal to submit the differences between Austria-Hungary and Serbia to a conference of the Ambassadors of Germany, France, and Italy under his chairmanship. We declared in regard to this proposal that we could not, however much we approved the idea, participate in such a conference, as we could not call Austria in her dispute with Serbia before a European tribunal.

France consented to the proposal of Sir Edward Grey, but it foundered upon Austria's declining it, as was to be expected.

Faithful to our principle that mediation should not extend to the Austro-Serbian conflict, which is to be considered as a purely Austro-Hungarian affair, but merely to the relations between Austria-Hungary and Russia, we continued our endeavors to bring about an understanding between these two powers.

We further declared ourselves ready, after failure of the conference idea, to transmit a second proposal of Sir Edward Grey's to Vienna in which he suggested Austria-Hungary should decide that either the Serbian reply was sufficient, or that it be used as a basis for further negotiations. The Austro-

Hungarian Government remarked with full appreciation of our action that it had come too late, the hostilities having already been opened.

In spite of this, we continued our attempts to the utmost, and we advised Vienna to show every possible advance compatible with the dignity of the monarchy.

Unfortunately, all these proposals were overtaken by the military preparations of Russia and France.

On July 29th, the Russian Government made the official notification in Berlin that four army districts had been mobilized. At the same time further news was received concerning rapidly progressing military preparations of France, both on water and on land.

On the same day, the Imperial Ambassador in St. Petersburg had an interview with the Russian Foreign Secretary, in regard to which he reported by telegraph, as follows:

"The Secretary tried to persuade me that I should urge my Government to participate in a quadruple conference to find means to induce Austria-Hungary to give up those demands which touch upon the sovereignty of Serbia.

"I could merely promise to report the conversation and took the position that, after Russia had decided upon the baneful step of mobilization, every exchange of ideas appeared now extremely difficult, if not impossible. Besides, Russia now was demanding from us in regard to Austria-Hungary the same which Austria-Hungary was being blamed for with regard to Serbia, i.e., an infraction of sovereignty.

"Austria-Hungary having promised to consider the Russian interests by disclaiming any territorial aspiration—a great concession on the part of a state engaged in war—should therefore be permitted to attend to its affairs with Serbia alone. There would be time at the peace conference to return to the matter of forbearance towards the sovereignty of Serbia.

"I added very solemnly that at this moment the entire Austro-Serbian affair was eclipsed by the danger of a general European conflagration, and I endeavored to present to the Secretary the magnitude of this danger.

"It was impossible to dissuade Sazonof from the idea that Serbia could not now be deserted by Russia."

In reply to various inquiries concerning reasons for its threatening attitude, the Russian Government repeatedly pointed out that Austria-Hungary had commenced no conversation in St. Petersburg.

The Austro-Hungarian Ambassador in St. Petersburg was therefore instructed on July 29th, at our suggestion, to enter into such conversation with Sazonof.

Count Szapary was empowered to explain to the Russian minister the note to Serbia, though it had been overtaken by the state of war, and to accept any suggestion on the part of Russia as well as to discuss with Sazonof all questions touching directly upon the Austro-Russian relations.

Shoulder to shoulder with England we labored incessantly and supported every proposal in Vienna from which we hoped to gain the possibility of a peaceable solution of the conflict. We even as late as 30 July forwarded the English proposal to Vienna, as basis for negotiations that Austria-Hungary should dictate her conditions in Serbia, i.e., after her march into Serbia. We thought that Russia would accept this basis.

During the interval from July 29th to July 31st there appeared renewed and cumulative news concerning Russian measures of mobilization. Accumulation of troops on the East Prussian frontier and the declaration of the state of war over all important parts of the Russian west frontier allowed no further doubt that the Russian mobilization was in full swing against us, while simultaneously all such measures were denied to our representative in St. Petersburg on word of honor.

Nay, even before the reply from Vienna regarding the Anglo-German mediation, whose tendencies and basis must have been known in St. Petersburg, could possibly have been received in Berlin, Russia ordered a general mobilization.

During the same days, there took place between His Majesty the Kaiser and Czar Nicholas an exchange of telegrams in which His Majesty called the attention of the Czar to the menacing character of the Russian mobilization during the continuance of his own mediating activities.

On July 31st, the Czar directed the following telegram to His Majesty the Kaiser:

"I thank you cordially for your mediation which permits the hope that everything may yet end peaceably. It is technically impossible to discontinue our military preparations, which have been made necessary by the Austrian mobilization. It is far from us to want war. As long as the negotiations between Austria and Serbia continue, my troops will undertake no provocative action. I give you my solemn word thereon. I confide with all my faith in the grace of God, and I hope for the success of your mediation in Vienna for the welfare of our countries and the peace of Europe."

Your cordially devoted,

NICHOLAS.

This telegram of the Czar crossed with the following, sent by H.M. the Kaiser, also on July 31st, at 2 P.M.:

"Upon Your appeal to my friendship and your request for my aid I have engaged in mediation between Your Government and the Government of Austria-Hungary. While this action was taking place, your troops were being mobilized against my ally Austria-Hungary, whereby, as I have already communicated to you, my mediation has become almost illusory.

"In spite of this, I have continued it, and now I receive reliable news that serious preparations for war are going on my eastern frontier. The responsibility for the security of my country forces me to measures of defense. I have gone to the extreme limit of the possible in my efforts for the preservation of the peace of the world.

"It is not I who bear the responsibility for the misfortune which now threatens the entire civilized world. It rests in your hand to avert it. No one threatens the honor and peace of Russia, which might well have awaited the success of my mediation.

"The friendship for you and your country, bequeathed to me by my grandfather on his deathbed, has always been sacred to me, and I have stood faithfully by Russia while it was in serious affliction, especially during its last war. The peace of Europe can still be preserved by you if Russia decides to discontinue those military preparations which menace Germany and Austria-Hungary."

Before this telegram reached its destination, the mobilization of all the Russian forces, obviously directed against us and already ordered during the afternoon of the 31st of July, was in full swing. Notwithstanding, the telegram of the Czar was sent at 2 o'clock that same afternoon. After the Russian general mobilization became known in Berlin, the Imperial Ambassador at St. Petersburg was instructed on the afternoon of July 31st to explain to the Russian Government that Germany declared the state of war as counter-measure against the general mobilization of the Russian army and navy which must be followed by mobilization if Russia did not cease its military measures against Germany and Austria-Hungary within 12 hours, and notified Germany thereof.

At the same time, the Imperial Ambassador in Paris was instructed to demand from the French Government a declaration within 18 hours, whether it would remain neutral in a Russo-German war.

The Russian Government destroyed through its mobilization, menacing the security of our country, the laborious action at mediation of the European cabinets. The Russian mobilization in regard to the seriousness of which the Russian Government was never allowed by us to entertain a doubt, in connection with its continued denial, shows clearly that Russia wanted war.

The Imperial Ambassador at St. Petersburg delivered his note to M. Sazonof on July 31st at 12 o'clock midnight.

The reply of the Russian Government has never reached us.

Two hours after the expiration of the time limit, the Czar telegraphed to H.M. the Kaiser, as follows:

"I have received your telegram. I comprehend that you are forced to mobilize, but I should like to have from you the same guarantee which I have given you, viz., that these measures do not mean war, and that we shall continue to negotiate for the welfare of our two countries and the universal peace, which is so dear to our hearts.

"With the aid of God it must be possible to our long tried friendship to prevent the shedding of blood. I expect with full confidence your urgent reply."

To this H.M. the Kaiser replied:

"I thank you for your telegram. I have shown yesterday to Your Government the way through which alone war may yet be averted.

"Although I asked for a reply by to-day noon, no telegram from my Ambassador has reached me with the reply of Your Government. I therefore have been forced to mobilize my army.

"An immediate, clear and unmistakable reply of Your Government is the sole way to avoid endless misery. Until I receive this reply, I am unable, to my great grief, to enter upon the subject of your telegram.

"I must ask most earnestly that you, without delay, order your troops to commit, under no circumstances, the slightest violation of our frontiers."

As the time limit given to Russia had expired without the receipt of a reply to our inquiry, H.M. the Kaiser ordered the mobilization of the entire German Army and Navy on August 1st at 5 P.M. The German Ambassador at St. Petersburg was instructed that, in the event of the Russian Government not giving a satisfactory reply within the stipulated time, he should declare that we considered ourselves in a state of war after the refusal of our demands.

However, before a confirmation of the execution of this order had been received, that is to say, already in the afternoon of August 1st, i.e., the same afternoon on which the telegram of the Czar, cited above, was sent, Russian troops crossed our frontier and marched into German territory.

Thus, Russia began the war against us.

Meanwhile the Imperial Ambassador in Paris put our question to the French Cabinet on July 31st at 7 P.M.

The French Prime Minister gave an equivocal and unsatisfactory reply on August 1st at 1 P.M., which gave no clear idea of the position of France, as he limited himself to the explanation that France would do that which her interests demanded.

A few hours later, at 5 P.M., the mobilization of the entire French Army and Navy was ordered.

On the morning of the next day France opened hostilities.

Source: *Source Records of the Great War, Vol. II, ed. Charles F. Horne, National Alumni, 1923.*

The German Book rests almost its whole case on the priority of mobilization measures. The way in which that case was carefully built up during the negotiations is shown by British Book No. 71, where the German Chancellor declares on July 28th that the Russian mobilization in the south endangered the efforts of the German Government to encourage direct communications between Vienna and Petrograd.

It will be seen that at the moment the Chancellor was speaking, Austria had already refused both direct discussions with Petrograd and Sir E. Grey's mediation proposals, before she heard of the Russian mobilization, and on the sole ground that she had herself declared war on Serbia.

It was after she heard of the Russian preparations that she resumed conversations on July 29th–30th. It will be observed that on July 28th Russia believed that the general Austrian mobilization had been ordered. As a matter of fact, in sifting any case based on mobilization reports there are several points to be remembered.

Mobilization measures as preliminaries to war are a German tradition. If anyone will refer to the account of the negotiations between Prussia and Austria from March 31 to May 8, 1866, before the

Prussia-Austrian War, given in Sybel's *Foundation of the German Empire,* he will see the example in this line set by Bismarck.

But a case based on priority of mobilization measures is never a strong one for several reasons. First, it is difficult enough to tell, "Who began it" when the negotiations are spread over months, but it is practically impossible to do so when, as here, it is a question of hours.

The actual mobilization measures are taken in the midst of a cloud of accusations and threats, and it is impossible to separate cause from effect. Secondly, in any attempt to state the facts, the minor accusations and innuendoes must be discarded as of slight importance, except as a guide to the psychology of the moment.

The same may be said of rumors of violations of frontier. They have their value, but to put them forward, as does the German and Austrian correspondence, as the actual ground for the commencement of hostilities is to assume the impossible position that the fate of nations is subject to the reported action of a roving patrol. A marked insistence on such reports, as in the German Book, shows a poor appreciation of the value of the evidence.

Thirdly, mobilization "orders" are not mobilization. The mobilization systems of different countries are radically different; the precise nature of those systems, the lines of the railways and a hundred other points must be taken into consideration in judging mobilization measures, and any statement which ignores these factors is a mere bid for uninformed public opinion.

The hard fact that though Germany only proclaimed "Kriegsgefalzrzustand" on July 31st and mobilization on August 1st, to take effect on August 2nd, the German troops were across the Luxemburg frontier at dawn on August 2nd, will probably be judged to be historical evidence of far more value than any isolated reports received during the crisis.

As to Russian mobilization, it was fully realized in Germany that the Russian system was so complicated as to make it difficult to distinguish the localities really affected by mobilization. Germany accuses Russia of mobilizing against Germany, not Austria, because she is reported to be mobilizing at Vilna and Warsaw, but both those towns are nearer to the Galician frontier than Prague is to the Serbian frontier, and Austria was reported to be mobilizing at Prague four days before she declared to Russia that she was only mobilizing against Serbia. The bare facts are of very slight value as evidence without knowledge of the points already mentioned.

If the charges as to the priority of Russian mobilization are examined in the light of these considerations, it will be admitted that the evidence for those charges is remarkably slight, and that, given the admitted extreme slowness of Russian, and the extreme rapidity of German, mobilization, a fact which is frequently alluded to in the correspondence, there is no indication in favor of, and an overwhelming presumption against, the theory that the Russian measures were further advanced than the German when war was declared on August 1st.

The charge that the Czar's telegram of July 31st was misleading, and that the mobilization orders issued about the time of its dispatch destroyed the effect of sincere efforts then being made by Germany to mediate between Russia and Austria, is also unestablished.

In the first place, a glance at the Czar's telegram is sufficient to show that this charge is, to put it frankly, of the flimsiest character. His Majesty gave his "solemn word" that, while it was "technically impossible to discontinue our military preparations," the Russian troops would "undertake no provocative action as long as the negotiations between Austria and Serbia continue."

There was no promise not to mobilize; there was nothing but a statement, which is almost word for word the same as that, contained in the German Emperor's telegram to King George twenty-four hours later—the statement that, under certain circumstances, mobilization would not be converted into hostilities.

As a matter of fact, a somewhat unscrupulous use, in effect though perhaps not in intention, has been made of the Czar's telegrams to substantiate the theory of "betrayal."

Take for instance the German Chancellor's statement on July 31st (British Book, No. 108), that "the news of the active preparations on the Russo-German frontier had reached him just when the Czar had appealed to the Emperor, in the name of their old friendship, to mediate at Vienna, and when the Emperor was actually conforming to that request."

The telegram referred to must be that of July 29th (German Book, No. 21), since this is the only one which mentions "old friendship"; but this telegram, though it asks the Emperor to restrain Austria, also says in so many words that popular opinion in Russia would soon force measures which would lead to war.

Source: *Source Records of the Great War, Vol. II, ed. Charles F. Horne, National Alumni, 1923.*

Chapter Thirty-Eight
August 8, 1914

On the other hand, I should like to state that I received all through this trying time nothing but courtesy at the hands of Herr von Jagow and the officials of the Imperial Foreign Office. At about 11 o'clock on the same morning Count Wedel handed me my passports—which I had earlier demanded in writing—and told me that he had been instructed to confer with me as to the route, which I should follow for my return to England. He said that he had understood that I preferred the route via the Hook of Holland to that via Copenhagen; they had therefore arranged that I should go by the former route, only I should have to wait till the following morning. I agreed to this, and he said that I might be quite assured that there would be no repetition of the disgraceful scenes of the proceeding night as full precautions would be taken. He added that they were doing all in their power to have a restaurant car attached to the train, but it was rather a difficult matter. He also brought me a charming letter from Herr von Jagow couched in the most friendly terms. The day was passed in packing up such articles as time allowed.

The night passed quietly without any incident. In the morning, a strong force of police was posted along the usual route to the Lehrter Station, while the embassy was smuggled away in taxicabs to the station by side streets. We there suffered no molestation whatever, and avoided the treatment meted out by the crowd to my Russian and French colleagues. Count Wedel met us at the station to say good-bye on behalf of Herr von Jagow and to see that all the arrangements ordered for our contact had been properly carried out. A retired Colonel of the Guards accompanied the train to the Dutch frontier and was exceedingly kind in his efforts to prevent the great crowds which thronged the platforms at every station where we stopped from insulting us; but beyond the yelling of patriotic songs and a few jeers and insulting gestures we had really nothing to complain of during our tedious journey to the Dutch frontier.

Before closing this long account of our last days in Berlin, I should like to place on record and bring to your notice the quite admirable behavior of my staff under the most trying circumstances possible. One and all, they worked night and day with scarcely any rest, and I cannot praise too highly the cheerful zeal with which counselor, naval and military attachés, secretaries, and two young attachés buckled to their work and kept their nerve with often yelling mob outside and inside hundreds of British subjects clamoring for advice and assistance. I was proud to have such a staff to work with, and feel most grateful to them all for the invaluable assistance and support often exposing them to consider personal risk, which they so readily and cheerfully gave me.

I should also like to mention the great assistance rendered to us all by my American colleague, Mr. Gerard, and his staff. Undeterred by the hooting and hisses with which he was often greeted by the mob on entering and leaving the embassy, his Excellency came repeatedly to see me to ask how he could help us and to make arrangements for the safety of stranded British subjects. He extricated many of these from extremely difficult situations at some personal risk to himself, and his calmness and *savior-faire* and his firmness in dealing with the imperial authorities gave full assurance that the protection of British subjects and interest could not have been left in more efficient and able hands.

No. 52.
From: **M. Yov. M. Yovanovitch, Minister at Vienna.**
To: **M. N. Pashitch, Prime Minister and Minister for Foreign Affairs.**
Nish
August 16, 1914.

Sir,

From June 17/30 the Serbian Legation at Vienna was practically surrounded by police and gendarmes, while the staff were under constant police supervision. Our movements and our communications with the outer world were, as you can imagine, rendered extremely difficult; the attitude of the population towards the Legation and its staff was inclined to be menacing. After the beginning of July, (o.s.) even telegraphic communication with you became difficult, while matters developed with such rapidity that I was unable to report to you some of the events, which preceded our armed conflict with Austria-Hungary. I accordingly do so now. Up to the end of June (o.s.), the whole question of the Sarajevo outrage appeared to be developing normally. At the commencement of July, however, a change took place as regards the question of the consequences of the Sarajevo affair. There were no tangible proofs that a radical change had taken place, but it was to some extent indicated by certain vague signs and symptoms, which betrayed the existence of some hidden intentions. First of all, the Vienna and Budapest press, in conformity with instructions issued by the Ministry for Foreign Affairs, ceased to publish reports of the magisterial enquiry relating to the Sarajevo outrage. The press began also to represent the whole matter as a question, which must be settled between Serbia and Austria-Hungary alone—eventually by war.

Moreover, statements to this effect were communicated to the leading Vienna newspapers by the German Embassy. Exceptions were: the semi-official *Fremdenblatt,* which was, in general, more moderate in the tone of its articles; *Die Zeit;* and the *Arbeiter Zeitung.*

Simultaneously with this new attitude on the part of the press, a very unsettled condition of affairs developed on the Bourse, such as it had not witnessed during the whole course of recent events in the Balkans. In private conversations also and in high financial circles the "settlement with Serbia" was declared to be the only way out of the general financial and economic crisis prevailing in Austria-Hungary ever since the annexation of Bosnia and Herzegovina. Under secret instructions, it was ordered that gold should be gradually withdrawn from circulation, and a corresponding rise in exchange took place.

A further indication was the clumsy explanation given of the reasons, which had induced the Minister for War, Krobatin, and the Chief of the General Staff, Hetzendorf, to interrupt their leave of absence and return to Vienna. The Chief of Staff constantly travelled to the south, east, and north of Austria, and at that time had had an interview with the Chief of the German General Staff, Count Moltke, in Bohemia, I believe, at Carlsbad.

All the reserves, which had been called out for the June maneuvers in Bosnia and Herzegovina, were kept with the colours beyond the stipulated period.

The number of soldiers belonging to the permanent establishment in Austria-Hungary allowed to go home on short leave of absence in order to gather in the harvest, and to attend to other private affairs, was much larger than is usually the case; at the same time those whose duties were of a military-administrative nature were called upon in ever increasing numbers.

Another indication was the non-committal nature of the answers given to several interpellations in the Hungarian Diet by the Hungarian Prime Minister, Count Tisza, a statesman who is very clear as a rule in his political statements.

The attitude of the Ballplatz was especially characteristic. None of the usual weekly receptions by Count Berchtold was held. They suddenly ceased at the Ballplatz to discuss the Sarajevo outrage with the representatives of foreign countries; or, if discussion did arise, it seemed as if instructions had been issued on the subject; that is to say, it was mentioned to everyone in such a manner as to dispel all apprehensions and suspicion that Austria-Hungary was preparing some serious step against Serbia. They acknowledged that some step would be undertaken at Belgrade as soon as the results of the magisterial enquiry should have sufficiently established the connection between Belgrade and the Sarajevo outrage. But, at the same time, it was said that this step would not be such as to give rise to any uneasiness. The Russian Ambassador, who spoke several times on the subject with Count Forgach, in the absence of Count Berchtold, was unable to discover the true nature of Austria's intentions. M. Schebeko told me that Count Szapary, the Austro-Hungarian Ambassador at Petrograd, who, for family reasons, was at that time stopping in Vienna, had said to him that the step to be taken at Belgrade would be of conciliatory character. According to M. Schebeko, Count Szapary had also assured M. Sazonof that the intended Austro-Hungarian Note to Serbia would not be such as to cause Russia any dissatisfaction. The French Ambassador, M. Dumaine, who, under instructions from his Government, had drawn the attention of the Ballplatz to the complications which might arise should the eventual demands which it was intended to make of Serbia not be of a moderate nature, was told by the principal Under-Secretary, Baron Macchio, that the Austro-Hungarian Government, appreciating the friendly and conciliatory action of the French Government, would only put forward such demands, embodied in a note to the Serbian Government, as Serbia would be able to accept without difficulty. I drew the attention of the Ambassadors of the Triple Entente to the fact that such an assurance might well conceal the true nature of the intentions of the Austro-Hungarian Government, and that the Powers of the Triple Entente might then be confronted by certain fiats' accomplish which Europe would be compelled to accept in order to avoid a general European war.

The line followed by the Ballplatz was, moreover, comparatively successful, as all those of my colleagues whom I saw during that period were more or less dissuaded from believing that Austria-Hungary contemplated any serious step which could provoke European complications. Many of the members of the diplomatic body were so firmly convinced of this that they were preparing at that time to quit Vienna on long leave of absence at various watering places.

Nevertheless, it was known that a note was being drawn up at the Ministry for Foreign Affairs, which would contain the accusations against Serbia, and also the demands of Austria-Hungary. This task was entrusted to Count Forgach, formerly Austro-Hungarian Minister in Serbia. At the same time, it was universally believed that of the foreign representatives, the German Ambassador, Herr von Tschirsky, was the only one who was kept informed of the note even in its minutest details, while I had reason to believe that he was also co-operating in drafting it. In view of the above, the representatives of the friendly Powers agreed with me in thinking that the note would impose very difficult terms on Serbia, but that there would be no inacceptable demands. When the contents of the note were published all of them were surprised, not to say dumbfounded.

In the same way as the contents of the note were kept secret, a similar amount of secrecy was observed in regard to the date of its presentation. On the very day that the note was presented at Belgrade, the French Ambassador had a prolonged conversation with the Principal Under-Secretary at the Ministry for Foreign Affairs—Count Berchtold was again absent at Ischl—on the subject of the note. Yet Baron Macchio did not tell M. Dumaine that the note would be presented at Belgrade that afternoon, and published in the newspapers on the following day.

On the publication in the Vienna papers on the morning of July 11/24 of the contents of the note, which Baron Giesl had presented to then Serbian Government, a feeling of dejection came over the friends both of Serbia and of the peace of Europe. It was only then realized that serious European complications might ensue, though it was not believed that it was the intention of the

Austro-Hungarian Government to provoke them. This feeling of depression was increased by the tone of the articles in the Viennese newspapers, with the exception of *Die Zeit* and *Arbeiter Zeitung* and by demonstrations in the streets, which clearly showed that war would be a most welcome solution—a war with Serbia, of course.

On that day, after having two or three conversations, I realized that an armed conflict between Serbia and the Dual Monarchy was inevitable, even should Serbia accept all the demands contained in the Austro-Hungarian Note, from the first to the last. The attitude of the people in the streets towards our Legation was such that I expected even personal attacks upon the members of the staff.

The French Ambassador, the British Ambassador, and the Russian Chargé d'Affaires held the view that the step taken by Austria-Hungary should be considered not as a note but as an ultimatum. They disapproved of the form, the contents, and the time limit of the note; they also declared it inacceptable.

In the course of conversation with them on the subject of the note I pointed out that those passages in it which dealt with the order by the King to the Army, with the dismissal of officers and Government officials, and especially that which referred to the co-operation of, Austro-Hungarian officials in the "Suppression of the subversive movement in Serbia against the territorial integrity of the Monarchy," would be inacceptable as not being compatible with the dignity and sovereignty of Serbia. Only a victorious war, I said, could enforce the acceptance of conditions, which were so humiliating to an independent State. In reply to their enquiry whether it would not perhaps be better to accept the conditions and avoid war for the present, I said that the Austro-Hungarian Note, which amounted in fact to a declaration of war upon Serbia, was worded in such a way that, even if Serbia should accept all the conditions without reserve,

Austria-Hungary would still find an excuse for her army to march into Serbia at any time. It was in the belief that the conflict would be limited to Serbia and Austria-Hungary that Austria-Hungary had drafted such a note.

To M. Dumaine, Sir M. de Bunsen, and the Russian Chargé d'Affaires, the unexpected character of the note was the cause not only of surprise but also of alarm, in view of the complications, which they feared might ensue. The Russian Ambassador M. Schebeko, previously to the presentation of the note, had stated on several occasions to his colleagues that Russia could not remain indifferent to any step taken by Austria-Hungary, which might have as an object the humiliation of Serbia. He also expressed the same view at the Ballplatz. Hence the apprehension felt by the three Ambassadors, who at once foresaw the possibility of war between Russia and Austria-Hungary.

The day after the note was presented; Prince Koudacheff went to see Count Berchtold to discuss the matter. In reply to his statement, that the note as it stood was inacceptable, and that Russia could not watch with indifference the humiliation of Serbia, Count Berchtold said that Austria-Hungary had been obliged to take this step as her very existence was threatened; that she could not withdraw nor alter the demands made in the note, and that he considered that the matter in dispute concerned Serbia and Austria-Hungary alone and that no other Power had any grounds for interference.

Count Berchtold's reply did not allow of any further doubts as to the intention of Austria-Hungary to chastise Serbia by force of arms without the consent of the European concert. From conversations which I had at that time with the Ambassadors of the Triple Entente—who, during the whole of that difficult period showed every kindness and attention to me and to the staff of the Legation—it seemed quite clear that Austria-Hungary had been assured, and felt convinced, that the Serbo-Austro-

Hungarian conflict would be localized, as she would otherwise not have decided upon a note which undoubtedly meant war. It was also clear that Austria-Hungary was confirmed in this impression especially—and perhaps solely—by Herr von Tchirsky, the German Ambassador in Vienna. Herr von Tchirsky was the only one who thought and even stated publicly, that Russia would remain quiet while Austria-Hungary carried out her punitive expedition against Serbia. He declared that the Russian Minister for Foreign Affairs would easily control the Panslavists, in the same way as he had done last year, and that Russia was not disposed at the moment to begin a discussion of the many vexed questions in Europe and Asia which were her main concern. It was necessary, according to Herr von Tchirsky, to give Serbia a lesson. Russia had no right to interfere. As far as Germany, he said, was concerned, she was in the fullest sense of the word conscious of what she was doing in giving Austria-Hungary her support in the matter.

These statements of Herr von Tchirsky have induced many to hold the opinion that Germany desired to provoke a European war, on the ground that it was better to have war with Russia before the latter had completed her military reorganization, i.e., before the spring of 1917. This point of view had formerly been freely discussed and even written about in Vienna. "The longer the matter is postponed, the smaller will become the chances of success of the Triple Alliance."

On the other hand, rumors from the most authoritative diplomatic sources in Berlin reached me in Vienna, to the effect that the Wilhelmstrasse did not approve of Austria's policy on this question, and that Herr von Tchirsky has exceeded the instructions given to him.

The Russian Ambassador, M. Schebeko, on his return from Petrograd, did his utmost at the Ballplatz to obtain an extension of the brief time limit given to the Serbian Government for a reply to the Austro-Hungarian Note, and to discover some way which might lead to an exchange of views between Vienna and Petrograd in regard to the whole question, but until July 13/26, when we met, his efforts had proved unavailing. From the conversations I then had with him, I gathered that the Austro-Hungarian Note, in its contents and in its form, was regarded as a challenge to Russia and not to Serbia and that Russia would not permit the humiliation of Serbia, even if war were to be the price.

On the day of my departure from Vienna, M. Schebeko told me that, in spite of the many great difficulties to be overcome, there was a prospect of arriving at a solution by which an armed conflict might be avoided by means of discussion between the Russian Government and Count Szapary. A feeling of depression, however, prevailed in Vienna as soon as reports began to be spread that the Austro-Serbian conflict would bring about a war between Russia and the Dual Monarchy.

No. 161.
Sir M. de Bunsen, British Ambassador in Vienna, to Sir Edward Grey.
London
September 1, 1914.

THE rapidity of the march of events during the days, which led up to, the outbreak of the European war made it difficult, at the time, to do more than record their progress by telegraph. I propose now to add a few comments.

The delivery at Belgrade on the 23rd July of the Austrian note to Serbia was preceded by a period of absolute silence at the Ballplatz. Except Herr von Tschirscky, who must have been aware of the tenure, if not of the actual words of the note, none of my colleagues were allowed to see through the veil. On the 22nd and 23rd July, M. Dumaine, French Ambassador, had long interviews with Baron Macchio, one of the Under-Secretaries of State for Foreign Affairs, by whom he was left under the impression that the words of warning he had been instructed to speak to the Austro-Hungarian Government had not been unavailing and that the note which was being drawn up would be found to contain nothing with which a self-respecting State need hesitate to comply. At the second of these interviews, he was not even informed that the note was at that very moment being presented at Belgrade, or that it would be published in Vienna on the following morning. Count Forgach, the other Under-Secretary of State, had indeed been good enough to confide to me on the same day the true character of the note, and the fact of its presentation about the time we were speaking.

So little had the Russian Ambassador been made aware of what was preparing that he actually left Vienna on a fortnight's leave of absence about the 20th July. He had only been absent a few days when events compelled him to return. It might have been supposed, that Duke Avarna, Ambassador of the allied Italian Kingdom, which was bound to be so closely affected by fresh complications in the Balkans would have been taken fully into the confidence of Count Berchtold during this critical time. In point of fact his Excellency was left completely in the dark. As for myself, no indication was given me by Count Berchtold of the impending storm, and it was from a private source that I received on the 15th July the forecast of what was about to happen which I telegraphed to you the following day. It is true that during all this time the *Neue Freie Presse* and other leading Viennese newspapers were using language, which pointed unmistakably to war with Serbia. The official *Fremdenblatt*, however, was more cautious, and till the note was published the prevailing opinion among my colleagues was that Austria would shrink from courses calculated to involve her in grave European complications.

On the 24th July the note was published in the newspapers. By common consent, it was at once styled an ultimatum. Its integral acceptance by Serbia was neither expected nor desired, and when, on the following afternoon, it was at first rumored in Vienna that it had been unconditionally accepted, there was a moment of keen disappointment. The mistake was quickly corrected, and as soon as it was known later in the evening that the Servian reply had been rejected and that Baron Giesl had broken off relations at Belgrade, Vienna burst into a frenzy of delight, vast crowds parading the streets and singing patriotic songs till the small hours of the morning.

The demonstrations were perfectly orderly, consisting for the most part of organized processions through the principal streets ending up at the Ministry of War. One or two attempts to make hostile manifestations against the Russian Embassy were frustrated by the strong guard of police, which held the approaches to the principal embassies during those days. The demeanor of the people at Vienna and, as I was informed, in many other principal cities of the Monarchy, showed plainly the popularity of the idea of war with Serbia, and there can be no doubt that the small body of Austrian and Hungarian statesmen by whom this momentous step was adopted gauged rightly the sense, and it may even be said the determination, of the people, except presumably in portions of the provinces inhabited by the Austro-Hungarian Minister for foreign Affairs and Austro-Hungarian Minister at Belgrade Slav races. There had been much disappointment in many quarters at the avoidance of war with Serbia during the annexation crisis in 1908 and again in connection with the recent Balkan war. Count Berchtold's peace policy had met with little sympathy in the Delegation. Now the floodgates were opened, and the entire people and press clamored impatiently for immediate and condign punishment of the hated Serbian race. The country certainly believed that it had before it only the alternative of subduing Serbia or of submitting sooner or later to mutilation at her hands. But a peaceful solution should first have been attempted. Few seemed to reflect that the forcible intervention of a Great Power in the Balkans must inevitably call other Great power into the field. So just was the cause of Austria held to be, that it seemed to her people inconceivable that any country should place itself in her path, or that questions of mere policy or prestige should be regarded anywhere as superseding the necessity which had arisen to exact summary vengeance for the crime of Sarajevo. The conviction had been expressed to me by the German Ambassador on the 24th July that Russia would stand aside. This feeling, which was also held at the Ballplatz, influenced no doubt the course of events, and it is deplorable that no effort should no effort should have been made to secure by means of diplomatic negotiations the acquiescence of Russia and Europe as a whole in some peaceful compromise of the Serbian question by which Austrian fears of Serbian aggression and intrigue might have been removed for the future. Instead of adopting this course, the Austro-Hungarian Government resolved upon war. The inevitable consequence ensued. Russia relied to a partial Austrian mobilization and declaration of war against Serbia by a partial Russian mobilization against Austria. Austria met this move by completing her own mobilization, and Russia again responded with results, which have passed into history. The fate of the proposals put forward by His Majesty's Government for the preservation of peace is recorded in the White Paper on the European Crisis. On the 28th July I saw Count Berchtold and urged as strongly as I could that the scheme of mediation mentioned in your speech in the House of Commons on the previous day should be accepted as offering an honorable and peaceful settlement of the question at issue. His Excellency himself read to me a telegraphic report of the speech, but added that matters had gone too far; Austria was that day declaring war on Serbia, and she could never accept the conference which you had suggested should take place between the less interested Powers on the basis of the Serbian reply. This was a matter, which must be settled directly between the two parties immediately concerned. I said His Majesty's Government would hear with regret that hostilities could not be arrested, as you feared they would lead to European complications. I disclaimed any British lack of sympathy with Austria in the matter of her legitimate grievances against Serbia, and pointed out that whereas Austria seemed to be making these the starting point of her policy, His Majesty's Government were bound to look at the question primarily from the point of view of the maintenance of the peace of Europe. In this way, the two countries might easily drift apart.

His Excellency said that he too was keeping the European aspect of the question in sight. He thought, however, that Russia would have no right to intervene after receiving his assurance that Austria sought no territorial aggrandizement. His Excellency remarked to me in the course of his conversation that, though he had been glad to co-operate towards bringing about the settlement which had resulted from the ambassadorial conferences in London during the Balkan crisis, he had never had much belief in the permanency of that settlement, which was necessarily of a highly artificial character, inasmuch as the interests which it sought to harmonize were in themselves profoundly divergent. His Excellency maintained a most friendly demeanor throughout the interview, but left no doubt in my mind as to the determination of the Austro-Hungarian Government to proceed with the invasion of Serbia.

The German Government claim to have persevered to the end in the endeavor to support at Vienna your successive proposals in the interest of peace. Herr von Tschirscky abstained from inviting my co-operation or that of the French and Russian Ambassadors in carrying out his instructions to that effect, and I had no means of knowing what response he was receiving from the Austro-Hungarian Government. I was, however, kept fully informed by M. Schebeko, the Russia Ambassador, of his own direct negotiations with Count Berchtold. M. Schebeko endeavored on the 28th July to persuade the Austro-Hungarian Government to furnish Count Szapary with full powers to continue at St. Petersburgh the hopeful conversations which had there been taking place between the latter and M. Sazonof. Count Berchtold refused at the time, but two days later (30th July), though in the meantime Russia had partially mobilized against Austria, he received M. Schebeko again, in a perfectly friendly manner, and gave his consent to the continuance of the conversations at St. Petersburgh. From now onwards the tension between Russia and Germany was much greater that between Russia and Austria. As between the latter an arrangement seemed almost in sight, and on the 1st August I was informed by M. Schebeko that Count Szapary had at last conceded the main point at issue by announcing to M. Sazonof that Austria would consent to submit to mediation the points in the note to Serbia which seemed incompatible with the maintenance of Serbian independence. M. Sazonof, M. Schebeko added, had accepted this proposal on condition that Austria would refrain from the actual invasion of Serbia. Austria, in fact had finally yielded, and that she herself had at this point good hopes of a peaceful issue is shown by the communication made to you on the 1st August by Count Mensdorff, to the effect that Austria had neither "banged the door" on compromise nor cut off the conversations. M. Schebeko to the end was working hard for peace. He was holding the most conciliatory language to Count Berchtold, and he informed me that the latter, as well as Count. Forgach had responded in the same spirit. Certainly, it was too much for Russia to expect that Austria would hold back her armies, but this matter could probably have been settled by negotiation, and M. Schebeko repeatedly told me he was prepared to accept any reasonable compromise.

Unfortunately, these conversations at St. Petersburgh and Vienna were cut short by the transfer of the dispute to the more dangerous ground of a direct conflict between Germany and Russia. Germany intervened on the 31st July by means of her double ultimatums to St. Petersburgh and Paris. The ultimatums were of a kind to which only one answer is possible, and German declared war on Russia on the 1st August, and on France on the 3rd August. A few days' delay might in all probability have saved Europe from one of the greatest calamities in history.

Russia still abstained from attacking Austria, and M. Schebeko had been instructed to remain at his post till war should actually be declared against her by the Austro-Hungarian Government. This only happened on the 6th August when Count Berchtold informed the foreign missions at Vienna that "the Austro-Hungarian Ambassador at St. Petersburgh had been instructed to notify the Russian Government that, in view of the menacing attitude of Russia in the Austro-Serbian conflict and the fact that Russia had commenced hostilities against Germany, Austria-Hungary considered herself also at war with Russia."

M. Schebeko left quietly in a special train provided by the Austro-Hungarian Government on the 7th August. He had urgently requested to be conveyed to the Romanian frontier, so that he might be able to proceed to his own country, but was taken instead to the Swiss frontier, and ten days later, I found him at Berne.

M. Dumaine, French Ambassador, stayed on till the 12th August. On the previous day, he had been instructed to demand his passport on the ground that Austrian troops were being employed against France. This point was not fully cleared up when I left Vienna. On the 9th August, M. Dumaine had received from Count Berchtold the categorical declaration that no Austrian troops were being moved to Alsace. The next day this statement was supplemented by a further one, in writing, giving Count Berchtold's assurance that not only had no Austrian troops been moved actually to the French Frontier, but that none were moving from Austria in a westerly direction into Germany in such a way that they might replace German troops employed at the front. These two statements were made by Count Berchtold in reply to precise question put to him by M. Dumaine, under instructions from his Government. The French Ambassador's departure was not attended by any hostile demonstration, but his Excellency before leaving had been justly offended by a harangue made by the Chief Burgomaster of Vienna to the crowd assembled before the steps of the town hall, in which he assured the people that Paris was in the throes of a revolution, and that the President of the Republic had been assassinated.

The British declaration of war on Germany was made known in Vienna by special editions of the newspapers about midday on the 4th August. An abstract of your speeches in the House of Commons, and also of the German Chancellor's speech in the Reichstag of the 4th August, appeared the same day, as well as the text of the German ultimatum Belgium. Otherwise, few details of the great events of these days transpired. The *Neue Freie Presse* was violently insulting towards England. The *Fremdenblatt* was not offensive, but little or nothing was said in the columns of any Vienna paper to explain that the violation of Belgium neutrality had left His Majesty's Government no alternative but to take part in the war.

The declaration of Italian neutrality was bitterly felt in Vienna, but scarcely mentioned in the newspapers. On the 5th August I had the honor to receive your instruction of the previous day preparing me for the immediate outbreak of war with Germany, but adding that, Austria being understood to be not yet at that date at war with Russia and France, you did not desire me to ask for my passport or to make any particular communication to the Austro-Hungarian Government. You stated at the same time that His Majesty's Government of course expected Austria not to commit any act of war against us without the notice required by diplomatic usage.

On Thursday morning, the 13th August, I had the honor to receive your telegram of the 12th, stating that you had been compelled to inform Count Mensdorff, at the request of the French Government, that a complete rupture had occurred between France and Austria, on the ground that Austria had declared war on Russia who was already fighting on the side of France, and that Austria had sent troops to the German Frontier under conditions that were a direct menace to France. The rupture having been brought about with France in this way, I was to ask for my passport, and your telegram stated, in conclusion, that you had informed Count Mensdorff that a state of war would exist between the two countries from midnight of the 12th August.

After seeing Mr. Penfield, the United States Ambassador, who accepted immediately in the most friendly spirit my request that his Excellency would take charge provisionally of British interests in Austria-Hungary during the unfortunate interruption of relations, I proceeded, with Mr. Theo Russell, Counselor of His Majesty's Embassy, to the Ballplatz. Count Berchtold received me at midday. I delivered my message, for which his Excellency did not seem to unprepared, although he told me that a long telegram from Count Mensdorff had just come in but had not yet been brought to him. His Excellency received my communication with the courtesy, which never leaves him. He deplored the unhappy complications, which were drawing such good friends as Austria and England into war. In point of fact, he added, Austria did not consider herself then at war with France though diplomatic relations with that country had been broken off. I explained in a few words how circumstances had forced this unwelcome conflict upon us. We both avoided useless argument. Then I ventured to recommend to his Excellency's consideration the case of the numerous stranded British subjects at Carlsbad, Vienna, and other places throughout the country. I had already had some correspondence with him on the subject, and his Excellency took a note of what I said, and promised to see what could be done to get them away when the stress of mobilisation should be over. Count Berchtold agreed to Mr. Phillpotts, till then British consul at Vienna under Consul-General Sir Frederick Duncan, being left by me at the Embassy in the capacity of Charge' des Archives. He presumed a similar privilege would not be refused in England if desired on behalf of the Austro-Hungarian Government. I took leave of Count Berchtold with sincere regret, having received from the day of my arrival in Vienna, not quite nine months before, many marks of friendship and consideration from his Excellency. As I left, I begged his Excellency to present my profound respects to the Emperor Francis Joseph, together with an expression of my hope that His Majesty would pass through these sad times with unimpaired health and strength. Count Berchtold was pleased to say he would deliver my message.

Count Walterskirchen, of the Austro-Hungarian Foreign Office, was deputed the following morning to bring me my passport and to acquaint me with the arrangements made for my departure that evening (14th August). In the course of the day, Countess Berchtold and other ladies of Vienna society called to take leave of Lady de Bunsen at the embassy. We left the railway station by special train for the Swiss frontier at 7 P.M. No disagreeable incidents occurred; Count Walterskirchen was present at the station on behalf of Count Berchtold. The journey was necessarily slow, owing to the encumbered state of the line. We reached Buchs, on the Swiss frontier, early in the morning of the 17th August. At the first halting place, there had been some hooting and stone throwing on the part of the entraining troops and station officials, but no inconvenience was caused, and at the other large stations on our route, we found that ample measures had been taken to preserve us from molestation as well as to provide us with food. I was left in no doubt that, the Austro-Hungarian Government had desired that the journey should be performed under the most comfortable conditions possible, and that I should receive on my departure all the marks of consideration due to His Majesty's representative. I was accompanied by my own family and the entire staff of the embassy, for whose untiring zeal and efficient help in trying times I desire to express my sincere thanks. The Swiss Government also showed courtesy in providing comfortable accommodation during our journey from the frontier to Berne, and, after three days' stay there, on to Geneva, at which place we found that every provision had been made by the French Government, at the request of Sir Francis Bertie, for our speedy conveyance to Paris. We reached England on Saturday morning, the 22nd August.

I have, &tc.

Primary Documents: Kaiser Wilhelm's Account of the Events of July 1914
Updated: Monday, 29 October 2001.

Reproduced from the English translation of his memoirs.

After the arrival of the news of the assassination of my friend, the Archduke Franz Ferdinand, I gave up going to Kiel for the regatta week and went back home, since I intended to go to Vienna for his funeral. But I was asked from there to give up this plan. Later I heard that one of the reasons for this was consideration for my personal safety; to this, I naturally would have paid no attention.

Greatly worried on account of the turn which matters might now take, I decided to give up my intended journey to Norway and remain at home. The Imperial Chancellor and the Foreign Office held a view contrary to mine and wished me to undertake the journey, as they considered that it would have a quieting effect on all Europe.

For a long time I argued against going away from my country at a time when the future was so unsettled, but Imperial Chancellor von Bethmann told me, in short and concise terms, that if I were now to give up my travel plans, which were already widely known, this would make the situation appear more serious than it had been up to that moment and possibly lead to the outbreak of war, for which I might be held responsible; that the whole world was merely waiting to be put out of suspense by the news that I, in spite of the situation had quietly gone on my trip. Thereupon I consulted the Chief of the General Staff, and, when he proved to be calm and unworried regarding the state of affairs and he asked for a summer leave of absence to go to Carlsbad, I decided, though with a heavy heart, upon my departure.

The much-discussed so-called Potsdam Crown Council of July 5th in reality never took place. It is an invention of malevolent persons. Naturally, before my departure, I received, as was my custom, some of the Ministers individually, in order to hear from them reports concerning their departments. Neither was there any council of Ministers and there was no talk about war preparations at a single one of the conferences.

My fleet was cruising in the Norwegian fjords, as usual, while I was on my summer vacation trip. During my stay at Balholm, l received only meagre news from the Foreign Office and was obliged to rely principally on the Norwegian newspapers, from which I got the impression that the situation was growing worse. I telegraphed repeatedly to the Chancellor and the Foreign Office that I considered it advisable to return home, but was asked each time not to interrupt my journey.

When I learned that the English fleet had not dispersed after the review at Spithead, but had remained concentrated, I telegraphed again to Berlin that I considered my return necessary. My opinion was not shared there.

But when, after that, I learned from the Norwegian newspapers—not from Berlin—about the Austrian ultimatum to Serbia, and, immediately thereafter, about the Serbian note to Austria, I started without further ado upon my return journey and commanded the fleet to repair to Wilhelmshaven.

Upon my departure, I learned from a Norwegian source that it was said that a part of the English fleet had left secretly for Norway in order to capture me (though peace still reigned!). It is significant that Sir Edward Goschen, the English Ambassador, was informed on July 26 at the Foreign Office that my return journey, undertaken on my own initiative, was to be regretted, since agitating rumors might be caused by it.

Upon my arrival at Potsdam I found the Chancellor and the Foreign Office in conflict with the Chief of the General Staff, since General von Moltke was of the opinion that war was sure to break out, whereas the other two stuck firmly to their view that things would not get to such a bad pass, that there would be some way of avoiding war, provided I did not order mobilization. This dispute kept up steadily. Not until General von Moltke announced that, the Russians had set fire to their frontier posts, torn up the frontier railway tracks, and posted red mobilization notices did a light break upon the diplomats in the Wilhelmstrasse and bring about their own collapse and that of their powers of resistance. They had not wished to believe in the war.

This shows plainly how little we had expected—much less prepared for—war in July 1914.

When, in the spring of 1914, Czar Nicholas II was questioned by his Court Marshal as to his spring and summer plans, he replied: *"He resterai chez moi cette année parce que nous aurons la guerre"* ("I shall stay at home this year because we shall have war"). (This fact, it is said, was reported to Imperial Chancellor von Bethmann; I heard nothing about it then and learned about it for the first time in November, 1918.)

This was the same Tzar who gave me, on two separate occasions—at Björkö and Baltisch-Port—entirely without being pressed by me and in a way that surprised me, his word of honor as a sovereign, to which he added weight by a clasp of the hand and an embrace, that he would never draw his sword against the German Emperor—least of all as an ally of England—in case a war should break out in Europe, owing to his gratitude to the German Emperor for his attitude in the Russo-Japanese War, in which England alone had involved Russia, adding that he hated England, since she had done him and Russia a great wrong by inciting Japan against them. At the very time that the Czar was announcing his summer war program I was busy at Corfu excavating antiquities; then I went to Wiesbaden, and, finally, to Norway. A monarch who wishes war and prepares it in such a way that he can suddenly fall upon his neighbors—a task requiring long secret mobilization preparations and concentration of troops—does not spend months outside his own country and does not allow his Chief of the General Staff to go to Carlsbad on leave of absence. My enemies, in the meantime, planned their preparations for an attack.

Our entire diplomatic machine failed. The menace of war was not seen because the Foreign Office was so hypnotized with its idea of *"surtout pas d'histoires"* ("above all, no stories"), its belief in peace at any cost, that it had completely eliminated war as a possible instrument of Entente statesmanship from its calculations, and, therefore, did not rightly estimate the importance of the signs of war.

Photograph courtesy of

Bibliography

1914, B. T. *Belgium Grey Book.*
1914, F. T. *French Yellow Book.*
1914, G. T. *German White Book.*
1914, H. E. *Austro-Hungarian Red Book.*
1914, R. T. *Russian Orange Book.*
1914, S. T. *Serbian Blue Book.*
Dallas, G. *At the Heart of a Tiger Clemenceau,* and Ne Carroll & Graf, New York, New York 1993
Scott Staine, Greenwood Histories. *The History of France.* Greenwood Press Oxford OR 2000
Horne, C. F. (1923). *Records of the Great War, Vol. 1, ed.* American Legion, Indianapolis In
Keegan, J. *First World War.* Random House, New York New York, c 2001
Kitchen, M. *Illustrated History of Germany.* Cambridge University Press, 2000
Radzinsky, E. *The Last Tsar.* Anchor, New York New York 1993
Rowland, P. *David Loyd George.* Barriet Jenkins, England 1996
Russia and the Russians.
Geoffrey Hostling, Bellknap Press, Harvard University, Cambridge Ma USA 2001

- Showalter, Dennis E. *Tannenberg: Clash of Empires.* Hamden, CT: Archon Books, 1991.
- Stone, Norman. *The Eastern Front, 1914-1917.* London: Hodder and Stoughton, 1975, quotes from p. 231.
- Strachan, Hew. *The First World War: To Arms.* Vol 1. New York: Oxford University Press, 2001.
- http://history.sandiego.edu/gen/ww1/1914i.html
- "Chapter 1, Toward World War, 1901–08." *http://www.tfo.upm.es/DOCENCIA/2006-07/ArtDeco/Europa1902.htm.*
- Smitha, Frank. "Chapter 2, Europe's Slide to War." Copyright © 1998. All rights reserved.*http://www.fsmitha.com/h2/ch04.htm.*
- Horne, Charles F. ed. *Source Records of the Great War, Vol. I, National Alumni, 1923.*

Retrospect

June 28, 1914! A day that is recognized has to what lead to World War 1, but in fact it was a day that started World War 1. What happens in the following weeks leading up to August 5, 1914 is what really started World War 1. Events like Gregori Rasputin, being almost murder on same day has the Archduke, or the celebration by the Serbian government. What really astonished me was how governments could condemn the murder of the Archduke but turn around and tell Austria that they have no right to seek justice for the murder. In today's society it is told that the blank check that Germany gave Austria is in fact support to get justice for the murder. I have put in the telegram that Wilhelm II tells Austria king that Germany would support Austria to get justice but would not support Austria if they showed any sign that they would attack Russia. Then there is the meeting between Russia, France and Japan in St Petersburg, this meeting shows from French Ambassador that what was discussed, was how to start hostilities with Germany. The telegrams that I put in this book also show how Russia and France discuss military mobilization, because the day French President leaves Russia. Russia and Serbia order military mobilization, this is August 25, 1914. On August 26, 1914 French President orders military mobilization of its army. Germany and Austria have not even considered this yet. The only thing Austria does, is give its demands to Serbia, by looking and studying these demands, it shows that Austria is harsh but the crime was harsher, and justice should be served. From July 27, 1914 to August 5, 1914, things get obscured and can be confusing, which one should be able to refer back to documents to see how the attitude has changed to Serbia being the victim and Austria is committing the crime and Germany is the aggressor, When in fact Germany was doing everything possible to resolve the issue outside military options. England is trying to play mediator to get this resolved. Russia is who through Minister for Foreign Affairs has not only helped the Serbian group Narodna Odbrana (Black Hand) commit the crime, but are trying to cover it up. Then you have England asking Germany and France to respect Belgium's neutrality at this time, remember France as ordered military mobilization Germany has NOT has of August 27, 1914. Remember by international law when a host countries military is involved with the assassination of a visiting foreign diplomat to include members of a royal family. That is a declaration of war, Serbia's military was involved. History over time seems to forget that Serbia did declare war on Austria on June 28, 1914. By August 1, 1839 Treaty of London article 9 is violated by Belgium over the next 3 days, Belgium will violate this treaty 3 more times, France and Russia will start military operations into Germany, but Germany has mobilized it's military by this time to its borders. Germany also notifies England that Belgium has violated the 1839 Treaty of London, but England delays on this notification which is another contributor to the Start of World War 1. The other underlying facts to the Start of World War 1 is events that have taken place up to 40 years in past history, like the Franco-Prussia War of 1871 and the Berlin Congress. These other contributing events will be shown in future books. No country has ever started a war on a whim it takes years of planning. My plan is to do a whole series how World War II was actually started.

Glossary

A

Albert, King: Belgian, King

Alexander, crown Prince: Serbia, Royal Family

Allize', M.: France, Minister at Munich

Archduke Franz Ferdinand: last Heir to the throne for Hapsburg Empire

B

Beaumont, Mr.: British, Charg'e d; Affaires at Constantinople

Bethmann-Hollweg, Theobold: Germany, Chancellor

Benckendorff, Count: Russia, Ambassador in London

Bienvenu-Martin, M.: France, Acting Minister for Foreign Affairs

Boschkovitch, M. M. S.: Serbia, Minister in London

Berchtold, Count: Austria

Bertie, F.: British, Ambassador at Paris

Beyerns, Baron: Belgian, Minister at Berlin

Bilinski, Ritter Von: Austria, Minister for Finance

Blank Check: Support Germany was giving Austria to get justice for Archduke assassination, not to wage war on Russia

Buchana, Sir G.: British, Ambassador at St. Petersburg.

Bunsen, M. de: British, Ambassador at Vienna

C

Cabrinovic, Nedeljko: Serbia, Black Hand member and assassin of the Archduke

Cambon, M. Jules: France, Ambassador to Berlin

Cambon M. Paul: France, Ambassador at London

Ciganowic, Milan: Serbia, Black Hand member, instructed assassin in how to shoot browning pistols and use hand bombs

Crackanthorpe: British, Charg'e d' Affaires at Belgrade

Cubrilovic, Vaso: Serbia, Black Hand member and assassin of the Archduke

D

Dacic, Zivojin: Serbia, Black Hand member
Davignon, M.: Belgian, Minister for Foreign Affairs
Dumaine, M.: France, Ambassador at Vienna
Dudzeele, Errembault de: Belgian, Minister at Vienna

E

Eyschen, M.: Luxemburg, President

F

Fallon, Baron: Belgian, Minister at the Hague
Fleuriau, M. de: France, Charg'e d' Affairs at London

G

Georgevitch, M. M.: Serbia, Charge D' Affaires at Constantinople.
Gieslingen, Baron Gisel von: Austria-Hungary
Goshen, Sir E.: British, Ambassador at Berlin
Grabez, Trifko: Serbia, Black Hand member and assassin of the Archduke
Grbic, Rudivoy: Serbia, Helped Black Hand smuggle weapons
Grey, Sir Edward: British, Prime Minister

H

Hoflehner, Herr: Austria, Consular Agent to Count Berchtold.
House, Colonel: U.S.A., Presidential Consul
Hoyos, Count: Austria, Councilor of Legation.
Humbold, Sir H: British, Charg'e d' Affaires at Berlin

J

Jaures, Jean: France, Socialist Congress, and a journalist, could have stopped Frances involvement in
        World War 1, gunned down 31 July 1914
Jehlitschka, M.: Serbia, Consul-General
Joseph, Franz: Austria, King

K

Klobukowski, M.: France, Minister at Brussels
Kragujevatz Army depot: Serbia, Depot that supplied bombs to Black Hand members
Krobatin, Ritter Von: Austria, Keeper of the minutes

L

Lalaing, Count de: Belgian, Minister at London
Lichnowsky, Prince: German, Ambassador at London

M

Maugin, M. d' Apchier le: France, Consul-General at Budapest
Manneville, M. De: France, Charg'e de Affaires at Berlin
Mehmedbasic, Mehemed: Serbia, Black Hand member and assassin of the Archduke
Mensdorff, Count: Austria, Minister at London
Michailovitch M. Ljub: Serbia, Minister at Rome

Mollard, M.: France, Minister at Luxemburg
Morgenthau, Henry T.: U.S.A., Ambassador to Turkey

N
Nicholas II: Russia, King
Narodna Odbrana: other name for Black Hand organization

P
Pal'eologue, M.: France, Ambassador at St Petersburg, Russia
Pashitch, M.N.: Serbia, Prime Minister and Minister for Foreign Affairs
Pellet, M. Marcelin: France, Minister at The Hague
Popovic, Cetres: Serbia, Black Hand member and assassin of the Archduke
Popowic, Rade: Serbia, Frontier Captain of Shabatz, helped Black Hand group smuggle weapons
      into Bosnia and Herzegovina
Pribicevic, Major Milan: Serbia, Army officer that supplied the assassins with weapons and bombs
Princip, Gravrilo: Serbia, Know member of Black Hand and assassin

R
Rasputin, Gregori: Russia, Private confidante to Nicholas II
Ritter Von Storck: Secretary Legation Serbia
Rodd, Sir R.: British, Ambassador at Rome

S
Saleske, Herr von Below: German, Minister at Brussels
Sasonof, M.: Russia, Minister of Foreign Affairs
Sophie, Dutchess: Austria, wife of Archduke Ferdinand
Spalaikovitch, Dr. M.: Serbia, Minister at Petrograd
Sturkh, Count: Austria, Premier
Sz'ecsen, Count: Austria,

T
Tankositch, Major Voija: Serbia, Army officer that helped Black hand group
Tisza, Count: Hungary, Premier
Tschirschky, Baron: Germany, Ambassador in Vienna Austria

V
Vesnitch, Dr. M. R.: Serbia, Minister at Paris
Villain, Raoul: France, Murdered Journalist Jean Juares
Villiers, Sir F.: British, Minister at Brussels
Viviani, M. Renée: France, President of Council, Minister for Foreign Affairs.

W
Wilhelm, Kaiser: Germany, Leader and member of Royal Family, related to Nicholas II of Russia
      and Queen Victoria of Great Britain.
Welle, M. Michotte de: Belgian, Minister at Belgrade

Y
Yovanovitch, M. Yov. M.: Serbia, Minister at Vienna.
Yovanovitch, Dr. M.: Serbia, Charg'e D' Affaires at Berlin

Index

Treaty between Great Britain, Austria, France, Prussia, and Russia, on the one part, and Belgium, on the other.[1]

Signed at London, April 19, 1839.

In the Name of the Most Holy and Indivisible Trinity.

Her Majesty the Queen of the United Kingdom of Great Britain and Ireland, His Majesty the Emperor of Austria, King of Hungary and Bohemia, His Majesty the King of the French, His Majesty the King of Prussia, and His Majesty the Emperor of all the Russias, taking into consideration, as well as His Majesty the King of the Belgians, their Treaty concluded at London on the 15th of November, 1831, as well as the Treaties signed this day between their Majesties the Queen of the United Kingdom of Great Britain and Ireland, the Emperor of Austria, King of Hungary and Bohemia, the King of the French, the King of Prussia, and the Emperor of all the Russias, on the one part, and His Majesty the King of the Netherlands, Grand Duke of Luxembourg, on the other part, and between His Majesty the King of the Belgians and His said Majesty the King of the Netherlands, Grand Duke of Luxembourg, their said Majesties have named as their Plenipotentiaries, that is to say :

[Here follow the names.]

Article I.

Her Majesty the Queen of the United Kingdom of Great Britain and Ireland, His Majesty the Emperor of Austria, King of Hungary and Bohemia, His Majesty the King of the French, His Majesty the King of Prussia, and His Majesty the Emperor of all the Russias, declare, that the

---

[1]   C. P. Sanger, and H. T. J. Norton, *England's Guarantee to Belgium and Luxemburg, with the Full Text of the Treaties* (New York: Charles Scribner's Sons, 1915), 139-141. [↵]

Articles hereunto annexed, and forming the tenour of the Treaty concluded this day between His Majesty the King of the Belgians and His Majesty the King of the Netherlands, Grand Duke of Luxembourg, are considered as having the same force and validity as if they were textually inserted in the present Act, and that they are thus placed under the guarantee of their said Majesties.

Article II.

The Treaty of the 15th of November, 1831, between their Majesties the Queen of the United Kingdom of Great Britain and Ireland, the Emperor of Austria, King of Hungary and Bohemia, the King of the French, the King of Prussia, and the Emperor of all the Russias, and His Majesty the King of the Belgians, is declared not to be obligatory upon the High Contracting Parties.

Article III.

The present Treaty shall be ratified, and the ratifications shall be exchanged at London at the expiration of six weeks, or sooner if possible. This exchange shall take place at the same time as that of the ratifications of the Treaty between Belgium and Holland. In witness whereof, the respective Plenipotentiaries have signed the present Treaty, and have affixed thereto the seal of their Arms.

Done at London, the nineteenth day of April, in the year of our Lord one thousand eight hundred and thirty-nine.

(L.S.) Palmerston.Lord Palmerston, British Foreign Secretary

(L.S.) Senfft.Senfft von Pilsach, Austrian Minister

(L.S.) H. Sebastiani.H. Sebastiana, French commander during Napoleonic wars. French Minister at the signing of the treaty.

(L.S.) Bulow.Gabriele von Bulow, Prussian Minister

(L.S.) Pozzo di Borgo.Carlo Andrea Pozzo di Borgo, Russian Diplomat

(L.S.) Sylvan van de Weyer.Sylvan van de Weyer, Belgian Ambassador to the United Kingdom.

Annex to the Treaty of London signed at London, on the 19th April 1839, between Great Britain, Austria, France, Prussia, and Russia, on the one part, and the Netherlands, on the other part.[2]

Article I.

The Belgian territory shall be composed of the provinces of

---

[2]   C. P. Sanger, and H. T. J. Norton, *England's Guarantee to Belgium and Luxemburg, with the Full Text of the Treaties* (New York: Charles Scribner's Sons, 1915), 127-139. [↵]

South Brabant;

Liege;

Namur;

Hainault;

West Flanders;

Antwerp; and

Limbourg; such as they formed part of the United Kingdom of the Netherlands constituted in 1815, with the exception of those districts of the province of Limbourg which are designated in Article IV.

The Belgian territory shall, moreover, comprise that part of the Grand Duchy of Luxembourg which is specified in Article II.

Article II.

In the Grand Duchy of Luxembourg, the limits of the Belgian territory shall be such as will be hereinafter described, viz.

Commencing from the frontier of France between Rodange, which shall remain to the Grand Duchy of Luxembourg, and Athus, which shall belong to Belgium, there shall be drawn, according to the annexed map, a line which, leaving to Belgium the road from Arlon to Longwy, the town of Arlon with its district, and the road from Arlon to Bastogne, shall pass between Messancy, which shall be on the Belgian territory, and Clemancy, which shall remain to the Grand Duchy of Luxembourg, terminating at Steinfort, which place shall also remain to the Grand Duchy. From Steinfort this line shall be continued in the direction of Eischen, Hecbus, Guirsch, Ober-Pallen, Grende, Nothomb, Parette, and Perle, as far as Martelange; Hecbus, Guirsch, Grende, Nothomb, and Parette, being to belong to Belgium, and Eischen, Ober-Pallen, Perle, and Martelange, to the Grand Duchy. From Martelange the said line shall follow the course of the Sure, the water way (thalweg) of which river shall serve as the limit between the two States, as far as opposite to Tintange, from whence it shall be continued, as directly as possible, towards the present frontier of the Arrondissement of Diekirch, and shall pass between Surret, Harlange, and Tarchamps, which places shall be left to the Grand Duchy of Luxembourg, and Honville, Livarchamps, and Loutremange, which places shall form part of the Belgian territory. Then having, in the vicinity of Doncols and Soulez, which shall remain to the Grand Duchy, reached the present boundary of the Arrondissement of Diekirch, the line in question shall follow the said boundary to the frontier of the Prussian territory. All the territories, towns, fortresses, and places situated to the west of this line, shall belong to Belgium; and all the territories, towns, fortresses, and places situated to the east of the said line, shall continue to belong to the Grand Duchy of Luxembourg.

It is understood, that in making out this line, and in conforming as closely as possible to the description of it given above, as well as to the delineation of it on the map, which, for the sake of greater clearness, is annexed to the present Article, the Commissioners of demarcation, mentioned in Article V, shall pay due attention to the localities, as well as to the mutual necessity for accommodation which may result therefrom.

Article III.

In return for the cessions made in the preceding Article, there shall be assigned to His Majesty the King of the Netherlands, Grand Duke of Luxembourg, a territorial indemnity in the province of Limbourg.

Article IV.

In execution of that part of Article I which relates to the province of Limbourg, and in consequence of the cessions which His Majesty the King of the Netherlands, Grand Duke of Luxembourg, makes in Article II, His said Majesty shall possess, either to be held by him in his character of Grand Duke of Luxembourg, or for the purpose of being united to Holland, those territories, the limits of which are hereinafter described.

1. On the right bank of the Meuse; to the old Dutch enclaves upon the said bank in the province of Limbourg, shall be united those districts of the said province upon the same bank, which did not belong to the States General in 1790; in such wise that the whole of that part of the present province of Limbourg, situated upon the right bank of the Meuse, and comprised between that river on the west, the frontier of the Prussian territory on the east, the present frontier of the province of Liege on the south, and Dutch Guelderland on the north, shall henceforth belong to His Majesty the King of the Netherlands, either to be held by him in his character of Grand Duke of Luxembourg, or in order to be united to Holland.
2. On the left bank of the Meuse; commencing from the southernmost point of the Dutch province of North Brabant, there shall be drawn, according to the annexed map, a line which shall terminate on the Meuse above Wessem, between that place and Stevenswaardt, at the point where the frontiers of the present Arrondissements of Ruremonde and Maestricht meet on the left bank of the Meuse; in such manner that Bergerot, Stamproy, Neer-Itteren, Ittervoordt, and Thorn, with their districts, as well as all the other places situated to the north of this line, shall form part of the Dutch territory.

The old Dutch enclaves in the province of Limbourg, upon the left bank of the Meuse, shall belong to Belgium, with the exception of the town of Maestricht, which, together with a radius of territory, extending twelve hundred toisesA unit of measure equaling about two meters. from the outer glacis of the fortress, on the said bank of this river, shall continue to be possessed in full sovereignty and property by His Majesty the King of the Netherlands.

Article V.

His Majesty the King of the Netherlands, Grand Duke of Luxembourg, shall come to an agreement with the Germanic Confederation, and with the Agnates of the House of Nassau, as to the application of the stipulations contained in Articles III and IV, as well as upon all the arrangements which the said Articles may render necessary, either with the abovementioned Agnates of the House of Nassau, or with the Germanic Confederation.

Article VI.

In consideration of the territorial arrangements above stated, each of the two parties renounces reciprocally, and for ever, all pretension to the territories, towns, fortresses, and places situated within the limits of the possessions of the other party, such as those limits are described in Articles I, II, and IV.

The said limits shall be marked out in conformity with those Articles by Belgian and Dutch Commissioners of demarcation, who shall meet as soon as possible in the town of Maestricht.

Article VII.

Belgium, within the limits specified in Articles I, II, and IV, shall form an independent and perpetually neutral State. It shall be bound to observe such neutrality towards all other States.

Article VIII.

The drainage of the waters of the two Flanders shall be regulated between Holland and Belgium, according to the stipulations on this subject contained in Article VI of the definitive Treaty concluded between His Majesty the Emperor of Germany and the States General, on the 8th of November 1785; and in conformity with the said Article, Commissioners, to be named on either side, shall make arrangements for the application of the provisions contained in it.

Article IX.

§ 1. The provisions of Articles CVIII to CXVII inclusive of the General Act of the Congress of Vienna, relative to the free navigation of navigable rivers, shall be applied to those navigable rivers which separate the Belgian and the Dutch territories, or which traverse them both.

§ 2. So far as regards specially the navigation of the Scheldt, and of its mouths, it is agreed, that the pilotage and the buoying of its channel, as well as the conservation of the channels of the Scheldt below Antwerp, shall be subject to a joint superintendence; and that this joint superintendence shall be exercised by Commissioners to be appointed for this purpose by the two parties. Moderate pilotage dues shall be fixed by mutual agreement, and those dues shall be the same for the vessels of all nations.

In the meantime, and until these dues shall be fixed, no higher pilotage dues shall be levied than those which have been established by the tariff of 1829, for the mouths of the Meuse from the high sea to Helvoet, and from Helvoet to Rotterdam, in proportion to the distances. It shall be at the choice of every vessel proceeding from the high sea to Belgium, or from Belgium to the high sea, to take what pilot she pleases; and upon the same principle, it shall be free for the two countries to establish along the whole course of the Scheldt, and at its mouth, such pilotage establishments as shall be deemed necessary for furnishing pilots. Everything relating to these establishments shall be determined by the regulation to be concluded in conformity with § 6 hereinafter following. These establishments shall be placed under the joint superintendence mentioned in the beginning of the present paragraph. The two Governments engage to preserve the navigable channels of the Scheldt, and of its mouths, and to place and maintain therein the necessary beacons and buoys, each for its own part of the river.

§ 3. There shall be levied by the Government of the Netherlands, upon the navigation of the Scheldt and of its mouths, a single duty of florins 1.50 per ton; A florin was a Dutch coin that is to say, florins 1.12 on vessels which, coming from the high sea, shall ascend the Western Scheldt in order to proceed to Belgium by the Scheldt, or by the Canal of Terneuze; and of florins 0.38 per ton on vessels which, coming from Belgium by the Scheldt or by the Canal of Terneuze, shall descend the Western Scheldt in order to proceed to the high sea. And in order that the said vessels may not be subject to any visit, nor to any delay or hindrance whatever within the Dutch waters, either in ascending the Scheldt from the high sea, or in descending the Scheldt in order to reach the high sea, it is agreed that the collection of the duty abovementioned shall take place by Dutch agents at Antwerp and at Terneuze. In the same manner, vessels arriving from the high sea in order to proceed to Antwerp by the Western Scheldt, and coming from places suspected in regard to health, shall be at liberty to continue their course without hindrance or delay, accompanied by one health guard, and thus to proceed to the place of their destination. Vessels proceeding from Antwerp to Terneuze, and vice versa, or carrying on in the river itself coasting trade or fishery (in such manner as the exercise of the latter shall be regulated in pursuance of § 6 hereinafter) shall not be subjected to any duty.

§ 4. The branch of the Scheldt called the Eastern Scheldt not being in its present state available for the navigation from the high sea to Antwerp and Terneuze, and vice versa, but being used for the navigation between Antwerp and the Rhine, this eastern branch shall not be burthened, in any part of its course, with higher duties or tolls than those which are levied, according to the tariffs of Mayence of the 31st of March, 1831, upon the navigation from Gorcum to the high sea, in proportion to the distances.

§ 5. It is also agreed that the navigation of the intermediate channels between the Scheldt and the Rhine, in order to proceed from Antwerp to the Rhine, and vice versa, shall continue reciprocally free, and that it shall be subject only to moderate tolls, which shall be the same for the commerce of the two countries.

§ 6. Commissioners on both sides shall meet at Antwerp in the space of one month, as well to determine the definitive and permanent amount of these tolls, as to agree upon a general regulation for the execution of the provisions of the present Article, and to include therein a provision for the exercise of the right of fishing and of trading in fish, throughout the whole extent of the Scheldt, on a footing of perfect reciprocity and equality in favour of the subjects of the two countries.

§ 7. In the meantime, and until the said regulations shall be prepared, the navigation of the Meuse and of its branches shall remain free to the commerce of the two countries, which shall adopt provisionally, in this respect, the tariffs of the Convention signed at Mayence on the 31st of March, 1831, for the free navigation of the Rhine, as well as the other provisions of that Convention, so far as they may be applicable to the said river.

§ 8. If natural events or works of art should hereafter render impracticable the lines of navigation mentioned in the present Article, the Government of the Netherlands shall assign to Belgian navigation other lines equally safe, and equally good and commodious, instead of the said lines of navigation become impracticable.

Article X.

The use of the canals which traverse both countries shall continue to be free and common to the inhabitants of both. It is understood that they shall enjoy the use of the same reciprocally, and on equal conditions; and that on either side moderate duties only shall be levied upon the navigation of the said canals.

Article XI.

The commercial communications through the town of Maestricht, and through Sittardt, shall remain entirely free, and shall not be impeded under any pretext whatsoever.

The use of the roads which, passing through these towns lead to the frontiers of Germany, shall be subject only to the payment of moderate turnpike tolls, for the repair of the said roads, so that the transit commerce may not experience any obstacle thereby, and that by means of the tolls abovementioned these roads may be kept in good repair, and fit to afford facilities to that commerce.

Article XII.

In the event of a new road having been constructed, or a new canal cut, in Belgium, terminating at the Meuse, opposite the Dutch canton of Sittardt, in that case Belgium shall be entitled to demand of Holland, who, on the other hand, shall not in such case refuse her consent, that the said road, or the said canal, shall be continued, according to the same plan, and entirely at the cost and charge of Belgium, through the canton of Sittardt, to the frontiers of Germany. This road or canal, which shall be used only as a commercial communication, shall be constructed, at the option of Holland, either by engineers and workmen whom Belgium shall obtain permission to employ for that purpose in the canton of Sittardt, or by engineers and workmen to be furnished by Holland, and who shall execute the works agreed upon at the expense of Belgium; the whole without any charge whatsoever to Holland, and without prejudice to her exclusive rights of sovereignty over the territory which may be traversed by the road or canal in question.

The two parties shall fix, by mutual agreement, the amount and the mode of collection of the duties and tolls which should be levied upon the said road or canal.

Article XII.

§ 1. From and after the 1st of January, 1839, Belgium, with reference to the division of the public debt of the Kingdom of the Netherlands, shall remain charged with the sum of 5,000,000 of Netherland florins of annual interest, the capital of which shall be transferred from the debit of the Great Book of Amsterdam, or from the debit of the General Treasury of the Kingdom of the Netherlands, to the debit of the Great Book of Belgium.

§ 2. The capitals transferred, and the annuities inscribed upon the debit of the Great Book of Belgium, in consequence of the preceding paragraph, to the amount of the total sum of 5,000,000 Netherland florins of annual interest, shall be considered as forming part of the Belgian National Debt; and Belgium engages not to admit, either at present or in future, any distinction between this portion of her public debt arising from her union with Holland, and any other Belgian national debt already created, or which may be created hereafter.

§ 3. The payment of the abovementioned sum of 5,000,000 Netherland florins of annual interest, shall take place regularly every six months, either at Brussels or at Antwerp, in ready money, without deduction of any kind whatsoever, either at present or in future.

§ 4. In consideration of the creation of the said sum of 5,000,000 florins of annual interest, Belgium shall be released from all obligation towards Holland, on account of the division of the public debt of the Kingdom of the Netherlands.

§ 5. Commissioners to be named on both sides, shall meet within the space of fifteen days in the town of Utrecht, in order to proceed to the transfer of the capitals and annual interest, which upon the division of the public debt of the Kingdom of the Netherlands, are to pass to the charge of Belgium, up to the amount of 5,000,000 florins of annual interest.

They shall also proceed to deliver up the archives, maps, plans, and other documents whatsoever which belong to Belgium, or which relate to her administration.

Article XIV.

The port of Antwerp, in conformity with the stipulations of the XVth Article of the Treaty of Paris, of the 30th of May, 1814, shall continue to be solely a port of commerce.

Article XV.

Works of public or private utility, such as canals, roads, or others of a similar nature, constructed wholly or in part at the expense of the Kingdom of the Netherlands, shall belong, together with the advantages and charges thereunto attached, to the country in which they are situated.

It is understood that the capitals borrowed for the construction of these works, and specifically charged thereupon, shall be comprised in the aforesaid charges, in so far as they may not yet have been repaid, and without giving rise to any claim on account of repayments already made.

Article XVI.

The sequestrations which may have been imposed in Belgium during the troubles, for political causes, on any property or hereditary estates whatsoever, shall be taken off without delay, and the enjoyment of the property and estates abovementioned shall be immediately restored to the lawful owners thereof.

Article XVII.

In the two countries of which the separation takes place in consequence of the present Articles, inhabitants and proprietors, if they wish to transfer their residence from one country to the other, shall, during two years, be at liberty to dispose of their property, movable or immovable, of whatever nature the same may be, to sell it, and to carry away the produce of the sale, either in money or in any other shape, without hindrance, and without the payment of any duties other than those which are now in force in the two countries upon changes and transfers.

It is understood that the collection of the droit d'aubaine et de detractionThis is French for "right to bargain and detraction." upon the persons and property of Dutch in Belgium, and of Belgians in Holland, is abandoned, both now and for the future.

Article XVIII.

The character of a subject of the two Governments, with regard to property, shall be acknowledged and maintained.

Article XIX.

The stipulations of Articles from XI to XXI, inclusive, of the Treaty concluded between Austria and Russia, on the 3rd of May, 1815, which forms an integral part of the General Act of the Congress of Vienna, stipulations relative to persons who possess property in both countries to the election of residence which they are required to make, to the rights which they shall exercise as subjects of either State, and to the relations of neighbourhood in properties cut by the frontiers, shall be applied to such proprietors, as well as to such properties, in Holland, in the Grand Duchy of Luxembourg, or in Belgium, as shall be found to come within the cases provided for by the aforesaid stipulations of the Acts of the Congress of Vienna. It is understood that mineral productions are comprised among the productions of the soil mentioned in Article XX of the Treaty of the 3rd of May, 1815, above referred to. The droits d'aubaine et de detraction being henceforth abolished, as between Holland, the Grand Duchy of Luxembourg, and Belgium, it is understood that such of the abovementioned stipulations as may relate to those duties shall be considered null and void in the three countries.

Article XX.

No person in the territories which change domination, shall be molested or disturbed in any manner whatever, on account of any part which he may have taken, directly or indirectly, in political events.

Article XXI.

The pensions and allowances of expectants, of persons unemployed or retired, shall in future be paid, on either side, to all those individuals entitled thereto, both civil and military, conformably to the laws in force previous to the 1st November, 1830.

It is agreed that the above-mentioned pensions and allowances to persons born in the territories which now constitute Belgium, shall remain at the charge of the Belgian treasury; and the pensions and allowances of persons born in the territories which now constitute the Kingdom of the Netherlands, shall be at the charge of the Netherland treasury.

Article XXII.

All claims of Belgian subjects upon any private establishments, such as the widows' fund, and the fund known under the denomination of the fonds des leges,This is French for "leges funds" or "law funds." and of the chest of civil and military retired allowances, shall be examined by the Mixed Commission mentioned in Article XIII, and shall be determined according to the tenour of the regulations by which these funds or chests are governed.

The securities furnished, as well as the payments made, by Belgian accountants, the judicial deposits and consignments, shall equally be restored to the parties entitled thereto, on the presentation of their proofs. If, under the head of what are called the French liquidations, any Belgian subjects should still be able to bring forward claims to be inscribed, such claims shall also be examined and settled by the said Commission.

Article XXIII.

All judgments given in civil and commercial matters, all acts of the civil power, and all acts executed before a notary or other public officer under the Belgian administration, in those parts of Limbourg and of the Grand Duchy of Luxembourg, of which His Majesty the King of the Netherlands, Grand Duke of Luxembourg, is to be replaced in possession, shall be maintained in force and validity.

Article XXIV.

Immediately after the exchange of the Ratifications of the Treaty to be concluded between the two parties, the necessary orders shall be transmitted to the commanders of the respective troops, for the evacuation of the territories, towns, fortresses, and places which change domination. The civil authorities thereof shall also, at the same time, receive the necessary orders for delivering over the said territories, towns, fortresses, and places to the commissioners who shall be appointed by both parties for this purpose.

This evacuation and delivery shall be effected so as to be completed in the space of fifteen days, or sooner if possible.

(L.S.) Palmerston.

(L.S.) Senfft.

(L.S.) H. Sebastiani.

(L.S.) Bulow.

(L.S.) Pozzo di Borgo.

(L.S.) Sylvan van de Weyer.

References

Sanger, C. P. and H. T. J. Norton. *England's Guarantee to Belgium and Luxemburg, with the Full Text of the Treaties.* New York: Charles Scribner's Sons, 1915.